D1081352

Services Management
An Integrated Approach

WITHDRAWN FROM
ST HELENS COLLEGE LIBRARY

Wate

This boo

- 3 J

RET

- f
RF

RETU

We work with leading authors to develop the strongest educational materials in management, bringing cutting-edge thinking and best learning practice to a global market.

Under a range of well-known imprints, including Financial Times/Prentice Hall, we craft high quality print and electronic publications which help readers to understand and apply their content, whether studying or at work.

To find out more about the complete range of our publishing, please visit us on the World Wide Web at: **www.pearsoned.co.uk**

SECOND EDITION

Services Management
An Integrated Approach

Edited by

Bart Van Looy
Paul Gemmel
Roland Van Dierdonck

 Prentice Hall
FINANCIAL TIMES

An imprint of **Pearson Education**
Harlow, England • London • New York • Boston • San Francisco • Toronto
Sydney • Tokyo • Singapore • Hong Kong • Seoul • Taipei • New Delhi
Cape Town • Madrid • Mexico City • Amsterdam • Munich • Paris • Milan

Pearson Education Limited

Edinburgh Gate
Harlow
Essex CM20 2JE
England

and Associated Companies throughout the world.

Visit us on the World Wide Web at:
www.pearsoneduc.com

First published in Great Britain in 1998
Second edition published 2003

© Financial Times Professional Limited 1998

© Pearson Education Limited 2003

All rights reserved. No part of this publication may be reproduced, stored in
a retrieval system, or transmitted in any form or by any means, electronic,
mechanical, photocopying, recording or otherwise, without either the prior
written permission of the publisher or a licence permitting restricted copying
in the United Kingdom issued by the Copyright Licensing Agency Ltd,
90 Tottenham Court Road, London W1T 4LP.

ISBN 10: 0 273 67353 X
ISBN 13: 978 0 273 67353 8

British Library Cataloguing-in-Publication Data
A catalogue record for this book is available from the British Library.

10 9 8 7 6
08 07 06 05

Typeset in 9.5/12 pt Stone Serif by 68
Printed and bound by Bell & Bain Limited, Glasgow

The publisher's policy is to use paper manufactured from sustainable forests.

CONTENTS

LIST OF FIGURES

LIST OF TABLES

LIST OF EXHIBITS

ABOUT THE AUTHORS

Werner Bruggeman is a professor in management accounting and control at the Vlerick Leuven Ghent Management School and at the faculty of Economics of the Ghent University in Belgium. He is also Chairman of the Competence Centre Accounting and Finance and Partner of B&M.

Dirk Buyens is the Academic Dean and Partner at the Vlerick Leuven Ghent Management School. As professor he is head of the Human Resource Management Department. His major fields of interest are strategic HRM, organization development and strategic career management.

Koenraad Debackere is professor in technology and innovation management at the Catholic University of Leuven and Managing Director of K. U. Leuven R&D. His major research interests include innovation strategy and the management of innovation in industry and the development of government policies to support innovation in industry.

Marion Debruyne is assistant professor of marketing at the Goizueta Business School, Emory University (Atlanta, USA). Prior to that, she was a visiting scholar at the Kellogg Graduate School of Management (Northwestern University) and the Wharton School (University of Pennsylvania). She holds a Ph.D. in Applied Economics, a Master's in Marketing and a Chemical Engineering degree, all from the University of Ghent. Her research interests involve competitive reactions, organizational imitation and the development of new markets.

Patrick De Pelsmacker is professor of marketing at the University of Antwerp and at Ghent University. He is also Dean of Universiteit Antwerpen Management School.

Steven Desmet studied applied economic sciences at the Ghent University, where he has been working as research assistant in operations management, service operations management, service productivity and quality. He currently works for IBM Business Consulting Services in the area of customer relationships management, focusing on the areas of customer service and field service.

Koen Dewettinck is connected to the HRM Centre of the Vlerick Leuven Ghent Management School. He holds a Master's degree in Work and Organizational Psychology from the University of Ghent. He has published research on HRM in the service sector; comparative HRM in Europe; and labour market oriented research. Since November 2001, Koen has been an ICM Doctoral Fellow. His Ph.D. project concerns the employee empowerment process and its link with service employee performance. Currently, Koen is a visiting scholar at the Marketing and Policy Studies Department of the Weatherhead School of Management, Case Western Reserve University, Cleveland, Ohio.

Kristof De Wulf studied applied economic sciences and holds an MBA (University of Antwerp). He is partner of the Vlerick Leuven Ghent Management School, where he heads the Competence Marketing Centre. His research focus is on customer relationship management, internet marketing, brand management, and database marketing.

Tim Duhamel is co-founder and CEO of InSites Consulting, a research and consulting company that specializes in online marketing strategies. InSites delivers value added research and advice to companies who want to optimize an interactive relationship with their clients.

Dries Faems holds a Master's degree in Commercial Engineering and works as a researcher at the Department of Applied Economics of the Catholic University of Leuven. His research focus is on organization studies, HRM, innovation management and inter-organizational collaboration.

Paul Gemmel is professor of service and hospital operations management at the Ghent University. His research focus is on operations management in different service sectors such as health care and banks. He is founder and scientific advisor for a research centre for hospital management at the Vlerick Leuven Ghent Management School.

Wim Grielens is a senior consultant with IBM Global Services. He has several years of experience in applying telecommunications, collaboration and portal technology for improved operational effectiveness. He specializes in the analysis of collaboration processes. He holds a Master's degree in applied economics.

Wilfried Grommen is General Manager for .NET in EMEA at Microsoft, where he manages the overall .NET adoption. Previously, he was a founding partner of Capco, a financial services company active in straight-through processing activities and e-finance solutions. Wilfried's expertise was developed at Cimad consultants/IBM Professional Services, where he headed technology competencies, including Internet, middleware, software factory and systems management activities, each of which was applied in several large projects. From Cimad, he became Industry Services Executive for Capital Markets Region West at IBM, where he managed a consulting team of over 300 people. Wilfried holds a B.S. in Civil Engineering and Electro-Mechanical Engineering with a specialization in microelectronics from the University of Leuven.

Aimé Heene is a professor in the field of strategic management at the University of Ghent and Antwerp University and a founding member and secretary of the Flemish Strategy Society. He has been a fellow of the China–Europe Management Centre at Fudan University (Shanghai). He specializes in competence based strategic management and management for social profit and public organizations.

Krist'l Krols is manager of the World Class Manufacturing Centre at the Vlerick Leuven Ghent Management School. In close collaboration with manufacturing companies, she undertakes research on state of the art topics with a focus on possibilities, conditions and actual status in Belgian industry.

Pedro Matthÿnssens is a manager of business development in the securities and capital markets team of IBM Global Services. He holds an MA degree in Classics, University of Leuven, Belgium and Computational Linguistics, University of Antwerp, Belgium (magna cum laude).

Niels Schillewaert is assistant professor of marketing at the Vlerick Leuven Ghent Management School. In addition, Niels is managing partner of InSites Consulting, a research and consulting firm specializing in e-business. He obtained his Ph.D. at Ghent University and studied at The Pennsylvania State University (USA) during his doctoral work. Niels has received several awards for his research and has published in leading scientific journals.

Walter Stevens has over 12 years of consulting experience with a strong focus on management development, competence management, organizational development and HR policy setting. He is one of the founders of The Competence Network (TCN) a network of experienced professionals who – starting from shared values like respect, authenticity, and integrity – deliver value to customers in the field of organizing and HRM.

Stefan Stremersch studied applied economics at Ghent University and obtained his Ph.D. at Tilburg University. He is currently assistant professor of marketing and research fellow at Erasmus University Rotterdam (The Netherlands). He specializes in new product growth and marketing of high-tech products.

Joeri Van Den Bergh studied applied economics at VLEKHO Brussels and is a Master in Marketing (SLM) at the Vlerick Leuven Ghent Management School. He is currently managing partner of the Internet research and consulting firm InSites.

Tine Vandenbossche received her Master's degree in psychology from Ghent University. She is scientific coordinator of the Competence Management Research Centre at the Vlerick Leuven Ghent Management School and is preparing a Master's Programme on European human resource management.

Roland Van Dierdonck is civil and industrial engineer (Ghent University) and Doctor in Business Administration, Harvard University (USA). He was an assistant professor at IMD, Lausanne, visiting research scholar at the University of North Carolina, Chapel Hill (USA) and visiting professor at INSEAD (France) and Rotterdam School of Management (The Netherlands) and various other schools and universities. He is Partner and professor of Vlerick Leuven Ghent Management School and at Ghent University. He is currently Dean of Vlerick Leuven Ghent Management School. His main research interests are supply chain management, manufacturing strategy and service operations management.

Bart Van Looy was responsible for the Service Management Centre at the Vlerick Leuven Ghent Management School from the beginning of 1996 until the end of 1997. Previously, he worked as a consultant in the field of HRM and organizational behaviour. He obtained his Ph.D. from K. U. Leuven where he is currently studying innovation processes at INCENTIM, a multidisciplinary research centre focusing on innovation strategy, innovation policies and knowledge intensive entrepreneurship.

Gino Van Ossel is visiting professor of marketing at the Vlerick Leuven Ghent Management School and at the Rotterdam School of Management. He is chairman of the Retail & Trade Marketing Research Centre at the Vlerick School. Prior to that, he was senior researcher of the Service Management Centre. He specializes in service management in general, and in retail and trade marketing in particular.

Kurt Verweire obtained his Ph.D. in 1999 on the topic of 'Performance consequences of financial conglomeration with an empirical analysis in Belgium and the Netherlands' at the Erasmus University in Rotterdam, the Netherlands. Since 1992, he has been working at the Vlerick Leuven Ghent Management School on strategic and marketing issues in the financial services industry. He is assistant professor at the Vlerick Leuven Ghent Management School. His fields of research focus on financial convergence, financial conglomeration, integration between banking, insurance and investment industry, and performance management. Kurt Verweire is also Programme Director of the MBA-FSI.

PREFACE

You are looking at the first pages of *Services Management: An Integrated Approach*. This book originated out of continuous discussions and research efforts that took place at the Service Management Centre of the Vlerick Leuven Ghent Management School. The first point of discussion is the notion of services and service management. All too often one is tempted to take well-established insights and know-how coming from manufacturing environments and apply them to services. However, services do have some characteristics that pose specific challenges and/or require special attention, for example: intangibility poses specific challenges to the communication and marketing effort; simultaneity – i.e. the presence of the customer during the service delivery process – implies a direct link between employees' feelings and behaviour and customers' perceptions of service quality; the perishable nature of service has serious implications for managing the service delivery system and the available capacity. Second, services are processes. They require an integrated and concerted approach; the operational service delivery system, employees and customers all need to be attuned to deliver value in a seamless way.

This awareness of the specific nature of services and, hence, service management inspired several companies, together with the Vlerick Leuven Ghent Management School, to establish a forum that allowed for exploration and in-depth discussion of the specific nature of service management. The centre followed a multidisciplinary approach from the start; people with an engineering, marketing or organizational behaviour background have been involved, and both academics and practitioners have collaborated in the discussions. Over the past years, workshops have been organized covering themes such as customer satisfaction, information technology, empowerment, the service profit chain, innovation, performance management, capacity management and waiting lines, to name just a few. In-depth case studies and survey research have also been part of these exploration efforts.

During these years of working together it became clear that services need to be approached in an integrated way: the operational service delivery system, employees' competencies, behaviour and feelings, and customer needs and preferences all need to be balanced, resulting in a configuration that eventually will lead to value creation and benefits for all stakeholders involved. In the light of this approach we have established the structure of this book as follows.

In the first part, we explore the nature and importance of services in today's economies. This will lead to the development of a first guiding framework – the service concept – and the delineation of its constituting elements (Chapters 1 and 2). Moreover, we will argue that the notion of services and hence of service management, is becoming an important issue for manufacturing companies as well (Chapter 3).

Next we focus on customers. We will look at the crucial relationships between customer satisfaction, customer loyalty and eventual profitability (Chapter 4); discuss ways of measuring customer satisfaction and improving it by means of complaint management and the introduction of service level agreements and guarantees (Chapters 7 and 8). Promoting and pricing services will also be considered (Chapters 5 and 6).

Employees play a decisive role in delivering service quality. Therefore, in the third part we look at the dynamics of the script underlying this crucial role (Chapter 9). Consecutively, we develop the notion of competencies and their development, the importance of collaboration and the relevance of empowerment (Chapters 10, 11 and 12). Finally, we focus on the specific issues related to job design and performance of front-line employees (Chapter 13).

In the fourth part we turn to issues related to the design and management of the service delivery system (chapter 14). As services are intangible they become perishable as well; there is no possibility of stockpiling services. Designing and managing capacity adequately will often affect directly the level of profitability in services. We devote a complete chapter to relevant approaches and techniques of capacity management as well as related concepts such as yield management (Chapter 15). In Part Four, we will also discuss location and facilities (Chapter 16), and explore the role information technology can play in the service delivery process (Chapter 17).

The fifth part is devoted to issues of a more integrated and dynamic nature; designing adequate performance measurement systems (Chapter 18); updating your service concept by means of innovation (Chapter 19); extending services across national boundaries (Chapter 20), and service strategy as an overreaching concept (Chapter 21).

Of course, we cannot cover all issues related to the different themes listed in the table of contents. Rather, we have tried to highlight those elements that relate directly to the nature of services or bear a crucial importance for service management. By placing service aspects in the spotlight, this book can be seen as complementary to other managerial texts focusing on a functional area or domain.

Bart Van Looy
Paul Gemmel
Roland Van Dierdonck

Ghent, September 2002

ACKNOWLEDGEMENTS

The work of the Service Management Centre resulted in *Services Management: An Integrated Approach*. Without the Service Management Centre, no such book would have been written, so we are grateful for the support, both financially and intellectually, of the partners involved in the Service Management Centre: *ABB Service*, part of the Asea Brown Boveri Group; *Electrabel*, the leading Belgian electricity, gas and cable TV company; *Generale Bank*, created in 1822, now part of the Fortis Group; *Schindler*, the worldwide market-leader in escalators and moving walkways; and, finally, *Digital Multivendor Customer Services (MCS)*, now part of the Compaq organization.

Just looking at the table of contents and the number of authors involved demonstrates that putting this book together extended beyond the efforts of the editors. We thank all contributors for the time and knowledge they put into this book, for the patience they have displayed when confronted with our comments and suggestions, and for their openness to explore the topics at hand with us. Some people contributed to this book in ways that went beyond writing the various chapter(s). When writing the first edition, Steven Desmet was there all the time as the silent, but vitally important, man behind the scenes, always prepared to pick up the loose ends when they created problems. Ann Coopman (first edition) and Isabelle De Ganck (second edition) coped with an endless stream of drafts and re-drafts and kept their good humour all the way through. Gino Van Ossel played a crucial role in the first years of the Service Management Centre and acted as the perfect convenor for the marketing department of The Vlerick Leuven Ghent Management School. Stratton Bull (first edition) and especially Anne Hodgkinson (first and second edition) were there during the whole process as 'ghostwriters', looking over our shoulders to watch the quality of the language in an extremely flexible and customer-oriented way. Rebekah Taylor, Rachel Owen and all other colleagues involved at Pearson Education were there as well to provide us with useful comments, suggestions and the necessary support to bring this book to its final stages. Thanks to all of you for these valuable contributions and your co-operation when putting together this book. Finally we are grateful for the continuous support and patience of Nicole, Veerle and Lucrece (first and second edition); this book is also indebted to the opportunities they provided for us to accomplish this work.

Bart Van Looy
Paul Gemmel
Roland Van Dierdonck

PUBLISHER'S ACKNOWLEDGEMENTS

We are grateful to the following for permission to reproduce copyright material:

Figure 1.2 from figure from Maslow, A. H., 'Motivation and Personality', Pearson Education, 1987; Figure 1.5 from figure from Maister, David H., *'True Professionalism'*, The Free Press, 1997; Figures 4.1 and 4.3 adapted and reprinted by permission of Harvard Business Review, from 'Putting the service-profit chain to work', Heskett, J. L., Jones, T. O., Loveman, G. W., Sasser, W. E. and Schlesinger, L., March–April 1994. Copyright © 1998 by the President and Fellows of Harvard College; all rights reserved; Figures 4.4 and 4.5 adapted and reprinted by permission of Harvard Business School Press, *The Loyalty Effect – the hidden force behind growth, profits and lasting value*, Reichheld, F. F., Boston, MA (1996), p. 39. Copyright © 1998 by Bain & Company, INC. Figure 4.2 from figure from Dick, A. S. and Basu, K. (1994) *Journal of the Academy of Marketing Science*, 22 (2), 99–113. Copyright © 1998 Sage Publications. Reprinted by permission of Sage Publications Inc.; Figures 4.6, 4.7 and 4.9 from figures from Jenkinson, A., *Valuing Your Customers: From Quality Information to Quality Relationships Through Database Marketing*, 1995, McGraw Hill Book Co. Ltd. (McGraw-Hill Education), reproduced with the kind permission of McGraw-Hill Publishing Company; Figure 5.2 from figure from Journal of Marketing, published by the American Marketing Association, Lavidge, R. C. and Steiner, G. A., 1961, Vol. 25, pp. 59–62, *'A model for the predictive measurements of advertising effectiveness by "further reading"'*; Figure 7.1 from figure from Hays, J. M. and Hill, A. V. (1999) 'The market share impact of service failures', *Production and Operations Management, An international Journal of the Production and Operations Management Society,* Vol. 8, No 3, pp. 208–20; Figures 7.2 and 7.3 from figures from TARP (1986) *Consumer Complaint Handling in America: An update study.* United States Office of Consumer Affairs; Table 9.1 from Schlesinger, L. A. and Zornitsky, J. (1991) reprinted with permission from *Human Resource Planning*, Vol. 14, No 2 (1991). Copyright © 1998 by the Human Resource Planning Society; Figure 10.1 and 10.2 and Table 10.2 are copyright © Quintessence Consulting Belgium; Table 10.1 based on information from *'Competentiemanagement: beheersen of begeleiden?'*, in *Tijdschrift voor HRM*, Vol. 3, 2002, No 2, pp. 31–59, Business Unit HRM, Kluwer B. V., (Faems, D., 2002); Figure 10.1 and 10.2 and Table 10.2 are copyright © Quintessence Consulting Belgium; Figure 11.1 based on Lewicki, R. J. (1996) 'Developing and maintaining trust in work relationships', in Kramer, R. and Tyler, T. (eds) *Trust in Organisations: Frontiers of theory and research.* Copyright © 1998 Sage Publications. Reprinted by permission of Sage Publications Inc.; Exhibit 11.1 is based on Marshall, H. (1972) 'Structural constraints in learning' in Geer, B. (ed.) *Learning to Work.* Copyright © 1998 by Sage Publications. Reprinted by permission of Sage Publications;

Figure 11.2 from figure from Bouwen, R. and Fry, R. (1996) 'Facilitating group development: interventions for a relational and contextual construction' in West, M. (ed.) *Handbook of Group Psychology*. Copyright © 1996 John Wiley and Sons Limited. Reproduced with permission; Figure 12.3 reprinted by permission of Sage Publications Ltd from Stewart, G. and Manz, C. (1995) 'Leadership for self-managing work teams: A typology and integrative model', *Human Relations*, Vol 48, No 7, pp. 747–70; Figure 13.1 is reprinted with permission from *Journal of Marketing Research*, published by the American Marketing Association, Singh, J. and Rhoads, G. K., 1991, Vol. 28, August, pp. 328–38; Figure 14.4 from figure from Ravi, S. and Chase, R. B., 'Service quality deployment: quality service by design' in Rakesh V. Sarin (ed.) *Perspectives in Operations Management: Essays in honour of Elwood S. Buffa*, Kluwer Academic Publisher, Norwell, Mass., 1993; Figure 15.7 from *The Decision Sciences Journal*, published by the Decision Sciences Institute, College of Business Administration, Georgia State University, Atlanta, GA.; Figure 15.11 from figure from *'An integrated system framework and analysis methodology for manpower planning'*, in *International Journal of Manpower*, Vol. 17, 1996, No 2, pp. 26–46, Emerald MCB University Press (Khoong, C. M., 1996), reprinted by kind permission of MCB University Press Ltd.; Table 15.1 and Figure 15.13 are from Pruyn, A. T. H. and Smidts, A. (1993) *De Psychologische Beleving van Wachtrijen*. Erasmus University; Table 15.2 © 1993 American Society for Quality Control. Reprinted with permission; Figure 16.1(a) from figure from *http://sedac.ciesin.org/plue/gpw/index.html?main.html&2*, Center for International Earth Science Information Network (CIESIN), Columbia University; International Food Policy Research Institute (IFPRI); and World Resources Institute (WRI). 2000. Gridded Population of the World (GPW), Version 2. Palisades, NY: CIESIN, Columbia University. Available at *http://sedac.ciesin.columbia.edu/plue/gpw*. Copyright © 2003 The Trustees of Columbia University in the City of New York; Figure 16.1(b) from figure *from www.meteo.be*, the Royal Meteorological Institute of Belgium; Table 16.1 reprinted by permission from *Nature* (1997) No 390, p. 132. Copyright © 1997 Macmillan Magazines Ltd.; Figure 16.3 from figure from *Journal of Marketing,* published by the American Marketing Association, Huff, D. L., 1964, Vol. 28, pp. 34–38, *'Defining and estimating a trade area'*; Figure 16.9 from figure republished with permission of the Academy of Management, from *'The locus of control in the R & D matrix'*, in *Academy of Management Journal*, Katz, R. and Allen, T., Vol. 28, No 1, pp. 67–87, 1985, permission conveyed through Copyright Clearance Center, Inc.; Figure 18.1 adapted and reprinted by permission of *Harvard Business Review* from 'The balanced scorecard – measures that drive performance', Kaplan, R. S. and Norton, D. P., Jan–Feb, 1992. Copyright © 1992 by the Harvard Business School Publishing Corporation; all rights reserved; Figure 18.2 has been reproduced with the permission of EFQM. Copyright © EFQM. The EFQM Excellence Model is a registered trademark; Table 18.3 based on Loveman, G. W. (1998) 'Employee satisfaction, customer loyalty and financial performance: an empirical examination of the service profit chain in retail banking', *Journal of Service Research*, Vol. 1, No 1, pp. 18–31. Copyright © 1998 Sage Publications. Reprinted by permission of Sage Publications Inc.; Figure 20.3 from figure from *Organisational Culture and Leadership, 1st Edition*, Schein, Edgar H., Jossey-Bass Publishers, Copyright © 1985 Edgar H. Schein, this material is used by permission of John Wiley & Sons, Inc. Figure 20.6 from figure from Bartlett, C. and Ghoshal, S. (1989) Managing Across Borders: the transnational solution, published by Random House Business Books.

PUBLISHER'S ACKNOWLEDGEMENTS

Reprinted by permission of The Random House Group Ltd.; Figure 21.1 reprinted from Long Range Planning, Vol. 30, No 6, Heene, A., 'The nature of strategic planning', p. 934 (1997) with permission from Elsevier Science.

In some instances we have been unable to trace the owners of copyright material, and we would appreciate any information that would enable us to do so.

PART ONE

The nature of services

Bart Van Looy · Roland Dierdonck · Paul Gemmel

Any book on services should start with an account of the nature of services. What makes services so special that a complete book should be devoted to managing services? In Chapter 1, we first outline the broader evolution of services in the world economy. Two trends emerge: services account for an ever-increasing part of wealth creation in economies all over the world, and services are becoming global to a greater extent. Next, we examine the different characteristics that distinguish services from goods. This leads on to the idea of service classifications; not all services are alike. Acknowledging differences among different types of services is crucial for managing service operations, as will become clear in Chapter 2. Within this chapter we will also stress the critical role of the service concept. Service firms face the challenge of developing a coherent and internally consistent concept that is targeted to a specific segment of a market. The definition of the service concept, together with the target market, is the starting point of the development of any service delivery system. In Chapter 2 we will outline the different elements that need to be adressed. We will also point out interrelationships between the constituting elements, each of which will be discussed in length within the chapters to be found in the remainder of the book. Finally, we will illustrate how different types of services might translate into differences in terms of designing and managing a service delivery system.

While these first chapters might suggest a sharp distinction between services and goods, it is becoming clear that boundaries between manufacturing companies and service providers are increasingly blurred. In Chapter 3, we look in depth at the notion of 'servitization' – that is, manufacturing companies which include services in their offering as well. As such, managing services becomes equally a challenge for manufacturing companies.

CHAPTER 1

The nature of services

Steven Desmet · Bart Van Looy · Roland Van Dierdonck

INTRODUCTION

John Lewis was feeling hungry after a long day's work. He particularly wanted to have a pizza. He was already picking up his phone to order one and have it delivered to his home, when he realized that he had other options which could satisfy his pizza needs.

1. He could go to the supermarket and buy the necessary ingredients such as flour, mushrooms, pepperoni, etc., to make the pizza himself. This would be the cheapest alternative for him, costing roughly £2.
2. Rather than buying the ingredients he could buy a frozen pizza in the same supermarket for £3.
3. He could indeed order the pizza and have it delivered to his home. However, the price tag attached to this alternative jumped to £4.
4. He could go and eat the same pizza in the restaurant operated by the same company that was delivering the pizza at home. The price would be about £4.25.
5. The option of going to the restaurant made him also consider going to Luigi's restaurant, a new Italian restaurant where customers are seated and served at the table, where tables are covered with tablecloths and Italian music is played by a live band. However, this option was pretty expensive. He imagined that he would easily pay £15 for the pizza and a glass of wine.

John was overwhelmed by the choices he had and did not know how to compare them. How did the various alternatives differ? What was the extra value he received for the higher prices he had to pay? He was particularly puzzled by the fact that somewhere along the spectrum from buying ingredients to visiting the Italian restaurant he had crossed the line from buying a good (i.e. a tangible product) to buying a service since, according to what he remembered from his course in economics, products like flour, mushrooms, etc., were classified as 'goods', while restaurants were classified as 'service' companies.

A lecture or a class is undeniably a service, but what if the same lecture is recorded on tape and sold? Does this fall into the category of goods or services? What is the difference between a pizza you buy in a store (a good) or the same pizza you eat in an Italian restaurant (a service)? What makes buying a truck different from leasing one? Is IBM a manufacturing firm or a service organization?

This is a book about service management and it is, therefore, important to understand what makes a service a service. What distinguishes services from goods? Are all services similar? If not, how can we understand these differences? What are the managerial consequences of this? These are all questions which will be addressed in this chapter. However, we will start by illuminating the growing importance of services for our economies and the driving forces behind this growth.

Next, we shall explore the defining characteristics of services and shall attempt a definition. We shall use the characteristics, intangibility and simultaneity, to distinguish different types of services and to develop some relevant classification schemes.

Objectives

By the end of this chapter, you should be able to discuss:

■ the importance and contribution of services to our world economy
■ the driving forces behind the growth of services
■ the characteristics that distinguish services from goods
■ the managerial implications of these specific characteristics
■ service classifications and their practical relevance

THE GROWING IMPORTANCE OF SERVICES

Economists like to divide our industries into three or sometimes even four broad sectors:

■ The *primary* sector – farming, forestry and fishing.
■ The *secondary* sector – the industrial sector, including gas, mining and manufacturing, electricity, water and construction.
■ The *tertiary* sector – a synonym for the service sector.

Some economists have mentioned an evolution to a *quaternary* sector, but there is some disagreement over which services are tertiary and which are quaternary. Some say the quaternary sector consists of the more intellectual services, while others say it comprises social services or non-commercial services. When speaking of the service sector, we actually mean the whole service sector including the quaternary sector. 'Services' therefore becomes a label covering a wide variety of business. As a result, further refinements can be useful.

Broadly speaking, a distinction can be made between the following categories of services:

■ *Distributive services* include transportation, communication and trade.
■ *Producer services* involve services such as investment banking, insurance, engineering, accounting, bookkeeping and legal services.

■ *Social services* include health care, education, non-profit organizations and government agencies.
■ *Personal services* include tourism, dry cleaning, recreational services and domestic services.[1]

The contribution of services to the creation of wealth

The service sector's contribution to our economy has long concerned economists and philosophers. Some economists feared that the transition from an industrial economy to a service economy would lead to a halt in economic growth. The view that service is less – or not at all – productive is not confined to the second half of the twentieth century, as can be seen from the following quotes:

'Productive is all labour which fixes and realises itself in a particular subject or vendible commodity . . . unproductive is all labour which generally perish in the very instant of their performance.'

(Adam Smith, 1776)[2]

'Services and other goods, which pass out of existence in the same instant that they come into it, are of course not part of the stock of wealth.'

(A. Marshall, 1920)[3]

Adam Smith, one of the founding fathers of economics as a science, stated in his book, *The Wealth of Nations*, that labour was only productive if it increased the value of the item for which the labour was employed. Therefore, the services of priests, lawyers and doctors, as well as labour in trade, were not productive. Marx and Lenin held similar views on the non-productivity of trade. This explains why in the formerly Socialist countries little attention was given to services and the service industry.

The majority of economists agree today that services make an important contribution to economic development. Producer services, for instance, have influenced positively the manufacturing sector's effectiveness. Moreover, value creation is not confined to producing and consuming goods; enhancing quality of life by means of services can be equally important. Indeed, this can be seen as one of the driving forces behind the growing importance of services as will be explained in the next section.

Service industries are now the largest contributors to employment and gross domestic product in most countries. This has not always been the case. Food production (agriculture and livestock breeding) was the world's main economic activity for many centuries and still is in many developing countries, especially in sub-Saharan Africa. Over the decades, however, there has been a clear shift towards the tertiary sector. After the Industrial Revolution in the second half of the eighteenth century, the secondary sector's share of economic activity started to increase, first in Europe and then spreading to the rest of the world. By the beginning of the twentieth century, it had become the largest sector. The service sector has grown steadily, and became the major contributor to GDP in the 1950s.

The service sector has thus experienced a steady increase in importance in the world economy. Although the significance of the service sector can vary significantly when comparing developed and developing countries, the rise of the service sector can be considered a general trend.

Table 1.1 Contribution of service sector* to GDP in some developed countries, 1970–99 (%)

	Belgium	France	Japan	Netherlands	United Kingdom	Average of developed countries	Average of developed countries: Europe
1970	56	–	47	–	–	53	55
1980	66	64	54	65	–	59	62
1990	69	70	56	68	67	64	68
1999	73	–	–	74	74	71	71

* Service sector defined by the International Standard Industrial Classification: wholesale and retail trade and restaurants and hotels (division 6); transport, storage and communication (division 7); financing, insurance, real estate and business services (division 8); community, social and personal services (division 9).

Source: UNCTAD (2001) *Handbook of Statistics on CD-ROM*; United Nations Conference on trade and development; United Nations, New York and Geneva: UNCTAD, Table 5.3.

Let us take a closer look at the figures, starting with the developed market economies (*see* Table 1.1). Services presently amount to an average of 70 per cent of GDP in these economies.

The situation is slightly different in the formerly Communist countries of Eastern Europe (*see* Table 1.2). In general, the service sector is following the same pattern as in the developed market economies – that is, the relative importance of services is increasing. However, the actual share of the service sector in GDP is still below the level of the developed market economies. In most of these countries, there was agricultural over-population until the 1960s[4] and in some countries, such as Bulgaria and Romania, the agricultural sector is still very large. The main explanation, however, is that during the Communist era more priority was given to the manufacturing sector. Some services were viewed as non-productive, in line with the thinking of Marx and Lenin, or labelled as bourgeois. Only a limited number of service activities was stimulated, notably those that were closely associated with the Socialist view of society – for example, social security, education, science and sports. This approach hampered the development of producer services as well as personal services, which are an important source of growth for the service setor in market economies. This explains why several services, such as financing

Table 1.2 Contribution of service sector* to GDP in some Eastern European countries, 1980–99 (%)

	Bulgaria	Hungary	Poland	Romania
1980	32	34	–	–
1990	31	46	44	30
1999	62	–	65	53

* Definition of service sector as in Table 1.1.

Source: UNCTAD (2001) *Handbook of Statistics on CD-ROM*; United Nations Conference on trade and development; United Nations, New York and Geneva: UNCTAD, Table 5.3.

Table 1.3 Contribution of service sector* to GDP in some developing countries, 1970–99 (%)

	Burundi	China	Egypt	India	Mexico	Average of developing countries
1970	19	24	42	34	55	41
1980	25	21	45	37	57	41
1990	25	31	52	41	64	48
1999	30	33	51	46	67	51

* *See* Table 1.1.

Source: UNCTAD (2001) *Handbook of Statistics on CD-ROM*; United Nations Conference on trade and development; United Nations, New York and Geneva: UNCTAD, Table 5.3.

and insurance, were and still are underrepresented, compared with the developed market economies. The almost total lack of producer services under the former Communist leadership has been cited as one of the main causes of economic stagnation in these countries.[5] With the breakdown of the Communist regimes and the transition towards market economies well underway, we observe a fast increasing contribution by the service sector to these economies, certainly during the last decade of the twentieth century.

The situation in the developing countries is much more varied (*see* Table 1.3). The service sector is also gaining importance here, but the level and pace of gain show some rather marked differences. In some countries, especially in sub-Saharan Africa, the primary sector still dominates the economy. In others, the secondary sector is the largest sector, but the service sector is the strongest. The developing countries have a notable backlog in the area of producer services. Whereas producer services are among the fastest growing segments in developed countries, generating at present some 20 per cent of GDP, the equivalent figure for low-income developing countries is around 5 per cent and not higher than 10 per cent for the higher-income developing countries.[6]

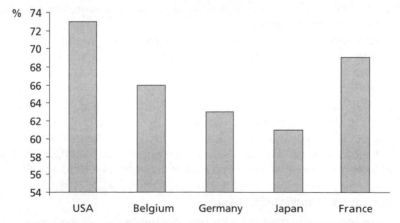

Figure 1.1 Contribution of service sector to employment, 1999 (%)

Source: UNCTAD (2001) *Handbook of Statistics on CD-ROM*; United Nations Conference on trade and development; United Nations, New York and Geneva: UNCTAD, Table 5.4.

This increasing importance of services for our economies is also reflected in the number of people working in the service sector. Figure 1.1 shows the contribution of the service sector to the employment in some developed countries.

Nowadays, over two-thirds of all employment in developed countries is in the service sector. The US also heads the list of the service sector's share in employment, with almost three-quarters of all 1999 employment in the service sector.

The service sector's increasing share of the economy can thus be seen as a universal trend. We have shifted from an industrial society of machine operators to a post-industrial society of service workers.[7] The dominance of the secondary sector has been eclipsed by the rise of the service sector. In the following section we shall take a brief look at factors which may explain this phenomenon.

Driving forces behind the growth of services

It is hard to pinpoint one determining factor in the service sector's growth; rather, a combination of different factors have all played a part in the sector's increasing importance. In general, two groups of factors can be determined.

- Increasing consumer incomes and sociological changes have led to a greater demand for services.
- Increasing professionalism in companies and technological changes have brought about the creation of new services, notably of producer services.

The impact of income changes on buying behaviour

In the nineteenth century, the statistician Ernst Engel observed a phenomenon which is now called *Engel's Law*. When people are poor, they have to allocate all or a large part of their income to the necessities of life – namely, food and shelter. When incomes rise, people spend more on food, but not all of the increase in income is spent on food, since this need can be saturated. As a result, the proportion of total spending on food diminishes as income increases. Instead of spending their extra income on food, people spend it on clothing, recreation, personal care, travel and luxury items. People with higher incomes tend to spend relatively more on services and less on goods.

Disposable incomes have risen in most countries in the last few decades. As a result, the demand for both social and personal services – such as leisure, private health care, hotels and restaurants – has increased. New consumer services, such as fitness services, have been developed in order to satisfy people's needs for services. Such a development can be explained by referring to the well-known Maslow pyramid of needs, where a distinction is made between basic and complementary needs (*see* Figure 1.2). People first seek food and shelter before they can satisfy other needs, such as leisure. If millions of people are unable to fulfil even their most basic needs, services directed at their secondary needs will be hard to sell.

Sociological and demographic changes

Many services once provided by consumers themselves or performed on a voluntary basis are now being outsourced to service providers – for example, food services, laundry services and beauticians.

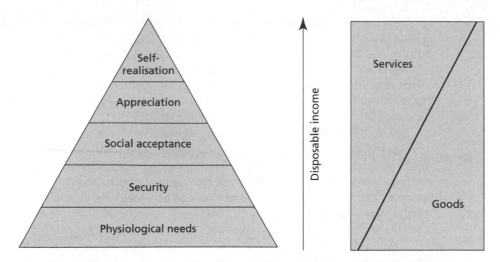

Figure 1.2 Maslow's pyramid of needs and its relationship to disposable income

Source: A. H. Maslow (1987) *Motivation and Personality* (Third Edition). Copyright © 1954, 1987 by Harper & Row, Publishers, Inc. Copyright 1970 by Abraham H. Maslow. Reprinted by permission of Pearson Education Inc., Upper Saddle River, NJ.

The traditional family of a working husband, a housewife and two children is being replaced by the dual-income family. Since such a family has less free time, it has to outsource many activities to service providers. Instead of eating at home or washing the car, the members of the family go to a restaurant or use a carwash. Furthermore, a higher percentage of women in the labour force leads to a greater demand for day-care nurseries and maid services. This phenomenon is sometimes referred to as 'doing each other's laundry'. Instead of you doing your own laundry, you pay someone else to do it and hence contribute to the increasing output of the service sector; basically, the only thing that has changed is a switch in service provider. However, many new services have been created to fulfil the changing needs of the different subgroups in our population. Since these dual-income families have a higher total income, they spend more money on services in line with the reasoning of Engel's Law.

Another trend is the increase in life expectancy, which is leading to a greying population. This has increased the demand for nursing homes, health care services and specialized travel agencies. These services are no longer organized from a voluntary perspective; they have become professional service industries.

Finally, legal advisers and income tax consultants have become necessary due to the increasing complexity of life.[8]

The growing importance of producer services

Growing disposable incomes, as well as changes in behaviour, certainly contribute to the growth of services, but nowadays it is clear that the role played by households is declining in importance.[9]

During the 1960s, social services were the biggest contributor to rising employment in the service sector. These services, mainly provided by the government under the label of state welfare provision, included health care, education and military services. During the 1970s and 1980s, the growth in these services slowed down and producer services became the fastest growing segment.[10] Producer services are the services used in the production process of both goods and services, as opposed to consumer services, which are directed at the final consumers. There has been an increasing demand for these producer services, in both manufacturing and service companies, leading to the creation of many service companies offering these services. Companies hire law firms for their legal counselling, consulting firms for their management problems, and advertising companies for their advertising campaigns. Other examples of producer services are maintenance, data processing, transport, R&D and surveillance. This growth in producer services indicates that services do not replace manufacturing, but rather contribute to the production of value added in manufacturing firms. These services not only facilitate, but also make possible, the goods-producing activities of the manufacturing sector.

However, it should be noted that at least part of the growing contribution of the service sector to our economies can be attributed to a reclassification of jobs. While many manufacturing firms previously executed these jobs themselves, they have now outsourced them to service companies. Therefore, while these jobs were previously considered a contribution to manufacturing output, these same tasks now provided by service firms are counted as a contribution to service output.

Technological developments

Technological progress has also been an important factor, especially in microelectronics and telecommunications. Although advances in information technology are not directly correlated to the rising importance of services, they have certainly made a contribution to the diversification of the services available and towards the creation of new services.[11] Technological development has made possible the creation of whole new service sectors like telecommunications, software development and engineering, to name just a few. This technological-evolution is also continuously affecting the way services are delivered – for instance, in banking, shopping and transportation. New technologies have created economies of scale and scope which have allowed completely new service products to move through established networks or systems with little added cost.[12] The impact of information technology and the use of the Internet are discussed in further detail in Chapter 17.

SERVICES: WHAT MAKES THEM SPECIAL?

Producing a definition of services is not an easy task. Several scholars have tried to define the notion. For example, you can define services by saying what they are not, as attempted by Quinn and Gagnon:

> 'Services are actually all those economic activities in which the primary output is neither a product nor a construction.'[13]

As defined by Kotler, a more positive and more substantive definition of services could be:

'Any activity or benefit that one party can offer to another that is essentially intangible and does not result in the ownership of anything.'[14]

This definition suggests that services centre around intangibility. There is more to it, however, as the following, more extensive definition by Grönroos suggests:

'A service is an activity or series of activities of a more or less intangible nature that normally, but not necessarily, take place in interactions between the customer and service employees and/or physical resources or goods and/or systems of the service provider, which are provided as solutions to customer problems.'[15]

A careful reading of this definition reveals that services are activities or processes characterized by two central notions: *intangibility* and *simultaneity*.

- *Intangibility* simply means that the result of a service transaction is not a transfer of ownership, as in the case of physical goods. A service is a process or an act.
- *Simultaneity* means that the realization of a service implies the presence of provider as well as customer; both play an active role in the realization of services. Production and consumption are intertwined and services come into being in the simultaneous interaction between consumer and provider.

Services can thus be defined as:

'all those economic activities that are intangible and imply an interaction to be realised between service provider and consumer.'

Both intangibility and simultaneity imply further characteristics:

- Intangibility implies *perishability*. Services cannot be kept in stock like goods. It is not possible to produce services at one moment in time, store them, and take them from the shelf to sell when appropriate, as it is with goods.
- Simultaneity implies *heterogeneity*. The fact that both provider and customer need to interact at a certain point within the service delivery process, opens up possibilities for variation. Customers, service providers, the surroundings and even the moment of interaction are all sources of variation; consequently, service delivery processes will tend to be characterized by increased heterogeneity.

Table 1.4 illustrates some of the differences between services and goods.

Table 1.4 Differences between services and goods

Services	Goods
■ An activity or process	■ A physical object
■ Intangible	■ Tangible
■ Simultaneous production and consumption: customers participate in production	■ Separation of production and consumption
■ Heterogeneous	■ Homogeneous
■ Perishable: cannot be kept in stock	■ Can be kept in stock

A CLOSER LOOK AT SERVICES

Intangibility

In the literature on the differences between goods and services, the intangibility of services is the characteristic most frequently cited. While goods are produced, services are performed. A service is an act or a deed that we cannot take home with us. What we can take home is the effect of the service. When you go to a cinema, you cannot take home the service you receive, but you should be relaxed or impressed by the experience. As a result, there is no transfer of ownership involved in the delivery of services as opposed to goods.

> 'Services by their very nature are physically intangible; they cannot be touched, tasted, smelt or seen. This contrasts with the physical substance or tangibility of goods. In addition to their physical intangibility, services can also be difficult for the mind to grasp and thus can be mentally intangible.'[16]

Of course, not all services show the same degree of intangibility; few services are 100 per cent intangible, just as few goods are 100 per cent tangible. Instead, many offerings[17] – both goods and services – have both tangible and intangible elements. They can be placed on a continuum ranging from low to high intangibility. In a fast-food restaurant, for instance, the tangible component of the offering – the food – plays an important role. In a three-star restaurant, on the other hand, the more intangible factors such as the behaviour of employees, the atmosphere and the image might be equally important. Services can also imply 'facilitating goods', i.e. tangible elements that embody the service offered, as in the case of car rental. Leasing companies offer financial services; however, these are linked inherently to physical goods, namely cars. The same is true for textbooks that support educational services.

What are the implications of this intangibility?

The intangibility of services makes products difficult, and sometimes impossible, to evaluate before and sometimes even after purchase. How can a customer try out an offering before it is purchased if it cannot be seen, heard, felt, smelt or tasted? Zeithaml[18] has developed a framework to clarify this issue. She distinguishes between three categories of qualities related to offerings:

1. *Search qualities* – attributes which a consumer can determine prior to purchase. Thus, search qualities include attributes such as colour, price, feel and smell. You can smell perfume or you can evaluate the colour or style of clothes and the decision as to which perfume or what clothes to buy is based on these qualities.
2. *Experience qualities* – attributes such as taste and wearability which can only be discerned after purchase or during consumption. Hairdressing services clearly fall into this category. You cannot evaluate the quality of a haircut before the hair has been cut. However, once your hair has been cut, you can decide whether you like it or not.
3. *Credence qualities* – attributes which the consumer may find impossible to evaluate even after purchase and consumption. When you pick up your car at the garage, do you have the skills to evaluate whether your brakes are properly aligned? The difference between credence and experience qualities is subjective. If you know a lot about cars, you will have no difficulties in evaluating the brake

alignment of your car. It then becomes an experience quality. However, most people do not have the skills to evaluate that service and thus it becomes a credence quality.

The intangibility of services means that experience and credence qualities will tend to dominate, whereas search qualities dominate in the choice of tangible products (*see* Figure 1.3). Clothes and cars can be evaluated and even tried out before being purchased. However, in many services, especially those provided by professionals and specialists, credence qualities dominate. Most customers do not possess the required skills to evaluate whether a doctor's medical diagnosis is correct or not.

The domination of credence qualities has serious implications, especially in terms of the marketing of services. Since customers cannot evaluate a service before consuming it, it is important to provide clues as to what can be expected during the service delivery process so that customers can make some kind of pre-purchase evaluation of the service. As a marketing strategist, you have to give credible proof of the competitiveness of your product; you face the challenges of '*making tangible the intangible*' to facilitate the evaluation process for the customer.[19] Consider, for instance, 'dress codes' used within consulting firms, which tend to induce an impression of seriousness, professionalism and technical expertise – that is, characteristics that are inherently linked to the nature of the service they are offering.

It should be noted that 'making the intangible tangible' is often quite the opposite strategy to that of a manufacturer of a good. Here, the intangible aspect of the offering tends to be stressed in the communication with the customer. As Rushton and Carlzon observe:

> '*Because at the centre of a tangible product there is something solid, something 'real', it seems that both customers and marketers are able to move to the realms of intangibility when it comes to identifying and assessing what the product can deliver.*'[20]

Many car manufacturers do this in their advertising campaigns, as shown by slogans such as BMW's 'freude am fahren', Smart's 'reduce to the max' or Volvo's 'the thinking man's car'.

Striking a balance between tangibility and intangibility is not simply a question of communication, however; it is also an issue of strategic importance. This will become clear when we discuss the notion of *servitization* – that is, the

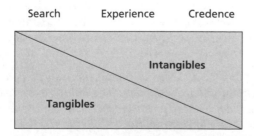

Search   Experience   Credence

Figure 1.3 The different kinds of qualities and their importance for tangible and intangible products

practice whereby manufacturing firms extend their offerings by including services. Service companies may go in the opposite direction. By including tangible components in their offering, they try to overcome the limitations of 'selling capacity'. This idea is explored further in the discussion on service strategy (*see* Chapter 21).

Simultaneity

A second common characteristic of services is the simultaneity of production and consumption. Whereas goods are produced first and then consumed, services are produced and consumed at the same time. The customer takes part in the production process and consumes the service as it is being produced. For example, when attending a lecture, the student listens and learns (i.e. consumes the service at the same time as the lecturer gives the lecture). The pilot flies a plane at the same time as the passenger is transported. While the movie is being shown, the audience is watching it. It should be stressed, however, that the degree of overlap can vary significantly from service to service, ranging from a small degree of overlap in a bank or a car repair shop to a high degree of overlap in a hospital or a smart restaurant. The at least partial overlap between production and consumption means that there is personal contact during the service delivery process: service employee and customer interact during the service delivery process. This is not necessarily the case with goods, since goods can be produced and consumed separately. This makes the human factor in services crucial.

Therefore, careful attention must be paid to the employees dealing with the customer. They represent the company providing the service and the customer will identify their actions and behaviour with the company. For certain services (for instance, entertainment and professional services), customers not only expect a high quality service, but are also interested in the person providing the service. Customers want to be serviced by a certain top accountant, chef or top professor; they do not want 'just anyone' to perform these services.

At the same time, in some cases, the customer must be just as 'educated' as the employee. How well certain services are performed depends not only on the performance of the service provider, but also on the ability of the customer to specify or perform his or her own part of the service. If a tax consultant does not receive the right information from the client, or if a customer is unable to specify clearly which haircut he or she desires, there could be disappointment with the outcome.

Where production and consumption occur simultaneously, clearly the customer has to be present at the place where the service is provided. This means that the service provider has to make the service accessible to the customer. Services are therefore '*place dependent*' and not all services can simply be 'traded'. As Bateson states:

> 'There is little point in McDonald's deciding to follow the lead of Ford or Procter & Gamble and build a huge, capital-intensive factory. The ability to produce one billion hamburgers a year in Michigan does not help consumers elsewhere in the world who are waiting for their food. Instead, place of consumption is important.'[21]

Service companies will thus require their own type of internationalization strategies. This is an issue we shall explore in Chapter 20.

Heterogeneity

Heterogeneity is related to the potential of variability in the performance of services. As already explained, services are processes implying simultaneity and, therefore, they bear a larger risk of being different depending on circumstances such as the employee involved, the particular customer, the physical setting or even the hour of the day.

Where does this heterogeneity come from? In general, there are three possible sources:

1. *The service provider.* Most services involve an (inter-)active role on the part of service employees. Humans are not robots, able to repeat consistently the same action day in and day out without error. Therefore, a first source of heterogeneity is the service employee involved in the service delivery process. Humans, consciously or unconsciously, vary their actions and sometimes make mistakes. People can be moody, which may lead them to treat the customer in a less friendly way. As a result, the outcome of the service delivery process is more susceptible to variation than in the case of goods, as evidenced in the following remark by an airline manager:

   'Two cabin crews can go through the same motions, do the same tasks, and yet the service given can be worlds apart. So much depends on how they do the things they do – what mood they're in – and that we just can't control, we can only try to influence.'[22]

2. *The customer.* The state of mind or the personal situation of the customer strongly influences his or her behaviour, as well as his or her perception of the service. As a result, each customer will experience the service rendered differently. In addition, it should be mentioned that a particular customer will be influenced by the presence and behaviour of other customers.
3. *The surroundings.* Several external factors may influence the customer's perception of the service – for example, whether you visit Disneyland on a rainy day or on a sunny day; whether there is a long or a short queue in the bank; or whether or not there is a lot of turbulence on a flight. These are all factors that will make a big difference to the customer. However, the problem is that many of these factors are difficult, if not impossible, for the service provider to control.

This heterogeneity of services creates one of the major problems in service management – that is, 'how to maintain an evenly perceived quality of the services produced and rendered to the customer'.[23] Even with a highly standardized service product, such as a McDonald's cheeseburger, variability will occur. The complexity of the service does not allow for control of all the process parameters, to ensure a consistent, high quality output. Even if the same ingredients and the same process parameters, such as time and temperature, are used all over the world, the McDonald's service in Paris might be experienced as different from that in London, Tokyo or New York, simply because the context is different in terms of type of customers, neighbourhood, social acceptance, etc. The fact that the outcome of the service delivery process is variable creates uncertainty and higher risk for the customer who wants to purchase a service. How, therefore, can a company make sure that it delivers consistently high quality services to its customers?

One option is to increase the quality control, just as manufacturing companies do, in order to detect 'bad service' and prevent it from reaching the customer. This can be done by performing a quality check when the service is produced but before it is delivered to the customer. Obviously, this is not as easy for services as it is for goods. First, service output is essentially intangible so what should be checked? Second, production and consumption of the service occur simultaneously, making it difficult to check the quality of the produced service before it is consumed. Bad quality can therefore in most cases not be detected and prevented before the customer 'consumes' the service.

Better planning of the service encounter – that is, the moment of interaction between service provider and customer – could reduce the degree of variability. Training employees to interact with the customer, to behave consistently and to deal with new situations can improve the homogeneity of their actions. Adopting uniform production procedures is also common practice in this regard. This means incorporating the principles and techniques of manufacturing firms into service organizations. The success of McDonald's, for example, can be attributed to a large degree to this approach.[24]

The downside of this industrial approach, however, is the lack of personalization of the service offering. Customers receive a standardized package, which is not always exactly what they would like to have. An alternative to reducing heterogeneity can lie in developing strategies that build on this inherent heterogeneity and making it into a strength. At most pizza chains, every customer is able to choose his or her own toppings. By providing their services in such a way, the heterogeneity of customer preferences is taken as a starting point, and the service delivery system is designed to cope with this variety of preferences.

Heterogeneity, then, has wide-ranging implications for the operational side of the service delivery system. Things become even more complicated when one realizes that services are also perishable.

Perishability

Unlike goods, services cannot be stored. This is not only due to their intangibility, but also due to the limitations of simultaneous production and consumption. Once a service has been produced, it has to be consumed, otherwise it is of no use. If a plane leaves the ground with empty seats, the sales are lost forever. They cannot be inventoried and sold the next day. Empty seats are of no value. The same applies to restaurants with empty tables, service maintenance engineers with no machines to maintain, or hairdressers with no clients. As Lovelock states:

> '. . . unused capacity in a service organisation is rather like a running tap in a sink with no plug: the flow is wasted unless customers (or possessions requiring servicing) are present to receive it.'[25]

If the demand for these services were constant, there would be no problem. If the number of passengers an airline had to fly from New York to Paris were 150 a day, every day, airlines would build planes with exactly 150 seats and there would be no empty seats. Of course, we do not live in a world where demand is constant. On the contrary, demand for most services is rather volatile and cannot always be predicted. In restaurants, peaks of demand occur at noon and in the evening; for public transportation services, peaks are just before and after office hours; the first frost is a peak for plumbers. The fact that services cannot be stored makes the volatility of demand a bigger problem for service producers than for goods producers. When demand is lower than production, goods can be stored. If demand is higher than production, the accumulated stock of goods can be sold to accommodate the surplus in demand. Thus, stock can be used as a buffer to demand variability. This is not the case for services.

Managing supply and demand in services is therefore dependent on capacity management, as we shall see in Chapter 15.

THE ROLE OF SERVICE CLASSIFICATIONS

Services are different from goods: intangibility and simultaneity imply heterogeneity and perishability. These elements pose specific challenges for the management of the service delivery process. Commercial policies, service employees and operational issues are all affected by these characteristics. However, not all services are alike. The management of a hairdressing salon will be different from the management of a consulting firm, just as the management of a fast-food restaurant will be different from that of a bank. Therefore, before developing a guiding framework to look at the managerial consequences of the different service characteristics, we need to refine our insights into services.

Service classifications are very helpful in this regard. There is a plethora of classification schemes depending on the particular combination of different dimensions. However, the relevance of certain dimensions will vary depending on the question asked. If, for example, the nature of skills required for customer-contact personnel is being considered, it will be more relevant to take into account dimensions that address the nature of the interaction between customer and front-line employees than to focus only on the degree of intangibility. When examining the impact of information technology on the service delivery process, it is necessary to look more at the character of the different exchange moments and less, for instance, at the fluctuations of demand over time.

In Exhibit 1.1, we have listed a number of dimensions that can be used to generate useful insights.

Exhibit 1.1

Methods of classifying services

Degree of intangibility
This dimension has already been discussed extensively. All services can be placed on a continuum ranging from low to high intangibility. The higher the intangibility, the more difficulties customers experience when evaluating the offering. Intangibility also poses problems for the operating system since intangible things cannot be stored. Intangible things are also difficult to standardize, making their quality much more dependent on the employee providing that particular service.

Degree of customer contact required
One of the characteristics of high-contact service organizations is the fact that demand for the service is often instantaneous and cannot be stored, and that a flaw in the service operating system will have an immediate, direct effect on the customer.[26] The interaction between the employee and the customer means that the service employees have to be both competent and communicative. Therefore, it becomes even more important to select and train employees that fit these criteria in order to perform their jobs well as front-office employees.

Exhibit 1.1 continued

Degree of simultaneity
This is not necessarily the same as the previous dimension. Production and consumption can occur simultaneously without the customer being present. Home-banking or phone-banking, for instance, allow the customer to consume the service without face-to-face contact with the service provider. Consequences of this dimension were discussed earlier in this chapter.

Degree of heterogeneity
Both the employee and the customer are a source of heterogeneity. As a result, there will be more heterogeneity in high customer contact organizations. Standardizing the operating system might be a way to reduce this heterogeneity.

Degree of perishability
This dimension is of course closely related to the degree of intangibility and the degree of simultaneity. The lower the goods component in the offering and the more consumption and production overlap, the higher the degree of perishability. As a consequence, these offerings cannot be stored. Managing the operation system by means of capacity management thus becomes more complex. Capacity management itself will influence both the employees and the customers. For example, capacity management approaches might be aimed at shortening waiting times for customers, but at the same time cause employees to adopt a more flexible approach.

Degree of demand fluctuation over time[27]
This dimension is related to the previous point. The more demand fluctuates, the more capacity management becomes important. In restaurants and hotels, for instance, this problem is more acute than it is in banks and insurance companies.

Degree of service customization[28]
Unlike goods, which are mostly purchased 'off the shelf', services can be much more customized. This is especially true when there is a high degree of overlap between production and consumption. The service provider can tailor the service to the needs of the customer. Professional services, hospitals and upmarket restaurants are examples of services where there is a high degree of customization. This certainly demands different employee competencies as opposed to more standardized services.

Degree of labour intensity[29]
Service businesses differ in their labour intensity. Communications companies, amusement and recreation companies, hospitals and transport companies are all examples of low or moderate labour-intensive companies. For instance, despite the fact that hospitals have many employees, there is a great deal of very expensive equipment present, thus increasing the capital intensity. Professional services and personal services represent the opposite end of the spectrum, having a high labour intensity. According to the labour intensity of a business, different challenges will arise. Managers in low labour-intensive service businesses have to think of capital decisions, technological advances and capacity management. Human resource management, including training, hiring, and rewarding, is a top priority in the management of high labour-intensive businesses.

Service direction: towards people or equipment[30]
Personal services, hotels, restaurants and schools are services where the recipients of the service are people, while freight transportation, accounting, and laundry services are aimed at tangible objects or intangible items. The management consequences of this include, for instance, the fact that people-oriented services require the presence of the customer and as a result employees need to have different skills.

Classification schemes should be relevant in practice, there is no point in making them just for the sake of segmenting the service sector into neat categories. Rather, classification schemes should generate insights that inspire managerial action. We will now take a closer look at some specific classification schemes.

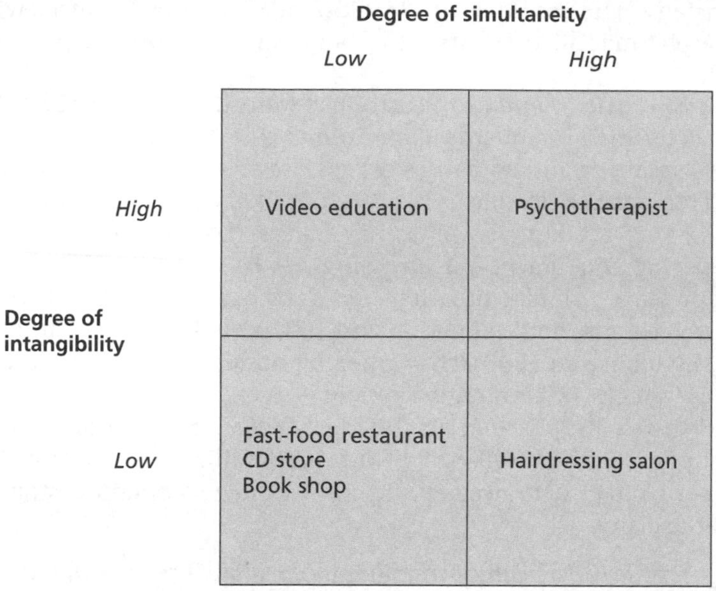

Degree of simultaneity

Low   High

Figure 1.4 **Service classifications based on intangibility and simultaneity**

Intangibility and simultaneity

A first and obvious classification is based on the dimensions of intangibility and simultaneity as these figure dominantly within our definition of a service (*see* Figure 1.4).

In the upper right-hand corner of the matrix are the pure services – that is, those customized services with a high degree of intangibility and a high degree of simultaneity. Typical labour-intensive services such as professional services fall into this category. In the bottom left-hand corner, we find the more tangible services. The boundaries between the latter category and goods become blurred sometimes, as in the case of CDs and books.

What does this classification teach us? As intangibility increases, marketing strategy might change – from stressing the intangible components to stressing the tangible components, for example. When simultaneity increases, there is greater interaction between consumer and service provider, leading to different skill requirements. Employees have to be competent and their attitude towards the customer also becomes important. They must possess good communication skills. This classification scheme can also be used to distinguish between different internationalization strategies for service firms,[31] as we will see when looking at internationalization strategies in Chapter 20.

Maister's framework: combining the degree of contact with the degree of customization

Although Maister has developed this framework specifically for professional service firms, it has a wider validity among different sorts of services firms. Here the degree of contact with the customer and customization of the process are used as dimensions. The result is the traditional two-by-two matrix with four situations: the pharmacist, the nurse, the brain surgeon and the psychotherapist (*see* Figure 1.5).[32]

In the case of the '*pharmacist*', customers want the service to be delivered according to strict technical standards at a minimal cost. Conformance to specifications is important, resulting in standardized processes with a limited degree of customer contact. Think of the retail activities of your bank: you want to be informed about the state of your account as well as having easy access to money, when necessary, without paying too much – if anything at all. Going to the pharmacist for an aspirin represents a similar situation: the client wants to buy well-established products and procedures, not innovation and creativity. It is clear that for these types of services, the industrial approach – whereby one relies on procedures, systems and technology – might be eminently suitable.

'*Nurses*' share with pharmacists the high degree of standardization that this category implies in terms of well-established and familiar services. However, the degree of customer contact here needs to be considerable to obtain customer satisfaction. As Maister explains:

> '. . . the nurse delivers relatively familiar (or "mature") services that do not require high levels of innovation. However, it differs from the pharmacist practice in that the emphasis is not only on the ability to make the pill (which still may be required), but also on the ability to counsel and guide. The client wants to be nurtured and nursed: "Help me understand what is going on; explain to me what you're doing and why; involve me in the decision making; help me understand my options. Be with me and interact with me throughout the process, until this is all over. I need a front-room advisor, not a back-room technician."'

	Standardized process (*Execution*)	Customized process (*Diagnosis*)
High degree of client contact. Value is rendered in the 'front room', i.e. during interaction with the client	**NURSE** **Key skill:** making client experience comfortable and user-friendy in going through pre-set process	**PSYCHOTHERAPIST** **Key skill:** real time diagnosis of complex, ill-specified problems
Low degree of client contact. Value is rendered in the professional's 'back room'. Client focus is on results only	**PHARMACIST** **Key skill:** supervision of low-cost delivery team	**BRAIN SURGEON** **Key skill:** creative, innovative solutions to one-of-a-kind problems

Figure 1.5 Maister's framework of service classification

It is crucial to pay enough attention to the moment of interaction for these services. Nurses are the example *par excellence* here, although some hospitals tend to forget this in attempts to cut down on personnel costs. As a patient, however, minimal, industrial treatment is often not appreciated, although it might be viable from a purely medical point of view.

The *'brain surgeon'* situation is characterized on the one hand by a high degree of customization, creativity and even innovation, but on the other hand involves rather low levels of customer interaction. Professional services like tax specialists, lawyers or doctors might fall into this category; as a service provider you offer the skills to solve the customer's complex problem. The customer, unaware of the technicalities of the service delivery process, does not engage in the technical processes to obtain the solution; he or she just wants you to deliver it. Professional technical skills, creativity and being at the frontiers of development are crucial here.

Finally, the *'psychotherapist'* combines these professional skills with a high degree of customer interaction; in this case one is faced with problems whereby the customer wants to be – and even must be – involved in the process to come to solutions. There is no use in paying a psychotherapist without also engaging in the process. The same applies to some consulting services – for example, when it is necessary to work with a management team to ascertain what can be done to get the company back on track.

So this framework starts to give us an idea about what might be important for managing services depending on what kind of service provider you want to be.[33] The nature of the interaction with the customers plays a crucial role. Before we develop a more systematic framework to look at managerial action, we will therefore discuss a last service classification scheme, based on the differences that might occur in terms of the nature and intensity of contact between customers and service providers.

The work of Mills and Margulies: focusing on the nature and intensity of contact

We have already identified simultaneity or interaction between the customer and the service delivery system as a dimension which characterizes and classifies services. However, there can be tremendous differences in the nature or intensity of interactions of particular services. If you go to a bank to withdraw money, the interaction is quite different from the interaction with your architect, which in its turn is different from the interaction with your psychotherapist. These differences have led Mills and Margulies[34] to develop a classification scheme around three basic types of interaction: maintenance-interactive, task-interactive and personal-interactive services.

Let us take a closer look at how Mills and Margulies define these different types of interactions.

Maintenance-interactive services

When you withdraw money from your account at the bank, the direct interaction between the employee and yourself as a customer is short and rather standardized. The interaction is basically a cosmetic one because it often goes no further than polite social niceties and gestures. Convenience or comfort is the main concern in this type of interaction. The amount of information transmitted between service employee and customer is often limited. The importance of the information input by the customer into the production function – as it pertains to the completion of the employee's task – is considerable, because the customer knows just what is desired. The employee in a maintenance-type organization tends to make few judgements and those that are made are generally of a simple nature. This is why the employee decision unit is capable of providing services for a relatively large number of customers. The direct interface between the employee and the customer allows widespread interchangeability of activities – that is, it is not necessary to have one employee serve the same customer repeatedly.[35] The pharmacist category of Maister's framework is clearly connected with this type of interaction.

Task-interactive services

In task-interactive services – for instance, interaction with an architect – there is uncertainty in the transaction. By uncertainty, we mean that customers are generally less precise, not about *what* they need, but *how* to obtain or accomplish it. To a very significant extent, the interaction revolves around the task to be performed. The client has no knowledge of the techniques required to provide adequate answers to the questions posed. Such techniques are almost exclusively in the domain of the service provider.

Generally, the information provided by the customer is not critical, a fact that reflects the client's relatively low level of awareness of the problem at hand. The duration of the relationship is generally relatively long, because the flow of information is extensive. The interaction is usually intensive, yet there is an expected termination of the relationship – for example, an engineering firm will give an estimate of the time required for a task. The decisions made by the employee are complex and sometimes require novel solutions to unusual and even unique problems.

In the task-interactive service firm, the client is perceived as being in a dependent position. This power disparity exists because the employee controls more information relative to the client. The relationship is intense and there is usually little substitutability of employees in the interaction as the extensive technical process implies switching costs. The similarities between this and the brain surgeon category, as defined by Maister, are clear.

Personal-interactive services

In personal-interactive services – for example, the case of the psychotherapist – there is not only uncertainty, but also ambiguity. Ambiguity means that one is not only looking for answers but that even the relevant questions seem unclear. The employees in these situations provide a personal service to clients/customers, who are typically unaware or imprecise about both what will best serve their interest and how to go about remedying a situation. A client with an emotional problem may seek help from an organization providing counselling, but may be unaware of the extent of the problem. Based on this information, customer and service provider engage in a process which involves tackling the ambiguity. Within this process the skills of the service provider are crucial; however, besides the technical expertise required like in the case of task-interactive services, in personal-interactive services, personal and social skills and competencies are equally crucial.

Given the complex nature of this type of interaction, the professional service provider tends to dominate during the interaction. This is evident in teacher–student and counsellor–patient relationships. The client/customer is in a subordinate role and the interaction is usually a personal one. The information provided by the client is often of a confidential nature, and it is unusual for employee substitution to take place in these organizations after a relationship between the employee and client has been established.[36]

The personal-interactive service firm is the most dynamic of the service organizations – dynamic in the sense that each task and even each episode requires novel solutions, with the decisions of employees tending to be complete and judgemental. The employee operates with considerable autonomy. Standards and guidelines are difficult to establish in this setting.

It is becoming clear that different types of services might imply different forms of management. Furthermore, within the same type of services, different approaches are possible: as a consultant you can position yourself as a technical expert (task-interactive) or as an integrated problem solution provider (personal-interactive). Such a choice will affect the way you have to design the components of your service organization, as will become clear in the next chapter and the remainder of this book.

CONCLUSION

Services are undeniably different from manufactured products or 'goods', as we like to call them. The distinguishing factors are the intangibility and the simultaneity of production and consumption. When managing service firms, these characteristics should be kept in mind.

We have seen how these characteristics have an impact on such marketing issues as promotion, product positioning and customer interaction. Similarly, these characteristics have clear operational and technological implications, more specifically in areas such as capacity management, process development, and facilities management. Likewise the relevancy of HR practices will be dependent on the characteristics of the service delivery system. In this chapter we also touched upon some strategy implications such as growth, internationalization and focus. These issues will be developed in more depth in the following chapters.

It should also be remembered that not all services are alike. There are various dimensions which distinguish different kinds of services and on which classification schemes can be based. Such schemes are only useful insofar as they give additional insights into how to manage these various types of firms.

The fact that services are different from manufactured goods does not mean that is always easy to distinguish manufacturing firms from service firms. We see manufacturing firms adding more and more service components to their product offerings. We will discuss this phenomenon in Chapter 3.

Review and discussion questions

- Discuss the following extract on the relative importance of manufacturing and services to economies.

  'The relative importance of manufacturing and services to economies, and the inter-relationship between the two have been the subject of much discussion through the years. Some have urged that the decline in manufacturing and the corresponding shift to services is unsupportable in the long run, since services depend critically on manufacturing for their existence. In the absence of manufacturing, service sectors are seen as collapsing. On the other hand, a forceful case was made at the Forum that services have become a major driving force in economic growth. Rather than services following and supporting manufacturing, manufacturing is seen as flowing to those countries and areas where the services infrastructure is efficient and well developed.'

  (*Source:* OECD, 2000)

- Based on the work of Mills and Margulies, discuss how the distinction between maintenance-interactive, task-interactive and personal-interactive services leads to influential approaches in services management (in terms of operations, marketing as HRM).

Notes and references

1 An overview of this classification can be found in Browning and Singlemann (1978).

2 Smith, A. (1776) *The Wealth of Nations*. Reprinted 1991. Loughton, Essex: Prometheus Books.

3 Marshall, A. (1920) *Principles of Economics*. Reprinted 1997. Loughton, Essex: Prometheus Books.

4 Caselli, G. P. and Pastrello, G. (1992) 'The service sector in planned economies of Eastern Europe: past experiences and future perspectives', *The Service Industries Journal*, Vol 12, No 2, Apr.

5 Illeris, S. and Philippe, J. (1993) 'The role of services in regional economic growth', *The Service Industries Journal*, Vol 13, No 2, Apr, 3–10.

6 Daniels, P. W. (1993) *Services Industries in the World Economy*. Oxford: Blackwell Publishers.

7 Hishorn, L. (1988) 'The post-industrial economy: Labour, skills and the new mode of production', *The Service Industries Journal*, Vol 8, No 1, Jan, 19–38.

8 Schoel, W. F. and Ivy, J. T. (1981) *Marketing: Contemporary concepts and practices*. Boston, MA: Allyn and Bacon.

9 Caselli, G. P. and Pastrello, G. (1992), op. cit.

10 Elfring, T. (1989) 'The main features and underlying causes of the shift to services', *The Service Industries Journal*, Vol 9, No 3, July, 337–56.

11 Daniels, P. W. (1993), op. cit.

12 Quinn, J. B. and Cagnon, C. E. (1986) 'Will services follow manufacturing into decline?', *Harvard Business Review*, Nov–Dec, 95–103.

13 Ibid.

14 Kotler, P. (1997) *Marketing Management: Analysis, planning, implementation and control.* Englewood Cliffs, NJ: Prentice-Hall.

15 Grönroos, C. (1990) *Service Management and Marketing: Managing the moments of truth in service competition.* Lexington: Lexington Books, p. 27.

16 Bateson, J. E. G. (1977) 'Do we need service marketing?', in Eiglier, P., Langeard, E., Lovelock, C. and Bateson, J. (eds) *Marketing Services: New insights.* Cambridge: Marketing Science Institute.

17 The word 'offering' is used here instead of 'product' to stress the difference between this and goods. In the remainder of the book we shall use the word 'product' to refer to services and goods.

18 Zeithaml, V. A. (1981) 'How consumer evaluation processes differ between goods and services', in Donnelly, J. H. and George, W. R. (eds) *Marketing of Services.* Chicago: American Marketing Association, pp. 186–90.

19 Levitt, T. (1981) 'Marketing intangible products and product intangibles', *Harvard Business Review*, May–June.

20 Rushton, A. M. and Carson, D. J. (1985) 'The marketing of services: managing the intangibles', *European Journal of Marketing*, Vol 19, No 3, 19–40.

21 Bateson, J. E. G. (1989) *Managing Services Marketing.* Orlando: The Dryden Press.

22 Rushton, A. M. and Carson, D. J. (1985), op. cit., p. 37.

23 Grönroos, C. (1990), op. cit., p. 30.

24 Interested readers are referred here to the work of Levitt who pioneered this approach in the 1970s and is still worth reading. *See* Levitt, T. (1972) 'Production-line approach to service', *Harvard Business Review*, Sept–Oct, 41–52 and Levitt, T. (1976) 'The industrialisation of service', *Harvard Business Review*, Sept–Oct, 63–74.

25 Lovelock, C. (1981) 'Why marketing management needs to be different for services', in Donnelly, J. H. and George, W. R. (eds) *Marketing of Services.* Chicago: American Marketing Association, p. 5.

26 Chase, R. B. (1981) 'The customer contact approach to services: theoretical bases and practical extensions', *Operations Research*, Vol 29, No 4, 698–706.

27 Lovelock, C. (1988) *Managing Services: Marketing, operations and human resources.* Englewood Cliffs, NJ: Prentice-Hall.

28 Haywood-Farmer, J. (1988) 'A conceptual model of service quality', *International Journal of Production and Operations Management*, Vol 8, No 6, 19–29.

29 Schmenner, R. W. (1986) 'How can service businesses survive and prosper?', in Lovelock, C. (ed.) *Managing Services: Marketing, operations and human resources.* Englewood Cliffs, NJ: Prentice-Hall, pp. 25–36.

30 Thomas, D. R. E. (1978) 'Strategy is different in service businesses', *Harvard Business Review*, July–Aug, 158–65.

31 Vandermerwe, S. and Chadwick, M. (1989) 'The internationalisation of services', *The Service Industries Journal*, Vol 9, No 1, 79–93.

32 Maister, D. H. (1996) *What Kind of Provider Are You?* Boston, MA: Maister Associates, Inc.

33 It should be clear that Maister's typology does not define specific services but rather different market segments.

34 Mills, P. K. and Margulies, N. (1980) 'Towards a core typology of service organisations', *Academy of Management Review*, Vol 5, No 2, 255–65.

35 Ibid. p. 263.

36 Ibid. pp. 263–4.

Suggested further reading

Edgett, S. and Parkinson, S. (1993) 'Marketing for service industries – a review', *The Service Industries Journal*, Vol 13, No 2, 19–39. This article gives a detailed review of the literature on the characteristics of services. It focuses on the four main characteristics – intangibility, simultaneity, heterogeneity and perishability. Each characteristic is explained in depth and implications for service management are discussed.

Kingman-Brundage, J., George, W. R. and Bowen, D. E. (1995) 'Service Logic: achieving service system integration', *International Journal of Service Industry Management*, Vol 6, No 4, 20–39. This article advances the multi-dimensional nature of service management. The service logic model provides a common language for a cross-functional discussion of service issues, by using the three management functions active in the creation and delivery of services: marketing, operations and human resources. Decisions taken in one domain cannot be considered in isolation from the other domains.

Levitt, T. (1972) 'Production-line approach to service', *Harvard Business Review*, Sept–Oct, 41–52. Service companies can learn a lot from manufacturing companies. If companies could stop thinking of service as servitude and personal administration, they would be able to improve its quality and efficiency drastically.

Lovelock, C. (1988) *Managing Services: Marketing, operations and human resources*. Englewood Cliffs, NJ: Prentice-Hall. This excellent book on service management devotes a chapter to service classifications. Besides explaining a number of classifications in detail, it also contains a literature review on service classifications.

Maister, D. (1997) *True Professionalism*. New York: The Free Press. An excellent discussion of the service concept and its managerial consequences for different types of services.

CHAPTER 2

Defining the service concept

Paul Gemmel · Bart Van Looy · Gino Van Ossel

INTRODUCTION

Martin Vanderbilt was enjoying a cool beer and the summer evening breeze on the terrace of his small cottage in the Ardennes. It had looked like a ruin when he bought it only a year before, but over the last couple of months he had spent every weekend turning it into a small holiday home. To save money, he had done most of the work himself, even though he had never been much of a do-it-yourself expert.

Now that the work was finished, he was reminiscing. There had been several evenings in January when he had visited the interior decorating shop to learn about all the different painting techniques. The staff had custom-mixed the paint to achieve precisely the colour he wanted.

Then there had been the bet with his colleague, Michael, who had talked him into installing the bathroom himself. His friend's belief that he would never be able to pull off the job had cost him a bottle of champagne. To his surprise, the people in the do-it-yourself shop had been extremely helpful. The book they had sold him, Plumbing for Dummies, had come in very handy.

The actual work had really started when he borrowed his cousin's van over the Easter weekend. In one day he made five round trips to an elegant-looking, yet relatively large discount store, loading the van with large amounts of building material. The dinner he had bought his cousin, in return for the use of the van, was paid for with the money he had saved that day.

Finally, there was the small shop down the road. It was definitely not cheap, but nonetheless he had become one of its best customers. Time and again he had discovered that he had forgotten to buy a particular type of screw or that he had run out of sandpaper and, to waste as little time as possible, he had rushed over to the small shop.

In Chapter 1 we discussed how services are processes and as a result are less tangible than physical goods. Nevertheless, service firms have to sell their products. They need therefore to make clear what the characteristics of the service offering are.

In this chapter we shall argue that, to be successful, a service firm needs to develop a service concept that is as focused as possible. The need for focus is a consequence of another crucial characteristic of services, namely heterogeneity. The variety of customers makes it impossible to create one shop which satisfies everyone's needs, as will become clear in this chapter.

Objectives

By the end of this chapter, you should be able to discuss:

- why service firms need a service concept
- how service firms define a service concept
- how service firms implement a service concept and the three steps that make up the implementation process

WHY DO WE NEED A SERVICE CONCEPT?

Somebody once defined a service as a 'product in the making'. This refers in particular to a service as an experience or a process. In service delivery there is no marked point at which a transaction of ownership of the product takes place. There is no clear end product on which all attention is focused. As with all products, services address a range of different customer needs.

As a result, any product should be defined in terms of customer needs. With tangible products these needs are translated into specific (technical) characteristics and product specifications. Once defined, product development, production and even marketing all focus on these characteristics and specifications. With services, such a natural central and focal point does not exist. This is one of the reasons why in the service sectors it is important to be more explicit about the nature of the 'product' or what we call the *service concept*.

The service concept is also important in the management of services because of the extent to which the service delivery system is in direct contact with the customer. In industrial sectors, those who are designing, producing and distributing the product are rarely in direct contact with the customer. They only influence the needs of the customers through the intermediary of the final (tangible) product. This is not the case in the service sectors. Much, if not all, of the service delivery system is in direct contact with customers and their many needs. The system in general, and the employees in particular, are part of the product. The system, including the competence, behaviour and attitude of the employees, has a direct impact on the fulfilment of the needs and are therefore part of the product.

Furthermore, we need to be more explicit about the service concept because of the much greater danger of dilution of the concept. As we shall see later, it is important in services to grant a level of autonomy to personnel, and in particular to the front-office personnel. However, variations in employee behaviour, competence, attitude, etc., can result in the service becoming diluted as it becomes randomly interpreted by field personnel. A second source of dilution is, of course, the customers themselves. It is clear from the example of the discount do-it-yourself store that some customers come to the shop for advice. If the limited number of employees all started to give extensive advice to the do-it-yourself customers, they would either have to neglect activities – such as making sure that racks were filled and helping people to locate material they were looking for – or the store would have to hire more personnel, losing its price advantage. The same is true in other sectors. International business schools are popular with students who are more interested in spending some time abroad, rather than being genuinely motivated by management, and are therefore not willing to do the hard work or do not possess the necessary (language) skills to participate effectively in the programme. Even in focused organizations, such as Club Méditerranée, employees are confronted with this phenomenon. What can you do with tourists who do not like the vacation philosophy of Club Med? To satisfy these customers, service workers may need to deviate from the defined service concept. This can mean that the service organization begins to lose its focus.

A service company has therefore to be very clear what its service concept is, both towards its customers, and also towards its own employees.

HOW TO DEFINE THE SERVICE CONCEPT

According to J. Heskett,[1] a service management expert at Harvard Business School, any definition of the service concept must answer the following three questions:

- What are the important elements of the services to be provided, stated in terms of results, produced for the customer, for the employee and the company?
- How are these elements supposed to be perceived by the target market segment? By the market in general? By the employee? By others?
- What efforts does this suggest in terms of designing, delivering and marketing the service?

For Martin Vanderbilt in our introductory case study, the important elements of service in a do-it-yourself shop are low price and a broad range of products. The do-it-yourself market can be perceived as the reliable discounter. With regard to the design, the delivery and the marketing of the service, the following efforts are required: efficient replenishment and a broad product range; few floor personnel; strong emphasis on self-service; drive-in option and good shop layout. The service concept of the do-it-yourself shop is completely different from that of the interior decorating shop, where advice and support are much more important elements of services than low price.

While it is clear that a service concept needs to address customer needs, it is also important that a service concept in service organizations addresses employee needs. Ultimately, service workers are carrying out the service concept and this is especially true for those who interact with the customer. In this respect, the service concept must involve a common set of values to which core groups of employees can subscribe. It is therefore important to note that Heskett also talks about the results for and the perception by the employees.

Exhibit 2.1

SMART: addressing parking needs

In the last quarter of 1997, SMART – a joint venture of Daimler-Benz and SMH[2] – introduced a new 'SMART' car. The SMART is a car enhanced with a very clear service concept – it is a safe small car that is a solution to the problems of mobility. 'Reduce to the max' is the slogan SMART uses to advertise its concept. In accordance with the service concept of the SMART, the joint venture developed the parking space concept. No car needs less space for parking than the SMART. It fits into every gap. However, when there are no gaps to be found, there are special SMART-sponsored parking spaces near railway stations and airports or in city centres.[3] The service concept is also reflected in the company's innovative distribution approach – for instance, its independent and autonomous sales network of 'SMART centres' (instead of large importers). One of the reasons for SMART working with dedicated and specialized dealers is to completely tune the sales network to the needs of customers.

Those working in maintenance and housekeeping functions commonly have a lack of self-respect and even satisfaction with their work. When firms such as ISS want their employees to have respect for the customer, they need to encourage employees to develop a sense of self-respect and personal satisfaction. As a result, the service concept in these firms must include 'improved self-respect, self-development, personal satisfaction and upward mobility'.[4]

In defining the service concept, we must think in particular about the impact on personnel, both in terms of skills and personal characteristics:

- *Skills*. Staff must be adequately qualified to serve specific customer segments. Investment brokers, for example, do not like to handle routine financial transactions, and, moreover, their time is too expensive for them to perform such tasks.
- *Personal characteristics*. In the example of ISS, the personal characteristics of the employees will determine whether or not they will be able to function within the organization. Someone who is not able to develop self-respect will possibly have to leave the company.

Finally, when defining the service concept, the requirements for the other elements of the service system and the perception of these elements by customers and employees must be considered. The setting should be adjusted to the needs of the customer. For instance, restaurants targeting different age groups find it challenging to select music, not to mention volume levels, that are acceptable to all.

When defining a service concept, a service firm must try to preserve consistency between the front- and back-office elements of the service system.[5] This involves alignment which is more than a simple extrapolation of policies which are appropriate in the 'front office' without questioning the necessity or even the desirability of these policies for the back office, and vice versa. One such problem occurs in day clinics within hospitals. Nurses and administrative personnel in such clinics are used to working from 9.00 a.m. to 5.00 p.m., while physicians do not always respect these time limitations. This leads to overtime work which can be the origin of dissatisfaction when it becomes structural. Working hours, shifts, quality control systems, the social skills of the workers and the physical environment are examples of elements which can involve alignment from the front office to the back office.

The service concept, once defined, becomes a blueprint that communicates to employees what service they should give and to customers what service they should expect to receive. The past success of Club Méditerranée partially depended on the very clear definition and communication of its service concept, both to (potential) customers and to employees. If you visit the website of Club Med, you are first asked to indicate which profile best fits you as a customer (family, single or couple). Furthermore, Club Med uses the site to explain its vacation philosophy very clearly. This vacation philosophy can only be realized when the employees of Club Med, the so-called GOs,[6] completely believe in it.

Once the service concept has been defined, it will have a major impact on the components of any service delivery system as one will notice as soon as one starts with implementation.

IMPLEMENTING THE SERVICE CONCEPT

Given the heterogeneity of the needs of customers and employees and the variability introduced through the interaction between customers and employees, implementing the notion of a service concept is a difficult balancing act. To do this successfully, three tasks are particularly crucial: segmenting the market, targeting the various customer segments and designing the delivery system, which includes both operations and technology as well as the role and competencies of employees.

Segmenting markets

Since different customers have different needs and expectations, it is essential to analyse the market and to define the different segments that exist. Each segment contains customers who have more or less the same needs and therefore can be treated as one single submarket. At the same time, each segment should be as differentiated as possible from all the other segments, so that it can be served differently (as it should be). In the tourist sector, for instance, a segmentation could be based on the purpose of travel – business or recreation.

In segmenting markets, two broad groups of variables are generally used:

- the benefits sought; and
- the customer characteristics.

The benefits sought are in principle the most important segmentation criterion. After all, underlying the segmentation effort is the fact that different groups of customers have different needs; they should therefore be treated differently and as a result require a different service concept. Segments should be as internally homogeneous as possible, so that customers belonging to the same segment are looking for the same benefit.

In principle, benefit segmentation should be the primary consideration of any marketer. However, from a managerial point of view, it is important to be able to set an indicator which allows allocation of individual customers to specific segments. Marketers therefore try to match the benefit segments to specific customer characteristics, such as their geographic and socio-demographic status. By considering a consumer's age and gender, or the size and industry of an organizational buyer, marketers will try to assess the customer's needs and consequently the benefit segment the customer belongs to. Other important customer characteristics in consumer markets are psychographic in nature, while business-to-business marketers will also consider operating variables and purchasing approaches.[7]

However, it is becoming increasingly difficult to match the benefit segment to customer characteristics. For example, situational segmentation criteria indicate that the same customer will have different needs depending on his or her buying situation. This is reflected in the introductory case study concerning Martin Vanderbilt and his building experience. He found himself in the following different buying situations:

- *Looking for ideas.* Consumers who have no clear idea of what solution they are looking for will explore the market to find some ideas. They will turn to a shop which offers a vast selection of goods, including the latest fashions in the market. Service and advice from the sales staff are equally important. That is why Martin Vanderbilt turned to a specialist interior decorating shop when buying his paint.
- *Facing a difficult job.* All do-it-yourself devotees may find themselves facing a job they have never done before, which requires special materials and advanced technical knowledge. Just as in the case of Martin's plumbing, the consumer does not want to run any risks and needs both good advice and materials of the best possible quality.
- *Requiring large quantities.* Occasionally, you may find yourself in need of a large quantity of do-it-yourself goods. As the total bill will be relatively high, you care

Table 2.1 Buyer expectations of various do-it-yourself stores according to the buying situation

Store characteristic	Buying situation				
	Urgent purchase	*Large quantities*	*Difficult job*	*Regular purchase*	*Get ideas*
1 The store is nearby	✓			✓	
2 I can get what I want quickly	✓				
3 I know that the store sells those products	✓			✓	
4 The store has low prices		✓		✓	
5 The store has a large enough stock of the product I want	✓	✓	✓	✓	
6 The store also offers good service after purchase			✓		✓
7 I can choose from different models of one product			✓		✓
8 The store is pleasant and elegantly designed					
9 The store carries the latest products					✓
10 The store carries very good quality products			✓		

about low prices. Every percentage point of a price reduction will result in more money saved. This is why Martin went to the large discount store in his cousin's borrowed van.

■ *Making urgent purchases*. Whenever a do-it-yourself customer forgets to buy or runs out of some item, his or her major concern is to be able to resume work as quickly as possible. This is why Martin went to the more expensive shop just down the road.

The buying situation is a characteristic that can be of high relevance for market segmentation. In studying the do-it-yourself retail industry we have discovered four different situations in addition to routine purchases. Table 2.1 clearly shows that the expectations regarding the store differ significantly depending on the buying situation.

Targeting market segments

As each segment has significantly different needs, the service offered should be customized for each segment. Competitors who try to be everything to everybody by offering a standardized service concept to all segments will find themselves to be the second best solution for each segment, whenever a more appropriate product is available.

In evaluating different markets, the firm must look at two factors: the overall attractiveness of the segment and its compatibility with the organization itself. The attractiveness of a segment depends on its size and on how well it is already being served. The latter reflects the willingness to pay premium prices as well as an opportunity for the firm to outperform competitors. There should also be a match between the segment and the organization, its core capabilities, its objectives and its resources.

Targeting always means making choices. The do-it-yourself chain targeting the average do-it-yourself devotee is trying to be everything to everyone. It builds large outlets with a wide and deep product range, has highly trained and readily available staff, a high penetration (always near the customer) and very competitive prices. However, it would find itself in a very difficult situation if confronted with more focused competitors. For instance, the unfocused chain will find it hard to balance the added value with the added costs. The large number of highly trained staff, combined with the many outlets and the ample product range, will involve relatively high costs and therefore will make it difficult for the chain to compete with a more focused store.

In the banking sector, very focused players seem to be achieving major successes at the expense of banks trying to offer everything to everybody:

■ *Urgent purchases*. Banks' market share in consumer credit is decreasing in favour of the sellers of durable consumer goods. Loans for buying a car, a TV set or a piece of furniture can often be obtained directly from the seller. As customers are eager to buy, they tend to choose the convenience of one-stop shopping and therefore do not even invite the bank to make a quote.

■ *Regular purchases*. Direct (home) banking offers the consumer the convenience of managing regular bank affairs from home, and at competitive prices. This is because the direct bankers have no need for a network of branch offices and therefore can achieve lower cost levels. Traditional banks have successfully responded to this threat by offering direct bank services which complement their existing distribution channels.

- *Large quantities*. For mortgages and standardized medium-sized investments – for instance, bonds and savings deposits of over 10 000 ECU – competitive prices prevail over service. As a result, specialist financial institutions, such as Crédit Lyonnais Belgium and the Hypotheker in the Netherlands, concentrate on these specific products. Like the direct bankers, they have developed a lower-cost distribution system than the traditional banks.

- *Difficult job and to get ideas*. Specialist banks and investment consultants, such as Paribas Belgium, target affluent customers. Again they have developed a distribution network with fewer branches than the traditional banks. As each individual affluent customer represents a high level of assets and thus of potential investments, they actually go to visit their customers rather than inviting them to come to their offices. Traditional banks have responded by creating a different segment for their affluent clients and by serving them in a similar way.

Another aspect of targeting is communication. The communication strategy of service companies should be particularly concerned with creating the right expectations and making sure that the 'right' customers are channelled to the right delivery system. In some cases, targeting can be implemented by explicit – or sometimes implicit – selection mechanisms. Shouldice hospital, mentioned in Chapter 1, applies a very explicit selection mechanism: patients have to fill in a questionnaire on the basis of which surgeons decide whether or not the patients are suitable for the 'Shouldice treatment'.

Focusing the service delivery system

The nature of services commonly introduces high variation in terms of customer needs or employee needs. Therefore a clear service concept needs a focus. When there is no focus, it is very difficult to develop a service delivery system which fits the heterogeneous needs. Examples of 'focused factories' in the service industry are McDonald's fast-food restaurants, Benetton and Club Méditerranée. These service firms all focus on a well-defined market segment and have designed their services in accordance with the characteristics of the customer needs or expectations in this market segment.

It should be made clear that focusing does not necessarily mean narrowing the product range. In some instances, it might be the opposite. One successful example of focusing is a cinema complex in Ghent, Belgium.[8] Despite the fact that in that city one cinema after another was closing its doors, an entrepreneur opened a complex of 12 cinemas in the early 1980s. Everybody predicted a short life for this organization. However, quite the opposite happened: it was and still is a tremendous success. The entire service delivery system was focused on the service concept of 'choice'. People do not go to the cinema with a specific film in mind, but make their decision after they have entered the system. The entrepreneur has repeated the success since then in various other Belgian and European cities.

The main challenge in focusing the service delivery system is keeping coherence among the various elements of the service delivery system and consistency over time. Important issues include:

- *Communication to, and selection and training of employees*. When the integrity of the service concept is to be maintained in a situation where it is either impossible or undesirable to control the customer input, we have to make sure that the employees are well informed about the service concept and their role in this concept. Service organizations should devote as much effort to internal communication as they do to external communication. In the case of SMART, it is important that the independent dealers are totally customer-oriented and that they are creative and innovative in dealing with customer needs. SMART can attain this objective by carefully selecting the dealers with which it works. It is also possible to train dealers into the SMART culture.
- *Separating front-office and back-office activities*. The presence of the customer in the service delivery system (front office) limits the degree of freedom in the design of the service delivery system. The skills of front-office workers are clearly different from those people who always work in the back office. Differences between the back and front offices increase the chance of the firm losing its focus. Nevertheless, it is important that there is consistency between the front-office and back-office elements when policies are formulated in the context of a service concept.

THE SERVICE CONCEPT AS A GUIDING FRAMEWORK: AN OVERVIEW OF ITS MAIN INGREDIENTS

As the previous paragraphs made clear, defining and implementing the service concepts is the essence of what services management is all about. Everything starts from the question: what value do we want to offer for whom? This idea of 'value' is hence situated centrally within Figure 2.1 which summarizes the different building blocks that make up any service delivery system. Defining the value one wants to

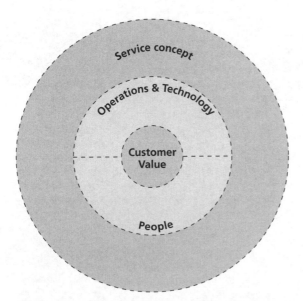

Figure 2.1 Service concept as guiding framework

create immediately brings us to the question what is exactly needed in order to create it. What kind of technology is necessary in order to deliver the services we have in mind? How to organize operations and capacity? What kind of people do we need and which competencies do they have to possess? What does an appropriate communication strategy look like? What about internationalization and keeping the initial idea alive and pushing it further by innovation? Actually, all these issues and more are on the table when starting to define and implement any service concept.

Fortunately, within this multitude of issues, some order is to be found. Broadly speaking, one can discern three different core building blocks of any service system: customers, operations, including technology, and finally the people who actually perform the services. And of course, all these core building blocks – each consisting in its turn of different elements – need to be designed and implemented in an integrated way in order to arrive at consistent and seamless service delivery processes. This again underlines the need for a coherent, sound and focused overall service concept. Figure 2.1 depicts this logic; around the core formed by customer value, one finds operations and technology as well as people; a sound service concept is needed to unite all the constituting elements.

As said, each building block in itself implies numerous issues and points of attention. Some major points of attention are listed in Figure 2.2. These will be dealt with systematically in the remainder of the book. The idea of customer's value brings the notions of customer relationships and loyalty to the forefront (Chapter 4). What kind of communication strategies (Chapter 5) and pricing approaches (Chapter 6) are relevant for service environments? How to assess customer satisfaction and handle customer complaints? (Chapter 7). How can the customer's value be made more tangible in service guarantees and service level agreements? (Chapter 8).

With respect to people, we will first discuss the crucial role employees play in terms of value creation (Chapter 9). Next we will explore the nature and relevancy

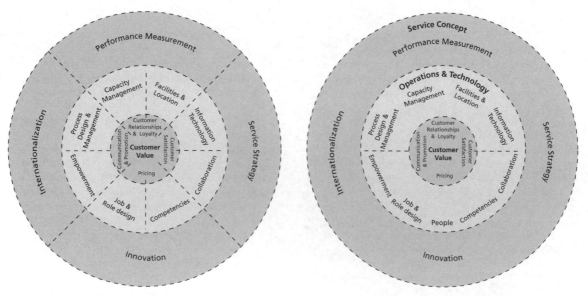

Figure 2.2   The service concept: main ingredients

of competencies (Chapter 10), and collaboration for services (Chapter 11). Likewise we will elaborate the concept of empowerment (Chapter 12) and discuss what role stress entails and how to minimize this in service settings (Chapter 13). On the level of operations and technology, we will address themes like process design (Chapter 14), capacity management (Chapter 15), design and location of facilities (Chapter 16) and examine the role (information) technology can play (Chapter 17). Finally, the idea of defining – and developing – a consistent service concept itself entails multiple issues. Successful implementing the service concept will become easier when supported by a performance measurement system that reflects the multiple issues to take into account (Chapter 18). Any service concept needs to become adapted or even rejuvenated: hence the need for innovation (Chapter 19). In addition, during the development of any service concept, questions will arise about extending activities beyond national boundaries; issues surrounding internationalization will be discussed in Chapter 20. And as has become clear by now, the service concept in itself should be looked upon as a strategic notion; so we will end this book by discussing the notion of strategy and the particularities it implies for service environments (Chapter 21).

WHY NOT ALL SERVICE CONCEPTS ARE ALIKE

A recurrent theme to be found throughout the book, relates to the relative importance of the elements that constitute a service delivery system. This importance varies with the nature of the services themselves. Recall how we discussed different service classifications in Chapter 1. Here it became clear that not all services are alike. We ended with discussing the differences between maintenance-interactive, task-interactive and personal-interactive services as outlined by Mills and Margulies. As this typology reflects the core of the service delivery process itself, we will use this framework throughout the book to illustrate how the specific nature of the service delivery process will affect the design of the service delivery system as a whole. At this stage, a few examples to clarify the logic we will apply. Recall that maintenance interactive services relate to 'standardized' interaction between service employees and customers; these interactions are aimed at eliciting an appropriate service delivery process. These processes lend themselves quite often to standardization and in a number of cases even to high levels of automation. This is much less the case for personal interactive services which imply, by definition, fuzziness and ambiguity. Addressing this ambiguity is in fact a crucial part of the added value sought in the service delivery process. But the very nature of this activity implies that the introduction of for instance technology which operates in an automated way is less relevant for this type of services. To illustrate this point more concretely, compare the extent to which retail activities taking place in banks become replaced by self-banking and home-banking technology with the technology intensity of complex financial advice provided by the same banks. In the latter case, the advent of internet has had far less impact than in the former case; nowadays the majority of banks in the industrialized world offers Internet-enabled banking services. A closer look reveals however that these services relate to payments, checking the status of your accounts and the like. Stated otherwise, automation pertains most to maintenance interactive services. Complex financial service transactions like deciding on an appropriate investment strategy, taking into consideration your professional and family situation as well as your personal attitude and preferences towards risk, are less common to be found in an automated way. As we will explain in Chapter 17, personal contact is often superior to handle this kind of complex service interaction. Hence, the importance of information technology and new developments in this field is much more pronounced in the case of maintenance interactive services than in the case of personal interactive services. Similar arguments will be developed in relation to different aspects of marketing, operations and human resources as will become clear in the following chapters. The idea that the relevance of different building blocks varies with the nature of services does not mean that the optimal characteristics of a service delivery system are *determined* by the characteristics of the service transactions involved. It is clear that the strategy pursued by the company will influence as well the relative importance of the different building blocks. In fact, as will become clear throughout this book, and especially in the chapter where we will discuss strategy (Chapter 21), the appropriate mix will be the result of the interplay between the nature of the service delivery and the competitive position strived for.

CONCLUSION

The nature of services requires service firms to be specific about the market segments they are going to serve and the needs they will address. A clear service concept identifies the 'what' and the 'how' of the focus. However, a service concept has to go further than simply identifying market segments; it addresses any aspects of the service organization's marketing, human resource management and operations management. The content and process of these areas of management are discussed in Parts Two, Three and Four of this book, respectively. In doing so, we will illustrate the relevancy of taking into account the nature of the service delivery process. This, together with the competitive strategy deployed by the organization will define eventually the appropriate service delivery system. Part Five deals with the strategic aspects of defining and developing the correct service concept.

As the experience with the SMART car shows (*see* Exhibit 2.1), the service concept is not a prerogative of service firms. Even when a tangible product exists, a clear service concept can be a crucial element in the positioning of the product. This is a first indication of the fact that service management also applies to manufacturing situations – the topic of Chapter 3.

Review and discussion questions

■ Do you believe service companies can be successful on the market without having a clear service concept? Can you give examples? Why is this the case (or not)?

■ In terms of impact on the design of service delivery systems, what is most influential in your opinion: the nature of the service delivery process or the strategic orientation of the firm? Why? Can you give examples of companies that illustrate your point of view? Are you aware of (successful) companies who have done things in a completely different manner?

Notes and references

[1] Heskett, J. L. (1986) *Managing in the Service Economy*. Boston: Harvard Business School Press and Heskett, J. L. (1987) 'Lessons in the service sector', *Harvard Business Review*, Vol 65, No 2, Mar/Apr, 118–26.

[2] SMH is known for, among other things, the watch brands Omega and Swatch.

[3] Although SMART is a product, the service concept underlying SMART illustrates the blurring boundaries between products and services, as will be explained in Chapter 3.

[4] Heskett, J. L. (1987), op. cit.

[5] Van Dierdonck, R. and Brandt, G. (1988) 'The focused factory in service industry', *The International Journal of Operations and Production Management*, Vol 8, No 3, 31–8.

[6] GO: 'Gentil Organisateur' or Gentle Organizer.

[7] A more thorough discussion of segmentation criteria can be found in any standard marketing book. One example is Kotler, P. (1997) *Marketing Management, Analysis, Planning, Implementation and Control*. Englewood Cliffs, NJ: Prentice-Hall International.

[8] Van Dierdonck, R. and Brandt, G. (1988), op. cit.

Suggested further reading

Heskett, J. L. (1987) 'Lessons in the service sector', *Harvard Business Review*, Mar/Apr, 118–26. This article gives a thorough discussion on the role of the service concept in creating a strategic service vision that integrates operations and marketing.

Kotler, P. (1997) *Marketing Management, Analysis, Planning, Implementation and Control*. Englewood Cliffs, NJ: Prentice-Hall International. This marketing book covers the themes of segmenting and targeting.

CHAPTER 3

Servitization: or why services management is relevant for manufacturing environments

Steven Desmet · Roland Van Dierdonck · Bart Van Looy

INTRODUCTION

A survey held in 2002 among executives in Germany and Belgium indicated that over 90 per cent of all manufacturing companies believe the further development of services is crucial for maintaining and improving their competitive position.

During the summer of 2002 IBM acquired Monday, the consulting arm of PriceWaterhouseCoopers (PWC). This deal reinforces the leading position IBM has in IT services. IBM's global services unit ranked already first in terms of revenue in 2001 (35$Bn) leaving behind companies like EDS (22$Bn), Fujitsu (17$Bn) and HP/Compaq (15$BN) but also service companies like Accenture (11$Bn) and Cap Gemini (9$Bn).[1] Moreover, IBM global services employed about 150 000 people worldwide, while PWC consulting counted 30 000 employees. Not bad for a manufacturing company who ten years ago made most of its money selling hardware.

In the previous chapters we have identified the specific characteristics of services. This may have given the false impression that manufacturing goods and delivering services are so different that this book will only be relevant to companies classified as being in the tertiary or services sector of the economy. This is an outdated view.

Traditionally, manufacturing companies supplied goods, while service was seen as having only minor importance. This attitude has changed. Services have become important for manufacturing companies. More and more of these companies are offering an integrated package of products and services. Sandra Vandermerwe, one of the leading scholars on this topic, has called this movement 'the servitization of businesses'.[2]

This change affects the management of traditional manufacturing companies. The offering to the customer has to be redefined to include this 'bundle' concept. As a result, manufacturing businesses and service companies are no longer so very different, and each has something to teach the other.

In this chapter we shall take a closer look at this change, describing the way in which servitization is evolving. We shall also examine some of the causes of this trend and some of the implications it has for a company's organization and its production processes.

Objectives

By the end of this chapter, you should be able to discuss:

- what is meant by the notion of servitization
- how servitization develops in different stages
- why more and more manufacturing firms are opting for the servitization approach
- what the crucial prerequisites are for achieving servitization

FROM GOODS TO SERVICES

Traditionally, the focus in manufacturing companies has been on making a good quality article. The objective has been to make a car that would take the customer from point A to point B, a lift that would go up and down, or a coffee machine that would make coffee. There is nothing wrong with this; we all want our cars to function smoothly or our coffee machines to make good coffee. Every manufacturer has to ensure that the goods – the substantive element of the product – work well. However, manufacturers have come to realize – often at the behest of customers – that the offering of a product is enhanced when it is complemented by services.

A classical form of customer service offered by manufacturing companies is after-sales service – the installation, maintenance and repair of goods sold. In so-called 'flexible factories', the notion of customer service also implies the introduction of breadth to the range of product offerings and the ability to customize the product to meet specific customer needs. It is apparent, however, that customer services in this context are seen as 'services that accompany goods' – for example, acceptable delivery time, after-sales repairs, correct installation, etc.[3] Services are seen as an add-on or sometimes even as a necessary evil, since in the minds of most consumers or salespeople, an intervention after the sale is often associated with a defect in the product.

This notion of service can obviously be extended. Servitization goes beyond the traditional approach of providing 'additional' services. In the case of servitization, the offer is defined as a 'bundle' consisting of both goods and services. Servitization thus requires a different mindset.

> *'Management must break out of the mindset that considers manufacturing (or goods production) as separate from the service activities that make such products possible and effective.'*[4]

Redefining 'products' will often mean taking a fresh look at customers' needs. Instead of trying to sell the item with the service as an add-on, we should address the problem that a particular product solves. This will often lead to the conclusion that the hardware is only part of the solution. Solutions are provided not merely by a good and some added-on services, but by means of a package which includes both goods and services. Both contribute to the fulfilment of customer needs.

Consider, for instance, the example of Schindler, the Swiss lift and escalator company. This company no longer sees itself as being in the business of manufacturing lifts and escalators, but rather in the business of *ensuring the mobility of the*

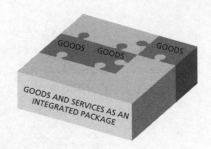

Figure 3.1 Goods and services: three stages of transition[5]

occupants of a building. This is done not only by designing, producing and installing the hardware, but also by providing customers with simulation tools to determine how many lifts a building should have, given the traffic patterns and acceptable waiting times, and performing preventative maintenance to minimize down-time, or even to guarantee in a service-level agreement the up-time of the installations. This clearly required a change of mindset at a strategic level, and a whole new kind of thinking about Schindler's product.

An examination of the different ways of defining the relationship between goods and services reveals three different approaches:

■ considering yourself as a mere goods manufacturer and supplier;
■ offering additional services; and
■ embracing the notion of servitization.

Often these three different approaches follow an evolutionary process, as depicted in Figure 3.1. A company may start with merely offering goods; it may then develop services as an add-on. The intrinsic value of services is then acknowledged in the following step.

WHY SERVITIZATION?

Why is it that manufacturing companies are becoming increasingly interested in giving their customers good service? Broadly speaking, there are two main reasons. First of all, most customers just want more service and are no longer satisfied with the good alone. They want the service that goes along with it – that is, the service that addresses the underlying needs. Second, offering a higher level of service than that of your competitors is a way of making your offering more attractive for your customers. It can differentiate you from your competitors.

Satisfying customer needs

Today's customers simply demand more services. They do not simply want to buy a computer or a car; they also want a guarantee that it works. They want ease of use, ease of repair, and a 24-hour information desk. This is not to say that the tangible element of the offering has become less important. Customers still want the same article, but they also want the services, so that they can get the most out of their purchase. Ultimately it comes down to satisfying a need, which often implies more than the availability of products.

Redefining an offering as a bundle of services and goods may, therefore, meet customers' expectations. However, there is a danger of misunderstanding this approach or executing it poorly. Many suppliers simply add layer upon layer of services to their offerings without even knowing whether customers really want them, whether these services should be added on to the standard package or offered as an option, or even what the costs associated with these services are.[6] The notion of the service concept, discussed in Chapter 2, is as important to bundling as it is to 'pure' services.

Customers are also increasingly taking the so-called *life-cycle cost* into account. They are no longer looking at the purchase price alone, but also at other costs incurred over the product's lifetime – for example, cost of use (fuel, parts and supplies, etc.) and maintenance. For many products, especially durable goods, the purchase price represents only a small fraction of the total life-cycle cost. The purchase price of an average car, for example, represents only about a quarter of the total cost. The remainder consists of fuel, maintenance, insurance and taxes. Providing good service to lower these additional costs can become an important aspect of competitive strategy. Mercedes-Benz recognized this and used it in advertising campaigns for their trucks. Customers were reminded that the price of a truck constituted only about 15 per cent of the total average lifetime cost of the truck. The company's sales directors thus advised potential customers to calculate these additional costs – that is the costs 'in use' – taking into account Mercedes-Benz fuel-saving systems, lease or finance terms, and especially the availability of a broad range of vehicles, high quality production and efficient after-sales service before choosing a supplier.[7]

Exhibit 3.1

Colora: selling solutions[8]

Colora, a Belgian chain of franchisee-operated paint shops, provides a good example. Imagine yourself having to paint the living room of your new home. You go to the local Do-It-Yourself shop to buy paint and a brush, only to find hundreds of different types of paint. You look for someone to help you choose, but either you can't find anybody or those you can find don't know anything about paint. Compare this with a typical Colora shop. It also has hundreds of different types of paint, but the employees are trained to help you. Based on the description of the type of wall in your living room, they advise you which is the best type of paint for your needs, or if that is not enough, they'll even come with you to your house to give information on the spot. Colora's management realizes that most customers entering a paint shop or DIY shop are not just looking for paint or a brush; instead they are looking for help in solving a problem. Colora thus sells more than just products; it sells solutions to customer problems – solutions which consist not only of goods, but also of a service which together satisfy the needs of its customers. Hence, providing goods and services based on the sound technical knowledge of the employees are the key to Colora's success.

Seeking differentiation

Traditionally, competition between manufacturing firms has tended to focus on the goods themselves. A company gained customers or increased its sales because its goods were better than those of its competitors. Now competition has shifted to another level, namely that of the product's service component. Many manufacturers only have limited competitive advantage in terms of their goods. Goods are rather easy to copy; patents often give only limited protection against copying. Goods are becoming more and more alike in terms of their quality and performance. Manufacturers are finding it difficult to differentiate themselves from their competitors on the strength of the goods alone, and thus have to find their source of differentiation elsewhere. Offering better service than the competition can become an important competitive advantage, as indicated in the findings of a survey of 138 German companies, where managers were asked their opinion on future opportunities for effective long-term differentiation: 76.9 per cent of those surveyed mentioned services.[9] This is a much higher percentage than for the other competitive factors, such as product quality, technology /innovation, price/performance, communication/image.

The computer industry provides a well-known illustration of this trend. Competition, especially in the business-to-business market, is now less focused on speed, capacity or other qualities of the computer, and more on the service offered – ease of use, after-sales service, etc. One of IBM's advertising slogans during 1985 was 'If everybody wants to have an IBM terminal, it is because IBM service is the best.' It is not that the tangible aspect of the offering is no longer important, but the fact that most manufacturers can make a high-quality, high-performance computer means that this does not differentiate anymore. It is as if the goods have become a 'qualifier', whereas the service offered has become the 'order winner'.[10] A good tangible product must be produced to even be in the running, but high margins are realized elsewhere. Focus has shifted from the core product towards the services because offering a mixture of goods and service components allows the company to differentiate and hence to create more satisfied and loyal customers. Satisfied customers are less eager to switch to the competition or less eager to do it themselves. By using services as a competitive tool, companies may also succeed in setting up barriers to entry to competitors and in creating switching costs.[11] Offering extended services can keep the competition away by making entry too costly and complex. Offering a bundle of services and goods also makes your competitive strength less transparent for competitors and hence more sustainable. We shall discuss this issue in more detail when talking about service strategy (*see* Chapter 21).

MAKING THE TRANSITION

It is clear that the trend towards servitization offers companies many opportunities for differentiation. However, redefining the service and good offered and seeing its potential benefits are only half of the story. Realizing the benefits of servitization will require effort: for example, relevant information systems need to be put in place and an adequate organization should be installed, often including the development of appropriate skills.

Setting up customer information systems

In order to increase customer focus and thereby enhance customer service, a company has to know more about customers and their needs, and be able to act on that information.

ABB's Metrawatt division has adopted just such a strategy. The Metrawatt division has a computer database where all relevant data on each client is stored including key contacts, type of purchase, frequency of purchase and maintenance required. This information is used to schedule preventive maintenance, even if the client does not have a maintenance contract. The company can then contact its client before the client calls in distress. The same information is also used to forecast periods when maintenance activities will be heaviest. We will discuss this issue in more detail in Chapter 5 when we focus on relationship marketing.

Organizing the service delivery system

In the traditional view of services, customer service strategies had little impact on the production system. Customer service was viewed merely as a supportive and buffering sub-system to the production sub-system, and the customer as a disruptive factor. Direct customer contact was avoided because it reduced efficiency. Everything was done to insulate the production process from its surroundings.

However, when shifting from the production of goods to the production of goods and services as an integrated package (*see* Figure 3.1), the interaction between the customer and the production system increases, since an important characteristic of services is its (at least partially) simultaneous production and consumption. This certainly requires a big change in mentality from managers. A 1992 study,[12] consisting of a series of in-depth interviews with 80 senior managers and group discussions with 388 senior managers in 16 US-based multinational firms, reported that this increased interaction with the client was seen as one of the major difficulties in the servitization process. Adapting to the dual role of the client as both customer and co-producer and managing this increased participation are thus seen as a serious challenge.

During the transition from being a manufacturing company to being a bundle-producing company, the customer should be made more visible, not only in front-office activities but in the whole design–manufacturing support chain. What is needed is a form of open system with direct and accessible linkages between the factory and its internal and external customers.[13] 'The four walls of a factory no longer limit the domain of manufacturing', as Chase[14] puts it.

This has not only physical implications, but also organizational consequences. The traditional breakdown into manufacturing, marketing and sales, product development, and field support divisions increasingly makes less sense. The vertical lines and structures should be replaced by horizontal lines including the interface between customers and suppliers. In particular, the interface between manufacturing and marketing and sales should be re-evaluated, since keeping the two functions separate will seriously hamper the fulfilment of customer needs. Manufacturing should not only be integrated upstream with, for instance, Research and Development, but also downstream. This is necessary because the front office is becoming more and more important and also because there is a need for tighter and more direct coupling of customer needs with the organization's capabilities.

The organization's front office will have to become larger because the customer is involved with a larger part of the operating system.

Putting the right skills in place

As a result of servitization, more and more workers will have direct customer contact, which will require changes in employees' skills as well as their behaviour. Much more attention will need to be given to the interpersonal skills of customer-contact personnel. Factory personnel, in addition to possessing technical knowledge, must be adept at communication and sensitive to customer needs. The personnel should have a *service orientation* – that is, a helpful, thoughtful, considerate, and co-operative attitude.[15]

The simultaneous production and consumption of most services also means that customer-contact employees will often need to make instantaneous decisions in the absence of their supervisor, in the same way that field-service engineers spend most of their time in the company of the customer firm. Personnel empowerment should be increased to enable them to make decisions and to act in the customer's interest on the spot. This notion of empowerment will be discussed in more detail in Chapter 14.

The virtual factory?

It is clear that servitization – that is, paying more attention to the service component of the product offering – may eventually lead to what has been called *the virtual factory*.[16] Generally speaking, a virtual factory is:

> *'a factory which attains its target of transforming materials and components into value for the customer by using resources outside the manufacturing function proper.'*

Customers both possess, and are themselves, important resources and therefore should be included in the network of resources which a virtual factory controls. In addition, when the product is enhanced, the manufacturing organization should 'control', but not necessarily 'own', its various activities. ABB does not own its customers' spare part warehouses, but rather controls them.

In a number of cases, pure manufacturing is becoming less important to competition. As a consequence, we might see more and more manufacturing firms subcontracting the manufacturing component and concentrating on the various service activities downstream and upstream of the actual manufacturing activity. This may eventually lead to the virtual factory becoming a reality.

If the service component of the offering represents the core of the company's competitive advantage, then traditional manufacturing companies may ultimately subcontract the tangible part and concentrate themselves entirely on the service component. The example of E&J Gallo Winery, the largest wine producer and distributor in the US, shows that this fourth stage is not as improbable as we may think. Gallo outsourced the growing of specialized grapes for its wine:

> *'an activity many vintners consider the core of their business. Gallo devotes its resources and management attention to maintaining the legendary marketing and sales strength that give the company its volume advantages and to using the deep knowledge base its 31 per cent market share can provide to purchase grapes with the precise quality its wines require.'*[17]

Exhibit 3.2

The development of ABB Services[18]

Asea Brown Boveri (ABB) provides an excellent example of a traditional manufacturing organization that came to recognize the importance of service and consequently broadened the definition of its offering.

ABB is the largest electrical engineering group in the world. It was created on 1 January 1988 when Percy Barnevik, who at that time was managing director of the Swedish company Asea,[19] announced the merger of Asea with the Swiss firm Brown Boveri. ABB is a $35 billion multinational company representing over 1000 working companies employing 213 000 people in 140 countries. More than half of ABB's activities take place in the European region, with around one-quarter in the Americas and a growing presence in the Asian Pacific.

Initially, in the 1950s and 60s, Asea's service activities were not so explicitly organized. Service jobs were being done in the plants. Asea began to observe that 'these annoying warranty repair jobs' were disturbing work flow, planning and focus in production. The broken transformers and generators coming in through the back door were making it difficult to respect delivery deadlines and quality. Unforeseen urgent repair work was filling expensive production areas. Priorities were getting muddled and people were becoming disorganized, with the resulting delays creating unsatisfied customers. It became clear that 'service' needed another management and different behaviour, tools, customer approach, and methods from 'production'.

Changes came about in the 1970s and 80s in part due to the ongoing expansion through acquisitions. Cost centres were transformed into profit centres: the total ABB organization was split up into 5000 profit centres. 'Service' became a separate business unit, a network of repair shops was installed, field engineers were sent to the customers, and the service offering was expanded through spare parts deliveries. This evolution implied first a shift in mindset; employees had to evolve from technical repairmen into entrepreneurs responsible for profits. However, the maintenance and repair activities offered were still mainly supportive and corrective and remained tied to ABB's products.

Things changed drastically in 1992–3 when ABB Service Worldwide was established to integrate the different local service organizations into a separate Business Area. ABB Service Worldwide belongs to the 'Industrial and Building Systems' business segment. This BA Service accounts for a $1.2 billion organization, and now employs a total of 10 000 people in over 50 countries all over the world. ABB Service also developed its own mission statement:

'To foster customer success through service which is professional, close to the customer and comprehensive, and all from a single dedicated ABB Service organisation.'

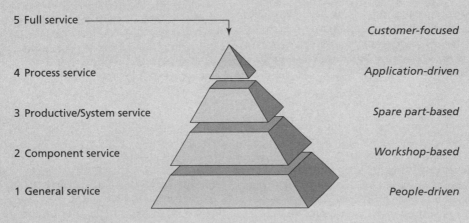

5 Full service — Customer-focused

4 Process service — Application-driven

3 Productive/System service — Spare part-based

2 Component service — Workshop-based

1 General service — People-driven

Figure 3.2 The ABB pyramid

Exhibit 3.2 continued

Note that no reference is made within this statement to ABB *products*.

ABB Service visualized its service concept with a pyramid (Figure 3.2). Within this concept the service market was divided into five market segments, from more generalized to extremely sophisticated maintenance services. Only upon closer inspection of this pyramid does it become clear that the notion of Full Service will eventually entail extending services beyond the add-ons, to where the work of optimizing operations is done in partnerships with customers. The focus shifts from service on specific machines to proactive maintenance.

ABB Service proactively redefined its attitude from 'fix it when it breaks' to 'the world-wide expert in maintenance'. Even though ABB Service still services ABB products, it is now more and more directed to the huge open markets. Let us take a closer look at this pyramid.

■ *General Service* denotes small repairs meaning largely standardized services. The main issue in this segment is cheap labour. Competition from independent local maintenance companies is very intense.

■ *Component Service* mainly involves the repair of products in an ABB Service workshop. This segment used to be 80 per cent of ABB Service's business, but by now it has dropped to less than 35 per cent, mainly due to the products' improved reliability. Name of the game is good lay-outs, time-based management, through put times, organization, etc.

Providing service in these first two segments does not differentiate ABB Service from competition, since they have become commodity services. If someone else is cheaper, ABB Service will lose market share.

■ The third segment is *Product/System Service*: on-site repair of ABB equipment by specialists. Margins are higher, but this is still a case of services as an add-on. Critical success factor here is availability of spare parts.

■ *Process Service* is mostly done by the plant operator. To perform this type of service, ABB Service must have specialists who know what petrochemical processes are, how cars are made, what quality steel

means, at what speed paper leaves the machine, and so on. Here the product loses focus; customers are demanding emphasis on their process. Although this segment is rather small, it is growing fast and margins tend to be higher. Moreover, service providers entrusted with these assignments hold key positions.

■ Finally, *Full Service* is a strategic service 'package' where ABB Service partially or completely takes over the responsibility of its customer's maintenance function. Since maintenance activities are not core businesses for the customer, ABB Service can not only provide these functions better, but in general also more cost-effectively than the customers. If ABB Service can expand the number of its Full Service contracts, it can develop the additional expertise and take advantage of economies of scale and scope. These contracts already account for $200 million in revenues per year in a business that did not exist three years ago. On top of that, these contracts generate at least $150 million additional service work and another $150 million pull-through of new ABB equipment.

This evolution towards Full Service again implies a change in mindset. This time the relationship with customers has to be reconsidered, as illustrated in Figure 3.3.

In the 1980s, ASEA Service was still acting like a fire brigade – the customer would call only after a breakdown. As a result, ABB made money when the customer lost money. The new idea was to turn the relationship with the customer into a win-win situation (*see* Figure 3.3). With its Full-Service contracts, ABB Service is being paid for its expertise in optimizing a customer's processes. By providing guidance during the design and development stage, by offering preventive maintenance, and so on, ABB Service creates value for the customer, resulting in increased availability. Integral customer cost starts to correlate negatively with ABB Service profit; indeed, added value for customers goes hand in hand with ABB Service profit. Similarly, ABB Service gave a new competitive edge to Component Service with Total Motor Management Contracts. Here, ABB Service takes the long-term responsibility for the customer's motor park and guarantees their availability

Exhibit 3.2 continued

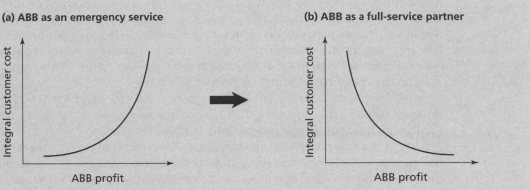

Figure 3.3 New view of customer service

24 hours a day, 365 days a year. This too is a win-win situation as both customers and ABB Service can aim for increased availability and optimize their profitabililty by doing so.

This focus on customer needs implies that ABB Service eventually will not only provide service on its own machinery, but on any piece of the customer's equipment. About 60 per cent of all services are now performed on non-ABB products. Following this line of evolution, ABB Service's latest offering is named 'Global Service Agencies': service activities for manufacturers, who do not have their own worldwide after-sales service.

It is clear from this example that ABB Service's product has experienced a continuous evolution. Starting from a point where only limited attention was paid to service, it gradually extended its offering to include more and more services, such as training, 24-hour spare parts logistics, and a help desk. As ABB Service continues to move in the direction of more Full Service contracts and Global Service Agencies, it is clear that the definition of its 'business' is becoming much broader than the original one: from repairing electrical motors, to managing entire maintenance functions with or without ABB equipment (*see* Figure 3.4).

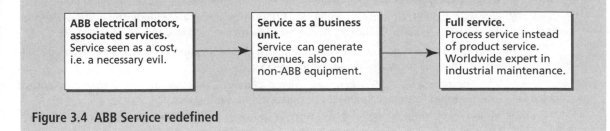

Figure 3.4 ABB Service redefined

CONCLUSION

In this chapter we have seen that the traditional boundaries between manufacturing and service companies tend to blur, as manufacturing firms adopt more and more service components in their offerings – a trend which has been labelled servitization. This trend towards servitization presents itself as a three-stage process: from offering merely goods, to adding services, and finally offering bundles of both tangible and intangible components.

The driving forces behind servitization are twofold. First, customers are asking for additional services as this will help to fulfil their own needs. Second, for manufacturing companies servitization implies the recognition that defensible competitive advantage usually derives from outstanding knowledge of customer needs, and linking these needs to human skills, logistical capabilities, knowledge bases and other assets and activities at various points on the value chain. This involves adding services to the offerings made to customers.

Finally, we have looked at some of the prerequisites for an efficient service delivery system: customer information systems, a well integrated service delivery system and, finally, the right competencies and skills.

Service management is, therefore, not only relevant to managers of service companies, but also to managers of manufacturing companies. The trend towards increasing the service component of the offering will certainly continue. Manufacturing managers who fail to recognize this trend will be in for a rough ride in the coming years.

Review and discussion questions

- Do you think manufacturing companies can afford not to offer any services? Why? Why not? Do you see differences in this respect in relation to the type of industry?

- Do you think the reverse also holds true, i.e. should service companies start thinking about offering products as well? Why? Why not? Can you come up with examples?

Notes and references

[1] Figures from *The Economist*, August 2002.

[2] Vandermerwe, S. and Rada, J. (1988) 'Servitization of businesses: Adding value by adding service', *European Management Journal*, Vol 6, No 4, 314–24.

[3] Bowen, D., Siehl, C. and Schneider, B. (1989) 'A framework for analysing customer service orientations in manufacturing', *Academy of Management Review*, Vol 14, No 1, 75–95.

[4] Quinn, J. B., Doorley, T. L. and Paquette, P. C. (1990) 'Beyond products: Service-based strategy', *Harvard Business Review*, Mar–Apr, 58–68.

[5] Van Dierdonck, R. (1993) *Post Lean Manufacturing: The importance of servitization*. Fourth International Forum on Technology Management. Berlin, Oct.

[6] Anderson, J. C. and Narus, J. A. (1995) 'Capturing the value of supplementary services', *Harvard Business Review*, Jan–Feb, 75–83.

[7] Mathe, H. and Shapiro, R. D. (1993) *Integrating Service Strategy in the Manufacturing Company*. London: Chapman & Hall, p. 23.

[8] Adapted from De Personeels Gids *De Standaard*, 18–19 Oct 1997.

[9] Simon, H. (1991) *Service Policies of German Manufacturers: Critical factors in international competition*. Research Report, Bonn: UNIC, in Mathe, H. and Shapiro, R. D. (1993), op cit, p. 39.

[10] A 'qualifier' is a quality your product must possess in order to even be considered by the customer. However, possessing such a quality will not give you any advantage over the competition. Only 'order winners' have that. For instance, a car with zero defects the first year is a qualifier, while one offering free air conditioning might be an order winner.

[11] Vandermerwe, S. and Rada, J. (1988), op. cit.

[12] Martin, Jr., Claude, R. and Horne, D. A. (1992) 'Restructuring towards a Service Orientation: the Strategic Challenges', *International Journal of Service Industry Management*, Vol 3, No 1, 25–38.

[13] Chase, R. B. (1991) 'The service factory: A future vision', *International Journal of Service Industry Management*, Vol 2, No 3, 60–70.

[14] Ibid.

[15] Bowen, D., Siehl, C. and Schneider, B. (1989), op. cit.

[16] De Meyer, A. (1992) 'Creating the Virtual Factory', *INSEAD Research Report*, Dec.

[17] Quinn, J. B., Doorley, T. L. and Paquette, P. C. (1990), op. cit.

[18] Based on an internal working document of ABB authored by J. Coene and B. Jonkers and 'Percy Barnevik's global crusade', *Business Week* (1993), 6 Dec, 59.

[19] On 1 January 1997, Göran Lindahl became president and CEO of ABB. Percy Barnevik still works at ABB as chairman of the board.

Suggested further reading

Chase, R. B. (1991) 'The service factory: a future vision', *International Journal of Service Industry Management*, Vol 2, No 3, 60–70. This article gives an excellent description of the service factory as opposed to the manufacturing company. The requirements and new roles for the organization are discussed.

Levitt, T. (1980) 'Marketing success through differentiation of anything', *Harvard Business Review*, May–June, 83–91. In this article, Levitt discusses the attributes of products (both goods and services) that give the marketer the opportunity to differentiate the product from its competitors. The total product concept is introduced in which the product is divided into the generic, expected, augmented and potential product.

Vandermerwe, S. and Rada, J. (1988) 'Servitization of businesses: Adding value by adding service', *European Management Journal*, Vol 6, No 4, 314–24. This is a definitive article since it introduces the notion of servitization. The traditional vision of products being either goods or services makes room for the bundle concept.

Vandermerwe, S. (1993) *From Tin Soldiers to Russian Dolls: Creating added value through services*. Oxford: Butterworth-Heinemann. This book from one of the leading authorities on servitization provides a good insight into its hows and whys.

PART TWO

Customer logic

Gino Van Ossel · Paul Gemmel · Bart Van Looy

When designing and managing services, it is very important that a company spends time getting to know its customers. Customers are being asked to consider a purchase that is very difficult to evaluate beforehand. Furthermore, because customers are participating in the production process, it is a much more intimate activity than simply buying an item of goods. A service company must find out the needs and the motivation of its customers.

It should not come as a surprise that the most important focus in service marketing is on building and maintaining relationships. Chapter 4 is therefore devoted to what is called *relationship marketing*. Building and maintaining relationships in service situations is directly related to the principle that customer satisfaction, customer loyalty and profitability are closely intertwined with each other.

An important element in building up trust between the service company and its customers is the task of 'making the intangible tangible'. This is the remit of those involved in service marketing and can be achieved by clearly promoting the service offering and by setting a price level which fits the competitive positioning of the service firm. These two marketing tasks are discussed in Chapters 5 and 6 respectively.

The single most important activity in promotion is communication. A service concept must be developed and then communicated in a clear and consistent way so that the risk to the customer when buying in a service situation is reduced. A good communication strategy will include a decision on communication channels and tools as well as a communication plan. The simultaneity of production and consumption in services means that the delivery system itself (and especially the employees) is a very important communication tool.

Pricing is another very 'tangible' aspect of service marketing. In Chapter 6 we develop a framework for setting the price of a service offering in service firms. Four steps are discussed: pricing objectives, pricing strategy, pricing structure

▶

and pricing levels/tactics. The choice of pricing strategy has an impact on many other aspects of service management. Not only is the competitive position of the service firm influenced by pricing, but price levels can also be used to manage service demand in accordance with the capacity of the firm.

In Chapter 7, we consider customer satisfaction and look at the match between customers' expectations about the service and the performance of the firm in delivering the service. Various methods of measuring customer satisfaction are discussed.

While satisfaction scores can give very valuable information about the way customers appreciate the product of the service firm, dissatisfaction is even more important to detect. Actively stimulating customers to reveal their complaints is a strategy which pays off, certainly in terms of customer loyalty. In Chapter 7, we also discuss how a system of complaints management can be set up so that the customer feels encouraged to complain, if necessary.

Customer satisfaction depends to a great extent on how well the service employees understand the customer expectations. This is why some service firms are making their performance standards more explicit by using service guarantees or service-level agreements – the subjects of Chapter 8. In this kind of arrangement, the service provider makes promises about the level or quality the customer may expect and sometimes backs up these promises with a pay-out. This kind of arrangement gives the service provider the opportunity to track service failures and to continuously improve the service offering. This again can be important in maintaining a long-term relationship with customers.

Throughout this part, it will become clear that customer retention is very important for service firms because of the fact that there seems to be a positive relationship between customer retention and profitability, leveraged by the lifetime value of the customer. The customer cannot be separated from the service delivery system and it is this crucial relationship that is the key to effective services management.

CHAPTER 4

Relationship marketing

Kristof De Wulf

INTRODUCTION

> *'He who wishes to be rich in one day, will be hanged in a year.'*
> Leonardo da Vinci

Building satisfaction, loyalty and profitability is not something that can be decided upon one day and implemented the next. It can only result from building and sustaining close and/or long-term relationships. This means that in services much attention must be paid to relationship marketing. Relationship marketing replaces the more traditional, transaction oriented, approaches of marketing by placing greater emphasis upon the creation of customer value by means of developing and sustaining relationships. This introductory chapter will show why building relationships with profitable customers deserves increasing attention. The links between company performance and traditional parameters such as market share, cost structure or company size are fading. By revealing key research findings, we shall point out how and why customer satisfaction, customer loyalty and profitability are so closely related to each other and hence why developing relationships is relevant.

Objectives

By the end of this chapter, you should be able to discuss:

- the importance of building and sustaining relationships – referred to as relationship marketing – as the most distinctive feature of marketing services
- the service profit chain model, highlighting the close links between customer satisfaction, customer loyalty and profitability
- how the lifetime value of the customer can be calculated
- the role of different relationship marketing strategies in enhancing customer loyalty
- the importance of a detailed knowledge of the purchasing patterns of a company's customer base, when developing a particular strategy

RELATIONSHIP MARKETING: NEW WORDS TO AN OLD TUNE?

Over the past few decades, we have witnessed several shifts in marketing focus. If the 1950s were the era of mass marketing, and the 1970s the era of market segmentation, then the 1990s represent the genesis of personalized marketing. Today we see an increased acceptance of the relationship concept which can be defined as all marketing activities directed toward establishing, developing, and maintaining successful relational exchanges.[1] Relationship marketing in itself is not a new concept. Two hundred years ago, the natural approach to the market was through relationships. Jacob Schweppes, who founded the soft drinks company bearing his name in 1790 in Geneva, had already built up close relationships with local doctors who provided poorer patients with his sparkling mineral waters.

The renewed attention to relationship marketing refocuses the traditional transactional marketing approach by placing a greater emphasis upon the creation of customer value. In transaction marketing, marketing managers are generally concerned with the day's sales and the year's top and bottom lines. In relationship marketing, a marketer's challenge is to bring service quality, customer service and marketing into close alignment, leading to long-term and mutually beneficial customer relationships.[2] We can find evidence of this in retail banking, for instance. Retail banks are well aware of the fact that it takes six years for some of their customer accounts to reach the break-even point. In the UK, attracting 150 000 new student/youth accounts could cost £3 million in advertising and another £20 per head in incentives, mailings, computer costs and administration. As a result, retail banks are adopting the long-term view of account retention.

The importance of relationship marketing is expected to grow as resellers have gained increased power and as communication and information technologies have put individual consumers in more direct contact with resellers and manufacturers. Such technological advances enable sellers to recognize individual consumer needs, to directly interact with consumers, to quickly respond to their preferences, and to differentiate product or service offerings towards them. In addition, other factors such as eroding repeat purchases, intensified competitive pressures, and the continuing growth of the service economy increase the need to apply relationship marketing. Technological, social and economic developments have encouraged marketers to redirect their attention:

■ *Technological developments*. Changes in information technology have permitted us to collect, store and manipulate a growing amount of raw data at an ever-increasing tempo. E5 Mode, a fashion retailer in Belgium, set up an information system which is able to track the demand pattern in an almost real-time way. Every customer has a personal card and every time the customer buys clothes, a number of items of information are registered. As a result, the firm has developed a database of almost 2 million customers and more than 100 attributes per customer. This database allows the company to study the factors which affect demand and allows it to form a relationship between products and customer attributes. The database can be used to produce aggregate figures, such as how many pairs of trousers are sold in a year. However, the database also allows insight at a very detailed level: does the company sell more 'shirts with collar buttons' than 'shirts without collar buttons'? The database is analysed daily and modifications to demand patterns are noted very quickly through changes in the inventory level of some of the products.

■ *Social developments.* With respect to the social environment, increased individualization is a widely noted change. Today's customers feel and assert their individuality and expect this to be recognized. The customer wants to be listened to and respected. The acceptance of cocooning leads the customer to look for a safe and familiar environment. An increasing number of customers are complaining and protesting when they feel their expectations are not being met.

■ *Economic developments.* These have changed the level of competition and, consequently, the marketer's view of the marketing process. Over the last decade, there has been an explosion in the number of distribution channels, products and services and the boundaries between them are disappearing. Tesco, a large UK supermarket chain, is selling personal computers. Nielsen's[3] estimates tell us that 100 new products are added to the French market every day. Head & Shoulders, the leading shampoo, has only a 9 per cent share of the market. Texaco, the second best-selling gasoline, has 7 per cent of the US gasoline market, and Exxon, the leader, has only 8 per cent. A BBDO worldwide survey of consumers in 28 countries found that two-thirds believed that no differences existed in the quality of brands in 13 different product and service categories.

These developments are forcing today's managers to address the principles of relationship marketing – that is, to create and maintain relationships of value. The following examples illustrate how some companies are emphasizing relationships in their marketing efforts:[4]

■ Free Spirit Travel, a Colorado-based travel agency, assigns frequent-traveller clients a special travel agent to co-ordinate all travel arrangements. Information, such as the preferred form of payment, the secretary's name, and flight and hotel preferences, are stored in computerized client files.

■ With a database of 13 million names (4–5 million are active members) containing variables such as tenure, tier status, past stay history and hotel spending over the past 12 months, the hotel chain Starwood is able to segment as few as 1000 customers with tailored e-mail offers, as opposed to the industry's more common one-size-fits-all promotions. 'At the end of the day, the ability to segment from your database is what's going to increase loyalty and profitability,' said Berra. 'As you begin to find strategies that work for you at some level, the next generation may take you into a more finite segmentation and to the point where you really are targeting a small population. But you have the insight to know that you're marketing to a group with the highest propensity to respond.'[5]

■ Senior executives at the US affinity credit card issuer, MBNA America, learn from their own disaffected customers. Each executive spends four hours a month in a special 'listening' room, monitoring routine customer service calls as well as calls from customers who are cancelling their credit cards.

■ In order to deliver the services that fleet managers desire and need, ExxonMobil announced the development of the new ExxonMobil Fleet Card Program. The program offers a number of valuable features including: greater control over driver's expenses, money-saving rebates on fuel purchases, special discounts on business-related products and services, innovative technology and the convenience of more than 16,000 Exxon and Mobil branded locations nationwide.[6]

- Harley-Davidson created a Harley Owners Club, which has about 200 000 members worldwide. Besides motorbikes, Harley-Davidson also has an insurance programme, a travel agency, an emergency roadside service, two magazines, member competitions and 750 local chapters.

LINKING CUSTOMER SATISFACTION, CUSTOMER LOYALTY AND PROFITABILITY

The fundamental importance of relationship marketing in services is directly related to the principle that customer satisfaction, customer loyalty and profitability are closely intertwined with each other. The creation of superior value for the customer is the key driver of satisfaction and loyalty. This is one of the most important elements of the '*service profit chain model*' of Heskett *et al.*[7] (*see also* Chapter 9). Profitability, customer loyalty, customer satisfaction, employee satisfaction, employee productivity and employee loyalty are all related to each other in this model (*see* Figure 4.1). By analysing several successful service organizations, Heskett *et al.* discovered that service capability or the quality of the internal service delivery system influences the level of employee satisfaction, that higher employee satisfaction leads to higher employee retention and productivity, that high employee retention and productivity have a positive influence on the value of the external service, that the high value of the external service helps to create customer satisfaction, that high customer satisfaction leads to customer loyalty, and that high customer loyalty creates growth, turnover and profits. The better the value of the external service, the more customers are satisfied and loyal; and the higher the level of growth, turnover and profits, the better the quality of the internal service and the level of employee satisfaction.

The rest of this chapter will especially focus upon the right-hand area of the service profit chain model (the left side will be covered in Chapter 9). We first define customer satisfaction and customer loyalty before considering the motivations for the links between the two concepts. Their relationship with profitability is then explained in detail. We discuss potential strategies for increasing customer satisfaction and customer loyalty and then describe how to set objectives and how to measure and evaluate satisfaction and loyalty strategies.

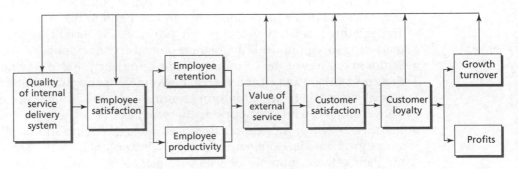

Figure 4.1 The service profit chain[8]

Source: Reprinted by permission of *Harvard Business Review*, from 'Putting the service-profit chain to work', Heskett, J. L., Jones, T. O., Loveman, G. W., Sasser, W. E. and Schlesinger, L., March–April 1994. Copyright © 1998 by the President and Fellows of Harvard College; all rights reserved.

Customer satisfaction and customer loyalty defined

Customer satisfaction is generally defined as:

'*the customer's feeling regarding the gap between his or her expectations towards a company, product or service and the perceived performance of the company, product or service.*'

If the perceived performance matches or even 'excites' customers' expectations, they are satisfied. If it does not, they are dissatisfied. This is why organizations need to manage the expectations of their customers well, so that there is no room for misunderstanding regarding what the organization intends to provide.

We define *customer loyalty* as:

'*customer behaviour characterized by a positive buying pattern during an extended period (measured by means of repeat purchases, frequency of purchase, wallet share or other indicators) and driven by a positive attitude towards the company and its products or services.*'

Since customer attitude is difficult to measure, for financial and practical purposes, *customer retention* is most widely used as an indicator of customer loyalty. However, attitude and behaviour can be very different (*see* Figure 4.2).

- *Truly loyal* customers are willing to seek out a particular service, location or brand.
- *Spuriously loyal* customers tend to be more motivated by impulse, convenience, and habit – that is, if the conditions are right.
- *Latent loyalty* applies to customers who are loyal simply because they have no other choice. In the 1970s, IBM owned the proprietary technology from which it

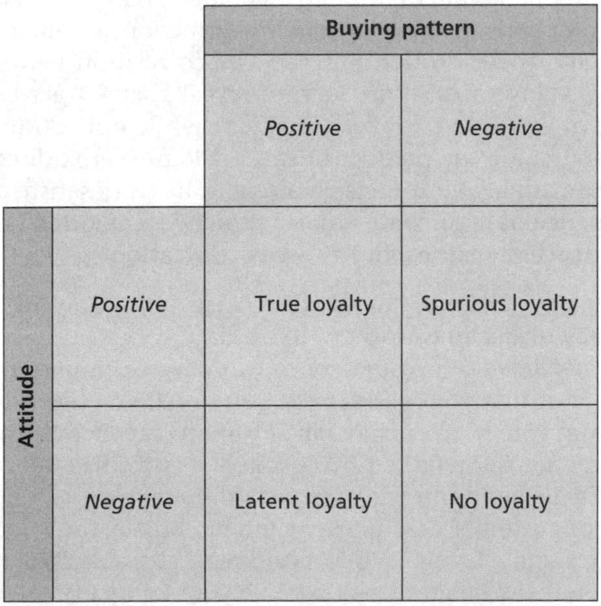

	Buying pattern	
	Positive	*Negative*
Attitude *Positive*	True loyalty	Spurious loyalty
Negative	Latent loyalty	No loyalty

Figure 4.2 The dimensions of customer loyalty[9]

Source: Dick, A. S. and Basu, K. (1994) *Journal of the Academy of Marketing Science*, 22 (2), 99–113.
Copyright © 1998 Sage Publications. Reprinted by permission of Sage Publication Inc.

was difficult and expensive to escape. Today, with some notable exceptions it is no longer morally acceptable or commercially possible to try to strait-jacket a customer.

■ *No loyalty*. Obviously there will always be some customers who display no loyalty to a particular company or brand.

The different loyalty types which appear in the matrix in Figure 4.2 can be matched with different forms of relationships: *interaction frequency* (long-term relationships) and *interaction profundity* (close relationships). While interaction frequency solely focuses upon the buying pattern of a customer, interaction profundity is strongly related to the attitudinal component of customer loyalty. The more profound the relationship between a service provider and its customers, the more positive the customers' attitudes are likely to be.

The relationship between customer satisfaction and customer loyalty

Customer satisfaction studies should form an integral part of the management of the service delivery process. Although many companies conduct such studies on an *ad hoc* basis, some actually measure customer satisfaction on a continuous basis. Rank Xerox is a well-known example. For the last few years, Xerox has tracked satisfaction ratings of 480 000 customers, with the aim of reaching '100% satisfied customers'. Xerox will settle for nothing less because it is well aware of the substantial impact of even a 1 per cent increase or decrease in satisfaction on its results. For example, only 8 per cent of British customers are actively dissatisfied with the goods and services they purchase by direct mail. However, since this is a £12 billion-a-year industry, that 8 per cent could be worth between £5 billion and £10 billion over five years. IBM found that a 1 per cent increase in customer satisfaction translated into $500 million in increased sales over five years.

Despite the common belief that customer satisfaction automatically translates into customer loyalty, there is often only a weak correlation between satisfaction scores and loyalty. Many satisfaction surveys reveal that 90 per cent of the customers questioned are 'satisfied' to 'very satisfied', while only 30 to 40 per cent of these customers repurchase the product or service. Rank Xerox discovered that the chance of repurchase among customers claiming to be 'very satisfied' was six times higher than the chance of repurchase among those who reported being 'somewhat satisfied'. There are several reasons for this weak correlation.

1. Positive and negative feelings can coexist. A customer may feel good about a company, but may dislike one aspect of its service.
2. Factors not directly related to your service can play an important role. It is not the restaurant's fault that your partner chooses to tell you over dinner there that he or she is leaving you, but you may never want to eat there again!
3. Satisfaction scores are self-reported by customers, and thus are to a great extent influenced by the unstable and temporary conditions the respondent is in.
4. Different levels of customer commitment might explain the large differences in satisfaction and loyalty levels. While customers characterized by a *calculative* commitment merely outweigh the extra value your company can offer compared to that offered by the competition, customers who show *affective* commitment truly have a deep relationship with their service provider. While calculatively oriented customers might well be satisfied with the service offerings, they can

turn out to be less loyal as a result of the fact that service offerings are easily copied by competitors. An affective relationship, on the contrary, is more protected from a competitor's actions. Again, the difference between 'interaction frequency' and 'interaction profundity' is related to notions of calculative and affective commitment.

These weaknesses in the measurement of customer satisfaction often lead to the suggestion that customer retention should be measured instead of customer satisfaction (see also Chapter 7). In our opinion, the fact that a measurement should be interpreted carefully does not mean it should be rejected. Satisfaction scores can provide very valuable information about the way customers appreciate the value proposition of a company. Moreover, they can be compared reliably over time.

A close relationship does exist between customer loyalty and high levels of customer satisfaction (*customer delight*). This implies that companies should not only meet their customers' expectations, but should try to 'excite' their customers in one way or another. Figure 4.3 shows the relationship between customer retention and customer loyalty. Very loyal customers can only be found in the affection zone, which also consists of very satisfied customers. *Apostles* are customers who are extremely loyal and delighted or extremely satisfied. *Terrorists* are extremely dangerous for your company: they grab every opportunity to complain about their bad experiences with you. The attrition zone contains customers who show low levels of satisfaction and as a result are also less loyal. Customers in the indifference zone show no true loyalty: their satisfaction level is only moderate.

Perhaps what matters even more than a customer's satisfaction with your service is what happens in a crisis, or when something simply goes wrong. Mistakes are an inevitable part of every service. Even the best service companies cannot prevent the occasional late flight, burnt steak or missed delivery. While companies may not be able to prevent all problems, they can still listen to their customers and learn to

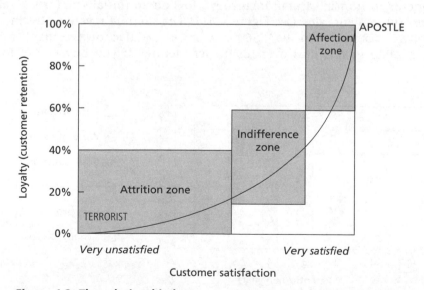

Figure 4.3 The relationship between customer satisfaction and customer loyalty[10]

Source: Reprinted by permission of *Harvard Business Review*, from 'Putting the service-profit chain to work', Heskett, J. L., Jones, T. O., Loveman, G. W., Sasser, W. E. and Schlesinger, L., March–April, 1994. Copyright © 1998 by the President and Fellows of Harvard College; all rights reserved.

recover from their mistakes. That is one of the reasons why service organizations are paying more and more attention to complaints and have developed a system to handle and manage complaints (*see* Chapter 7).

LIFETIME VALUE: THE LINK WITH PROFITABILITY

A US study[11] discovered that half of a company's customers disappear in five years (10 to 30 per cent attrition) and half of a company's employees disappear in four years (15 to 25 per cent attrition). At these rates, disloyalty is claimed to be limiting company performance by 25 to 50 per cent. Defections cost British companies £100 billion per year in sales and another £100 billion in recruiting new customers to replace those lost. How do we explain this strong relationship between customer loyalty and company performance? There are two arguments:

1. Strategies directed at increasing loyalty help to plug the leaky bucket: higher customer retention, given the same number of new customers, leads to a volume effect.
2. Customers become more profitable over time: in addition to a reliable base profit, your turnover per customer will increase and your operational costs will go down thanks to productivity and cost advantages; a more positive word of mouth will be generated and price sensitivity will drop.[12]

By understanding and measuring both of these dynamics, you can calculate the lifetime value of your customers. This figure represents the net present value of the profits you will generate from your customers over a number of periods (usually four to five years). By computing the average lifetime value of your customers, you will be able to determine how much you can invest in attracting a potential new customer. The basic principle is to look upon customers as investments in human capital: incurring a loss on an initial sale for the sake of profits on subsequent sales (*see* Figure 4.4).[13] The lifetime revenue stream from a loyal pizza customer can be £5600. A loyal Cadillac owner may easily generate £232 000 in revenues over his or her lifetime. If you buy £70 of food products

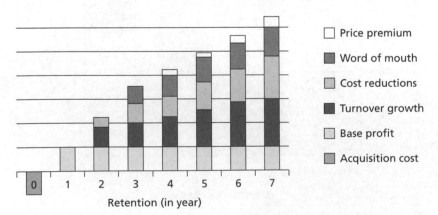

Figure 4.4 Sources of profitability in relation to customer retention

Source: Reprinted by permission of Harvard Business School Press, *The Loyalty Effect – the hidden force behind growth, profits and lasting value*, Reichheld, F. F., Boston, MA (1996), p. 39. Copyright © 1998 by Bain & Company, INC.

every week and you are loyal to your supermarket, you will spend £36 000 over a period of ten years. A moderately frequent flier who travels between the US coasts once a month will generate £15 000 or more in revenues for the airline over a five-year period. To a news vendor in Manchester, a customer who buys every daily edition of *The Times* and the *Sunday Times* is worth £10 000 in lifetime revenues. A newborn baby can soil £1000 worth of single-use nappies in its first year.

You can carry out your own lifetime value calculation by following the simple steps described below:

■ Select a group of customers, all of whom became regular customers at about the same time in the past (four to five years ago).
■ Calculate the retention rate by determining how many of these customers were still buying a year later. If there is enough data, determine the second-year retention rate as well. If not, estimate it for subsequent years (50 per cent attrition is not unusual for some companies).
■ Determine the average amount of money that these customers spend in a single year.
■ Determine the percentage of revenue that must be allocated to direct costs.
■ Determine the discount rate that applies to the business (a sound rule is to double the market rate of interest).
■ Put all of this data into a spreadsheet, projecting the customer lifetime value for five years.
■ Try out some 'what-if' analyses – i.e., try to predict the effect of several marketing scenarios on the customer lifetime value.
■ Keep the spreadsheet active. After trying a few marketing initiatives, check their results against the spreadsheet, thereby improving your company's forecasting ability.

By following these steps, you will end up with a spreadsheet similar to that shown in Table 4.1.

Table 4.1 Calculation example of lifetime value

Revenue	Year 1	Year 2	Year 3	Year 4	Year 5
Customers	1000	400	180	90	50
Retention rate (%)	40%	45%	50%	55%	60%
Average yearly sale	$150	$160	$170	$180	$200
Total revenue	$150 000	$64 000	$30 600	$16 200	$10 000
Costs					
Cost (%)	50%	48%	46%	44%	42%
Total costs	$75 000	$30 720	$14 076	$7 128	$4 200
Profits					
Gross profit	$75 000	$33 280	$16 524	$9 072	$5 800
Discount rate (20%)	1	1.2	1.44	1.73	2.07
NPV profit	$75 000	$27 733	$11 475	$5 244	$2 802
Cumulative NPV profit	$75 000	$102 733	$114 208	$119 452	$125 056
Lifetime value (NPV)	**$75**	**$103**	**$114**	**$119**	**$125**

In the example in Table 4.1, the following assumptions were made:

- The retention rate increases each year as a result of the fact that customers who have shown loyalty in the past also have a higher chance of remaining loyal in the future.
- The average annual sales increase each year as a result of the fact that customers tend to spend more money if they show higher loyalty.
- Costs drop each year as a result of the fact that loyal customers require less operational handling and acquisition costs have disappeared.
- A discount rate of 20 per cent was used.

Bain & Co. have studied the relationship between retention rate and lifetime value in a number of different industries. Their study of the US credit card industry shows that if a credit card customer leaves after the first year, the average business suffers a loss of $21. If it can keep the customer for four years, the customer's net present value to the company rises to about $100. If the credit card company cuts its defection rate from 20 per cent to 10 per cent, the lifespan of its customers goes up from 4 to 10 years and the lifetime value more than doubles – jumping from $134 to $300![14]

The US affinity credit card issuer, MBNA, even found that 5 per cent reduction in defection rates improved the average customer value by more than 125 per cent. The research projects undertaken by Bain & Co. (Consultants) show that keeping 5 per cent more customers each year can boost profits by 25 to 85 per cent, depending on the sector (*see* Figure 4.5). The results of reducing customer defection are especially spectacular in the credit card and branch deposits business (75 per cent and 85 per cent respectively).

Not all customers should be made loyal, however. Reichheld stresses the importance of seeking the right customers in the first place (*see* Reichheld, 1996). Customers differ inherently with respect to loyalty, profitability and 'fit' with your organization. Different customers have different profit profiles.[15] According to

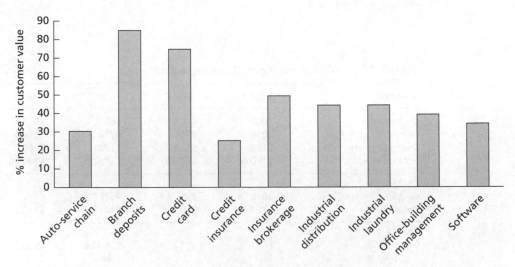

Figure 4.5 Percentage increase in customer value (profitability) as a result of a 5 per cent decrease in customer defection[16]

Source: Reprinted by permission of Harvard Business School Press, *The Loyalty Effect – The hidden force behind growth, profits and lasting value*, Reichheld, F. F., Boston, MA (1996), p. 36. Copyright © 1998 by Bain & Company, INC.

James Vander Putten, vice president for information management at American Express, the best customers outspend others by ratios of 16 to 1 in retailing, 13 to 1 in the restaurant business, 12 to 1 in airlines, and 5 to 1 in the hotel/motel industry. It makes no sense to build up a loyal but unprofitable relationship.

With the Pareto principle in mind (a relatively small number of customers generate a relatively high percentage of the total sales volume of a company), it follows that you should allocate 80 per cent of your time and effort to 20 per cent of your customers. It is not uncommon for approximately 50 per cent of the customers in a retail bank's database to be unprofitable. However, it is not always possible to know whether a currently unprofitable account might generate a future profit stream, given investment in that particular customer. Research by Ogilvy & Mather Direct shows that making fickle customers loyal may be more difficult than switching loyal purchasers of another's brand to a new trustworthy partner. Loyal customers may be hard to win over, but once you do, they are worth the investment. Therefore, care must be taken if a commission system is in operation that rewards sales personnel for acquiring customers – the easiest prospects are those with the lowest loyalty potential. The secret of profitable customer acquisition is not to find new bargain-sensitive customers, but to seek and reward loyal ones. Practical experience from a variety of industries shows, for example, that referrals are better prospects than people who respond to advertisements, that people who buy at the standard price are better than promotion shoppers, that risk-averse people are better than experimenters, and that long courtships are better than short ones.[17]

HOW TO INCREASE CUSTOMER SATISFACTION AND CUSTOMER LOYALTY

In a customer's relationship with a particular company, he or she can progress from being a prospect to being a customer, client, supporter and, at the top of the ladder, an advocate (*see* Figure 4.6). Advocates are so deeply embedded in your organization

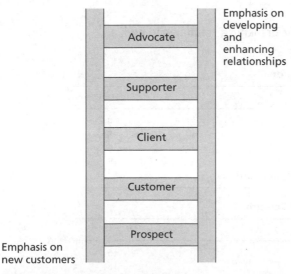

Figure 4.6 Customer loyalty ladder[18]

Source: From Jenkinson, A., *Valuing Your Customers: From Quality Information to Quality Relationships Through Database Marketing*, 1995, McGraw Hill Book Co. Ltd., reproduced with the kind permission of McGraw-Hill Publishing Company.

that they are not only very loyal long-term purchasers themselves, but also influence others through positive word of mouth. Too often marketers stop short, being satisfied with having converted a prospect into a customer. Considering loyalty as the natural consequence of selling is the essential flaw in our management of customer relationships. The romantic ideal of courtship as a series of steps leading to marriage and eternal happiness applies to relationship marketing as well. The real value of your customers will only manifest itself when they can be nurtured further up the loyalty ladder. The aim of any company should be to encourage its customers as far up the ladder of customer loyalty as possible. Each rung of the ladder represents a development of mutual commitment. In order to reach this objective, specific strategies for developing and enhancing customer relationships should be adopted.

A first requirement for sound relationship marketing is to make sure that customers do not fall from the loyalty ladder. High levels of customer service quality are vital in achieving this objective: by creating an offering that is distinctly superior to that of your competitors, you will win customer loyalty. Most research seems to confirm that customers are five times more likely to switch suppliers because of perceived service problems and lack of attention[19] than price concerns or competitive actions in general. Table 4.2 gives an overview of the results of studies conducted by McGraw-Hill Research and Forum Research.

Jan Carlzon, president and CEO of Scandinavian Airlines System (SAS), was one of the first managers to popularize the importance of customer contacts in fulfilling the promise of a product or service. He realized that each of SAS's 10 million annual customers came into contact for approximately 15 seconds with an average of five SAS employees during a flight. He referred to these encounters as 'moments of truth'. A crucial ingredient in the turnaround of SAS from its status as an $8-million-a-year loser to a $71-million-a-year winner was its focus on those 50 million 'moments of truth'.

Table 4.2 Reasons for breaking a relationship with a supplier

(a) Results of Forum Research

Reason	Percentage
Move away or die	4
Personal relationship	5
Competitor activity	9
Product dissatisfaction	15
No contact, indifference, poor attitude	67

(b) Results of McGraw-Hill Research

Reason	Percentage
Better product	15
Cheaper product	15
Too little contact and individual attention	20
Poor quality of attention and service	49

Keeping customers at the same rung of the loyalty ladder is not sufficient, however. They should be boosted as high as possible up the ladder. An article in the *McKinsey Quarterly* states:

'Our lessons reflect the simple truth that excellence in marketing has always flowed from understanding how to deliver what customers need – profitably. Many retailers offer discounts, rebates or goods if customers present loyalty cards at every purchase, yet they fail to use the resulting information to tailor their offerings to individual customers' tastes, buying patterns, or value to the company.' [20]

In today's business practice, examples of relationship marketing practices are widespread. Ritz-Carlton is well-known for its personalized welcome and farewell of guests, using the guest's name when possible. Loyalty programs initiated by airlines consist of rewarding the most valuable customers in the form of mileage prizes, but also of showing recognition and providing special privileges. In general, the literature distinguishes between two levels of relationship marketing. [21]

Level one relationship marketing

A first level relies on pricing incentives to secure customer loyalty and is often referred to as 'level one relationship marketing'. Level one relationship marketing implies providing customers with rewards that rely primarily on pricing incentives and money savings to secure their loyalty. Examples of tangible rewards customers get as a means of appreciating their patronage are frequent flyer miles, customer loyalty bonuses, free gifts, or personalized money-off coupons. Also trying to earn points – on such things as hotel stays, cinema tickets, and car washes – would help customers to remain loyal, regardless of service enhancement or price promotions of competitors offering discounts, rebates or goods. However, it is considered to be the weakest level of relationship marketing because competitors can easily imitate price. Reward programmes are frequently regarded as being cheap promotional tools, short-term fads which give something for nothing. Initiatives such as Mobil's Premier Points may help boost sales – 25 per cent in the case of Mobil – but do little to lock in the highly promiscuous consumer. American Express raised its sales by 20 per cent or more in certain markets with its Membership Miles scheme. Reward systems can and do affect customer behaviour (*retention*), but they cannot change attitudes (*loyalty*). Real loyalty comes from real differentiation. The danger exists that consumers are enticed by the promotions, rather than being attracted to the products or the service. From this point of view, loyalty cannot be bought; it must be earned. [22] An old American joke clearly points out the danger of using rewards in order to stimulate loyalty. An old man was being insulted every day by a group of ten-year-olds, who would tell him how stupid, ugly and old he was. Instead of shouting at them, he called them together and told them that any of them who shouted a him the next day would get a dollar. Excited and amazed, they all came round, hurled abuse and collected their dollars. 'Do the same tomorrow,' he said, 'and I'll give you a quarter for your trouble.' The children thought this was still pretty good, and turned out again to insult him and earn their reward. The man apologized and told them that on the following day, he could only afford to give them a penny. 'Forget it,' they said – and that was the end of his problem! Removal of rewards leads to a decline in desirable responses and a return to baseline performance levels. The loss of reward is a source of dissatisfaction capable of shifting the buying habit. National Westminster Bank offered one point per £10 spent, then one point per £20 spent, but what could it do next? When Shell stopped distributing free savings stamps to its customers in the Netherlands, their reactions were so fierce that the company was obliged to reintroduce them. Notice that 'level one' relationship marketing seems to be especially relevant for maintenance-interactive services,[23] task and personal-interactive services might benefit more from level two initiatives (*see* Chapter 6).

Level two relationship marketing

A second level of relationship marketing focuses at the social aspects of a relationship exemplified by regularly communicating with consumers. These socially inspired tactics are usually bundled into what is called 'level two relationship marketing'. In general, it is recognized that buyer–seller communication enhances the prediction of behaviour of the other party and clarifies each other's roles and by doing so increases the probability of beneficial behaviours. In addition, communication leads to the discovery of similarities and encourages feelings of trust, special status, and closeness. Moreover, especially differentiated communication is assumed to positively influence relationship strength. Sheth and Parvatiyar[24] recognized that 'implicit in the idea of relationship marketing is consumer focus and consumer selectivity – that is, all consumers do not need to be served in the same way.' The nature of services affords many service firms the opportunity to customize the relationship. By learning about the specific characteristics and requirements of individual customers, and then capturing this information for use as needed, service firms can more precisely tailor service to the situation at hand. Consider the simple example of a person who called a local independent florist to arrange for flowers to be sent to his mother on her birthday.[25] The following year, three weeks before his mother's birthday, he received a postcard from the same florist, reminding him that his mother's birthday was coming up, that he had sent spider lilies and freesias the year before for a certain price, and that a phone call to the specified number would put another beautiful bouquet on his mother's doorstep. The only tools the florist needed were a PC and a large measure of common sense. The possibilities for relationship customization are especially impressive when personal service capabilities are combined with electronic data-processing capabilities. A Ritz-Carlton hotel in California stores all information from guest registration cards in a computerized system. This information is immediately displayed on terminals used by front-desk personnel when a repeat guest visits the hotel. The guest's assigned room can be pre-stocked with the brand of whisky, newspaper and hairdryer that were requested on a previous visit.

SETTING OBJECTIVES IN SERVICE MARKETING

'Managers only need to concentrate on strategy and vision, not on measurement' is a familiar expression. However, a sound strategy can only be realized by using the right measurement systems (we shall return to this in Part Five). What a company measures, communicates its values, channels the thinking of its employees and clarifies management priorities.

When managers talk about objectives, they usually mention profits, return on investment, market share, growth or other indicators showing the financial consequences of their decisions. All of these financial indicators are generated from one single source – customers. Marketers need to think increasingly in terms of share of customer, rather than share of market.

Let's suppose you are such a manager. If you have a 10 per cent market share, then for every pound spent on your product or service, you receive about 10p. Perhaps every single consumer in your market spends an equal amount on your product or service, and perhaps every single one buys your brand about 10 per cent of the time. This means you will receive 10 per cent of the business from each of them. However, it is more likely that your business is coming from about 20 per cent of consumers who are buying your product or service about 50 per cent of the time.[26]

During each planning period, you should try to set specific objectives for prospects and customers:

- Which prospects are you looking for?
- Which prospects do you want to convert to customers?
- Which customers do you want to keep?
- Which customers do you want to develop?

Unless you are confident enough to rely upon your own intuition and experience, information you have assembled about your customers' past behaviour will guide you through this planning process. Many companies already have access to some of this information through consumer panels or repeat purchase studies. Moreover, more and more companies are exploring the opportunities database marketing provides for analysing profiles of existing customers on the basis of demographics, purchase behaviour or other information.

The construction of your customer portfolio thus begins with determining meaningful customer classifications based on actual purchase patterns. Your portfolio segments can be measured in terms of number of customers, number of purchases, recency of purchases, demographic and psychographic profiles and

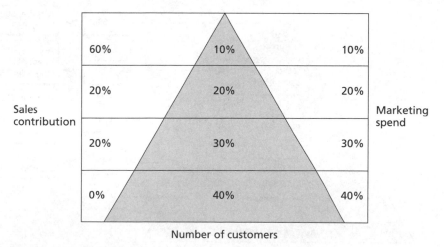

Figure 4.7 Distribution of marketing costs over customer segments[27]

Source: From Jenkinson, A., *Valuing Your Customers: From Quality Information to Quality Relationships Through Database Marketing*, 1995, McGraw Hill Book Co. Ltd., reproduced with the kind permission of McGraw-Hill Publishing Company.

contributions to sales or profits. You can visualize the type and number of customers in each portfolio using a *customer pyramid* (*see* Figure 4.7). This pyramid represents the structure of your customer base and could be composed, for example, of top customers, medium customers, small customers, prospects and suspects. In a typical case, 10 per cent of customers generate about 60 per cent of sales and over 60 per cent of profits. However, when marketing and customer service expense is analyzed, these costs are frequently shared equally across the customer base. Do you believe in spending 70 per cent of your budget to generate only 20 per cent of your business? It makes economic sense to redistribute your marketing costs according to the value (sales contribution or profits) customers are bringing in.

Let's suppose you decide to define your top customers as customers generating a yearly turnover of more than £3500 (630 customers), your medium customers as those yielding between £1400 and £3500 in revenues (1720 customers), and your small customers as those bringing in less than £1400 per year (6310 customers). Moreover, your suspect market consists of 14 020 potential customers and you have 1370 prospects. In Figure 4.8, targets are set for each customer category by determining how many customers should move in, stay or move up. For example, looking at the category of small customers, the objectives are to acquire 700 new small customers, to keep 4690, to move 250 to the category of top customers and to move 420 to the category of medium customers.

Another way of setting objectives is by modelling the value spectrum of your customers. *Value-spectrum modelling* is based on two fundamental dynamics: loyalty and value. The simplest model can be represented as a two-by-two matrix (*see* Figure 4.9). The basic principle is that high-value loyal customers should be retained, low-value loyal customers should be upgraded, high-value disloyal customers should be converted and low-value disloyal customers should be rejected. This model is especially useful in business-to-business and service markets where both value potential and loyalty can be measured reasonably well.

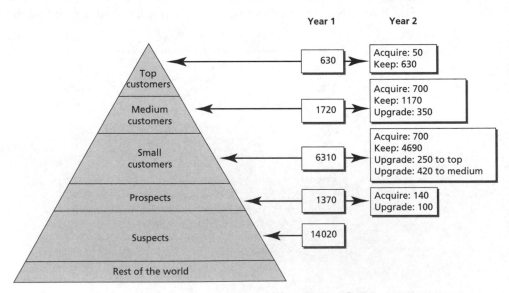

Figure 4.8 Setting marketing objectives one customer at a time[28]

Source: MSP Associates Amsterdam, Curry, J., Wurtz, W., Thys, G. and Zÿlstra, L. (1998) *Customer Marketing – How to improve the profitability of your customer base*.

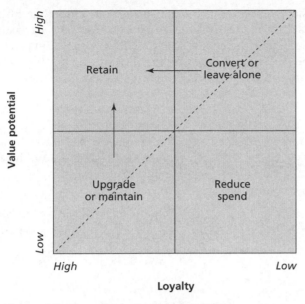

Figure 4.9 The value-spectrum model[29]

Source: From Jenkinson, A., *Valuing Your Customers: From Quality Information to Quality Relationships Through Database Marketing*, 1995, McGraw Hill Book Co. Ltd., reproduced with the kind permission of McGraw-Hill Publishing Company.

CONCLUSION

Today, the new marketing environment and improvements in information technology have brought about a return to the relationship approach.

The relationship between customer satisfaction and loyalty measurements is not straightforward, but nevertheless very important. Although strong relationships are found only between high levels of customer satisfaction and loyalty, a 1 per cent increase in customers satisfaction may translate into a substantial increase in sales over five years. Dissatisfaction is equally, if not more important. Actively stimulating customers to reveal their complaints is a strategy which pays off (*see* Chapter 7).

The relationship between customer loyalty and profitability is very strong. Customer loyalty not only results in a business volume effect through diminishing customer attrition, it also leads to increased business per customer. The value of customer loyalty can be measured by calculating the lifetime value of customers. Superior value creation for the customer is the key driver of satisfaction and loyalty. It is important to link this insight with the findings on how employee satisfaction, productivity and employee loyalty are related to value creation (*see* Chapter 9).

How can a company move customers up the loyalty ladder? Most research seems to confirm that a customer's decision to switch from one supplier to another is five times more likely to be based on perceived service problems and lack of attention, than on price concerns. In addition to providing what is promised and keeping to contacts, companies commonly use two approaches: building learning relationships with customers and rewarding customers for their loyalty with hard benefits. Keeping customers solely on the basis of hard benefits is, however, not a sustainable long-term strategy.

One of the basic requirements for activating the loop that links satisfaction, loyalty and profitability is creating delighted customers by exceeding customers' expectations. In the remaining chapters of Part Two, we shall explain how the right expectations can be created and how an organization can be stimulated and steered towards meeting and sometimes even exceeding these expectations.

Review and discussion questions

- One could argue that loyal customers will often be less profitable; one reason for this is that they expect a reward for their loyalty. What do you think of this statement? Does a reward mean the same as 'less profitable'? Why? In what kind of situations does it hold true?

- What kinds of data are needed in order to decide whether or not customer relationship management (CRM) might be profitable? What does this mean in terms of CRM databases?

Notes and references

[1] See Morgan and Hunt 'The Commitment-Trust Theory of Relationship Marketing', *Journal of Marketing* July 1994, Vol 58, No 3, 20–38 (1994, p.22).

[2] Christopher, M., Payne, A. and Ballantyne, D. (1994) *Relationship Marketing: Bringing quality, customer service and marketing together*. Oxford: Butterworth-Heinemann (2nd edn).

[3] Nielsen is a company which tracks how many products are being sold in retailing through inventory checking.

[4] Reichheld, F. F. (1996) *The Loyalty Effect – The hidden force behind growth, profits, and lasting value*. Boston: Harvard Business School Press.

[5] 'Marketers of the next generation: Jim Berra' *Brandweek*; New York; Apr 8, 2002; Mike Beirne.

[6] 'ExxonMobil Corporation introduces new fleet card program Fleet Equipment'; Lincoln-wood; Mar 2002; Anonymous.

[7] Heskett, J., Sasser, E. W. and Schlesinger, L. (1997) *The Services Profit Chain*. New York: Free Press.

[8] *See* Heskett *et al.* (1997); Heskett, J. L., Jones, T. O., Loveman, G. W., Sasser, W. E. and Schlesinger, L. (1994) 'Putting the service profit chain to work', *Harvard Business Review*, Mar–Apr, 164–74.

[9] Adapted from Dick, A. S. and Basu, K. (1994) 'Customer loyalty: toward an integrated conceptual framework', *Journal of the Academy of Marketing Science*, Vol 22, No 2, 99–113.

[10] *Source*: Heskett *et al.* (1994), op. cit.

[11] Reichheld, F. F. (1996), op. cit.

[12] Ibid.

[13] Reichheld, F. F. and Sasser, W. E. (1990) 'Zero defections: quality comes to services', *Harvard Business Review*, Sep–Oct, 105–11.

[14] Reichheld (1996), op. cit.

[15] See in this respect also the article of Dowling (2002) Customer Relationships Management: in B2C Markets, Often Less is More. California Management Review, 44, 3.

[16] Reichheld (1996), op. cit.

[17] Ibid.

[18] Jenkinson, A. (1995) *Valuing Your Customers: From quality information to quality relationships through database marketing*. London: McGraw-Hill.

[19] It is clear that paying more attention to customers requires resources; hence one should focus on increasing attention in so far as one is able to compensate for the efforts this requires; for a further extension of this point, we refer as well to the work of Dowling, op. cit.

[20] Child, P., Dennis, R. J., Gokey, T. C., McGuire, T. I., Sherman, M. and Singer, M. (1995) 'Can marketing regain the personal touch?', *The McKinsey Quarterly*, No 3, 113–25.

[21] Based on De Wulf, Kristof, Gaby Odekerken-Schröder, and Dawn Iacobucci (2001) 'Investments in Consumer Relationships: A cross-country and cross-industry exploration', *Journal of Marketing*, Vol 65, No 4, 33–50.

[22] Molenaar, C. N. A. (1995) 'Loyaliteit kun je niet kopen', *Tijdschrift voor Marketing*, Nov, 24–7.

[23] The definition of these different types of services is to be found in Chapter 1.

[24] Sheth, Jagdish and Atul Parvatiyar (1995) 'Relationship Marketing in Consumer Markets: Antecedents and Consequences', *Journal of the Academy of Marketing Science*, Vol 23, No 4, 255–71.

[25] Peppers, D. and Rogers, M. (1993) The One-to-One Future. Building business relationships one customer at a time. London: Piatkus.

[26] Peppers, D. and Rogers, M. (1993), op. cit.

[27] Jenkinson, A. (1995), op. cit.

[28] Curry, J., Wurtz, W., Thys, G. and Zÿlstra, L. (1998) *Customer Marketing – How to improve the profitability of your customer base*. Amsterdam: MSP Associates.

[29] Jenkinson, A. (1995), op. cit.

Suggested further reading

Dowling (2002) 'Customer Relationships Management: in B2C markets, often less is more', *California Management Review*, Vol 44, No 3. In this article, Dowling is rather critical regarding applying the idea of relationships 'anytime, anywhere'. As such, this article becomes very valuable in terms of pinpointing the how and when of relationships marketing. A 'must check' for anyone interested in developing profitable relationships with their customers.

Peppers, D. and Rogers, M. (1993) *The One-to-One Future: Building business relationships one customer at a time*. London: Piatkus. The core theme of this book is customer-focused thinking. Using many examples, Peppers and Rogers show that the one-to-one future offers the best chances to build up long-term relationships with customers.

Reichheld, F. F. (1996) *The Loyalty Effect – The hidden force behind growth, profits and lasting value*. Boston: Harvard Business School Press. This book describes how the performance of the firm is linked to the loyalty of the customers, employees and investors. The general message is to create a maximum customer value. The statements are supported by figures from diverse business sectors which focus on loyalty.

CHAPTER 5

Promoting services

Patrick De Pelsmacker · Joeri Van Den Bergh

INTRODUCTION

This chapter looks at communication and the promotion of services. We devote particular attention to this topic because services have their own peculiarities that merit our attention. We shall first sketch out these points of interest to highlight why promotion is different for services. Some basic building blocks and insights will then be examined that aid the understanding of the management of promotional activities. Once equipped with these building blocks, we can start thinking about service-specific models for promotion.

Objectives

By the end of this chapter, you should be able to discuss:

- the special characteristics of the promotion of services
- what promotion entails – the communication process, communication effects and hence the link with the service concept through the notion of customer needs
- some common communication errors
- the service delivery process and what the different steps of this process entail in terms of promotional activities
- a guiding framework to develop the outline of a promotion plan

WHAT IS SO DIFFERENT ABOUT PROMOTING SERVICES?

There are a number of distinct characteristics of services that determine the rules about their communication or promotion.[1] Not surprisingly, these particular points stem directly from the nature of services – that is, their intangibility and simultaneity.

Services are at least partially intangible, which leads to difficulties for customers when trying to evaluate services before consuming them (an issue already touched upon in Chapter 1). This does not mean that customers do not try to carry out an evaluation before engaging in the service delivery process. They tend to observe the tangibles associated with a service in a search for 'clues' about the service's quality. For this reason, service communication has to strive to give concrete visual clues that reflect the needs and concerns of the targeted customer segment – for example, by showing the facilities in which a service is performed or by creating a personality symbol that represents the service idea.

Another way in which customers acquire information is by looking at the experiences of other customers. In high-involvement situations – that is, when the consequences of buying a low quality service are perceived to be serious – consumers are especially receptive to word-of-mouth communication. This propensity may be used in communication in the following ways:

- by means of testimonials, that is, persuading satisfied customers to let others know of their experience;
- by targeting communication to opinion leaders; or
- by guiding prospective customers in soliciting word-of-mouth communication.

Intangibility is not the only feature of services that plays a part; the simultaneity of production and consumption in services implies that the service transaction process itself is part of the communication process. Hence, the importance of thinking about – and designing – the physical setting as well the appearance of the staff.

Within services environments the importance of alignment between internal and external communication needs to be stressed. A service is a performance that involves the co-operation and co-ordination of several parties. The quality of the service rendered is inseparable from the quality of the service provider. A rude or slow waiter, for example, can ruin what otherwise might have been perceived as a fine meal. This means that communication effort will not only have to encourage the customer to buy but, by means of internal communication, will also have to encourage the employee to perform. However, it is important that this internal flow of information and communication is in line with the external communication. Otherwise, the disparity between the inside and the outside of the service organization will lead rather quickly to friction. Customer-contact personnel are an important 'second audience' for service communication.

Promising only what is possible is a good general principle of communication. Service company employees pay attention to their own company's ads and are influenced by them, albeit not always positively. When promotional communication promises more than what is possible, the seeds of problems are sown. Expectations raised by promotional messages are brought to the service encounter by customers who find themselves faced with desperate or cynical front-line employees, who then set about creating their next 'dissatisfied' customer. Raising expectations too high may easily lead to dissatisfied consumers, since a reinforcing effect is expected. Service employees may feel betrayed by their organization's service concept as they are not backed up by adequate support.

So, the communication or promotion of services has its own particularities. Before developing some guiding frameworks to deal with these issues, we will first look at some of the basic building blocks for promotional activity.

THE BASIC BUILDING BLOCKS OF PROMOTION

Since promotion is communication, we shall first look at a basic model of communication. The notion of reference groups is important in this context as we already know that the intangibility of services will lead customers to search for social clues to assess the service characteristics.

The process of communication

A general model of the communication process – the two-step flow model[2] – is presented in Figure 5.1. Communication requires a sender and a receiver. The sender is the marketer who wants to convey a message to a receiver – that is, the target group(s). The first stage in the communication process is the encoding of communication ideas into communication symbols such as words, sounds or illustrations. The encoded symbols become the message, which is sent through a number of media. A medium is a communication channel that can be personal or mass-oriented. If and when the message is received, it is decoded. Decoding means that reference groups and/or the receiver try to give a meaning to the symbols received.

Reference groups are individuals, groups of individuals or organizations that influence a consumer's decision in a certain direction. A distinction can be made between:

1. membership groups (all the customers of my bank) and non-membership groups (all the clients of an insurance company of which I am not a client); and
2. positive groups (that serve as examples and inspire certain behaviour) and negative groups (not imitated at all, quite the contrary).

Communication campaigns should thus be aimed at both types of reference groups. Opinion leaders may be important target groups as such, since they are very often also innovators and early adopters of new products. They can make or

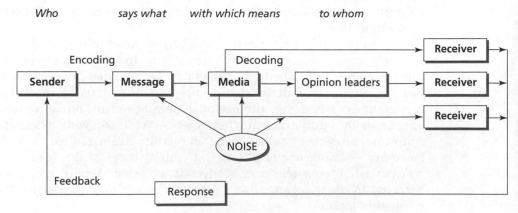

Figure 5.1 A two-step flow communications model[3]

Source: Adapted with the permission of The Free Press, a division of Simon & Schuster, from *Personal Influence: The part played by people in the flow of mass communications*, Elihu Katz and Paul Lazarasfeld. Copyright © 1955 The Free Press; Copyright renewed 1983 by Patricia Kendall Lazarasfeld and Elihu Katz.

break a new product introduction and it is therefore worthwhile convincing them to try the new product. For example, the first stage of phone and home banking promotion was targeted at innovators; similarly, banking via the Internet will be used initially by early adopters of new media.

The whole process is potentially biased by 'noise' – that is, all those elements that can cause disturbances between the sender and the receiver. Examples include misunderstandings between the advertiser and the advertising agency, a competitor's communication in the same media, or a noisy environment during exposure.

The effects of communication

The aim of communication is always to provoke an effect of some kind. Most models relating to the effects of communication[4] assume three categories of effects: cognitive, affective and behavioural effects.

- In the *cognitive stage*, consumers become aware of a product and get to know it.
- In the *affective stage*, the consumer develops a positive attitude towards the product and perhaps a preference for it.
- In the *behavioural stage*, the consumer tries the product and adopts it.

Although the final objective of all marketing activity is to make people buy a product, the effect of communication is assumed to be gradual, a progression with one effect leading to another. Consumers are assumed to make decisions in a number of stages. Marketers can influence consumer decisions by guiding the consumer through these stages using the appropriate messages.

The most frequently used model is the Lavidge and Steiner model,[5] which describes the adoption process of the consumer as having six stages (*see* Figure 5.2).

1. *Awareness*: the consumer knows that the product exists; he or she has to be able to recognize and later recall its name.
2. *Knowledge*: the consumer is able to link the product to its distinctive characteristics or benefits as communicated; in other words, the consumer has an idea of the positioning of the product.
3. *Liking*: consumers develop a favourable attitude towards the product.
4. *Preference*: consumers prefer that particular brand over all other brands.
5. *Conviction*: consumers develop firm beliefs about the product, as a result of which they are inclined to buy the product and nothing else.
6. *Purchase*: consumers buy the product.

This model assumes a 'learning–liking–doing' sequence of effects. This structure may be true for high-involvement decisions (decisions concerning product categories

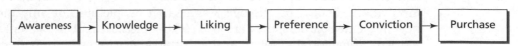

Figure 5.2 The Lavidge and Steiner model of the customer adoption process
Source: From *Journal of Marketing*, published by the American Marketing Association, Lavidge, R. C. and Steiner, G. A., 1961, Vol 25, pp. 59–62.

that are very important to the consumer and for which the consumer perceives a high risk of some kind), but may not always be as relevant to decisions in which the consumer is not very involved. In these cases, other series of effects may occur.

The 'dissonance–attribution' hierarchy is an example of such an alternative model. In this model, the following stages in consumer behaviour – and as a result, communication objectives – are distinguished:

- brand awareness;
- purchase;
- knowledge/attitude;
- repeat purchase.

Building awareness remains a primary communication objective, but in contrast to the high-involvement situation, this awareness is sufficient for a consumer to try the product. As a result of using the product, the consumer gets to know it and, eventually, to like it, bringing opinion (liking the product) into line with behaviour (buying the product). As a result, the product is purchased again. In terms of communication strategy, this implies that advertising efforts will have to be targeted at building awareness rather than knowledge and attitude, and that sales promotion aimed at stimulating trial purchase will be relatively more important than in the high-involvement case.[6]

The content of communication

Of course, communication needs a content; the more promotion appeals to the needs of customers, the more effective it will be. Think back to the service concept discussed in Chapter 2. The service concept involves a clear view of the needs that should be addressed with the service offer. These needs form the basic starting point for designing the promotional efforts. This is the case in the advertisement for Bank Julius Baer shown in Figure 5.3; here a customized approach is strived for and hence communicated.

When deciding on the content of promotional materials, it is important to consider what motivates a consumer to buy a service. What kind of motivational cues can be used in communication to convince consumers to buy?

To answer these questions, we first need to know what the customers' needs are. Of course, if we approach customer needs from the standpoint of specific products or services, we will be confronted with an almost endless list of buying motives. For example, people going for a meal in a restaurant might look for convenience, excellent food, a reasonable price/quality ratio, or a convivial atmosphere, to name but a few. An investigation of reasons or motives for taking out an insurance policy or opening a bank account will lead to further lists.

Fortunately, broader categorical schemes of needs are available. One of the basic distinctions that can be made is the one between negatively and positively oriented motivations. Today, psychologists agree that people are not only motivated by a negative state of affairs; they are also seeking pleasure and enjoyment as well.[7] This has led promotional scholars to the distinction between informational and transformational buying motives (*see* Table 5.1). *Informational motives* are negatively oriented while *transformational motivations* are positively oriented.[8]

Since no two investors are ever completely alike, standardized solutions for capital preservation can sometimes lead to frustration.

At Bank Julius Baer, where personalized private banking is our philosophy, there are few standardized client investment strategies.

Portfolios are individually structured by a Baer financial advisor skilled at analyzing your current situation and then mobilizing the resources of the entire Julius Baer Group to tailor a creative package that goes beyond traditional asset management services. A snug fit for long-term, after-tax performance.

At Bank Julius Baer, wealth management is our strength. Personalized service is our commitment. Just call

Zurich:
Joseph A. Belle (+41-1) 228 55 59
Geneva: (Société Bancaire Julius Baer)
Candace Wehbe (+41-22) 317 64 18
London:
Julian Yorke (+44-171) 623 42 11

**Most off-the-rack
investment solutions
belong here!**

JB°°B

BANK JULIUS BAER

The Fine Art of Swiss Private Bankin

Group Presence: Zurich Geneva London New York
Frankfurt Lugano Monaco Guernsey
Montreal Grand Cayman Palm Beach Los Angeles
San Francisco Mexico Hong Kong

Regulated by the SFA

Figure 5.3 Advertisement for a Swiss bank in which the customers' needs for individual service are addressed

Table 5.1 Addressing needs: making a distinction between negatively and positively oriented buying motives

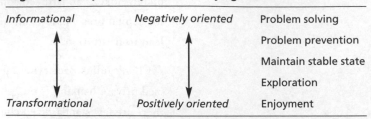

Informational	Negatively oriented	Problem solving
↕	↕	Problem prevention
		Maintain stable state
		Exploration
Transformational	Positively oriented	Enjoyment

Source: Based on Rossiter, J. R. and Percy, L. (1987) *Advertising and Promotion Management*. New York: McGraw Hill, and Fennell, G. (1978) 'Customers' perceptions of the product-use situation', *Journal of Marketing*, Apr, 38–47.

Fennell[9] was among the first to apply such a broad distinction and to point out its relevance for promotional activities. She distinguishes between five basic motives: problem solving, problem prevention or avoidance, normal depletion, interest opportunity and, finally, sensory pleasure opportunity. The first two are clearly negatively oriented buying motives. Normal depletion is situated somewhere inbetween – consumers have rather a minimal interest in the product category they consume; the consumption of the product is seen as a routine part of daily life. Interest and sensory pleasure opportunity are positively oriented buying motives; consumers are looking for fun, novelty, enjoyment or sensory pleasure. One example makes this distinction clear. Figure 5.4 shows an ad for Thai Airways International in which transformational needs are addressed.

We can clarify this with the example of having lunch or dinner out:

- *Problem solving*. Suppose you have a busy life. You are running late with everything and on a particular night you have promised your kids you will cook for them. You come home an hour late and find the kids nagging and your spouse welcoming you with the 'it's always the same with you' look. You have a time management problem. One way to solve this problem is to pay for a dinner in a (fast-food) restaurant or to order some (home-delivered) Chinese food or pizzas. It is clear that several service providers have developed a service concept that fits this need and that the providers' communication or promotion appeals to this need ('home delivered in 30 minutes').
- *Problem prevention*. The night before you hope to have a little peace and quiet to watch an interesting film or soccer game on television, you take everybody out for a real family dinner. You are allowed to watch television the following day but your reputation for being a good parent is intact.
- *Normal depletion*. You have lunch in the company's restaurant; you are there anyway, it is not too expensive, and all your colleagues are going.
- *Exploration and enjoyment*. You can also look for opportunities for fun and exploration ('let's go to this new Cambodian restaurant to try out something different') or sensory pleasure ('let's go to this excellent Italian restaurant where they still know what real Italian food is like').

What this example also makes clear is that the same product or service can be purchased by some people based on a negatively oriented motivation and by others

IN THAILAND, THERE
ARE OVER 3,600
GREENS TO LAND ON.
SMOOTH AS SILK.

Thailand boasts over 200
golf courses. Many are
championship standard.
Ask about Thai's Royal
Orchid Holidays golf packages in Thailand. Then
fly our colours to some of
the best greens on earth.
Thai. Smooth as silk.

Figure 5.4 Advertisement with transformational needs as basis of message

based on a positively oriented motive. What drives the consumption of a particular service will depend on the complex interaction between the consumer as a person (preferences, prior experiences, values, self-concept and so on), his or her specific context (family and/or professional situation, environmental factors and so on) and the market dynamics (available brands, marketing communications, word-of-mouth communication, etc.).[10]

What we need to find out here is what drives groups of people to consume a particular service. This brings us back to the need for focus and the notions of segmenting, positioning and targeting (*see* Chapter 2). This knowledge then becomes a starting point for defining the content of the promotional campaign; the needs to be addressed by the developed service concept should be the basis of the promotional efforts. Just look at some restaurants in your neighbourhood: the appeal of some is their speedy delivery; some offer a family experience; some use fashionable and exotic characteristics to attract customers; and others stress the exceptional quality of the food itself.

Different needs will imply different service concepts and in turn will mean that the content of the promotional message will also differ. Once you know the needs you want to address with the service concept, you can start working on your promotional campaign. However, this simple principle of good communication practice is often leading to what can be labelled as communication 'errors'. Exhibit 5.1 considers some classic examples.

Exhibit 5.1

Some errors in communication

The success of transmitting the desired message about a service can be compromised by errors made in the communication process. Often a mismatch between the needs and the context of the target segment, and the way the message is formulated or sent, underlies these failures.

- *Unnecessary distraction.* To convey an effective message, the attention of the reader/listener/viewer must not be overly distracted. Using sex appeal or humour, for instance, can make an advertisement pleasant to look at, but it can also ruin its effectiveness. Brand and message recall could be low because the wit or the beautiful girls refocused attention away from what the advertiser actually wanted to say.
- *Incorrect audience targeting.* The choice and use of the media to reach a selected group of (potential) customers are crucial factors for communication effectiveness. Service marketers must link their communication messages with their knowledge of which media can reach the selected groups. If the company wants to appeal to, for example, hard-working business people, distributing leaflets in the afternoon in a busy shopping mall is a waste of time and money; it will not find its customers there at that time.

- *Incorrect timing (radio and TV) and placing (print media).* When and where the advertisement is placed in a medium is just as important as the creative work. To determine the most suitable times and places for a service's advertisement, the marketer must study the various ratings to determine what and when their target group is watching.
- *Crowded and complicated ads.* One of the most common mistakes is to place too much information in one ad. The average consumer only spends two seconds reading an advertisement. This means that the ad must be clear at first glance: one or two unique selling propositions must be stressed that appeal directly to the needs the company wants to address. The advertisement must be kept simple and easy to process. Another very common mistake is a message that is too complicated to be readily understood. Such advertisements fail to grab the attention of the reader/listener/viewer, who will often simply ignore the ad.[11]

▶

Exhibit 5.1 continued

■ *Poor identification.* The potential customer must quickly become aware of the advertiser's identity. It is crucial to include a strong identification in the advertisement, otherwise there is a chance that the reader/listener/viewer will attribute the ad to the market leader or the advertiser with the highest share of voice. This problem is called 'brand confusion'. Recent research on brand confusion[12] found, for instance, that print ads for smaller banks which used the same colour codes as the market leader were wrongly attributed to that leader.

DESIGNING A MARKETING COMMUNICATIONS STRATEGY FOR SERVICES

Now that we have an insight into the basic building blocks of promotion and recognize the notion of service concept as a crucial starting point, we can look at how services can be best promoted. Since services are processes, we should first develop a model linking the different stages of the service process with the different communication tools at our disposal:

■ one-way communication or advertising;
■ public relations activities;
■ two-way communication or personal interaction;
■ point-of-sales communication; and finally
■ word-of-mouth communication.

Linking service communication with the service consumption process

The service consumption process looked at from a promotional point of view can be depicted as consisting of several phases or stages[13] (*see* Figure 5.5). During the *orientation* or *awareness* stage, (potential) customers gather information, evaluate possible service providers and choose one to interact with. They then open the interaction. During the *alignment and specification* stage, the problem is defined,

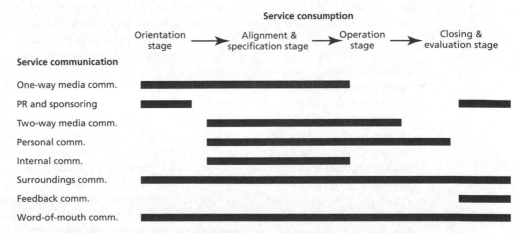

Figure 5.5 The service delivery process and the relevance of promotional channels[14]

Source: Based on Pieters, R., Roest, H. and Koelemeijer, K. (1995) 'Ze zei mener tegen me. Servicecommuniatie in Serviceconsumptie', *Tijdschrift voor Marketing*, Oct, 30–45.

possible solutions are explored and an agreement reached on one or more of the solutions. During the *operation* stage, the actual service is being delivered. The *closing and evaluation* stage consists of ending the interaction between the service provider and the served customer and evaluating the balance between expectations and experiences. The result of this exercise is an adaptation of the customer's expectations.

Different promotional media may be used, depending upon the stage in the service consumption process.

- *One-way media communication.* This includes the traditional marketing communication elements: advertising, sales promotions, sponsoring and direct marketing. They are one-way because the customer cannot interact with the service provider. One-way media are often used to influence the customer's orientation stage to attract customers to the next stages. They can also be used in the specification stage – for example, a printed catalogue of a mail order company.
- *Interactive media.* New technologies, such as the Internet or telephone banking, are systems that allow customers to have direct contact with the service organization without human (personal) interference. This two-way media communication is particularly useful at the operations stage – for example, buying airline vouchers on the Internet, but it is clear that these media can be used as well for other stages within the process (e.g. creating awareness of new offerings by means of e-mail).
- *PR and sponsoring.* Activities here relate to the collection of communication initiatives aimed at creating a desired image with the larger public, including customers and opinion leaders.
- *Personal communication.* This involves the interaction between front-office personnel and the customer and is important in all service consumption stages. These contacts help to make services more tangible and allow expectations about the service to be adjusted during its delivery.
- *Internal communication.* This includes all communications between personnel. This kind of communication should be seen as part of the promotion process; simultaneity implies that the service encounter is one of the most important parts of the communication processes taking place between customer and service provider. Internal communication contributes significantly to achieve consistency between the messages put forward in advertising campaigns and what actually happens during the service encounter.
- *Surrounding communication.* This deals with all kinds of communication related to the physical environment in which services are consumed. These are important during all stages of the consumption process, including the orientation phase as customers often lack other tangible clues. Not only are interior elements, such as music, temperature and furnishing, important; exterior elements, such as parking space, and personal elements, like personnel clothing, also communicate something to customers.
- *Feedback communication.* After service consumption, the customer compares experiences with expectations, and may express incomplete satisfaction to the front-office personnel, to management, or worse, to other customers or third parties such as consumer organizations. It is advisable to structure feedback communications and to actively play a role in this evaluation process – for

example, by using suggestion boxes, evaluation cards or service departments. (*See also* Chapter 7 on measuring customer satisfaction and complaint management.)

■ *Word-of-mouth communication.* As stated already, the intangible nature of services makes it more difficult to assess qualities and effects before consuming them. As such, customers will talk about experiences and will actively solicit opinions of people who went through the 'service experience'. Notice that this word-of-mouth communication can appear throughout the entire service delivery process.

We shall next focus more systematically on the most important issues.

One-way communication and advertising

Advertising can be defined as impersonal mass communications in mass media (television, radio, newspapers, magazines, advertising hoardings/billboards, cinemas) for which an identified sender (the advertiser) defines the content and pays the price. In a service context, advertising is the appropriate tool to inform clients, prospects and employees about the service and the role all parties play in the service process.

Is the information a service manager needs to provide different from that of a goods producer? Both need to be clear about the need(s) they want to address. However, research findings seem to confirm that consumers expect different kinds of information from service advertising. There are differences in content and in execution.

Differences in content

In a recent study, Butler and Abernethy[15] asked 550 respondents to rate the importance of 25 different types of information (determined by a pre-test) for both services and goods advertisements. Ten types of information were seen to be especially important for services advertising: phone number, opening hours, diversity of services, capable personnel, years of experience, concerned and helpful personnel, independent qualifications, safety, and ability to solve problems. In short, three major factors seemed to make a difference: value, personnel and availability (for detailed results, *see* Appendix 1).

Abernethy and Butler[16] also studied whether service industries actually used those elements of information. They drew a distinction between pure service industries (financial services, hotels and phone services), mixed companies offering bundles of services and goods (hardware and software providers, airlines and car repair) and companies selling goods (garments, food, cars and furniture). Table 5.2 shows in how many of the advertisements the information types were used.

Advertising for 'pure' services only rarely contains information concerning the category of 'within reach'. However, because of the simultaneous consumption and production of services, the number of contacts between client and service provider is far higher than in goods industries. This would suggest the need for information on location, phone numbers and opening hours. Appendix 1 actually states that it is precisely that kind of information a services customer needs. Service industries with a mixed approach (goods and services) seem to have understood

Table 5.2 Research results showing how often certain items of information appeared in newspaper advertisements

	Services	Services + Goods	Goods
Within reach	35.5%	71.8%	60.4%
Components	16.1%	57.3%	51.4%
Phone number	50.5%	25.2%	8.5%
Address	7.5%	0.0%	1.1%
Price	19.4%	73.8%	78.7%
Guarantees	18.3%	39.8%	15.8%
Method of payment	2.2%	22.3%	15.6%

Source: Abernethy, A. M. and Butler, D. (1992) 'Advertising information: services versus products', *Journal of Retailing*, Vol 68, No 4, 411–13.

this and use more of these types of information in their ads. Another remarkable difference is that service advertising uses fewer price indications. Since most services are customized, it is quite difficult to calculate standard prices. Advertising for services needs to use more guarantees, as the perceived risk is higher than in goods industries. Table 5.2 illustrates that the mixed service industries use the most guarantee claims, but that fewer than one in five 'pure' service advertisers do the same.

Research by FHV/BBDO,[17] a Dutch advertising agency, confirmed Butler and Abernethy's findings and added that advertising for services puts more emphasis on the company image. A strong corporate image augments the tangibility and clarity of services and diminishes the perceived risk.

Differences in execution

The same BBDO research found the following differences in execution:

■ Services advertising uses more text and fewer images. Intangibility makes services harder to comprehend and thus requires more explanation, which also reduces perceived risk.
■ Services advertising uses fewer colours. This might simply be a result of lower communication budgets in service industries; it could also be the result of the inclination to make more serious ads.
■ Advertising for services has longer headlines – again the need for more explanation.

On the other hand, when advertising for services, creativity can overcome the need for long texts and explanation. Remember that one picture can say more than 1000 words. If an image can be found that reflects the service concept, this can make words obsolete – as can be seen from the Swissair ad in Figure 5.6.

The service advertiser should choose the media that have the best reach and coverage within the target group and which support the communication objectives. Newspapers are actively read for information about recent events and for control over the world surrounding the reader. These characteristics make newspapers a rationally approached medium. Services are often serious matters over which consumers like to feel a degree of control – for example, loans, investments, insurance, health, justice. Service marketers should try to offer as much certainty and confidence as possible. With their image of seriousness and truth, newspapers have

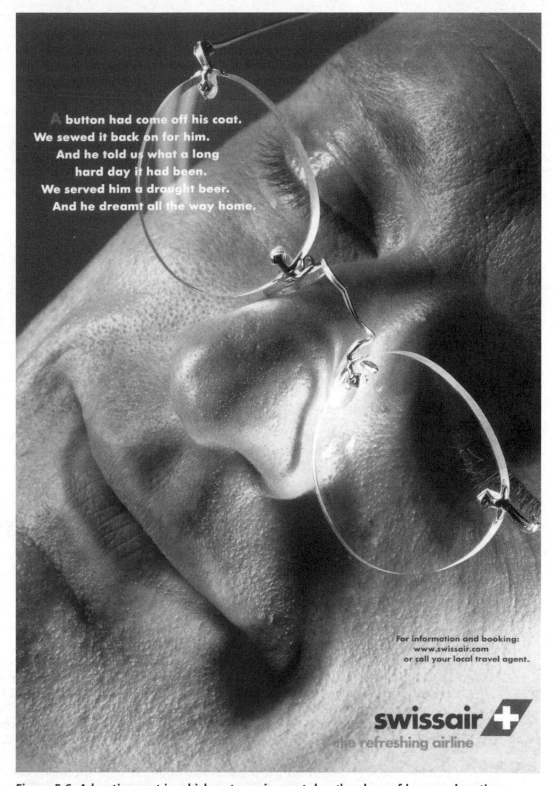

Figure 5.6 Advertisement in which a strong image takes the place of long explanations

positive source effects for the service advertiser. Magazines have the same quality as newspapers for the service marketer. They are read more slowly than newspapers, and so ads in magazines can be more complex – for instance, include more text. They are also aimed towards selected target groups and can easily be used to reach a well-defined public. Although magazines are less actively read, they are still approached in a rather rational way.

By contrast, watching television is an activity people reserve for their leisure time. It is a medium that is approached much more emotionally. Television is therefore an excellent medium for image building. Service marketers frequently use radio advertising to reach young target groups. This medium is consumed passively and emotionally, but offers interesting market segmentation opportunities.

Billboards are a highly visual medium and cannot be used to give much textual information. This is probably the reason why this medium is not as popular with service marketers. However, research conducted by Donthu[18] indicates that billboards are more effective for service advertising than for goods. Especially effective are colour billboards giving directional clues such as 'Take a left at the next lights'.

Service marketers often use newspapers and magazines to promote new products. These media are more flexible (radio and television media time has to be reserved far in advance) and can be used to provide more explanation. Older and more well-known products are communicated through radio and television. Television is also used for communicating promotional activity and for image advertising.

Public relations, exhibitions and sponsoring

Palmer defines public relations as 'the deliberate, planned and sustained effort to establish and maintain mutual understanding'.[19] It is a collection of techniques used to optimize the relationship between a company and the public. PR is important for services for two reasons.

1. It has to communicate and guard a good corporate image.
2. Services are evaluated in a subjective way (personal experiences) and this evaluation is rapidly diffused through word-of-mouth information exchange processes. PR makes sure that the service organization is playing an active role in this process and can prevent negative rumours circulating about the company or its products/services.

It should be noted that in a service company – due to simultaneity – everyone is responsible for public relations. The crucial role of personnel (especially front-office personnel) will be discussed in the next section.

Publicity is defined by Kotler and Armstrong[20] as 'securing editorial space (i.e., not paid space) in all media read, viewed or heard by a company's customers or prospects, for the specific purpose of assisting in the meeting of the goals'. Publicity is stimulated by press events, press releases and press conferences. It is cheap, has high coverage and comes from a reliable and independent source. On the other hand, publicity is almost uncontrollable and thus can turn out to be negative. Therefore, good relations with the press and experienced PR people are necessary.

Service companies often participate in exhibitions with the objective of generating awareness, rather than selling. A service exhibitor's stand should make the intangible tangible; the exhibitor should lower the risk and give clearly understandable explanations of the rendered services. A service company can also organize events to obtain press attention (free publicity) and to increase awareness.

Consumers today pay more attention to culture, environmental issues and general welfare. Service industries have understood this and are sponsoring related organizations and events. Sponsoring culture is popular among service marketers because it has positive associations – quality, seriousness and importance. Sponsoring sports is also attractive as it can lead to increased exposure, can support corporate images or alter negative attitudes towards a company. Sponsoring offers some segmentation possibilities. By choosing the right events, certain target groups can be reached very effectively (e.g. youth and music events).

Personal communication

Personal communication aimed at selling the service offered, is defined as 'the oral presentations and/or demonstrations to one or more (potential) buyers for the final purpose of making sales'. Often called 'the backbone of service marketing', its importance is based on the following factors:

- the quality of services is hard to evaluate;
- buying services implies risk;
- buying services is less pleasant than buying goods;
- the image of the service company strongly influences the decision to buy;
- prices are less frequently compared;
- the salesperson has a great influence on the client;
- the impact of advertising is smaller, but personal recommendations are more important;
- for some services, the customer's involvement is higher;
- the customer's satisfaction is influenced by salespeople's behaviour;
- salespeople often have to reassure their clients.

Personal selling can fulfil two functions that facilitate the more effective selling of services:

- *servicing* – that is, front-office personnel informing and advising customers, and by doing so addressing specific points of concern (remember the notion of heterogeneity, discussed in Chapter 1);
- *monitoring* – that is, front-office personnel trying to detect customer needs and problems and reacting appropriately.

Furthermore, personal selling has advantages compared to other communication tools as it offers opportunities for establishing relationships. Frequent, and sometimes confidential contacts between personnel and clients can lead to the formation of close relationships which will in return lead to loyalty. Cross-selling opportunities may also arise as a result. With closer personal interaction, employees can detect additional customer needs and can provide information on other services. A prerequisite here is a good knowledge of the complete range of services and of the customers' needs.

Of course, the personal contact between service provider and customers does not end at the moment of sale. Customers see the contact personnel as a personification and an integral part of the services they pay for. Personnel is a tangible element for them, and thus much easier to evaluate. Employees of a service company are thus responsible for the corporate image.

This also has implications for the alignment of front and back office. For example, an employee at the counter may speak the customer's language and understand his or her needs, but when the back office produces incomprehensible documents or invoices, anything gained by such efforts will be lost. This highlights the need for good employee motivation, education and an integrated process view. Every service must first be sold to a company's own employees before it can be sold to consumers.

Surroundings: the importance of the point of sale

Bateson remarks on the importance of the point of sale, store, office or outlet.[21] The architecture, lighting, temperature, furnishings, layout, colour and artefacts present in the firm's facilities all communicate non-verbally to the customer how the firm sees itself and how it wishes the customer to behave when entering the premises.

This is of course due to the physical presence of the customer during the service encounter. The service company's facilities have a great influence on the perception of its quality and its corporate image.[22] For this reason, service companies are often housed in large, imposing buildings. Final purchase decisions are said to be made during the last three footsteps. This indicates that the information a consumer gathers during these last steps is crucial and must be convincing. The point of sale should be well appointed: posters, brochures, and even furnishing should be recognizable and remind the consumer of the advertising he or she has seen (*see also* Chapter 16 on facilities and location).

Word-of-mouth communication

Word of mouth, seen as both reliable and independent, is one of the most important communication channels for services. Its effect on purchase decisions may be even greater than other elements such as advertising. As we pointed out earlier in this chapter, word of mouth can be stimulated and influenced by the other communication tools. Unfortunately, the precise content of word-of-mouth 'advertising' is difficult to control or monitor. Negative experiences are said to be communicated to at least twice as many listeners as positive ones.

To create positive word of mouth, it is important to have the consumer feel that he or she is understood and that the service company is working out solutions, offering an honest and realistic view of what to expect. Service organizations can adopt a proactive approach towards worth-of-mouth communication by encouraging (potential) customers and customers to exchange experiences and insights. Discussion meetings, customer meetings, workshops or conferences can be organized on topics of interest. Some companies have even set up special organizations to handle this area of their activities.[23]

Establishing the right mix

The different communication instruments described in the last section are called the *communications mix*. This means that the service marketer must strive for an optimal integration of all these tools in order to fulfil the marketing communications goals. Finding the right combination of elements has a great influence on the success of the communication campaign. Each element has its specific advantages and disadvantages and each has a different price.

After the previous explanation, it should come as no surprise that the effectiveness of the individual elements of the communications mix is different for services. A survey which looked upon the importance of different communication elements to induce buying behaviours found important differences between goods and services[24] (*see* Figure 5.7).

Front-office management and personnel are typical communication tools for a service environment. The absence of impulse purchase decisions for services means that sales promotions are used more often for advertising goods rather than services. The effect some sales promotions have on impulse purchases explains the upward curve of the goods line. Sales promotions are used in services to stimulate repeat purchases and to balance out demand and supply. However, publicity and PR are more commonly used in services. A strong corporate image is needed to compensate for the lack of tangible product characteristics. This observation can become extended to the importance of the physical settings or surroundings as well as word-of-mouth communication, elements not included in this survey. Given the intangible nature of services, both the location and design of the service facility (*see also* Chapter 16) as well as the physical appearance of the staff will be more important when deciding to purchase services than products. One can extend this reasoning even further in order to delineate differences between different types of services. It will come as no surprise that we enter at this moment the three different types of services delineated by Mills and Margulies: maintenance-interactive, task-interactive, and finally personal-interactive services (*see* Chapter 2). Whereas maintenance-interactive services are most like products, given the lower levels of uncertainty involved, the appropriate communication mix can be seen as more in line with the one suited for goods (*see* Figure 5.7); for task and personal-interactive services the relative importance of personal communication and word-of-mouth

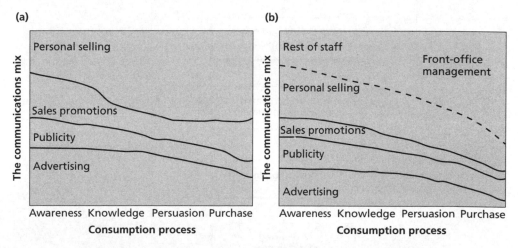

Figure 5.7 The relative importance of the individual elements of the communications mix (a) for goods and (b) for services

Source: Tettero, J. H. and Viehoff, J. H. (1994) 'Marketing voor dienstverlenende organisaties', *Beleid en Uitvoering*. Deventer: Kluwer.

will be higher. Finally, it should be stressed that all the elements of the communications mix interlink with each other. And given the observation that simultaneity is an inherent characteristic of any service organization, this remark equals with a plea for an integrated view on designing and managing the service delivery system. It is easier for a salesperson to sell a certain service if the company has a good reputation thanks to advertising and PR. Advertising will have a greater effect if it is supported by in-store communications. Sales promotions have to be communicated to generate action. Customers will only rely on the services of an advertised company if they have confidence in the capabilities of front-office employees and vice versa. Hence, promotion points our attention again to the need for an integrated and holistic approach towards designing and operating the service delivery system. Let us now take a look at a framework for drawing up an outline promotion plan.

DRAWING UP A PROMOTION PLAN

The different stages in building up a communication plan are presented in Figure 5.8.

Setting objectives

The objectives of a communication plan, or the messages that are to be conveyed, depend upon a number of factors. First of all, in a marketing communication campaign, the objective of the campaign will target one particular level in the hierarchy of effects:

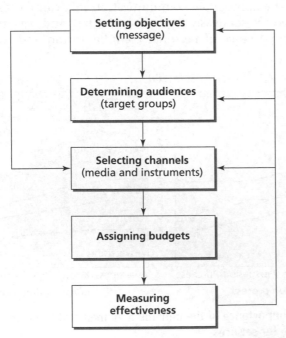

Figure 5.8 The stages in drawing up a communication plan

- creating the need for the product category;
- building brand awareness;
- spreading information;
- developing a favourable attitude, purchase intention, behaviour facilitation and trial purchase;
- inducing loyalty; or
- enhancing customer satisfaction.

Furthermore, the actual product characteristic or benefit to be stressed will depend upon the strengths and weaknesses of the product promoted, the target group at which the product is aimed, and the positioning decision that has been made. In other words, the definition of the service concept – 'a desired unique place in the mind of the consumer' – comes first, and the communication strategy should then be based on it.

In the case of a corporate campaign, communication objectives will be based on the (desired) corporate identity, the actual corporate image and the gap between the two. Corporate campaigns always serve the purpose of bringing or keeping the corporate image in line with the desired corporate identity. As such, the message of a corporate campaign will be based on the image attribute(s) – that is, the aspects of the company's identity and image that are considered to be important and that the company wants to stress. Corporate communication objectives are mostly long-term and image-oriented. The ultimate objective of these campaigns is to create goodwill for the company.

Determining audiences

The nature of communication objectives largely depends on the target groups. In marketing communication, the target groups may be segments of final customers, opinion leaders, reference groups or members of the distribution channel. In corporate communication, the nature and the number of audiences are much more heterogeneous. Indeed, companies may be interested in creating goodwill with a large number of audiences such as the government, potential employees, the competition, corporate buyers, local communities, the media, employees, suppliers, shareholders, analysts or the general public. Since not all audiences will be equally important, part of the communication plan will consist of a selection or ranking of the most important audiences. Two audiences are important in almost every corporate campaign – the media and the company's employees – because they both serve as intermediate groups for the other audiences. Therefore, internal communication and communication with the media are extremely important, especially in a service environment in which personal contacts and reputation are important determinants of perceived quality.

Selecting channels

Next, communication channels and instruments have to be selected. Communication media and instruments were discussed earlier in this chapter. It is important to stress once again that 'the medium is the message' – that is, that the instruments and media used have to be consistent with the message conveyed and its target groups; the two have to support each other. Furthermore, a strict timetable has to be adopted which is in line with the objectives of the communication campaign.

Assigning budgets

Various methods may be used to determine a communication budget. Unfortunately, many companies still use 'percentage-of-sales', 'availability-of-funds' or 'imitate-the-competition' methods of determining a budget. All these methods have the disadvantage that there is no relationship between the budget and the communication problem at hand. The best way of setting a communication budget is the 'objective-and-task' method in which communication objectives are defined as precisely as possible, the necessary media and instruments are decided upon, and a budget is calculated based on the efforts necessary to reach the objectives. To apply this method, a clear idea of the communication objectives and the necessary input is required.

Measuring effectiveness

The effectiveness of a communication campaign can be measured in two ways, directly and indirectly. Direct measurement of effectiveness implies measuring the impact of the campaign itself: Do members of the target groups recall having seen the communication? Did they pick up the important elements of the message? Did they understand it? Did they consider it credible or personally relevant? Although direct measurement provides interesting data for campaign evaluation and further campaign development, indirect brand-level or company-level measurement is perhaps more relevant.[25] In indirect effectiveness measurement, the effect of the campaign on the product or company is assessed. A communication campaign has been effective if it has realized its objectives. As a result, measuring effectiveness boils down to comparing the situation of a product or a company before and after the campaign with respect to the objectives of the campaign in terms such as awareness, knowledge, attitude towards the brand, company image and purchase intention. The results of the effectiveness measurement will be input into the next communication campaign, together with the necessary market and customer research, leading to new or adjusted objectives.

CONCLUSION

In this chapter we have looked at the specific characteristics of the promotion of services. Both intangibility and simultaneity have an impact on the promotional approach. Making the intangible tangible, word-of-mouth communications, the role of internal communication and its alignment with external communication are all issues meriting our attention.

We looked at the basic building blocks of the promotion process; here it became clear that a good promotion campaign builds on the defined service concept. Furthermore, during the service delivery process a varying mix of promotional activities can be most appropriate. This mix entails a different emphasis when compared to goods; but also the nature of the service delivery process plays a role here as well. This chapter ended with an overall framework which allows to outline a promotion plan.

Review and discussion questions

- Benetton is famous for – amongst other things – the way it has been promoting its products. Would you consider the 'Benetton' approach relevant for services? Why? When?

- How important are the physical surroundings in which service transactions take place? Would you rate its importance equal for all types of services? And for all phases of the service 'consumption' process? Why?

Notes and references

[1] George, W. R. and Berry, L. L. (1981) 'Guidelines for the advertising of services', *Business Horizons*, July–Aug.

[2] Katz, E. and Lazarsfeld, P. F. (1955) *Personal Influence: The part played by people in the flow of mass communications*. New York: Free Press.

[3] Ibid.

[4] Colley, R. H. (1961) *Defining Advertising Goals for Measuring Advertising Results*. New York: Association of National Advertisers.

[5] Lavidge, R. C. and Steiner, G. A. (1961) 'A model for the predictive measurements of advertising effectiveness by "further reading"', *Journal of Marketing*, No 25, 59–62.

[6] Batra, R., Ray, M. L. (1983) 'Advertising situations: the implications of different involvement and accompanying affect responses', in Harris, R. J. (ed.) *Information Processing Research in Advertising*. Hillsdale, NJ: Lawrence Erlbaum.

[7] *See* Warr, P., Barter, J. and Brownbridge, G. (1983) 'On the independence of positive and negative effect', *Journal of Personality and Social Psychology*, Vol 44, No 3, 644–51.

[8] Rossiter, J. R. and Percy, L. (1987) *Advertising and Promotion Management*. New York: McGraw-Hill.

[9] Fennell, G. (1978) 'Customers' perceptions of the product-use situation', *Journal of Marketing*, Apr, 38–47.

[10] *See* Fennell (1978), op. cit. for a more extensive discussion.

[11] An exception here are ads aimed at creating confusion by not being very clear. As the reader is puzzled, this enhances the amount of cognitive processing devoted to the ad. This has a positive impact on memory retention. However, it is clear that these ads are working at the level of creating awareness, as they do not address a specific need directly. However, they do create a positive attitude within the segment of interest to opportunity seekers.

[12] De Pelsmacker, P. and Van den Bergh, J. (1997) *Merkverwarring in printreclame* (Brand confusion in print advertising). Research Paper 6, Marketing Communications Centre, The Vlerick School of Management.

[13] Based on Pieters, R., Roest, H. and Koelemeijer, K. (1995) 'Ze zei meneer tegen me. Servicecommuniatie in serviceconsumptie', *Tijdschrift voor Marketing*, Oct, 30–45.

[14] Ibid. p. 34.

15 Butler, D. D. and Abernethy, A. (1994) 'Information consumers seek from advertisements: Are there differences between advertisements for goods and services?', *Journal of Professional Services Marketing*, Vol 10, No 2, 75–91.

16 Abernethy, A. M. and Butler, D. (1992) 'Advertising information: Services versus products', *Journal of Retailing*, Vol 68, No 4, 398–419.

17 FHV/BBDO (1983)

1891 George Batten sets up the first agency engaged in the compilation of advertisements. 1928 George Batten decides to join up with threesome Bruce Barton, Roy Durstine, and Alex Osborn, and thus BBDO is born.

1962 Giep Franzen, Nico Hey, and Martin Veltman introduce a new business concept in which a horizontal relationship between creativity and marketing forms the basis for its service proposition. 1970 BBDO starts the expansion of its network outside the confines of the United States, and is the first to cooperate with FHV. This cooperation forms the basis for participation with other creative and locally strong agencies throughout the whole world. 1981 FHV/BBDO is the first full service agency in the Netherlands, offering a total range of integrated communication disciplines. 1997 FHV/BBDO transforms into a creative marketing agency, covering the full range of all marketing and communication disciplines.

FHV/BBDO is a full service communication agency based in The Netherlands. Since 2000 it has been known by the name FHV Group.

18 Donthu, N. (1994) 'Effectiveness of outdoor advertising of services', *Journal of Professional Services Marketing*, Vol 11, No 1, 33–43.

19 Palmer, A. (1994) *Principles of Services Marketing*. London: McGraw-Hill.

20 Kotler, P. and Armstrong, G. (1991) *Principles of Marketing*. Englewood Cliffs, NJ: Prentice-Hall.

21 Bateson, J. (1992) Managing Services Marketing: Text and readings. Chicago: Dryden Press.

22 Bitner, M. J. (1992) 'Servicescapes: The impact of physical surroundings on customers and employees', *Journal of Marketing*, No 56, Apr, 57–71.

23 For example, DECUS, a customer organization set up by Digital. DECUS publishes a magazine and regular conferences and workshops are held related to all sorts of IT issues of interest to customers. Through DECUS, Digital is keeping in touch with customer needs and considerations, and is playing an active role in the word-of-mouth communication process.

24 Tettero, J. H. and Viehoff, J. H. (1994) 'Marketing voor dienstverlenende organisaties', *Beleid en Uitvoering*. Deventer: Kluwer.

25 *Source*: Ibid. p. 118. Jacoby, J. and Chestnut, R. W. (1978) *Brand Loyalty. Measurement and management*. New York: Ronald Press/John Wiley.

Suggested further reading

Butler, D. D. and Abernethy, A. (1994) 'Information consumers seek from advertisements: are there differences between advertisements for goods and services?', *Journal of Professional Services Marketing*, Vol 10, No 2, 75–91. This and the previous work cover particular points of interest for the promotion of services.

Fennell, G. (1978) 'Customer's perceptions of the product-use situation', *Journal of Marketing*, Apr, 38–47. This work includes a clear treatment of the distinction between informational and transformational needs.

George, W. R. and Berry, L. L. (1981) 'Guidelines for the advertising of services', *Business Horizons*, Jul–Aug.

Rossiter, J. R. and Percy, L. (1997) *Advertising and Promotion Management* (2nd edn). New York: McGraw-Hill. This book provides a comprehensive insight into promotional issues.

CHAPTER 6

Pricing services

Marion Debruyne · Stefan Stremersch

INTRODUCTION

George Downey, business unit manager of a large multinational company offering telecommunication services, is working on next year's business plan. The launch of a new project which is planned for next year is his main preoccupation, as it will determine the company's future competitive position. The company is planning to enter a new and potentially rewarding market as an Internet access provider.

After numerous discussions and meetings with his colleagues and co-workers, they finally agree on most of the points. There is only one item to be settled: the issue of price. The opinion of the financial manager is clear: he wants a high unit contribution. To achieve this, the company should set the price high. The sales manager, on the other hand, argues that this is unrealistic. Since many competitors are entering the market, the only way to gain a significant market share is by pricing low, perhaps with the new service bundled into a package along with regular services. Others claim that the price should be adjusted for different customer segments, allowing separate price structures for corporate and individual customers.

All these arguments leave the business unit manager with nothing but a new set of questions. Should he price high or low? How will competitors react? Could the sales revenue be guaranteed at high prices? How will this affect the other services the company offers? Should he allow for price reductions, and if so, in which cases? Should he charge a fixed monthly subscription rate or should he charge by the hour?

This chapter aims at providing answers to all these questions by offering a general step-by-step framework to guide pricing decisions.

Objectives

By the end of this chapter, you should be able to discuss:

- the setting of pricing objectives as the starting point for any price-setting decision for services
- the three basic strategies for setting prices in accordance with a certain objective – cost, customers (value) and competition (the 3 Cs)

Objectives continued

- the choice of strategy – skimming or penetration – to reflect the fact that the customer value of a service is not stable over time and such changes in value must be reflected in price setting

- decisions regarding how a pricing structure is made up, which price level will actually be charged, and why and when short-term promotional price initiatives are used

DEVELOPING A FRAMEWORK FOR PRICING DECISIONS

The questions raised in the introductory case study perplex many service marketers. Of the classical four Ps of the marketing mix (product, place, promotion, and price), it is price that usually receives the least attention, even though the pricing decision probably has the greatest impact on a company's profits.

We can use the price structure in Figure 6.1 to illustrate the leverage effect price has on profits. If prices drop by five percentage points, profits are cut by half, from 10 per cent to 5 per cent. To keep the same profit, the volume sold should increase by 20 per cent, which is very unlikely considering the concept of price elasticity.[1,2] Generating a 20 per cent increase in volume, when prices drop by 5 per cent, requires that the price elasticity should exceed −4. By comparison, the price elasticity of cola in Belgium is −0.44, indicating that a price decrease of 1 per cent causes a volume increase of 0.44 per cent.

In addition to this leverage effect on profits, pricing behaviour affects customer satisfaction and customer loyalty, thus impacting on the long-term profit potential. Research[3] indicates that 'pricing' – for example, prices, rates, fees, charges, penalties, coupons, price promotions and price deals – ranks third on the list of reasons for switching service provider (after core service failures and failed service encounters). When asked 'Why did you switch service providers?' more than 30 per cent of all respondents who had switched service providers answered that this was due to a price issue, such as high prices, price increases, or unfair or deceptive pricing practices.

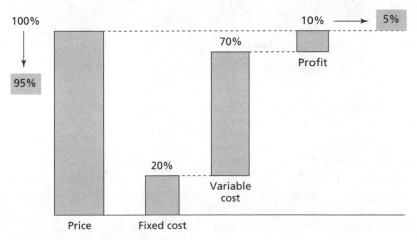

Figure 6.1 A price structure

In spite of its obvious importance, not many service marketers deal with the pricing issue in a structured or creative way. One major cause of this neglect is that many separate issues are involved in pricing decisions. It is not surprising that George Downey in our case study cannot find a solution to his problem, since the questions he is asking himself are all concerned with different issues. These questions all relate to price, but they cannot all be handled in the same way.

To develop an effective approach to pricing decisions, the service provider has to consider the different stages in the decision-making process. Figure 6.2 illustrates the various steps necessary in setting the price of a product or service.[4]

The first question a service marketer ought to ask is what he or she wants to achieve with the pricing strategy. This seems obvious, but it is often completely overlooked in practice. Determining the *objective* you want to obtain by setting a price is the first step of the pricing process, and can clear up other questions at an early stage. George Downey could relieve much of his worry by just thinking about what he wants to accomplish. Every pricing decision can then be seen in the light of that objective. He should consider, for example, whether he wants to achieve a considerable market share immediately after the launch or if he wants to build it up step by step.

The second step in the pricing process is about determining which *pricing strategy* the company will follow. A pricing strategy provides general guidelines that relate to all the pricing decisions about a single product line or company. The company can of course alter the pricing strategy to adapt to changing circumstances. There are three main determinants on which the pricing strategy can be based – referred to as the three Cs – cost, customer and competitor. Each of these will be discussed later in this chapter.

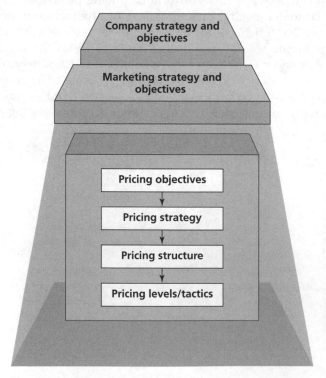

Figure 6.2 The pricing process

Once the pricing objective and strategy are clear, decisions have to be made on the *pricing structure*. This means the service provider has to decide:

- which aspect of the service will be priced;
- what will be included for that price;
- on which unit the price will be based;
- if there will be a differentiation among customers; and
- what the payment conditions will be.

Imagine, for example, that you are the manager of a restaurant. Would you charge for food and drinks separately? Are you going to provide a fixed-price meal, with wine included, as a bundle? Would you charge extra for the service, or would it be included? Can the customers eat as much as they want or will they pay by the portion? Would you allow student discounts? Do the customers have to pay cash?

All these questions concern the price structure. Once this structure has been established, the service marketer has a clear overall framework into which decisions concerning pricing level and tactics have to fit. The *price level* is the actual price that is asked for a service. *Price tactics* refer to periodic price promotions or other short-term actions.

A service marketer therefore has to go through several steps to develop a pricing policy – from determining a pricing objective and strategy to the price structure, level and tactics. Obviously, the price element of the marketing mix cannot be isolated from the other three Ps. The pricing of a service has to be embedded in the marketing strategy and must be consistent with the other marketing activities relating to this service. The pricing process, as illustrated in Figure 6.2, is overshadowed by the overall marketing strategy and is in continuous interaction with other marketing measures. We shall now discuss each of the stages of the pricing process in greater detail and the specific issues involved in pricing services.

PRICING OBJECTIVES

Let us return to the case study described in the introduction to the chapter, and in particular the argument unfolding between the sales manager and the finance manager. The focus of their argument is the decision on whether to set prices high or low. It is clear that they have different objectives, making consensus around the pricing topic virtually impossible. It is therefore necessary for them to first discuss pricing *objectives*, before beginning to discuss different pricing *strategies*.

Reaching maximum profit is not always the key objective. Many others are possible, such as:

- stabilizing the market;
- acquiring a desired market share;
- maximizing long-term profit;
- maximizing short-term profit;
- avoiding cannibalizing other service offers;
- achieving the speedy exit of marginal competitors;
- being the price leader;
- avoiding price wars;
- generating traffic;

- communicating a particular image;
- making a fast recovery of investments;
- crowding out new market entries;
- regulating demand;
- securing key accounts;
- using spare capacity.

These pricing objectives can be divided into two categories: *short-term tactical moves* and *long-term strategic moves*. The decision to lower prices temporarily to make better use of existing capacity is a decision which can be taken further down the line than decisions which will shape the future of the company, such as setting the price at such a level as to reach the desired market share.

The choice of a pricing objective is usually influenced by the dominant form of regulation within the market. A service company can be:

1. subject to *government regulation* (for example, railways, post offices and universities);
2. subject to a certain amount of *self-regulation* (for example, lawyers and doctors); or
3. services where the *market mechanism* decides (for example, cleaning services, hotels and catering).

Companies in the first category – those subject to government regulation – will have to consider the specific task in society for which they are sustained by government. Social and political goals will influence the pricing objective. For example, the Belgian government decided to take measures against ozone pollution. To discourage car use, they stimulated railway travel by offering special train fares during the summer period, when ozone levels are at their highest. Clearly, the pricing objective for these tickets was not to maximize profits, but to realize an environmental goal (reducing ozone pollution) as well as a political one (creating goodwill with the public).

The second category of services – those subject to a certain amount of self-regulation – will try to establish a stable market situation and fair prices. Their pricing policy is devoted to continuity and stability. Doctors, for example, agree on general tariffs, in consultation with the doctors' association, social security agencies and the government.

The last category of services deals with a total free-market situation. The number of possible pricing objectives in this situation is almost endless. The choice of pricing objective in this case is primarily influenced by the company's strategy and objectives. Suppose the company pursues a niche strategy. The pricing objective has to be in line with that strategy. Maximizing market share would be a useless pricing objective in this case. On the other hand, if the company follows a strategy of cost leadership, it would be an appropriate goal.

Finally, the current market situation will also affect pricing objectives. Pricing objectives have to be realistic and feasible, and they will often involve intimate knowledge of the market and the competitors presently in the marketplace.

PRICING STRATEGIES

A pricing strategy establishes a general framework for pricing decisions and determines the way in which the price will be set. There are three main determinants on which the pricing strategy can be based – cost, competitor and customer. Although we discuss cost-based, customer-based and competition-based pricing strategies separately, a combination of the different perspectives seems to be necessary to compensate for the weaknesses each pricing perspective entails. In addition, price limits set by government through regulation must of course also be taken into account when setting prices.

Cost-based strategies

Marketers most often set their prices in accordance with the cost of the product or service. This means they focus entirely on the cost of providing a service to determine the price that is asked for it. A study by Morris and Fuller reveals that in industrial services, the process of estimating and covering costs is perceived by managers as far more important when setting prices than competitor- or customer-based considerations.[5] Mark-up pricing and target return pricing are the most common cost-based pricing strategies.

Mark-up pricing is probably the easiest way to set a price based on costs. A fixed margin is added to the service's cost to determine the price. The price is then calculated as follows:

$$\text{Mark-up price} = \frac{\text{Unit cost}}{1 - \text{Desired mark-up \%}}$$

Take, for example, a unit cost of £1600. A desired mark-up of 20 per cent sets the price at:

$$\frac{1600}{0.8} = £2000$$

Target return pricing is based on the desired return on investment (ROI):

$$\text{Target return price} = \text{Unit cost} + \frac{\text{ROI} \times \text{Investment}}{\text{Expected number of units sold}}$$

An investment of £1 000 000, a desired ROI of 15 per cent, and an expected volume of 1000 would construct a price of:

$$1600 + \frac{1\,000\,000}{1000} = £1750$$

Cost-based strategies are fast and easy, and they can reveal the minimum price level necessary for the company to remain profitable. As such, cost-based price strategies do have their uses. However, cost-based strategies also show some major disadvantages from a marketing point of view:

- If the price is based on cost alone, then the pricing objective can only be to reach a certain profit level, because that is an integral part of the price formula (mark-up percentage or ROI). As has been explained above, many other pricing objectives exist for which, consequently, cost-based pricing is not effective.
- Cost-based strategies require an estimation of the number of units likely to be sold. It is clear, however, that this number will be greatly influenced by the price itself, taking into account the price elasticity of demand. In the case of high elasticity, using the sales volume to determine the price is pointless.

■ Service managers should also take into account the *price cross-elasticity of demand*. This is the relative change in demand of one service caused by the change in price of another service. This price cross-elasticity could be important for additional services linked to a primary service or product. For example, the demand for computer training will be greatly influenced by the demand for computers and thus by the price of new computers.

■ Cost-based strategies assume that the cost of providing a service or product has something to do with the value of the product or service. However, different organizations can have different costs for producing the same service, depending on their efficiency. The cost of a service therefore reflects more the efficiency or inefficiency of the service provider than the value of the service delivered. Consequently, different companies, although providing the same service and thus creating the same value for the customer, will set different prices if they rely on their internal cost structure.

■ Cost-based strategies have an entirely internal focus and do not in any way take market considerations into account. Obviously, in reality, customers are not in the least interested in what it costs the company to deliver a service; they are only interested in the benefits and values it offers them. Prices obtained by looking only at cost ignore market demand and can be much lower or higher than the customer is prepared to pay.

The cost of a service delivery is difficult to measure, due to the intangible nature of services. It is therefore crucial to monitor all the processes involved to keep track of costs incurred for every service offered (*see* Chapter 18 on performance management). The cost of a service is not a static concept. Economies of scale and learning effects influence the cost and can change it over time.

It is clear from the above list of disadvantages that the cost of producing a service cannot be used as the sole determinant of price. However, it is still very important to have a detailed insight into costs, not only to determine the bottom price level, but also to be able to monitor and analyse every service offered. Service marketers can consider the cost of providing a service when setting the price, but it should also be correlated to the actual value the service delivers to the customer. In other words, their pricing strategy should also be based on the customer value.

Customer-based strategies

Customer-based pricing focuses entirely on the market. The basic concept is that the price should be commensurate with the value the service really delivers to the customer. In the end, it is the customer who will judge whether the price is fair or not and use it as a primary decision and evaluation criterion. Consequently, customers must feel they are receiving value for money.

Some service marketers measure the value construct as an equation incorporating the features and benefits of the service, with each additional benefit involving a price increment. However, this does not always correspond with the value as it is perceived by the customer. Consumers define value in four different ways:[6]

■ '*Value is low price.*' Some consumers equate value with low price, indicating that what they give up in terms of money is most salient in their perceptions of value.

■ '*Value is whatever I want in a service.*' Some consumers emphasize the benefits they receive from a service as the most important component of value.

- *'Value is the quality I receive for the price I pay.'* Some consumers see value as a trade-off between the money they give up and the quality they receive.
- *'Value is what I receive for what I give.'* In this definition, the customer not only weighs up the quality and benefits of the service, but also takes into account sacrifice components other than the price (for example, time and effort).

In one overall definition, perceived value is:

'the consumer's overall assessment of the utility of a service, based on perceptions of what is received and what is given.'

In any case, the key is to determine the perceived value of the service to the customer, and set the price according to this value. The concept of 'perceived value' has been explored by Zeithaml, using the model shown in Figure 6.3. As can be seen, the concept of perceived value is related to a number of other concepts.

1. *Intrinsic and extrinsic attributes.* The specific features of the service will influence the perceived value. Take the example of a sports centre. This centre's attributes would be its name, the opening hours, which sports can be practised there, the location, the availability of parking, the infrastructure, the professional qualifications of the instructors, and so on.

   There is a distinction between intrinsic and extrinsic attributes. *Intrinsic* attributes cannot be changed without altering the nature of the service itself. They are part of the delivered service. In the case of the sports centre, the infrastructure and the skills of the instructors are examples of intrinsic attributes. *Extrinsic* attributes are not really part of the service the customer consumes. As such, they are not really an essential part of the service, but are secondary variables that determine the total framework in which the service is offered. Objective price and brand name are the most important extrinsic attributes. The advertising of the sports centre is another example of an extrinsic attribute.

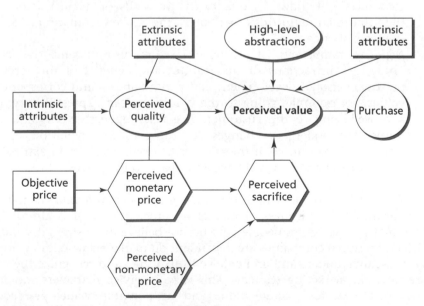

Figure 6.3 The model of 'perceived value'[7]

Source: Zeithaml, V. A. and Bitner, M. J. (1996) *Services Marketing*. Reproduced with Permission of the McGraw-Hill Companies.

2. *Objective and perceived prices*. The *objective price* of a service is the actual price asked. This objective price often differs from the *perceived monetary price* because customers forget or misunderstand prices, or simply do not pay attention to them. For example, you could presume a bus ticket cost 0.87 euro, even though in reality it now costs 1.12 euro.

Service marketers should also understand that service buyers pay a *non-monetary price*, in addition to the monetary price. The monetary price should already take into account, and compensate for, this non-monetary price. These non-monetary customer costs result primarily from the fact that consumption and production of services coincide, and thus that customer participation is required. The customer has to invest time and effort to be able to receive the service, which implies *opportunity costs* (the customer is prevented from doing something else in the meantime) and *convenience costs*. The customer also has to invest time and effort, or *search costs*, to select the right service. *Psychological costs* are also incurred resulting from the uncertainty felt while selecting, consuming, and evaluating a service. Search costs and psychological costs can be quite high because of the intangibility of services!

The various types of non-monetary costs can be illustrated with the example of visiting a restaurant. The customer:
– looks for an appropriate restaurant (*search costs*);
– worries whether the price/quality will be all right (*psychological costs*);
– goes to the restaurant (*convenience costs*);
– waits to be served (*opportunity costs*).

3. *Perceived sacrifice and quality of service*. The perceived monetary and non-monetary price combine to form the *perceived sacrifice*. This includes everything the customer has to lose in order to obtain the service. This sacrifice is compared with the *perceived quality of the service*, which is determined by the intrinsic attributes, the brand name and the perceived monetary price. The sports centre's customers will judge its quality by the skills of its instructors, the state of the infrastructure (intrinsic attributes), the centre's reputation (brand name), and the level of prices.

4. *High-level abstractions*. High-level abstractions also influence the perceived value. These are abstractions of the features and benefits of the service – such as prestige, personal development and performance – and correspond to universal values. For example, going to the hairdresser can express beauty, personal care and well-being to the customer. The resulting perceived value is clearly not stable, but undergoes changes according to the evolution of the defining elements. For example, if the advertising level, which is an extrinsic attribute of the service, changes, it will have an impact on the perceived value.

The service provider can also influence the perceived value of the service. Take, for example, the business of market research. Clearly, it is almost impossible to sell market research to people who do not believe in its strengths and possibilities. Market research companies are dependent on marketers who know how to use market research, understand and believe in its value, and recognize the role of market research in marketing strategy. This is why service marketers should distinguish between a service's actual value and its potential value. The actual value is the value customers perceive at this moment. The potential value is the value the service provider could attain with continuous marketing efforts. For example, the customer could need more 'education' to fully understand the benefits a service offers. The intangible nature of services can make it more difficult to explain their uses and benefits.

Value-based pricing is based on the fact that the 'perceived value' is a fundamental consideration in setting a price, and this price as such already communicates a certain value to the customer. As can be seen from the model in Figure 6.3, the actual price influences the perceived value. This is a concept explored by Berry and Yadav.[8] They identify three different strategies that aim at capturing and communicating the value of a service, according to what value means to the buyer:

- satisfaction-based pricing;
- relationship pricing; and
- efficiency pricing.

Satisfaction-based pricing

Satisfaction-based pricing eliminates the uncertainty that accompanies the purchase of a service. These kinds of strategies primarily aim to reassure the customer that he or she cannot go wrong when buying this service. Service providers can do this in several ways.

- *Benefit-driven pricing*. Service companies can explicitly price the aspect of the service that directly benefits customers. The underlying principle is that customers feel less uncertain and more satisfied if the unit in which the price is measured seems logical to them and the price is related to the benefits the service provider delivers. Benefit-driven pricing could certainly be beneficial for professional services such as legal services, which cause a great deal of uncertainty for the client, especially when lawyers charge by the hour. The cost–benefit analysis of a legal procedure cannot be estimated in advance, since the costs are not related to the benefits. Uncertainty when shopping for legal assistance is greatly reduced when prices are set according to the benefits delivered – for instance, by charging a percentage of the awarded claim (benefit) – especially when the outcome of the lawsuit is unpredictable.
- *Flat-rate pricing*. Of course, there are cases in which customers are more or less certain about the benefits they will receive, yet uncertain about the costs. To relieve this uncertainty, prices are agreed upon in advance. Flat-rate pricing only makes sense if the flat-rate price is attractive to the customer, compared to what he or she would expect to pay normally, and the company has to dispose of a cushion for unanticipated costs, through a highly efficient and streamlined cost structure. Lawyers, for instance, could also opt for flat-rate pricing instead of benefit-driven pricing. This could prove especially useful in lawsuits where the outcome is largely foreseeable.
- *Service guarantees*. These also belong to the category of satisfaction-based pricing. They are certainly the most extreme form of value-based pricing. Statements like 'If you're not completely satisfied, we don't expect you to pay' (Hampton Inns) guarantee service delivery of high perceived value (*see also* Chapter 8).

Relationship pricing

Relationship pricing encourages long-term relationships with the company that the customer views as beneficial. This pricing technique should not be confused with flat-rate pricing. Flat-rate pricing concerns the price of one project, while relationship pricing should encourage the customer to expand his or her purchases, both in time and in volume. The two most important pricing issues in relationship marketing are long-term contracts and price bundling.

- *Long-term contracts*, which offer customers price and non-price incentives to enter into relationships lasting several years, can change the buyer–seller relationship into a partner alliance based on mutual trust and collaboration ('win–win' philosophy).
- *Price bundling* aims at an extension of the relationship in terms of volume instead of time, by selling two or more products/services bundled together. We shall discuss price bundling in greater detail later in this chapter, when we address the price structure decision.

Efficiency pricing

Efficiency pricing is based on understanding and managing costs, in order to accomplish cost reductions which are then passed on to the customer. The 'efficiency pricer' must find a continuous challenge in eliminating non-value adding activities and hence streamlining the service processes by constantly questioning the way in which things are done. By working on the cost side in this way, the service provider can then offer the lowest price. A typical example of efficiency pricing is McDonald's. Costs can be minimized through a production-line approach to the service delivery. As we have already stated (*see* cost-based strategies), understanding costs is particularly difficult for service companies. Moreover, attempts at improving efficiency might have a negative impact on the quality of service delivery.

Exhibit 6.1

Pricing service innovations throughout the life cycle

The customer value of a service is not stable; it changes over time and differs between separate customer segments. Service marketers should keep this in mind when setting the price of a *new* service. They have to consider the price's evolution over time, together with the service life cycle.

For example, George Downey in our introductory case study is wondering about the price of an Internet connection. Should he begin with low prices, in order to gain a large market share right from the start, or should he aim for a select public and start out at a high price? Such concerns centre around a choice of strategies: penetration pricing and skimming pricing.

Skimming strategy

A skimming strategy is characterized by a maximum price setting at every stage of the life cycle. The basic premise is that there is always a group of customers willing to pay more for a service than others. The perceived value of the service is higher for these customers. The service price is then set at this level to maximize unit contribution. Over the life cycle, the price is decreased, to gradually win the customers with a lower perceived value who want to pay less. As the life cycle progresses further, the market is developed, step by step.

A skimming strategy has several advantages:

- The total profit is maximized over the life cycle of a service. At every point, the service provider asks for the maximum price, fully exploiting the perceived value of each segment.
- Price skimming supports the long-term development of the market, gaining the market step by step.
- The introductory price communicates a quality image, reassuring the customer and taking away any doubt about the performance to be expected. Since the price itself is already an indi-

Exhibit 6.1 continued

cation of value, and influences the perceived value, it can sustain the image of a high quality service. This is particularly important since the intangible nature of services makes them harder to judge before purchase.

- Investments are quickly regained, aided by the high unit contribution.
- Starting with a high price allows for reductions later.
- Since the market is not fully attacked from the beginning and only a fraction of the potential customers are prepared to pay the introductory price, the necessary capacity can be limited at first and then be built up gradually. The service provider does not need full capacity from the start.

A skimming strategy does have some disadvantages, however:

- A skimming strategy involves a higher risk, since there is a possibility that the service will not be accepted at all due to its high price.
- New market entries are stimulated by the creation of an attractive market with high margins and growth potential.

With a skimming strategy, severe competition can be expected right after the introduction of the new service, when a number of competitors, attracted by the profits to be gained, also enter the market. This will cause pressure on prices. Setting a low price from the beginning could discourage new market entries and avert price wars. A good illustration of this is the Belgian cellular telephone market. Belgacom launched its product and services lines under the umbrella of their expiring monopoly. After the entrance of a second provider, Mobistar, prices dropped dramatically, indicating clearly the skimming practices adopted first by Belgacom.

Penetration strategy
Introducing a new service at a low price in order to obtain a rapid market penetration is called penetration pricing. This pricing strategy is used to gain a large market share in a short time. If the service can be quickly imitated, penetration pricing can be beneficial. Furthermore, if the hesitations of customers to try out the new service need to be overcome, offering the new services at the lowest price possible or even for free is advisable. The introduction of automatic teller machines (ATMs) is a good example of this. At first, this service was offered by most of the banks for free; once customers got acquainted on a large scale – which is necessary for the ATM-network to become sustainable in the long run – pricing was introduced in many countries.

A number of conditions need to be fulfilled and so it is essential that the implementation of a penetration strategy is handled carefully.

- The market has to adopt the service quickly, without a long test period.
- The elasticity of demand should be high, providing a high demand at low prices. If the demand does not vary with the price, there will be no point in offering low prices, since this will only damage the profitability of the service provider.
- The service provider should be aware of the possibility that the low price will communicate low quality and value to potential customers. This, combined with the fact that many services are difficult to evaluate before purchase (or even after it) could create uncertainty and doubt. Contrary to the service provider's intentions, this could actually inhibit fast, large-scale adoption. Take the example of market research studies. No one would want a study that only costs $100, since the price would indicate that this study could not possibly have been executed thoroughly and professionally.
- The necessary capacity to sustain a rapid market development should be present from the outset.

Competition-based strategies

This category of pricing strategies is entirely based on the firm's actual and desired competitive position. The prime motivation for this kind of pricing strategy is to reach a desired position within the competitive field. Such a position can be reached through the following pricing strategies: *experience-curve pricing, going-rate pricing, price signalling* and *price leadership*.

Experience-curve pricing

Let us consider a competitive market with experience effects – for instance, the market for Internet access providers – as shown in Figure 6.4.

When company A sets prices at or even below current costs, the price-sensitive customers of companies B and C will switch to company A. This will make it possible for A to gain experience more rapidly, thus outpacing the competition and eventually driving competitors out of the market. In addition, company A's low price can encourage more customers to enter the market, once again giving company A the opportunity to exploit economies of scale.

Experience-curve pricing – that is, pricing aggressively at or even below current costs – can be used when:

- experience effects are strong;
- the firm has more experience than its competitors;
- customers are price-sensitive.

Going-rate pricing

This pricing strategy involves charging the most prevalent price in the market. In some service markets, demand is so price-sensitive that a firm would risk losing most of its business if its prices became higher than those of competitors. On the other hand, charging lower prices would result in immediate retaliation from competitors. Within going-rate pricing, a distinction can be made between 'naive' and 'sophisticated' going-rate pricing.[9]

In *naive going-rate pricing*, a firm automatically sets its prices at the same level as the competitors, without analysing demand or costs. An example of this situation can be found in a busy tourist zone where a number of restaurants 'cluster' together. To attract price-sensitive tourists, restaurants will set the 'Daily Special' at the going rate, while more specialized dishes, for which competition is more 'fuzzy', are priced at a premium.

In *sophisticated going-rate pricing*, a 'follower' follows the pricing decisions of the 'leader'. This can be observed in the banking sector, where the leader determines the rate changes in a specific segment (mortgage loans, deposit accounts, etc.) and is then followed by smaller banks within that segment.

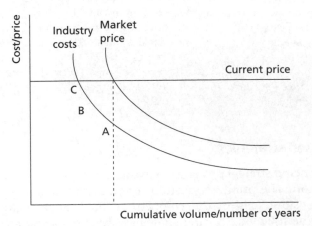

Figure 6.4 Chart showing relative positions of companies in a competitive market

The use of going-rate pricing has two main advantages for service businesses:

1. *Simplicity*. It is much easier to make price decisions on the basis of the going rate than to set prices according to customer value or cost, given the difficulties in measurement in a service environment.
2. *Price peace*. Going-rate pricing prevents price wars.

Price signalling

Service offers often differ in quality and average total cost. Suppose there are only two different quality levels, high and low, and associated with these quality levels are average total costs of $100 and $120 respectively. Service firms can choose from three different strategies:

1. charging $100 for low quality;
2. charging $120 for high quality service; and
3. charging $120 for low quality.

The third option is called price signalling.

There are three underlying conditions necessary for price signalling to be an equilibrium strategy.[10]

- Consumers must be able to obtain information about price more easily than information about quality. In many service businesses this will be the case, since the inherent intangibility of services makes it more difficult for customers to gain information about the quality of the service.
- Customers must want the service enough to risk buying the higher-priced service even with no guarantee of high quality.
- There must be a sufficiently large number of informed consumers who can understand quality and will pay the high price only for the high quality service. This ensures a sufficiently positive correlation between price and quality, so that uninformed consumers who infer quality from price will find it, on average, worthwhile to do so.

The restaurant business is a typical service business where these three conditions are fulfilled. Consumers can gain access to price information by looking at the menu, which is often placed outside at the entrance to the restaurant, but information about the quality of the food served inside is more difficult to obtain. However, there will be a sufficiently large number of customers who can understand quality, thus ensuring a positive correlation between price and quality. Finally, many customers want the high quality enough to take some risks.

Although this pricing strategy will maximize short-term profits, it will be disastrous for most businesses in the long run, because it is based on cheating the customer. Duped customers will go away unsatisfied, spreading their bad experience by word of mouth, which makes acquisition of new customers ever more difficult. And since customers are constantly being fooled, development of a loyal customer base is impossible. However, there are certain service providers for whom a price signalling strategy can be beneficial, even in the long term. What visitor to the Piazza della Signoria in Florence or the banks of the Canal Grande in Venice has not felt cheated by the local restaurant keepers? Restaurants in tourist hot spots such as these do not need loyalty to be profitable. They just need one shot at every tourist visiting these cities. There is thus no need for loyalty or positive word of mouth.

Price leadership

A price leader exerts a dominant influence on market prices for a service delivery, giving direction to market price levels and patterns by initiating price increases or decreases. The price leader is commonly a market leader, the biggest selling service firm in that specific service segment. For example, in mortgage loans, the price leader will determine interest levels for mortgage loans. The price leader will often behave very aggressively towards competitors when they are, in its opinion, misbehaving. Further characteristics of the price leader include:

- it is often a low-cost producer;
- it has strong distribution channels;
- it is often recognized as being in the technical forefront of service development;
- it has superior financial resources.

Handling fierce price competition in a service environment

Since the fixed/variable cost ratio is high in a considerable number of service businesses, the marginal profit contribution is almost equal to the revenue obtained. In the presence of competition, the result can be an intense price war, since price cuts are immediately matched by competitors. Considering the enormous impact of prices on the company's profits, the result can be devastating. The huge price war raging in the English Channel crossing market is a case in point. Since the construction of the railway tunnel ('the Chunnel'), the price of crossing the Channel has collapsed. The three main players (ferries, airlines and the tunnel) are competing by using ever cheaper offers to tempt potential customers, up to the limit where crossing the Channel by ferry can cost next to nothing. Clearly, this price war has brought few benefits to the competitors. No single price advantage is maintained for any length of time, since it is always being matched by a competitor's offer. The impact on the value perceived by customers is also detrimental. Customers' perceptions of the 'normal price' to cross the Channel are completely distorted by the continuous price cuts. The suppliers' emphasis on price in their messages to the customer only enhances this price sensitivity.[11]

In waging a price war, two key issues must be watched closely: *security* and *flexibility*. A sufficient degree of security against enemy attack is essential if an offensive strategy is to be pursued. Key customers must be looked after, with attention concentrated where the bulk of the business is done. In military terms, defend your vital targets at all costs. In Pareto terminology, fight to retain the 20 per cent of your customer base that delivers 80 per cent of your sales. In this case, price discrimination can offer interesting perspectives. Besides security, flexibility is a key issue in waging a price war, since prearranged plans may have to be altered to meet changing situations.

In most cases, none of the parties engaged in a price war is a winner in the end. Thus, preventing a price war seems at least as important as fighting it. This can be achieved in the following two ways:

1. *Threats*. Competitors are left in no doubt that price attacks will be retaliated against immediately.
2. *Price agreements*. Explicit or implicit agreements excluding price competition between competitors in oligopolistic markets enhance profits for all parties.

An example of the second option can be found in the Belgian telecommunications industry. Proximus (Belgacom, AirTouch) was the only cellular phone operator in Belgium until 1996, when a second operator, Mobistar (France Télécom), entered the market with very low prices. Proximus responded by dropping its prices to some 4 per cent above Mobistar's. The combination of the price drop with press releases from Proximus, stating that the GSM market was big enough for both competitors to be profitable, averted a price war. Consequently, Mobistar also stated its intention to prevent a price war under any circumstances.

Finding a balance between the different pricing strategies

The three determinants of price (cost, competitor and customer value) are clearly all important and ignoring any of them could be a major mistake.

The cost of providing a service determines the bottom price level. The perceived value of the service by the customer determines the top level. The competitors' price is the moderating variable that forces service providers to strike a balance between cost and customer value. However, determining how each of the three determinants will affect price must be examined in the light of the pricing objective.

To clarify this, let us return to the situation described at the beginning of the chapter. George Downey, who is responsible for a telecommunications company's expansion into providing Internet access, has to determine the price for this service. With profit optimization as his objective, he will aim at the segment that has the highest perceived value and is prepared to pay the most for an Internet connection. This way, he can skim the market incrementally, continuously looking for those high-value customers. This would be the ideal way to work in a monopoly situation, but as more and more competitors enter the market, each fighting for its share of the cake, there will doubtless be more and more pressure on prices. Furthermore, as Internet access becomes more common, the perceived value will erode. Lowering prices will further this erosion.

Another scenario would be to depart from a market objective – to develop the market as quickly as possible. The cost then will determine the bottom price level. George Downey should aim at the mass market and lower the threshold as far as possible. He should achieve this by not only setting low prices, but also by taking away any customer doubts – by allowing a free test period, for example.

No matter what pricing objective George Downey chooses, there is one factor he should never lose sight of: his pricing strategy has to be embedded in the total marketing strategy. The process of segmenting, targeting and positioning determines who the customers are, as well as who the direct competitors of the company are (aiming at the same segment). Consequently, George Downey should regard service value only through the eyes of his target group, and study the actions of those competing for the same segment. This also means that the pricing strategy must be in line with the service strategy and the implied service concept.

In line with the arguments developed in the first chapters of this book, it can be also noted that the nature of the service delivery process itself plays a role here. Recall the typology stemming from Mills and Margulies outlined in Chapter 1. A distinction has been made between maintenance interactive, task interactive and personal interactive services. These services vary in terms of the amount of uncertainty and complexity entailed in the service transaction itself. The standardized nature of maintenance interactive services implies that cost-based and competition-based considerations might dominate the final outcomes in terms of pricing strategy. As these types of services are much easier to compare cost and competitive considerations will prevail. Also, and this will become clear in Chapter 17, these type of services are often more capital- and hence technology-intensive. This phenomenon might inspire to emphasize experience-curve pricing like outlined above. Such phenomena are less to be observed in the case of task and especially personal interactive type of services. Characterized by high levels of uncertainty or even ambiguity, pricing these types of services will be much closer related to the dynamics outlined by Zeithaml (*see* Figure 6.3) whereby intrinsic and extrinsic attributes or of a less tangible nature than in the case of maintenance interactive services.[12] Notice as well, that for these types of services, one often does not pay for a certain transaction or outcome. Rather fees depend directly on the time spent by the service provider; think about counselling but also about professional consulting services. And while this phenomenon, which can be linked directly to the uncertain nature of these service delivery processes, might create transparency in terms of budget (one can compare hourly/daily fees), the heterogeneity of both inputs and process ingredients will in the end lead again to idiosyncratic value perceptions. So finding a balance in terms of pricing strategy requires to take into account both the competitive strategy and the nature of the service delivery process.

Government policies restraining pricing policy

We stated above that pricing decisions can be studied from three perspectives: a cost perspective, a customer perspective and a competitor perspective. In most Western economies, however, government policies aimed mainly at protecting the consumer will also play a large part in pricing strategies. In economics, it is a widespread belief that competition is the most effective way to achieve low consumer prices. In practice, however, services are more likely than goods to be supplied in non-competitive environments. This has forced many Western governments to intervene directly in pricing decisions. These interventions take the following forms:[13]

- *Price agreements*. Since many service industries are oligopolistic in nature, companies can enhance profitability through price agreements. These in fact eliminate competition, which results in higher prices for the consumer. Such activities have been declared illegal by many European countries, both individually and in combination through European legislation (Articles 85 and 86 of the Treaty of Rome). In the UK, an agreement between the four largest betting shop operators not to compete on price was declared illegal in 1986. In Belgium, the government determines maximum price levels for petrol.
- *Monopoly pricing*. In order to protect customers from exclusion, governments might want to avoid competition for some services. Nonetheless, to keep prices within certain bounds, governments can use regulatory bodies which determine the level and structure of charges made by these service companies. British Telecom, British Gas and the regional water companies are controlled by Oftel, Ofgas and Ofwat, respectively. Article 86 of the Treaty of Rome prohibits exploitation of a monopoly situation through the charging of unfair prices.
- *Price communication*. Governments can specify the manner in which prices should be communicated. For instance, the Belgian government, through The Consumer Protection Act of 1991, requires that all prices should be communicated with VAT included. For financial services, there are specific requirements about the communication of debit and credit rates, exchange rates, and so forth.

■ *Tie-in sales*. Most governments, recognizing that some forms of bundling (*see* later in this chapter), in particular some forms of tie-in sales, inflict substantial harm on the general public, have forced companies to limit the use of these techniques (in the US by the Clayton Act, in the European Union by directives of the European Commission). These cases are mostly related to limiting the use of bundling due to anti-competitive pressures.

PRICING STRUCTURE

The pricing structure takes into account a set of product, customer and purchase characteristics which will have an effect on price levels.

Price discrimination

Price discrimination can be defined as the charging of different prices to different market segments. Price discrimination should not be confused with price differentiation, which involves the service provider charging lower prices due to economic factors, such as extra-large orders. Nor should price discrimination be confused with the efforts of managing demand, since price discrimination is not meant to shift demand to off-peak periods. It is meant rather to augment profits from price-insensitive segments, and to generate more business from price-sensitive segments.

Service providers can discriminate between segments with different price sensitivities, charging high prices to customers almost insensitive to price changes, and charging low prices to price-sensitive customers. Price discrimination is only possible when:

■ different segments have different price sensitivity;
■ the different segments are identifiable, and a mechanism exists to charge them different prices;
■ the different segments are fully separated – that is, individuals in the low-price segment cannot pass their right to use the service on to another segment;
■ the segments are large enough to make the discrimination worthwhile;
■ the cost of the price discrimination strategy does not exceed the incremental revenues obtained;
■ the use of different prices does not confuse customers;
■ competition is limited (preferably a monopoly).[14]

The time-dependent nature of services makes price discrimination possible. Different prices at different times of the day are often feasible because demand is also time dependent. Rail companies, for instance, can charge higher prices during peak hours (since commuters cannot shift to off-peak hours), thus increasing profits obtained from these segments.

It should be noted that price discrimination is not always meant as a profit-enhancing mechanism. In many public utilities, for instance, it is common to give discounts to certain customer segments – senior citizens, minors, large families – for social reasons.

Price-line decisions

When making price-line decisions, two important factors should be studied: price consistency and price lining.

Since services are by their nature intangible, the service offerings of different providers cannot easily be compared. Thus, the price of the service offering itself will often communicate the service level of the provider. When pricing different services or products, the service provider has to keep the overall targeted position in mind. This is called *price consistency*. For instance, imagine the confusion of a guest in a five-star hotel if he or she were to see that breakfast cost only $1.95.

Price lining, on the other hand, involves dividing the product assortment into different price ranges. Clothing stores, for instance, will sell raincoats in the price categories of $200, $150 and $120. Through this pricing method, a service provider can maximize sales by offering different value (price–quality) propositions. The Marriott Hotel group, for instance, covers four different value propositions: Marriott Marquis (premium price–superior quality), Marriott (high price–good quality), Courtyard (average price–standard quality) and Fairfield Inn (low price–low quality). Marriott is thus able to enlarge its customer base by offering a hotel for every segment. Moreover, Marriott eliminates loss of a customer's lifetime value, if they want to move up or down to a different price category.

Pricing complementary services

Companies that offer complementary products or services sometimes take a small profit margin on the main purchase, such as a car, but take a high margin on complementary products or services (accessories or maintenance). This pricing approach can be very profitable, unless there are more focused competitors, selling those complementary services at a lower margin. In industrial markets, for instance, installations sometimes are sold at low margins, which is compensated for through high margins on maintenance services. This technique is called *installed base management*. The low margins on installations boost sales (penetration), thus enlarging a company's installed base, and thus enlarging the potential market for the service department. Since the high margins on services will attract entrants to this market, one has to be able to build and sustain a competitive lead to secure these high margins.

Price bundling

Price bundling is the practice of marketing two or more products and/or services in a single package for a special price and is sometimes called *'package' pricing*.[15] It is a potentially powerful method to exploit profit potentials and to maximize profits in any company which offers multiple products and/or services.

Bundled accounts which roll together credit cards, checking accounts, certificates of deposit and consumer loans, have become big sellers for many banks. One of the biggest selling points is their convenience. The marketing angle aside, these accounts are intended to reduce the overhead and support costs of taking in new deposits and making loans.[16]

There are two possible approaches to price bundling: pure or mixed price bundling.

1. In *pure price bundling* (or 'tie-in sales'), the services and/or products are available only in bundled form, and cannot be purchased separately. Pure price bundling is only applicable in the rare cases in which a firm holds monopoly power over one of the components of the bundle.
2. In *mixed price bundling*, the customer is offered the opportunity to either buy the bundle or to buy its different components separately. Typically there is some price incentive for purchasing the bundle, although bundling can simply take the form of add-on services. There are two forms of mixed price bundling: mixed-leader price bundling and mixed-joint price bundling.[17]
    – In *mixed-leader price bundling*, the price of one (or several) of the services/ products is discounted while the other is purchased at the regular price. For example, some theatres and opera houses offer discounts for parking, with the theatre ticket serving as proof. This type of price bundling is not very frequent in service industries, compared to the mixed-joint form.
    – In the *mixed-joint* form, a single price is set when the different services are purchased jointly. In 1994, De Generale Bank introduced the G-Global Club in Belgium. A large number of banking transactions are free of charge for members of the club, as are debit and credit cards (including Eurocheques), in exchange for a monthly fee of 5.58 euro. Examinations of the charges to non-members show that a club membership costs about 24.79 euro more per year than the fees charged by the bank to non-members. This difference is more than compensated for through large discounts offered to the members of the club by hotels, restaurants and even a travel agency. Although this price bundling effort has been profitable for De Generale Bank (the club had 150 000 members in 1996), it does not necessarily mean that it will be profitable for all banks. Two of the bank's biggest competitors, BBL and ASLK, have stated that they have no intention of copying De Generale Bank's bundled offer in the foreseeable future.

A price bundling approach (mixed or pure) is only profitable when the following conditions are met:

1. *Government regulation permits price bundling.* Tie-in sales, for instance, are illegal in many European countries.
2. *The value offered by the bundle to the customer exceeds the value of the different components of the bundle*, where value is defined as 'what a customer gets for what he sacrifices'. Here are a few cases where this condition is fulfilled:
    – customers believe that substantial time and effort will be saved in one-stop shopping (*convenience*);
    – customers who have little knowledge about the bundled product(s) or service(s) believe that buying the bundled offer is less risky (*risk reduction*);
    – the bundle is offered at a *price discount*.
3. *Customer needs are similar*, and thus can be satisfied with one bundled offer. When customer needs are diverse, the bundled offer might not fully satisfy customers and consequently may create opportunities for more focused companies.

Pure price bundling is very common in the computer and software industry, for instance. PCs are delivered with a software package already installed. If most customers want to use another supplier's software, however, this bundled offer does not increase value for the customer, and eventually results in higher prices for the customer and/or lower margins for the supplier. In consequence, this customer can be tempted to switch to more focused ('unbundling') suppliers.

Although it is not strictly speaking a condition, proprietary control over one of the components of the bundle greatly reduces the risk of duplication in the case of pure price bundling.

A successful price bundling effort can enhance profits and support the competitive position of a firm in several ways. First, it may enable the firm to gain a *cost advantage*, especially when bundled offers are standardized, since standardized bundled offers cost less to produce than several customized individual products or services. Second, when using a mixed-price bundling strategy, price bundling can be used as a *discrimination* device, charging different prices to different customer segments, based on their buying behaviour. Finally, price bundling may enable the firm to offer a *differentiated product or service*, by providing an overall solution to the customer's needs.

Managing demand

The nature of services, with characteristics such as intangibility, simultaneity and, above all, perishability, coupled with capacity constraints, suggests that demand should be managed in an effective way to maximize profits. Most service industries are characterized by varying demand curves over time, which follow a daily, weekly, annual, seasonal, cyclical or random pattern. These fluctuations in demand foster the need to manage capacity (*see* Chapter 15). In the case of rail services, for example, workers and students must generally arrive at work or school at a specified time, which creates peaks around certain time periods. Resort hotel demand will be higher during prime vacation months than it is in the off-season, while capacity is more or less fixed. Furthermore resort hotel demand curves show that the market is much less price-sensitive during prime vacation months than it is in the off-season.

Profits can be maximized through setting prices according to price sensitivity. In high season, the price for a room per night can be double the off-season price. Thus, tourists taking their holidays outside prime vacation months due to price discounts level out demand, with higher profits for the hotel as a consequence through better capacity utilization.

In addition, when different customer segments have different demand patterns over time, targeting these segments and thus expanding business through other segments can also significantly enhance profitability. Exploiting these other segments will often require a different price positioning effort. Capacity utilization of fast-food restaurants, for instance, is very low during the afternoon, yet this is the preferred time for children to have birthday parties. Arranging children's birthday parties can thus enhance capacity utilization, and in this manner augment profitability for fast-food chains such as McDonald's. Of course pricing decisions will also be of great importance in attracting this additional business. Demand management can also be addressed in the broader context of yield management, which will be discussed extensively in Chapter 15 on capacity management.[18]

PRICING LEVELS AND TACTICS

Price levels refer to the actual price that is charged for a service, including any specific promotions being offered. Price tactics involve short-term promotional price initiatives. The aim of such actions can differ from case to case and promotional pricing can be tailored to suit a particular objective. Examples of promotional goals and their complementary actions are:

- *Quantity discounts*. The service provider offers a discount to customers dealing in greater volume – for example, transportation companies offering discounts for every additional truck engaged.
- *Temporary discounts* (time shift). Prices are lower at certain times or on certain days – for example, off-peak hours in a squash centre, or hotel discounts at weekends.
- *Promotional discounts* (generate trial). The service can be set at a lower price for a limited period of time to attract new customers.

Promotional pricing is difficult for services, however, when customers lack precise reference prices. If such price transparency does not exist, promotional discounts become quiet useless. This transparency of price information is determined by three factors:

1. *The availability of price information* – can I get information about the price of a particular service?
2. *The effort it costs to get that information* – what do I have to do to receive it?
3. *The clarity of the price information* – is it understandable?

Another important criterion – *the comparability of competing service offers* – can be defined using the same three variables as above:

1. *The availability of information on the result of a service offer* – can I get information about the performance of a particular service offer?
2. *The effort it costs to compare service offers* – what do I have to do to be able to compare service offers?
3. *The clarity of the comparison* – is it possible in any way to compare, even when I have the necessary information?

The combination of these two criteria – transparency of price information and comparability of the results – creates a framework in which every kind of service can be represented (*see* Figure 6.5).

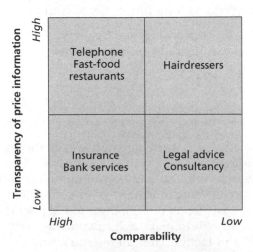

Figure 6.5 Matrix representing criteria for implementation of discount pricing

Services that are easily comparable and that possess a high transparency of price information are most appropriate for discount pricing actions. The customers of these services are more likely to know reference prices and can judge the promotional price compared to it. The effect of price discounts on services with low transparency of price information is questionable. The price discount can create a greater clarity (which is not always beneficial to the service provider) but it can also confuse the customer who cannot distinguish the discount price from the regular price. For services with a low degree of comparability, it is more important for the customer to receive assurance of quality, since the result of the service is difficult to judge beforehand.

The framework in Figure 6.5 does more than determining when discount prices can be useful. Given that the basic aim of discounting prices is to obtain more income by lowering the price, discounting assumes that decreasing the price will have a positive effect on sales. In reality, the usefulness of price discounts will be determined by the price competition that exists in the market, and the vulnerability of the service provider when it comes to pricing.

Clearly, markets with a high transparency of price information and a high degree of comparability experience greater price competition, and are forced either to use price discounts (in order to keep or attract customers) or to expand their sales volume. The matrix in Figure 6.5 provides a means of escaping this trap, making price discounts obsolete.

1. *Reducing the transparency of price information.* Creating complicated price structures is a possible way to lower the transparency of the price information. However, this is a dangerous path to walk alone since it can increase the insecurity of the customer, who prefers to know what to expect. De Generale Bank takes this approach with its G-Global Club which, in one way, enhances transparency by attaching a clear, fixed price to a bundled set of services. On the other hand, the individual services can no longer be distinguished, making it impossible to know what they cost.
2. *Reducing the comparability of the offer.* The service provider can implement this by differentiating its offer from that of its competitor's. Customization of the service is one possible way to do this. Clearly, when the offer is completely adapted to a customer's needs, it becomes difficult for him or her to compare several offers.

According to the framework described, there are two ways to escape from severe price pressure: by making it more difficult to see through the pricing or by making it more difficult to see through the offer.

CONCLUSION

In this chapter we have provided you with an overview of the major elements playing a role in pricing services.

It is important to take time to think at the beginning of the pricing process. Determining in advance what you want to achieve with your pricing strategy is a necessary, but often neglected, first step in developing a sound pricing approach.

Within the pricing process, it helps to make a distinction between pricing objectives, strategy, structure, level and tactics. They all refer to a single pricing process, but consider separate questions.

In terms of pricing strategy, the costs, competition and the value as experienced by customers should all be taken into account. Also, the nature of the service delivery process itself might affect the relevancy of these different elements. It is important to know exactly what drives costs and to make sure that the pricing strategy is in line with the overall marketing strategy. Pricing is a valuable instrument when targeting a particular segment and positioning the company in relation to competitors. Perhaps the most difficult task is determining what value means to the customer and adapting the pricing strategy to reflect this. What value means for customers is dynamic as well, which become clear when discussing pricing strategies for innovations.

Anticipating competitors' moves and avoiding price wars by differentiating your product from that of the competition are important tactical considerations. Regulations governing the market dynamics are another issue to be taken into account.

Finally, being clear about your prices is more important than developing all kinds of promotions.

Review and discussion questions

- Being first in the market allows deploying different pricing strategies; which one would you prefer under which conditions?

- The idea of price bundling is not only very fashionable, but also very controversial (e.g. Microsoft). Under what conditions would price bundling be relevant and acceptable?

- With respect to e-business, pricing seems to be extremely difficult. What do you consider as relevant approaches to price the (different?) services the Internet entails? And which part should be paid by whom? Would bundling be a relevant concept in this respect?

Notes and references

[1] Considering that the fixed costs can be spread over a larger volume, an increase of 20 per cent in volume will be sufficient to cover the price decrease.

[2] Price elasticity is defined as the ratio of the relative change in volume to the relative change in price:

$$\text{Elasticity} = ((\delta V/V)/(\delta P/P)).$$

Depending on the price elasticity of the service, the total demand will vary more or less according to the price. If the price elasticity is high, the demand will increase relatively more than the price decreases, and vice versa.

[3] Keaveney, S. M. (1995) 'Customer switching behaviour in service industries: An exploratory study', *Journal of Marketing*, Vol 59, Apr, 71–82.

[4] Morris, M. and Cantalone, R. (1990) 'Four components of effective pricing', *Industrial Marketing Management*, Vol 19, 321–9.

[5] Morris, M. H. and Fuller, D. A. (1989) 'Pricing an industrial service', *Industrial Marketing Management*, Vol 18, 139–46.

[6] Zeithaml, V. and Bitner, M. J. (1996) *Services Marketing*. New York: McGraw-Hill, pp. 496–8.

[7] Ibid.

[8] Berry, L. and Yadav, M. (1996) 'Capture and communicate value in the pricing of services', *Sloan Management Review*, Summer, 41–51.

[9] Giletta, M. (1992) 'Prix: de la maîtrise des prix à la maîtrise des coûts', *Vuibert Gestion*, p. 22.

[10] Tellis, G. J. (1986) 'Beyond the many faces of price: An integration of pricing strategies', *Journal of Marketing*, Vol 50, Oct, 146–60.

[11] Garda, R. and Marn, M. (1993) 'Price wars', *McKinsey Quarterly*, Issue 3.

[12] A point we will further explore in Chapter 17.

[13] Palmer, A. (1994) *Principles of Services Marketing*. New York: McGraw-Hill, pp. 257–8.

[14] Bateson, J. E. G. (1989) *Managing Services Marketing*. The Dryden Press, p. 363.

[15] Guiltinan, J. P. (1987) 'The price bundling of services: A normative framework', *Journal of Marketing*, Vol 51, Apr, 74–85.

[16] Radigan, J. (1992) 'Bundling for dollars', *United States Banker*, Vol 102, No 9, Sept, 42–4.

[17] Guiltinan, J. P. (1987), op. cit.

[18] Yield management is the process of allocating the right type of capacity to the right kind of customer at the right price so as to maximize revenue or yield – Kimes, S. E. (1989) 'Yield management: A tool for capacity-constrained service firms', *Journal of Operations Management*, Vol 8, No 4, Oct, 348–63.

Suggested further reading

Berry, L. L. and Yadav, M. S. (1996) 'Capture and communicate value in the pricing of services', *Sloan Management Review*, Summer, 41–51. This article focuses on the specific aspects of pricing for services and deals with the characteristic features of services compared to physical products and how you can take these into account in pricing.

Dolan, R. J. and Simon, H. (1997) *Power Pricing*. New York: The Free Press. This is the most recent and comprehensive book on pricing. Highly recommended.

Leszinski, R. and Marn, M. (1997) 'Setting value, not price', *The McKinsey Quarterly*, Issue 1. This is a very interesting article on the issue of value-based pricing with clear real-life examples.

CHAPTER 7

Customer satisfaction and complaint management

Gino Van Ossel · Stefan Stremersch · Paul Gemmel

INTRODUCTION

The management of a chain of family restaurants were presented with the results of a market research study. When they read the findings on the freshness of the salad bar at two different sites, they were very surprised to see that customers surveyed inside one of the two locations tested expressed dissatisfaction with the freshness of the salad bar in the restaurant. This was not in line with what the restaurant's management had expected. In fact, the number of meals served in the restaurant with the supposedly inferior salad bar was about 40 per cent higher than the number in the other restaurant. This salad bar therefore required more frequent refills and was objectively the fresher of the two.

The managers were then shown photographs of the two salad bars. The salad bar causing dissatisfaction was in one of the chain's oldest and most successful restaurants. The age was reflected in its servicescape: the decoration looked worn and the lighting was sombre. In these surroundings the salad bar simply did not look fresh, while in the other restaurant, which had opened more recently, the salad bar's presentation increased its perceived freshness.

In this chapter we shall introduce a service satisfaction framework which will allow us to link different concepts such as service quality, customer satisfaction, complaints and service recovery. We shall further discuss the measurement of customer satisfaction and complaint management in more detail.

Objectives

By the end of this chapter, you should be able to discuss:

- the difference between service quality and customer satisfaction
- why customer satisfaction measurement in services is important
- the basics of setting up a system of customer satisfaction measurement – including what to measure, whose satisfaction to measure, what the appropriate organizational unit is, and how to decide on a benchmark

Objectives continued

- the notion of moment of truth
- how the notion of quality can be broken down into quality dimensions
- how a systematic process of complaint handling can be implemented
- how the complaint threshold can be lowered and what the advantages of such an action is
- the importance of a speedy and appropriate response to complaints
- how complaints can benefit the company by generating improvement projects and improving the customer orientation

SERVICE QUALITY AND CUSTOMER SATISFACTION

The distinction between customer satisfaction and service quality is a very important one. Service quality is a form of attitude representing a long-run, overall evaluation, whereas satisfaction represents a more short-term, transaction-specific judgement. The level of customer satisfaction is the result of a customer's comparison of the service quality expected in a given service encounter with perceived service quality. This also means that satisfaction assessments require customer experience while quality does not.[1]

Service quality as perceived by the customer may differ from the quality of the service actually delivered. A patient can be very dissatisfied about a visit to a doctor because he felt that the doctor did not spend enough time communicating the diagnosis of a fatal disease. The patient could not understand how the doctor could take only two minutes to give a life-changing diagnosis. Nonetheless, from a medical point of view the diagnosis was totally correct. This leads to the distinction between technical quality, or 'what' is perceived by the customer, and 'functional' quality, or 'how' a service is provided:

> 'The latter [functional quality] is the most critical aspect and is concerned with the psychological interaction taking place during the exchange transaction. It is based on the customer's perception and is therefore extremely subjective and encompasses all the cues that the customer picks up during the transaction.'[2]

These cues not only emanate from the server but are also based on perceptions of the whole service environment (*see* the 'servicescape' in Chapter 16). Passengers on the Titanic were delighted with the ship's accommodations. If the ship had reached its destination, many passengers would have been satisfied customers. But, as we all know, the ship sank due to the crew's lack of competence in navigating such a large ship through an ocean full of icebergs. If nothing had happened, this lack of competence (an aspect of technical quality) would never have been perceived by the customer. Therefore it is said that measuring service quality cannot end with measuring customer satisfaction. Technical quality, which is based on the ability of people and the service system to deliver good (professional) quality, must also be monitored. In the manufacturing industry, monitoring process capability is one of the oldest basic principles of quality management. In the service industry, process capability is considered in a very limited way due to the fact that the variability of processes is taken for granted. Nevertheless we believe that technical quality is a major issue in many service environments, and we will therefore spend a separate chapter on managing processes (*see* Chapter 14), and will emphasize the role of employees in realizing a service quality experience.

In trying to explain the gap between expected service quality and perceived service quality, Parasuraman *et al.* came up with a 'gap model' consisting of four causes leading to this gap:[3]

- The gap between management perception of consumer expectations and expected service by the customer. For instance, field service engineers sometimes know very well what their customers want, but this kind of information is not always fed back to the company, with the result that management has an inadequate idea of customer expectations. In the long run, this may lead to role conflict at the level of the field service engineer. Market research can help to close this gap.
- The gap between management perception of consumer expectations and the translation of those perceptions into service quality specifications. The quality specifications (which can be enshrined in quality systems such as ISO 9000) are not fine-tuned to customer expectations.
- The gap between service quality specifications and the actual service delivery. Lack of resources can make it impossible for employees to meet the quality specifications. Other factors contributing to the closing of this gap are teamwork, employee-job fit, technology-job fit, perceived control, supervisory control systems, role conflict and role ambiguity.[4]
- The gap between the actual service delivery and the way the organization communicates about it. External communication of what the customer can expect through advertising can be important in reducing this gap.

The conclusion is that customer satisfaction is a subjective concept, not only because of the perception filter but also because expectations will vary from customer to customer. Our introductory case study is a clear illustration of this. Any organization trying to assess how well it is performing should distinguish between measuring customer satisfaction, customer perceived service quality and technical quality. This distinction is particularly important in services, given their inherent simultaneity and intangibility. In an industrial environment, at least in those sectors where the tangible component in the product plays a dominant role, making this distinction is less relevant.

This chapter is particularly concerned with customer satisfaction measurement. Such a measurement is part of a (balanced) performance measurement system (to which we shall return in Chapter 18).

A SERVICE SATISFACTION FRAMEWORK

Satisfaction and dissatisfaction are seen as two ends of a continuum, where the location is defined by a comparison between expectations and outcome. A customer will be satisfied if the outcome of the service meets his or her expectations. When the service quality exceeds the expectations, the service provider is in the happy position of having a delighted customer. A customer will be dissatisfied when the perceived overall service quality is below his or her expectations.

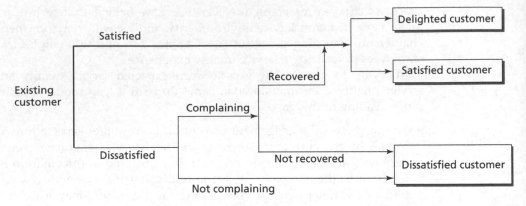

Figure 7.1 A service satisfaction framework

Source: Based on J. M. Hays and A. V. Hill (1999) 'The market share impact of service failures', *Production and Operations Management, An international Journal of the Production and Operations Management Society*, Vol 8, No 3, pp. 208–20.

The service satisfaction framework (*see* Figure 7.1) shows that only a certain percentage of customers who are dissatisfied voice their complaints, while others do not. Complaints should be considered gems for the company, as they provide information helpful for continuous improvement, as well as opportunities to recover customers. Service recovery in itself is a big opportunity to make customers even more loyal than those consistently satisfied with the firm's service. Customer retention through effective complaint management creates more value than attracting new customers.

Customers who do not complain cannot be recovered. These customers tell everyone how bad the service is, and it is these customers who can deeply damage the business.

Customer satisfaction management, and therefore measurement, and complaint management are important ingredients of any strategy to increase customer loyalty and thus increase profits. As we discussed earlier, this can be done by minimizing customer defections, service recovery and maximizing repeat business. In addition, a company will want to maximize sales through referrals. In this chapter, we will discuss customer satisfaction measurement and complaint management as basic building blocks in achieving service satisfaction.

MEASURING CUSTOMER SATISFACTION

Introduction

Measuring is an important part of management. One of the reasons for this is that what gets measured gets done. However, measurement is just a start. In their never-ending battle against kilos and calories, obese people who want to lose weight typically start by buying a bathroom scale and a book with a title like '*How to lose 10 kilos in 4 weeks without feeling hungry*'. Weighing oneself and reading about successful dieting methods, however, rarely results in weight loss. Most people on diets fail to lose weight, even though they genuinely want to, because of a lack of willpower to resist the continual temptation of tasty foods and drinks. This is the secret of the success of 'Weight Watchers'. Instead of trying to stick to a diet all alone, a 'Weight Watchers' member has the opportunity to meet with fellow overweight people. During the weekly gatherings, everyone is invited to step on the scales, which creates peer pressure to sustain one's dieting efforts.

Organizations often make the same mistake. Their managers read books and attend seminars on customer focus. They make satisfaction measurement systems part of their customer focus efforts and invest heavily in buying the best possible scales – that is, a highly sophisticated customer satisfaction measurement system. All too often, however, it turns out that the books, seminars and measurement system do not trigger the desired improvement projects. These organizations are experiencing the obese person's lack of willpower. They too can benefit from the 'Weight Watchers' approach by creating peer pressure within the organization. This typically requires:

- measuring customer satisfaction for specific organizational units rather than for the organization as a whole;
- making the satisfaction data available to everyone in order to create peer pressure and healthy internal competition;
- linking a manager's appraisal to the customer satisfaction data.

Another reason for measuring customer satisfaction is being able to balance the score card. As we shall argue later, performance measurement systems tend to be biased in favour of financial measures.

Need for a benchmark

In order for a measure to have any impact, a reference point is required – a standard according to which an employee or company can judge performance, whether it is good or bad, better or worse. In other words, a benchmark is what is needed.

In customer satisfaction measurement, the most common benchmarks are:

- development over time;
- the different organizational units (for instance, branches, subsidiaries or business units);
- competition.

Evolution over time is the best indicator of whether an organization's customer focus efforts are paying off. Therefore, most customer satisfaction measurements assess the rate of improvement. Since comparisons are only possible if the measurement system is standardized over time, conceiving a customer satisfaction measurement system should be carried out with the utmost care. Indeed, adjusting the system regularly will hinder comparisons. This does not mean that temporary performance measures linked to improvement projects and/or individual or team performance cannot be used at certain points in time.

Quite often, a service organization operates multi-site facilities with different branches or service units at different places. This often makes it possible to carry out inter-organizational benchmarking. Special techniques such as Data Envelopment Analysis have been developed to carry out such benchmarking.[5] Measuring customer satisfaction across different service units is necessary to create peer pressure and internal competition, in order to create a willingness in all units to improve customer satisfaction.

In a competitive environment, outperforming competitors may yield more than simply achieving the highest possible performance. Therefore it is common to benchmark customer satisfaction scores against those of the competition, both in terms of the actual performance and in terms of the rate of improvement.

Whose satisfaction to measure?

This looks like an easy question to answer. Is it not the customer's satisfaction? This is the correct answer, but are we interested in *all* the customers, and who is 'the customer' anyway?

We have already explained that loyalty and referrals result from customer delight, while defections and negative word of mouth arise from dissatisfied customers. Consequently, in customer satisfaction surveys the focus should be on the percentage of dissatisfied and delighted customers, rather than on average satisfaction scores. The question remains as to whether the company should calculate these percentages for its average customer or for the customer representing the highest turnover, potential turnover or profit.

Key accounts or all customers?

If the Pareto principle applies and 20 per cent of the customers account for 80 per cent of company's sales and profits, delighting these 20 per cent is far more important than delighting the other 80 per cent. If a company surveys a representative sample of all its customers, however, the results will mainly reflect the satisfaction of that 80 per cent, which accounts for only 20 per cent of its business. This is one argument for a company surveying only its biggest customers. On the other hand, the biggest customers often receive to all intents and purposes the same service as the smaller ones.

In deciding which customers to survey, the following guidelines should be followed:

■ *Percentage of delighted customers*. It is desirable to be able to calculate the percentage of delighted customers for key accounts separately from the other customers. The more important the key accounts are, the more special attention they should get. This may even necessitate a significant cash outlay to delight individual customers. Spending that money on key accounts will usually be more profitable than spending it on the average customer. Achieving customer delight among key accounts is the best defence against competitors. On the other hand, it is useful to monitor the overall percentage of delighted customers, as this percentage will indicate the company's potential for referrals. This is not an absolute necessity, however.

■ *Percentage of dissatisfied customers*. The reasons for dissatisfaction are usually the same for large and small customers alike. Working on structurally improving the service process and offering will usually benefit all customers. However, since the large customers are limited in number, analysing only the (hopefully limited number of) dissatisfied key accounts may not provide a good insight into the root causes of customer dissatisfaction. That is why surveying all customers rather than only key accounts will probably offer more information on the areas for improvement. However, a single dissatisfied big customer poses a much bigger threat than a small one. It is thus desirable to calculate the percentage of dissatisfied key accounts separately from the overall dissatisfaction rate.

Furthermore, and equally important, identifying dissatisfied customers is the first step in the service recovery process. The organization has to ensure that it can identify all key accounts which are dissatisfied.

Who is the actual customer?

A second question to be answered in an organizational buying situation is 'who is the customer?' In business-to-business marketing, the familiar concept of the decision-making unit refers to all the individuals involved in the buying process. The company has to decide for which members of the decision-making unit they want to know the degree of satisfaction and dissatisfaction. These individuals can perform one or more of the following roles:

- *Users* – members of the organization who will use the product or service.
- *Initiators* – those who initiate the buying process.
- *Influencers* – those who affect the buying process, for instance by setting specifications (prescribers), providing information for evaluating alternatives.
- *Buyers* – those with the formal authority to select the vendors.
- *Deciders* – those who actually make the final decision on which vendor to choose.
- *Approvers* – those with the formal authority to veto the deciders.
- *Purchasers* – those who do the actual buying without having the formal power to decide anything.
- *Gatekeepers* – those who control the flow of information, particularly the stream of salespeople, mailings and sales material which targets the other members of the decision-making unit, thus indirectly influencing which vendors are selected.

As a general rule, it is obvious that the survey should focus in the first place on the members of the decision-making unit who have the biggest impact on the selection of the vendor. They will defect when dissatisfied and generate repeat business when delighted. However, in the long run, their satisfaction will also be affected by the satisfaction of the other members of the decision-making unit. Although it is dangerous to generalize, investing in their delight will usually not be profitable, but in the long run not preventing dissatisfaction may make the customer defect.

Whose performance to measure?

Another question to be answered before the details of a measuring instrument can be designed, is which organizational unit's performance should be assessed. Our recent studies have proven that the aggregate results for an organization as a whole do not generate actionable and relevant results. The smaller the unit of measurement, the richer the information will be; unfortunately, the effort and therefore cost are also proportionally greater.

In retail banking, for instance, it could be assumed that customer satisfaction with the bank's actual products (for instance, its savings account) would be the same across all branches, since these products are standardized within the bank. However, the service relating to the product is being delivered ('produced') at the branch level. Consequently, customer satisfaction may vary from one branch to another. In deciding which organizational unit's customer satisfaction will be measured, three elements should be taken into consideration:

- *The unit as seen by the customer*. The customer will only be able to judge a unit which he or she perceives as such.
- *The managerial unit*. Organizations aiming at improving their performance want to collect data for a manager and his staff. This managerial unit can be the organization as a whole (top management and all staff), the smallest unit possible (a crew leader and his crew), or something inbetween.
- *Costs*. As mentioned earlier, the smaller the unit for which we measure, the more expensive the survey becomes. However, we have come across several organizations that, mainly for cost reasons, calculated customer satisfaction scores only at the national level. These results turned out to be useless as they revealed nothing that could be used for improvement projects.

The compilation of statistics involves drawing a sample at the smallest level for which you want to make the analysis. Data can always be consolidated for a larger unit of measurement; it can never be broken down for sub-units.

What to measure?

As customer satisfaction affects customer loyalty and as this loyalty may eventually result in referrals, a measurement instrument will typically cover these three aspects: overall satisfaction, customer loyalty and referrals.

Overall satisfaction

Customers should be asked explicitly about their overall satisfaction with the organization's performance. A distinction should be made in measuring satisfaction between what some people call *relationship satisfaction* and *transaction satisfaction measurement*. Transaction satisfaction refers to satisfaction with respect to usually the most recent interaction with sharp focus on the core part of the service. Relationship satisfaction refers to a more general feeling of satisfaction with the organization as a whole. For instance, a business school could ask the question 'How satisfied are you with the course you just attended?' It could also ask the question 'How satisfied are you with our business school in general?' There is of course a relationship between the two measures.

All too often, however, organizations simply report average scores, in the best case complemented with standard deviations. Not surprisingly, these scores indicate that the average customer is satisfied with the organization's offerings. This will always be the case in practice, since dissatisfied customers defect and thus will always make up only a limited part of the surveyed sample.

Customer loyalty

Establishing a customer loyalty measure allows us to assess the relationship between satisfaction and loyalty in the organization. Ideally it will eventually be possible to assess the impact of individual improvement projects on customer loyalty and ultimately on the bottom line. This assessment will help to justify investments in customer satisfaction. However, measuring customer loyalty is not easy. In multiple-supplier situations it is even difficult to define customer loyalty.

Let us begin with the simplest of situations, where the customer only buys from one supplier. In that case the customer is either loyal (buys 100 per cent from you) or is not (buys 0 per cent from you). If the company has a database and if the survey is not anonymous, the company can link the customer satisfaction score to the actual loyalty history. In all other cases it becomes much more difficult to define and measure loyalty. If customers buy the same service from different suppliers, loyalty can be defined either according to the customer's intent or behaviour.

- *Intent.* Customers are loyal to a supplier if they consider this supplier to be their preferred supplier. For instance, few people buy all their clothes from the same store or only go to one restaurant. That is why one fast-food chain has decided to define a loyal customer as the customer who, when visiting a fast-food chain of that kind, will always go to one of its restaurants, whenever there is one in the immediate neighbourhood.
- *Behaviour.* Obviously, a more powerful concept of loyalty is based on the customer's actual buying behaviour. The most typical measure is the share of wallet or the percentage of the customer's business the company is enjoying. An alternative is to look at the number of visits to an outlet rather than at the actual spending. In industries where the average sale is more or less stable, both measures will result in the same outcome.

A final option is to score customers depending on what products they buy from you.

In these complex cases, linking the satisfaction survey data to the company's database is not always a solution. Even if the company tracks the customer's spending and number of visits, it does not necessarily have information about the customer's spending habits at, or visits to competing outlets. Consequently, it is difficult to determine this customer's loyalty.

Questions about loyalty are typically biased and overstate the actual loyalty, as respondents typically want to please the surveyor and are not in a real buying situation. This also means that justifying investments in improving customer satisfaction by using the above questions as the only measure of loyalty is not without risk. However, asking these questions makes some sense as it is safe to assume that the measurement error is stable over time and, on average, across the respondents. Consequently, it is possible to analyse trends and relationships between loyalty and other measures.

Referrals

Delighted customers may refer other customers to your service organization. It is therefore intriguing to link satisfaction and loyalty measurements to these referrals. However, since it is very difficult, if not impossible, to link these measures to actual referrals, it is common to measure the intent to refer instead.

Measures relating to specific aspects of the service

The overall satisfaction, loyalty and referral measures are complemented by measures relating to specific aspects of the service. When considering the more specific aspects of the service, the whole service can be broken down according to two types of frameworks: the moments of truth and the quality dimensions of the service.

Moments of truth

In deciding on what aspects of the service to measure, the most common approach is to follow the customer through the service process. Listing the moments of truth in customer experiences will result in a comprehensive inventory of the service attributes. However, one of the major pitfalls of this so-called attribute-based method of measuring customer satisfaction is the inclusion of too many service aspects and consequently too many questions, in a fruitless attempt to be exhaustive. The true challenge is to reduce this comprehensive list down into a more concise and workable one.

The main reason why so many satisfaction surveys are too long is that managers are (rightly) obsessed with getting results that can be acted upon. They assume that corrective actions will deal with specific aspects of the service rather than with the service as a whole, and consequently they want to cover all aspects of the service. What they seem to overlook is the fact that in ongoing research, it is simply too expensive to cover all aspects in a detailed enough manner to trigger immediate corrective actions.

Quality dimensions of the service

Another way to list and then to measure specific service aspects is to break the service down into its quality dimensions. Any service provider should do market research to try to determine the core needs of its customers. The quality dimensions are related to these needs.

Many researchers have tried to discover which dimensions influence the quality, as perceived by the customers. Not only did they try to identify these dimensions, but they also tried to assign relative weights to these dimensions. In an ideal model, the various dimensions should be a *comprehensive set*: it should be possible to explain differences in quality perceptions as a result of differences in one or more quality dimensions. The model should also be *universal* – that is, the various dimensions should be valid, albeit with different weights, across a wide spectrum of services. The dimensions should further be *independent*, or at least measure different aspects of service quality perception. They should also be *homogeneous* and *unambiguous*. Finally, the number of dimensions should be limited.

We have to admit from the start that the ideal model meeting all these criteria does not exist yet; however we shall describe one model which seems to be widely accepted: the servqual model.

The Servqual model

The Servqual model was developed by Parasuraman, Zeithaml and Berry,[6] and has been presented as a service quality measurement instrument. Originally these researchers listed ten determinants or dimensions of service quality: reliability, responsiveness, competence, access, courtesy, communication, credibility, security, understanding/knowing the customer and tangibles. Exhibit 7.1 defines each of

Exhibit 7.1

Ten components of service quality

(1) Reliability involves consistency of performance and dependability. It also means that the firm performs the service right the first time and keeps its promises. Some specific examples it may involve are:

- accuracy in billing;
- performing the service at the designated time.

(2) Responsiveness concerns the willingness or readiness of employees to provide service. It may involve:

- mailing a transaction slip immediately;
- calling the customer back quickly;
- giving prompt service (e.g. setting up appointments quickly).

(3) Competence means possession of the skills and knowledge required to perform the service. It involves:

- knowledge and skill of the contact personnel;
- knowledge and skill of operational support personnel;
- research capability of the organization.

(4) Access involves approachability and ease of contact. It may mean:

- the service is easily accessible by telephone;
- waiting time to receive service is not excessive;
- convenient hours of operation and convenient location of the service facility.

(5) Courtesy involves politeness, respect, consideration, and friendliness of contact personnel (including receptionists, telephone operators, etc.) It includes:

- consideration for the customer's property;
- clean and neat appearance of public contact personnel.

(6) Communication means keeping customers informed in language they can understand, and listening to them. It may mean that the company has to adjust its language for different customers. It may involve:

- explaining the service itself and how much the service will cost;
- explaining the trade-offs between service and cost;
- assuring the consumer that a problem will be handled.

(7) Credibility involves trustworthiness, believability and honesty. It involves having the customer's best interests at heart. Contributing to credibility are:

- company name and reputation;
- personal characteristics of the contact personnel;
- the degree of hard-sell involved in interactions with the customer.

(8) Security is the freedom from danger, risk or doubt. It may involve:

- physical safety;
- financial security and confidentiality.

(9) Understanding/knowing the customer involves making the effort to understand the customer's needs. It involves:

- learning the customer's specific requirements;
- providing individual attention.

(10) Tangibles include the physical evidence of the service:

- physical facilities and appearance of personnel;
- tools or equipment used to provide the service;
- physical representations of the service, such as a plastic credit card.

Source: Francis Buttle (1996) 'Servqual: review, critique, research agenda', *European Journal of Marketing*, Vol 30, No 1, pp. 8–32.

these dimensions and gives some examples. This list was drawn up as a result of focus group studies with service providers and customers. Later they found a high degree of correlation between communication, competence, courtesy, credibility and security and therefore merged them into one dimension, which they called *assurance*. Similarly they found a high correlation between access and understanding which they merged into *empathy*.

This has led to the well known and widely used five dimensions of service quality:

- *Tangibles* – the appearance of physical facilities, the personnel, the tools or equipment used to provide the service and communication material.
- *Reliability* – consistency of performance and dependability. This means that the firm performs the service correctly the first time and that the firm honours its promises.
- *Responsiveness* – the willingness to help the customer and to provide prompt service.
- *Assurance* – knowledge and courtesy of employees and their ability to inspire trust and confidence.
- *Empathy* – caring, individualized attention to customers.

The researchers claimed that the dimensions were sufficiently generic that they could cover a wide spectrum of service sectors.

Since this pioneering work, many others have tried to duplicate these findings in a variety of service settings. Some researchers have confirmed these findings and therefore the model; however, most failed to do so. It was particularly difficult to find the same five generic quality dimensions – that is, the various sub-dimensions did not aggregate as in the Parasumaran *et al.* studies. Furthermore, the comprehensiveness of the five dimensions could not always be supported. In other words, it was doubted whether the service quality construct could be composed of five dimensions. One study suggests that the Servqual dimensions are likely to be industry specific.[7]

The criticism voiced towards the Servqual dimensions was also related to more fundamental methodological issues and even conceptual issues, such as the presence of conceptual inconsistency in the dimensions. 'Tangibles' and 'responsiveness', for instance, are entirely different concepts. Tangibles are part of the service package, but are not a quality dimension. The 'quality' of the tangibles (their appearance, availability, operating characteristics such as comfort, etc.) no doubt influences the perceived quality just as much as the 'quality' of the personnel (their appearance, competence, care, etc.). Like personnel, tangibles are not a quality dimension, but an important quality-determining element influencing dimensions such as reliability, credibility and others. Another conceptual problem is related to the homogeneity of the generic dimensions. For instance, it is difficult to understand how 'factors' like courtesy and competence would always correlate and therefore be grouped into one category, as they are both such different concepts.[8]

Notwithstanding the many criticisms of the Servqual tool, this tool has been adapted to measure service quality in a variety of service settings such as healthcare, retail chains, banks, fast-food restaurants, etc. Exhibit 7.2 shows one example of an adaptation of the Servqual tool to measure service quality in an ambulatory care (outpatient) nuclear medicine clinic.

Exhibit 7.2

Measuring service quality at an outpatient nuclear medicine clinic[9]

A survey comprising 22 questions was taken in 2001 to measure patients' perception of service quality.[10] Altogether, 416 patients received the questionnaire, of which 259 were completed and returned (response rate: 62 per cent). Using factor analysis, it became clear that the items could be grouped into five dimensions. Table 7.1 shows these dimensions, the different items and the average and the standard deviation of their scores on the dimensions. Four items were not retained in

the analysis due to a large number of missing values.

When looking at the results, a first remark is that the dimensions in this study are not the same as in the basic Servqual framework. It is generally accepted that different service environments can generate different service dimensions.

A second remark is that only the perception part of the Servqual was measured. Expectations

Table 7.1 The results of a Servqual perception measurement in a Nuclear medicine clinic

Item analysis of patients' service quality perception	
Item in each dimension	Mean and standard deviation (SD) of patients perceptions
Tangibles-Assurance	
Has up-to-date equipment	5.99 (SD = 1.04)
Physical facilities are visually appealing	4.88 (SD = 1.60)
Employees are neat in appearance	6.13 (SD = 0.91)
Physical facilities in accordance to service	5.17 (SD = 1.49)
Shows sincere interest in solving your problems	5.99 (SD = 1.07)
Employees can be trusted	5.95 (SD = 0.99)
Feels safe in your interaction with employees	6.08 (SD = 0.93)
Reliability	
When promises to do something, it does so	5.50 (SD = 1.38)
Provides services at the time it promises	5.35 (SD = 1.56)
Responsiveness	
Tells you when the services will be performed	4.68 (SD = 1.88)
Gives prompt services	4.65 (SD = 1.83)
Personnel is always willing to help	5.77 (SD = 1.44)
Never too busy to respond to your requests	4.61 (SD = 1.83)
Empathy	
Gives individual attention	5.01 (SD = 1.68)
Employees give personal attention	5.35 (SD = 1.52)
Employees understand your specific needs	5.03 (SD = 1.57)
Convenience	
Has operating hours convenient to you	5.65 (SD = 1.41)
Has your best interests at heart	5.90 (SD = 1.40)
Not Included in the analysis	
The personnel perform the service right the first time.	
The department keeps its records accurately.	
The personnel is consistently courteous.	
The personnel get adequate support from the University Hospital.	

Source: Stefanie De Man, Paul Gemmel, Peter Vlerick, Peter Van Rijk and Rudi Dierckx (2002) 'Patients' and personnel's perceptions of service quality and patient satisfaction in nuclear medicine', *European Journal of Nuclear Medicine and Molecular Imaging.*

Exhibit 7.2 continued

were deliberately not measured because there is a lot of disagreement about the added value of measuring expectations when perceptions are already measured.

Patients give the highest score to the tangibles-assurance and convenience dimension. They have the perception that the opening hours are convenient and that employees care about their patients. The lowest scoring items are all situated within the responsiveness dimension. Patients perceive that they do not get prompt service and that they don't know when the service will be performed. One of the problems patients are confronted with in an outpatient clinic in hospitals is the waiting time. To better serve customers, management needs to pay more attention to the responsiveness dimension.

The relative importance of the various aspects of the service

Parasumaran and his colleagues also found that in all service settings reliability was the most important dimension, followed by responsiveness, assurance, empathy, and finally tangibles as the least important dimension. This finding has also been questioned. Many researchers could not duplicate these results.

Johnston and his colleagues did not claim that the factors they suggested were universally important.[11] However, what they found was that the various dimensions could be classified into three categories: some were *predominantly satisfiers*, some were *predominantly dissatisfiers*, while others had *both satisfying and dissatisfying effects*. A variable is a dissatisfier when the performance or absence of the desired feature leads to dissatisfaction and results in complaining behaviour. Higher levels do not result in compliments. A variable is a satisfier if the contrary is the case – that is, when unusual performance elicits strong feelings of satisfaction, while low performance does not necessarily cause negative feelings. In a bank study they found, for instance, that attentiveness, care and friendliness were satisfiers, while integrity, reliability, availability and functionality were dissatisfiers. Responsiveness was both a satisfier and a dissatisfier.

Integrating customer satisfaction with other customer feedback

A common mistake is to deal with the customer satisfaction survey independently of all other customer feedback systems. If the aim is to prioritize improvement projects, the best results will be achieved when other sources of information are used, including more qualitative ones. Indeed, a satisfaction measure rarely reveals the underlying drivers or causes of a certain level of satisfaction. If 15 per cent of the customers rate the meals on board a certain flight as poor, it is difficult to ascertain the reasons for this from this statistic alone. Similarly, if 15 per cent of the customers are delighted with the meals, it is still unclear why.

Using other sources of customer feedback can be very revealing.

1. *The complaints and congratulations a company receives.* All complaints or congratulations will help to explain what the possible satisfiers and dissatisfiers are. Comparing both complaints and congratulations on the one hand, and satisfaction scores on the other hand, for different organizational units, can be extremely revealing. (We shall deal with complaints, and to a lesser degree with congratulations, further on in this chapter.)

2. *The invoked guarantees.* By inviting customers to explain why they are invoking the offered guarantee, and by linking these explanations to the satisfaction scores, a more refined insight into the underlying drivers of satisfaction scores can be obtained. Again, a separate chapter is devoted to the topic of service guarantees (*see* Chapter 8).

3. *User groups and qualitative market research.* By explicitly asking customers to discuss the strengths and weaknesses, as well as their likes and dislikes, in a more qualitative manner, valuable information can be obtained.

4. *The front-line staff.* Obviously, front-line personnel can provide very useful information in assessing what the major areas for improvement or the few vital priorities are.

Putting it all together

Taking all the above considerations into account, we can now construct a blueprint for the contents of a customer satisfaction performance measurement survey.

1. *The organization's strategic performance measures.* Questions related to these performance measures provide the data on customer satisfaction for use in the organization's balanced scorecard (to be discussed in Chapter 18). The questions should be asked in the same format over a long period of time.

2. *The organizational unit's strategic performance measures.* The organizational unit that is being measured will also have its own strategic performance measures. These are called strategic because they reflect that unit's core activities, functions and processes. These questions should also be asked in the same format over a long period of time. Typically, these unit strategic performance measures should coincide at least partially with those of the organization as a whole. However, they are usually more detailed and reflect more aspects of the service.

3. *Measures related to improvement projects.* The strategic performance measures may trigger improvement projects on specific aspects of the service. To monitor the effect of the improvement projects, the survey should temporarily include more detailed performance measures on those projects and the service aspects to which they relate. Since improvement projects may differ from one organizational unit to another, these temporary performance measures should also reflect these differences.

4. *Measures assessing the competitive performance* (optional). Questions on how well the organization is doing compared to its competitors, should only be asked for the strategic performance measures. Temporary measures do not merit these competitive questions, as the answers would yield too detailed information.

5. *Measures assessing the relative importance of service aspects* (optional). As explained earlier, in certain circumstances it is possible and even advisable to assess the relative importance of the respective service aspects indirectly.

6. *Open-ended questions.* These can be included in order to clarify the actual scores in a more qualitative manner. These questions can compensate for the more general wording of the strategic performance measures, particularly if no improvement projects are scheduled for this specific performance measure. For instance, if only a general question on the flight attendants' service is being asked, the open-ended question on 'what can be done better in the future' may yield additional information on the nature or cause of any dissatisfaction

occurring with that service, and can compensate for the lack of more detailed questions on each service aspect. As a result, the number of questions can be smaller.

7. *Questions on respondent.* Questions that allow the respondents to be segmented according to their buyer/user status and their socio-demographics can be of great value.

If following this blueprint eventually results in the survey having too many questions, it is possible to alternate certain questions – that is, not to ask all questions on all surveys. For instance, it is possible to ask for the relative importance of the service aspects in only 50 per cent of the surveys, while the questions on the competitive performance can be asked in the other 50 per cent. The disadvantage of this approach is that the number of respondents for these questions is halved; this means either the size of the sample has to be doubled or the analysis might no longer yield statistically meaningful results at the lowest unit of measurement.

COMPLAINT MANAGEMENT

Introduction

The famous Dutch singer Vanessa was flying business class from Curaçao to Holland. When she ordered a sherry for her husband and a tomato juice with a dash of tabasco for herself, the steward replied that tabasco and sherry were only available in first class and that he couldn't bend the rules. In the commotion that followed, the steward exclaimed that she shouldn't be ordering first-class drinks if she couldn't afford a first-class ticket. When the airline's top management heard about the incident, they apologized to the singer and sent her a bottle of sherry and a bottle of tabasco. At the same time, however, they informed cabin staff that the rules would stay the same.[12]

In the following parts of this chapter we deal with the handling of complaints – that is, the setting up of a complaint management system. We shall discuss the advantages of lowering the complaint threshold and the importance of responding quickly and appropriately, before going on to discuss how a systematic complaint handling process should be set up. At the end we shall explore how complaints can be used to steer improvement projects and how they affect an organization's orientation towards customers.

Why manage complaints?

The above example might not have made the national press had the victim not been a celebrity. Yet it fully illustrates the importance of complaints and how to deal with them.

■ *Customer retention.* Since complaints are the expression of dissatisfaction, the way the organization deals with complaints will determine whether it will retain or lose the complaining customer. Moreover, since negative word of mouth is very likely to result from customer dissatisfaction, the business (earnings) at risk can be more than those from the complaining customer alone.

■ *Continuous improvement.* Customers will only go to the trouble of complaining if the service defect is important to them. Therefore, complaints provide valuable information on what is important to customers and on the frequency with which specific service failures occur. A complaint is a 'gem', as it provides an opportunity for learning and continuous improvement.

■ *Building a customer-focused organization.* The way top management treats complaints sends clear signals to all staff on how important it considers customer satisfaction and retention.

In a service context, the simultaneity of production and consumption makes quality errors, and consequently dissatisfied and/or complaining customers, more likely. The result, of course, is that customers will defect. The well-known TARP (Technical Assistance Research Programs Institute) studies indicate that the percentage of customers who stated that they will definitely/probably repurchase/recommend is significantly lower among customers who have experienced a problem than among the customers that did not experience problems (*see* Figure 7.2).[13]

The handling of those complaints is more difficult to manage in services, as up to 90 per cent of all customers complain directly to the contact personnel serving them.[15] Therefore, developing complaint handling skills through training cannot be limited to a central customer service department, but should be offered to all contact personnel.

Finally, the business at risk goes beyond the dissatisfied customer him- or herself. Complaining customers are likely to create twice as much word-of-mouth (in this case bad) advertising as satisfied customers.

All this should lead service organizations into paying attention to complaints and into systematizing their complaint management.

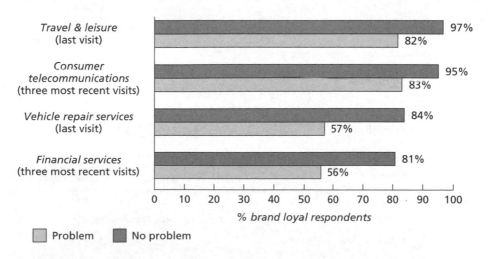

Figure 7.2 Percentage of brand-loyal customers in various sectors[14]

Source: TARP (1986) *Consumer Complaint Handling in America: An update study.* United States Office of Consumer Affairs.

Lowering the complaint threshold

The first step in complaint handling is to encourage dissatisfied customers to complain. If they do not complain, the service provider may not be aware of the existing dissatisfaction and consequently will have no opportunity for service recovery. Dissatisfied customers who do not complain may 'vote with their feet' and simply switch to another service provider. Several studies have revealed that the actual complaints are only the tip of the iceberg. Complaint submission rates in different studies are as low as 9 per cent. One of the objectives of complaint management is therefore to maximize the number of complaints (while minimizing the number of actual service problems).

Indeed, research has indicated that among customers experiencing a problem, complainants are more likely to rebuy than non-complainants, even if the complaint is not entirely resolved. The same TARP studies have indicated this quite clearly (*see* Figure 7.3).

Whether or not customers who experience a problem complain, depends on a variety of factors:

- *The problem characteristics.* Customers are more likely to complain about severe problems and when the (potential) financial loss is significant. This is partly dependent on the type of, and involvement and experience with the product or service. The level of (un)articulated complaints also depends on whether the seller, the buyer or chance is to blame.
- *The customer characteristics.* Assertive and self-confident people, who are socially active, sensitive to declining product quality, and have positive prior experiences (mainly with other companies) are more likely to complain. Less important factors are socio-demographics, although the average complainer has a high income, is relatively young, well educated and has a high professional job status.
- *The expected redress.* Customers also balance the perceived trouble involved in complaining with the expected outcome. The complaint submission rate is much higher if customers know where and how to complain, if they believe the supplier to be responsive, and if they think the outcome will be worthwhile.

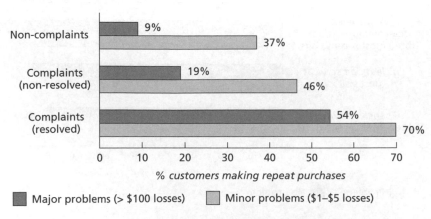

Figure 7.3 Repeated purchases for dissatisfied customers[16]

Source: TARP (1986) *Consumer Complaint Handling in America: An update study*. United States Office of Consumer Affairs.

■ *The height of the complaint threshold.* The level of the threshold consists of the sum of all perceived physical, emotional or monetary trouble (or encouragement) involved in formulating a complaint.

By improving the expected redress and lowering the threshold, service business should encourage the silent majority of dissatisfied customers to identify themselves. The most common ways to lower the threshold are:

1. communicating explicitly how the organization can be contacted; or
2. proactively inviting customers to complain if they have any problems.

Research in 1996[17] among 350 service companies in Belgium revealed that customer complaint cards and surveys are the most commonly used techniques (*see* Figure 7.4). Yet, very strikingly, over one-third of all companies did not try to lower the threshold in any way.

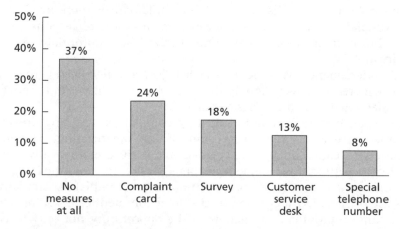

Figure 7.4 Percentage of service organizations using different techniques to lower the threshold to complain

Communicating how the organization can be contacted

Establishing a call centre that can be reached free of charge with a toll-free number is one option. Alternatives are customer complaint cards in hotel rooms or on the tables in restaurants. Personal visit complaints, signs directing customers to the complaint handling office and greeters who direct consumers and handle simple complaints in a store are also very effective.

Proactively inviting customers to react

Customers can also be asked proactively to react, whether or not they have any problems. Mercedes Belgium, for instance, in its customer satisfaction survey, asks customers explicitly whether they are experiencing any problems. To this end, it invites customers to fill out their names and contact information, if they wish Mercedes to contact them regarding a problem they have experienced or a question or concern they might have.

Similarly, Rank Xerox Belgium sent all its customers a card encouraging them to complain. Approximately 2.5 per cent of the customers returned the card. About 80 per cent of the responses were complaints which had not been made before. The remaining 20 per cent were either existing complaints already known to Rank Xerox, or customers inquiring why they had received the card, as they were basically satisfied.

Soliciting complaints too explicitly may provoke dissatisfaction which would otherwise not exist. Sometimes managers are concerned that customers may become too demanding on trivial issues. In their opinion, the provocation of complaints about minor problems should be avoided at all costs. Since these problems are minor, non-complaining customers are seen as contented; once customers complain about these problems, they expect an appropriate reaction. If the complaint is not being dealt with properly, they will become more dissatisfied than if they had not complained in the first place. In short, managers believe that in the case of minor problems companies should 'let sleeping dogs lie'. There is no real empirical evidence to support the validity of this concern. The TARP studies indicate that a dissatisfied non-complainant is more loyal than a dissatisfied complainant who did not receive an appropriate response. On the other hand, however, a complainant who received an appropriate response became very loyal.[18]

This phenomenon is sometimes called *the frustration effect* – that is, expressing feelings increases satisfaction if the outcome is positive, but causes even more dissatisfaction if the outcome is negative.

There can be a downside to soliciting complaints. Focusing on negative issues can encourage a negative perception of the organization. Therefore, inviting customers to complain is often carried out more diplomatically. The complaint handling department is renamed 'customer service' to avoid the image of an unreliable organization that has to deal with numerous complaints. Similarly, complaint cards are often called suggestion or customer comment cards. A further tactic is for a company to provide customers with the opportunity not only to complain but also to praise.

Responding quickly

The key driver of satisfaction or dissatisfaction with complaint handling is the response time. A formal study indicated that only 8 per cent of Germans are willing to wait for an answer for more than one week after filing a complaint.[19]

Satisfaction with complaint handling can therefore only be achieved through a quick response. Several elements help to accomplish this:

- anticipating complaints;
- empowering front-line staff;
- acknowledging the receipt of a complaint;
- routing complaints;
- prioritizing complaints.

Anticipation

When a service provider is aware of a problem that affects several customers in the same way, the organization can maximize its chances of service recovery by anticipating the complaints. The customer can be contacted before he or she contacts the company. This will not only permit a timely reaction, but will also involve the potentially non-complaining customers in the service recovery efforts.

Anticipation is particularly relevant and feasible in the following situations:

- *New services*. The likelihood of defects is much higher for new services than it is for existing ones. For instance, when the new Brussels air terminal was opened in 1995, the extremely sophisticated and fully automated luggage handling system was not compatible with the tags on luggage issued at certain other airports. As a consequence, these pieces of luggage were not automatically removed from the back-office conveyor belt but required manual intervention. Lead times of up to an hour were not uncommon. The operation could have anticipated these problems and, by doing so, could have avoided a large number of angry customers.
- *Recurring problems*. By tracking the nature and frequency of all complaints (see below), organizations can assess which problems merit a standardized approach. For instance, the airline industry is so often confronted with lost and/or damaged luggage that all operators have legally agreed upon a standard level of compensation.
- *Predictable problems*. A couple of years ago, we were to give a training seminar in Lithuania. We had booked a flight from Brussels to Copenhagen, where we would change airlines and board an SAS flight to Vilnius. Unfortunately, the Brussels–Copenhagen flight was delayed. At worst, we feared we would miss our connection and arrive 24 hours late for the seminar. At best, we hoped we would be able to change terminals and catch our flight, but it was extremely unlikely that our luggage would arrive in time. The cabin crew of our flight had warned SAS of our problems, however, and, much to our surprise, an SAS employee was waiting for us at the gate. He took us to a car on the tarmac, asked what our luggage looked like, and collected it from the airplane. He then drove us to our connecting flight, where the other passengers were already boarding. He made one telephone call, and put our luggage on the conveyor belt loading the airplane. Finally, he apologized for the fact that since it was too late to obtain a boarding pass for us, we would have to wait in the car until all the other passengers had boarded.

Empowering front-line staff

Empowerment will be discussed in Chapter 12. Empowerment means providing service employees with enough autonomy to allow them to handle unforeseen problem situations such as complaints.

Acknowledging the receipt of a complaint

Although it is preferable to solve complaints immediately, sometimes finding a solution and deciding on the proper compensation may take a great deal of time. In those circumstances, it is vital to inform the customer that his complaint has been received and is being dealt with. Ideally, the confirmation specifies the name and telephone number of the person handling the complaint, and the deadline by which the final answer can be expected.

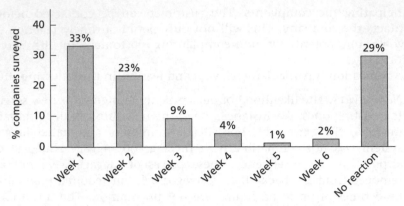

Time between receipt of complaint and reaction

Figure 7.5 Time taken for companies to react to complaint

Advertising Age[20] ran an experiment in the US. Twenty-six car companies received an identical letter of complaint. Only two managed to respond within one week, 15 companies responded during the second week and seven companies did not respond at all. This result is supported by an experiment we witnessed in January 1996.

One of our students sent out decoy letters of complaint to 80 companies and monitored very carefully how the companies responded.[21] Figure 7.5 gives an overview of the response delay. Note that after six weeks 29 per cent of all companies had not responded at all and only one-third replied within one week. Contrast this with the experience of a Dutch friend of mine who sent a written complaint to the headquarters of the Dutch subsidiary of McDonald's, and received a response by telephone the following day. The call was made by the manager of the restaurant where the incident had occurred. After having been informed about what had actually happened, the manager asked whether the complainant would agree to accept vouchers for a free meal as compensation for the inconvenience. The vouchers arrived by post the following day.

The fastest way to respond is by telephone. In the research illustrated in Figure 7.5, only 28 per cent of the reactions were by telephone. Two-thirds of the reactions came by post, and 5 per cent of the companies actually sent a sales representative. Interestingly, about one-third of the telephone reactions related to letters which did not contain the complainant's telephone number, indicating that some organizations had gone to the trouble of looking it up themselves.

Routing and prioritizing complaints

As a result of the simultaneity of production and consumption, complaints regarding services can be addressed to anyone at any level within the organization. Consequently, even if the organization empowers its front-line staff and tries to anticipate complaints as much as possible, the person receiving the complaint will not always be able to solve the problem. In those circumstances, much time can be lost transferring the complaint to the person or department which eventually has to handle it. Moreover, some complaints may merit a higher priority; the routing should therefore be different from one complaint to another.

In assessing whether a complaint should receive priority or not, the criterion should be the business at risk. This depends on the following factors:

■ *Problem characteristics*. The more serious the problem is, the bigger the chances are that the customer will defect. Moreover, a customer who has experienced a serious problem is generally more demanding. Therefore, prioritizing may be justified.
■ *Customer characteristics*. Key accounts represent more sales and profit than smaller customers. Consequently, complaints from important customers deserve preferential treatment.
■ *Expected action by the complainer*. Customers put business at risk not only by defecting themselves, but also by creating negative word of mouth and/or by incurring costs. Often priority is given to complainers threatening to write letters to the press, to inform consumer organizations or to take the service provider to court.

In addition, it is very important to set up instructions about what to do when very serious complaints arise. Often the way they are handled will be outside the traditional complaint handling system. Some organizations instruct front-line employees to notify senior management.

The actual response

Complainers not only demand a quick response, they also expect proper redress. Customers judge the redress by three criteria:

■ *The compensation*. The customer expects to be compensated for the problem he or she has experienced.
■ *The sincerity*. The organization should care for the customer and the problem he or she has experienced. The customer wants to be taken seriously.
■ *The follow-up*. Customer satisfaction with complaint handling can be increased by encouraging feedback from the customer afterwards.

The compensation

Granting the customer compensation requires balancing the costs and benefits of the compensation to the organization with the fairness of the compensation to the customer.

The costs and benefits to the organization

Organizations will grant compensation to retain the customer and to avoid negative word of mouth. The compensation should therefore always be smaller than the business at risk. Estimating the business at risk may require the assessment of the lifetime value of the complainant (*see* Chapters 4 and 6). Compensation can be higher for key accounts than for smaller customers.

To illustrate this issue, we can refer to the furniture store which receives a complaint concerning a scratch on a brand new leather couch. If the customer asks for a new couch, it is very unlikely that the same customer's future purchases will compensate the store for the cost of the new couch. The store will therefore not be inclined to give the customer a new couch, but will instead offer to repair the couch for the customer. In some circumstances, however, the company should replace the couch because it should also take the cost of negative word of mouth into account. This cost is admittedly much more difficult to assess.

The fairness to the customer

The complainer who is experiencing a problem wants to be compensated, and the compensation has to be perceived by the complainer as fair. Figure 7.6 lists some types of compensation and the frequency of their use.[22]

Setting a fair compensation is not easy, particularly when the complaint is non-monetary. Moreover, in services, rework or repair is not always an option. For instance, if a meal is not satisfactory, a restaurant can offer to drop the bill, but what if the same problem occurs on board an airplane? Refunding the full fare would be overcompensating the passenger. What is a fair compensation?

In the case of minor complaints, companies may be tempted to offer mere apologies. However, doing so can be perceived as dishonest if it is not followed by a tangible outcome. The provision of symbolic compensations is therefore recommended for minor complaints.

For instance, a couple of years ago we sent a case study by mail to participants in a training seminar. Due to exceptional circumstances, the value of the stamps on the package was insufficient, and so the participants had to pay a postage due fee of less than one euro. We were afraid that our actually refunding the money would make things worse, as some people could have been offended because of the extremely low amount, and yet we wanted to go beyond a mere expression of apology. We eventually decided to create vouchers which looked like a huge stamp with a face value matching the penalty. On the final day, we distributed these to the participants, explaining that we wanted to compensate them for the inconvenience, and that they could exchange their vouchers for a free drink at the bar. The gesture was appreciated, as our customers understood that we had gone to some effort to make the vouchers. It is worth nothing that the customers were expecting to receive a free drink anyway, as they had already been invited to the farewell cocktail party on the first day of the programme weeks before the actual incident.

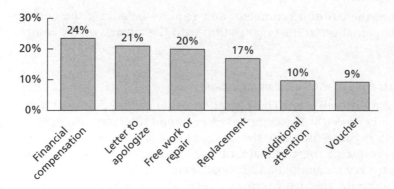

Figure 7.6 Types of compensation used by service organizations

For more severe complaints, issuing vouchers which can be redeemed only by the service provider offers the advantage over a reimbursement that the customer has to make use of the company's services again in order to cash the voucher. Furthermore, the cost to the company of a voucher is usually lower than the actual reimbursement. Customers may find a financial compensation the fairest solution.

In judging the fairness of the compensation, it is also important to think of the inconvenience that the customer has suffered. If a customer's clothes are stained in a restaurant, paying only for the cost of dry-cleaning them does not make up for the time and effort invested in getting the clothes clean. Again, a token of apology – for instance, a complimentary drink – on top of the financial compensation, can work wonders.

If customers receive unequal compensation because of differences in business at risk, this may be perceived as unfair. Overall, customers believe they are being treated more fairly when they believe the provider is following company procedures, and that there are no special favours granted to specific customers.

A final consideration is that the compensation should not depend on whether the complaint is justified. If the customer perceives that the seller made a mistake, he or she wants to have compensation. The seller can try to convince the buyer that the seller is not responsible for the problem experienced, but when not successful, the dissatisfaction will remain. Again, balancing the costs and benefits to the organization should guide management's decision. Compensating for an unjustified complaint may result in retaining an otherwise lost customer.

The sincerity

If a business operates with 0.1 per cent defects, it means that one out of every 1000 customers will be confronted with a defect. That one customer, however, perceives that business and purchase as a 100 per cent defect. The 0.1 per cent defect statistic is not very convincing. That customer expects the company to deal with the particular problem with sincerity and empathy. This is not an easy endeavour. Each customer considers his or her problem to be unique and of the highest priority, whereas the complaint handler perceives it as a routine situation or even very exceptional and therefore negligible. Therefore, managing how the organization deals with complaining customers – whether in a specialized customer service department or by front-line employees – is an organizational issue.

Front-liners

Front-line employees should possess the social skills needed to deal with irate customers. These social skills are partly inborn and partly developed through training. Consequently, social skills will be a very important selection criterion when hiring front-line employees. The best way to further develop these skills is through simulated real-life situations and role playing. The airline KLM, for instance, organizes workshops around the world for its desk personnel to improve skills such as creativity and communication skills. A crew of actors simulate real-life situations that require creativity. This role play is recorded and afterwards discussed.

Specialized complaint handlers

Organizations that have to deal with many complaints set up specialized complaint handling cells, separate from front-line staff. The complaint handlers working in these cells should not only possess all the social skills mentioned above, but they also require additional technical skills. They should have a clear understanding of the organization as a whole, of the service delivered to the customer, and of the processes that exist within the entire service delivery system.

Complaint handling at Club Med, for instance, can involve requests for information to departments such as transport, marketing and sales, and local villages as well. Consequently, a broad understanding of Club Med's operations is required to answer complaints. At Club Med, this is achieved by job rotation.[23]

Job rotation is useful in general, as most complaint handlers suffer from burnout after a few years, and develop a very negative image of the company. At British Airways, people are kept in the complaint handling department for a maximum of two years. A transfer to another department becomes inevitable to maintain the quality of complaint handling. Transferring complaint handlers after a few years to another department also increases the company's overall sensitivity to consumer problems. Replacing this staff is preferably done through in-company recruitment, because of the required knowledge of the business.

It is important to find a balance between technical and social skills. Case-based research in the Belgian tourist industry revealed that seven out of eight companies had staffed their complaint handling departments only with lawyers, indicating a defensive and argumentative attitude to complaint handling.[24]

Since service in complaint handling is of major importance and since complaint handling is very demanding, it can only be achieved by high-quality personnel. Therefore some organizations find treating complaint handling as a stepping stone to promotion a very effective means of attracting and ensuring high-quality staff.

Centralized versus decentralized receiving and handling

An organization cannot always control where complaints will be received, because it is the customer who makes that decision. However, the customer can be directed. Complaints can be received locally (in local agencies or stores), by front-office personnel, by customer service personnel, or centrally (in corporate offices) by the complaint handling office. Therefore, a major decision is whether to encourage customers to complain centrally or to the front-liners serving them. Equally important, the resolution of the customer's problems can also be entrusted to specialists in a central department or delegated to the front-line staff as much as possible.

Collecting complaints

Collecting complaints centrally offers more control. Logging, classifying and tracing the complaint handling is much easier. Furthermore, in the case of oral complaints, trusting the communication to specialists who are trained in dealing with irate customers can result in a better quality service. A central point of entry might also be helpful in lowering the complaint threshold. For instance, customers may be reluctant to drop a customer complaint card in a suggestion box inside a restaurant or shop, preferring to mail it to a central address. In addition, a central point of entry satisfies the desire of most customers to complain to a higher authority.

Organizations that are confronted with many complaints sometimes set up specialized customer service desks. This allows them to provide encouragement to customers to complain locally, while at the same time providing customers with complaint specialists.

Solving complaints

As already discussed, having specialists deal with complaints can offer the advantage of a broader view of the business and better technical skills. However, there are also major disadvantages. Often the 'specialists' have to call upon front-liners to explain the customer's background as well as to find out what really happened, which may cause unnecessary delays. In addition, having front-liners deal with complaints themselves makes them more aware of the importance of delivering quality service. There is thus good reason to divert the solving of complaints to the front-line staff, particularly for minor problems. If the complaints are serious, a central approach can be recommended. Another reason to centralize is if many complaints are very similar. This allows for a standardized approach resulting in economies of scale.

Consequently, there are four possible scenarios (*see* Figure 7.7). In some cases, they can all occur within one organization, but usually one situation or a certain type of complaint handling is predominant.

The follow-up

Not all customers are very satisfied with the way complaints are handled. Therefore, after the compensation has been given to the customer, organizations can try to maximize the service recovery effort by adding some sort of follow-up. The customer can be informed about the service recovery. Furthermore, measuring the degree to which the customer is satisfied with the complaint handling will help to fine-tune the complaint handling process itself. The follow-up of complaints can be exhaustive or selective. Companies which receive a large number of complaints

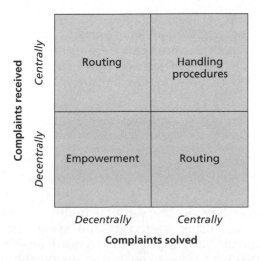

Figure 7.7 Centralized and decentralized handling and receiving of complaints

sometimes limit the follow-up to the most severe complaints or to complaints received centrally. There are a number of ways in which complaints can be followed up:

1. The first type of follow-up consists of calling up or writing to the customer afterwards to remind him or her of how the complaint was dealt with and what the actual compensation was. Reminding the customer can increase customer loyalty, particularly if the complaint was settled very quickly and/or if the compensation was perceived to be very fair. This type of follow-up should always attempt to ascertain whether everything is now according to the customer's wish. If it is, the customer is reminded of that fact. If not, the organization has a second chance at service recovery.
2. A more powerful alternative is to communicate to the customer that, partly based on his or her complaint, corrective actions have been taken to prevent the problem from recurring. Not only will this result in the greater involvement of the customer with the organization, it will also strengthen the image of an organization constantly trying to improve the quality of its service. It may yield both higher customer loyalty and positive word of mouth.
3. A final option is to measure the customer's satisfaction with the way his or her complaint has been handled. Again, dissatisfied customers will be identified, allowing a second attempt at service recovery. Furthermore, customers may perceive the measurement as an expression of the organization's concern for its customers and their complaints. This option is also interesting, as it allows for a comparison of the satisfaction regarding the complaint handling process with the overall customer satisfaction.

Designing a complaint handling system

Many service organizations handle complaints on an *ad hoc* basis. Whenever they receive a complaint, they find out more about the incident and handle the complaint, without following any explicit procedures. This approach has two main disadvantages:

1. Similar complaints may not receive similar treatment, which may lead to a perception of the organization as inconsistent or disorganized.
2. No learning takes place in terms of timeliness, efficiency and effectiveness of the complaint handling process. The organization keeps reinventing the wheel.

We recommend therefore that companies set up a comprehensive complaint handling system.

Tackling the root causes

Complaint management goes beyond the simple handling of individual complaints in order to retain dissatisfied customers and avoid negative word of mouth. The complaints should also inspire improvement projects in order to eliminate the root causes that led to the complaints in the first place. Complaints are particularly valuable as they relate to incidents which are so critical to the customer that he or she has gone to the trouble of filing a complaint. This explains why maximizing the number of complaints helps to minimize the number of problems.

Tackling the root causes involves expanding the remit of the complaint handling scheme, by three major steps:

■ classifying the complaints by their nature;
■ analysing the business at risk; and
■ executing the improvement projects.

Building a customer-oriented organization

The final objective of any complaint management system is to build a customer-oriented organization. The way an organization deals with complainants is more symptomatic of its customer orientation: it actually strongly influences the company culture as it signals to all staff what priority top management attaches to customers and their concerns.

The organization's management system should therefore include the following complaint handling performance measures:

■ number of complaints, possibly as a ratio to compliments, and/or limited to those centrally received;
■ the speed of handling complaints, often measured as average number of days required and percentage of complaints taking more than X days;
■ customer satisfaction with the complaint handling process;
■ number of (successful) improvement projects resulting from complaint analysis.

By discussing the statistics during board meetings, by publishing them in the annual report or in internal magazines, and by portraying employees who deal with complaints in an outstanding fashion as employee of the month, complaint management will be taken more seriously throughout the organization.

By way of contrast to Exhibit 7.3, an airline cabin attendant told us about how the management of her company reacted to the way she settled complaints. Although she was supposed to be empowered to compensate passengers for

Exhibit 7.3

Involving the entire company

A fine example of how this can be achieved is the way the complaint card was used by Hewlett-Packard in the Netherlands. All its customers received a yellow card stating:

'I give Hewlett Packard the yellow card because I am not satisfied. Please contact me.'

The card had to be returned to the attention of the general manager. Much to the surprise of both employees and customers, the members of the board actually took turns calling the complaining customers. Customers were surprised and delighted, and several of them immediately explained that the problem was not so important that the director had to get involved.

The impact on the employees was even more impressive. If complaints are so important that they merit senior management's time and attention, then certainly all staff should treat complaints as a priority.

problems they experienced, she was very reluctant to do so. The main reason was that on the two previous occasions when she had issued a voucher, her manager had asked for an elaborate report on the exact circumstances of the incident. She had expected to be congratulated for serving the customer well, but ended up feeling that she had had to defend herself.

Again, top management can offset these situations by monitoring the number of vouchers issued by each team. Teams issuing too few vouchers are either operating at zero defects (which is unlikely) or are too stringent in compensating passengers.

CONCLUSION

In this chapter, we have focused on two aspects related to service satisfaction: measuring customer satisfaction and handling complaints, based on an integrated service satisfaction framework.

Measuring customer satisfaction (and acting upon the results of these measurements) benefits from having a benchmark. Other crucial considerations when setting up a customer satisfaction measurement system relate to determining whose satisfaction to measure, as well as whose performance to take into account. Equipped with some guiding principles to tackle these issues, one can start thinking about what exactly to measure: overall satisfaction, loyalty and referral measures, as well as measures that relate to specific aspects of the service. In order to set the step towards action, it might also be interesting to collect data on competitors' customers, relate the findings towards different segments and integrate them with other (customer) information. As such, this chapter offers a blueprint for getting your own customer satisfaction measurement system going.

In this chapter we have also looked extensively at why complaints should be managed and how to manage them. Simultaneity and the importance of word-of-mouth advertising make complaint management of particular interest for services. Designing an adequate complaint management approach consists of lowering thresholds, responding quickly, giving a proper response and finally systematizing complaint handling. The ultimate goal of working on complaints is to create a more customer-oriented service company by tackling the root causes and improving services.

Review and discussion questions

- Take the list of ten components of service quality in Exhibit 7.1 and discuss what they particularly mean in a context of a specific service environment (such as a restaurant, a bank office or a post office).

- In the case of the nuclear medicine ambulatory care clinic (Exhibit 7.2) who is the actual customer? Is the current way of measuring customer satisfaction an adequate one? Should you use other performance measures of customer feedback?

- Why is it important to register complaints in a systematic way?

- There are some commons issues in complaint handling and implementing service guarantees (see next chapter). By reading the following chapter identify the common issues?

Notes and references

[1] Caruana, A., Money, A. H. and Berthon, P. R. (2000) 'Service quality and satisfaction – the moderating role of value', *European Journal of Marketing*, Vol 34, No 11/12, 1338–53.

[2] Ibid.

[3] Parasuraman, A., Zeithaml, V. A. and Berr, L. L. (1985) 'A conceptual model of Service quality and its implications for Future Research', *Journal of Marketing*, Vol 49, 41–50.

[4] Zeithaml, V. A., Berry, L. L. and Parasuraman, A. (1988) 'Communication and Control processes in the delivery of service quality', *Journal of Marketing*, Vol 52, Apr, 35–48.

[5] *See* Chapter 18 for more details on these techniques.

[6] Parasuraman, A., Zeithaml, V. A. and Berry, L. L. (1985) 'A conceptual model of service quality and implications for further research', *Journal of Marketing*, Vol 49, Fall, 45–50; and Parasuraman, A., Zeithaml, V. A. and Berry, L. L. (1988) 'Servqual: A multiple item scale for measuring consumer perceptions of service quality', *Journal of Retailing*, Spring, 22–40.

[7] Asubonteng, P., McCleary, K. J. and Swan, J. E. (1996) 'SERVQUAL revisited: a critical review of service quality', *The Journal of Services Marketing*, Vol 10, No 6, 62–81.

[8] For a further critical review of Servqual, *see* Buttle, F. (1996) 'Servqual: review, critique, research agenda', *European Journal of Marketing*, Vol 30, No 1, 8–32.

[9] De Man, S., Gemmel, P., Vlerick, P., Van Rijk, P. and Dierckx, R. (2002) 'Patients' and personnel's perceptions of service quality and patient satisfaction in nuclear medicine', *European Journal of Nuclear Medicine and Molecular Imaging*, Vol 9, No 29, 1109–17.

[10] It is important to note that in this study only perceptions are measured and no expectations. There is a lot of scientific discussion about whether or not it is useful to measure expectations.

[11] Johnston, R. (1995) 'The determinants of service quality: Satisfaction and dissatisfaction', *International Journal of Service Industry Management*, Vol 6, No 5, 53–71; and Johnston, R., Silvestro, R., Fitzgerald, L. and Voss, C. (1990) 'Developing the determinants of service quality', *Proceedings of the first International Research Seminar in Service Management*, La londes les Maures, France.

[12] *Het Laatste Nieuws*, 5 Aug 1989.

[13] TARP (1986) *Consumer Complaint Handling in America: An update study*. United States Office of Consumer Affairs.

[14] Ibid.

[15] Ibid.

[16] Ibid.

[17] Bourgeois, S. (1996) *Klachtenmanagement in de dienstensector* (Complaint management in the service sector). Unpublished final paper, University of Ghent, Faculty of Economics.

[18] TARP (1986) op. cit.

[19] Meyer, A. and Dornach, F. (1995) *The German Customer Barometer: Quality and satisfaction.* German Marketing Association and German Post AG.

[20] Kauchak, T. (1991) 'A little service please!', *Advertising Age*, 21 Jan, S8–S10.

[21] Blontrok, V. (1996) *Klachtenbehandeling in België. Een empyrisch onderzoek* (Complaint Handling in Belgium: An empirical investigation). Unpublished paper, De Vlerick School voor Management.

[22] Bourgeois, S. (1996), op. cit.

[23] Verhaeghe, K. (1996) *Klachtenbehandeling in diensten: een profielschets van enkele sectoren* (Complaint handling in services: a profile of some service sectors). Unpublished paper, De Vlerick School voor Management.

[24] Ibid.

Suggested further reading

Hart, C. W. L., Heskett, J. L. and Sasser, Jr, W. E. (1990) 'The profitable art of service recovery', *Harvard Business Review*, Jul–Aug.

Maister, D. (1993) *Managing the Professional Service Firm*. New York: The Free Press. In his book on professional service, David Maister devotes a chapter to satisfaction measurement. Highly recommended for the 'personal-interactive' type of services.

TARP (1985) *Consumer Complaint Handling in America: An update study*. A how-to-do-it manual for implementing cost effective consumer complaint handling procedures. United States Office of Consumer Affairs, September 30. To my knowledge, no good books on complaint management do exist. Further reading should definitely include this work, although there is a significant overlap with the contents of this chapter.

Zeithaml, V. A., Parasuraman, A. and Berry, L. L. (1990) *Delivering Quality Service: Balancing customer perceptions and expectations*. New York: The Free Press. This book on service quality introduces the so-called Servqual method of assessing customer satisfaction, which has been the standard in satisfaction measurement in services for years. Today its methodology has been challenged, but it still functions as an interesting source of inspiration in listing service attributes to be covered in a satisfaction survey.

CHAPTER 8

Service guarantees and service-level agreements

Gino Van Ossel · Paul Gemmel

INTRODUCTION

In 1989 the Dutch telephone company, PTT Telecom, needed to change. Business would never be the same again. The European telecommunications industry was being deregulated, abolishing all competitive restrictions in all European-Union member states. As in most European countries, PTT Telecom had previously enjoyed a national monopoly as a government-owned utility, resulting in high costs for calling and long lead times for having telephones connected and/or repaired. The Dutch government privatized PTT in order to maximize the chances of success for a major change management programme. PTT was now to become more market-oriented in order to face future competition. Total quality management became a core value at PTT. Customer satisfaction surveys and other market research helped management to monitor how PTT's progress was perceived by its customers.

Five years later, although the efforts had resulted in a significant improvement in the delivered service, service levels were still unreliable and the general public perceived PTT as performing less well than was actually the case. PTT Telecom's management made a bold decision. It decided to guarantee its customers that, as of February 1995, a new telephone would always be connected within three working days (which in March 1994 occurred just 40 per cent of the time). Similarly, PTT intended to guarantee that all repairs to telephone lines would be completed within 1.5 working days (which was the case only 70 per cent of the time). If PTT could not keep its promise, customers would be refunded two months' basic service fee.

Management strongly believed that setting up such an extraordinary service guarantee would help to steer the organization towards increased customer satisfaction and would trigger a quantum leap in both service level and service reliability improvements.[1]

In pursuing customer satisfaction, every organization tries to balance its customers' expectations with the delivered service. As this service is to a great extent based on the efforts of the organization's employees, customer satisfaction largely depends on the employees' understanding of the customers' expectations.

Service guarantees and service-level agreements – related and yet different concepts – are attractive to companies because they render the sometimes abstract service concept into a concrete and measurable performance standard.

A service guarantee promises the customer a certain service quality and backs up this promise with a payout. Of particular interest are the so-called extraordinary guarantees whose promises go beyond what is usually expected.[2]

A service-level agreement is an agreement between the service provider and its customers quantifying the minimum acceptable service to the customer.

By communicating this performance standard to its employees, an organization can genuinely focus on what is really important to the customer. Moreover, since service guarantees and service-level agreements make services more 'tangible', they have become important communication tools that can facilitate customers' search and purchase processes by reducing the perceived risk of purchasing something. The presence of a service guarantee or service-level agreement can support the perception of service reliability, which is one of the most critical determinants of customer satisfaction.

With both concepts, service quality is made measurable. This allows all service failures to be tracked and used as input for future improvement projects.

Objectives

By the end of this chapter, you should be able to discuss:

- the components of service guarantees and what is meant by extraordinary service guarantees
- the effects of service guarantees
- how to implement service guarantees
- the core characteristics of service-level agreements
- the basic building blocks of service-level agreements and when to use them
- internal service guarantees and service-level agreements and how to implement them

SERVICE GUARANTEES

In this section the key components of a service guarantee will be discussed, as well as the possible advantages of their use. Organizations can aim for external marketing effects as well as for internal improvements, for which the payout functions as an incentive. Special attention is also paid to the implementation of service guarantees. This is important not only to maximize the desired improvements but also to manage the business risks inherent in promising a payout in case of a service failure.

A service guarantee makes the customer a meaningful *promise* and specifies a *payout* and an *invocation procedure* in case the promise is not kept. Each of these elements is equally important in making a guarantee successful.

The promise

By introducing a service guarantee, an organization is making a meaningful but credible promise to its customers. In the introductory case study, PTT Telecom promised to connect new telephones within three working days and to fix telephone lines within a day and a half. This promise is meaningful in a European context, where shorter lead times are among consumers' top desires. The promise can be classified along two dimensions. In terms of content, it can either promise total satisfaction or be more specific. In terms of communication to the customer, the promise can be either explicit or implicit.

Content of the promise

A good promise is meaningful to the customer, that is, it goes beyond what is normally expected. A distinction can be made here between total satisfaction and specific promises.

The most powerful type of service guarantee is the total satisfaction guarantee. The customer is guaranteed total customer satisfaction. For instance, a training institute guarantees its course participants that they will be satisfied or they can obtain a refund. Similarly, Holiday Inn makes a 'Hospitality Promise':

> 'We promise that throughout your stay with us, we will endeavour to meet the high standards that you expect from Holiday Inn Hotels. However, should anything not be to your satisfaction, don't hesitate to tell us, . . . as you are not expected to pay for unsatisfactory service.'

Unconditional total satisfaction guarantees are rare. The main reason for this is that service providers fear (massive) abuse by their customers (*see* later in this chapter).

The most common type of service guarantee – *the specific service guarantee* – focuses on one or more service aspects. There are two possible reasons for offering this type of guarantee:

1. It is possible that the core customer satisfaction criterion can be boiled down to one specific service aspect. For instance, Federal Express guarantees that all documents and packages that are sent from Europe to the US will be delivered the next day before 10.00 a.m. As reliable overnight delivery is the single most important quality criterion, the guarantee is limited to this service aspect.
2. The risk of abuse and/or the unreliability of the delivered service quality sometimes discourages organizations from offering total customer satisfaction guarantees. Therefore they guarantee one or several service aspects that are meaningful to the customer.

PTT Telecom sees its guarantee as a first step on a difficult journey towards a possible total satisfaction guarantee. By focusing on the connection and repair times, specific service aspects which are important to the customer are guaranteed.

Sometimes it is worthwhile to communicate information about the service process improvement put in place to attain the promised service level. For instance, a bank promising a wait of no more than five minutes in its service guarantee can gain credibility by also communicating in the guarantee that the bank has doubled the number of tellers working at peak hours.[3]

In defining the promise, a company should be very careful not to promise what would be expected anyway. This can send the wrong message, as the guarantee may signal that service failures are more likely to occur than would normally be expected. However, this is less harmful than launching a promise which is too limited in scope – that is, those that guarantee only less important service aspects or that are highly conditional, excluding all major causes of service failures. Lufthansa guarantees that its customers will make their connecting flights if there are no delays due to weather or air-traffic control problems. Yet these two problems cause in total 95 per cent of all flight delays. Furthermore, the guarantee only applies if all flights, including the connecting flights, are with Lufthansa.[4]

Additional information in a service guarantee must always be treated carefully because the information may erroneously be considered part of the guarantee itself. This does not mean that conditional guarantees are never successful. PTT Telecom has excluded service failures due to strikes and natural disasters from its guarantee, but this is acceptable to its customers as these causes are truly exceptional.

Communication of the promise

Promises and therefore guarantees can be communicated explicitly to the customer; on the other hand, it is also possible to define a guarantee and not communicate it to the customer. Such implicit guarantees are less powerful than explicit ones, but they offer certain advantages.

Explicit service guarantees are the best known and most powerful type. They are communicated clearly to customers. The customer may choose the service provider over another because of the guarantee. Furthermore, the guarantee may lower the complaint threshold and can therefore be an excellent tool in a relationship marketing strategy.

Implicit service guarantees are the least powerful type, as the promise is not explicitly communicated to the customers. Consequently, there are fewer positive effects. The marketing effect is limited to possible service recovery benefits in case of complaining customers. Similarly, the number of payouts will be lower than with explicit service guarantees. Consequently, the smaller amount of the payout functions as a less powerful incentive for positive change. The smaller number of reported service failures also provides less information for improvement projects.

Implicit guarantees do offer certain advantages.

1. They minimize the risk of an excessive payout coming through, because the risk of a service failure is too great. In the PTT Telecom example, the service guarantee was operational as of December 1994, yet its existence was only communicated to the general public in February 1995. PTT Telecom opted for a two-month test period during which the guarantee was implicit only. If the payout had been too large to bear, revoking the guarantee would still have been possible without any negative publicity.
2. Their use prevents abuse. A Belgian chain of book and CD shops applies an implicit unconditional satisfaction guarantee. All books and CDs can be returned for a refund for any reason, even without producing any proof of purchase. However, in order to avoid being used as a library where the latest books and CDs can be borrowed at no cost, this retailer prefers to use an implicit guarantee.

3. By communicating a guarantee, the organization is actually indicating that service failures may occur. In Lufthansa's service guarantee, the company promises its customers that their luggage will arrive with them. Although this is meaningful to customers, as luggage does get lost occasionally, the perception may have been created that lost luggage is more of a problem with Lufthansa than it is with its competitors. In this case an implicit guarantee would have been more appropriate.

It seems that professional services have to be particularly careful not to send the wrong message. Customers may start wondering why it is necessary to announce a guarantee in the first place.

The effectiveness of communicating a service guarantee is also dependent on the source of the message, particularly if a firm has a history of service problems. It will be difficult for a service firm with a bad service reputation to send out a credible message.[5]

The payout

When the promise is not kept, the customer will receive a *payout*. This payout will encourage the customer to communicate all service failures, which has a double effect:

- *Service recovery*. The customer who claims his payout is less likely to defect. Service recovery becomes possible.
- *Service quality improvement*. Each claim not only represents valuable information about quality errors and their possible causes, but the avoidance of future payouts functions as an incentive to all staff to participate in improvement projects.

In order to achieve service recovery, the payout has to be meaningful to the customer. It should make up for all the damage and inconvenience that he or she has suffered. It should make the customer 'whole'.

For instance, if a Federal Express document or parcel sent overseas to the US has not been delivered by 10.00 a.m. the following day, there is no charge to the customer. However, this payout is not a solution for the customer whose partner on the receiving end did not receive the promised delivery. To be fair to Federal Express, we have to stress that an acceptable solution is not easy to find. On the one hand, the late delivery has occurred and cannot be rectified. On the other hand, compensating for the damage is also very difficult. The actual damage to the customer is difficult to assess, as it varies widely from one case to another and may occasionally be so high that it has an impact on Federal Express's financial results – for example, in the case of transporting human organs for transplantation.

By contrast, the payout offered by the Dutch bus service organization, Interliner, makes their customers 'whole'. They guarantee that passengers boarding their buses will make their connecting buses and trains. Again, a refund would not adequately compensate the passenger who has just missed a connection. Therefore, every passenger who has had to wait for more than 15 minutes for a connection due to a delay by Interliner can be taken to his or her destination by taxi at Interliner's expense.[6]

A payout can also be too high. Domino's Pizza offered customers its pizzas free of charge if they were not delivered within 30 minutes from ordering. Much to Domino's surprise, fewer people made use of the guarantee than expected. Market research showed that consumers felt sorry for the delivery boy. They feared that if they did not pay for the pizza he could get fired, and thereby declined the payout. Consequently, the service guarantee did not trigger the expected customer feedback on late deliveries. Domino's has therefore reduced the payout to a discount if the pizza is delivered between 30 and 45 minutes after ordering. A refund or a fresh pizza is offered only if the pizza is more than 15 minutes late. Consequently, customers who now perceive that the 'punishment fits the crime' have started using the guarantee, providing Domino's with valuable information on the actual frequency of late deliveries.

The invocation procedure

The final component of the service guarantee is the invocation procedure. How can customers notify the organization that it has not kept its promise, and what do they have to do to collect the payout?

Invoking a guarantee should be either very easy or even proactive. Supermarkets Hoogvliet (the Netherlands) and Match (Belgium) both promise short queues at their checkouts. If all tills are not manned and if you are the third (Hoogvliet) or fourth (Match) customer in a queue, you do not have to pay (Hoogvliet) or you receive a significant discount (Match).

The invocation procedure itself is the major difference. At Match, the customer has to step out of the queue and press a bell, which focuses all attention on the 'complaining' customer. Social pressure prevents customers from using the bell. The guarantee is hardly ever invoked and queues have not decreased. In contrast, Hoogvliet customers do not have to do anything at all. If they find themselves third in line, the person manning the till will proactively tell them that their groceries are free of charge.

A fine example of an unconditional satisfaction guarantee which is easy to invoke is Superquinn's Goof Card system. Superquinn is the leading supermarket chain in the Greater Dublin area. Periodically, all customers who participate in its loyalty saving system called 'Superclub' receive a so-called Goof Card. The card explains to the customers that each time Superquinn 'goofs' – that is, produces a service failure – the customer simply has to point this out to any member of staff, and he or she will receive 30 Superclub bonus points worth about £1.

The guarantee offers unconditional satisfaction, as customers can define the goofs themselves, but in order to further help their customers, Superquinn lists ten examples of goofs. Included are products which have passed their sell-by date, prices at the checkout which do not match the prices marked on the shelf, wobbly trolleys, and labels being out of stock at the fruit and vegetable scales.

The invocation of PTT Telecom's guarantee is proactive as well. After each connection or repair, PTT Telecom makes an after-sales call to the customer. During that call, PTT Telecom tries to assess the customer's satisfaction. If the promise of a timely connection or repair was not kept, the customer is informed immediately of the payout.

The effects of a service guarantee

Service guarantees can serve different purposes. First, such a guarantee has major internal effects on an organization's operations and staff. The payout catalyses improvement projects which focus on the guaranteed promise. As such, guarantees have proven to be a highly effective tool in steering organizations towards maximum customer satisfaction.

The internal effects should indirectly translate into marketing benefits – more precisely, increased customer loyalty and positive word of mouth. Some organizations also use guarantees to reduce the customer's perceived risk. By guaranteeing a specific outcome, the organization hopes to increase its business and to acquire new customers. It conveys the image of a reliable supplier. A side effect of this is improved customer loyalty through service recovery in case of service failure.

The internal effect on the organization's operations and staff

The benefits of service guarantees are in many ways similar to those of complaint management systems. The payout and the easy invocation procedure lower the threshold for customers to report any service failure and seize the opportunity for service recovery. Furthermore, these service failures are reported and analysed, and used to set up improvement projects aimed at eliminating their root causes.

Service guarantees seem to be more effective than complaint procedures. The payout penalizes each failure and seems to mobilize all staff to switch to prevention mode. If Holiday Inn's guests were generally dissatisfied or if Domino's delivered too many pizzas late, they would simply go out of business. As Intuit's founder, Scott Cook, has put it, 'They are operating without a safety net.' The guarantee is a very effective way for management to communicate to its staff that customer satisfaction truly is a number one priority.[7]

A second advantage of a service guarantee over complaint management systems is that the promise helps to highlight what is important to the customer. This is particularly true for specific service guarantees. As the promise is related to certain aspects of the service, all staff involved will focus on these service aspects.

The PTT Telecom example clearly shows the operational effect of implementing a service guarantee. The decision to set up a guarantee was made in February 1994. The first measurements were carried out in March 1994. After a pilot phase in four regions, the guarantee was launched implicitly but nationwide in December 1994. In February 1995 it was announced to the general public. The improvement of the service level was striking (*see* Figure 8.1).

Service guarantees which are not clearly linked to the organization's service concept, or that put emphasis on aspects which are of secondary importance to the

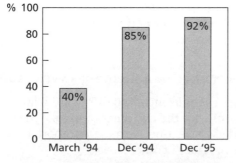

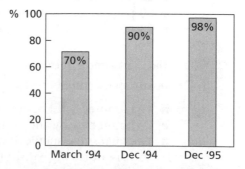

(a) % of connections within 3 working days   **(b)** % of repairs within 1.5 working days

Figure 8.1 The effect of the introduction of a service guarantee at PTT Telecom

customer, may send the wrong signal to the staff. Similarly, aiming at zero defect operations should not be done at any price.

A fine case in point is Domino's. The service guarantee promises the delivery of a pizza to the customer's address within 30 minutes. While very meaningful to the customer, the guarantee may encourage the delivery staff to risk their own safety in order to meet the 30-minute target. Moreover, the delay may have been caused while cooking the pizza and not during the delivery. Domino's has come up with a very simple solution.

1. Pizzas are only delivered to customers within an eight-minute drive from the outlet.
2. Ten minutes (or a two-minute margin) is allowed for delivery.
3. Pizzas leaving the kitchen more than 20 minutes after the order was taken, are automatically stickered as 'discounted for late delivery'. The effect is threefold:
   – Back-office staff are directly confronted with service failures and the resulting payout. This increases their involvement with the service guarantee.
   – The delivery staff cannot avoid the payout by speeding and thus risking their safety, in order to make up the time lost in the kitchen. The sticker already awards the penalty.
   – The invocation procedure is made proactive.

The Domino's example also shows another effect of the promise, namely that it sets clear performance standards. The snappy but non-committal 'Quick delivery' becomes '20 minutes from order-taking to start of delivery' and '10 minutes to deliver'. All staff know exactly what is expected of them.

A final internal effect of service guarantees is increased employee satisfaction and a greater staff empowerment. By advertising the guarantee, the employees perceive their organization as delivering a high quality and very reliable service. As such they find the working environment more pleasant and their satisfaction increases. The constant customer feedback encourages a natural feeling of empowerment. With no formal 'empowering' effort, employees are allowed, expected and willing to take more initiative in trying to avoid service failures incidentally and in setting up improvement projects to tackle root causes structurally.

Hampton Inn, which guarantees its customers total customer satisfaction, has researched the guarantee's impact on its staff:[8]

- 69 per cent say it makes the company a better place to work.
- 90 per cent say it motivates them to do a better job.
- 93 per cent say it motivates others to do a better job.

The marketing effects

In summary, the following factors affect the influence of a service guarantee:

- A guarantee must be stated in a simple and straightforward way;
- It should be easy and worthwhile for the customer to invoke the guarantee;
- The guarantee should include service aspects that are important to the customer and are normally within the provider's control.

The payout and the easy invocation procedure encourage customers to express their dissatisfaction because of a service failure. Not only will more customers complain, but their efforts and aggravation are minimized as the invocation procedure can actually be proactive. Guarantees are therefore a valuable tool in service recovery.

Service guarantees can produce some very specific marketing effects. They are a particularly powerful way to reduce the customer's perceived risk of buying and can therefore attract new customers and/or new business. For example, some restaurants advertise that they can serve a three-course business lunch within an hour or it will be free. The guarantee reduces the risk for time-conscious business people that they will waste too much time sitting in a restaurant. Similar guarantees are offered by restaurants in train stations and airports, allowing customers to judge very precisely if they have time to order a meal before their train or plane leaves.

Risk reduction is particularly useful for 'high-risk' services. Dining out at a low-priced restaurant carries a lower risk than dining at a higher-priced (i.e. high-risk) restaurant. A study looking at the impact of service guarantees on the choice of restaurants by students showed that service guarantees have marginal added value in ensuring a good dining experience for low-priced restaurants. Higher-priced restaurants seem to benefit more from service guarantees.[9]

The degree of risk depends partly on the predictability of the outcome and of the possible consequences of an undesirable outcome. The outcome is less predictable with new suppliers and/or with initial purchase situations, hence the use of guarantees to attract new customers. The consequences are typically related to the actual service: the late arrival of a package delivered by Federal Express or of a bus operated by Interliner may have major consequences.

Service guarantees make the service promise more tangible, but it is important to remember that breaking the service promise is the single most important way in which service companies fail their customers.[10]

Implementing a service guarantee

The Spanish national railway company, RENFE, launched a service guarantee which promised a refund to all passengers in the case of any delay exceeding five minutes. Within 24 hours of the launch, RENFE revoked the guarantee, as technical difficulties had caused delays to 900 passengers, who were paid refunds totalling approximately £65 000. Apart from the short-term financial loss, by revoking the guarantee RENFE actually reinforced its image as an unreliable service provider, which obviously was exactly the opposite of what it wanted to achieve.

This example clearly illustrates that implementing a guarantee has to be carried out with the utmost care. The consequences of an unsuccessful implementation can be very diverse. In the best case, a failure has simply been a waste of resources. This happens if the guarantee is never or rarely invoked. Payout consequently is limited, but so is the feedback to the organization on service failures. There is no real incentive to set up improvement projects and there are no opportunities for service recovery. The benefits of the guarantee are zero, while resources have been invested in its conception, advertising and implementation.

RENFE illustrates the worse case. The organization suffered significant financial losses because of the excessive failure rate and resulting payout. Eventually the organization had to revoke the guarantee, sending a clear signal to both its customers and its staff that management accepts that the organization cannot guarantee a reliable service.

In order to minimize the risk and to maximize the chance of success, we recommend the following approach:

Step 1   Assessing the impact of the guarantee
Step 2   External analysis and conception of the guarantee
Step 3   Internal analysis and feasibility study
Step 4   Pilot stage and launching the guarantee implicitly
Step 5   Full implementation and follow-up

We will now discuss each of these steps in greater detail.

Step 1 Assessing the impact of the guarantee

Although the potential benefits of service guarantees are abundant, they will not be realized by all organizations. Before committing major resources to conceiving and implementing a guarantee, senior management should consider to what degree it will improve the organization's competitive position. Three major factors should be taken into account:

- *The industry in which the organization is operating.* Since guarantees help to reduce the customer's perceived risk, 'high-risk' industries will benefit more from establishing guarantees than others. For instance, public utilities, which often have a monopoly, tend to be perceived as more product- than customer- or performance-oriented – hence, PTT Telecom's launch of a service guarantee to overcome this negative image. In general, service industries are risk intensive because offerings are to a certain extent intangible, making it difficult for customers to judge the quality of the service prior to purchase. Medical services are the ultimate example. A patient will only find out after the operation whether or not he or she has chosen the right doctor. Even if the operation failed, it would be difficult to judge whether another surgeon would have been more successful. Indeed, the failing surgeon could disclaim all liability because of 'medical complications' which could not have been anticipated.
- *The actual level of risk intensity.* This depends on the predictability as well as on the consequences of a service failure. If you show up at a hotel looking for a room for the night, you can ask to see the room before actually taking it. As such, the risk is much more predictable than that involved in booking through a travel agent or the Internet. There is no way you can judge in advance what 'a comfortable room with view' will really be like. Only on arrival will you be able to see whether it is above a nightclub or not, and if the quality of the mattress meets your expectations. The possible impact of a service failure is just as important as the predictability of the outcome. A surgical operation may result in the patient's death. Nothing can compensate for the avoidable loss of a human life. The impact is therefore clearly linked to the possibility of redress. Finally, the company may be competing in an industry or in a segment in which failures are simply not expected or accepted. As discussed earlier, the company may actually send out the wrong signal by offering a guarantee. A surgeon who explicitly guarantees a payout in case of the loss of a patient would be suggesting that there is a real risk of dying. In these cases, only implicit guarantees should be considered.

- *The organization's performance.* Obviously guarantees are only an option for reliable service providers. The organization's performance should be judged both in an absolute manner and relative to its competitors. The organization's absolute performance can be measured by the number of service failures. Too many failures would trigger too high a payout. Several studies have recognized the need for a company to raise its service level before implementing a guarantee to avoid excessive payout, negative publicity and ultimately loss of customer goodwill. As PTT Telecom's experience has shown us, establishing a guarantee may actually result in a significant increase in the service level. Consequently, judging the performance goes beyond the mere calculation of the current service level. It requires the assessment of the possible (positive) internal effects of a guarantee. Actually, service guarantees typically yield the most internal benefits in case of good but not yet excellent performance. The guarantee becomes a means of achieving excellence.

- Equally important is *performance relative to competition.* As the concept of a guarantee can easily be copied by anyone offering at least the same service level, only the better performing organizations should launch a guarantee. In fact, the best performer can either make the most meaningful promise or offer the most attractive payout.

By now it should be obvious that service guarantees will yield most benefits to a high-performing organization in a high-risk industry, which wants to move from being a good service provider to an excellent one. Service guarantees will only allow an organization to differentiate itself from competition if it is outperforming them. If all or several competitors are more or less equally reliable, organizations may look for aspects of the service which are meaningful to the customer and in which they perform better than their competitors. The guarantee then becomes an instrument the company can use to distinguish itself from its competitors.

And what about the risk of abuse?

The simultaneous nature of consumption and production justifies service managers' concern for the risk of abuse. If a satisfied guest at Holiday Inn abuses the guarantee to obtain a free stay, he cannot be forced to 'return' the goods. This is less important with tangibles. For instance, if a customer buys a television set and is not satisfied, the invocation procedure of an unconditional satisfaction guarantee will usually require the customer to return the rejected television. This discourages abuse, as the customer wanting a TV would have to procure a new set anyway.

The importance of abuse is difficult to assess. Although total satisfaction guarantees are more likely to be abused than specific ones, the risk of abuse seems to be industry- and culture-dependent. Eastern Airlines, for instance, had to revoke its 100 per cent satisfaction guarantee after five months as customers complaining about details were receiving full refunds. Hampton Inn, an American hotel chain, spotted a guest who invoked its guarantee 18 times within one year. They put this customer on a blacklist.

On the other hand, if the number of abusers is limited, the vast majority of honest customers should not be punished because of a small minority of abusers.

There are different ways to manage the risk of abuse:

- *Testing the guarantee.* By using a pilot phase – explained below in Step 4 – it is possible to assess the actual abuse.
- *Adjusting the invocation procedure.* Both the training institute which guarantees its participants unconditional total satisfaction and Holiday Inn try to combat abuse by inviting their customers to report any dissatisfaction during the consumption of the service. At the training institute, a refund can only be obtained if the participant decides to leave the one-day course before noon. Abusers punish themselves, as they have their money back, but cannot attend the course in full.
- *Using an implicit guarantee.* The risk of abuse can be minimized by not communicating the guarantee explicitly to the customers. The earlier example of the book and CD shop which gives refunds for whatever reason and without a proof of purchase illustrates this approach.

Step 2 External analysis and conception of the guarantee

Once senior management is committed to the idea of a service guarantee, the actual implementation can begin. The first step involves conceiving the guarantee. A first draft of the guarantee should be developed by balancing customers' needs with the offer and service level of all competitors.

Market-oriented organizations which invest heavily in customer perception studies and competitive analysis should find it easy to define what is meaningful to the customer. However, conceiving a guarantee may require additional information.

First, the promise needs to be specific. PTT Telecom had to go beyond promising that a connection would be made 'quickly'; it actually had to set the specific lead time of three working days as a promise and performance standard. Moreover, the promise is often subject to a list of restrictions. Market research is needed to assess what restrictions are acceptable to the customer, what payout is considered to be a fair punishment, and what invocation procedure is perceived as easy.

At this stage, it is common to consider the ideal guarantee as well as other scenarios. PTT Telecom may have learned that customers prefer to obtain a telephone connection within 24 hours without any restrictions, and a payout of a year's free service. However, during the 'internal analysis stage', it may turn out that this is simply not feasible. It therefore makes sense to test different variants of the promise, the restrictions, the payout, and the invocation procedure with customers.

Benchmarking can prove to be an important source of information during the external analysis stage. For instance, PTT Telecom learned that similar service guarantees existed in the UK, Germany and Sweden and eventually set up an alliance with their Swedish colleagues to learn from their experiences.

To maximize the chances of successful implementation, it is important to involve as many employees as possible in conceiving the guarantee. They will not only be able to provide interesting insights, but their early involvement will also result in maximum commitment. In larger organizations it may not be possible to involve everyone, but at least the opinion leaders should be involved.

Step 3 Internal analysis and feasibility study

Once the service guarantee, including some different scenarios, has been conceived, the internal analysis should reveal the effect on the organization's profitability.

The first step typically consists of calculating the additional out-of-pocket expenses of launching a service guarantee. Multiplying the suggested payout by the current number of service failures, taking into account alternative performance standards and restrictions, results in the expected total payout. Adding the other out-of-pocket expenses, such as advertising the guarantee and training the staff, concludes the easiest part of the internal analysis.

The potential benefits are much more difficult to assess. The guarantee may attract new customers through the lower perceived risk. Moreover, each payout may prevent a current customer from defecting. The guarantee should also result in fewer service failures, and therefore in higher customer loyalty as well as a lower than expected payout. Experience has also shown that service guarantees also trigger improvement projects which cut costs. Finally, employee satisfaction may increase.

The challenge is, of course, to assess these benefits accurately prior to introducing the guarantee. It seems that at one point launching a guarantee is more a question of faith than of facts and figures.

The internal analysis may reveal a too high failure rate, indicating that it is not yet feasible to launch a guarantee. However, this should not necessarily mean that the idea of a guarantee has to be scrapped, but rather that a plan of action is developed to improve the service reliability to a level where a guarantee becomes feasible.

Step 4 Pilot stage and launching the guarantee implicitly

To minimize the risks involved, organizations often launch a guarantee implicitly and/or on a limited scale. For instance, PTT Telecom first tested its guarantee implicitly and in only four regions, later launching it (still implicitly) nationwide. Eventually, two months after its launch, a national advertising campaign made the guarantee explicit.

The advantages of such an approach are obvious. The assessment of the costs and benefits during the internal analysis stage can be made in a real-life situation. Note that the benefits are usually underestimated as the guarantee is implicit only.

Testing the guarantee implicitly may be difficult if the invocation procedure is not proactive. The outcome of the test can be very misleading. If the employees do not pay out when they should according to the guarantee, the number of service failures can be grossly underestimated.

Testing the guarantee explicitly but on a limited scale, for instance in just one region, solves this problem. However, if the eventual guarantee will be communicated through mass media, it will be difficult to explain to customers that the guarantee is only being offered in the test region. The pilot stage usually results in fine-tuning the guarantee and in setting up nation-wide improvement projects.

Step 5 Full implementation

Full implementation is started once the pilot stage delivers acceptable results.

SERVICE-LEVEL AGREEMENTS

A service-level agreement is an agreement between the service provider and its customers quantifying the minimum acceptable service to the customer.[11] This definition reflects three core characteristics:

■ It is an agreement and thus requires the approval of both parties. This is the first basic difference between a guarantee and a service-level agreement. A guarantee is unilateral. The supplier decides on the promise, the restrictions, the payout and the invocation procedure. The supplier should of course take into account the customers' points of view in conceiving the guarantee, but it does not need their formal approval.

By contrast, a service-level agreement is bilateral. Both the supplier and the customer have to approve it, which can necessitate compromise. For instance, on the one hand the supplier may promise to achieve certain service levels, and, on the other hand, the customer may commit to providing accurate volume forecasts and respecting specified deadlines.

As a result, elements which affect the supplier's promise but which are within the customer's control become the customer's promise in a service-level agreement. In a guarantee they would typically take the form of 'restrictions'.

An important consequence of the 'mutual' nature of a service-level agreement is that it is by definition tailor-made. Instead of offering a standard contract with standard clauses, as a service guarantee does, customer and supplier sit down together to draft an agreement which addresses both parties' needs and interests.

■ The agreement specifies the minimum acceptable service, taking into account the mutual interest of both parties. For instance, a company servicing copiers may guarantee that its repair staff can be on all their customers' premises within 60 minutes in case of a malfunction. Such a guarantee sets a clear performance standard but is not necessarily the optimal intervention time. Some customers may consider 120 minutes or 24 hours equally acceptable. Since reducing the response time typically results in higher costs, the service-level agreement allows supplier and customer to define the minimum acceptable service level at which the total cost to both parties is minimized. A service-level agreement should prevent unnecessary and expensive over-provision of quality.

■ The agreement also quantifies the service. As such, it sets clear performance standards for both supplier and customer. For instance, a supplier of information systems may promise to limit the down-time of a multi-computer service. When conceiving such an agreement, the customer's expectations have to be clearly defined. In this case, this requires defining 'availability' of the system: is it available or unavailable if one of the computers is down, or if only 5 per cent of all users cannot access it? The timing of the availability has also to be discussed. Average availability figures may hide the fact that the system is too often down when it is really needed. The same degree of clarity is of course required on the customer's part.

Table 8.1 summarizes the main differences between service guarantees and service level agreements.

Developing service-level agreements creates better awareness of customer needs and enables a company to better manage its customer expectations. As with service

Table 8.1 The main differences between service guarantees and service-level agreements

	Service guarantee	Service-level agreement
The needs of the customer	Identified by the manager	Communicated by the customer
The promise	Unconditional	After negotiation
The content	Standardized	Customized
The responsibility	Supplier	Supplier and customer
Number	One guarantee for all customers	One SLA for each customer
Changes	Unusual	Possible with consent of supplier and customer
The kind of customer	B-to-B and B-to-C	B-to-B
Communication of the promise	Not in the case of implicit service guarantees	Through negotiations
The payout	Proactive or when the customer asks for it	When there is a deviation from the norm
The nature of the payout	Rather a fine	A fine or a reward
Feedback on the perceived service delivery	Unidirectional	Bidirectional
The source of information for feedback	The invocation procedure	Reports and meetings

guarantees, the internal processes should be stable enough to make the SLAs feasible. The SLAs also help to optimize allocation of scarce resources to competitive needs, for instance, by not delivering service at an unreasonably high level. Ultimately, SLAs should have a positive impact on customer retention and the development of a long-term relationship with the customer.

Setting up service-level agreements

A service-level agreement is a tool which can be used to help a company move towards the delivery of a service of a quality appropriate to the needs of the business. It provides an objective indication of whether the service is being delivered at a minimum acceptable level; furthermore, if such a service is not being delivered, it provides what is needed to bring the service to that level.

The following mechanisms should underlie any service-level agreement:

1. The minimum acceptable service level must be specified, as well as the commitment from the customer.
2. The degree to which the mutual promises are kept must be measured.
3. The root causes of failures should be sought and improvement projects set up.
4. Review meetings should be set up to discuss progress and to see whether the initial commitments need fine tuning.

When to use service-level agreements

Service-level agreements require a considerable amount of resources. First, they have to be conceived, then measurement systems have to be installed and, finally, review meetings have to be held. Moreover, as a service-level agreement is custom-made, the investment has to be repeated for each individual customer. Service-level agreements also make demands on the customers' resources, as they also have to participate in the start-up negotiations and review meetings.

As a result, the benefits of service-level agreements can only outweigh the costs for major and long-lasting customer–supplier relationships, which yield a high dividend for the supplier and high cost implications for the customer. This illustrates a major difference between service guarantees and service-level agreements. As a guarantee is a unilateral concept which can be applied to all customers in a standardized manner, it is more suitable in a mass-marketing context.

Common pitfalls when implementing service-level agreements

Many service-level agreements fail during implementation. The most common mistake is to assume that, once the agreement has been signed, the work is basically over. In reality, drafting and signing an agreement is only the first step. Its success depends on the way the agreement is managed afterwards. The following pitfalls are often encountered during the implementation of service-level agreements.

- *Poor handling of service failures*. As the objective of a service-level agreement is to develop a communication platform on areas for improvement, service failures have to be treated as a valuable source of management information, and must be dealt with constructively. One of the most common pitfalls is for customers to treat the agreement as an unconditional guarantee. Each failure is presented as a major cause of dissatisfaction. This creates a defensive attitude on the part of the supplier, who starts focusing on avoiding the reporting of failures rather than on tackling their root causes. A clear symptom of this problem is when the agreement is drafted as a legal contract. Contracts are considered binding, while a service-level agreement is a basis for future co-operation, including future reviews of the agreement itself.
- *Inadequate definitions and poor measurements*. Inadequate definitions and poor measurements turn the focus of the review meetings from the root causes of failures to the accuracy of the service failure data.
- *Unclear definition of 'availability'*. In the previous example of a multi-computer system, we stressed the importance of a clear definition of 'availability'. If this definition is inaccurate, several review meetings will be required to come up with more accurate definitions and appropriate measurement systems. Moreover, supplier and customers may have different interpretations of the initial agreement, so that fine-tuning the definitions may result in an agreement which is unacceptable to one of the parties.
- *Poor measurements*. Similarly, poor measurements will result in debates on the validity of the number of reported service failures. If penalties are part of the agreement, it is particularly important that the validity and impartiality of the measurements are accepted by all concerned. Otherwise, the agreement, which has already consumed a fair amount of resources, will fail to yield early

benefits. Eventually this may result in an overall failure. Some have misinterpreted this point by drafting very elaborate and detailed service-level agreements up to 30 pages long. As the agreement is not a contract, but a platform for communicating, clarity and specificity are more important than degree of detail. A good service-level agreement should take no more than one or two pages.

■ *Lack of mutual benefits*. As a service-level agreement is demanding on both customer and supplier, both have to benefit from it. If not, the commitment of one of the partners is bound to gradually diminish.

■ *Lack of commitment of both senior management and front-line staff*. Service-level agreements are expensive. They need constant resourcing. Consequently, senior management has to be committed in order to keep the agreements alive. On the other hand, the organization will only reap the benefits if front-line staff are also involved. By having them participate at the conception stage as well as in the review meetings, one can avoid the discussion of the service-level agreements being confined to management meetings.

Exhibit 8.1

Service-level agreements at Securis[12]

Security is one of our most basic needs. Many companies have been paying more attention to creating a secure environment, especially since 11 September 2001. In most cases, security services are bought from an external supplier. One of these suppliers is Securis.

Securis was founded as a Belgian aviation security company in 1985. In later years the company diversified into permanent and mobile security. In 1999 Securis was taken over by the Swedish holding company Securitas AB, a world leader in the area of security. Securis has 4000 employees working in five divisions.

SLAs were introduced in Securis several years ago following an explicit request from a customer to develop such an agreement. Securis only develops an SLA when a business customer explicitly asks for it. Each SLA has a duration of three to five years and is developed to meet the customer's specific needs. This requires an intensive process of negotiation between Securis and the customer about the specified quality level, the dimensions of quality to be measured, the measurement method and the consequences. The consequences may be a fine or a reward for the supplier (Securis) depending on whether or not the specified quality level is attained.

The 'A' of 'Agreement' in SLA is of great importance for Securis. In the negotiations a situation acceptable to both supplier and customer is striven for and a balance is made between price and quality. This aspect of mutual interest, which is so important in developing a SLA at Securis, is also recognized as one of the most difficult to realize in practice.

According to Securis's COO, customers do not have any experience in working with SLAs, so it can happen that some customers tend to abuse the SLA to their advantage.

The SLAs at Securis do not specify the outcome of the service delivery, but the resources and the efforts which are necessary to perform it. An agreement about outcomes carries too much risk, certainly when the supplier has insufficient input in the customer's business. Securis's limited number of years of experience with SLAs and its uncertainty about the consequences of using SLAs results in a rather cautious approach.

Compliance with the specifications in a SLA is only possible when the company has a well-functioning quality assurance system in place. Management at Securis is convinced that a good level of service quality is a conditio sine qua non for implementing SLAs. SLAs do not lead to an improvement in quality, only to a change in perception of quality. An SLA is very useful in making the quality perception more objective. The performance measurement system specified in the SLA permits an objective assessment of whether or not the service delivered corresponds with what has been agreed upon in the SLA. When this performance evaluation is positive, the operational

▶

Exhibit 8.1 continued

management in charge of the execution of the SLA is rewarded at the end of the year.

Management at Securis believes that the use of SLAs can lead to a future competitive advantage if the service company proves that it is able to develop and implement a well-functioning SLA. The SLA has a positive impact on the relationship between the customer and the company. The increased transparency and objectivity in the relationship means that customers react in a less emotional way to any problems. An SLA also creates some dependency in the relationship between supplier and customer, since the cost of shifting to other suppliers increases.

A properly functioning SLA creates trust in the relationship between customer and supplier and leads in the end to greater customer loyalty. But a SLA is also a double-edged sword, according to Securis management: the customer learns about the positive but also about the negative points of the company. Customers must learn to handle this kind of information.

Discussion questions
- *Securis applies SLAs in their own particular way. What are the differences between the theory and the practice of developing and implementing SLAs at Securis?*
- *What are the opportunities and threats of using SLAs in a service company such as Securis?*

INTERNAL SERVICE GUARANTEES AND SERVICE-LEVEL AGREEMENTS

The first service-level agreements were developed not between service providers and their external customers, but between electronic data processing (EDP) departments and their internal customers. Information technology solutions have all too often been conceived by headquarters specialists operating from their 'ivory towers' and unaware of their users' real needs and concerns. The dissatisfaction of the end users, who after all are ultimately paying for all central functions, has resulted in EDP departments developing service-level agreements in order to become more (internal) customer-oriented.

The concept of the internal customer has proven to be very difficult to bring to life. Despite its popularity in managerial literature, organizations have learned that it is hard to establish a culture in which the internal customer is being treated with the same respect as the external one. The underlying reason for this is that the internal supplier traditionally has had a monopoly, since the internal customer has no alternative source of supply. In recent years, organizations have attempted to break this monopoly, either by outsourcing some of the support functions or by allowing the internal customers to buy from external suppliers if they can get a better service.

It is not surprising, therefore, that most internal service-level agreements and service guarantees have been developed by so-called off-stream internal service providers – that is, those departments that require no handover of work in order to allow the internal customers to continue their work. Customer and supplier are not contributing directly to the same stream of work. For instance, finance and accounting may be responsible for invoicing, but if invoices are sent out late, the sales representatives are not directly affected in their work.

Today we are witness to a second generation of internal service guarantees and service-level agreements, namely those centred around the in-process handoff. Whenever the internal service provider is performing a task that must be completed before the internal customers can do their work, they are contributing directly to the same stream of work. The provider-to-customer handoff is an in-process hand-off. The idea that 'the next process is your customer' was proposed by Ishikawa[13] in the 1950s. For instance, contact personnel in a bank cannot write a quote for a loan if the credit department has not approved the loan application. Similarly, the credit department cannot approve the loan if the contact person has not properly filled out the loan application form.

Unfortunately for the in-process handoff, outsourcing is not a valid alternative, and so the service provider in effect has a true monopoly. In recent years, organizations have learned that internal service guarantees and service-level agreements are a powerful tool in bringing the concept of the internal customer to life.

In deciding whether to use service guarantees or service-level agreements internally, the same arguments apply as to external ones: agreements require efforts from both the supplier and the customer. They also consume more overall resources. Therefore, agreements only make sense if there is a clear mutual benefit which outweighs the costs to both parties. Typically, they will apply to services with a very wide scope and a major impact on the overall costs.

Exhibit 8.2

Filling vacancies

This example involves a service guarantee between an off-stream service provider and its internal customers in the human resources department of Marriott's Bethesda Hotel. At the time the guarantee was introduced, the hotel was doing very well and required constant hiring of new staff to keep up with growth. However, all kinds of administrative work prevented the human resources department from investing enough time in finding and selecting new staff members. As a result, it was taking too long to fill vacancies.

To focus more clearly on the internal customers' needs, the human resources department launched an internal service guarantee. It promised that within two weeks of a vacancy being reported to them, qualified applicants would be found. If not, the human resources department would hire temps at its own budget's expense. After introducing the guarantee, the number of vacancies decreased from 45 to 4.

The implementation process

Internal service guarantees and service-level agreements are built on the same mechanisms as external ones – that is, they trigger non-compliance reports. They make errors measurable and allow for improvement projects.[14]

There are very important differences, however, between internal and external service guarantees and service-level agreements. By describing the consecutive steps in setting up guarantees and agreements, these differences will become clear. Those steps are:

- creating organization-wide commitment;
- selecting the services;
- identifying the internal customer's expectations;
- conceiving the guarantee or agreement;
- trial run.

Creating organization-wide commitment

Under normal circumstances errors are threatening to individuals and departments within an organization. Whenever an error is discovered, the quest for the guilty begins. Consequently, covering up errors is a more common attitude than looking for the underlying root causes in an attempt to look for structural solutions. Argyris[15] puts it thus:

'Organizational defensive routines make it highly likely that individuals, groups, inter-groups and organizations will not detect and correct errors that are embarrassing and threatening because the fundamental rules are to (1) bypass the errors and act as if that were not being done, (2) make the bypass undiscussible, and (3) make its undiscussibility undiscussible.'

The first step in launching internal service guarantees and service-level agreements therefore is explaining the need to reveal and communicate errors. Process improvement is clearly error-activated. It should also be made clear how service guarantees and service-level agreements can help in achieving better service quality.

A common way to achieve organization-wide involvement is by establishing a steering committee whose task is to market the concept internally. It is recommended that all hierarchical levels be represented. Representatives of middle and line management should be joined by other employees and at least one top manager. This committee should also manage the implementation process.

Selecting the service(s)

The second step is to select the service or services for pilot guarantees and service-level agreements. As any new initiative is usually greeted with scepticism, it is essential to gain credibility as fast as possible. It is common, therefore, to select services which are at the same time highly visible and for which the guarantee or agreement is likely to succeed. The chances of success are limited whenever delivering quality service depends largely on factors beyond the service provider's control. Furthermore, when the department offering the service is not functioning well, it is unlikely that a guarantee or an agreement will deliver the expected results. Finally, it is worth noting that the closer the internal service is to the external customer, the easier the impact will be to measure.

Identifying the internal customer's expectations

This step is the first contribution of internal guarantees and agreements that truly adds value. The concept of the internal customer begins to come to life, as internal market research typically gives new insights into the internal customer's expectations.

The benefits of this stage are numerous.

1. The service providers have to consider their role in the overall service delivery process to the external customer.
2. The internal customers have to decide on what they need to perform their service. It is not uncommon for the service requirements to be overstated. The key question, however, is in what way internal customers will be helped to serve

their customers better if their expectations are met. As a result, expensive over-provision of quality has to be prevented.

3. Internal customers often start to make suggestions for service improvements themselves.

The best way to discover the internal customer's expectations is to set up group meetings. One-to-one interviews are a complementary technique.

Conceiving the guarantee or service-level agreement

A service-level agreement by definition has to be conceived by the service provider and customer together. Therefore it is not always easy to distinguish between the 'expectations identification' and the 'conception' stages.

As guarantees are unilateral, it is the service provider who will have to decide on the promise, the invocation procedure and the payout. Although these components are similar to those of the external guarantees, the actual agreements are very different.

1. Internal service providers are more likely to *promise* unconditional total customer satisfaction, particularly during the trial stage and for in-process handoffs. By making the promise unconditional during the trial stage, each invocation is an indication of the internal customers' true needs. As such, invocations can provide additional insights which may enrich the internal market research.

2. With internal guarantees, the *risk of abuse* is close to zero.

3. The *invocation procedure* typically requires the use of a standard form. This form should ask for the nature of the dissatisfaction. It should be very simple in order not to make the invocation procedure too demanding on the internal customer, and ideally should be proactive.

4. The *payout in the case of an in-process handoff* has to be symbolic. In the trial stage it may even be absent. With external guarantees, the payout is a compensation for the customer's damage and it has to make the customer 'whole'. With internal customers, this works differently. Since customer and service provider are actually colleagues, a payout which compensates for the damage at the provider's expense is less likely to be invoked. The internal customer may unconsciously expect that the payout functions as a punishment for his fellow service provider.

    Therefore the payout is usually symbolic, for example: 'At the discretion of the account manager, the account executives will either enter the job (into the computer) themselves, take the account manager out to lunch, or sing a song of the account manager's choice at the next sales meeting.'

    In certain cases, it is possible to make the service provider 'owner' of the problems resulting from the non-compliance. For instance, if the night crew in a hotel fails to prepare the information required to make up a guest's bill, they may have to assist with the early check-out during their own time.

5. The *payout in the case of off-stream services* can be, but is not necessarily, more punishing. It can be more punishing if the relationship between customer and provider is not too close to prevent the customer from invoking the guarantee. Particularly in large organizations, the support functions are almost like external suppliers.

    An example of a more punishing payout can be found at the human resources department of the Marriott Bethesda Hotel. We have already said that it pays for temporary workers out of its own budget if vacancies are not filled within two weeks. The same HRM department guarantees all employees that their income statement is correct and that all requests for information will be handled within 24 hours. If not, the employee is given a dinner for two, paid for out of the department's bonus fund.

The trial run

As these guarantees or agreements involve a much smaller risk than external ones, it is possible to start them up much more quickly. Unfortunately, this also implies that fine tuning will be needed after the formal launch. This is why trial runs are necessary. For service-level agreements, it means that the frequency of the review meetings will be much higher during the first couple of months. For guarantees, the payout may be absent. Rather than trying to assess the achievable service level prior to launching the guarantee, it is simply launched and the service level is measured in the process. Furthermore, the promise is not yet final. Often the initial promise is for total satisfaction. After the final reckoning, the promise can be made more specific.

Common pitfalls of internal guarantees and agreements

The major risk in implementing internal service guarantees and service-level agreements is that after the initial enthusiasm, they fade out and die a silent death. For instance, in the case of a service guarantee with a merely symbolic payout, the internal customer has only a limited incentive to invoke the guarantee. For service-level agreements, the required efforts are much higher. A lack of initial results may discourage service provider and internal customer from continuing the review meetings. The risk of fade-out is particularly great in the following circumstances:

- *Lack of a support structure and/or a facilitator.* Setting up service-level agreements and service guarantees requires a certain expertise. By establishing a steering committee, this expertise is gradually developed as more agreements and/or guarantees are launched. Moreover, the interest is kept alive by marketing these concepts internally and by formally asking for the achieved results. The facilitator should be available for daily support. Particularly in large organizations, his or her function can be compared with that of a quality manager or of a quality coach reporting to the quality manager.
- *All initiatives are isolated.* If such a support structure is lacking, guarantees and service-level agreements are often isolated initiatives of individual departments. Particularly for in-process handoffs, the chances of early fade-out can be reduced by launching a series of linked guarantees or agreements, gradually moving further away from the external customer. Some organizations use such an integrated but gradual approach as a preparation to launching an external guarantee.
- *Lack of integration in everyday working procedures.* Often the guarantee and the service-level agreement add to the normal workload. For instance, they may require an additional reporting system. By integrating them into the existing working procedures, and replacing existing tasks with new ones, the workload of the employees concerned is less affected. Particularly for service-level agreements that require a great deal of effort from both customer and supplier, the existing reporting system should be largely replaced by the mechanisms of the agreement.

CONCLUSION

Service guarantees and service-level agreements can be valuable tools to realize customer satisfaction by creating explicit customer expectations. Moreover, they allow difficulties due to the intangibility of service to be overcome; when it comes down to making tangible the intangible, service guarantees and service-level agreements can play a crucial role. In this chapter, we have discussed extensively the important issues to consider when defining and implementing both service guarantees and service-level agreements. It has become clear that the success of implementing either one depends heavily on the joint efforts of the total organization. Although this no doubt sounds like a platitude by now, the intertwined nature of what happens inside the service organization and what customers eventually will experience cannot be stressed enough as the examples and the pitfalls described in the chapter amply illustrate. Implementing service guarantees and service-level agreements will require dedication and a well balanced plan. We identified the major building blocks and guiding principles of the implementation process.

Both service guarantees and service-level agreements can be powerful devices to link the service delivery processes to customer satisfaction. They can help to:[16]

- Reduce customer buying risk and ensure outstanding service delivery
- Ensure an adequate service recovery, which results in a more favourable image for the firm in terms of quality and value
- Establish a company's competitive image in the customer's mind as the superior service provider
- Enhance customer feedback, both positive and negative.

Review and discussion questions

- What are the major differences between service guarantees and service-level agreements?

- Look up an example of a firm using a service guarantee and evaluate it (for example, does it contain all the necessary information to be a service guarantee?) What is the purpose of the service guarantee? Is it effective?

- If you want to use internal service guarantees or SLAs in your company, what kind of service process are you going to start with?

Notes and references

1 The PPT Telecom example that we use throughout this chapter has been discussed in Thomassen, J. P. (1996) *Buitengewone service- en tevredenheidsgaranties* (Extraordinary service and satisfaction guarantees). Deventer: Kluwer bedrijfswetenschappen.

2 Hart, C. W. L. (1988) 'The power of unconditional service guarantees', *Harvard Business Review*, Vol 66, No 4.

3 Marmorstein H., Sarel, D. and Lassar, W. M. (2001) 'Increasing the persuasiveness of a service guarantee: the role of service process evidence', *Journal of Services Marketing*, Vol 15, No 2, 147–59.

4 Lufthansa Airlines, advertisement in the *Wall Street Journal*, 9 Mar 1987.

5 Ibid.

6 www.interliner.nl

7 'Customer service: The last word', *Inc. Magazine*, Aug 1992.

8 Rust, R. T., Zahorik, A. J. and Keiningham, T. J. (1996) *Service Marketing*. New York: Harper Collins College Publishers.

9 Tucci, L. A. and Talaga, J. (1997), 'Service guarantees and consumers evaluation of services', *Journal of Services Marketing*, Vol 11, No 1, 10–18.

10 Kandampully, J. and Butler, L. (2001) 'Service guarantees: a strategic mechanism to minimize customers' perceived risk in service organizations', *Managing Service Quality*, Vol 11, No 2, 112–20.

11 Hiles, A. N. (1994) 'Service level agreements: Panacea or pain', *The TQM Magazine*, Vol 6, No 2, 14–16.

12 The case information is based on a study developed by Darline Vandaele in her graduation thesis 'The impact of Service Level Agreement on the operational system of service companies' under the supervision of Paul Gemmel. Many of the information has been captured in an interview with Mr Kris Van Den Briel, COO of Securis.

13 Ishikawa, K. (1996) Guide to Quality Control, Quality Control, New York.

14 Hart, C. W. L. (1995) 'The power of internal guarantees', *Harvard Business Review*, Vol 73, No 1, Jan–Feb, 64–73; and Epelman, M.S. (1994) 'Internal service guarantees. A constructive approach to errors', *Proceedings of the 3rd International Research Seminar in Service Management*, IAE, Aix-en-Provence, France.

15 Argyris, C. (1990) *Overcoming Organizational Defences*. Needham Heights: Allyn & Bacon.

16 Kandampully, J. and Butler, L. (2001) op. cit.

Suggested further reading

Hart, C. W. L. (1993) *Extraordinary Guarantees: A new way to build quality throughout your company and to ensure satisfaction of your customers*. AMACOM. Anyone who wants to learn more about service guarantees should turn to this book, which is definitely the most complete work on the topic. It is very accessible thanks to the numerous examples.

Hart, C. W. L. (1995) 'The power of internal guarantees', *Harvard Business Review*, Vol 73, No 1, 64–73.

Hiles, A. (1993) *Service Level Agreements. Managing cost and quality in service relationships*. London: Chapman & Hall. This concise book is of practical help when drawing up service-level agreements. It contains plenty of checklists which help managers to avoid common pitfalls.

Marmorstein, H., Sarel, D. and Lassar, W. M. (2001) 'Increasing the persuasiveness of a service guarantee: the role of service process evidence', *Journal of Services Marketing*, Vol 15, No 2, 147–59. In this article, the effects of service process evidence, compensation and prior beliefs about the service providers are investigated in the context of service guarantees. It is an example of the kind of research currently being done.

PART THREE

Human resources in service organizations

Bart Van Looy

Services are processes involving both service employees and customers. The simultaneity of services leads to an inherent link between employees' behaviour, their motivation, competencies, satisfaction and commitment, and customers' perceptions of service quality and hence satisfaction. As a result, human resources (HR) practices play a crucial role in the management of service operations. These are discussed extensively in Chapter 9, where we introduce three crucial notions which service-oriented HR practices should address: competencies, collaboration and empowerment.

In Chapter 10, we address competencies by taking a broader look at an integrated HR framework, which is centred around the notion of competencies. Ways of defining and assessing competencies are discussed.

Of course, not all services are alike (as has been argued in Chapter 1) and so we introduce in Chapter 10 three different forms of competencies: behavioural repertoire, technical skills and personal characteristics and link them to the three different types of services described in Chapter 1 maintenance-interactive, task-interactive and personal-interactive services. Competence development strategies will vary with the nature of the competency, so we conclude with an integrated framework connecting the nature of the service process, the relative importance of the different forms of competencies and hence the relevance of competence development actions.

When talking about competence development, it is tempting to look upon this process from an individual perspective. However, competence development has a highly relational side. We highlight the importance of collaborative relationships in Chapter 11, thereby completing our overview of competencies and their development.

In Chapter 12, we discuss the notion of empowerment. Two levels can be discerned here – empowerment at the individual level and at the organizational level. Empowerment at the individual level is linked closely to the notion of motivation. We will examine closely the meaning of empowerment as a motivational construct and will also look at the implications for leadership. With empowerment at the organizational level, redistributing power, rewards, information and knowledge are seen as crucial. It will become clear that organizations functioning in this way tend to achieve higher levels of employee and customer satisfaction, and even profitability. This brings us back to where we began: HR practices do make a difference in services. The same message can be found in Chapter 13 where we will discuss the notion of role stress and its consequences. Front-line employees, in particular, are regularly confronted with multiple and sometimes conflicting requirements. This observation stems directly from both the simultaneity and heterogeneity that characterizes services. Hence addressing the phenomenon of role stress becomes a specific point of attention for service environments.

CHAPTER 9

The role of human resource practices in service organizations

Bart Van Looy · Koen Dewettinck · Dirk Buyens · Tine Vandenbossche

INTRODUCTION

Imagine you are shopping in a large department store in one of Europe's many famous shopping streets.

You arrive at the counter with several items you would like to buy and you think you are lucky: there are no customers waiting at the desk and there are three members of staff just waiting to serve you. At least that idea crosses your mind for a moment. As you approach, you notice that they are talking to each other. Is this a staff meeting perhaps?

You put all the items on the desk in front of the lady you like the most (at first sight) and you smile. Important issues are obviously being discussed; your presence is hardly noticed. After a minute you take off the smile and try a small cough. Too modest. The discussion continues, but now another staff member joins the debate.

'Is it here that I have to pay?' you try finally, choosing English so as to avoid language disputes. One of the three employees half turns, picks up the pile of goods, takes out scissors and continues the discussion with her colleagues. You sigh with relief; things are at least progressing. Tickets are detached by means of the scissors and put on a pile. Suddenly there are two piles – goods and tickets. Job done, scissors put away, discussion continues.

The two who have dominated the discussion leave; end of discussion you hope. Silence falls – for a moment. Number two takes the goods and starts to organize them so they fit nicely into a bag. You have your credit card ready when you notice that the tickets are still there in their nice pile. The conversation starts up again. No, it is not about new ways of organizing floor space, recent changes in working conditions or the latest initiatives aimed at improving customer satisfaction. No, it is about one of the colleagues having an affair with someone working in the warehouse.

You tap your credit card on the desk. An employee looks up. 'Can I pay with this card?' 'Yes', she replies. 'And when?' you enquire. A name is yelled through the store. Customers all start to look in your direction. You start to sweat a little and produce a weak smile. The employee who had left a couple of minutes before starts to move in your direction again – only slowly as the story of the affair has to be related to a colleague filling the racks. You produce the 'I don't want to be annoying, but I have a plane to catch' routine. Another yell.

Now you start to consider the possibility of just walking out. You hesitate just too long; someone picks up the pile of tickets. Between ticket three and ticket four, a short break seems appropriate; the colleague filling the racks is in need of some details.

Finally, you can pay. You stumble out of the store. Out on the street you open up the bag to see the clothes you bought. They look great; it was all worth it. Then your eye falls on the pair of socks you just bought, more specifically the place where the ticket was removed, or rather the large hole where the ticket was removed. The scissors.

For a moment you consider the possibility of going back into the shop. Then you look upwards and see that it is a beautiful day, too nice a day to spend in a department store.

The human resources of a service provider and the way in which they work are the most crucial factors in the company's performance. The intrinsic nature of services leads to a clear relationship between the role of employees, on the one hand, and the success of the service delivery, on the other. We will look in this chapter at the findings of several studies which have documented and refined this relationship.

This will allow us to establish crucial elements that are central to the management of human resources in service environments – competencies, collaboration and empowerment – which will be further explored in Chapters 10 to 12. In addition, Chapter 13 will tackle the issue of role stress as it relates directly to the notions of simultaneity and heterogeneity that characterizes services.

Objectives

By the end of this chapter, you should be able to discuss:

- how the nature of services, in particular its simultaneity, explains the crucial role of HR practices for services

- how the relationship between employees' behaviour and feelings and customer satisfaction eventually will affect service firms' profitability

- relevant HRM models that can be used as the basis for designing relevant HR practices

- the identification of key elements of HR practices for service firms – competencies, collaboration and empowerment

THE NATURE OF SERVICES

In practice, it is difficult in a service operation to distinguish clearly between the service, the process of providing the service, and the system and procedures which deliver it. One of the unique attributes of services is the customer's participation in its production, which we called simultaneity in Chapter 1. The service itself always concerns an act involving the customer; as a result quality will also be perceived by the customer in terms of this interaction.

Simultaneity as an inherent characteristic of services means that service organizations have a permeable boundary between themselves and their customers. There is both psychological and physical closeness between service providers and consumers. Service employees and consumers frequently work together, observe each other and interact. As a consequence, what employees experience in their work is communicated to consumers. Dissatisfied, unmotivated or frustrated employees bring their feelings with them when interacting with the customer, and these feelings are transmitted during interactions. We can all tell stories about how the behaviour of service employees in a restaurant affects our global impression of the overall service quality. Whereas in some the customer is given the impression that he or she is lucky to be served at all, in others the customer emerges after the meal feeling totally spoiled and well looked after.

Schneider and Bowen have documented this relationship extensively.[1] In a series of studies on the relationship between the experiences of employees at work and customer perceptions of service quality, the findings point to the same conclusions over and over again. The way employees feel and act has an impact on the quality of the service delivered: satisfied people deliver good-quality service!

Let's take a closer look at one of their studies. To examine the relationship between employees' perception of and satisfaction with HR practices, and customers' evaluation of service quality, data was gathered from 28 branches of a service company. Employees could express their satisfaction with features such as work facilities, supervisory characteristics and development opportunities. At the same time and independently, data was collected on customers' perceptions of service quality. Both elements of the study were strongly correlated. We would like to stress that the data stemmed from the same company. The type of service and the overall routines within these 28 branches were the same. It was the difference in employee satisfaction, therefore, that became the single crucial element that accompanied – or put more strongly, caused the differences in – customer perception of service quality.

Heskett, Schlesinger and Sasser[2] also stress the connection between employee and customer satisfaction within the service profit chain model, developed at the Harvard Business School (introduced in Chapter 4). Here the relationship between employee and customer satisfaction is called the 'satisfaction mirror'. Empirical evidence supporting this effect is abundant: data collected at Rank Xerox or MCI Communications, to name but two, reveals positive relationships between the two elements. Employees feeling enthusiastic about their job not only communicate this feeling both verbally or non-verbally, but are also eager to work hard towards satisfying their customers. Customers treated in this way start to act reciprocally, increasing employee satisfaction even further. Moreover, employee loyalty is crucial; employees who stay on the job long enough not only develop their skills to a high level, but also start to know customers and their specific interests and needs. This will allow them to provide an even better, personalized and customized service. This creates more value which in turn will increase customer satisfaction.

We can conclude from these authors, therefore, that much of what happens inside a service organization cannot be hidden from the customer with whom the organization's employees interact. Achieving high levels of service quality and customer satisfaction implies that consideration is being given to employee satisfaction as well.

Linking employee and customer satisfaction with profitability

It can be argued that, despite the link between employee and customer satisfaction, neither is a final goal for service companies. A link is needed with the notion of profitability. Otherwise, the notion of happy employees relating to happy customers will only be thought of as a pleasant side effect which is a 'plus' but not 'essential' to doing business.

Here the work of Heskett, Sasser and Schlesinger provides us once again with crucial insights. They connected employee satisfaction, customer satisfaction and profitability in the well-known service profit chain. It all starts from the notion of service:[3] service capability influences employee satisfaction. Employee satisfaction in turn will lead to employee loyalty and will affect the service employees' efforts to achieve productivity and quality requirements. This in turn will affect the value created for and perceived by the customer. Value creation will lead to satisfied customers and eventually loyal customers, and this loyalty will in turn contribute to profitability.

Schlesinger and Heskett[4] demonstrate very clearly this dynamic interplay between the 'inside' and the 'outside' of the service firm – that is the interplay between employees' satisfaction and behaviour and customers' perceptions of service quality and hence satisfaction – when describing different 'cycles' that may occur in managing services.

As a first example, the *'cycle of failure'* is summarized here (*see* Figure 9.1). This cycle very often begins when an organization is looking for cost reductions in the short run.

As an attempt to reduce costs in the short run, companies start by looking for people who are willing to work for wages marginally above statutory minimum levels. Jobs are reduced to a series of simple and boring tasks that require almost no training, since training costs money. Involving people in the company itself – in decisions, or simply more in their own jobs – costs time and effort as well, so it is easy simply not to bother. Technology is used to install some degree of quality control.

The rationale goes something like this:

'Of course, people are not really motivated when working in such a system and yes, they do leave the company frequently and after a short period of employment, but who cares? The pool of unemployed people out there is large, and we can easily find new employees.'

What becomes clear here is that while in the short run employee costs might be minimized, the effects in the long run are disastrous. The dynamics installed at the employee level lead to indifferent attitudes towards customers. These in turn translate into poor perceptions of service quality by the same customers, which results in a further increase in employee dissatisfaction, and leads to lower sales and profit margins. This will eventually inspire the next 'squeezing round' and everything will start all over again.

Several factors explain how companies can get 'seduced' into this cycle. Technology is assumed to be the saviour that will allow a company to reduce the unpredictability of human behaviour, so investing in technology is seen as more important than investing in people. It is clear, however, that while the use of technology for some service industries will increase in the future, it will be difficult

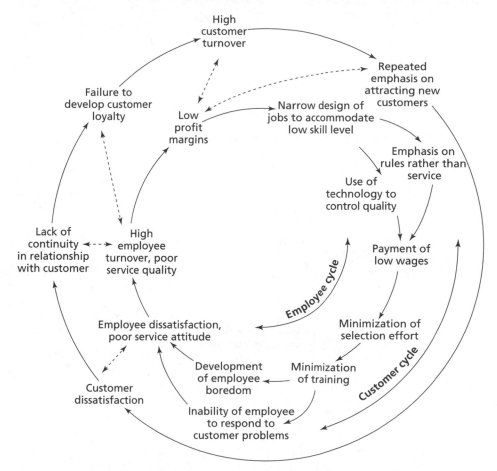

Figure 9.1 The cycle of failure

Source: Reprinted from 'Breaking the cycle of failure in services', Schlesinger and Heskett, *Sloan Management Review*, Spring 1991, by permission of the Publishers. Copyright © (1998) by Sloan Management Review Association. All rights reserved.

for many services to replace the human factor completely. We will discuss this issue in greater detail in Chapter 17 when we examine the relevance of IT developments for service encounters.

It is also argued that factors such as the inadequate level of talent in the labour pool, the failure of educational systems and the loss of past values, such as the work ethic, force companies to take such an approach. What we tend to forget here is that companies do play a role in society and that the concepts and views with which they approach the labour force tend to be self-reinforcing.

Perhaps most important in creating the cycle of failure are the pressures for short-term performance, and linked to this, the lack of accurate information. Too many companies still fail to compute or are unable to compute the impact of employee turnover on customer retention, or how customer acquisition costs relate to customer retention costs. The costs of wages and training, on the other hand, can be calculated exactly. The short-term savings become clear from a look at the accounts. While improving recruitment, training and development, and rewards and recognition are all acknowledged to be important, the budget has to be managed.

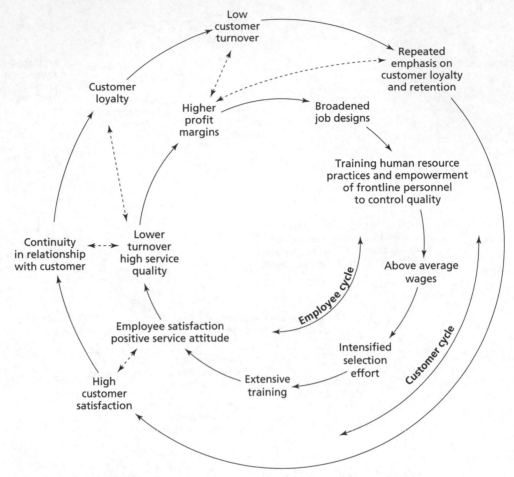

Figure 9.2 The cycle of success

Source: Reprinted from 'Breaking the cycle of failure in services', Schlesinger and Heskett, *Sloan Management Review*, Spring 1991, by permission of the Publishers. Copyright © (1998) by Sloan Management Review Association. All rights reserved.

Long-term trends occur more slowly and less dramatically and hence are usually at the bottom of managers' lists of priorities. Since it is hard to quantify the impact of long-term events on intermediate earnings, efforts put into improving the quality of the workforce tend to be minimal. Moreover, since 'only what gets measured gets managed', the impact of the inner part of the cycle of failure is often not known or calculated.[5]

These dynamic relationships can also take on a positive face. Schlesinger and Heskett juxtapose the cycle of failure described above with its counterpart, *the cycle of success* (*see* Figure 9.2). Here the dynamics going on inside the company positively affect what goes on outside, and vice versa.

Operating in the services sector, therefore, without devoting a great deal of effort to service employees is like noticing the car is nearly out of gas and starting to drive faster. The longer you go on with this attitude the worse it will get.

Since managing human resources is of vital importance, let us take a look at what is most important in terms of human resources management for service firms.

Exhibit 9.1

Rising sales at Au Bon Pain[6]

Au Bon Pain is a chain of French bakery-cafés on the East coast of the United States. Initially, store managers were being paid salaries marginally above local market averages and were allowed very little discretion regarding how they managed their stores. A 'carousel' pattern of high manager and employee turnover was normal for the firm.

To turn things around, new contracts were developed which involved the company and store managers splitting any profits above a certain target. At the same time, managers were given freedom to modify procedures, staff policy, and even the layout of the store.[7] Headquarters started to redefine their own role. Instead of putting emphasis on control, field coaching and consulting became the priority. In a number of cases this led to a doubling of sales volume.

One local manager, taking things even further, started to look for people willing to work 50 to 60 hours per week. The increased productivity and the longer work hours allowed him to reduce head count by about 70 per cent. Absenteeism dropped to nearly zero (as a missed day meant lost overtime pay). Turnover for the low-skilled, entry-level jobs went down to 10 per cent, where as 200 per cent is quite normal in this industry. Sales soared as customers noticed the changed atmosphere and started to develop relationships with the people they saw every day behind the counter. His front-line employees earned approximately double the industry norm.

HUMAN RESOURCE MANAGEMENT FOR SERVICES

HRM: what is it?

The concept of human resources management (HRM) began in the 1970s. Formerly, employees were regarded more or less as a cost, but with the evolution of human capital theory it was argued that people could be seen as an asset as well. Later on in the 1980s, it was seen that human resources management could and should be tied into a company's business strategy, since committed personnel were shown to make a substantial difference in an era of increasingly stiff global competition. This position has now been widely accepted and is the main difference between HRM and 'classical' personnel management. The traditional tasks of personnel management have been enlarged from a basic managing of the workforce to larger, more global issues – such as the organization's culture, new types of training and contributing to or even forming organizational direction.[8]

Different models can be found within the domain of human resources management. We will discuss three of these models, each of which we believe makes a valuable contribution to our understanding of HRM. Considered together, they provide us with an integrated view of HRM.

- The *Michigan model* stresses the idea of strategic matching and the basic building blocks of HRM.
- The *Harvard model* directs our attention towards the diversity of stakeholders involved and introduces the four Cs of HRM.
- The work done at *Warwick* (UK) results in a view of HRM in which process takes its proper place.

The Michigan model: linking HR practices and business requirements

In this model the resource side is emphasized. People in organizations are resources and should be managed in a way that is consistent with organizational requirements. Congruence with organizational strategy and effectiveness is crucial; we should look for the 'fit' between human resources and business strategies. Human resources management should be in line with and supportive to achieving business goals. Being supportive means developing appropriate HRM systems – such as selection, performance appraisal, rewards and development.[9]

This way of thinking stresses the importance of developing strategic contingencies, whereby human resource practices are designed according to the type of strategy being adopted. For instance, if a company is striving for differentiation by means of innovation, creative and innovative people should be selected, and the company should invest in a broad range of competencies, foster cross-functional co-operation, and design dual-ladder careers.

While this approach may be attractive at first sight, it has its shortcomings. HRM is here cast rather reactively; once the strategy is defined, the human resources are 'adapted' to it. Such an HRM approach reduces the importance of the human factor to a large extent – not necessarily the most appropriate course of action in a service environment.[10] The quality of service delivery will depend on the commitment of the service employees to the defined service concept. Casting your employees in a mere 'compliance' role does not seem the best way to create this commitment. That is why it is important to address HR values and practices when defining the service concept (*see* Chapter 2) – a process in which employees could also be involved.

It is also worth noting that within this model strategy is approached as a rational process with generic typologies of strategy as valid starting points.[11] However, generic strategies such as cost leadership or differentiation are not as mutually exclusive as was once thought. Moreover, strategy has as much to do with process as with content. Strategy formation and change often form an incremental process which has its own, often not so rational, logic. Within this change process, HR practices can also play a role. In this context defining HRM as selection, performance appraisal, rewards and development is too narrow a definition.

We need therefore to complement this view with other models that do more justice to the complexity faced.[12]

The Harvard model: stakeholders working on the four Cs

A less prescriptive model was developed at the Harvard Business School.[13] Here the human aspect of HRM is stressed. HRM is defined here as:

> *'all management decisions and actions that affect the nature of the relationship between the organization and the employee.'*

This implies a broader range of areas than in HRM as defined by the Michigan school. Beer and his colleagues define four HRM policy areas: human resource flows, reward systems, employee influence and work systems.

1. *Human resources flows* are comprised of activities related to managing the flow of people in, through and out of the organization: recruitment and selection, placement, development, performance appraisal, promotion and termination.
2. *Reward systems* imply everything that is related to attracting and retaining employees: pay systems, motivation, and benefits.

3. *Employee influence* refers to the levels of (employee) authority and power and the way in which they are designed within the organization.
4. Finally, *work systems* refers to the way that work is designed and the arrangements of tasks and technology which achieve optimum results.

The Harvard model recognizes different stakeholders, each with their own interests: shareholders, management, employees and unions, government and the community. Outcomes that need to be achieved within these different policy domains and among the different stakeholders involved are called the four Cs:[14]

- *Commitment* of employees to their work and organization.
- *Congruence* between the objectives of the different stakeholders – employees and their families, the organization and its objectives, shareholders, community and society at large.
- *Competence* now and in the future – to what extent can one attract, keep and develop the skills and knowledge of the people involved.
- *Cost effectiveness* – what are the consequences of certain policies in terms of wages, benefits, turnover, motivation, employment and so on? Costs can be considered at the individual, organizational or even societal level.

Within this model, management's role is stressed. General managers need to develop a vision or viewpoint about how they wish to see employees involved in and developed by the organization. This model integrates all stakeholders as well as the content and process of HRM and strategy, but it still stresses this integration more in terms of strategy implementation than in terms of strategy formation. As such, the model tends to be moving in one direction only – from strategies to HRM practices to employee behaviours with the manager as the driving force. Warwick contributes a more balanced view.

Warwick: bringing in context and process

Academics at Warwick University[15] take a process-oriented view of HRM in which the importance of context is also stressed. Sparrow and Hiltrop[16] adopt the following starting points for their work:

- Strategy should not really be seen as a ready-formed output to which HRM can be easily moulded. Changes in structure, culture or other areas of HRM can precede strategic change and therefore shape the way that the organization thinks about strategy. Strategy can be as much bottom-up as top-down.
- As changes in strategy and HRM tend to occur over a longer time frame, the process of change becomes as significant as the content of change. HRM systems should not be designed in an overly rational way when the processes that create the need for them are anything but rational.

Given these observations, the human resources policy framework as developed by the Harvard scholars was extended. While adopting the different policy domains (the HRM content) from Harvard, the Warwick model includes the context in which HRM and the organization as a whole are situated.

When studying organizational change processes and HRM practices, it becomes clear that taking a number of different pathways can achieve the same end result. These pathways will always be context-specific and influenced by the organization's history. Learning by doing is important. Proponents of this model are HRM champions when it comes down to successfully implementing new HR practices, such as building engagement and involvement, creating commitment for new practices, mobilizing support within the organization and maintaining initiative.

As such, this model becomes less prescriptive in terms of defining what needs to be done, since what is best for one company will not necessarily be best for another. This point is made explicitly by Schneider and Bowen[17] in relation to services in their discussion of the recruitment process and what kind of service employees to engage, when they write:

'. . . it is not necessary to hire the best people: it is necessary to hire the best people to meet the expectations and needs of your market.'

Does this mean that the final word on the human factor in services is that everything will depend on the individual situation? The answer is both yes and no:

- *Yes, in the sense that there is no single best way.* Appropriate action will always be context-specific. Following by-the-book rules and action plans developed by others will result in formulas that will at best be copies of the 'real thing', since the initial ingredients and circumstances will always be different for every organization.
- *No, in the sense that lessons can be learned from others.* Insights and concepts can be valuable starting points and even inspiring guidelines for working out actions within specific contexts. However, they will always require adaptation and modification during the process, resulting in new concepts and models as well.

HR practices for services: competence, collaboration, empowerment

Three tendencies are especially important for all service organizations: paying attention to competencies and their continuous development, establishing collaborative relationships, and empowering service employees. All three elements should be reflected in HR practices for services.

How did we arrive at this conclusion? We will turn again to the Harvard Business School. You will remember that the service profit chain kicks off at the left side with the notion of service capability. Service capability is defined by Heskett *et al.*[18] as being composed of several elements:

- the latitude in delivering results to customers;
- a clear expression of boundaries within which front-line employees are permitted to act;
- excellent job training;
- well-engineered support systems, such as service facilities and information systems;
- recognition and rewards for doing jobs well, determined at least partially by the levels of customer satisfaction achieved;
- rigorous recruitment and selection practices.

Where did this definition come from?

Intrigued by the strong relationship between employee and customer satisfaction – described earlier as the mirroring effect – the Harvard scholars began an investigation into the sources of employee satisfaction. A study by Schlesinger and Zornitsky[19] revealed that about two-thirds of employee satisfaction levels were caused by just three factors: the latitude given to employees by their management to meet customer needs, the authority given to them to serve customers, and finally, possession of the knowledge and skills needed to serve customers.

Table 9.1 Sources of employee satisfaction

Determinants of employee satisfaction	Explanatory power*
Latitude is given to meet customer	36.6%
I have the authority to serve the customer	19.2%
I have the knowledge and skills to serve the customer	12.9%
Rewards are provided for serving the customer well	7.3%
Customer satisfaction is a high priority with the director/manager	4.2%
Production requirements are reasonably balanced with serving the customer	3.1%
Supervision overall is satisfactory	2.8%
Underwriting training is satisfactory	2.1%
13 other determinants	11.8%
TOTAL	100.0%

* Each figure represents the proportion of the total R^2 (correlation between determinants and general feelings about capability to do the job) explained by each determinant. Explanatory power represents the amount of variance explained by the antecedents.

Source: Schlesinger, L. A. and Zornitsky, J. (1991) Reprinted with permission from *Human Resource Planning*, Vol 14, No 2 (1991). Copyright © 1998 by The Human Resource Planning Society, 317 Madison Avenue, Suite 1509, New York.

When looking at these findings, two central notions are clear: competence and empowerment.[20] This is seen from an examination of the top three elements of Table 9.1. Latitude refers to the freedom employees are given to act as the situation requires. The idea of having authority to serve the customer is closely linked to latitude. These two together read like a textbook definition of empowerment. Knowledge and skills clearly bring the word 'competence' to mind.

Thus, competence and empowerment form the core of the human side of service capability, and hence are crucial when discussing relevant HR practices for service firms. We will go into these two concepts in greater detail in Chapters 10 and 12.

We have also inserted the idea of collaboration, however. Why do we want to stress this? First of all, services are often provided by means of an interplay between a number of service employees; collaboration can help to deliver seamless service. Teamwork is often a prerequisite for success in services.[21] In some cases, clear arrangements, task division and allocating responsibilities might also do the job. However, as discussed extensively in Chapter 1, services are characterized by a certain degree of heterogeneity. In other words, as a service employee you will from time to time be confronted with the unforeseen, in many cases also the unknown. At these moments support from and collaboration among service employees become crucial. Collaboration also plays a crucial role in terms of competence development; learning and improving are social processes as well, something often forgotten. This is an issue deserving specifically the attention of service scholars and managers given the nature of services.

The notion of heterogeneity, stemming from simultaneity, directs our attention as well to the phenomenon of role stress; front-line employees, in particular, are vulnerable in this respect as will become clear in Chapter 13. Because of the simultaneity of services, service employees might become confronted with conflicting demands. The tension between satisfying customers and at the same time meeting productivity and quality goals emerges as a frequently encountered issue in the daily operations of front-line employees. The American Institute of Stress went as far as to categorically identify a customer service worker as one of the ten most stressful jobs in America.[22] It is therefore worthwhile to discuss this role stress phenomena and ways to handle it, since there is a direct impact on the behaviour of employees and the attitudes and intentions of customers and employees.

CONCLUSION

In this chapter we have looked at why HR practices matter for service organizations. Given the simultaneity of services, there is a 'mirror' effect – that is, the behaviour and feelings of service employees are reflected in customer perceptions of service quality and hence will affect customer satisfaction. This interdependence between what is going on inside a firm and how customers and the market perceive and react to it, becomes very clear when the cycles of failure and success developed at the Harvard School are considered. The Michigan, Harvard and Warwick models were discussed in some detail. With these models in mind, three central notions were established – competencies, collaboration and empowerment – which are key elements of HRM practices in the services sector. In addition, and closely related to these central notions, role stress, especially in relation to front-line employees, deserves our specific attention. These key elements are discussed in greater detail in the remaining chapters of Part Three.

Review and discussion questions

- Despite the crucial role of human resources, and hence human resources management, in relation to value creation, a lot of companies still do not adopt HR practices accordingly. Why is this the case? What is needed to arrive at a more widespread implementation of HR investment principles?

- The dynamics and relationships outlined here stem from research in service firms. Would you consider these findings to be relevant for manufacturing environments as well? Why (not)?

Notes and references

[1] *See* Schneider, B. and Bowen, D. (1985) 'New service design, development and implementation and the employee', in George, W. and Marshall, C. (eds) *New Services*. Chicago: The American Marketing Association; Schneider, B. and Bowen, D. (1993) 'Human resource management is critical', *Organizational Dynamics*, 39–52; and Schneider, B. and Bowen, D. (1995) *Winning the Service Game*. Boston: Harvard Business Press.

[2] For an excellent overview, *see* Heskett, J., Sasser, W. and Schlesinger, L. (1997) *The Service Profit Chain*. New York: Free Press.

[3] 'Service capability' refers to all elements that constitute the operational service delivery system.

[4] Schlesinger, L. A. and Heskett, J. (1991) 'Breaking the cycle of failure in services', *Sloan Management Review*, Spring.

[5] Given the importance of adequate performance measures, we have devoted a complete chapter to this issue (Chapter 18).

[6] For more details on this example, *see* Schlesinger, L. A. and Heskett, J. (1991), op. cit.; Heskett, J., Sasser, W. and Schlesinger, L. (1997), op. cit.

[7] Of course, one should stay within certain standard parameters.

[8] For a more extensive and excellent discussion on these developments, *see* Sparrow, P. and Hiltrop, J. M. (1996) *European Human Resources Management in Transition*. Prentice Hall.

9 *See* Tichy, N., Fombrun, C. and Devanna, M. (1982) 'Strategic human resources management', *Sloan Management Review*, Vol 23, No 2, 47–61; and Fombrun, C., Tichy, N. and Devanna, M. (1984) *Strategic Human Resources Management*. New York: Wiley.

10 In fact, we do not believe in this approach for manufacturing firms either.

11 Sparrow, P. and Hiltrop, J. M. (1996), op. cit.

12 Besides the models we discuss here, we refer the interested reader as well to the ideas developed by Creed and Miles on HR investment principles, as well as the work of Ulrich on adding value to HR practices: Miles, R. and Creed, W. (1995) 'Organizational forms and managerial philosophies – a descriptive and analytical review', *Research in Organisational Behaviour: An annual series of analytical essays and critical review*, Vol 17, 333–72; Ulrich, D. (1997a) *Human Resource Champions, The Next Agenda for Adding Value to HR-practices*, Harvard: Harvard Business School Press; Ulrich, D. (1997b) 'Measuring human resources: an overview of practice and prescription for results', *Human Resource Management*, Vol 36, 302–20. Ulrich, D., Brockbank, W., Yeung, A. and Lake, D. G. (1995) 'Human resource competencies: an empirical assessment', *Human Resource Management*, Vol 34, No 4, 473–95; and Yeung, A., Brockbank, W. and Ulrich, D. (1995) 'Lower cost, higher value: Human resource function in transformation', *Human Resource Planning*, Vol 17, No 3, 1–16.

13 Beer, M., Spector, B., Lawrence, P., Mills, D. and Walton, R. (1984) *Managing Human Assets*. New York: Free Press; and Beer, M., Lawrence, P., Mills, D. and Walton, R. (1985) *Human Resources Management*. New York: Free Press.

14 Beer, M., Lawrence, P., Mills, D. and Walton, R. (1985), op. cit.

15 Hendry, C. and Pettigrew, A. (1986) 'The practice of strategic human resource management', *Personnel Review*, Vol 15, 3–8; and Hendry, C. (1991) 'International comparisons of human resources management: putting the firm in the frame', *International Journal of Human Resources Management*, Issue 2, 415–40.

16 Sparrow, P. and Hiltrop, J. M. (1996), op. cit., p. 16.

17 Schneider, B. and Bowen, D. (1995), op. cit.

18 Heskett, J., Sasser, W. and Schlesinger, L. (1997), op. cit., p. 114.

19 Schlesinger, L. A. and Zornitsky, J. (1991) 'Job satisfaction, service capability, and customer satisfaction: an examination of linkages and management implications', *Human Resource Planning*, Vol 14, No 2, 141–9.

20 Despite the objections of Heskett *et al.*, we do use the notion of empowerment.

21 For a very convincing plea for teamwork in professional services, *see* Maister, D. (1997) *True Professionalism*. New York: Free Press.

22 Miller, A., Springen, K., Gordon, J., Murr, A., Cohen, B. and Drew, L. (1988) 'Stress on the job', *Newsweek*, 25 April, 40–45.

Suggested further reading

Schlesinger, L. A. and Heskett, J. (1991) 'Breaking the cycle of failure in services', *Sloan Management Review*, Spring. This article provides a clear account of the dynamic interplay between employees and customers in services.

Schneider, B. and Bowen, D. (1995) *Winning the Service Game*. Boston: Harvard Business Press. An overview of how the human factor is interwoven into the process of delivering services and how HR practices should reflect this.

CHAPTER 10

Competencies and service organizations

Walter Stevens · Dries Faems · Bart Van Looy · Tine Vandenbossche ·
Dirk Buyens

INTRODUCTION

HR practices need to be balanced and integrated in order to reflect the specific context, as became clear when looking at the different HRM models in the previous chapter. Moreover, competencies play a crucial role in HR practices for service firms. As a result, we need to address issues related to competency-based HR practices: what are different types of competencies and how does their importance relate to the types of services? How can one work on competence development? We shall go into this in more detail in the next section. First, however, we shall indicate how the notion of competencies can find its own place in an integrated HR approach. Complementary to this overall framework, we shall focus on some operational approaches to work with competencies: how to inventory competencies, how to develop profiles of them, and how to assess them.

Objectives

By the end of this chapter, you should be able to discuss:

- the general outline of competency-based HR practices
- characteristics of different deployment processes and their implications
- how one can start to operationalize the notion of competencies and what relevant tools might look like to proceed here; both on the level of identifying relevant competencies as on gathering information on existing competencies
- the different types of competencies one can distinguish between, and how their importance relates to different types of services
- what the process of developing competencies looks like at the individual level
- different development strategies and what they might imply
- appropriate competence development strategies for different types of competencies

DESIGNING COMPETENCY-BASED HR PRACTICES

A competency-based HR framework

HR practices balance between – and connect – employees and the organization. They act as an interface between organizational goals and characteristics (e.g. structures) and the individual, working within the firm. In the past, the organizational characteristics tended to dominate the discussion; most of the efforts in designing an operational HR system went to job design, task profiles, recruitment procedures, and so on. Introducing the notion of competencies offers possibilities to create more balance between organizational requirements and the functioning of employees.[1] More specifically, competency systems can be developed to link the strategic core competencies of the organization with the individual competencies of the employees. Following Prahalad and Hamel (1990) core competencies have to be defined as 'specific combinations of internal resources that can constitute a competitive advantage for the organization'. Individual competencies, on the other hand, are defined here as human characteristics related to effective performance. These characteristics can be seen as indicating ways of acting, behaving or thinking. These individual competencies are considered more or less generalizable over situations and enduring over a period of time.[2]

Figure 10.1 outlines such an approach. Both organizational goals and structure as well as the individual competencies and performance find a place here. Developing the match between them is the continuous challenge for HR practices.

The organizational mission and vision, and their translation into the firm's structure bring us eventually to different roles and jobs. Roles and jobs are not the same: roles are situated more directly in concrete activities (e.g. selling projects) whereas jobs are (often) a combination of roles. It is crucial here to explain not

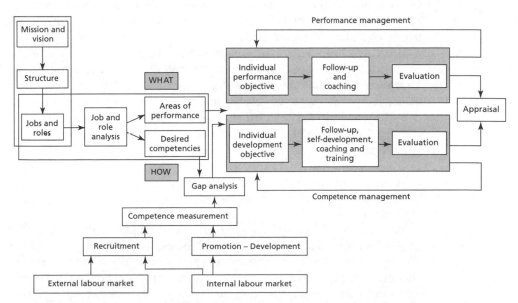

Figure 10.1 Quintessence Performance and Competency Management Model[3]

Source: © Quintessence Consulting Belgium.

only what needs to be done, the areas of performance, but as well to indicate *how* one can achieve this and what kind of competencies are needed with regard to the areas of performance.

Take the example of a sales engineer selling sophisticated technical systems to professional users. In terms of areas of performance, one can stipulate that the sales engineer should promote the systems in question, sell them, and take care of the customer relationships established. These areas can be complemented by specific performance objectives, such as realizing a certain turnover in new sales and achieving an adequate level of customer retention and loyalty (e.g. at least one out of two existing customers should place an order again within the next year).

However, these elements – areas of performance and objectives – do not say anything about how to 'go for it'; that is, which competencies are needed to succeed as an individual within the job. So defining necessary or required competencies explicitly adds value to HR practices. The notion of roles integrates both elements: areas of performance and competencies necessary to achieve results.

When competencies are made explicit, they offer a guiding framework for both recruitment practices and development actions when complemented with a gap analysis. Let us return to our sales engineer. Required competencies here include, among others, customer orientation, interpersonal understanding, empathy, initiative, technical expertise, and persuasion. Comparing the level of the required competencies with the information gathered during the recruitment or promotion/mutation process allows one to make relevant decisions both in terms of hiring and in terms of instruction and/or development programs.

Working on the tension between desired and actual competencies is not only relevant for recruitment or promotion/mutation. Given the ever increasing rate of change companies face today, it should become a 'daily' routine. This can be achieved by complementing the 'classical' performance management process which focuses on the realization of objectives, with a competency management process addressing competency levels and their evolution over time as depicted in the upper right half of Figure 10.1.

We just have illustrated why gap analysis can be seen as a useful approach for comparing the desired and actual competency levels of employees. However, this approach can entail the risk of 'organizational rigidity', a risk which is not implied as such in the 'system' itself, but rather in the process characteristics of the deployment trajectory. Recall that everything starts with the mission and vision of the organization, which we called the service concept (*see* Chapter 2). As one starts to organize competencies accordingly, i.e. in line with the required service strategy, one bears the risk of reducing what is needed to what is needed *today*. Stated otherwise, one might arrive at a situation in which too much 'homogeneity' has been created, which limits the potential of the organization to adapt to changing circumstances.

Within today's changing environments, organizations have to reconsider the desired competencies on a regular basis, in order to be able to respond to changes that challenge the competitive position of the organization. So, one should not push the use of the aforementioned approach (Figure 10.1) to the extreme where only competencies are to be found within the organization that reflect the '*hic et nunc*' strategic position of the company. Keeping open possible avenues towards the future will imply – besides allocating some resources to 'playground' activities (*see* Chapter 19 on innovation) – adopting a more process-oriented approach towards competencies. Such an approach[4] goes beyond the 'control' logic that can easily become infused in HR systems. It stresses the context-specific nature of strategy which in turn is considered a continuous process (see the Warwick view on HRM discussed in the previous chapter). Within the framework of competencies, a more process-oriented orientation implies several points of attention. First of all, 'meta-competencies' enter the stage. Such meta-competencies relate to capabilities to change and redefine existing competencies. On the organizational level this introduces notions like 'double loop learning' or even the idea of the learning organization.[5] On the individual level, one can easily see the relevance of competencies which relate to learning and innovation. Conceived like this, it becomes possible to achieve an appropriate balance between stability or continuity (identity) on the one hand and novelty or change (flexibility) on the other hand. Secondly, a more process-oriented approach will benefit from adopting principles rather than strict rules,[6] a direct consequence of the co-evolving nature of strategy processes and their deployment. Finally, and in line with the previous remarks, it will come as no surprise that a process-oriented approach will advocate designing definition and implementation projects with respect to competencies as a joint effort between line management and HR staff. Such a stance will ensure the relevance, transparency and, hence, the acceptance of any system. Table 10.1 summarizes some of the key characteristics to be found in control-oriented versus process-oriented approaches regarding competencies.

By now we hear you thinking, 'OK, this might be a nice overall framework which includes some relevant accompanying guidelines with respect to deployment processes, but how can it work in practice? How can you make this notion of competency concrete so that it can become a practical aid for linking organizational goals with employees' functions and be an integral part of HR practices? And what do approaches that can identify and assess competencies look like?'

Identifying and assessing competencies

To make competencies as a notion workable within HR practices one needs a vocabulary, defining competencies and their gradations as well as adequate techniques for collecting relevant information on the presence of these competencies.

As stated above, competencies can be seen as human characteristics related to effective performance. These characteristics can be seen as indicating ways of acting, behaving, or thinking.

Relevant techniques include assessment centres as well as behaviourally-oriented interviews. Both approaches start from concrete behaviour in order to assess the presence of a competency. As such, they tend to differ rather significantly from more classical 'paper and pencil' instruments used in assessment contexts, such as personality questionnaires or IQ tests. Not that these become obsolete; in practice combining more classical tools with competency-based approaches will yield the most complete insights.

But before digging into these concrete competency instruments, we first have to say something about developing a relevant vocabulary or a competency dictionary.[7]

Table 10.1 Characteristics of Competence Management deployment processes

	Control-oriented model	Process-oriented model
Strategy		
Strategic vision	Strategy as a planning process aimed at 'adapting' to the (industrial) environment, resulting in a rather static view on competitive advantages	Strategy as a learning process in which 'co-evolving' processes figure prominently. Competitive advantage looked upon as inherently dynamic
How is strategy created?	Autonomous decision of management	Continuous interaction between different stakeholders
HRM		
HRM objectives	Create an 'external' fit between HRM and strategy by designing HR tools and designs that reflect the current strategy	Support and facilitate the definition and deployment of the strategic process, enabling organizational change
Function of HRM	Controlling (steering, governing and controlling)	Facilitating (supporting, facilitating and mobilizing)
Competencies		
On an organizational level	Core competencies as the translation of the strategy defined at the top	Core competencies as a context-specific translation of the core activities of the organization. In addition, meta competencies are introduced as operational principles that allow to combine stability and flexibility
On an individual level	Generic defined individual competencies that reflect the current core competencies and hence bear the risk of neglecting the role of change and transformation	Context specific individual competencies that reflect as well development related competencies (reflection, innovation, learning and transformational capabilities, . . .)
Competency system	Top-down linkage between strategy and individual competencies via core competencies	Interaction between meta competencies, core competencies and individual competencies that stimulate evolutionary development of strategy
Used by HRM as	Controlling instrument	Facilitating instrument

Source: Based on Faems, 2001.

Identifying relevant competencies

We face two challenges here: defining specifically what is meant by a particular competency and its constituting elements, and then identifying varying degrees within a certain competency. Take, for instance, customer service orientation. Here focusing on the client's needs and a willingness to act on it are crucial. Within this competency one can distinguish different levels, as illustrated in Table 10.2.

How does one arrive at the delineation of these competencies and their levels? Starting from scratch implies a rather intensive exercise. By looking at 'model' behaviour within a certain situation by means of observation or behavioural event interviews (*see below*), one starts to identify and describe as precisely as possible relevant behaviours reflecting the meaning of the competency. Working with contrasting exemplars is useful: Who is a role model for our idea of customer orientation and who demonstrates just the opposite? Once a list of relevant behaviours is developed,

Table 10.2 Customer orientation as a competency

Level	Description
Level 1	Shows consideration for customers, behaves in a friendly manner
Level 2	Investigates the needs and desires of customers; takes time to gain an insight into customers' problems
Level 3	Takes concrete actions to meet customers' preferences or to solve customers' problems
Level 4	When undertaking actions, the specific needs or requests of customers are taken into account explicitly: the action undertaken reflects the problem at hand and the specific concerns of the customer
Level 5	Provides customer with systematic feedback on the steps undertaken and the progress of the process
Level 6	Looks for ways to improve customer service based on concrete experiences with customers, their requests and the experienced problems

Source: © Quintessence Consulting Belgium.

degrees need to be identified. This can be done by ranking different descriptions referring to the same competency in terms of intensity, completeness or scope. Such varying degrees of the competency in question allow one to define more precisely what is meant, for instance, by customer orientation (*see* Table 10.2).

It should be clear that this description, brief as it is, covers a great deal of work: gathering data (descriptions) on relevant competencies, analysing them in terms of content and gradation, or working on issues such as reliability and validity by means of statistical analysis. In practice it will not always be possible to develop these kinds of definitions completely on one's own. Hence it is advisable to turn to specialized agencies or sources that offer workable models and instruments and eventually modify and adapt these to particular needs.

Once relevant competencies, including sub-dimensions and gradations, have been defined, one is well equipped to develop competency profiles. Working with a team of experts on certain activities and roles (supervisor, organization specialists from the HR or Quality department, employees themselves) allows one to determine the relative importance of different competencies for a particular job as well as the required levels for each competency. The different activities and roles one has to perform form the starting point here.

One can as well turn to examining – by observing – the best practices and translating these into a competency profile. The following figure gives a concrete example of the result of such an exercise carried out in a distribution company. Starting from a dictionary containing 36 different competencies, an iterative process was undertaken whereby different experts within the distribution company become involved in judging the relevance of the different competencies for the activities and roles of front-line employees, as well as the desired level for each competency, resulting in the profile that can be found in Figure 10.2. Determining the appropriate competencies is achieved here by confronting the experts with different descriptions of specific behaviour.

Progress monitoring, customer orientation and oral presentation are a few crucial competencies for the front-line employees in this company. The ability to develop a broader vision or analysing complex problems are less important competencies here.

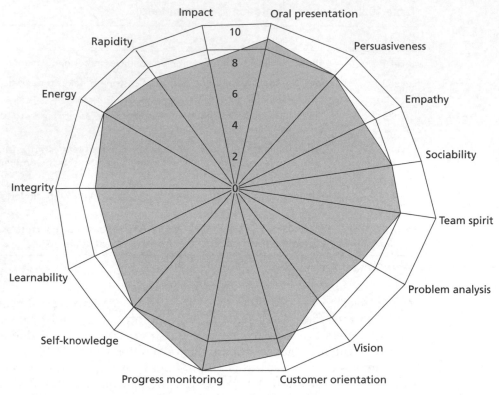

Figure 10.2 Most important competencies for front-office personnel in a distribution company
Source: © Quintessence Consulting Belgium.

This profile can then serve as a guiding framework for the processes of recruitment and promotion/mutation, as well as for development. Here the profile must be compared with the actual presence and degree of the competencies at hand. This also requires data on existing competencies, and an approach to gathering relevant information.

Before explaining how information on existing competencies can be gathered, we want to stress that, in order for competency profiles to become an effective part of daily practice, they have to be as context-specific as possible. As an example, Table 10.3 shows the definitions of three competencies, used in the competency profile of salespeople.

Although these definitions seem to be quite good at first sight, a more detailed analysis of the different functions that are present within the sales department makes it clear that these competencies are too abstract and therefore rather unpractical. After all, a large number of functions are present within the sales department. The job descriptions of two of these functions, 'key account manager' and 'presales consultant', are mentioned in Table 10.4. Based on interviews with employees that performed these jobs, one can obtain a more detailed description of the competencies mentioned above for each function. These alternative competency descriptions are also illustrated in Table 10.4.

Table 10.3 Definitions of three competencies for 'salespeople'

Competency	Definition
Knows products and services	Demonstrates breadth and depth of knowledge about ChipX's product and service offerings
Communicates effectively	Structures and conveys ideas and information to individuals and groups in a way that brings about understanding
Inspires trust	Projects a personal image of credibility and reliability that inspires confidence

By comparison with the original definitions, these competency descriptions are much more job-specific. Moreover, these alternative competency descriptions clearly illustrate that the content of the two functions is different, although both functions are part of the same sales department. Therefore such context-specific competency descriptions are much more useful when the organization wants to implement a competency-based HRM to improve the effectiveness and efficiency of the core activities that employees have to perform.

Table 10.4 Detailed definitions of three competencies for 'salespeople'

	Key Account Manager	*Presales Consultant*
Job description	The Key Account Manager is responsible for the relationships with a number of important customers. He/she has to contact these customers on a regular basis and try to discover sales opportunities	The Presales Consultant is a technical specialist who possesses extended knowledge with regard to a number of products from the portfolio of the company
Competencies		
Knows products and services	The Key Account Manager must possess enough knowledge about products and services of the company. By this he/she must be able to offer the customer an accurate picture of the portfolio of products and services that the company can deliver	The Presales Consultant must possess the necessary technical knowledge to answer technical questions of customers and/or colleagues with regard to the products in which he/she is specialized
Communicates effectively	The Key Account Manager must be able to communicate effectively and efficiently with the management of the customer	The Presales Consultant must be able to communicate effectively and efficiently with the technical specialists of the customer
Inspires trust	Externally, the Key Account Manager must be able to convince the customer to buy total integrated solutions of the company	Externally, the Presales Consultant must be able to convince the customer of the technical superiority of the product in which he/she is specialized
	Internally, the Key Account Manager must be able to convince colleagues from different teams to invest time and effort in projects for which he/she is responsible	Internally, the Presales Consultant must be able to promote products in which he/she is specialized

Gathering relevant information on existing competencies

Many techniques are available for assessing competencies or capabilities. We shall focus here on some new techniques – or at least relatively new – focusing on people's behaviour more than on their 'talk'. Since competencies underlie people's characteristics, indicating ways of behaving or thinking, they must somehow be observable in practice. By taking actual practice, i.e. behaviour, as a starting point, one can avoid the pitfalls of more traditional approaches (for instance, focusing on overall personality traits that might be of minor relevance for the concrete tasks at hand, or mistaking what is said for what is actually done).

The most straightforward way to make inferences about competencies is simply to observe behaviour. One needs to observe in a systematic way, however. Techniques used in 'assessment centres' have been flourishing in recent years. One can also try to derive the presence of competencies by means of interviews. Here again, specific approaches are developed. Let us look at these two techniques.

Assessment centres

In an assessment centre, simulations are set up that correspond to the actual role to be performed. Contextual elements can be brought in as well. For instance, in the case of the front-line employee within the distribution company, one can create a desk situation whereby customers and potential customers enter at random, telephones start to ring at the worst possible moment, and so on. Observing actual behaviour of people in these types of situations allows one to assess the actual competency levels. The defined competencies and their gradations are the guiding framework here. By linking actual behaviour to those definitions, one starts to sketch a profile of existing competencies. When, for instance, during such a simulation exercise people start to connect different elements they are confronted with, a certain level of the 'problem analysis' competency is indicated: they are now able to relate different aspects of a certain problem.

Although this might sound rather straightforward, in practice one should not underestimate the efforts it requires. First of all, one needs to design a relevant situation that allows the people involved to demonstrate relevant behaviour and hence competencies. Designing 'real' situations is the challenge. Secondly, making the link from behavioural observations to a specific level of a particular competency asks for certain skills as well: the behaviour must be registered as correctly as possible, then the observed behaviour must be linked with its most adjacent competency, and finally, the level of the competency inferred must be judged. Multiple observations are often required to accomplish this. These different steps require some skill; assessors most definitely need to be trained! On the other hand, the benefits of this approach are great: it yields information that is highly relevant for the activities in question, while at the same time one is not obscured by more general psychometric data often not easily accessible or relevant, and sometimes even contradictory. This approach is highly recommendable, especially for front-line employees, as the behaviour here is directly experienced by customers.

Behaviourally oriented interviews

Assessment centres are of course not cheap; they require a serious investment in time and resources if one wants valuable information. Interviewing is in this respect more 'efficient'. Different approaches have been developed recently in an attempt to combine the best of both, gathering data on concrete behaviour and obtaining this information by conducting interviews. We will discuss two approaches here: behavioural event interviews[8] and interviewing by life themes.[9]

Within behavioural event interviews one does not ask questions such as 'How many people did you manage?', 'How did you feel?' or 'Why did you do this or what would you do in the future?' Although these types of questions might reveal much about facts, emotional states, and after-the-fact rationalizations, they often teach us little about actual skills or competencies. The core of behavioural event interviewing consists of focusing on concrete events that have taken place within the professional activities of the interviewee. These might be successes as well as failures (to get a balanced view, both types should be included). Next, one asks for a detailed description of the event: 'What happened?', 'Who was involved?', 'What did you think, feel, or want to do during the course of the event?', 'What did you actually do?' and 'What was the outcome?' By gathering this kind of concrete situated data it becomes possible to assess actual competency levels. The procedure here is roughly the same as described in the case of assessment centres.

Just as it can be advisable to record the observation by means of videotapes in concrete simulations like assessment centres, here, taping the interview can be worthwhile, allowing one to recheck certain conclusions and even to bring in different assessors – not present at the interview – to eliminate interviewer biases. Also, recorded material can be very useful for the person involved as well: it can be introduced within the development process in order to involve him or her to recognize, understand, accept and assess development needs.

A variation on this approach has been developed whereby the focus is on 'life themes': by identifying star performers, distinctive characteristics connected to life themes are established; the emphasis is here on attitudes and values (e.g. customer orientation, flexibility) more than on technical skills and specific knowledge. The development of specific questions around these life themes provides a basis for holding interviews, which can then be recorded. After being transcribed, the interviews are analysed by experts to derive a life-theme profile. Several companies have even started to use telephone interviews to obtain this type of data. Although this sounds like a very efficient way to collect data, it has some drawbacks. When using telephone interviews, the starting tools need to be very well developed (structure of interview, type of situations, what-if rules to decide when to ask additional questions), implying a great deal of effort in terms of development. This makes the technique more relevant when one needs to hire on a large scale for the same job (e.g. 500 crew members for fast-food restaurants) as compared to looking for only one particular employee. Moreover, it tends to limit the amount of information passed through. While this might reduce the impact of some biases it also can mean not noticing relevant aspects in (non-verbal) behaviour. So while it is true that this approach is used more and more in service industries, especially in the US,[10] its relevance will depend on the specific situation. Relying solely on this type of information will be hazardous, which is in fact the case with every technique.

Besides assessment centres and behaviourally oriented interviews, many organizations use surveys to measure the competency level(s) of their employees. In this kind of survey employees have to rate themselves on a number of questions, which should result in an image of the extent to which the respective employee masters the different competencies that are mentioned in the profile. Although this method has considerable cost advantages, we do want to express some cautions regarding the systematic use of this approach. After all, it will be impossible to circumvent all the possible biases that come along with this kind of self-assessment. Moreover, the use of surveys implies that more often than not, an abstraction has to be made of the working environment. Hence such surveys make it very difficult to execute a detailed and context-specific analysis of the competencies that are stressed in the profile. Hence, this method bears the risk of resulting in an approach whereby one throws the baby out with the bathwater.

So far, we have discussed how the notion of competencies can be integrated in an overall HR approach. We have also been looking at how to identify and assess relevant competencies. Equipped with this background we are ready to address the next issues: what types of competencies are important for services and how can one develop them.

COMPETENCIES FOR SERVICE ORGANIZATIONS

Distinguishing between different types of competency

Broadly speaking, three types of competencies can be distinguished: a person's behavioural repertoire, technical competencies including skills and knowledge, and finally, personal characteristics such as motivations, traits and self-identity.

- *Behavioural routines* are those competencies situated more 'on the surface', including traits such as politeness and friendliness. They refer to the behaviours displayed in brief encounters – for example, looking at customers when addressed, or a cheerful manner when speaking on the telephone.[11]
- *Technical competencies* refer to the sometimes broad range of knowledge and skills required to perform a certain task or job. Knowledge relates to the information a person holds in specific content areas, whereas skills are the actual ability to perform a certain physical or mental task. A surgeon's knowledge of nerves and muscles in the human body, a service technician's grasp of the lift's electrical circuits, a dentist's skill in filling a tooth without damaging nerves, and a computer programmer's ability to organize thousands of lines into a smooth-running computer program are all examples of technical competency.
- *Personal characteristics* are a mixture of motivations, traits and a person's self-concept. As such they form the core of an individual. *Motivations* are forces that move people to act in certain ways; they drive, direct and select action. Achievement orientation is an example of a motive; achievement-motivated people set more challenging goals for themselves and take personal responsibility for accomplishing them. They believe that their personal actions make a difference and want to realize certain objectives as well. *Traits* refer to more or less consistent responses to situations or information; they range from mere physical attributes, like good eyesight or adequate psychomuscular abilities, to more complex psychological traits like emotional self-control, or ability to cope with stress. Finally, the notion of *self-concept* refers to a person's values and self-image; how the person perceives him- or herself and others. Service employees who see people and hence customers as seeking short-term profit at others' expense will approach customers with a basic attitude of mistrust, unlike those people who see the interaction between providers and customers as a potential win–win situation.

These different layers of competencies are depicted in Figure 10.3. These three types of competencies vary in terms of profoundness. While the behavioural repertoire can

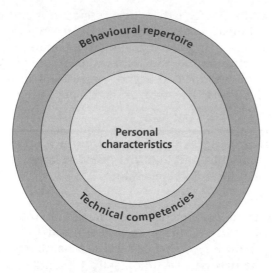

Figure 10.3 The three layers of competencies

be seen as situated more on the surface, personal characteristics really form the core of the person.

Of course, these three types of competencies are also interrelated and influence each other reciprocally. Personal characteristics can affect the development of technical competencies, as in the case where achievement orientation results in making the sacrifices necessary to become an engineer. Adopting new behaviour can lead to a modification of one's self-concept – for example, when someone discovers that she has a gift for public speaking after simply having done it. Acquiring behavioural skills therefore influences a person's sense of identity.

Linking competencies to services

The relative importance of each of the three different types of competencies is not the same for all forms of service encounter. Whereas bank tellers need to be polite and have to possess the necessary skills for handling customer transactions, they are usually not involved in the service transaction on a deeper, more personal level. Under normal circumstances, neither bank tellers nor fast-food restaurant employees are expected to explore ways of looking at the world or engage in discussions relating to their own opinions or self-image with customers in order to deliver an adequate level of service to them. Therapists, career counsellors or process consultants, on the other hand, do address these issues. These professionals not only need technical expertise but they are also involved with their customers at a more personal level during the interaction process. Here personal characteristics do play an important or even decisive role.

The service classification framework developed by Mills and Margulies[12] (explained in Chapter 1) can be useful in understanding the relative importance of the different competencies in relation to the nature of services.

As you may recall, Mills and Margulies made a distinction between three sorts of service transactions: maintenance-interactive, task-interactive and personal-interactive.

- *Maintenance-interactive services* imply rather short interactions and the complexity of the task is rather limited – for example, the work done by bank tellers, hotel receptionists and service employees in fast-food restaurants or shoe stores.
- *Task-interactive services* centre around the technicality of the task, where the customer has a definite question but does not have the knowledge or skills necessary to provide the answers. This type of service provider needs to handle uncertainty. Examples of these services are tax consultancy or computer programming.
- In *personal-interactive services* the provider engages in a much deeper process with customers to clarify, circumscribe and fulfil the needs at hand, which are often situated at a more personal level. Job counselling, legal advice and therapy are examples of these services.

Obviously all three sorts of competencies – behavioural routines, technical competencies and personal characteristics – are present and to a certain extent important for all three types of services. When serving a hamburger one needs to be polite, as well as have the necessary technical skills to handle the food served. Moreover, having a positive attitude when interacting with people facilitates being friendly and helpful. Computer programmers need to be technical experts, but friendliness and being able to take a customer's viewpoint into account are also assets in this job. Therapists will benefit from having a mature and healthy personality, but being polite and friendly as well as having a profound knowledge of human nature are also essential here. It cannot be said, therefore, that a certain type of competency is irrelevant for some types of services. However, their relative importance certainly differs for each of the three types of services (*see* Figure 10.4).

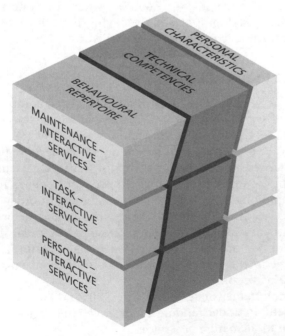

Figure 10.4 The relative importance of the three types of competencies in different types of services

In maintenance-interactive services, the behavioural repertoire plays a dominant role. Technical knowledge and skills are necessary, but are less important. Personal characteristics merely have a facilitating role. In task-interactive services, technical competency plays a major part. In personal-interactive service encounters the personal characteristics of the service employee become equally important.

This framework should not be used, however, to design uniform competency development strategies for the service organization as a whole. A bank, for instance, has employees performing tasks that fall into the category of maintenance-interactive services as well as highly specialized people performing task-interactive services. Branch managers might even take on the role of counsellors for certain customers. This framework should be used to look at the relevance of different sorts of competency to the diversity of roles often present within the whole service organization. Having said this, it seems time to take a closer look at competency development.

Competency development

The competence development process implies different stages. Experiential approaches to education made it clear that adults learn best if they are exposed to a process consisting of four different steps that are linked as shown in Figure 10.5.[13] Abstract conceptualization can lead to active experimentation, whereby concrete experience is gained. Reflection upon these experiences can lead to new insights.

Furthermore, development requires the presence of three different conditions:

■ dissatisfaction with an existing condition (actual situation);
■ clarity about a desired condition (ideal situation); and
■ clarity about what to do to move from the actual to the ideal.

This means that, at the individual level, different steps or phases can be acknowledged during the development process:

1. self-assessment, involving recognition, acceptance and understanding of the need for development;
2. practice or application to acquire new competencies; and
3. follow-up.[14]

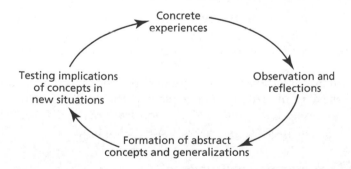

Figure 10.5 Kolb's learning cycle[15]

Source: Organisational Psychology: Readings on human behaviour in organisations (4th edition), Kolb, D., Rubin, I. and McIntyre, J. © 1979. Reprinted by permission of Prentice-Hall, Inc, Upper Saddle River, NJ.

The *self-assessment phase* implies recognition, acceptance and understanding. *Recognition* simply means that learners need to recognize that certain types of competencies do exist and are relevant to them. *Understanding* implies the creation of a clear insight into the level of competency at hand. During the recognition and understanding stage, the person will also face issues of acceptance. *Acceptance* is not always evident, especially when speaking of personal characteristics. Early attempts to teach achievement motivation to stimulate economic development in Third World countries were criticized for being attempts at 'brainwashing'. Critics felt that psychologists had no right to 'muck about with people's minds'. These critics were assured that in fact a person's motivation cannot be changed unless its validity is accepted – that is, the person really sees it in his or her own self-interest to change. Brainwashing does not work: competency learners must want, and work hard, to develop a new competency.[16] Self-assessment relates therefore to obtaining an accurate view of one's own level of competency.

Practice has to do with experimenting with the competency behaviours in realistic simulations, whereas *application* refers to the application of a new competency to real job situations. Finally, *follow-up*, *support* and *feedback* close the circle.

It is also clear that developing competencies will require different efforts, depending on the type of competency. As they vary in terms of profoundness, different types of competency often imply a different time frame and will require different developmental approaches. Whereas competencies related to the behavioural repertoire can often be easily trained and are adopted quite quickly, the development of technical skills and knowledge can imply longer time periods. Personal characteristics are often the most difficult to develop, as they are formed and fixed during childhood and early adult years.

Moreover, competency development strategies can take on different forms. Whereas behaviour modelling is more appropriate for developing one's behavioural repertoire, technical training and education seem to be more suited for gaining technical expertise. The development of personal characteristics will often demand more intense forms of change and training, such as sensitivity training. So once the relevant competency areas to be developed are identified, the company can choose from a number of different kinds of training or development strategies.

Choosing appropriate development strategies

Competence development can be seen as a set of activities providing the opportunity to acquire and improve competency. A variety of methods and approaches exists, and a brief overview of the main types of competency development activities is included here.

The most common methods and approaches applied are lectures and programmed instructions, behaviour modelling and role-playing, team building efforts and personal assessment programmes, case studies and action learning, and finally simulation or vestibule training, which comes very close to on-the-job training.

Lectures and programmed instructions

Lectures, where an instructor presents material to a group of learners, are the mainstay of higher education, so they are perhaps all too familiar. The accepted shortcomings of lectures include the predominance of one-way communication;

insensitivity to learner differences in learning style, ability and interest; and lack of feedback to the learner.

Although this method communicates the same message to large groups of people, it suffers from time and space constraints, as the student needs to be present at the same time as the teacher. Recent technological developments have allowed some of these constraints to be overcome. The course content gets translated into programmed instructions and is subsequently made available on PCs, networks or CD-ROM. Self-paced or programmed instruction approaches present the learner with a series of tasks, allow for evaluation of success at intervals throughout the training, and provide feedback about correct and incorrect responses as the learner advances through the training. Instruction programs can proceed through a fixed sequence of experiences or they can skip from one point to another, depending on how well the learner is grasping different parts of the material. These programmed instructions are being made more and more available via electronic media.

Computer-based training (CBT) includes both computer-assisted instruction (CAI) and computer-managed instruction (CMI). CBT is most commonly used to deliver training about computers, but a wide range of other topics can also be addressed.

- CAI developed out of the programmed learning texts of the 1960s. In these applications, the computer simply presents a block of information and then asks the trainee questions to assess his or her mastery.
- CMI is much more complex. In this type of program, the computer assesses the trainee's initial level of competency and then provides a customized set of learning modules and exercises. The trainee's performance is assessed frequently, and the training content is modified continuously in line with the learner's progress.

It will become clear that this approach and these methods are most suited to teaching technical knowledge and insights, and are less appropriate for developing behavioural routines or personal characteristics. Moreover, programmed instruction will always be limited to what is known; it cannot anticipate new and unforeseen problems.

Behaviour modelling and role-playing

Behaviour modelling training is based on the social learning theory which states that most people learn by observing others and then copying their behaviour, when appropriate. Learning from others reduces the need for trial-and-error learning. Behaviour modelling training typically follows a fixed sequence of steps.

1. The trainer introduces a single interpersonal skill, perhaps in a short lecture that conveys some of the principles underlying the skill.
2. Trainees view a videotape of someone performing the skill correctly. Then the trainer plays the tape again, highlighting key principles, or steps, called learning points.
3. Trainees practise the skill by role-playing with other trainees.
4. Trainees receive feedback on the effectiveness of their role-playing behaviour.

Practice continues until the trainees feel confident with their new skill.

Team building and personal assessment programmes

Many organizations invest in team building and personal assessment programmes in order to develop the capacity of individuals and work groups to interact more effectively. Team building often starts with a data collection phase, utilizing questionnaires or individual interviews with team members. The trainer looks for information about how the group works together, what problems exist, and what norms are followed. This information is summarized and fed back to the group so that they can take an objective look at the way they work together and decide how they wish to change it. The facilitator helps the team understand the feedback and develops action plans for improving group processes. These plans may include training in specific skills such as active listening, problem analysis and group decision making, consensus seeking and conflict resolution. Team building without the feedback but with a heavy emphasis on group problem-solving skills is also commonly provided to new teams when self-directed work groups are set up.

Personal assessment programmes focus on the personal characteristics that people apply in their interaction with work and the social environment. Issues addressed here include coping with stress and personal organization, but some programmes dig even further into self-image or identity and how it relates to functional or dysfunctional behaviour. It is clear that these programmes are more profound on the personal level. Issues such as acceptance are crucial here.

Case studies and action learning

The *case study method*, developed at the Harvard Law School in the 1920s, presents the trainee with a written description of an actual or hypothetical problem in an organizational setting. The trainee is required to read the case, identify the problem and recommend solutions. The case study method has several intended purposes:

- It shows trainees that there is usually no easy solution to complex organizational problems.
- It helps trainees realize that different perspectives and solutions to the same case may be equally valid.
- It helps managerial trainees develop their problem-solving skills.
- Since case studies can often be worked out in groups, the development of behavioural and personal characteristics can also be addressed when cases are explored in depth over a longer time period by several people. Team building and collaboration, negotiation, and presentation skills then all become involved.

Case studies allow complex issues to be tackled in a concise format, but they remain studies; real practice is still out there in the real world. Action learning attempts to overcome this by combining formal training with practical experience. *Action learning* is an increasingly common method for middle and upper management development which combines on- and off-the-job learning in innovative ways. The underlying idea is that formal training is good at conveying programmed knowledge (facts) but poor at teaching the student to question insights (the ability to seek out and use knowledge to solve real problems in innovative ways); yet it is precisely the latter that is most crucial to managerial success. Action-learning programmes usually feature some classroom instruction along with an applied project tackled by a team of trainees (or occasionally by individual trainees). As these projects actually take place, they are richer in terms of 'real life' context and complexity. On the other hand, as these projects are often limited in time and resources, they tend to not be as rich in terms of content as case studies.

Simulation and vestibule training

Simulation techniques create a facsimile of elements of the work setting, in which trainees try out different behaviours or strategies. The objective is to have trainees learn from their own actions, as well as from the group discussion that follows the simulation in a debriefing session. Simulations can be as simple as two-person role-playing or as complex as a sophisticated computer simulation of business processes.

Many experiential exercises are designed for more than two people. Large-scale behavioural simulations represent an increased level of complexity. These involve simulated organizations of up to 20 people in different roles, lasting from six hours to several days. Simulations at this level of complexity are typically used with executives rather than lower-level supervisors because sophisticated interpersonal and decision-making skills are prerequisites for learning from such an extremely complex situation.

Another simulation technique is the computerized business game. A business simulation or game may be defined as a sequential decision-making exercise structured on a model of a business operation, in which the trainee's role is to manage the simulated operation. In the game, the trainee or group of trainees is asked to make decisions about organizational matters such as investment in R&D, pricing or entering new markets. Based on these decisions, the program provides computer-generated feedback on how the organization has performed. With this new information at hand, the trainee is asked to make another series of decisions, which are used in the next run of the simulation. The primary objectives of these business games are to teach general management skills such as decision making, setting priorities, long-range planning and effective use of time, personnel, and equipment.

Like on-the-job training, *vestibule training* requires trainees to do the whole job, using the same tools and machines that are used on the job. However, the training takes place in a vestibule, or separate workshop used just for training. Examples are flight simulators for pilots or test restaurants for hamburger chains. A trainer is present at all times, and the trainees are protected from the hustle and pressure that occur on the job itself.

In Table 10.5, the different forms development programmes can take are linked with the different types of competency defined above. Behaviour modelling and

Table 10.5 Different training approaches and their relevance for developing different types of competencies

	Behavioural repertoire	Technical competency	Personal characteristics
Behavioural modelling and role-playing	XXX		
Lectures and programmed instruction		XXX	
Team building and personal assessment sessions			XXX
Case studies and action learning	XXX	X	X
Simulation and vestibule training	XX	XX	XX

role-playing are most suitable when addressing the development of the behavioural repertoire. Lectures and programmed instruction are most relevant for developing technical competency, whereas team building and personal assessment sessions focus on personal characteristics. The other forms can be relevant for developing a range of competencies simultaneously. The relative importance of the different learning objectives can be used as a guideline when deciding which form to use. Finally, on-the-job and apprenticeship training can be seen as valid approaches to developing different sorts of competency.

CONCLUSION

We started this chapter by positioning competencies within an integrated HRM model. Some techniques and approaches that can be used to apply the concept of competencies to organizational practice were described, including the process of defining competencies and the role of assessment centres and behavioural event interviews.

Equipped with this more general background we developed a more detailed view of competencies and their relevance for services. Three types of competencies were distinguished: behavioural repertoire, technical competencies and, finally, personal characteristics. Although these three types of competencies are intertwined and will present themselves together in almost any situation, the importance of these different types of competencies varies, depending on the type of service activities under consideration. The behavioural repertoire is most important for maintenance-interactive services, while technical competencies are dominant when discussing task-interactive services. Finally, personal characteristics are crucial for personal-interactive services.

We then looked at competence development. Here it became clear that different sorts of competencies require different development initiatives. The framework within which the relative importance of certain competencies was linked to the type of services provided, was then expanded to accommodate different types of competence development actions.

So far we have presented the notion of competencies as being rather individual-oriented, suggesting thereby that competency development is a rather individual activity. It is not. Learning, that is competence development, has a highly relational side – something we turn to in Chapter 11.

Review and discussion questions

- Would you agree with the statement that certain competencies are irrelevant for certain service jobs (e.g. personal characteristics for service employees working in cleaning companies)? If yes, can you give examples?

- It is often said that people are the most valuable assets of an organization. What are the consequences of this statement for competency management within service organizations? Would this imply as well forms of 'competence accounting' and 'competence valuation'?

Notes and references

1 Possibilities are no guarantees; one can also design competency profiles from a one-way perspective (from the organization towards the individual who has to comply). Acknowledging competencies, however, brings back employees (instead of jobs) in the picture.

2 Definition adapted from Spencer, L. and Spencer, S. (1994) *Competence at Work*. New York: Wiley & Sons.

3 *Source*: Quintessence Consulting Belgium.

4 *See*, for instance, Whittington, R. (1993) *What is Strategy and Does it Matter?* London: Routledge; or Hendry, C. and Pettigrew, A. (1986) 'The practice of strategic human resource management', *Personnel Review*, Vol 15.

5 On single and double loop learning, see Argyris, C. (1994) *On Organisational Learning*. Oxford: Blackwell Publishers; on learning organizations, see Senge, P. (1990) *The Fifth Discipline*. New York: DoubleDay.

6 A point stressed by Janssens, M. and Steyaert, C. (1996) 'Culture & HRM practices: operational and ethical principles'; Tijdschrift voor Economie en Management, Vol 41, No 3, 327–54.

7 *See* Spencer, L. and Spencer, S. (1994), op. cit.; Van Beirendonck L. (1998) Beoordelen en ontwikkelen van competenties (Assessing and developing competencies), Acco, Leuven.

8 *See*, for a fuller description, Spencer, L. and Spencer, S. (1994), op. cit.

9 *See also* Heskett, J., Sasser, W. and Schlesinger, L. (1997) *The Service Profit Chain*. New York: Free Press.

10 *See* Heskett *et al.* (1997), op. cit.

11 Smiling when speaking on the telephone makes your voice more cheerful.

12 Mills, P. K. and Margulies, N. (1980) 'Towards a core typology of service organisations', *Academy of Management Review*, Vol 5, No 2, 255–65.

13 Wolfe, D. and Kolb, D. 'Career development, personal growth, and experiential learning', in Kolb, D., Rubin, I. and McIntyre, J. (1979) *Organisational Psychology: Readings on human behaviour in organisations*. Englewood Cliffs, NJ: Prentice-Hall.

14 Adapted from Spencer, L. and Spencer, S. (1994), op. cit.

15 Kolb, D., Rubin, I. and McIntyre, J. (19) *Organisation Psychology: Readings on human behaviour in organisations*. Englewood Cliffs, NJ: Prentice-Hall.

16 Spencer, L. and Spencer, S. (1994), op. cit.

Suggested further reading

Spencer, L. and Spencer, S. (1994) *Competence at Work*. New York: John Wiley & Sons. This book provides an excellent overview on what competencies mean and imply for HR practices; besides underlying frameworks and operational methods, this work also contains an extensive competency dictionary.

CHAPTER 11

Collaboration: integrating work and learning

Bart Van Looy

INTRODUCTION

Alice has a problem: her machine reports a self-test error, but she does not quite believe it. So many of the parts of the control system in this machine have failed that she suspects there is some other problem that is producing the failures. She is unwilling to accept that so many failures could be independent of each other. We are going to lunch at a restaurant where many of her colleagues eat to try to persuade Fred, the most experienced of them, to look at the machine with her. If this fails, she will try to get the team technical specialist to look at it. She makes copies of the information from the error log and service log to take with us. In the parking lot, she recognizes the cars of the colleagues, including that of the one she wants to recruit to help . . .

When she succeeds in getting him and the others interested, they listen to the list of problems the machine has and begin to talk about noise problems or communication problems. She repeats that she wants help, that she does not understand this series of problems, and Fred tells her she has to fix it. He looks at the logs and tells her ways of approaching the problem as a noise issue; he also tells her she cannot ignore the error code. They figure out which board the error code is actually indicating, where it is in the machine. She repeats that she wants help; he repeats that he is not going to help her, but he will tell her how to approach the problem. He shows her how to check the communication lines, and they all laugh at one of the suggested remedies for persistence of the fault – swapping all the boards in the machine, one at a time.

Fred asks her again about the error code: she tells him, adding that it is persistent, and the machine will do nothing. He says that in that case she should be able to solve the problem right away with the procedure associated with the error code, and why is she bothering him? She reminds him again of the number of previous failures and the number of modules replaced. He asks about a specific one as she recites the list, and yes, she has replaced that one too. One of the other technicians points out that that only means that the part is new, not that it is necessarily functional, and all the others agree.

Alice repeats that she thinks there is something about that machine that is causing the failure of all these components; the other technicians all tell her just to fix the problem. Alice reminds Fred that some of the components have been replaced twice in recent months. Fred starts to tell her about running the noise test, and then says that she probably cannot do it if the machine will not run at all. Alice doubts that the machine will run long enough to do the noise test, although she has managed to read the error log; if she can't do that, she may be able to use some of the other diagnostic programs. He starts to tell her about testing communication lines . . .(J. Orr)[1]

In this chapter we will explore the importance of collaboration and its implications for people management in service organizations. We will first look at some recent observations related to the work practice of service technicians, which highlight the benefits of collaboration. Collaboration enables people to find solutions for new and unforeseen problems as well as to create and transfer knowledge and insights – in other words, it enables people to learn. Although we start by considering the work of service technicians, we will argue that these findings are also relevant to a broader range of service situations. Learning and collaboration are not only linked in the case of well established teams of professionals; collaboration also plays a role in the learning process of novices and apprentices. Finally, given the central role of collaboration, we will examine the development process of such collaborative relationships.

Objectives

By the end of this chapter, you should be able to discuss:

- the relationship between collaboration and learning
- why and for what type of services these dynamics are important
- the specific requirements learning poses regarding relational characteristics in connection with the learning processes of newcomers and apprentices
- how collaboration can be seen as a central concept
- the nature of collaborative relationships and how they can develop

THE BENEFITS OF COLLABORATION IN THE WORKPLACE

The recent study by Orr,[2] from which the introductory case study was taken, can be described as an in-depth anthropological analysis of service technicians – or, as he calls it, an 'ethnography of a modern job'. It certainly provides us with some interesting findings. Over a period of several years, Orr studied the work and behaviour of service technicians working on copying machines simply by participating in their daily activities. His findings reveal the importance of collaboration for service work. The characteristics of the interaction with customers, as well as with fellow technicians, have an important influence on the effectiveness of technical repair jobs.

These findings are in sharp contrast with the predominant view of technicians, who are often portrayed as 'lonesome cowboys' working alone in the field, with technical skill and expertise their only tools besides manuals and technical documentation. Technicians' work is commonly defined as merely the diagnosis, repair and maintenance of machines. Orr concludes that the social side of work is at least of equal importance:

'. . . a large part of service work might better be described as repair and maintenance of the social setting'.

From Orr's description of Alice in the introductory case study, technical service work appears highly relational; talk is a crucial dimension of the practice of the group of service technicians to which Alice belongs. Diagnosis is aided by and in some cases takes place through a communication process involving the creation of a coherent description of the machine in question. These descriptions become the basis for technicians' discussions about their experience. During these discussions knowledge and insights are shared and new approaches are developed. The circulation of anecdotes among technicians is the principal means by which they stay informed of the developing subtleties of machine behaviour. Let us examine this phenomenon more closely, by looking in detail at Orr's observations.

Socializing customers . . .

The starting point of diagnosis is usually a situation in which the customer has concluded that the machine has malfunctioned. The customer must then describe this situation when requesting a service call. Technicians receive a description of the problem which is the joint product of the customer and the call operator. The technician's task when diagnosing a problem is to produce a satisfactory representation of the problem in order to allow a course of repair to be identified.

The customer who first experiences the problem is the first source of information. However, these customers may need to be trained in describing the ways of the machine. This is done by the technicians, who encourage the customers to note significant incidents relating to the machine and to talk about them in appropriate language – that is, the technicians' language. Customers are taught to create lucid representations of the situation, which the technician can use to create a coherent picture of the situation so that it can be remedied. This socialization of the customers is a substantial part of the social work of services. Technicians focus on maintaining the relations between their customers and the machines, and this is accomplished through the technician's relationship with both.

. . . and exchanging war stories with colleagues

There is a class of problems for which the machine provides no direct diagnostic information. In such cases, diagnosis is accomplished by piecing together clues gleaned from the machine and the customers. These clues do not clearly indicate a specific cause of the problem. Their significance is in what they show about patterns of machine behaviour. If interpreted correctly – and various interpretations are possible – such clues might suggest further areas of investigation which could produce a definite cause.

Some of these diagnoses actually fall into the 'known-and-recognized' class, in that the connection between the clue and the problematic behaviour is long established and well known to technicians. Creating this stock of common knowledge is achieved by technicians circulating 'war stories' among themselves. These stories are anecdotes of experience narrated with an appropriate level of context and technical detail. These stories start to circulate and through them experience becomes reproducible and reusable.

Other diagnoses are more problematic. Technicians may find themselves confronted with problems which have some familiar elements, but where the facts do not add up to a clear picture of the problem – as in the situation Alice faced in the case study. In cases like this, technicians almost invariably start looking for colleagues and a story-telling cycle ensues. Comparable stories are told or retold in the consideration of the problem. Exchanging stories of similar experiences is a way of pushing the facts around, trying new perspectives to see if they suggest other interpretations. As a result of this process, new approaches and solutions are developed and constructed and at the same time transferred. This process can also be called '*learning*'.

Before delving into this idea of learning and its relationship to collaboration, however, we should first clarify the role of service documentation, often seen as the prime resource for learning. This will also allow us to explore and establish the broader relevance of the dynamics described by Orr.

The use of service documentation

Orr's findings clearly indicate that both interaction with customers and exchanging information and discussing problems with colleagues are crucial ingredients of the service technician's work. This finding contrasts with the prevalent practice in providing support for service technicians, which emphasizes adequate manuals or 'knowledge systems'.

Should these knowledge systems be considered obsolete in the light of these findings? Of course not; they play a supportive and hence valuable role, but this role will always be limited. Service manuals cannot replace the role discussions play when solving *new* and *unknown* problems that occur within a specific context of use. Nor do they succeed in providing a complete understanding of the machine, which is crucial in creating confidence both in the minds of customers and technicians. Let us explore both these issues.

A service manual is usually perceived as a collection of descriptive information about the machine in question. The assumption is that the technicians deduce the source of the machine's problems by obtaining information about it from the manual, which they consult whenever there is a problem with a machine. However, documentation is not simply a representation of the machine. A service manual is a device which one person (or group of people) constructs to convey information to someone else. Choices of inclusion and exclusion significantly constrain what can be done using the manual.

Often this documentation is designed not to provide information about the machine and its problems, but to direct the technician to the solution through a minimal decision tree. This approach is legitimate given efficiency considerations, but not without consequences. The directions in this type of document are intended to prescribe the technician's behaviour from arrival at the customer site to departure. The premise is that following the instructions carefully from beginning to end will lead to the resolution of problems more quickly than could be accomplished by the technicians reasoning from their understanding of the machine alone. Such directive documentation provides only the information believed necessary for following the instructions and may omit information that would contribute to a better understanding of the problem. The effectiveness of such information depends on the success of the documentation designer in correctly anticipating and providing for the problems that actually arise in the field. Success also depends on the users' and the technicians' understanding of how the documentation should be used, and making appropriate use of it.

Even with all these elements in place, however, it is clear that it is not possible for instructions to be completely stand-alone. The knowledge relevant to the job of diagnosis cannot be set out exhaustively. The documentation mechanism is limited in its prescriptive ability. It is composed of representations and instructions which require interpretation by their users in the *context* of their application. The scope of problems and their solutions will always be limited to the already known. As a result, certain new problems will arise out of the interplay between machines and the situations in which they are used.

Accordingly, the technicians must inevitably be prepared to solve new and unanticipated problems; they must therefore develop as comprehensive an understanding of the machine as possible. When technicians use the documentation, they contrast their analysis of what the documentation is trying to convey with their own analysis of what might be wrong with the machine. They pursue those paths in the documentation which seem consonant with their hypotheses. If this is not successful, colleagues are used as a more 'flexible' source of information. Fellow technicians are probably better able to contribute to new perspectives and the iterative process of diagnosis and technical problem solving.

Moreover, the technicians use the documents in pursuit of their own goals, and these are not entirely the same as those of the documentation's designers. A technician's primary goal is to keep the customer happy and this includes, but is not limited to, fixing the machine as necessary. An important component of this goal is keeping the customer assured that the situation is under control; this involves being able to tell the customer what the machine is doing and to say when it was fixed and what was fixed. The customer must be made aware that the technician has repaired the machine in order that they will feel confident that the machine can be repaired in the future, should the need arise. Thus a system that fixes the machine without either customer or technician knowing how or why is unlikely to be acceptable. This is why 'war stories' are becoming so important. Cause-and-effect links can be discussed, taking into account the context of use and pointing out reasonable courses of action.

These observations can also be of use in the design of relevant service manuals. Besides documenting well-known standard errors and common problems, they should also provide users with insights and understanding about the logic of the equipment at hand. Conceiving service manuals in this way makes them supportive and complementary to the collaboration process. The latter remains a crucial method of dealing with unforeseen, new and context-specific problems.

THE BROADER RELEVANCE OF COLLABORATION TO SERVICES

By now, we hear you say, what does all this mean for services in general, or for our service operations and employees in particular? Do these insights apply to all services and all situations?

As already discussed, the process of solving unforeseen, new and context-specific problems benefits greatly from interaction or collaboration. This idea is the guiding principle for determining the broader relevance of these social dynamics for services. If you can plan everything in advance and if there are no unforeseen circumstances or uncertain situations to be faced, these dynamics are irrelevant. You just make everything explicit, translate it into procedures, prescriptions, manuals and so on, and make sure people stick to them. Collaboration has only a social, motivational or mere distraction function; it does not directly affect the job to be done.

In all other cases, these dynamics are important. As a result, these dynamics are important for many service situations. In Chapter 1 we concluded that heterogeneity or variability was one of the core characteristics of services. Unforeseen situations occur, in which service employees need to puzzle out the situation at hand. In these cases, having support from colleagues is often an advantage. Consider the airline customer who arrives at the check-in desk asking if he can change the destinations and times of his complex flight scheme. Other parties become involved when you start to make changes: waiting times will shift, luggage problems might arise. A brief exchange of viewpoints with colleagues before choosing the most appropriate action can be very useful. Alternatively, think of IT consultants who may be facing a new complex problem when working for a particular customer. As soon as they get back to the office they may start discussing viable approaches to the problem with colleagues.[3]

Of course, the extent of heterogeneity is a very broad guideline when it comes to deciding how relevant collaboration is to a particular service. The framework of Mills and Margulies[4] provides us with more detailed insights. The different types of services – maintenance-interactive, task-interactive and personal-interactive – differ in terms of the level of uncertainty or ambiguity confronted with during the service encounters.

- For *maintenance-interactive services*, the level of uncertainty or ambiguity is low; hence technicians can rely more on systems, procedures or manuals.
- In the case of *task-interactive services*, uncertainty increases.
- For *personal-interactive services*, both increased uncertainty and increased ambiguity have to be taken into account.

Hence for these last two types of services, the relational dynamics described here become more and more vital. Neglecting them can have a profound effect on performance because the essential, social ingredient of the learning process is left out.[5] This is clear not only when observing how colleagues extend their existing knowledge by exchanging, discussing and interpreting novel experiences, as described by Orr, but also when looking at the learning process of novices or apprentices.

THE ROLE OF COLLABORATION IN LEARNING

Whereas conventional explanations of learning stress internalization – whether discovered, transmitted from others or experienced – real learning implies more. Learning also means becoming a practitioner within a community.[6]

This concept of community is crucial to any understanding of the relational side of learning. A community can be seen as a set of relationships among people and activity over time, characterized by a certain common understanding about what constitutes good work practice. Communities are characterized by a degree of homogeneity in terms of interest, theory and methodology. Examples of this type of community are lawyers, physicians, engineers or butchers.

Such a community of practice is an intrinsic condition for the existence of knowledge because it provides the necessary interpretative support. Activities, tasks, functions and understandings do not exist in isolation. They only have meaning as part of broader systems of relationships. These systems arise out of and are reproduced and developed within social communities. The individual defines and is defined by these relationships.[7]

Learning thus implies not only a relationship to specific activities, but also a relationship to social communities. It implies becoming a full participant, a member, a whole person – learning to function in a community, whether it is a community of physicists, engineers, classmates or scholars in philosophy or organizational behaviour.

This process of becoming a practitioner ideally takes on the form of '*legitimate peripheral participation*', as argued convincingly by Lave and Wenger.[8] The notion of legitimate peripheral participation denotes the particular mode of engagement of a learner who participates in the actual practice of an expert, but only to a limited degree and with limited responsibility for the outcomes.

Peripheral participation leads to the creation of knowledge in practice when it is approached as more than an observational lookout post; it involves participation as a way of learning. An extended period of peripheral *participation* provides learners with opportunities to take on board the culture of the practitioners. A general idea of what constitutes a community's practice is assembled piece by piece: who is involved, what is done, and what everyday life is like; how experts walk, talk and work; how people who are not part of the community of practice interact with it; what other learners are doing; and what learners need to learn to become full practitioners. It includes an increasing understanding of how, when and about what old-timers collaborate, collude and collide and what they enjoy, dislike, respect and admire. It provides paradigms, including masters, finished products and more advanced apprentices in the process of becoming full practitioners, which are grounds and motivations for learning activity. This means that legitimate peripheral participation is much more than creating initial impressions. Viewpoints from which to understand the practice evolve through changing participation in different tasks, changing relationships with ongoing community practices, and changing social relationships within the community.

This participation should be *peripheral*. Expecting the same results from newcomers as are expected from experts is asking for trouble. Conditions of participation should reflect this idea of peripherality. Space and time should be allocated to experimenting with and reflecting upon activities. Without such reflection and experimentation, no 'internalization' takes place. If a trainee has no time to live through experiences by means of reflection, discussion with other apprentices or masters, and so on, these experiences will remain superficial. Moreover, asking too much too soon can result in stress, burn-out and many quality problems.

Finally, having opportunities to participate peripherally – that is, having full access to all kinds of activities involved in practice – bring with it the idea of *legitimacy*, that the apprentice should be allowed to enter the field or the community. Introducing learning into work practice therefore implies certain characteristics of interaction. Conditions that place newcomers in adversial relations with their managers or colleagues, or that imply exhaustive over-involvement in daily operations, partially or completely distort the prospects for learning in practice.

Exhibit 11.1, which describes the learning process of becoming a butcher in a supermarket, highlights how things can go wrong. It provides us with many examples of how access can be denied. The trade school and its shop exercises did not stimulate the essential procedures of meat cutting for supermarkets, much less make them accessible to apprentices. The on-the-job training was not much of an improvement; worse yet, the master butchers confined their apprentices to jobs that were completely removed from activities rather than peripheral to them. By doing so, newcomers are prevented from peripheral participation and thus very little learning actually takes place. Opportunities for learning are thus also given structure by work practice.

Exhibit 11.1

Failing apprentices in the butcher trade[9]

A butcher's apprenticeship in the UK consists of a mix of trade school and on-the-job training. This programme was initiated by the Meatcutters' Union and culminated in the granting of a certificate. The certificate corresponded to six months of the apprenticeship and entitled the holder to receive journeyman's pay and status after two and a half years on the job . . . In preparing trainees for the certificate, the trade school class is run along traditional lines, with book work and written examinations in class and practice in shop. The work follows the same pattern, year after year, without reference to the need for apprentices to learn useful things not learned on the job. Teachers teach techniques which were in use when they worked in retail markets and which are readily adaptable to a school setting . . . Most assignments are not relevant to the supermarket. For instance, students learn to make wholesale cuts not used in the stores and to advise customers on how to cook meat. These skills are not particularly in demand, and as a result few students bother to learn them . . . Apprentices are more interested in the shop period, where they become familiar with equipment they hope to use some day at work. However, the shop also has tasks useless in a supermarket. One of the first things learned is how to sharpen a knife – a vital task, but only in the past. Today, a company delivers sharpened knives and collects dull ones from meat departments at regular intervals . . .

On the job, learning experiences vary with certain structural dimensions of the work settings. A supermarket meat department manager tries to maximise the difference in value between the total volume of sales for the department and the wholesale meat order, plus his costs for personnel and facilities. To do this, the manager ensures that his skilled journeymen can prepare a large volume of meat efficiently by specialising in short, repetitive tasks. He employs apprentices where they can work for him most efficiently. Diverting journeymen from work to training tasks increases the short-run cost of selling meat. As a result, journeymen and apprentices are so occupied with profit-making tasks that apprentices rarely learn many tasks . . . The physical layout of a work setting is an important dimension of learning, since apprentices can gain a great deal from observing others and from being observed. Some meat departments are laid out so that apprentices working at the wrapping machines cannot watch journeymen cutting and sawing meat. An apprentice's feeling about this separation came out when a district manager in a large local supermarket told him to return poorly arranged trays of meat to the journeyman:

I'm scared to go in the back room. I feel so out of place there. I haven't gone back there in a long time because I just don't know what to do when I'm there. All those guys know so much about meat cutting and I don't know anything.

When he arrives at a store, an apprentice is trained to perform a task, usually working the automatic wrapping machine. If he handles this competently, he is kept there until another apprentice comes. If none comes, he may do this job for years almost without interruption. If a new

Exhibit 11.1 continued

apprentice comes, he trains him to wrap and then learns another task himself . . . Stores offer the kind of meat customers in their area will buy . . . In poorer neighbourhoods, apprentices have more opportunity to practise cutting meat than in wealthy neighbourhoods. Where there is high volume, a division of labour among a relatively large

number of workers increases efficiency . . . in this situation, not only apprentices but also journeymen will seldom learn the full range of tasks which was once integral to their trade.

Source: Based on Marshall, H. (1972) 'Structural constraints in learning', in Geer, B. (ed.) *Learning to Work.* ©1998 by Sage Publications. Reprinted by permission of Sage Publications.

COLLABORATION AS THE CENTRAL THEME

Now that we have an insight into the relational dynamics at play in both work practice and learning processes for apprentices, we can start thinking about the crucial points of attention. The work of Brown and Duguid is helpful here.[10] After examining the work of Orr, they identify two crucial aspects of work practice:[11]

1. *The extensive narration used.* This refers to the exchanging of stories. Stories help to diagnose the problem at hand and they also become a means of preserving knowledge, as they function as repositories of accumulated wisdom circulating within the community of practitioners.
2. *The notion of collaboration.* The narrative process is collective, and not an individual process. Faced with difficult problems, people like to work together and to discuss problems together. This makes working an inherently social process that benefits from collaboration.

Brown and Duguid here make an analogy with the concept of 'bricolage' – that is, the ability to 'make do with whatever is at hand' – as developed by Lévi-Strauss:[12]

'. . . *what one needs for bricolage are not the partial, rigid models of the sort directive documentation provides, but help to build, ad hoc and collaboratively, robust models that do justice to particular difficulties in which they find themselves.*'

Exchanging, developing and adapting stories all play a crucial role in the process of augmenting knowledge, expertise and skill. However, this implies the free floating of these stories, the willingness to share, to listen and to engage in constructive dialogue. In short, this implies collaboration. Collaboration can therefore be seen as the enabling condition here.

When summarizing the different elements at play in the learning process depicted as legitimate peripheral participation, three ideas must be stressed:

1. *It is important to create a variety of learning situations.* The range of activities central to being a practitioner needs to be reflected in the learning curriculum. Job variety and rotation are crucial during this learning period.
2. *Participating in a variety of activities should take the form of peripheral participation.* Space and time should be reserved for experimenting with and reflecting upon the activities engaged in. If experiences are not reinforced by means of reflection, discussion with other apprentices or masters, and so on, the chances are high that these experiences will remain superficial. No thorough understanding is

built up when short-term demands interrupt this process of 'sense-making'. When no time is left for discussion, reflection and narration – in other words making sense of everything – people will start feeling insecure and helpless, suffer from stress, and will muddle through with their unsatisfactory understanding (because it has been experienced as incomplete), adding to what is known as the cycle of failure (*see* Chapter 9).

3. *Learning implies eventual legitimacy*. An apprentice has to be allowed to participate, to gain access, and this comes down again to establishing collaborative relationships between apprentices and masters, or between employees and their managers. If collaboration is absent, the goodwill, the patience and time, so crucial for feed-back and reflection, will also be.

Collaborative relationships are therefore seen as crucial prerequisites for the learning process to evolve. We should now take a closer look at what collaborative relationships mean and how they develop over time.

ESTABLISHING COLLABORATIVE RELATIONSHIPS

Collaborative relationships are crucial for learning. Working relationships characterized by openness, reciprocity, support and recognition are an essential element of the learning process. This idea has been around for quite a while and yet continues to pose serious challenges in practice.[13] A distinction can be made between different types of relationships: *dyadic relationships* involving just two persons or *team-oriented relationships* involving more people. Establishing collaborative relationships is somewhat different depending on which form of relationship is in question:

- On the level of dyadic relationships, the notion of trust can be seen as an integrating concept.
- As for teams, things are a little more complicated as more parties are involved. It is important to consider the development process taking place in this context.

Establishing trust within dyadic relationships

A distinction can be made between '*cognition-based*' and '*affect-based*' trust.[14]

1. Trust can be seen as *cognitive-based* when people act for what they take to be 'good reasons', balancing between 'total ignorance' and 'total knowledge'. Available knowledge and good reasons serve as a foundation for trusting behaviour. The extent of reliable role performance, the similarity between two parties and professional credentials are seen as factors positively influencing cognition-based trust.

2. *Affect-based* trust refers to emotional bonds between people.[15] Determinants of affect-based trust are related to insights gained in the motives of partners in the relationship; behaviour recognized as personally chosen and demonstrating care and concern (as opposed to self-interest) is seen as critical to the development of affect-based trust. Affect-based trust shows strong similarities with the concept of 'organizational citizenship behaviour' – that is, behaviour intended to provide assistance and support *outside* an individual's work role.

These two concepts are the building blocks of the process of developing trust. Four stages can be identified (*see* Figure 11.1).[16] The cognitive elements are prominent when speaking of calculus-based and knowledge-based trust. By contrast, the emotional dimensions are most critical in identification-based and diversity-based trust.

- *Calculus-based trust* can be seen as the outcome of a calculation whose value is derived by determining the outcomes resulting from creating and sustaining the relationship relative to the costs of severing it.
- *Knowledge-based trust* is closely related to the notion of predictability – that is, knowing the other sufficiently well so that the other's behaviour can be anticipated.
- *Identification-based trust* involves identification with another's desires and intentions: 'trust exists because the parties effectively understand and appreciate each other's wants; this mutual understanding is developed to the point that each can effectively act for the other'.

When a relationship develops, trust is seen as evolving from calculus-based trust towards cognition-based and (possibly) identification-based trust.

- Finally, *diversity-based trust* can be seen as the most complex form. Constructive collaboration means taking the perspectives of others into account. Tolerance of differences or dealing with diversity thus becomes an inherent part of working together. In this regard, total identification with the other cannot be the final stage, since learning ultimately would be limited to the other's knowledge and competence.[17] Difference is needed in order to develop new insights and to take steps forward. In this sense, identification-

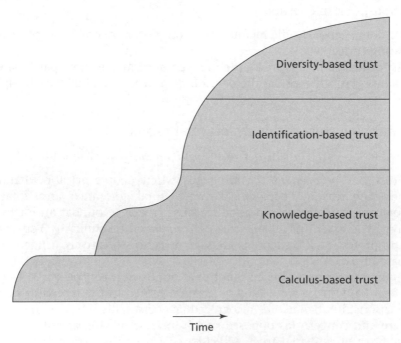

Figure 11.1 The stages of trust development

Source: Adapted from Lewicki, R. J. and Bunker, B. (1996) 'Developing and maintaining trust in work relationships', in Kramer, R. and Tyler, T. (eds) *Trust in Organisations: Frontiers of theory and research.* © 1998 by Sage Publications. Reprinted by permission of Sage Publications Inc.

based trust as a characteristic of working relationships is developed further to the next stage wherein differences are accepted and taken as a starting point for development.

Achieving collaboration within teams

Collaboration within teams is more complicated, as more parties are involved. The team or group developmental process can be depicted as involving a number of stages, with intermediate stages implying the development of collaborative relationships and trust, followed by 'productive' stages.[18]

A number of points should be kept in mind when considering how a team develops. In most cases a team is formed around a common goal. Teamwork also implies taking up different roles and establishing working procedures. Finally, working together involves interpersonal relationships as well. In Figure 11.2, these different elements are linked to the different phases that can be observed in the development process of groups.

1. In the first phase, dependency on authorities and issues concerning acceptance and inclusion are central. A well-known phenomenon when starting a new team is everybody looking at everybody else and asking themselves whether they will be accepted in the team and what needs to be done. Reliance on authority is then an easy way of making first steps. Moreover, conflicts are avoided as being accepted is preferable to being rejected, both from the point of view of the team members and from that of the supervisor.

   However, this period of superficial harmony does not last long. When engaging in different activities as a team, individual members become aware that they are saying yes to a certain way of working, to a certain own role, and the team's activities. This raises doubts as to whether members really want to go along with the implicit agreements made at the start.
2. Hence, the second phase is characterized by counter-dependency and fighting; role issues, control and ways of operating are debated with less attention paid to the task in hand. While these phases seem to be less productive at first sight, they are a crucial step in arriving at the commitment and acceptance required for the final stage. The challenge here is to arrive at an open two-directional way of dealing with differences of opinion. The one-sided use of power, in which opinions are forced through, might settle the issue in question but it will also signal a return to the first mode of working, where acknowledging the technical expertise of others often plays the role of stepping stone. It is a preliminary way of expressing 'I am OK, you are OK'.
3. By the fifth and final stage, trust is established whereby respect for the other as a person – including the differences from one's own perspective and/or capabilities – is realized and a working structure has been installed, allowing the team to be productive.

Whereas this model suggests a certain linearity, it should be thought of more as a spiral; going back is often easier than moving forward. Teams struggling with the third stage often 'regress' to the first stage by allowing 'authority' to settle the ongoing disputes. Furthermore, arriving at the fifth stage does not mean that the team will remain there. Achieving this means devoting continuous efforts to the team process.

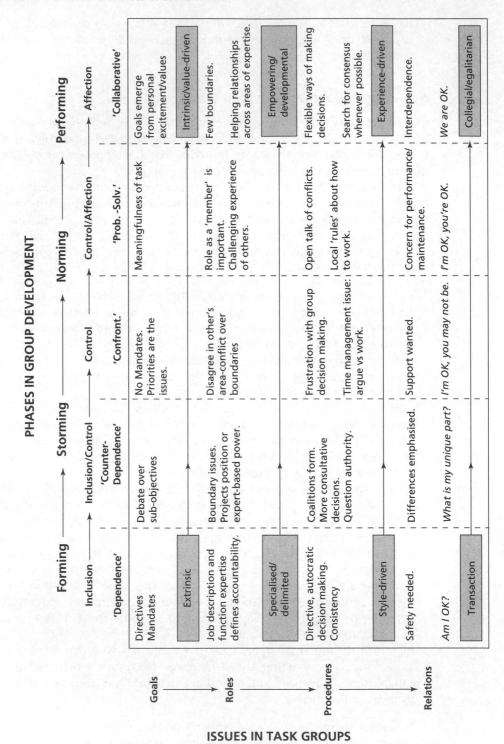

Figure 11.2 Phases in group development[19]

Source: Bouwen, R. and Fry, R. (1996) 'Facilitating group development: interventions for a relational and contextual construction', in West, M. (ed.) *Handbook of Work Group Psychology*, Wiley.

CONCLUSION

In this chapter we have discussed the relevance of collaboration for service environments. Collaboration is important because it relates directly to building and sharing knowledge; collaboration is linked to learning. This holds true especially in situations which involve new or unforeseen events; in situations where this is not the case, (expensive) interactions can be substituted by procedures or manuals. However, services are characterized by heterogeneity; moreover certain types of services involve by definition high levels of uncertainty or even ambiguity. Collaboration therefore deserves our attention, both in the daily work practice and in the learning process of newcomers or apprentices. We concluded this chapter by discussing the development process of such collaborative relationships.

Review and discussion questions

- Herbert Simon once said that 'all learning takes place within an individual's head'. Would you agree? How does this idea relate to the social dynamics outlined here?

- If these social dynamics are indeed crucial in terms of knowledge creation and diffusion, how might supportive HR practices look like? How might they complement the principles outlined in the previous chapter?

Notes and references

[1] Orr, J. (1996) *Talking About Machines: An ethnography of a modern job*. Cornell University Press, pp. 39–40.

[2] Ibid.

[3] As noted by Weick (1979), ambiguity, or equivocality as he calls it, drives interaction: the more ambiguity one experiences, the more one feels the need to interact with other people to make sense of the situation at hand. As 'universal' laws are rare within social sciences, this might just be one. We highly recommend Weick's work on this topic to interested readers: Weick, K. (1979) *The Social Psychology of Organizing* (2nd edition). New York: Random House; or, more recently, Weick, K. (1995) *Sensemaking in Organizations*, Sage.

[4] Mills, P. K. and Margulies, N. (1980) 'Towards a core typology of service organisations', *Academy of Management Review*, Vol 5, No 2, 255–65.

[5] As Maister stresses again and again when discussing professional services: teamwork is crucial. *See* Maister, D. (1997) *True Professionalism*. New York: The Free Press.

[6] Lave, J. and Wenger, E. (1991) *Situated Learning: Legitimate peripheral participation*. Cambridge University Press.

[7] Ibid., pp. 50–6, *see also* Giddens, A. (1984) *The Constitution of Society*. Cornwall: Polity Press.

[8] *See* Lave, J. and Wenger, E. (1991), op. cit.

[9] Adapted from Marshall, H. (1972) 'Structural constraints on learning', in Geer, B. (ed.) *Learning to Work*. Beverly Hills, CA: Sage.

[10] Brown, J. S. and Duguid, P. (1991) 'Organisation learning and communities of practice: toward a unified view of working, learning and innovation', *Organisation Science*, Vol 2, 40–57.

[11] In fact they also mention a third category; 'social construction'. This latter notion is however strongly linked with the notions of narration and collaboration. It does add the idea of (social) identity – by becoming a member, through exchanging stories and collaboration, one develops one's own identity. This identity also reflects values and visions of the community in which one is participating.

[12] Lévi-Strauss, C. (1966) *The Savage Mind!* Chicago: University of Chicago Press, p. 174.

[13] *See*, for instance, Argyris, C. and Schön, D. (1974) *Organisational Learning: A theory of action perspective.* Reading (Mass): Addison Wesley. The interested reader is referred to Argyris, C. (1994) *On Organisational Learning*, Oxford: Blackwell Publishers, which gives an excellent overview of more than 30 years of this scholar's work on the relationship between ways of working and collaborating and their impact on learning.

[14] McAllister, D. (1995) 'Affect- and cognition-based trust as foundations for interpersonal co-operation in organisations', *Academy of Management Journal*, Vol 38, No 1, 24–59.

[15] Note the distinction made by Johnson-George and Swap (1982) between reliability and emotional trust. *See* Johnson-George, C. and Swap, W. (1982) 'Measurement of specific interpersonal trust: construction and validations of a scale to assess trust in a specific order', *Journal of Personality and Social Psychology*, Vol 43, No 6, 1306–17.

[16] The first three stages of this typology have been developed by Lewicki and Buncker (1996) and are based on previous work by Saphiro, Sheppard and Cheraskin (1992). Based on discussions with M. Janssens we added the fourth dimension. The three forms of trust identified by Lewicki and Bunker are: deterrence-based trust, knowledge-based trust, and identification-based trust. *See* Lewicki, R. J. and Bunker, B. (1996) 'Developing and maintaining trust in work relationships', in Kramer, R. and Tyler, T. (eds) *Trust in Organisations: Frontiers of theory and research*. Thousand Oaks, California: Sage.

[17] Taking this reasoning to its limits even means that learning is not possible.

[18] Wheelan and Hochberger (1996) depict, for instance, four phases. We are limiting our discussion here to the work of Bouwen and Fry (1996), as they comprehensively integrate the work of their predecessors. *See* Wheelan, S. and Hochberger, J. (1996) 'Validation studies of the group development questionnaire', *Small Group Research*, Vol 27, No 1, 143–70; and Bouwen, R. and Fry, R. (1996) 'Facilitating group development: Interventions for a relational and contextual construction', in West, M. (ed.) *Handbook of Work Group Psychology*, Wiley.

[19] Bouwen, R. and Fry, R. (1996), op. cit.

Suggested further reading

Bouwen, R. and Fry, R. (1996) 'Facilitating group development: interventions for a relational and contextual construction', in West, M. (ed.) *Handbook of Work Group Psychology*, Wiley. These authors offer an excellent overview and integration of the issues involved when trying to develop groups.

Brown, J. S. and Duguid, P. (1994) 'Organisational learning and communities-of-practice: toward a unified view of working, learning and innovation', in Tsoukas, H. (ed.) *New thinking in Organisational Behaviour*. Oxford: Butterworth-Heinemann. These authors offer an excellent overview of the dynamics at play within communities and how social practices affect what is going on.

Lave, J. and Wenger, E. (1991) *Situated Learning: Legitimate peripheral participation*. Cambridge University Press. A must for people interested in the dynamics of learning processes.

Orr, J. (1996) *Talking About Machines: An ethnography of a modern job*. Cornell University Press. This book contains an extensive account of what is involved in the practice of service work nowadays; those interested in the tension between formal and informal practice should not hesitate to read it. It is also recommended to those involved in technical service jobs.

CHAPTER 12

The role of empowerment in service organizations

Bart Van Looy · Krist'l Krols · Dirk Buyens · Tine Vandenbossche

INTRODUCTION

During an ongoing change process, blue-collar workers in a computer firm's logistics department decided that they were as capable of taking initiatives and making decisions as their colleagues in engineering. At an after-hours meeting, they decided to ask their superiors for a mandate to handle the forthcoming move of their warehouse on their own. They formed a self-regulating project team and succeeded in transferring every piece of stock without management interference and, perhaps more importantly, without a financial loss.

After two years of discussion, it was agreed that the blue-collar workers in a tyre factory were to be allowed more discretion and autonomy in their jobs. As a result, several new teams started working without supervisors. During the first month, one of these semi-autonomous production teams stopped the machines for safety reasons. According to the engineers, the total cost of stopping the machines amounted to the gross yearly salary costs of three supervisors. Supervisors were re-installed after this incident.

A front-line airline employee was confronted with a queue of 30 people waiting for a trans-continental flight scheduled to leave in 15 minutes. He saw that he only had 12 places left. He also knew that the Concorde flight, due to leave 10 minutes later, still had plenty of capacity. There was no superior in the area. The last 18 passengers had the time of their lives, flying on Concorde using an economy ticket.

In a Brazilian company,[1] employees can participate in deciding the level of their wages. They are expected to decide by themselves the appropriate salary level, based on the following considerations: the amount of money they can earn elsewhere, the salary levels for similar jobs in other companies, the amount of money their friends and acquaintances with a similar background earn, and finally the amount of money they feel they need to live on. When this principle was introduced for the first time, problems occurred in only six cases, five of which involved people giving themselves a salary too low, according to their peers and supervisors.

In a large service organization, each employee has to define the objectives and direction for his or her own job every year. After extensive preparation, all the employees gather together for two weeks to discuss and integrate their different objectives and directives. If supervisors and employees disagree on whether to include a certain object-ive or to pursue in a certain direction, employees are allowed to explore the proposed direction. After a six-month experimentation period, a joint decision is made whether to continue or not. In the recent past, suggested objectives have resulted in a new product line, the formation of two new subsidiaries, and numerous quality improvements and cost reductions. Fifteen per cent of an employee's gross salary is contingent on achiev-ing his or her own goals.

These examples make it clear that today's organizations are experimenting and sometimes struggling with new ways of collaborating. The notion of *autonomy* – the degree to which people can and do make decisions on their own within their working context – seems to be central. An increase in autonomy and taking initia-tive is labelled as *empowerment*. However, empowerment also goes beyond the individual employee's specific work situation. Empowerment has implications for the organization as a whole: it affects the way of working, the way of organizing, and the relationships between employees and managers. Empowerment cannot be treated as an 'add-on'; rather, it implies changes in the design of authority, respon-sibility, learning and benefits.

The notion of empowerment is not completely new. In the past, we have encountered concepts such as participative management, involvement of the work-force, quality of working life, the role of autonomy for job satisfaction. However, there are some significant differences. The debate on empowerment strongly emphasizes results. Empowerment is today essentially seen as a way of improving a company's performance in terms of quality and customer satisfaction, whereas in the past the individual employee's well-being received equal or greater attention. The market demands quick responses to specific requests, technology allows for fast communication and flat structures and people ask for more involvement and autonomy. Everything seems to point to more participation of all employees in today's organizations, on a larger scale than ever before. Empowerment could be here to stay.

Empowerment can be approached on two levels.

1. *The level of the relationship between the individual employee and supervisor*. Here, individual motivation and leadership style will be crucial.
2. *The level of the broader system, the organization*. What is important at the organiza-tional level when speaking about empowerment? How must organizations be structured to allow for and reinforce empowerment?

Both levels will be explored in more depth in this chapter.

Objectives

By the end of this chapter, you should be able to discuss:

- the relevance of the notion of empowerment for service organizations
- what empowerment means at the level of the individual employee
- the implications of empowerment for leadership
- the implications of empowerment for the organization as a whole
- the consequences of empowerment for organizations in terms of outcomes

THE RELEVANCE OF EMPOWERMENT FOR SERVICE ENVIRONMENTS

Given the specific nature of service delivery, empowerment seems to be an issue especially important for service organizations. You will remember our discussion of the simultaneity of services in Chapter 1. Both customers and employees work simultaneously on the delivery of service. This means that employees play a crucial role in the experiences and satisfaction of the customer. Services also imply heterogeneity, part of which stems from the customer and becomes apparent only at the moment of the service delivery. This means that employees need a certain degree of autonomy during the service encounter. Standard operating procedures will not account for every customer–employee contact situation in most service organizations. As a result, the contact employees themselves play an important role in handling the customer interaction.

The significance of this autonomy will vary, however, according to the type of service activities, as well as the strategy followed.

Bowen and Lawler[2] developed a contingency model of empowerment within services. As a starting point, they observe that a number of ways of delivering services can all be very successful. These delivery methods are described by means of a continuum – with the 'production-line' approach at one end and the 'empowerment' approach at the other.

- The *production-line approach*, or the industrial way of delivering services, is characterized by simplification of tasks, clear division of labour, substitution of equipment and systems for employees, and little decision-making discretion afforded to employees.
- With the *empowered approach*, less emphasis is put on the systems surrounding the service employees, who are given more discretion and autonomy.

The empowerment approach can involve quicker on-line responses to customer demands during service delivery or when problems arise. Empowerment can also lead to higher levels of employee satisfaction, better quality of customer interaction, and higher levels of commitment, resulting in employee involvement, quality improvement and innovation.

However, empowerment requires greater investment in selection and training, resulting in higher labour costs. Empowerment can also possibly lead to customer impressions of not being treated correctly (because they are treated in a non-standardized way) and implies the risks of 'give-aways' and bad decisions by front-line employees.[3]

In the light of these benefits and costs, empowerment cannot be seen as the one best way to approach service industries. Bowen and Lawler define five contingencies including strategic, commercial, technological, environmental and workforce dimensions (*see* Table 12.1). Organizations, for which the description in the production-line column seems appropriate, will gain few benefits from empowerment. Costs will probably outweigh the benefits.

Although this framework offers guidance on how important empowerment can be at an *organizational* level, we believe that empowerment can be relevant for *individual* employees in almost every situation. Consider, for example, the blue-collar workers who formed a self-managing team to handle the forthcoming move of the warehouse. Within this project they acted autonomously: they drew up a project plan,

Table 12.1 Contingencies of empowerment

Contingency	Production-line approach	Empowerment approach
Basic business strategy	Low cost, high volume	Differentiation, customized, personalized
Tie to customer	Transaction, short time period	Relationship, long time period
Technology	Routine, simple	Non-routine, complex
Environmental	Predictable, few surprises	Unpredictable, many surprises
Types of people	Theory X manager, employees with low growth needs, low social needs and weak interpersonal skills	Theory Y manager, employees with low needs, high social needs and strong interpersonal skills

Source: Reprinted from 'The empowerment of service workers: What, why, how and when' by Bowen, D. and Lawler, E. *Sloan Management Review*, Spring 1992, by permission of publishers. © (1998) by Sloan Management Review Association. All rights reserved.

defined the individual steps, divided tasks and allocated responsibilities; they even worked out the budget and made decisions on necessary expenditures. However, about 85 per cent of their daily activities could be described as routine; procedures and quality regulations existed and had to be followed strictly. Nevertheless, among these employees the experience of empowerment was very high.

We can look at the functioning of a fire department in the same way. When an emergency occurs, everyone has to act quickly and central co-ordination – that is, one commander – is required. When a house is burning down, who needs a group discussion on how to approach the fire? However, in preparing actions or evaluating past performance and methods, everyone's input can be valuable. At these times giving employees the freedom and autonomy to think, speak and act can be extremely worthwhile.

EMPOWERMENT: THE EMPLOYEE AND THE SUPERVISOR

Empowerment at the level of the individual employee

Empowerment involves giving more autonomy, more freedom to employees to take decisions. Why should we do this?

The most important reason at the level of the individual employee is the belief that autonomy motivates people – that is, that people are willing to take initiatives and make decisions and that they prefer this above situations where everything regarding their jobs is dictated to them. Empowerment involves giving power and power means energy, so empowerment can be read as energizing people and increasing their motivation.

Motivation is not only a matter of autonomy, however. Intrinsic work motivation involves the elements within an individual, pertaining directly to the task, that produce energy, enthusiasm and satisfaction. Five elements seem to be crucial when talking about individual work motivation:[4]

- *Meaning* can be seen as the value of a work goal, as perceived by the individual in relation to his or her own ideals or standards. It implies that there is some sort of congruence between what an individual actually does and what he or she believes or values. The better the fit, the higher a person's motivation will be.

■ *Competence* has to do with an individual's belief that he or she is able to perform the required activities adequately – that is, confidence in one's own ability to perform the tasks skilfully. Competence is also related to motivation: the more an individual feels competent, the more motivated he or she will be.

■ *Self-determination* is linked with the individual's sense of having a say in initiating and regulating actions, work methods, productivity and so on. It involves the extent to which an individual can influence the way his or her activities are performed, which affects motivation.

■ *Strategic autonomy* pertains to the individual's freedom to influence the content of the job. Whereas self-determination refers to the influence on the *how* of the job, strategic autonomy refers to the extent to which people can influence the *what* of the job – that is, the content and direction of activities within their jobs. The case of the blue-collar workers handling the move, described in the introduction to this chapter, involves *operational autonomy* only. Once decisions are taken regarding what can be done, the workers have the freedom to define the way the move is organized. The example of the service company which allows its employees to define their own objectives and direction involves *strategic autonomy*.

■ Finally, *impact* can be viewed as the degree to which an employee can influence outcomes at work. It has to do with having a say regarding what is going on in the direct work environment, what happens in the department, and also how it happens.

All five elements contribute to intrinsic task motivation. The more they are present in the experiences of an individual in relation to his or her job, the higher the level of motivation will be. Self-determination, strategic autonomy and impact are obviously related to autonomy. However, motivation can be seen as something broader than autonomy; it also involves finding a job meaningful and having confidence in one's own competence.

It is important, therefore, when discussing empowerment at the individual employee level to keep in mind that empowerment has to do with motivation and that levels of motivation are determined by several different factors or elements. The more these elements are present in an individual's work experience, the more empowerment will be experienced and the higher motivation will be. Table 12.2 summarizes the five elements.

Now that we have identified the building blocks of empowerment at the individual level, we can start thinking about putting empowerment into practice.

When the five dimensions within the notion of empowerment are examined more closely, we observe that they are related to each other in the following way:

Table 12.2 The five dimensions of empowerment as a driving force behind individual work motivation

Meaning	The extent to which an individual experiences a task as personally meaningful
Competence	The extent to which an individual feels confident about his/her capabilities to perform the task
Self-determination	The degree of influence that an individual has on how to perform the job
Strategic autonomy	The degree of influence an individual has on the content of the job
Impact	The degree of influence an individual has on the direct work environment

Figure 12.1 Empowerment as a pyramid

competence and *meaning* seem to be necessary pre-conditions of *self-determination, impact* and *strategic autonomy.* High levels of both competence and meaning are required before high levels of autonomy can be achieved. In other words, low levels of meaning and competence are seldom seen in combination with moderate or high levels of autonomy.[5] As a result, empowerment can be pictured as a kind of pyramid, the foundations of which are formed by competence and meaning (*see* Figure 12.1).

These findings have serious managerial implications, since, when implementing change processes directed towards empowerment, looking at autonomy alone can be deceptive. Sufficient degrees of meaningfulness and competence should also be present; otherwise, the seeds of autonomy will be sown on dry ground. Empowerment is a gradual process, starting with the creation of meaning and feelings of competence, and evolving towards levels of self-determination, impact and even strategic autonomy.

Empowerment has been shown to have a significant impact on employee morale and behaviour. Research[6] has indicated clearly that employees with high levels of empowerment are more satisfied, show higher levels of commitment and higher degrees of problem-solving and innovative behaviour compared with colleagues for whom empowerment is not available (*see* Table 12.3).

Table 12.3 Comparison of employees with high and low levels of empowerment*

	Low empowered (mean)	High empowered (mean)
Job satisfaction	4.39	5.66
Commitment	4.61	5.76
Innovative behaviour	4.01	5.13

* Variables are rated on a seven-point scale and differences in means are significant at $p < 0.001$

Leadership and empowerment: an impossible marriage?

As we have shown, empowerment can be defined as increasing an individual's autonomy and degree of freedom. It involves giving employees more latitude in

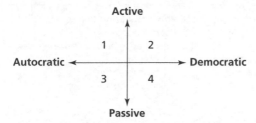

Figure 12.2 A general model of leadership

terms of decision making and actions. Does this mean that managers will become obsolete? The answer seems to be no. Setting goals and developing trust between employees and supervisors[7] will continue to be the preserve of the supervisor or manager. It is expected, however, that new forms of leadership will be developed; empowerment will have implications for the leadership style.

Before we examine and define more clearly this new style of leadership, we shall consider a general model of leadership (*see* Figure 12.2).[8] Leadership practices can be categorized on a continuum ranging from entirely autocratic to purely democratic. *Autocratic leadership* is displayed by leaders who look for sole possession of power and control; *democratic leadership* is characterized by sharing authority and power between superiors and employees.

Leadership styles can also be described according to a second dimension ranging from active to passive. A *passive* or laissez-faire leader is usually not involved in the daily activities of his or her employees, and thus exercises little influence. An *active* leader is highly involved in employees' activities, which leads to high visibility of the leader for the employees.

These two dimensions can be combined into a two-by-two framework which allows us to explore the notion of leadership in relation to empowerment in greater depth. In fact, Stewart and Manz[9] merged this framework with the notion of empowerment. Their integrated framework can be found in Figure 12.3.

As can be seen in Figure 12.3, some leadership styles do not seem compatible with the notion of empowerment:

■ *Overpowering leadership* – i.e., the combination of active and autocratic behaviour – tends to overwhelm the initiatives of employees, thus inhibiting empowerment.

■ *Powerless leadership* combines an autocratic orientation with a passive attitude. Here the probability that distance will occur between employees and their superior is high. This leads to leadership behaviour where little direction is given and only sanctions are taken. This will often cause stress and certainly does not seem a good foundation for building trust and support, let alone empowerment.

■ *Power-building leadership* includes encouragement in terms of skill development and co-operative networks. However, within this approach leaders still retain significant control over what is going on, as employees rely on the leader to set the overall direction.

■ *Empowering leadership* combines a democratic approach with a more passive way of acting. Within this approach, the requirements seem to be fulfilled for empowering employees in an enduring way. Here one can truly speak of achieving forms of 'strategic autonomy'.

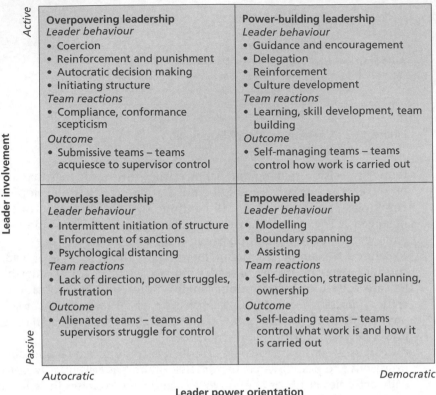

Figure 12.3 An integrated framework of leadership and empowerment[10]

Source: Stewart, G. and Manz, C. (1995) 'Leadership for self-managing work teams: A typology and integrative model', *Human Relations*, Vol 48, No 7, 747–70.

Exhibit 12.1

Empowerment at Taco Bell

The changes in leadership style involved inempowerment are revealed in the following account of the change process taking place within the Taco Bell corporation, a US fast-food chain offering Mexican cuisine.[11]

In this company a new market approach was introduced in the mid-1980s, stressing the idea of value. Value was to be understood as delivering food quickly, accurately, hygienically and at the appropriate temperature and this in combination with the lowest costs possible. This approach involved above all a change in the mindset of both managers and employees: quality characteristics and low costs were to be seen as mutually reinforcing elements, not contradictory items. To arrive at this reconfiguration of the business, changes were introduced at several levels. New production

techniques were developed, restaurant space was redesigned, a fully decentralized information system was introduced and even recipes were reformulated so as to allow fast delivery. These changes at the level of the supporting operational systems were complemented by training and development efforts as well as the introduction of empowerment at the level of the employees and the managers.

In the past a strong emphasis had been placed on managerial responsibility: any problem occurring in a restaurant had to be dealt with by the manager in charge, whether it involved a major breakdown of the technical equipment or a short-changed customer. This hierarchical approach was thrown out. As a first step, the jobs of restaurant manager and district manager – supervising several restaurants – were redesigned. In the past the

Exhibit 12.1 continued

district manager had played a policing role – including 'white gloves' inspections of the physical restaurants and audits of the financial books. This changed drastically: the span of control was increased from six to 20 restaurants. This implied an (intended) revision in the management skills and styles necessary for a market manager, as district managers were now called. Coaching and developing took the place of controlling.[12]

 This could only be realized by redefining the role and competencies of the restaurant manager, whose job title was changed to restaurant general manager. As more and more decision making was delegated, managers with broader skills were required, who could take care of profit and loss, are decisive and take ownership. Training and support to help with this transition were available. The compensation and benefits package was also redesigned as to reflect this new approach: the base salary was increased and the bonus element started to reflect the idea of ownership. These changes had a significant impact: sales and profits increased (doubled or tripled) over a five-year time period and employee and customer satisfaction evaluations did the same.

 In the early 1990s, this logic was even extended by introducing 'team-managed units' (TMUs) – teams of employees sufficiently trained to manage the store without a full-time manager. Crew members were seen as the experts in delivering value to the customers. It was crucial in this respect to create a shared ownership of problems among the crew members and the skills to solve these problems. The team-managed unit concept was introduced in 1992 and was enthusiastically embraced by restaurant general managers and market managers. By the end of 1993 there were TMUs in 90 per cent of the company stores. This transition also implied the commitment of resources to competence development; a restaurant manager had to spend about a year being trained in how to create a self-sufficient team. However, stores operating this system did perform better.

 The responsibilities of the restaurant general manager also increased. Once they were freed from most of their daily activities – such as scheduling labour, ordering inventory, interviewing applicants, handling cash and making deposits, opening and closing stores – they started to take on responsibility for the new distribution channels Taco Bell has been developing, including lunch-school programmes, and shopping mall restaurants. As a result of these changes, the span of control of market managers increased from 20:1 to 56:1. During these changes customer satisfaction increased steadily, as did sales and profits.

The Taco Bell story in Exhibit 12.1 shows that empowerment might be an important element in designing future HR practices. It motivates people and hence has a positive impact on sales and profits. However, empowerment is not something to be implemented overnight. It implies a serious rethinking of leadership approach and style. Moreover, the case of Taco Bell also illustrates that changes are not limited to the employee's motivation or the managerial style of the supervisor. Superiors and employees do not work in a vacuum; they are working within a broader organization. The changes taking place within Taco Bell would not have been successful without considerable training and development efforts and without the installation of new operating systems and remuneration packages. Empowerment implies changes at the level of the organization as a whole.

EMPOWERMENT: THE ORGANIZATION

People cannot become empowered when they are not supported by an environment that stimulates actions such as initiative taking and autonomy. We cannot expect employees to show dedication, responsibility, autonomy and initiative within their daily activities without first creating an environment in which this behaviour can be developed. What is needed is an *empowered organization*.

Empowered organizations have everything in place to facilitate the 'pushing down of information, knowledge, rewards and power'.[13] We have already discussed power in this chapter when we considered the autonomy of individuals within the organization. But what is meant by information, knowledge and rewards?

Sharing information

The sharing of information is extremely important; empowerment cannot work without people being informed. To be able to take the right decisions and initiatives, employees need to be informed. Information on a range of subjects is required.

- *The service concept.* Employees need to have a clear view of the service concept they want to achieve – that is the company's objectives and values (*see* Chapter 2). A good knowledge of these values and how they relate to daily activities are pre-requisites, if employees are to act according to the desired service concept. How can employees correctly evaluate the quality remarks of a displeased customer when the quality policy of the company is not clear to them?
- *The service delivery process as a whole.* Information should not be limited to an individual's own functional area; employees should have some insight into the total service delivery process and their own role within it. Otherwise, it becomes extremely difficult for people to assess the impact of their actions on the final customer experience. Withholding this broader information runs the risk of creating problems further down the service delivery process.
- *Past and current performance as well as future targets.* Employees are also entitled to be openly informed of the performance of the organization as a whole. Moreover information is not only important in relation to how to act in the future; information on current and past activities is equally crucial. Without this kind of information employees will not know whether they are doing well – whether their actions are appropriate or not.
- *The setting of goals.* Goal setting is crucial as well. Empowerment does not involve supplying information to employees and then leaving everything open. An attitude of 'let's see what happens with these guys now they are empowered' would be disastrous. Empowerment means giving people all relevant information as well as clear objectives so that they can achieve success. Whereas employees want enough latitude to be able to deliver results, they also like to have a clear picture of their authority. Employees who know what is expected of them and who have the right information to act to achieve these goals are simply more empowered.

Heskett, Sasser and Schlesinger[14] distinguish between two different modes of setting goals:

1. With *the traditional approach*, goals define what an individual is allowed to do. Everything else is discussed with management. So as long as employees stay within the 'box', they are free to act.
2. *The non-traditional approach* simply defines what needs to be done. Additional actions to achieve better results are allowed and even encouraged as long as the 'bottom line' is respected. It is this second approach that was introduced within Taco Bell (*see* Exhibit 12.1) and Au Bon Pain (discussed in Chapter 11).

The traditional approach is more hands-on. It implies a rather exhaustive definition process of what is allowed and what is not. Emphasis is refocused on conformance to rules and regulations and control. In this respect, the second is the preferred approach. However, it will demand more from employees in terms of competencies, maturity and integrity. The actual nature of the workforce will determine which of the options is chosen. To achieve real empowerment, an evolution towards the non-traditional approach will be inevitable.

Knowledge and competence development

It is clear that the successful implementation of empowerment requires competent employees with an extended range of skills. It is no longer sufficient to execute a limited number of tasks perfectly. An individual should be able to evaluate the way of working, to discover opportunities for improvement, to generate ideas and communicate them, to work in teams, to listen to colleagues and to take responsibility for the results obtained. The reverse relation also holds true; if an employer wants employees to develop these competencies, empowerment is the only option. Of course, this involves an element of change or even a transformation.

This transformation needs to be supported by a broader competence base; training programmes addressing technical skills as well as personal and behavioural characteristics will become essential. Business and management courses also need to be introduced on a larger scale. The crew members within Taco Bell had to master inventory control techniques, labour scheduling approaches or interview techniques to assess the competencies of new applicants. Increasing technical skills is not enough, however; personal characteristics, such as a customer orientation and good citizen behaviour, are also crucial as employees will have to make more frequent decisions on their own.

It is therefore crucial for today's service companies to develop continuously the competence base of their employees. Ways of developing these competencies have been explored extensively in previous sections. It is important to stress again here the relevance of the notion of 'useful slack'. Development involves time (just think back to our discussion of the idea of peripherality when addressing the notion of 'legitimate peripheral participation' in Chapter 11). In the stream of reorganizations, downsizing, cost-cutting programmes and rationalization, organizations are sometimes reducing themselves to a minimal level that could be harmful to future development. By looking at organizations as mere mechanical constructions and by seeking only immediate results, companies might cut out their own future – the human potential. In order to face the problems and opportunities of tomorrow's markets, employees need to understand, to learn continuously, to develop a critical spirit, to look for improvements and to adapt to change. This way of working is only possible if some 'slack' is left in the organization – room for teamwork, forethought and learning. It is impossible for people to develop a mutual learning process, to discover areas for improvement or to apply all their talents when they are *continuously* fully occupied and experiencing the stress of operational activities.

Redistributing rewards

Eventually, when employees are being asked to act like 'local' managers, a rethink of recognition and rewards is inevitable. There are two reasons for this:

1. People cannot be expected to act like responsible entrepreneurs engaging themselves fully in the achievement of results within their own activity domain, if the old employer–employee logic is applied when these same results are divided among the different stakeholders. Empowerment involves the idea of variable pay; a larger part of the salary will be linked more closely to results.
2. Broadening the competence base will also affect base salary levels. Whereas increasing people's competencies and abilities is rewarding in itself, there should also be some monetary rewards – a tendency justified by the increased role employees play in the value creation process.

Is empowerment worth it?

Empowerment cannot be regarded as a quick fix.[15] It is important to consider whether all the efforts required to achieve empowerment – for example, rethinking organizational functioning, developing competencies, introducing new ways of leadership – are worth pursuing.

Empirical evidence seems to show such efforts are worthwhile. The work on the service profit chain, extensively discussed throughout this book, provides us with the necessary conceptual links between empowerment and profitability. Service capability defines employees' satisfaction which in its turn has a positive effect on service quality and productivity, and hence customer satisfaction and profitability. Several studies have empirically demonstrated the robustness of these links. Companies involved include Taco Bell, Southwest Airlines, American Express, to name but a few.[16]

Our own research data confirms this view. Employees with a high level of empowerment are more satisfied and committed and hence will contribute more to productivity, quality and in the later stages customer satisfaction, loyalty and hence profitability.

An impressive study was also undertaken recently by Lawler *et al.*[17] to investigate how involvement efforts related to business performance. About 40 per cent of the Fortune top 1000 companies were involved in this study.

The relationship between organizational practices aimed at creating the involvement of the employees and performance was investigated systematically. With regard to involvement initiatives, a distinction was made between actions aimed at sharing information, increasing knowledge, redistributing rewards and finally delegating power and decision authority within the organization. Performance outcomes were examined at three levels: direct outcomes like quality and productivity, profitability (also compared with competitors) and employee satisfaction. The results are clear – despite the huge amount of interfering variables not included in this analysis. A strong positive relation occurs over and over again between the degree of involvement and the level of the results.

It is clear that concentrating on competence development and introducing empowerment are rewarding strategies even on a broader level than the purely economic.

CONCLUSION

In this chapter we have been looking extensively at the notion of empowerment. At the level of the individual, empowerment can be seen as a motivational construct involving more than just autonomy: meaning and competence are crucial building blocks, while impact, self-determination and strategic autonomy complete the picture. Empowerment will have an impact on employee–manager relationships – involving a shift from active and autocratic management styles towards more democratic and even passive forms of leadership. Moreover, the impact of empowerment extends beyond the hierarchical relationship; empowerment has implications at the level of the organization as a whole. Delegating power, sharing information, developing competencies and distributing rewards in line with actual performance are the main ingredients of an empowered organization.

It is clear that empowerment has many positive implications, both at the level of the individual employee and in terms of organizational outcomes.

Review and discussion questions

- Would you agree with the statement that empowerment is not relevant for low skilled employees? Why (not)?

- Does the road towards empowerment lead eventually towards strategic autonomy (at the individual level)?

- In terms of implementation, what are according to you crucial prerequisites and/or ingredients of (change) programs aimed at introducing – or further developing – empowerment within the organization?

Notes and references

[1] The company referred to is Semco. For a full description of the 'Semco-style', *see* Semler, R. (1993) *Turning the Tables*. New York: Time Books.

[2] Bowen, D. and Lawler, E. (1992) 'The empowerment of service workers: What, why, how and when', *Sloan Management Review*, Spring, 31–9; Bowen, D. and Lawler, E. (1995) 'Empowering service employees', *Sloan Management Review*, Summer, 73–84.

[3] Bowen, D. and Lawler, E. (1992), op. cit.

[4] Four of these dimensions are developed by Thomas and Velthouse (1990): meaning, competence, self determination and impact. Spreitzer (1995, 1996) later developed a scale to assess these four dimensions. Recent research on the notion of empowerment added the fifth dimension: strategic autonomy (*see* Van Looy, B., Desmet, S., Krols, K. and Van Dierdonck, R. (1998). *See* Thomas, K. W. and Velthouse, B. A. (1990) 'Cognitive elements of empowerment: an "interpretive" model of intrinsic task motivation', *Academy of Management Review*, Vol 15, No 4, 666–81; Spreitzer, G. (1995) 'Psychological empowerment in the workplace: Dimensions, measurement and validation', *Academy of Management Review*, Vol 38, No 5, 1442–65; Spreitzer, G. (1996) 'Social structural characteristics of psychological empowerment', *Academy of Management Journal*, Vol 39, No 2, 483–504; and finally Van Looy, B., Desmet, S., Krols, K. and Van Dierdonck, R. (1998) 'Psychological empowerment in a service environment', in Swartz, T., Bowen, D. and Brown, S. (eds) *Advances in Services Marketing and Management*, 7, JAI Press.

[5] This relationship between the different empowerment sub-dimensions has been tested in a more rigorous way. Results were statistically significant. For more details the reader is referred to Van Looy *et al.* (1998), op. cit.

[6] For more details the reader is referred to Van Looy *et al.* (1998), op. cit. Within this study highly significant differences between high- and low-empowered employees, related to more satisfaction, commitment and degree of innovative behaviour have been found. The sample contained nearly 500 service employees and managers.

[7] Empirical evidence can be found again in Van Looy *et al.* (1998), op. cit. Here it became clear that high-empowered employees differed from low-empowered employees in the sense that they had a more precise view of their goals. Also high-empowered employees had more trustworthy relationships with their managers.

[8] This framework was developed originally by Bass and Associates in the early 1990s. Given the wide empirical validation as well as acceptance, this framework is chosen as our starting point. The interested reader is referred to Bass, B. M. (1990) *Leadership and Performance Beyond Expectations*. New York: Free Press.

[9] Stewart and Manz developed this framework in the context of team functioning. Here some adaptations are made to make the model applicable to the supervisor–employee relationship. *See* Stewart, G. and Manz, C. (1995) 'Leadership for self-managing work teams: a typology and integrative model', *Human Relations*, Vol 48, No 7, 747–70.

[10] *Source*: Ibid.

[11] *See* extensive case studies developed at Harvard Business School (*Taco Bell Corp.*, 9–692–058, *Taco-Bell*, 1994, 9–694–076) as well as Heskett, J., Sasser, W. and Schlesinger, L. (1997) *The Service Profit Chain*. New York: Free Press.

[12] This does not mean, however, that Taco Bell did not monitor the operational performance of the restaurants any more. To ensure adherance to quality standards, different 'safety nets' were installed: a complaint line, mystery shoppers and regular market surveys. Information brought back to the restaurant general managers and market managers was to start working on improvement. Information was also used to assess the appropriate level of bonus.

[13] Lawler *et al.* (1995) define four characteristics of – what they call – 'high involvement' organizations: sharing information, developing knowledge, rewarding performance and, of course, redistributing power. For more details, *see* Lawler, E. E. III, Mohrman, S. and Ledford, G. (1995) *Creating High Performance Organisations*. San Francisco: Jossey-Bass publishers.

[14] Heskett, J., Sasser, W. and Schlesinger, L. (1997), op. cit.

[15] *See* in this respect as well the work of Blanchard, K., Carlos, J. and Randolph, A. (2001) *Empowerment Takes More Than a Minute*. San Francisco: Berrett-Koehler Publishers.

[16] Ibid.

[17] Lawler, E. E. III, Mohrman, S. and Ledford, G. (1995b), op. cit.

Suggested further reading

Bowen, D. and Lawler, E. E. III (1992) 'The empowerment of service workers: What, why, how and when', *Sloan Management Review*, Spring, 31–9.

Bowen, D. and Lawler, E. E. III (1995) 'Empowering service employees', *Sloan Management Review*, Summer, 73–84. These two works provide an excellent discussion on empowerment for service environments.

Lawler, E. E. III, Mohrman, S. and Ledford, G. (1995) *Creating High Performance Organisations*. San Francisco: Jossey-Bass. If you want to see some real empirical evidence that HR practices do make a difference in terms of financial returns, we strongly recommend the work of Lawler *et al.*

Stewart, G. and Manz, C. (1995) 'Leadership for self-managing work teams: A typology and integrative model', *Human Relations*, Vol 39, 483–504. The work of Stewart and Manz is very revealing in relation to the implications of empowerment for leadership.

CHAPTER 13

Role stress among front-line employees

Koen Dewettinck · Dirk Buyens

INTRODUCTION

Ariane is a customer service rep in a call centre. Almost every day, her manager emphasizes that the number one priority in her job is customer satisfaction. Being committed to the company, her department and her manager, she tries to create customer satisfaction as much as possible. For example, when she feels a customer needs some more detailed information on a certain topic, she's very happy to provide it. However, Ariane is not recognized as being a top performer because according to the company's appraisal system, her average 'calls handled' count is not up to the departmental standard. . .

Mark is a consultant who regularly has dinner with important customers. He does so because he knows that these dinners strengthen the relationship and make the customers happy. Sometimes, when Mark has come home very late yet again, his wife Carol wonders whether he is married to her or to his customers. . .

Joe works in a fast-food restaurant. Yesterday, a customer asked for a burger without any vegetables. Because the full-option burgers roll from the kitchen to his desk, Joe didn't immediately know how to respond. Once, the restaurant manager told him that quick delivery is the company's interpretation of qualitative service. 'But to have the burgers delivered quickly, we can't take specific requests from customers into consideration,' the manager added. Joe realized that this answer was not what the customer was waiting for, but it didn't matter any more, since the customer was already on his way out, shouting that he 'would try at the snack bar around the corner'. . .

Angela is a cleaning lady in a large community hospital. Her boss has told her that she is not expected to talk to visitors when she's busy sweeping the floor. Every time when a visitor asks for directions to a particular department, she feels very unsure about how to respond. . .

What do Ariane, Mark, Joe and Angela have in common in the above situations? They all are experiencing confrontations with various expectations of their roles as service employees. Although these single incidents may not have such a deleterious effect on their well-being or performance, the continual feeling of being torn apart by conflicting and unclear expectations from different constituencies they come into contact with (management, customers, family, colleagues. . .) clearly does. Those feelings have been called 'role stress' and are the central point of interest in this chapter.

Objectives

By the end of this chapter, you should be able to discuss:

- the relevance of the idea of role stress for service organizations
- what role stress means for the individual employee and which forms it takes
- how the work context can influence front-line employees' experience of role stress
- how role stress can be minimized for front-line employees

RELEVANCE OF ROLE STRESS FOR THE SERVICE ENCOUNTER

Front-line employees are employees involved in customer work. The term refers to special types of organizational service positions that involve interaction with both the organization and its customers.

As we stressed in the introductory chapter on the nature of services, simultaneity is an inherent characteristic of service work. This means that quite often the customer takes part in the production process and consumes the service as it is being produced. The (at least) partial overlap between production and consumption implies that there is personal contact during the service delivery process; customers and front-line employees are simultaneously involved in the service delivery process. Front-line work thus involves job expectations that arise from both the organization and the customers, whether in the context of closing a transaction or offering post-transaction problem-solving and/or technical support.[1] So one of the key characteristics of services, i.e. simultaneity, might imply the presence of multiple and sometimes even conflicting expectations. Bateson[2] even went so far as to suggest that a service encounter can be viewed as a 'three-cornered fight', with the customers, the server and the service firm all vying for control. He argues that front-line employees seek to control the service encounter as a means of safeguarding their mental and physical health. Yet, customers also seek to control the encounter since they not only consume the service, but also help to produce the service. Meanwhile, the organization itself seeks to control the encounter through its systems of policies, procedures and supervision. It is in this context of the service encounter, which can be considered a compromise between partially conflicting parties, that role stress takes shape. As argued by Singh,[3] the apparent conflict between satisfying management and customers and of meeting productivity and quality goals emerges as a consistent underlying theme in the study and management of front-line employees.

ROLE STRESS DEFINED

Role theory in organizations

The central theoretical framework for understanding role stress in organizations was developed by Kahn *et al.* (1964).[4] Although their work dates from the 1960s, it is still extremely relevant today, especially for those studying front-line service jobs.

The origins of role theory emphasize its focus on interactivity within social exchange patterns. Role theory would argue that the social exchange which occurs between two or more people demonstrates certain patterns which are determined to a large extent by the role expectations and actual roles which each person adopts. The life of the individual can thus be seen as an array of roles played in the particular set of organizations and groups to which he or she belongs. These groups and organizations, or rather the subparts of each, which affect the person directly, together make up his or her environment. Characteristics of these organizations and groups (company, union, church, family and others) affect the person's physical and emotional state, and are major determinants of his or her behaviour.

Different kinds of role stress

According to role theory, role demands and performance expectations from one or more people or groups towards a focal person can take the form of different role stressors. The three major role stressors that were identified are *role conflict, role ambiguity* and *role overload*.

Role conflict

Role conflict occurs for an actor when the actor perceives that sets of demands from two or more constituencies to which an actor is held accountable (a) are incompatible or inconsistent with one another in such a way that both sets cannot be met and (b) are simultaneously pressed on the actor.

Kahn and his colleagues made a distinction between different types of role conflict:

- *Intra-sender role conflict* refers to different prescriptions and proscriptions from a single constituent that may be incompatible. For example, a supervisor may request a subordinate to acquire material which is unavailable through normal channels and at the same time prohibit violating normal channels.
- *Inter-sender conflict* refers to the situation when pressures from one role sender oppose pressures from one or more other senders. The pressures on a foreman for close supervision from his superiors and for looser supervision from his subordinates provide an example of inter-sender conflict.
- *Inter-role conflict* refers to the situation when role pressures associated with membership in one organization are in conflict with pressures stemming from membership in other groups. Demands from role-senders on the job for overtime or take-home work may conflict with pressures from one's spouse to give undivided attention to family affairs during evening hours. The conflict arises between the focal person's roles as worker and partner/parent.
- *Person-role conflict.* An example of this is the conflict that may exist between the needs and values of a person and the demands of his or her environment. It can occur when role requirements violate a person's moral values or needs and aspirations.

All these types of role conflict have one major characteristic in common: members of a role set exert role pressures to change the behaviour of a focal person. Since the focal person is already 'in role', already behaving, and already maintaining some kind of equilibrium among the disparate forces and motives which he or she experiences, the generated pressures represent new and additional forces with which he or she must cope. In this sense, these pressures threaten an existing equilibrium. Moreover, the stronger the pressures from role senders toward changes in the behaviour of the focal person, the greater the conflict created for him or her.

Role ambiguity

Role ambiguity,[5] on the other hand, can be defined as the degree to which information is lacking regarding:

- the scope and limits of one's responsibilities;
- expectations associated with a role and the methods and behaviours for fulfilling one's job responsibilities;
- which expectations take priority or stated otherwise, which elements of the role are most important;
- the standards by which one's performance is appraised.

Each member of an organization must have certain kinds of information at their disposal if he or she is to conform to the role expectations held by members of the work environment. A person may be uncertain about many facets of their social or physical environment. Organizations have several frequently encountered areas of ambiguity which people often find stressful. Singh and Rhoads[6] found that front-line employees may experience uncertainties about the expectations of the organization, their manager and managers of other departments, their colleagues, customers and families and, finally, expectations concerning ethical behaviour. These authors thus found seven facets of ambiguity in front-line employees' jobs (see Figure 13.1). For example, front-line employees may experience uncertainties towards customers about how to behave when customers complain, but they may also be uncertain about which positive attributes of their products to highlight when presenting them to customers. Finally, front-line employees may also be uncertain about how to interact with their customers.

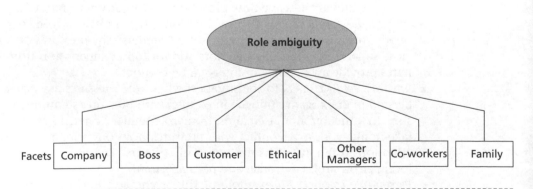

Figure 13.1 Ambiguities faced by front-line employees[7]

Source: Based on Singh, J. and Rhoads, G. K. (1991) 'Boundary role ambiguity in marketing-oriented positions: a multidimensional, multifaceted operationalization', *Journal of Marketing Research*, Vol 28, August, 328–38.

Role overload

Role overload, finally, occurs when an employer demands more of an employee than he or she can reasonably accomplish in a given time, or when the employee simply perceives the demands of work as excessive.[8]

To understand role overload, it is useful to distinguish between quantitative and qualitative overload. When quantitative overload is experienced, the employee is fully capable of meeting role demands. The problem is that there are too many role demands (e.g. too many customers within a given period of time) for the employee to handle. Given more time, and perhaps resources, the employee who is quantitatively overloaded could meet these role demands. On the other hand, when an employee is qualitatively overloaded, the demands of the role exceed his or her skills and abilities. In this case, even with more time and resources, the employee will not be able to meet the role demands. In the case of qualitative overload, individuals' skills and abilities do not allow them to meet their role demands adequately.

HANDLING ROLE STRESS FOR FRONT-LINE EMPLOYEES

Role stress's subversive effects

Numerous studies have focused on the relationship between the occurrence of role stress and the feelings and behaviours of those experiencing it.[9] One conclusion that can be drawn from these studies is that role stress clearly has a negative impact on employee satisfaction and employee commitment. Furthermore, it has been shown that role stress also negatively influences employees' willingness to stay in the organization.[10] Given the ideas behind the service profit chain discussed in previous chapters, one could even state that too much stress will affect customer satisfaction, and hence loyalty and even profitability.

Looking at the behavioural consequences there is evidence that role stress not only has a negative impact on employees' productivity but also on the quality of the services delivered by those employees. The relationship between role stress and performance has been predicted by both cognitive and motivational explanations.[11] From a cognitive perspective, role stressors hinder performance because with them the individual faces either a lack of knowledge about the most effective behaviours to engage in or an almost impossible situation in which to achieve everything expected. Therefore, regardless of the amount of effort expended, behaviours are most likely to be inefficient, misdirected or insufficient. A motivational perspective would predict that performance being negatively correlated with role stressors because they are negatively associated with effort-to-performance and performance-to-reward expectations.

Given the subversive impact of role stress on service employees' feelings and behaviours, it is worthwhile for managers in a service context to try to minimize role stress as much as possible. It has been shown that a mixture of different elements within the work context influences the level of role stress experienced by service employees. These relate to leadership, empowerment and formalization. We will review those different elements first; next we will point out some directions to choose an approach which fits your service organization.

Leadership and role stress

Since the supervisor plays an integral part in a service employee's role performance, for instance by providing key resources and by motivating personnel, it is important to take leadership into account when considering the work context in which role stress occurs.

Leadership behaviour has been extensively studied for several decades.[12] The focus was primarily on identifying and categorizing what the leader does – i.e. his or her behaviour. Different researchers have found a differing number of factors underlying leadership behaviour, varying from one to five. Nevertheless, although sometimes called different names, the same two major dimensions of leadership consistently emerged: leader initiating structure and leader consideration.[13]

Leader initiating structure relates to the way in which a supervisor guides employees, provides a psychological framework that clarifies roles, monitors subordinates' activities and stimulates them to display better performance. Leader initiating structure thus refers to the leader's task-oriented activities.

Leader consideration, on the other hand, is the degree to which a supervisor creates an atmosphere of affective support and socio-emotional concern for the well-being of subordinates. Leader consideration thus refers to the leader's people-oriented activities.

Both these dimensions of leadership behaviour have shown to affect role stress.[14] Task-oriented leadership behaviour provides employees with information about what is expected in their role. Consequently, these behaviours allow the leader to reduce role stress among front-line employees. As may be expected, task-oriented leadership behaviour is especially effective in reducing front-line employees' role ambiguity. Apparently, leader initiating structure helps clarify roles but does little to reduce conflict. Providing expectations unilaterally may preclude the subordinate from resolving conflicts that become clear in response to initiating structure.

People-oriented leadership behaviour, rather than exclusively serving a social or emotional role, appears to also serve an instrumental or task role. As employees gain knowledge about what behaviours are rewarded, indecision as to which role expectations to fulfil and which to ignore may diminish, thus reducing conflicts that may have arisen due to unclear role priorities. In contrast with task-oriented leadership behaviours, leader consideration may include some level of participation (e.g. the supervisor asks about and shows concern for subordinates) that affords subordinates the opportunity to discuss and resolve conflicts.

In summary, it seems that both task-oriented and people-oriented leadership behaviours have a reducing impact on role stress. When considering the role of service managers and others who take up a leadership role in the service organization, it is therefore important that these people not only be trained to be able to clarify what they expect from their subordinates, but they should also know that showing consideration and affective support clearly has a diminishing impact on front-line employees' role stress level.

Minimizing role stress by empowering employees . . .

As discussed in the previous chapter, empowerment assumes that to a large extent employees are capable of co-ordination, planning and control of service quality. As such, empowerment is also referred to as the 'involvement model'[15] and can be achieved by implementing practices that distribute power, information, knowledge and rewards throughout the organization. Employees experience greater autonomy and freedom to take initiatives. The empowerment approach thus strives for competent, motivated employees who experience autonomy and consequently can take the necessary actions to satisfy customers' needs during the 'moment of truth'. As such, empowerment might contribute to front-line employees confidence to handle the heterogeneity encountered during service encounters; if employees feel competent and find themselves within an organization that provides the necessary information and support, as discussed in the previous chapter. If these conditions are not satisfied, one bears the risk of ending up with merely an increase in job stress because of the lack of clear guidelines or prescriptions on how to behave in all kinds of situations.

. . . or by formalizing?

The idea of formalization reflects the production-line approach, a still popular view of managing service employees.[16] The production-line approach for services suggests that a technocratically conceived service process is the best way to serve the customer. This approach emphasizes:

1. task simplification;
2. clear task division;
3. replacement of human labour with equipment (hard technology), systems (soft technology) or a combination of the two (hybrid technology); and
4. little decision-making power for employees.

Although the idea of the production-line approach to services stems from the 1970s, it is still a very relevant viewpoint which is highly visible in contemporary service organizations. The is McDonald's approach is the most eloquent example. Another context where the production-line approach can be clearly recognized is the call centre industry. Call centre operators' response to customers is quite standardized. Employees usually have a clear idea of what to do and service levels are enhanced using high-tech solutions.

Central to these service contexts is the idea of formalization. Formalization is the extent to which work activities are governed formally by administrative rules, policies and procedures. The degree of formalization of the work context will influence service employees' role stress. Written rules and procedures governing the work activities theoretically make it clear to service employees what is expected of them. In this sense, formalization ought to reduce role stress, since it serves to specify legitimate role senders and ways of behaving. This reducing impact, however, will manifest itself only to the extent customers comply with these 'prescriptions'. This is more often than not the case for front-line employees involved in service work such as serving fast-food. For other workers involved in less standardized services and who hence have to respond immediately to customers' requests and sometimes improvise, the existence of written rules and procedures may have a counterproductive effect on their levels of role stress. This may be especially the case when those rules and procedures are not fitting the situation at hand, but also when these rules are in conflict with the solution the service employee has come up with.

Choosing the right way to handle role stress

Empowerment and formalization reflect two major perspectives on service employee management. As described above, both empowerment and formalization can reduce or increase feelings of role stress among service employees. But when to choose one over the other? Already glimpsing around the corner is the idea that choosing either one approach will depend on the nature of the service encounter which can be characterized by the degree of service interactivity. As you may remember from the first chapter, Mills and Margulies[17] identified service interactivity as an important dimension characterizing services. They identified three basic types of interaction between the customer and the service provider: maintenance-interactive, task-interactive and personal-interactive services. These three types of service interaction mainly differ according to:

- the degree to which the initial problem and possible solutions are clear to the customer and/or the service provider;
- the amount of input required from the customer into the service delivery process;
- the amount and type of judgements to be made by the service employee.

If we integrate this classification scheme into our empowerment versus formalization debate, a clear picture starts to emerge on how to address role stress within different service encounters. Let's take a closer look at a typical maintenance-interactive service job, that of a waiter/waitress in a restaurant. Both the restaurant customer and the server have a fairly clear view of the service delivery process. They both know what the initial problem is (the customer is hungry or thirsty) and possible solutions (the server can offer the customer a range of dishes and drinks). Furthermore, the customer only has to make a choice and communicate it to the server (information input from the side of the customer is rather limited). Finally, the server knows what to do once the customer has made a choice: he or she must inform the kitchen of the new order, and should be as friendly as possible when serving the customer. The server is thus not required to make many decisions.

The service delivery process in the restaurant situation described above is rather standardized. Some kind of fixed scenario applies to all service deliveries. In such a context, it is important that the service employee has a clear view of this scenario and how he or she should behave. This can be done by providing the server with some rules and procedures. In this particular situation, formalization seems to be the key to diminishing ambiguity and conflict about the server's role, and thus is the key to minimizing role stress for these kinds of service encounters.

For contrast, let's take a closer look at the job of a business consultant. The service encounter between the business consultant and the customer is very often characterized by a great deal of uncertainty and ambiguity. In such personal-interactive encounters, both the consultant and the customer may lack a clear view of what the concrete problem is and how this problem should be solved. In such situations, the customer and service provider engage in a process that involves tackling these kinds of ambiguities. The interaction between the service provider and the customer shapes the solution to the problem and thus the service delivery process. In these situations the input of the client is of crucial importance for reaching a satisfactory solution, and the consultant is required

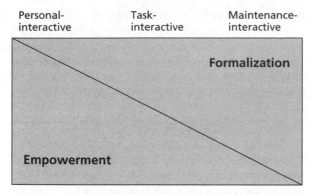

Figure 13.2 Minimizing service employees' role stress through formalization or empowerment, by degree of service interactivity

to judge how the customer can best be helped through a complex series of decisions.

In these kinds of service encounters, one may expect that providing the service employee only with an exhaustive set of specific rules and procedures will not be sufficient. Instead, trusting in the consultant's professional standards, i.e. empowerment, will be a better option. The – competent and motivated – employee is then given the freedom to behave using his or her personal knowledge to judge how the customer may best be served. In these situations, empowerment will be a better option for dealing with service employees' role stress.

Returning to our initial question, we may conclude that service interactivity is an important aspect of the service task to be taken into consideration when deciding how to deal with and minimize role stress among service employees. The rationale we developed is that formalization may be most appropriate to address role conflict when service encounters are of a maintenance-interactive nature. The more the encounter evolves towards personal-interactive services, however, the more the empowerment approach may become the better option for minimizing role stress. Figure 13.2 illustrates this idea.

Impact of co-worker support on role stress

As mentioned in this book's first chapter, one core characteristic of service work is its heterogeneity or variability. Since services are processes where customers and employees interact with each other, the encounters carry a greater risk of difference depending on circumstances such as the particular employee or customer involved, the physical setting or even the time of day. As a result of this variability, front-line employees are frequently confronted with unforeseen situations. In cases where service employees need to deal with the situation at hand, as argued in the chapter on collaboration, having support from colleagues is often an advantage.

It has indeed been proven that having the opportunity to share experiences with others in generically similar positions and to profit from similar experiences clearly diminishes role stress as experienced by service employees.[18] Kahn and his colleagues[19] argued that these kinds of professional and quasi-professional identifications may provide the person with referent group support in the conflicts and ambiguities he or she faces. They can provide either techniques for resolving such stressors, or simply reassurance that the person's difficulties are not so much the result of personal short-comings as the common fate of those who occupy an organizational position that involves interacting with customers.

Establishing collaborative relationships among service employee teams thus seems to be a core issue in striving for role-stress-free and thus satisfied and productive employees. However, as argued in Chapter 11, establishing those relationships in a team, with more parties involved, may be complicated and may take some time. When trying to achieve collaboration and co-worker support in a team, one should approach this effort as a developmental process in which trust must be gradually established.

CONCLUSION

This chapter focused on role stress. Role stress refers to the feeling of being torn apart by conflicting and/or unclear expectations from different constituencies service employees come into contact with (management, customers, family, colleagues, etc.). We showed that role stress clearly has a negative impact on employee satisfaction, commitment and willingness to stay in the organization. Furthermore, we discussed role stress' negative impact on service performance (i.e. both service quality and service productivity).

Given the subversive effects of role stress, we argued that minimizing role stress should be a core aspect of any strategy for improving service performance. We dealt with four main characteristics of service employees' work environment that are relevant in this respect: leadership behaviour, degree of formalization, degree of empowerment, and co-worker support. Regarding leadership behaviour, we made it clear that both task-oriented and people-oriented leadership behaviours are crucial in attempting to minimize service employees' role stress levels. We further pre-sented formalization and empowerment as two important ideas to consider when reflecting on the work context in which role stress occurs. We saw that both empowerment and formalization, although they reflect two different and almost contradictory viewpoints on how service employees should be managed, can decrease or increase role stress. The degree of interactivity between the service provider and the customer was demonstrated to be an important work characteris-tic that can inform the decision about which of these two approaches to take in order to minimize role stress. Finally, we emphasized that co-worker support, which can be established through a developmental team-oriented process, can contribute significantly to reducing role stress levels.

Review and discussion questions

- Is role stress a variable that should be 'reduced to zero'? Why (not)?

- For some managers, stress is just an individual 'problem'; do you agree? What arguments do you see in favour of this view? And which corroborate the opposite? What are the implications of these viewpoints for HRM practices?

Notes and references

1 Troyer, I., Mueller, C. W. and Osinsky, P. I. (2000) 'Who's the boss? A role theoretic analysis of customer work', *Work and Occupations*, Vol 27, No 3, 406–69.

2 Bateson, J. E. G. (1985) 'Perceived control and the service encounter', in Czepiel, J. A., Solomon, M. R. and Surprenant, C. F. (eds) *The Service Encounter: Managing employee/customer interaction in the service business*. Lexington & Toronto: Lexington Books, pp. 67–82.

3 Singh, J. (2000) 'Performance productivity and quality of front-line employees in service organizations', *Journal of Marketing*, Vol 64, No 2, 15–35.

4 Kahn, R. L., Wolfe, D. M., Quinn, R. P., Snoek, J. D. and Rosenthal, R. A. (1964) *Organizational Stress: Studies in role conflict and ambiguity*. New York: John Wiley & Sons.

5 The reader may recall from the first chapter that one of the main characteristics of personal-interactive services, according to Mills and Margulies' definition of different service types, is ambiguity. Mills and Margulies approach the idea of ambiguity from the perspective of the customer. In personal-interactive services, the customer is typically unaware or imprecise about both what will best serve his or her interest and how to go about remedying a situation. Within the context of role stress, (role) ambiguity refers specifically to an unclear situation about how to perform a role within the organization, from the perspective of the employee.

6 Singh, J. and Rhoads, G. K. (1991) 'Boundary role ambiguity in marketing-oriented positions: a multidimensional, multifaceted operationalization', *Journal of Marketing Research*, Vol 28, August, 328–38.

7 Ibid.

8 Jones, B., Flynn, D. M. and Kelloway, E. K. (1995) 'Perceptions of support from the organization in relation to work stress, satisfaction, and commitment', in Sauter, S. L. and Murphy, L. R. (eds) *Organizational Risk Factors for Job Stress*, Washington, DC: American Psychological Association, pp. 41–52.

9 For on overview of evidence on the impact of role ambiguity on employees attitudes and behaviours, see two meta-analytic studies: Jackson, S. E. and Schuler, R. S. (1985) 'A meta-analysis and conceptual critique of research on role ambiguity and role conflict in work settings', *Organizational Behavior and Human Performance*, Vol 36, 16–78; and Tubre, T. C. and Collins, J. M. (2000) 'Jackson and Schuler (1985) revisited: a meta-analysis of the relationships between role ambiguity, role conflict and job performance', *Journal of Management*, Vol 26, No 1, 155–70.

10 Brown, S. P. and Peterson, R. A. (1993) Antecedents and consequences of salesperson job satisfaction: a meta-analysis and assessment of causal effects, *Journal of Marketing*, Vol 30, 63–77; Fisher, C. D. and Gitelson, R. (1983) A meta-analysis of the correlates of role conflict and ambiguity, *Journal of Applied Psychology*, Vol 68, No 2, 320–33.

11 Jackson, S. E. and Schuler, R. S. (1985), op. cit.

12 House, R. L. (1971) 'A path-goal theory of leader effectiveness', *Administrative Science Quarterly*, Vol 16, Sept, 321–9.

13 Wetzels, M. G., De Ruyter, K. and Lemmink, J. (1999) 'Role stress in after-sales Service Management', *Journal of Service Research*, Vol 2, No 1, 50–67.

14 Jackson, S. E. and Schuler, R. S. (1985), op. cit.

15 Bowen, D. E. and Lawler, E. E. (1995a) 'Empowering service employees', *Sloan Management Review*, Vol 37, Summer, 73–84; Bowen, D. E. and Lawler, E. E. (1995b) 'Organizing for Service: Empowerment or Production Line?' in Glynn, W. J. and Barnes, J. G. (eds) *Understanding Services Management*, Chichester: John Wiley & Sons, pp. 269–94.

16 Levitt, T. (1972) 'Production-line approach to service', *Harvard Business Review*, Vol 50, Sept–Oct, 41–52; Levitt, T. (1976) 'Industrialization of service', *Harvard Business Review*, Vol 54, Sept–Oct, 63–74.

[17] Mills, P. K. and Margulies, N. (1980) 'Towards a core typology of service organizations', *Academy of Management Review*, Vol 5, No 2, 255–65.

[18] *See*, for example, Wetzels, M. G. (1998) *Service Quality in Customer-Employee Relationships: An empirical study in the after-sales services context*, Doctoral Dissertation, University of Maastricht; Newton, T. J. and Keenan, A. (1987) 'Role stress reexamined: an investigation of role stress predictors', *Organizational Behavior and Human Decision Processes*, Vol 40, 346–68; Schaubroeck, J., Cotton, J. L. and Jennings, K. R. (1989) 'Antecedents and consequences of role stress: a covariance structure analysis', *Journal of Organizational Behavior*, Vol 10, 35–58.

[19] Kahn, R. L., Wolfe, D. M., Quinn, R. P., Snoek, J. D. and Rosenthal, R. A. (1964), op. cit.

Suggested further reading

Kahn, R. L., Wolfe, D. M., Quinn, R. P., Snoek, J. D. and Rosenthal, R. A. (1964) *Organizational stress: Studies in role conflict and ambiguity*. New York: John Wiley & Sons.

Troyer, I., Mueller, C. W. and Osinsky, P. I. (2000) 'Who's the boss? A role theoretic analysis of customer work', *Work and Occupations*, Vol 27, No 3, 406–69.

PART FOUR

Operations management in service organizations

Roland Van Dierdonck · Paul Gemmel

In Part Four of this book we will deal with issues and problems which relate to the field of operations management or logistics. We will be addressing questions such as what should the capacity of the service delivery system be, how can we make sure that we utilize the various types of capacity resources efficiently, what kind of process type should we choose, what will be the role of automation technology, in particular information technology, where should a service facility be located and how should it be designed.

Most of these issues are well documented and researched for industrial firms. As a matter of fact, the fathers of the so-called 'scientific management' movement in the early twentieth century were very much concerned with these issues. One of them, F. Gilbreth, even succeeded in transferring the application of certain approaches (in particular, time and motion principles) to services, in particular hospitals. An endless number of models addressing the questions identified above have been developed since. With respect to services, an early school of thought supported the transfer of the industrial approaches to services. The most well-known advocate was perhaps T. Levitt with his *Harvard Business Review* article 'Production-line approach to services'. In this article Levitt developed the argument that companies should adopt a manufacturing approach to their service activities. As a result many service companies successfully 'industrialized' their service processes and achieved significant increases in productivity and quality dependability.

However, blindly following the path of industrialization could be dangerous. A company could end up with a very efficient process, but with totally alienated customers (not to mention alienated employees). As a result of the simultaneity of production and consumption, it is important, when dealing with the various issues already mentioned, to take the customer explicitly into consideration.

After all, as J. Carlzon of SAS stated:

'We are flying people, not airplanes.'

In the same way, it can be said that not following the path of industrialization can also be dangerous. Some service companies use the presence of the customer as an excuse for not managing the processes. This sometimes leads to situations where the basic processes are not in place. What is the added value of handing out hors d'oeuvres on silver platters to skiers on a hill in a ski resort, when the customers have severe difficulty in finding the resort at arrival because of poor signage?[1]

A good balance must be found between the industrial approach and the customer approach. The models which we will discuss are therefore inspired as much by the marketing literature as the operations management literature.

Part Four begins with a chapter on process management. In many cases the service process cannot be distinguished from the service product. It is therefore important to design and manage service processes in such a way that they are reliable. In Chapter 7 we saw that reliability is one of the most important service quality dimensions. To be reliable, the occurrence of problems must be avoided as much as possible. This means that one has to think about how to design the service process and especially how to bring in customer needs and preferences in this design.

One of the most important problems in process management is dealing with (inherent) process variability. Although services are inherent variable to some extent, a more systematic approach to monitor and evaluate processes can reduce the process variability. These and other issues related to process management are discussed in Chapter 14.

In Chapter 15 capacity management is discussed. Not only is capacity management extremely important to the financial success of the service firm, but, in addition, its outcome has a direct impact on the customer. It affects waiting times for the customers, but more importantly, capacity is part of the product. Capacity management is not only very significant but it is also quite often more difficult to deal with, given the simultaneity and intangibility of the service. Capacity management involves managing not only supply, but also demand. With the particular problems of managing supply and demand in services, customer waiting times are often inevitable. As a result, Chapter 15 includes a section on the psychology of waiting. The chapter concludes with a description of two techniques that can help us analyse capacity management problems: queuing theory and simulation.

Chapter 16 focuses on what is called facilities management – an important area of operations given the specific nature of services. Customers have to be brought to the service process or the service process has to be brought to the

[1] Sheppard, M. and Johnsons, F. (2000) 'Blue Mountain Resorts: the service quality journey', Case Study, Richard Ivey School of Business, 9B00D16.

customer. Furthermore, the customer 'senses' the facilities. Facilities are part of the product and are often used as surrogates to evaluate the quality of the service to be received or delivered. The chapter begins with a comparison of back-office and front-office activities. We then focus on the front office, addressing questions such as where to locate the service unit, and how the servicescape with which the customer comes into contact should be designed.

In Chapter 17 we deal with technology, in particular information technology. IT is important because most services are rich in terms of information exchange. We therefore discuss the impact IT might have on services and service processes, including how IT has transformed the physical marketplace with the introduction of its 'virtual' counterpart – the market space. The impact these IT developments have on service transactions will vary according to a number of factors: the behaviour of customers and service providers, as well as the nature of the service transaction itself.

CHAPTER 14

Service process design and management

Paul Gemmel

INTRODUCTION

Professor Jacob, a university economics professor, said 'Good morning' to his secretary Mr Thompson as he arrived at the office on Monday morning. But Mr Thompson, who had only been working for Prof. Jacob for three months, could tell that something was wrong when he saw Prof. Jacob's face. 'This looks bad for me', thought Mr Thompson. 'What did I do wrong?' 'Mr Thompson,' Jacob began, 'You know, I had that presentation last weekend at this big seminar about total quality management. Guess what happened after the presentation? At least three participants came to me and complained about the quality of my hand-outs. Six slides on one page makes them almost illegible and there were also several typing and spelling errors in the slides. How could this happen? This is unacceptable.' Mr Thompson felt treated like a naughty schoolboy. He agreed that it was embarrassing to present bad slides at a TQM seminar, but was it really his fault? What did he know about the participants' preferences as to the presentation of the hand-outs? He had thought that putting six slides on one page would reduce the number of pages of what looked like a long presentation. Furthermore Prof. Jacob had handed him a hand-written manuscript two days before the seminar. As a new secretary, Mr Thompson was not used to his boss's handwriting and there was no one he could ask when he had questions. He had had just enough time to make the slides in PowerPoint, print them out and read them himself, and finally copy them. He wondered how to avoid this in the future. At least he had learned that he also had an important but invisible role in meeting the expectations of the customers.

This is just one of many examples of avoidable errors in service delivery. It is far too simple to state that the presence of the customer in the service delivery process makes it impossible to manage service processes. Some share of many service processes is performed in the back office. In many cases, this back office is a service factory where quality assurance principles can be applied. Professor Jacob and Mr Thompson could have avoided their problems if they had clearly specified in advance just what constitutes a good presentation (for example, never putting six slides on one page). In the back office, quality is conformance to specifications just as much as in a manufacturing company. In services, this kind of conformance thinking in the back office is less important than thinking in terms of meeting or exceeding customer expectations. This frequently leads to promises being made to the customer which cannot be kept because the basic processes are not in place. What is the added value of, for instance, handing out hors d'oeuvres on silver platters to skiers on a hill in a ski resort, when the customers have great difficulty even finding the resort because of poor signage.[1] Without having the right basic processes in place, it is very difficult for a service company to meet customer expectations, let alone exceed them.

Many service companies are becoming aware that process management is the weak point in achieving service (or business) excellence. Process management has always been the basic concern of continuous quality improvement. Therefore, the management of processes (both back and front office) in service firms will be discussed here from an internal or operations point of view. This means that we will emphasize the 'conformance to specification' view of quality and try to integrate the expectations of the customer into this perspective.

An adequate process management starts with the choice of process type. This choice must reflect the service concept. Next, the process must be designed as a sequence of several tasks. When Jacob and Thompson look at the process of making slides, they will become aware that one important step is missing: Prof. Jacob's checking the slides for errors.

In a service environment, one must be sure that customer needs and preferences are designed into these processes. For instance, the format in which Prof. Jacob's slides are printed for the hand-outs is quite important. Six slides on one page diminishes the readability of the slides for the participants.

The monitoring of processes is another challenge. How do we know when a process gets out of control? Customer complaints are of course one source of information (Professor Jacob's reaction followed the complaints from participants in the programme about the quality of the hand-outs), but can complaints be avoided in the first place by monitoring the processes? A simple book of procedures could have helped Mr Thompson to know that slides are never printed six to one page.

The processes should be evaluated. Customer satisfaction and complaints are of course important tools for this task. Are there also evaluation tools which are much better related to the process and provide better insight into performing the different steps in the process?

The continuous monitoring and evaluation of processes must lead to process improvement. At some moment, it may be advisable to rethink processes from scratch. Process improvement and process re-engineering close the circle. Perhaps from now on, Professor Jacobs can make up his slides himself on the computer, and Mr Thompson can do the final lay-out.

Objectives

By the end of this chapter, you should be able to discuss:

- the different types of service processes and how the choice of a certain process impacts the management of service processes
- how a process should be designed as a set of logical, related tasks to bring about a predetermined output
- how to monitor service processes, especially using ISO 9000 norms

Objectives continued

- how to evaluate service processes, from a customer point of view as well as from an internal quality point of view
- the need for process re-engineering

PROCESS CHOICE

A three-star French restaurant looks quite different from a fast-food restaurant such as McDonald's for a variety of reasons. Both of these restaurants in their turn are quite different from a Benihana restaurant,[2] a Japanese-style restaurant where the meal is prepared in front of the customers on a hibachi cooking table. One of the major differences is the process type. The French restaurant has many characteristics of a so-called '*job shop process*' and has a functional layout; the fast-food restaurant has many characteristics of a *line process* and has a line layout; the Benihana restaurant, with its insistence on grouping customers in 'batches' of eight in the bar before preparing and serving the meal, seems more like a *batch process*. These differences demonstrate that the traditional distinction in manufacturing between different processes applies equally to service companies. As with manufacturing firms, the main determinant of the type of process is the transaction volume. The higher the volume, the more a line process will be appropriate; the lower the volume, the more a job shop process will be used. In extreme cases such as management consultancy, a project approach might be desired. This relationship between process type and volume is illustrated in Figure 14.1.

The matrix in Figure 14.1 as it applies to manufacturing sectors has the process type as a multi-dimensional construct. Several different manufacturing dimensions are combined. Correlated with process type are such variables as:

- product range (from narrow to broad);
- size of the (customer) order (from large to small);

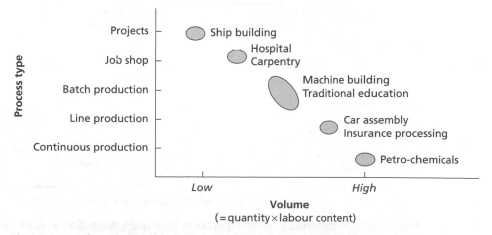

Figure 14.1 The relationship between process type and transaction volume

Source: Silvestro, R., Fitzgerald, R., Johnston, R. and Voss, C. (1992) 'Towards a classification of service processes', *International Journal of Service Industry Management*, Vol 3, No 3, 62–75.

- degree of product change accommodated (from standardized products to completely customized products);
- degree of innovativeness (from low to high);
- degree of automation (from highly automatic to purely manual work); and
- capital intensity *versus* labour intensity.

Something similar has been proposed by Silvestro *et al.*,[3] whose conclusions are illustrated in Figure 14.2. These researchers propose using the number of customers (or customer files) processed by a typical unit per day as a volume measure. On the y axis they have a composite variable composed of the following sub-variables:[4]

1. *Equipment/people focus.* Equipment-focused services are those where the provision of certain equipment is the core element in the service delivery. People-focused services are those where the provision of contact staff is the core element in service delivery.
2. *Customer contact time per transaction.* High customer contact time per transaction is where the customer spends hours, days or weeks in the service system, per transaction. Low customer contact is where the contact with the service system is a few minutes.
3. *Degree of customization.* A high degree of customization is where the service process can be adapted to suit the needs of individual customers. A low degree of customization is where there is a non-varying standardized process; the customer may be offered several routes but the availability of routes is predetermined.
4. *Degree of discretion.* A high degree of discretion is where front-office personnel can exercise judgement in altering the service package or process without referring to superiors. A low degree of discretion is where changes to service provisions can be made only with authorization from superiors.

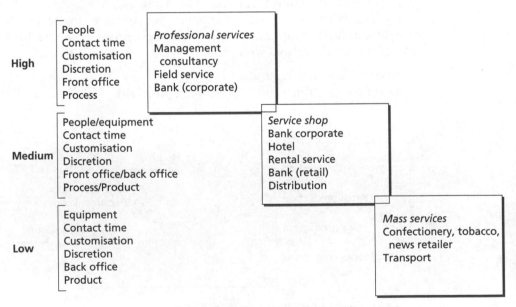

The number of customers processed

Figure 14.2 Relationship between process type and transaction volume, according to Silvestro *et al.*[5]

Source: Silvestro, R., Fitzgerald, R., Johnston, R. and Voss, C. (1992) 'Towards a classification of service processes', *International Journal of Service Industry Management*, Vol 3, No 3, 62–75.

5. *Value-added back office/front office.* A back-office oriented service is where the proportion of front-office (customer contact) staff to total staff is low. A front-office oriented service is where the proportion of front-office staff to total staff is high.

6. *Product/process focus.* A product-oriented service is where the emphasis is on what the customer buys. A process-oriented service is where the emphasis is on how the service is delivered to the customer.

Integrating these variables leads to a construct which, combined with volumes, results in three types of service processes: professional services, service shops and mass services (*see* Figure 14.2). Some other scholars propose a fourth type of service process, 'the service factory'.[6] The service factory is situated close to the mass services, but is differentiated from it in its rather high degree of capital intensity.

The different types of service processes lead to different challenges for management on the operations, HRM and marketing side.

For instance, on the operations side of mass services, service specifications are determined prior to the service delivery to the customer. In professional services, the service specifications are developed together with the customer during the service delivery.[7] While the challenge of the mass service provider is to identify customer needs and to build them into the service process, the challenge of the professional service provider is to be able to adapt to the changing customer needs during the service process. The development of clinical guidelines in the medical world is useful to make best practice more explicit, but they need to be adapted to the needs of the specific patient facing the physician.

Different styles of HRM fit the different service offers best where the styles can be differentiated by the amount of employee involvement and participation in shaping the service encounter. Social and interpersonal skills are less important in a fast-food restaurant than in a three-star restaurant.

From a marketing point of view, we recall the example of service guarantees where we pointed out that it can be dangerous for a professional service provider (such as a physician) to use such a guarantee, since it can create doubts about the provider's competence and reliability. In mass services, service guarantees (if applied in the right way) are considered a competitive advantage driving internal improvement and customer orientation.[8]

PROCESS DESIGN

A process (as a sequence of activities) must deliver the expected outcomes in a reliable way and at a satisfactory level of quality. In manufacturing, systematic analytical methodologies are used to design processes that are reliable and satisfactory. In services it is much less common to design processes in a systematic way. Services are put together haphazardly, relying on a mixture of judgement and past experience.[9]

Much of the work in service process design was done by G. Lynn Shostack, who introduced an analytical tool for process design and mapping, called service blueprinting. To illustrate this, consider the example in Figure 14.3 of a discount brokerage, a financial service process.[10,11]

The first step is to identify the different activities which together constitute the service process. The customer makes a telephone call, asking to open an account.

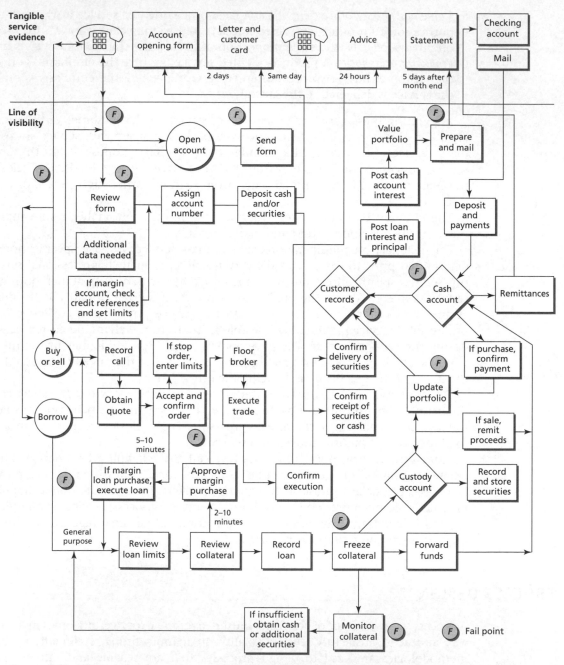

Figure 14.3 The service encounter: a blueprint for discount brokerage[12]

Source: Reprinted with permission from Shostack, G. L. (1985) 'Planning the service encounter', in Czepiel, J. A., Solomon, M. A. and Surprenant, C. F. (eds) *The Service Encounter: Managing employee–customer interactions in service businesses*, Fig. 16.1 (p. 245). Copyright © 1985 by Jossey-Bass Inc., Publishers. First published by Lexington Books. All rights reserved.

The back office then processes that request and decides to grant or deny an account. If accepted, the customer can place different orders, obtain advice and receive a monthly financial statement. All activities should be mapped – the activities which the customer actually sees (front office) as well as the back-office activities. Front- and back-office activities are separated in this approach by a *line of visibility*, indicating where the customer intervenes in the service delivery process.

In the service business, the interaction with the customer is an extremely important aspect influencing both productivity and quality. We should therefore rigorously identify the points of interaction, which J. Carlzon (former president of SAS) called 'the moments of truth' and others call *service encounters*. The customer is an important source of heterogeneity in the service delivery process and if the process is not adequately planned (if employees are not prepared for that heterogeneity or if they do not have the resources to deal with it) problems can occur.

Increasingly, service scholars are proposing the use of more systematic approaches to designing customer needs into the service processes. One of these approaches, borrowed from the manufacturing industry, is quality function deployment (QFD). QFD translates customer needs and preferences into operational goals for the firm. In a manufacturing context, QFD is very popular as it creates a bridge between the engineer and the customer. Applications of this technique have considerably reduced the cost of design and development of new products. The service applications of QFD are rather limited, but nevertheless are promising.[13] Figure 14.4 shows an example of the best known QFD matrix, the House of Quality,[14] applied in the environment of an auto service firm. In this House of Quality, the customer quality criteria are linked to some service company facets such as the skills and training of the employees and the availability of resources (equipment). For instance, it is impossible to diagnose a problem correctly without the right equipment and knowledgeable people. The customer criteria were originally defined in terms of the five Servqual dimensions: reliability, responsiveness, assurance, tangibles and empathy. (This figure only shows the reliability element.) The value in each cell is the multiplication of the following elements:

- the relative importance, indicating how important this quality criterion is compared with the other Servqual criteria;
- the strength of the relationship (this refers to the second part of the Figure 14.4 where a strong relationship is equal to 9, a medium relationship is equal to 6 and a weak relationship is equal to 3);
- the critical incidents, indicating the number of fail points in a certain period of time (see further in this chapter);
- the competitive benchmarking, indicating how important these quality criteria are for competitors;
- the Servqual scores.

For row 1, column 2 of the relationship grid (value for 'correct problem diagnosis' and 'resources (eqpt)') the value of 76 is calculated as follows: $5 \times 9 \times 2 \times 3 \times 0.28$.

One study argues that QFD is particularly promising in extended service transactions delivered by airlines, resort hotels, leisure activities, education and healthcare services.[15] Other scholars are much more careful in their evaluation of the use of QFD in services, questioning whether the subjective customer needs in a service context can be defined objectively. There is no magic formula for translating the customer needs into characteristics of service processes. Moreover, there is the danger that designers may make a subjective interpretation of the customer needs which then starts to live its own life.[16]

(a)

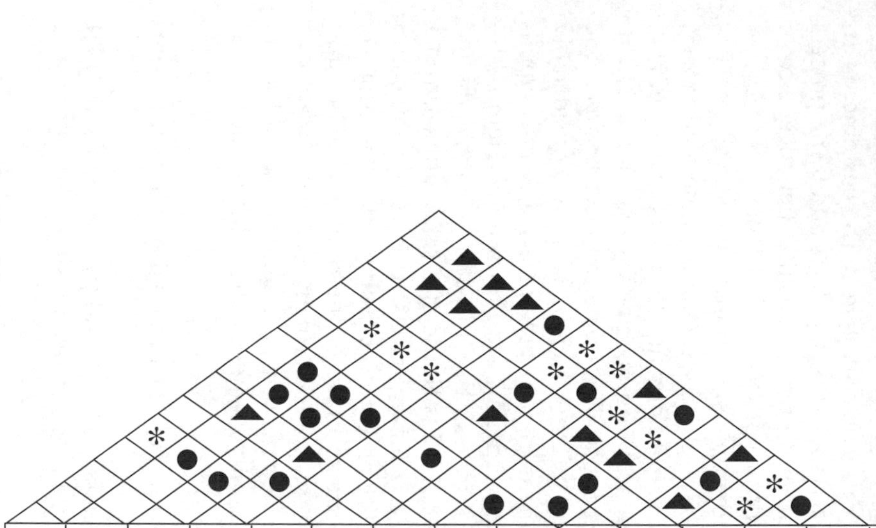

What? Customer quality criteria			Relative Importance	Layout	Resources (eqpt.)	Resources (pers.)	Systems capacity	Housekeeping	Consumer handling	Car handling	Information handling	Routine/nonroutine situations	Inventory	Job/personnel scheduling	Selection	Skills training tech/interpersonal	Attitudes/Morale	Critical incidents	Competitive benchmarking	SERVQUAL scores
Pr.	Secondary	Tertiary																		
Reliability	Accuracy	Correct problem diagnosis	5		76	76										76	8	2	3	−28
		Work right first time	5		917	306					917			917	306	917	102	7	8	−37
		Correct billing	5		130						389					389		6	3	−48
	Maintaining records	Clear statement of work done	5		138						414	138				414		5	4	−46
		Update maintenance book	5								77					77	26	3	1	−57
	Honouring promises	Do work mentioned by customer	5		558	558			558		558		62		62	186	62	7	3	−59
		Car ready at promised time	5		149	149	149				17		17	149		17	50	5	3	−22
		Keep promised appointments	5						478		478					478	159	6	3	−59
Absolute importance					1968	1089	149		1036		2850	469	79	1060	393	2554	407			
Relative importance					3	4	10		6		1	7	11	5	9	2	8			

Service company facets — How?

Figure 14.4 Partial QFD for an auto-service firm[17]

Source: Ravi S. Bahara and R. B. Chase, 'Service quality deployment: quality service by design' in Rakesh V. Sarin (ed.) *Perspectives in Operations Management: Essays in honor of Elwood S. Buffa*, Kluwer Academic Publisher, Norwell, Mass., 1993.

(b)

Pr.	Secondary	Tertiary	Relative Importance	Layout	Resources (eqpt.)	Resources (pers.)	Systems capacity	Housekeeping	Consumer handling	Car handling	Information handling	Routine/nonroutine situations	Inventory	Job/personnel scheduling	Selection	Skills training tech/interpersonal	Attitudes/Morale
Reliability	Accuracy	Correct problem diagnosis			*	*						●			●	*	▲
		Work right first time			*	●					*	●		*	●	*	▲
	Maintaining records	Correct billing			●						*					*	
		Clear statement of work done			●						*	●				*	
		Update maintenance book									*					*	●
	Honouring promises	Do work mentioned by customer			*	*			*		*	▲		▲	●	▲
		Car ready at promised time			*	*	*					▲	▲	*	▲		●
		Keep promised appointments							*		*					*	●

Strength of relationship

* Strong   ● Medium   ▲ Weak

Figure 14.4 continued

Source: Ravi S. Bahara and R. B. Chase, 'Service quality deployment: quality service by design' in Rakesh V. Sarin (ed.) *Perspectives in Operations Management: Essays in honor of Elwood S. Buffa*, Kluwer Academic Publisher, Norwell, Mass., 1993.

PROCESS MONITORING

Process variability is part of life in service environments. The interaction of customer and service provider, and the impact of the servicescape (*see* Chapter 16) means that no two customers are served in the same way. It is said that service processes are inherently variable, but not all variability in service processes is inherent and some variability can be taken away. Service processes can be out of control in the same way as manufacturing processes. The question is how to detect, or better still, prevent, out-of-control processes.

Preventing a process from getting out of control assumes the implementation of a quality assurance system such as ISO 9000. An ISO 9000 quality management system requires that customer expectations be documented as specifications, methods of measurement be defined, and the service process be monitored to ensure that the services conform to these specifications. A growing number of service firms apply ISO 9001 as part of their quality management initiatives. DVV, an insurance company in Belgium, received an ISO 9001:2000 certification in 2001 for two of their departments. Their quality management handbook documents all core, supporting and decision processes. DVV recognized the advantage of uniformly structured documents in making the organization more transparent not only for their own employees, but also for their customers. The implementation of ISO9001:2000 can be seen as one way to make the service concept more tangible. Other examples of the application of ISO 9000 can be found in many service companies delivering maintenance-interactive services such as maintenance, catering and security. ISO 9000 is also implemented in personal-interactive services (such as healthcare), but in most cases only in the back office. For instance, in one hospital, only the pharmacy was awarded ISO 9001 certification.

The importance of applying ISO 9000 principles in the front office may not be evident at first sight. Customers and employees usually do not have a common understanding of the specifications of the service. Consequently it is difficult to measure conformance to specifications. This does not mean that a service firm with predominantly front-office operations cannot benefit from an ISO 9000 certification. One study found that ISO 9000 certification creates a better balance between the quality management perspectives in the back and front offices.[18] Quality certification leads a high-contact service (with a large front office) to shift their unilateral emphasis on external quality dimensions (as defined, for example, by Servqual), to a more balanced emphasis on both external quality and technical quality. This better balance also supports the consistency of quality management policies and more generally of the service concept in the back office and the front office.

The application of ISO 9000:2000 in service organizations assumes performance measures for evaluating the service delivery. Measuring customer satisfaction and developing a complaint handling system can be very useful in this respect (*see* Chapter 7).

One method of detecting whether or not a process is out of control, commonly used in manufacturing, is Statistical Process Control (SPC). The goal of SPC is to check whether process parameters are within the natural control limits and thus only vary due to common causes of variation. The main purpose is to detect special causes of variation such as bad set-up or a machine overheating. Figure 14.5 shows an example of a control chart used to monitor the overall course evaluation. The variation around the expected value of a certain parameter is calculated using the standard deviation of the process parameter. A process is under control when these variations do not exceed some predetermined upper and lower control limits. In general these limits are calculated by adding three times the standard deviation to the expected value. This means that if only random behaviour is present, there is a 99.7 per cent probability that the value of a parameter lies within these limits. There are several kinds of control charts. The selection of a certain control chart depends on the kinds of process parameters used (continuous variable parameters versus attribute parameters) and the sample size. For further discussion of these specific control charts, we refer to the extensive literature on operations and quality management.[19]

Control charts are used much more in manufacturing than in services. Nevertheless, these charts can be useful in a service situation, for instance, to monitor the overall evaluation of a course as in Figure 14.5, or to identify when waiting times are getting out of control in a bank branch[20]. In Figure 14.5 weeks 1, 10 (from bottom chart), 16 and 22 should be reviewed to understand why the ratings are outside the control limits.

PROCESS EVALUATION

During the last few years, several techniques for assessing the service process have been put forward. For instance, mapping the service process and the different service encounters (as in the service blueprint in Figure 14.3) allows the company to identify the critical issues and highlight *fail* or *risk points*. It is essential to find out where things *can* go wrong. Can an activity be improved to prevent things going wrong? If things go wrong, what can be done to rectify the situation? For instance, the activity 'send form' in the blueprint of Figure 14.3 is a potential fail

X & R Chart
Overall Course Evaluations

n = 10 evaluations randomly sampled each week

1-Not at all 2-Not very 3-Moderately 4-Very 5-Extremely

WK #	1	2	3	4	5	6	7	8	9	10	11	12	13	14	15	16	17	18	19	20	21	22	23	24	25	Ave.
$\bar{x}$	3.76	4.21	4.29	4.36	4.13	3.77	4.17	4.21	4.22	4.00	4.30	4.20	4.32	4.18	4.02	3.71	4.08	3.98	4.46	3.96	3.63	4.48	4.30	4.29	4.13
R	1.01	1.27	0.48	1.32	1.52	1.03	1.15	1.07	0.70	2.05	0.95	0.99	1.06	1.21	1.33	0.78	1.21	1.23	1.08	1.64	1.20	0.98	0.91	1.19	1.03	1.14

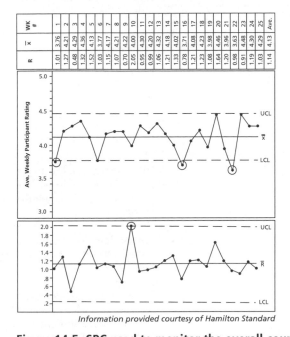

Information provided courtesy of Hamilton Standard

Figure 14.5 SPC used to monitor the overall course evaluation over time[21]

Source: M. Brassard and D. Ritter (1994) The Memory Jogger II, a pocket guide of tools for continuous improvement and effective planning, Frits Philips Institute for Quality Management, p. 51.

point since the form may be sent to the wrong person. The customer's perception or interpretation cannot be neglected in identifying a fail point. If customers themselves report that something 'unexpected' has happened, the fail point is called a critical incident. Methods to analyse critical incidents have been proposed. The main problems with this approach are that critical incidents and failures are reported in the same way, and that the whole context of the service delivery is not taken into account. One way to involve customers more actively is to ask customers whether or not they have encountered a mistake, error or failure at each step in the service blueprint. The problem with this method is that customers only mention the failures they really remember and find worthy of mention. Furthermore, the evaluation is more oriented to the service blueprint rather than to the service process itself.[22]

A technique which tries to rectify many flaws of the previous described methods is Service Transaction Analysis (STA).[23] Service Transaction Analysis is a technique where mystery shoppers, independent advisers or consultant-customers walk through the actual process to assess how real customers might assess each transaction.[24] Besides the assessment, the surrogate customers also give interpretations of how they arrived at their evaluations. These reveal the symbolic and subtle messages given off by the services.

SERVICE TRANSACTION SHEET				
Organization	**Disneyland Paris**			Service concept of Disneyland Paris:
Process	**Indiana Jones and the Temple of Peril: Backwards!**			An exiting ride through the jungle and the temple, which turns the world on its head
Customers type	**Adventurers**			
Transaction	Score			Message
	+	0	−	
◆ Noticing the attraction		0		Only one sign, 'maybe searching is part of the adventure?'
◆ Indication of waiting time			−	Only indication, but not very accurate according to us; 'don't they want to tell the truth?'
◆ Decor	+			'We are really in the jungle'
◆ Waiting lines		0		'This looks like a labyrinth, very confusing'
◆ Getting in	+			Quick change of passengers and control by cast members; 'they take care of us'
◆ The tour	+			'This is really an adventure'
◆ End of the tour	+			Again a smooth change of passengers 'this is well organized'
◆ Exit	+			Clear signs and close to exit which makes it easy to find the people who stayed outside.

Conclusion: The attraction was a pleasant adventure, but indications of direction and waiting time could be better.

Figure 14.6 Service Transaction Analysis of the 'Indiana Jones and the Temple of Peril Backwards' attraction in Disneyland Paris

Figure 14.6 shows an example of STA of the 'Indiana Jones and the Temple of Peril Backwards' attraction in Disneyland Paris. The first step in the analysis is to define the service concept of the organization, in this case Disneyland Paris. Without knowledge of this service concept, it is impossible to evaluate the attractions. In the next step, mystery shoppers evaluate each step (transaction) in the process, while giving some indication about the message sent out by each transaction. For example, the indication of the waiting time at the access of the attraction seemed to be not very accurate, which sent a negative message, that of not being honest with the customer.

The advantage of STA is that it goes a step further than evaluation of perceptions. It tries to understand why customers have some negative or positive experience. In some instances, STA reveals totally unexpected causes of a certain evaluation.

When a mistake or failure affecting the customer's perception is detected in the process, actions should be taken to recover the damage. Service recovery is defined as 'a process that identifies service failures, effectively resolves customer problems, classifies their root cause(s), and yields data that can be integrated with other measures of performance to assess and improve the service system'.[25] This process-oriented definition of service recovery fits completely with a quality management perspective and is much broader than complaint handling (*see* Chapter 7). Effective service recovery assumes the identification of fail points in the service process, the elicitation of a customer reaction following an incident (this can be a complaint), the identification of a response to the service failure and an analysis of the data to determine the root causes of the failure and the effectiveness of the recovery. The final goal is to improve the service delivery process.

There is some evidence that effective service recovery has an impact on customer satisfaction and loyalty as well as employee satisfaction (*see* Chapter 7).

Considering the potential flaws in the design of the service process in advance and establishing procedures to prevent them from happening will seriously affect the service quality perceived by the customer. Service recovery seems to be an important determinant of trust and commitment, but only when it is very effective.[26] Service recovery also has its impact on employee behaviour. One study showed that recovering is an emotionally difficult task for employees to perform.[27] Therefore it is important that management support employees in reducing their feelings of helplessness, to avoid a negative impact on job satisfaction. The negative feelings of the employee may need to be recovered by management. This is called internal service recovery. Service recovery has an impact on many different aspects of the service profit chain (*see* Chapter 4) : the internal service capability, employee satisfaction, customer satisfaction and customer loyalty.

PROCESS RE-ENGINEERING

Process re-engineering is 'the fundamental rethinking and radical redesign of business processes to bring about dramatic improvements in performance'.[28] The basic idea behind process re-engineering is to think 'outside of the box' and to reconsider the basic assumptions underlying the current process.

A company that wants to re-engineer processes has to walk through the 6 Rs: Realization, Requirements, Rethink, Redesign, Retool and Re-evaluate.[29] Each of these steps are illustrated below using the example of a CT scanning process in a hospital.[30]

Realization

In the realization phase, a company must become aware that continuous and radical improvement of processes is a condition *sine qua non* for survival in a competitive environment. Data must be gathered in order to convince decision-makers to start up a re-engineering process. It is also impossible to re-engineer without the support of the whole company.

For example, referral physicians are a very important customer group in the case of CT scanning. Easy access to the facilities and receiving feedback soon after examination are important basic needs for these physicians. Data on these needs must be collected.

Requirements

Before changing processes, it is important to clearly define the organization's mission, vision, values and the most important requirements in order to meet (or exceed) customer expectations. The customer's voice must be brought in and criteria for measuring process performance must be defined. These performance criteria must be in line with the strategy of the firm. The Balanced Scorecard (*see* Chapter 18) is a very useful way to define these performance measures.

In the case of the CT scanning, R.O.I, cash flow, reliability, quality of the medical diagnosis, patient satisfaction, process innovation, utilization rate, set-up times between patients, throughput time and waiting time are examples of performance measures from the financial perspective, the customer perspective, the internal process perspective and the innovation and learning perspective. Table 14.1 shows the examples of some operational performance measures of the CT scanning process in two different hospitals. Hospital B is able to serve customers more quickly than hospital A while at the same time obtaining a higher utilization rate.

Table 14.1 A comparison of operational performance measures between two hospitals

	Hospital A	Hospital B
Utilization rate of CT-scan	81%	91%
Ratio of real examination time to total throughput time	23%	34%
Total throughput time (room out – room in)	66 minutes	43 minutes
Average waiting time before CT	23 minutes	13 minutes
Set-up times	2.48 minutes	1.25 minutes

Drivers	Waiting on transport	Transport time	Waiting before preparation	Preparation time	Investigation time	Waiting on transport	Transport time
Architecture		X					X
Peparation Room				X	X		
Appointment System			X				
Communication System	X					X	
Transport time			X				

Figure 14.7 Time-drivers in the CT-scanning process

Rethink

In the rethink stage, the current and existing working conditions of the organization are studied. Current processes are evaluated and compared with the objectives and expectations. The causes of the operational weaknesses in the organization and variability are looked for. Every activity or process that does not add value in the realization of the product or service is labelled as waste.

Figure 14.7 shows the relationship between different time components in the CT scanning process and the factors driving the time.[31] It is important to study the non-value-adding activities, waiting and transport, in more depth. One of the important drivers of transport time is the architecture of the building, in particular the presence (or absence) of an elevator. In a tall building where patients and employees need an elevator to go to the radiology department, there seems to be no relationship between the distance (from the room to the department) and the total transport time. Because of the unpredictability of the transport time, patients are transferred to the radiology department earlier.

Redesign

A process is considered to be a set of logical, related tasks executed to bring forth a predetermined output. When redesigning the most important processes, every task is analysed. This redesign can be radical, i.e. old processes are replaced by totally new processes.

In studying the CT scanning process, it was found that in several hospitals, patients are prepared for CT while already lying on the CT scanner. This preparation seemed to be the most variable time component of the whole investigation. One possible solution could be to install a separate room where patients can be prepared before entering the scanner room. Because this reduces the variability of the time on the scanner remarkably, a higher utilization rate can be achieved without substantially increasing the waiting time.

Retool

Radical change is not possible without having the right tools (equipment, machines and other critical instruments).

It is quite clear that installing a separate preparation room for CT scanning requires some hospital space (which is very scarce in many instances). Another point is that an efficient lay-out of the radiology department is crucial to efficient use of the CT scanners. Having a work room between two scanner rooms is much more appealing than having two scanner rooms in separate locations.

In the example of the CT scanner it is possible to simulate the proposed changes and to get some insights into the change in performance before implementing the changes in reality. Computer simulation is a tool which allows the behaviour of production or service systems to be imitated, so that several designs of the process can be compared. For example, in production, the lay-out of warehouses can be studied before changes are implemented. In the CT scanning example, the effect of introducing a preparation room can be simulated before implementation. Computer simulation has been described in many different books and is extremely useful in those situations where a buffer exists, such as a queue in a service situation or an inventory in a production situation (*see* Technical Note 3 on simulation).

Re-evaluate

After redesigning and retooling, the complete process is re-evaluated in order to find out whether or not this has led to better performance. This assumes the availability of evaluation criteria such as throughput time, quality, productivity, customer satisfaction, employee satisfaction, market share and profitability.

After implementing changes (such as installing an examination room), it is important to re-evaluate the performance of the new processes.

CONCLUSION

In this chapter we argued that it is important in services to develop a comprehensive approach to design and manage processes. Such a comprehensive approach includes:

- selecting process types and being aware of the managerial consequences of each selection;
- designing customer needs into the service processes;
- monitoring processes in order to minimize process variability;
- evaluating processes and involving customers in doing so;
- re-engineering processes or rethinking the existing processes.

A systematic approach such as this must ensure that the basic processes are in place. Only then can a service company start thinking about how to exceed customer expectations.

Review and discussion questions

- Take an example of a service company (or take the service company you are working for) and determine the dominant process type. What are the consequences of this type of process for the design and the management of the processes?

- Discuss the advantages and the disadvantages of using QFD, ISO 9000 and SPC in service companies. Is there any relationship between the process type (mass service, service factory, etc.) and the possibilities of using these kinds of tools?

- How do you incorporate customer needs or customer preferences into service process design?

- What is the particular added value of Service Transaction Analysis compared to other evaluation tools such as service blueprinting?

Notes and references

[1] Sheppard, M. and Johnsons, F. (2000) 'Blue Mountain Resorts: the service quality journey', Case Study, Richard Ivey School of Business, 9B00D16.

[2] Benihana case, *Harvard Business School case study*, 9-673-057, 1972.

[3] Silvestro, R., Fitzgerald, R., Johnston, R. and Voss, C. (1992), 'Towards a classification of service processes', *International Journal of Service Industry Management*, Vol 3, No 3, 62–75.

[4] Ibid.

[5] Ibid.

[6] Schmenner, R. W. (1995) *Service Operations Management.* Englewood Cliffs, NJ: Prentice Hall, pp. 10–11.

[7] Silvestro, R. (1999) 'Positioning services along the volume-variety diagonal. The contingencies of service design, control and improvement', *International Journal of Operations and Production Management*, Vol 19, No 4, 399–420.

[8] Ibid.

[9] Ramaswamy, R. (1996) *Design and Management of Service processes: keeping customers for life.* Addison-Wesley Publishing Company, p. 16.

[10] Shostack, G. L. (1985) 'Planning the service encounter', in Czepiel, J. A., Solomon, M. A. and Surprenant, C. F. (eds) *The Service Encounter: Managing employee–customer interactions in service businesses.* New York: Lexington Books.

[11] Many process mapping techniques exist, and process mapping has many other purposes. This goes beyond the scope of this book. The reader interested in learning more about process mapping can refer to, for instance, the structured analysis and design technique and the service logic map. For references, *see* Congram, C. and Epelman, M. (1995) 'How to describe your service: An invitation to the structured analysis and design technique', *International Journal of Service Industry Management*, Vol 6, No 2, 6–23; and Kingman-Brundage, J., George, W. and Bowen, D. (1995) 'Service logic: Achieving service system integration', *International Journal of Service Industry Management*, Vol 6, No 4, 20–39.

[12] *Source*: Shostack, G. L. (1985), op. cit.

[13] Dubé, L., Johnson, M. D. and Renaghan, L. M. (1999) 'Adapting the QFD approach to extended service transactions', *Production and Operations Management*, Vol 8, No 3, 301–17.

[14] Hauser, J. R. and Clausing, D. P. (1988) 'The House of Quality', *Harvard Business Review*, Vol 66, No 3, May–June, 63–73.

[15] Hauser, J. R. and Clausing, D. P. (1988), op. cit.

[16] These scholarly opinions are based on an informal e-mail discussion about QFD with the following people: Mr Frede Jensen, Prof. Glenn Mazur, Dr Lary Menor, Prof. J. A. Fitzsimmons, Prof. A. Johne.

[17] Bahara, R. S. and Chase, R. B. (1993) 'Service quality deployment: quality service by design', in Sarin, R. V. (ed.) *Perspectives in Operations Management*: Essays in honor of Elwood S. Buffa. Norwell, MA: Kluwer.

[18] Dick, G., Gallimore, K. and Brown, J. C. (2001) 'ISO 9000 and quality emphasis: an empirical study of front-room versus back-room dominant service industries', *International Journal of Service Industry Management*, Vol 12, No 2, 114–36.

[19] Evans, J. R. and Lindsay, W. M. (1999) *The Management and Control of Quality.* South-Western College Publishing, pp. 723–51.

[20] Gardiner, S. C. and Mitra, A. (1994) 'Quality control procedures to determine staff allocation in a bank', *International Journal of Quality and Reliability Management*, Vol 11, No 1, 6–21.

[21] Brassard, M. and Ritter, D. (1994) *The Memory Jogger II, a pocket guide of tools for continuous improvement and effective planning.* Frits Philips Institute for Quality Management, p. 51.

[22] Johnston, R. (1999) 'Service Transaction Analysis: assessing and improving the customer's experience', *Managing Service Quality*, Vol 9, No 2, 102–9.

[23] Ibid.

[24] Johnston, R. and Clark, G. (2001) *Service Operations Management*. London: Prentice Hall, pp. 162–4.

[25] Tax, S. S. and Brown, S. W. (2000) 'Service recovery: research insights and practices', in Swartz, T. A. and Iacobucci, D. (eds) Handbook of Services Marketing and Management, Sage Publication, Chapter 16, pp. 271–85.

[26] Ibid.

[27] Bowen, D. E. and Johnston, R. (1998) 'Internal service recovery: developing a new construct', *International Journal of Service Industry Management*, Vol 10, No 2, 118–31.

[28] Hammer, M. and Stanton, S. (1995) *The Reengineering Revolution: The Handbook*. London: Harper Collins, p. 336.

[29] Edosomwan, J. (1996) *Organizational Transformation and Process reengineering*. St. Lucie Press and the Quality Observer Corporation, p. 5.

[30] Gemmel, P. (2000) *Beheersen en herdenken van processen: op zoek naar de patiënt* (Managing and redesigning processes: looking for the patient). Dossier Ziekenhuiswetgeving, Kluwer.

[31] Ibid.

Suggested further reading

Rohit Ramaswamy (1996) *Design and Management of Service Processes: keeping customers for life*, Addison-Wesley Publishing Company, Inc. 424 pp. This is one of the few books discussing design of service processes in depth. Using an overall framework of designing and managing service processes, the author discusses in more depth many of the topics mentioned before: Quality Function Deployment, Service blueprinting, simulation and measuring performance.

Silvestro, R. (1999) 'Positioning services along the volume-variety diagonal. The contingencies of service design, control and improvement', *International Journal of Operations and Production Management*, Vol 19, No 4, 399–420. In this article, Silvestro develops a diagnostic tool for evaluating the strategic coherence of service operations based on the volume-variety diagonal. Several elements are discussed, such as the design of the operations, planning and control and improvement.

CHAPTER 15

Capacity management

Roland Van Dierdonck

INTRODUCTION

The change in value of EuroDisney stocks more than anything else illustrates the difficult introductory period of Disneyland Paris. The initial euphoria disappeared very quickly after the opening of the park in April 1992. Financial restructuring and management changes have now put the company (it is hoped) on the path to profitability, but no one can deny that the company has not been the success envisaged at the start. What went wrong?

As usual, it was probably a mixture of various factors: financial, cultural, marketing and many others. Poor capacity management certainly played a part. The park was designed to have a maximum capacity of 50 000 visitors per day. Admission gates were to be closed after this figure was reached, with additional visitors being admitted as visitors left the park for the remainder of the afternoon and evening. For instance, on one occasion in the opening three months, the gates of the park were closed from 11.00 a.m. to 3.00 p.m. because the park had reached capacity; a large number of additional guests were admitted only after 3.00 p.m. The result was long queues at certain times[1] and a great deal of customer dissatisfaction.

While it may be true that Europeans in general, and the French in particular, are less tolerant of queues and are less disciplined while queuing, compared with Americans, it is undoubtedly true that there was a capacity problem. Take, for example, the 50 000 person peak-capacity design. With 29 rides and attractions in its first phase, this meant that at peak times there were 1724 (50 000/29) customers per ride per day. Compare this with the peak capacity of 90 000 at Disney World in Florida, where there are 72 attractions, leading to an average of 1250 customers per ride per day. No wonder the queues at Disneyland Paris were longer than visitors were used to in Florida. For an organization for which repeat business and word-of-mouth advertising are very important, this causes a serious problem.

Another capacity issue was that to break even there needed to be 11 million visitors a year. This meant an average of about 30 000 per day. Given the high seasonality of the business and a peak capacity of 50 000, an average of 30 000 seemed unrealistic. How many visitors could reasonably be expected in the winter season in Paris? Not only did winter visitors have to put up with the sometimes inclement weather, but adding insult

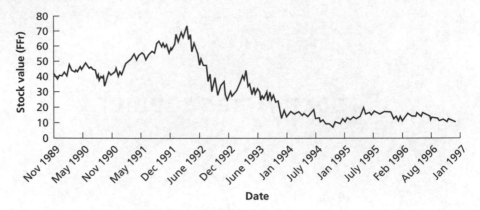

Figure 15.1 The value of EuroDisney stock, Nov 1989 to Jan 1997

to injury, they came to the conclusion that, in order to reduce costs, Disneyland Paris had closed many attractions for the season. It is highly probable that visitors felt cheated because the 'service concept' had been ruined.

Disneyland Paris made serious mistakes in its capacity management. However, the case is certainly not unique. Capacity management is crucial to almost all service businesses. The purpose of this chapter is to explore some of the issues related to capacity management. We shall identify typical problems and describe solutions – or at least approaches to tackling such problems.

We begin by defining 'capacity,' and identifying the essence of capacity management. We go on to deal with the issue of capacity planning – that is, determining the size of the capacity or providing an answer to the question of how much capacity should be made available. In order to do this, it is important to understand the relationship between capacity and service level; we shall therefore explain this relationship.

We shall also deal with capacity scheduling, which differs from capacity planning in that in planning we determine the capacity level, while in scheduling we decide how to utilize the existing predetermined capacity. We shall see that this distinction is somewhat artificial: what is scheduling at one level becomes planning at a lower – that is, more detailed and more short-term oriented – level. As a result, we concentrate on integrated systems for managing capacity – that is, for combining both planning and scheduling. In particular, we shall discuss service requirements, planning systems, and the utilization of Just-In-Time principles in capacity management.

An alternative to scheduling capacity is to try to influence demand so that it matches capacity as far as possible – a process known as demand management. This is also described in this chapter.

When managing capacity, the consequences of capacity shortage or excess must be considered. One of the consequences of a shortage is that customers will have to wait. As we shall see, however, waiting is not a purely rational issue: we shall look at the psychological factors involved in managing capacity.

We begin with Exhibit 15.1 which considers the problems faced by an organization involved in inspecting car emissions. Throughout the chapter, we shall refer back to Exhibit 15.1 to illustrate the application of concepts or techniques that can help us to analyse the problems and provide solutions.

Objectives

By the end of this chapter, you should be able to discuss:

- the specific nature of capacity management in services and why it is important
- ways of determining how much capacity to make available, given a certain demand pattern
- how to schedule the available capacity facing a variable demand pattern
- how capacity management involves the management of demand, and how the demand pattern can be influenced
- the concept of yield management
- how waiting in a service organization is inevitable and how the perception of the waiting experience can be managed

CAPACITY AND CAPACITY MANAGEMENT

Exhibit 15.1

The Belmont case[2]

Karel Verschaeve was coming to the conclusion that something had to be done about the capacity of his car-emission inspection stations. Over the preceding few months the number of complaints by customers as well as by employees had drastically increased. In particular, professional drivers had become visibly more irritated by the long waiting times at the inspection stations. The Ministry of Transport had even forwarded him a couple of letters of complaint.

Inspection of car emissions
Since 1 July 1992, the emission norms had become much more severe in an attempt to protect the environment and in particular to reduce the ozone concentration in summer. All cars, regardless of their age, had to be inspected for composition and level of emission of various pollutants. In the past, such inspection had been part of the general technical inspection. For private cars, this meant that they were only inspected three years after having been purchased.

The existing vehicle inspection stations could not handle the increased volume of business and, furthermore, the existing equipment was not suited to the more severe norms. The new equipment required a high level of investment and special expertise was required to operate the equipment, and so the authorities had decided to build specialized emission-control centres. In order to limit the total investment, the number of centres had been limited to one for every large metropolitan area.

Karel Verschaeve was the general director of all inspection centres. He was happy about this appointment, especially because the Minister of Transport had promised him a large degree of autonomy. Both the Minister and Verschaeve wanted to make a 'showcase' of the inspection centres. In particular, they wanted to demonstrate that an operation did not have to be privatized to be run efficiently and effectively. He recalled very vividly the political resistance which arose when the Minister decoupled the emission inspection centres

▶

279

Exhibit 15.1 continued

from the general technical inspection centres. The latter were operated by private institutions.

Belmont

Belmont was the largest city and the capital of the country. There was one inspection centre for the entire metropolitan area. The complaints referred to earlier were mostly related to this inspection centre. In this centre there was a total of 11 inspection lines to test the emission gases of the car. The test itself was rather short: between two and five minutes. However, it was clear that the test itself was the bottleneck. The steps that preceded and followed the test were of an administrative nature and went very smoothly thanks to automation. The two steps in the process lasted four and two minutes respectively. For these administrative processes there were in total 24 stations (see Figure 15.2).

It was estimated that in the Belmont metropolitan area there were about 260 000 cars registered, which all had to come to the inspection centre at least once a year. Roughly 20 per cent of the visits were repeat visits. When a car was refused, it had

to be presented for re-inspection within two weeks of the first visit. The opening hours of the inspection centre were between 8.00 a.m. and 4.00 p.m. on weekdays, over 50 weeks per year, excepting statutory holidays.

The demand was not evenly spread over the year. From February to May the average demand was about 10 per cent higher than the annual average. There were also clear fluctuations during the day. The peak occurred early in the morning shortly after opening. The variable cost of an inspection was about 3 euro, the bulk of this amount (around 80 per cent) being direct labour costs. The customers paid 8 euro per inspection.

Karel Verschaeve assumed that it would be very difficult to increase the number of inspection lines. The investment required to install an additional line was estimated to be at least 250 000 euro. The funds needed for such additional equipment had not been budgeted for. Although he did not want to exclude any particular option, he was convinced that he had to look for other, more creative solutions to solve the capacity problem.

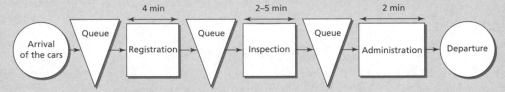

Figure 15.2 Flowchart showing the inspection process at Belmont

Source: Belmont case in Hill, A. (1991) *Minnesota Pollution Control Agency*. University of Minnesota.

Capacity as a measure of output

The concept of capacity is used in our everyday language quite frequently. The capacity of my fuel tank at home is 5000 litres; the capacity of the boot of my car is 466 litres, while the car can transport five people; the university hospital has 1100 beds; the aeroplane on the daily flight between Brussels and New York contains 320 seats; the Belmont inspection centre has 11 inspection lines. This notion of capacity is very close to the dictionary definition of capacity:

'the ability to hold, receive, store or accommodate a certain volume'.

This definition of capacity is inappropriate in most organizations for a variety of reasons:

1. It refers to capacity of input resources: the trunk of the car, the size of the tank, the number of beds or seats, or the number of parallel lines. It does not necessarily tell us anything about the output. The output is of course a function of the

'capacity' of the input resources, but usually of a particular combination of input resources. For example, in a hospital, resources include not only beds, but also nurses, surgery rooms and various materials.

2. Service times are frequently inherently variable, so that although a certain resource might usually be the cause of the bottleneck, on some occasions the problem might lie elsewhere. In the Belmont case, for example, although the inspection lines are the bottleneck, the registration process could also slow things down, as sometimes for a particular reason and sometimes for no reason at all, many customers may need a good deal of help in doing the paperwork.

3. The traditional input resources definition of capacity lacks the time dimension. It is a static concept and it is a dynamic concept that is needed. We do not know the capacity of a restaurant unless we know the average time customers stay there. It is clear that the capacity of a restaurant with 120 seats is much higher in the case of a fast-food restaurant with a throughput time per customer of 20 minutes or less, than in the case of a traditional French restaurant with a throughput time per customer of 120 minutes. To calculate capacity, we must incorporate a time dimension appropriate to the use of the assets. Capacity is therefore most appropriately expressed in so many 'output' units per hour, per day, per week, per month or per year.

Returning to the Belmont case in Exhibit 15.1, we can say that the capacity should be expressed in 'cars per day'. Assuming an eight-hour day and assuming that the inspection lines are in fact the bottlenecks, we can say that the capacity is 188.57 cars per hour or 1508 cars per day (*see* Figure 15.2).

Since time is an integral part of the capacity concept, capacity can be increased or decreased by influencing the processing time. In the Belmont case, if the time required to test the car increases by 20 per cent (from an average of 3 minutes 30 seconds to 4 minutes 12 seconds) the capacity of the inspection centre will decrease by 20 per cent to 1257 cars.

This reduction in capacity resulting from an increase in processing time has recently become particularly clear in the Belgian prison system. As in almost every other country, Belgian prisons are overcrowded (because of a lack of capacity). In order to solve the problem, the Belgian Justice Department adopted the policy of granting earlier parole. This seemed to be a much 'cheaper' solution to the capacity problem than building more prisons.

Fixed *versus* variable capacity

When we refer to capacity, we usually mean the fixed or installed capacity of the operating system. In the Belmont case, capacity is a function of the number of inspection lines. However, to achieve a capacity of 1508 cars per day an adequate number of inspectors is also required. If for one reason or another, only ten inspectors are available, the effective capacity will only be 1370. Nevertheless, most people will express capacity as a function of the number of inspection lines, because the inspection line resource is of a more fixed nature than the inspector resource. The inspector resource is presumed to be more variable. What is fixed or what is variable depends very much on the time horizon. Changing the number of inspection lines requires a long-term perspective as such a decision would require a long-term forecast of capacity needs. Likewise, the number of rooms in a hotel would not be changed without an examination of capacity needs over the following year or more, since this type of decision requires large financial commitments which are also more or less irreversible. If a capacity need is only going to last a week or so, it will probably not be necessary to change the number of lines in an inspection centre or the number of beds in a hotel.

In the long run, all capacity is variable, of course. The shorter the time horizon, the more constrained an organization is by the fixed and limited capacity of the resources. Considered in the long term, capacity management in a supermarket chain will mainly be concerned with the number of stores and their location; in the shorter term, capacity management will be concerned with the size of the store in the form of incremental additions or partial closures. As the time horizon decreases further, concern will be focused in turn on the number of check-outs, the opening hours and, finally, the staffing schedules.

Capacity management in services

The nature of capacity management is illustrated in Figure 15.3. In essence it involves two decisions:

1. How much capacity to make available (= capacity planning).
2. How to utilize the existing capacity (= capacity scheduling).

These two questions are hierarchically related – that is, the answer to the first question is the starting point for the second. This problem can also be considered within the framework of differentiating time horizons. The first question poses a capacity problem in terms of a long-term horizon. This restricts the shorter time-horizon capacity problem with which the second question is concerned. A supermarket, for instance, wants to decide how many check-out counters to install. Once installed, it starts to think about utilizing this resource effectively, by deciding on the staffing level and opening hours, but also by trying to influence the demand pattern. In the Belmont case, the number of inspection lines will probably be arrived at based on long-term patterns of demand; only afterwards will such issues as opening hours, staffing, and influence-demand patterns be addressed.

However, the decisions are not strictly sequential; there is usually a high level of interaction between these two levels. When there is a difficulty in changing opening hours or influencing the demand patterns in a certain period, a company might go back to the first decision and adapt the number of lines. Alternatively, a company might come to the conclusion that changing opening hours or influencing the demand patterns is the easier choice, and accordingly it would then go back and change the number of inspection lines.

There are of course many similarities between the capacity management problems in the service industry and in manufacturing industries. We can learn a great deal from the systems which have been developed in these fields and the experience that has been gained. However, there are a number of particularities, resulting from the fact that services are intangible and consumption and production occur simultaneously, that must be kept in mind when managing capacity in services.

■ *Intangibility*, for instance, means that services cannot be stored. Excess capacity cannot be utilized when there is no demand. Excess capacity is lost when the

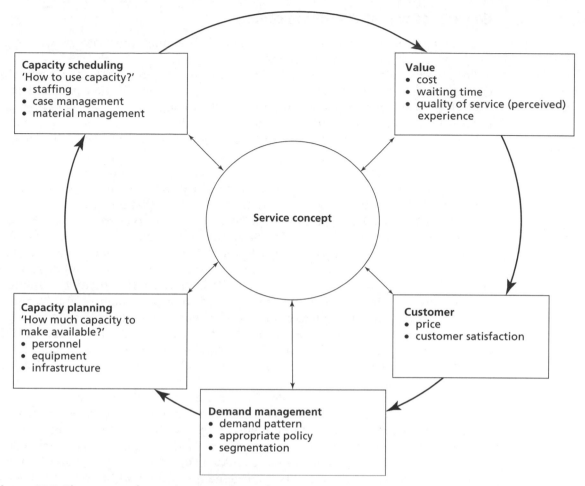

Figure 15.3 The nature of capacity management[3]

demand is not there. Output cannot be put into stock to be sold later. An airline that has scheduled a Boeing 747 between Amsterdam and New York with only 240 passengers loses forever the unoccupied excess of some 120 seats, or at least the profit potential of these excess seats.

■ *Simultaneity* also means that inventories cannot be used to balance supply and demand or – even better – to absorb demand fluctuations. This is the case both for seasonal and random fluctuations in demand. Statistical variation in demand patterns cannot be 'absorbed' by safety or other buffer stocks: the uncertainty in demand patterns penetrates (part of) the operating system. Expressed in technical terms, the arrival pattern in many services is *stochastic*: capacity management must inherently deal with uncertainty. Like the arrival pattern, the service pattern is stochastic: the time it takes to process a customer or a request varies statistically. This is mainly a result of the *heterogeneity* of services.

Uncertainty is thus inherent in the capacity management problem in services.

Capacity as part of the service concept

The way a service organization answers the two basic questions however will determine the value of the product we offer to the customer.

Simultaneity also means that imbalances in capacity and demand are visible to customers and will affect them. When the capacity is limited, the customer has to wait. The customer will perhaps be turned off by long waits, especially when the queues are not managed correctly. At the other end of the scale, excess in capacity might also have a negative effect on the atmosphere and therefore the quality experienced by the customer.

In many instances, capacity may be seen as part of the product. The atmosphere in a football stadium is very much influenced by the number of people in the stadium relative to its capacity. Watching football in a stadium with a capacity of 100 000 with only 10 000 spectators is a totally different experience – and therefore a totally different product – from watching the same game with the same number of spectators in a stadium with a capacity of 10 000. The experience and therefore the 'product' in a restaurant that is only one-third full is a different experience from that in a restaurant that is close to its effective capacity. An empty restaurant will also probably be seen by the customer as a sign of poor quality, while a restaurant that is fully occupied will be perceived as a good restaurant.

The opposite is true in an aeroplane environment. An aeroplane that is fully occupied offers a hustled, nervous type of experience, while an aeroplane that is only half full not only gives you greater physical comfort, but also projects an atmosphere of calm and relaxation.

The absolute size of capacity also has an impact on the customer or on the customer's perception of the service encounter. Coming back to our restaurant example, it is clear that the restaurant with 50 places is much more intimate, exclusive and relaxing than a restaurant with a capacity of 200 places. The latter creates the impression of being a mass-production kitchen; it looks impersonal and standardized. It is clear that the capacity management solutions will have an impact on the cost of the service and therefore on the price the customer has to pay.

Demand management

Given the direct interaction between capacity and customer, it is clear that capacity management should not only deal with the supply side, but also with the demand side. This means that it is important in capacity management to understand demand patterns and to try to influence them, because it might be easier or at least more cost effective to adjust the demand to the given capacity on the short term.

All these factors demonstrate that capacity management in service industries is not a numbers issue or a purely technical problem. It is a question beset with many intangible, difficult to quantify issues, which require a good understanding of the psychology of the customer. When designing a service, it is important to keep in mind the way in which a customer will 'feel' the capacity.

Capacity as a strategic weapon

Services are intangible, which makes it very difficult to take out a patent on a product to protect against imitation. A process can sometimes be patented, but very frequently another means is needed to protect against imitation when that process is successful. Economists speak of 'barriers to entry'. By this, they mean obstacles that make it difficult or unattractive for potential competitors to enter the market. A patent could be such a barrier. However, capacity and the way in which capacity is or is not built up can be another factor that will influence the entry behaviour of potential competitors. If a new service is successful it will certainly draw attention to itself and, if the market is large enough, will quickly lead to imitation. In order to protect against such imitation, the service organization sometimes has very little choice but to build up capacity very quickly, thereby closely following the evolution of the demand. By so doing, the innovating company turns its time advantage (being the first one) into another, such as location or reputation; above all, this makes it risky for a potential competitor to enter the market. If the innovating company lacks the financial needs or management talent to build up capacity quickly, it will often resort to franchising, which provides not only capital but also the management capacity to manage dispersed operations.

It is clear that a capacity strategy to deter competition is not without risk. The new service concept might enjoy temporary, short-lived success. Many theme restaurants have experienced this fate.

CAPACITY PLANNING

Capacity, service level and waiting

In the Belmont case, customers were complaining about long waiting times, a situation not unique to this organization. We have all been in situations where we have had to wait against our will and were frustrated by the length of the waiting time and/or by the circumstances under which we had to wait. Table 15.1 is based on a Dutch study[4] and gives an overview of the frequency of various waiting situations and average waiting times. Various studies have indicated that in many services the final level of customer satisfaction will depend to a great extent on the length of waiting times and on how waiting has been perceived by customers. The utility

Table 15.1 Various categories of waiting situations: frequencies and average waiting times

	Frequency	Average waiting time
1. Check out counters in supermarket, small stores, etc.	22.1%	7.6 min
2. Appointments with friends, business associates, etc.	13.6%	22.0 min
3. Public transport	12.4%	11.0 min
4. Bars, restaurants, etc.	10.6%	13.0 min
5. In traffic	9.5%	10.4 min
6. Services with a counter (banks, post office, etc.)	8.5%	7.7 min
7. Services with reservations	5.0%	26.0 min
8. Cultural/sports events	2.7%	12.1 min
9. Other	15.6%	19.9 min

Source: Pruyn, A. and Smidts, A. (1992) *De Psychologische Beleving van Wachtrijen.* Erasmus Universiteit. Based on diaries of 243 persons with 3566 waiting situations.

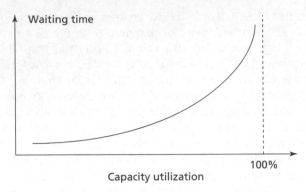

Figure 15.4 Capacity utilization and waiting time

company, Florida Light and Power, came to the conclusion that there was a strong correlation between waiting time on the telephone and the level of satisfaction[5] (*see* Table 15.2).

Services and service processes are inherently stochastic, therefore waiting is almost inevitable in service organizations. However, there is a strong relationship between capacity utilization and the length of the waiting time (*see* Figure 15.4). The relationship is usually exponential.

For instance, in the Belmont case, applying the queuing theory (*see* Technical Note 2), we can prove that with an average capacity utilization of 90 per cent, the average waiting time will be 2 minutes 5 seconds and the average number of customers waiting will equal 5.9. On the days or moments of the day, however, when the arrival rate is 10 per cent higher – that is, the utilization is 99 per cent – we can expect an average waiting time of 29 minutes 6 seconds and an average number of customers waiting of 90.6.

In a study in a Belgian bank we were able to establish a clear relationship between waiting time and capacity utilization. We produced simulation models for a number of branches in order to determine the optimal number of employees staffing the counters, taking into account the customer arrival patterns and the bank's service levels in terms of acceptable customer waiting times. Figure 15.5 depicts the relationship between capacity utilization and average waiting time for one particular branch. With three employees, the average waiting time for the customer is only 12 seconds. This is quite obvious given the low capacity utilization of only 37 per cent. With two employees and a capacity utilization of 57 per cent,

Table 15.2 Mean satisfaction rating by length of time on hold

Mean rating*	Time on hold
1.32	Less than 30 seconds
1.57	30 seconds to 1 minute
1.67	1 to 2 minutes
2.14*	2 to 3 minutes

* On a scale from 1 to 5, where 1 = very satisfied; 5 = very dissatisfied

© 1993 American Society for Quality Control. Reprinted with permission.

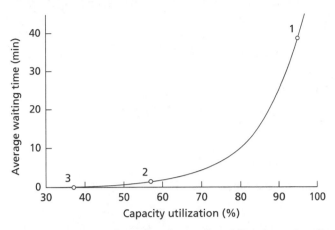

Figure 15.5 Capacity utilization and waiting times in a bank

the average waiting time increases slightly to 1.4 minutes. It can be clearly seen that employing only one person is totally unacceptable in terms of customer waiting times. The high capacity utilization of 95 per cent leads to average waiting times of 38 minutes. The acceptable level of capacity utilization seems to be in this case between 60 and 70 per cent, since beyond this point, an exponential growth will occur in customer waiting times.

If customers have to wait, they experience the general service level as low and become dissatisfied. In other circumstances, waiting is simply not feasible. When there are too few rooms in a hotel or too few seats on an aeroplane, customers have to be turned away. Not only is the gross profit potential lost as the customers are turned away, but there is also a loss of future earnings as the customers might never return.

When customers are able or willing to wait, service level can be defined as:

$$P = 100\% - \text{probability of an excessive wait}$$

When the customer is not willing to wait, service level can be defined as:

$$P = 100\% - \text{probability of having to turn away a customer}$$

What constitutes an excessive wait in the first case depends on the situation. Thirty seconds waiting for someone to pick up the telephone is usually considered excessive, while most of us are willing to wait for 30 minutes in a hospital to see a particular specialist. Each organization has to determine what an excessive wait is.

Let us assume that in the Belmont case 20 minutes is considered excessive. With a capacity utilization of 90 per cent, the probability of a certain customer having to wait 20 minutes is rather small. At peak times with a capacity utilization of 99 per cent, however, the probability of an excessive wait is equal to 54 per cent,[6] leading to a service level of 46 per cent.

Determining the capacity level

Cost of waiting is known

The first question in capacity management is how much capacity should be made available given a certain 'expected' demand pattern. This decision is basically a

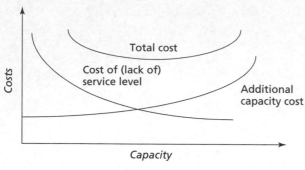

Figure 15.6 Determining the capacity level

trade-off between the cost of additional capacity on the one hand and the value of a higher service level or the cost of a lack of service level on the other (*see* Figure 15.6). The optimal capacity level depends very much on the evolution of both cost curves. Economists will tell us that it makes sense to increase capacity as long as the marginal cost of adding a capacity unit is lower than the marginal benefit of increasing the service level.

In the Belmont case, an additional inspection line requires an investment of 250 000 euro. Assuming the usable lifetime of this equipment to be five years, the annual equipment costs are 50 000 euro. An operator must be hired to run the line and paid 15 euro per hour. Standard queuing theory (*see* Technical Note 2) teaches us that by adding a twelfth line the average waiting time per customer will drop in peak months from 5 minutes to 1.2 minutes. However, assuming a morning peak during which the demand is 5 per cent higher than average, the average waiting time will drop from 1 hour to 2.2 minutes or a gain of 57.8 minutes. Let us then assume that we add an inspection line that is operated part-time from 8.00 a.m. to 10.00 a.m. for the period February to May, costing in total 21 000 euro (15 euro/hour × 14 weeks × 5 days × 2 hours). 50 000 euro is the depreciation charge for the installation, so the total yearly cost of increasing the capacity is 71 000 euro. The benefit is a reduction in waiting time of 57.8 minutes per customer during that period. This drop will affect 26 278 (= 187.7 customers at peak/h × 14 weeks × 5 days × 2 hours) customers.

If we assume that the 'value of waiting for the customer' is 12.5 euro/hour, the increased value for customers is therefore:

$$26\,278 \times \frac{57.8}{60} \times 12.5 = 316.430 \text{ euro}$$

Given that this value is higher than the marginal cost of expanding the capacity, it is worthwhile expanding the capacity to 12 lines. Expanding the capacity from 12 to 13 lines has the same marginal cost, but the marginal benefit in terms of reduced waiting times is a drop in average waiting time of only 1.4 minutes. The value of this reduced waiting time is:

$$26\,278 \times \frac{1.4}{60} \times 12.5 = 7.664 \text{ euro}$$

Therefore, it does not seem to be worthwhile expanding to 13 lines.

Often the benefit to the customer or, conversely, the cost of waiting to an external customer, is difficult to determine. However, if we are speaking of internal customers – that is, the organization's own employees – the cost is easier to determine. For instance, in the case of a large hospital that is considering investing in an additional lift to reduce personnel waiting time, the cost of waiting is simply the salary cost associated with the waiting time.

An interesting study in which the cost of waiting was traded off against the cost of increasing capacity was carried out by Mark Davis.[7] He first established a relationship between waiting time and customer satisfaction in a fast-food restaurant. In a second step, he established a relationship between customer satisfaction and the return behaviour of the customer, with which he could associate an increase or reduction in revenue and margin. Combining the two relationships he was able to define a cost function related to waiting time:

$$w(t) = 5.47 + 16.54t$$

where the cost of waiting $w(t)$ is expressed in dollars and the waiting time in minutes.

He concluded that each minute the customer had to wait cost about $16.54. This had to be traded off with the cost of installing capacity $C(t)$. In this case, adding capacity was mainly a matter of adding more personnel paid at $7.50 per hour. Applying standard queuing theory, one can establish a relationship between the number of workers and the average waiting time. Including the labour cost in the equation leads to a relationship between $C(t)$ and the waiting time:

$$C(t) = 52.98 \times t^{-0.09}$$

The total cost is therefore:

$$T(t) = 5.47 + 16.54t + 52.98 \times t^{-0.09}$$

As can be derived from Figure 15.7, the minimum total cost is reached for $t = 0.32$ minutes. In order to achieve this, eight servers were required.

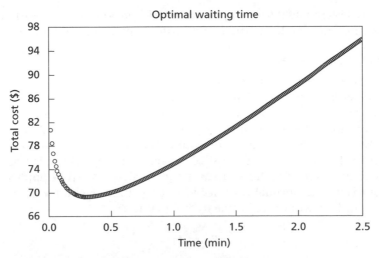

Figure 15.7 Optimal waiting time in a fast-food restaurant

Source: The Decision Sciences Journal, published by the Decision Sciences Institute, College of Business Administration, Georgia State University, Atlanta, GA.

Cost of waiting is not known

When dealing with external customers and when it is impossible to determine the cost of waiting, the problem can sometimes be approached from the other direction. Usually, it is easy to determine the cost of expanding capacity. Theoretically, as stated earlier, capacity should be increased as long as the marginal cost is lower than the marginal benefit of an increased service level. If service level is expressed as an average waiting time, the question then becomes whether or not the marginal cost of increasing capacity is lower than the reduction in total average customer waiting time multiplied by the cost of waiting per time unit. As a formula this becomes:

$$a < b \times \Delta_w \times N$$

where:

a = marginal cost of capacity expansion
b = cost of waiting per time unit and per customer
Δ_w = the marginal reduction of average waiting time per customer
N = total number of customers whose average waiting time will be reduced over the time horizon considered

As long as $b > \dfrac{a}{\Delta_w \times N}$, expansion is worthwhile.

If $b < \dfrac{a}{\Delta_w \times N}$, expansion should not take place.

While it is difficult to estimate the exact value of b in many cases, it is possible to evaluate whether this value is higher or lower than $\dfrac{a}{\Delta_w \times N}$.

For instance, in the Belmont case, we concluded that a = 71 000 euro, Δ_w = 57.8 minutes and N = 26 278, therefore:

$$\frac{a}{\Delta_w \times N} = \frac{71\,000}{57.8 \times 26\,278} = 0.047 \text{ euro}$$

As long as b is estimated to be higher than 0.047 euro/minute, expansion can go ahead. If b is estimated to be lower than 0.047 euro, expansion should not be considered.

Customer is turned away

Until now we have assumed that lack of capacity leads to waiting time – that is, that the service level could be related to waiting time. In many situations, customers cannot or do not want to wait when there is insufficient capacity. Customers go to the restaurant next door when they see that there is a long queue. Similarly, when a hotel or airplane is fully booked, the customer has to look for an alternative. In these cases, the cost of capacity shortage is the lost margin. In these instances, an approach referred to as marginal analysis can be applied. According to this approach, the optimal capacity level C^* is that level for which the probability that demand (D) will exceed capacity is equal to:

$$P(D > C^*) = \frac{C_o}{C_s + C_o}$$

where C_o is the cost of having one capacity unit in excess and C_s is the cost of having one capacity unit too few.

Here is an example to illustrate this concept. A hotel has to decide how many rooms to provide in a new hotel at a certain location. Management know the demand at that location is normally distributed with an average of 250 rooms per night and a standard deviation of 20. If on a particular day the hotel has to turn away a customer because it is fully booked, it loses the gross margin on the room of 50 euro (C_s is therefore 50 euro). They also know that if the hotel has one room unoccupied on a particular day, it has a cost which is equal to the depreciation of the capital invested in the room per day and the cost of the upkeeping of that room (cleaning, heating, etc.). This cost is estimated to be 12.5 euro (C_o in this case is therefore 12.5 euro). In this case the optimal capacity – that is, the optimal number of rooms $C*$ – will be such that:

$$P(D > C*) = \frac{12.5}{50 + 12.5} = 0.2$$

In other words, the capacity of the hotel should be such that there is a 20 per cent probability that the demand on a given day will be higher than the available capacity. Statistical calculations teach us that in order to have a 20 per cent chance of exceeding the level $C*$, the capacity should be equal to 267.[8]

SCHEDULING CAPACITY

Given a certain 'fixed' or 'structural' capacity level, it is important to work out how we should utilize capacity to maximize service to the customer on the one hand and minimize costs on the other. The assumption is that the 'fixed' capacity is given. Furthermore, in order to serve the customer, the organization has to provide other resources, such as materials and human resources. This is referred to as '*service resources planning*'. The key role of human resources in services means accurate scheduling of these resources so that they match the demand patterns as closely as possible is of crucial importance. Exhibit 15.2 illustrates the experience of capacity scheduling at McDonald's.

Exhibit 15.2

Capacity scheduling at McDonald's[9]

At McDonald's, the objective is to keep a customer waiting no longer than two minutes in a queue and no longer than 60 seconds at the counter. A restaurant is 'producing' meals to stock – or, more precisely, assembling (collecting the sandwich, the fries, etc.) – and to order. A stock (or a bin) of sandwiches divides the back office from the front office. Each restaurant has its own historical overview of the distribution of sales during the week and during the day. Tables 15.3 and 15.4 give examples of these distributions.

Based on historical data of weekly volumes, these distributions make it possible for the

Table 15.3 Distribution of sales throughout the week at a typical branch of McDonald's

	Percentage of week's customers
Sunday	14.0
Monday	12.3
Tuesday	12.4
Wednesday	13.2
Thursday	14.8
Friday	16.3
Saturday	16.8
	100.0

Exhibit 15.2 continued

Table 15.4 Distribution of sales throughout the day at a typical branch of McDonald's

For hour ending at . . .	Percentage of day's sales
8.00 a.m.	3.4
9.00 a.m.	4.1
10.00 a.m.	4.0
11.00 a.m.	3.9
12.00 noon	7.5
1.00 p.m.	14.9
2.00 p.m.	9.1
3.00 p.m.	5.0
4.00 p.m.	3.5
5.00 p.m.	5.5
6.00 p.m.	9.1
7.00 p.m.	8.4
8.00 p.m.	5.6
9.00 p.m.	5.3
10.00 p.m.	4.6
11.00 p.m.	3.4
12.00 p.m.	2.5
	100.0

restaurant manager to predict the work volume (expressed in $) for any moment of the day. With these data the manager determines the staffing schedule each Wednesday for the following Sunday through Saturday, using the guidelines shown in Table 15.5.

When the volume at a certain time is estimated to be $240, for instance, eight employees are scheduled in total: two at the grill, two at the counter, two at the drive-thru windows, one at the bin, and one with a flexible task (the floater). The bin plays an important role in the actual production scheduling (i.e. deciding which and how many hamburgers to make at a particular moment). The bin acts as the interface between the back-office personnel in the kitchen and the front-office personnel at the counter and at the drive thru windows. If hourly sales volume exceeds $240, a person is specially assigned to 'run' the bin. This person manages the flow of products into the sandwich-holding bin, calling for production as needed, wrapping the sandwiches when they are passed up, and keeping the bin stock organized and fresh. The person 'on the bin' uses certain rules of thumb to determine how much stock is appropriate. For instance, when volume is between $600 and $700/per hour, 20–24 hamburgers, 20–24 cheeseburgers, 9 Big Macs, 3–4 Quarter Pounders, 3–4 Quarter Pounders with Cheese, and 6–7 Filet o' Fishes are kept in stock. The distribution per type of sandwich is pretty well known and relatively stable over the week and during the course of the day.

Table 15.5 Staffing at McDonald's

	Total number of staff	Workstations						$ per hour volume guidelines
		Grill	Windows	Drive-Thru	Bin	Fry	Floaters*	
Minimums to open	4	1	1	1	–	–	1	$120
	5	1	1	1	–	–	2	150
	6	2	1	1	–	–	2	180
	7	2	2	1	–	–	2	210
	8	2	2	2	1	–	1	240
	9	2	2	2	1	–	2	275
	10	3	3	2	1	–	1	310
	11	3	3	2	1	1	1	345
	12	3	3	3	1	1	1	385
	13	4	3	3	1	1	1	425
	14	4	3	3	1	1	2	475
	15	4	4	3	1	1	2	525
	16	5	4	3	1	1	2	585
Fully staffed	17	5	5	3	1	1	2	645

* Floaters 'help the cause': patrol the car park, entrance and toilets; restock; cover on breaks.

Service requirements planning

In the Belmont case in Exhibit 15.1, it is clear that, in addition to the inspection lines and registration desks, there is also a need for people to staff these stations and for supplies, such as the filters and documents used at these workstations.

At first sight, scheduling the human resources in this case would appear to be very easy. One inspector is needed per line and one administrative employee per desk. However, given the seasonality of the demand pattern, it is not always necessary to staff all the lines and all the desks at 100 per cent capacity. The availability of human resources could be adapted to the expected demand pattern, as the restaurant manager does at McDonald's (*see* Table 15.5).

Successful completion of an inspection requires supplies – that is, various documents and materials consumed during the actual inspection. In this case, the cost of the supplies will probably be small compared to the cost of the other resources. Management will therefore pay little attention to optimizing the availability of these supplies, making sure that there are always sufficient levels in stock. A high safety stock will be maintained. In other cases, such as restaurants like McDonald's, the materials are relatively important not only because their share in the total cost of the service is high, but also because freshness is an important quality factor.

Independent versus dependent demand

An important concept to consider when managing the 'other resources' in service organizations is the notion of *independent, dependent, pseudo-independent* and *pseudo-dependent* demand items.

- *Independent demand items.* In a supermarket, sugar is in most cases an independent demand item – that is, the demand for sugar is not (directly) dependent on the demand for any other item in the supermarket. Therefore, the availability of the sugar can be managed independently of any other resource.
- *Dependent demand items.* In a catering company, conversely, the demand for sugar is dependent on the type and number of meals. If the planned production of meals over a certain time horizon is known, the demand for sugar can be derived from this planned production.
- *Pseudo-independent demand items.* On an airplane, the demand for sugar is theoretically a dependent demand item, dependent on the number of passengers and their preference when drinking coffee or tea. However, few airlines will derive the demand pattern for sugar from the planned number of passengers. They will probably always have a fixed supply of sugar on the plane, regardless of the number of passengers they have on board. The cost of managing the availability of sugar on board more precisely by deriving it from the scheduled number of passengers will probably be higher than the cost of excess stock of sugar they carry by managing it independently. Sugar is therefore a pseudo-independent demand item – that is, it is managed as if it were an independent item.
- *Pseudo-dependent demand items.* A pseudo-dependent demand item is an item which is not directly and deterministically dependent on the demand of another item, but where there is some sort of relationship which can be used to determine the demand more precisely. For instance, the demand for tennis facilities at a vacation resort can be derived from the number of villas or bungalows which are occupied.

Managing independent demand items

When the demand for a resource is independent, or when a company wants to manage it as if it were an independent item (i.e. it is a pseudo-independent demand item), and when the resource is a non-material resource, such as equipment or human resources, the approach discussed earlier can be used. When we are talking about a material resource, however, like the sugar in the supermarket, the various existing inventory management models can be used. We refer the reader to the standard textbooks on inventory management or production management for a detailed discussion of these models.

Management of dependent demand items using the MRP logic

When managing a dependent demand item, an approach called '*service resources requirements planning*', analogous to the manufacturing resources planning (or MRP) approach utilized in manufacturing organizations, can be used. Figure 15.8 depicts the framework of such an approach in a hospital.

The key elements of this approach are the *master schedule* (in the hospital application, the master admission schedules), the *bill of resources*, and the *data file on availability of resources*.

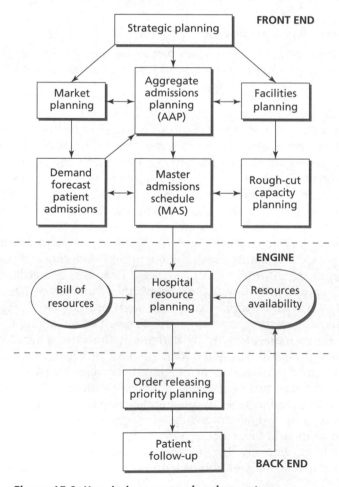

Figure 15.8 Hospital resource planning system

- The *master schedule* expresses the known or forecast demand for so-called 'end products'. In the case of a hospital, for instance, this is the planned admission schedule or the planned discharge schedule of patients. For an airline catering company, this might be the actual and/or forecast number of passengers on a certain flight.
- Returning to the case of the hospital, each type of patient can be assigned a certain *bill of resources*. This is a projection of the amount and timing of resources that will be consumed by this type of patient during his or her stay in hospital. In order to do this, patients are classified into different groups – the so-called DRGs or diagnostic-related groups. In the airline catering company, there is typically a contract where the type of meals in each passenger class is specified. A further distinction has to be made between vegetarian and non-vegetarian meals, and sometimes kosher and non-kosher meals. When the actual or planned number of passengers in each of the categories on a certain flight is known, the number of each type of meals needed can be derived, as can, subsequently, the number of intermediate products, ingredients, and, over time, even human resources (*see* Figure 15.9).

Exhibit 15.3 illustrates how this concept has been implemented in a New Orleans restaurant.

Exhibit 15.3

MRP in a New Orleans restaurant[10]

The procedure starts with an aggregate daily forecast expressed in monetary terms. The forecast is estimated mathematically based on a regression analysis using trend and a series of dummy variables to account for the seasonal patterns within the week.

This aggregate forecast is disaggregated into forecasts for the various meals on the menu based on a distribution of the individual meals over the last eight months. This process was carried out for each of the 46 meals on the menu, resulting in a master production schedule.

For each of the meals a 'product structure' or 'bill of resources' is constructed (a kind of Recipe). Figure 15.10 depicts such a product structure for the 'Veal Picante' meal type. This structure includes not only material resources, but also human resources. This structure together with the master production schedule allows the organization to calculate a time-phased resources plan, for instance the 'cream' item #40011. This leads to the so-called requirements for the cream over the entire planning horizon.

Taking into consideration the *scheduled receipts*, i.e. the expected orders of cream that will be delivered, and the cream *'on hand'* one can calculate the net requirements – that is, the

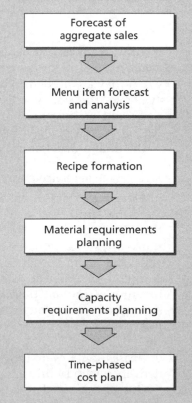

Figure 15.9 The resources planning procedure

Exhibit 15.3 continued

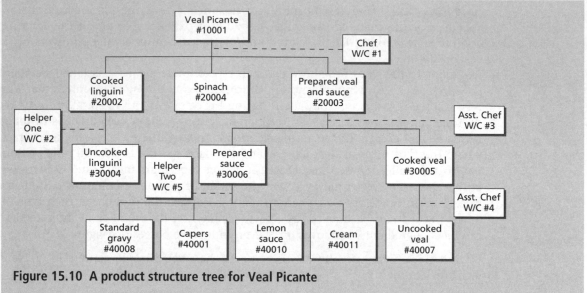

Figure 15.10 A product structure tree for Veal Picante

quantities of cream that should be ordered to avoid a stock out. Taking into consideration the delivery lead time and the order quantities. One can calculate the so-called 'planned orders', which are orders that have to be issued to the supplier of cream.

The advantage of a service resources requirements planning approach is that the availability of resources is much more integrated. The resources are available only when they are needed. When for one reason or another a particular resource is not available, the system tells us that the other resources normally required for the same end product are not needed either. Another advantage is that information regarding how much of the resource is required, and when it is required, is linked to the final product and kept up to date.[11]

Just-in-time in service environments

Just-in-time (JIT) is a production philosophy originally applied in Japanese manufacturing firms, but increasingly used by Western manufacturers. According to this philosophy, the objective is to eliminate waste – that is, the activities, such as transport, storage, quality inspection, waiting and setting up machines, that do not add value to the product. All these non-value-added activities have one thing in common: they all lead to unnecessary inventories. Just-in-time therefore targets the inventories and has the material delivered exactly when needed – 'just in time' to be utilized and in the quantities needed at that time. Applying the JIT philosophy not only leads to lower inventories and therefore reductions in costs and working capital, but by forcing companies to eliminate the non-value-added activities it decreases costs even further, providing the opportunity to improve quality and delivery dependability and to increase delivery speed and flexibility.

One of the key elements of JIT is the application of the so-called *pull principle* to the issuing of work and purchase orders. Using the pull principle as a tool to initiate production or purchase orders means that the signal to start producing or delivering a certain item comes from the place or the workstation where the item is being used or consumed. The signal does not come from a central planning department, but from the 'next' workstation. A typical example of the application of this principle is the relationship between the Volvo plant in Ghent and ECA, the supplier of seats located about 15 kilometres north of the plant. ECA starts producing a car seat after it has received an (electronic) message from Volvo that the car is at the final assembly stage. ECA has eight hours to produce and deliver the seats before they are installed in Volvo's final assembly plant.

Examples of pull systems in service environments can be found in hospitals where a pull relationship is established between the central pharmacy and the operating theatres for the delivery of medicines and supplies. A cart filled with a limited amount of supplies is the communication device. As soon as one cart is emptied, it is wheeled back to the central pharmacy where it is filled up and brought back to the operating theatre. Similar pull systems have been established between outside suppliers and various units in a hospital – for instance, for the delivery of linen.

The scheduling system of McDonald's is another example of such a pull system. The back office is told to make additional sandwiches when the number of sandwiches in the 'bin' drops below a certain minimum. This minimum is dependent on the time of the day, as we have already described.

The JIT principles can equally be applied to service, even if the material and therefore the physical stocks are negligible or non-existent. Rather than taking inventories – which are nothing more than 'queues' of materials – as a central point of reference, a queue of customers or files can be considered.

Staffing and scheduling in a service environment

In many service systems, human resources are the single most important asset and have a predominant role in the service delivery process. Available staff should be deployed in such a way that good (or excellent) service delivery can be obtained. This is not easy in an environment which is known as inherently stochastic.

The planning and scheduling of personnel should be integrated with the management of other resources and can be positioned within a larger framework of manpower planning (*see* Figure 15.11). However, in this section we will treat human

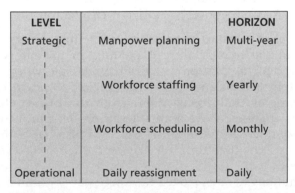

Figure 15.11 An integrated framework for manpower planning, staffing and scheduling[14]

Source: Khoong, C. M. (1996), reprinted by kind permission of MCB University Press Ltd.

resources as a somewhat separate area. First of all, as with capacity in general, it is necessary to divide the task of planning and scheduling into different hierarchical levels. As Figure 15.11 indicates, the highest level is the strategic level. At this level, the *manpower requirements* – i.e. the type and quantity – over a multiple-year horizon are determined.[12] Strategic decisions on the design of the service operating system have a severe impact on this decision. Other decisions, such as the number and types of operating units and the days and hours each unit will operate, determine the required manpower levels.[13]

Once these overall manpower requirements have been determined, they are annually adjusted in a *staffing plan*. This plan takes into account estimates of staffing requirements as produced by individual department managers. The department manager uses overall forecasts of demand and/or subjective estimates of the current workloads in order to determine the staffing requirements of his or her department. Normally this occurs once a year at the time of budgeting. These department level estimates are aggregated into a company figure which may be compared with the multi-year manpower requirements. Based on this information, a (re)allocation of the available personnel to the different departments or units can take place.

The staffing plan should also include policies regarding how predicted fluctuations in required human resources over a certain seasonal period will be handled. The available human resources capacity can be stretched (e.g., by means of overtime) or new interim labour resources can be acquired. These policies are generally embedded in a wider human resource management plan.

Once the human resources are allocated to a department, a *workforce schedule* specifies when (on which day and at which time) each of the allocated personnel is going to work (*see* Exhibit 15.2). Developing workforce schedules is particularly important in those service environments where a 24-hour service delivery is guaranteed through different shifts – the police, for example. By specifying the on-duty and off-duty periods for each employee over a certain period of time, an organization tries to match capacity with demand over a short time horizon. In many service firms, the development of a workforce schedule is considered to be a very complex (and time-consuming) task due to the many constraints which must be taken into account:

1. the available (allocated) staff;
2. the wishes of the individual employees as to when they want to work;
3. the demand pattern for services over a (shorter) cycle of a week or a day.

The nature of services and characteristics, such as the simultaneity of production and consumption and the impossibility of holding an 'inventory' of services, means that it is important to develop a workforce schedule where capacity and demand are well matched. Imbalances will become clear through fluctuations in the workload of the employees. It has been proven that in high-contact services, a work intensity that is sustained above normal levels can lead to increased fatigue, burnout and eventually increased turnover,[15] which in turn has an impact on the availability of personnel. The high turnover may be the start of 'a cycle of failure', as described in Chapter 11.

Many different operations research models have been developed in order to find an 'optimal' workforce schedule in specific situations.[16] The complexity of a workforce schedule also makes it an interesting application for automated decision support. Exhibit 15.4 describes the application of a software package for scheduling nurses.

The last level in the manpower planning framework is that of the *daily reassignments of personnel* due to sudden sickness leave of employees or unexpected peaks in demand. In order to cope with these daily changes, some degree of flexibility in workforce staffing and scheduling is required.

Exhibit 15.4

Staffing and scheduling nurses in an acute care hospital[17]

A hospital nurse staffing and scheduling survey in American hospitals (348 nurse managers) reveals that the three most important objectives of nurse managers are:

1. achieving and improving quality of care;
2. having satisfied nurses with a low turnover rate; and
3. assigning equitable workload to nursing staff by matching required staff to actual number on duty.

These objectives overrule other goals such as cost containment and productivity improvement. How do nurses typically deal with the nurse staffing and scheduling problem?

At the annual budgeting round, the nursing director is asked to project the next year's staffing needs. On average, the nursing director will develop estimates of the nursing staff needs by

- gathering data on patient days and admissions, and sometimes on forecasts of these data;
- studying trends in the utilization of nursing services; and
- using her experience.

The nursing director must also determine how many nurses will be allocated to the different nursing departments. While the number of patients on the unit is an important indicator of staffing, the nursing director must be aware that a patient day does not have the same meaning for every nursing department. A critical care unit needs a higher level of nursing resources per patient day than a non-critical care unit. In order to take these differences into account, the average amount of nursing care per patient for each nursing department must be known. This assumes the development of time standards for a type of patient. Several methods such as work sampling and expert opinion can be used to collect time standards. Applying time standards requires the development of a patient classification system that identifies different types of patients. Besides these quantitative differences, the qualifications of a nurse working in an intensive-care unit may be different from one working in a non-critical care unit.

The staffing needs of a nursing department at a certain time are thus a function of among others the kind of patient cared for. This makes it extremely difficult for the nursing director to allocate a fixed number of nurses to one department for a longer period of time (for instance, one year). The changing needs demand flexibility in the allocation of nurses. One way to deal with this problem is to use a pool of floating nurses who can be reallocated as needed.

The staffing budget specifies how many nurses with a specific qualification are needed for each nursing unit. This budget is the input into the nursing scheduling decision. The head of the nursing unit determines which nurses will work at which shift and on which day. A scheduling policy will specify the rules of schedule development. The scheduling policy includes decisions on the following topics: the time period of the schedule (two, four or more weeks), the number of shifts per 24 hours, how nurses rotate (or do not rotate) between shifts, how nurses are assigned to shifts, how many hours a nurse works per shift (day), the pattern of days on and off.

An example of a (traditional) scheduling policy is a cyclical schedule of an eight-hour shift, five-day working week.[18] These shifts are usually from 7.00 a.m. to 3.30 p.m., from 3.00 p.m. to 11.30 p.m. and 11.00 p.m. to 7.30 a.m. A cyclical schedule is one which repeats itself after some period of time (for example, six weeks). Many more complex scheduling rules have been developed – for example, a cyclical schedule of ten-hour days and four-day working weeks. Scheduling policies vary in terms of allowable scheduling patterns and wage rates and so the

Exhibit 15.4 continued

cost of implementing alternative scheduling policies is also different.[19]

An attractive scheduling policy seems to be an important factor in retaining nurses; it must take into account the individual wishes of the nurses. Common requests include working a maximum of seven consecutive days, never working on Wednesday afternoons, working only two week-ends per month and this for the whole weekend. These wishes are further complicated with very specific requirements such as requests for a particular day off.

Scheduling nurses is a complex calculation problem with many different goals, decision parameters and constraints. In order to solve this complex computational problem, several

automated scheduling procedures or systems have been developed.

On a shift-by-shift basis, non-predictable changes will occur, for instance, due to sudden sickness. Some policies must be available to deal with these daily problems. For instance, one nursing department uses a combination of overtime work, on-call staff, a pool of floating nurses from outside and the floating of nurses between nursing units. These reassignment mechanisms assume some kind of staffing and scheduling flexibility and do not all have the same costs and benefits. Hiring nurses from outside the hospital is clearly more expensive. Floating nurses between nursing units is sometimes limited by the special skills needed.

MANAGING THE DEMAND SIDE

Until now we have assumed that the demand pattern was a given – that is, that it could not be influenced by the organization. However, most service organizations, explicitly or implicitly, try to influence the demand pattern to provide a better match between demand and supply (the available capacity). It can sometimes be easier and/or less costly to work on the demand side of the service equation, rather than attempting to control supply. This is certainly the case in organizations with high capacity-related fixed costs, such as airlines, hotels and professional service organizations.

Influencing the demand patterns

Influencing the demand pattern involves changing the natural demand pattern – that is, the pattern that occurs if the customers do not have any incentive to adapt the timing or quantity of the demand. Demand management therefore involves offering customers an incentive to change their behaviour or otherwise changing the drivers of demand. Effective demand management therefore involves understanding this behaviour and the demand drivers.

Understanding demand patterns

In the Belmont case in Exhibit 15.1, there are two 'seasonal' patterns. There is a *daily pattern* whereby drivers prefer to arrive early in the morning, and there is the *yearly pattern* whereby more drivers tend to bring in their car for inspection in the first four months of the year than in the other eight. The yearly cycle is tied to the timing of car purchases. It appears that in this case people, for a variety of reasons, prefer to buy their new cars in the first months of the year. As long as the visit to the inspection station is tied to the date of purchase of the car, these peaks at the beginning of the year will persist, whatever the incentive the inspection station gives its customers to come later in the year. To change the yearly pattern, these dates must be decoupled, which in this case requires legislative action.

This situation is fairly clear in the Belmont case, but it is not always so in other cases. The notion of dependent and pseudo-dependent demand is useful in this context. The demand for car inspection services can be considered to be dependent on the purchase of the car. The demand for train seats is influenced at peak times by the opening and closing times of schools and workplaces.

Often the demand is composed of different segments which vary in terms of demand drivers or in their degree of sensitivity to incentives to change the demand pattern. In an ambulatory care facility, demand is made up of patients with an acute problem on the one hand and patients whose problems can be dealt with on an appointment basis on the other. One such facility analysed its demand pattern and came to the conclusion that on Monday mornings there were significantly more patients with acute problems than on any other day of the week. To avoid excessive demand on Mondays, a policy was introduced which did not allow patients to make appointments for Monday mornings. The capacity was made available exclusively for the treatment of acute problems.

The demand pattern must be understood not only to see if the demand can be influenced, but also to see the extent to which it can be influenced. For instance, price sensitivity might differ from segment to segment. Tourists are more sensitive to price reduction than businessmen and are therefore willing to stay over the weekend, if offered a cheaper plane fare. Businessmen usually prefer to return home as soon as business is over, no matter what the price is.

In the Belmont case, there are at least two segments: private individuals and professionals. A professional – such as a truck driver, taxi driver or travelling sales-person – drives his or her car as a part of the job. Statistics tell us that early morning peaks in demand come mainly from private drivers. The daily pattern for the professional driver is much more evenly spread. This is explained by the fact that private individuals who have to bring in their car in the middle of the day have to take at least half a day off. If they can come in early in the morning, these drivers do not have to take so much time off. At most, they will be an hour late for work. The 'cost' (in terms of time off) clearly varies depending on the time of the day. For the professional driver, the cost during the day is much more even since it is not dependent on the time of the day or tied to a particular time slot.

Introducing price incentives

Price incentives (or disincentives) are the most obvious way to change the demand pattern, as was already discussed in Chapter 7. Prices for ski lift passes are obviously more expensive during the Christmas break and the winter school holidays than they are, for instance, for the rest of the months of December or January. The price for electricity is lower at night than during the day. The same is true for a telephone conversation. Before applying price incentives, however, one has first to estimate the price sensitivity – not an easy task in many cases.

Price sensitivity is an expression of the relationship which exists between demand and price. In most cases when the price drops, demand will increase. The demand is said to be 'price-elastic'. More people will be tempted to buy the product or the service when the price is lower (see Figure 15.12). For example, taking the Disneyland Paris case described in Exhibit 16.1, one of the actions taken by management after the rather disastrous first year was to drop prices.

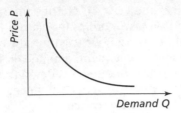

Figure 15.12 A demand curve

Demand can be very *elastic* – producing a curve that is very steep (as it is in Figure 15.12) – it can be *inelastic*, implying an almost flat curve. For certain products such as luxury goods, the demand can even be positively related to the price.

Before experimenting with lower prices, companies should be aware that the different segments in the market may have a different price sensitiveness. Very frequently, there is a segment in the market which is very price sensitive and another which is less so. If a price incentive is offered, regardless of the segment, it goes without saying that the less price-sensitive segment will also take advantage of the price discount and therefore the company will lose gross margin.

The key question is therefore how a market should be segmented. Airlines have done it very cleverly by requiring low fare (see chapter Yield Management) travellers to stay over the weekend.[20] The Belgian railways offer so-called 'GO Passes' for younger people in off-peak hours and are thereby reaching a market segment that otherwise would not take the train, certainly not during off-peak hours. Hotels that otherwise depend very much on business travellers or conventions offer special rates at weekends.

Segmentation and price incentives can become very complex in certain businesses, particularly if there is a dynamic policy. This leads to the practice of yield management, as we shall explain later in this chapter.

Promoting off-peak demand

Another approach to altering the demand pattern is promoting off-peak demand. This entails seeking out different sources of demand at various periods. Seaside hotels compete vigorously during the period between October and March for conventions and business meetings. A ski resort, on the other hand, will offer a full range of summer sports like mountain biking, archery, hiking trips and white water rafting.

Offering alternative services

When the demand for a certain service becomes too high, a part of that demand can be reassigned to an alternative service. For instance, a holiday resort offered puppet shows and other entertainment for children at the times when there was peak demand for the subtropical swimming pool area.

Altering the product

When trying to alter the demand pattern, price need not be seen as the only variable. The other elements of the so-called 'marketing mix' – product, promotion and place – should also be considered. An interesting example is offered by a US resort.[21] Faced with far greater demand for tennis facilities than they could handle at peak hours, they transferred part of that demand to the early morning hours by creating what became known as the Early Bird Club. People who played tennis early in the morning were offered a free breakfast at the tennis court and started to get to know one another, teaming up for singles or doubles games. The product had become entirely different.

Advertising

Promotion might also be effective in changing the demand pattern, for example, by announcing that certain periods of the day, week or year are going to be very busy. In the United States the postal service starts early – immediately after Thanksgiving – with its campaign to stimulate people to send their Christmas cards. This is reminiscent of the summer campaign by the coal industry in the 1950s and 1960s to 'buy coal in the summer'.

In the Belmont case, a promotional campaign could be launched to let the public know that mornings are very busy.

Installing reservation systems

An effective way to influence the demand pattern is to introduce a reservation system. A reservation system pre-sells the potential service. One can deflect additional demand to other time slots at the same facility or to other facilities of the same organization. Reservations also benefit the customer by reducing waiting and guaranteeing service availability. A problem with reservation systems is that consumers may fail to honour the reservation. We shall discuss this problem later in this chapter.

Another problem is of course dealing with the inherent uncertainties – those related to arrival, as well as those related to service times. In many service organizations, service times may vary considerably. Patients seeing a doctor or a dentist are sometimes difficult to schedule because of the (seemingly) random variations in service times. This is an even bigger problem because a customer who has made a reservation does not expect to wait and will be quickly dissatisfied when he or she has to wait beyond the scheduled time.

Yield management

What is yield management?

The next time you are sitting in an aeroplane, ask your neighbour what price he or she paid for the trip. There is a good chance that a different price was paid for the same seat and surrounding service package. If the price you have paid is higher, you probably won't be very happy about it. However, don't start writing a letter of complaint to your local consumer protection agency. The airline's differentiated price practice will not be seen as unfair. You are just the victim of the yield management system of that airline. If you question your neighbour a little further you will probably find out that he or she booked much earlier than you did, is required to stay over the weekend, or is a member of a bird watching association on the way to its annual convention in Orlando, Florida.

You could have the same experience if you stay in a hotel, rent a car or even attend a hospital. These are all examples of service organizations that practise so-called 'yield management'.

When an airline schedules a plane on a certain day for a certain route, the capacity for that day on that route is fixed. While the airline wants to sell that capacity to passengers who are willing to pay full fare, it probably knows that on that day there are insufficient passengers willing to pay the full price. Given the fixed nature of the capacity and the fixed nature of the cost of operating an airline, where variable costs are low, the airline will of course be tempted to reduce its sales price to fill up the remaining seats. However, it has to make sure that the passengers who are willing to pay full fare do not take advantage of this price reduction, but on the other hand, make sure that they do not feel cheated or unfairly treated by the airline. The problem is more complex in the case of an airline, since it normally cannot take a wait-and-see attitude (i.e. wait to see how the airline fills up and depending on the occupation rate decide to drop prices). It has to make the decision on what prices to charge to which type of customers well in advance. This means that it has to decide beforehand what maximum capacity it will set aside for the lower paying categories. Exhibit 15.5 describes a simple example of a yield management system.

Exhibit 15.5

Yield management at Transpacific Airlines

Let us assume that 'Transpacific Airlines' (TPA) has scheduled a flight between London and Sydney on a particular day. The plane has a capacity of 300 passengers. The airline knows that there are two categories of customers interested in this trip. A first category – Category A – is willing to pay £1000, while the marginal cost to serve this type of passenger is only £100. The second category – Category B – is only willing to pay £500, while the marginal cost is £80. The airline also knows that on that particular day an average of 175 passengers is willing to pay full fare. However, the actual number may fluctuate. Let us assume that the actual number is normally distributed with a standard deviation of 50 passengers. Similarly, TPA knows that on average 150 passengers are willing to pay the lower fare and that the standard deviation of the demand in this group is 25. How much capacity should TPA set aside for Category B?

It can be shown that the optimal number of seats to set aside for the lower paying category is such that the expected marginal revenue for both categories is the same. If we assign a fixed number of 120 seats to Category B, the remaining 180 are assigned to Category A. The probability that demand will exceed 180 in Category A is 46 per cent. Therefore, the expected marginal contribution of this seat is therefore $0.46 \times 900 = £414$. The probability that the demand in Category B will exceed the assigned number of seats is equal to 88 per cent. Therefore the marginal contribution of the seat above 120 is $0.88 \times 420 = £370$. The latter category is below the marginal contribution of the former one, and so the number of seats assigned to Category B should be reduced. When we reduce the number of seats to 116.1, the expected marginal revenue for both categories is the same (= £405). The optimal (static) policy is therefore to allocate 184 seats to Category A and 116 seats to Category B.

Defining yield management more precisely

Yield management has been defined as:

'the process of allocating the right type of capacity to the right type of customer at the right price so as to maximize revenue or yield'.

Yield is defined as:

'the ratio of revenue realized over revenue potential'.

Let us illustrate this with the TPA example.

Exhibit 15.5 continued

The total capacity of the aeroplane is 300 seats and the maximum yield per seat is £900 or the maximum total yield is $900 \times 300 = £270\,000$ or 100 per cent. If at a certain time the aeroplane is filled with 200 passengers paying full fare (£900) and 90 passengers paying the reduced fare, the yield becomes:

$$\frac{(200 \times £900) + (90 \times £420)}{(300 \times 900)} = 80.6\%$$

In this simple problem, yield management appears to be a fairly static process. The lower-fare passengers will be accepted as long as the total number of passengers (300) (called the booking limit) and the number that has been set aside for this category beforehand have not been exceeded. For the high-fare paying passengers, the rule is simple. Passengers are accepted as long as there is an empty seat on the airplane (ignoring the fact for a moment that most airlines will probably overbook).

In reality, however, the problem is much more dynamic. The booking limit (number of seats set aside for the lower category) changes over time depending on the forecast of demand for the high category. If the conclusion is reached that the booking for the high category is slow – that is, that fewer higher-fare paying passengers are expected than originally planned – the booking limit will rise. On the other hand, when the demand for the high-fare tickets is much higher than expected, the booking limit will be reduced. To add to the complexity, there could be more than two categories. Another source of complexity is that customers who have made reservations could fail to show up. This shows how difficult it is to develop yield management systems. We refer the reader to the literature for further details.

Yield management is an issue in service organizations in the following circumstances:

1. *When the organization is operating with a relatively fixed capacity* – that is, capacity which cannot be quickly changed.
2. *When it is possible to segment markets*. It must be possible to effectually segment the markets into different types of customers. For example, the airline industry distinguishes between time-sensitive and price-sensitive customers by requiring that discounted fares involve a Saturday night's stay.[22] A hotel distinguishes between transient guests who walk in and request a room and, for instance, corporate travellers who usually make reservations. The first group pays a higher price than the second group.
3. *When the capacity is perishable*. This is one of the basic characteristics of services. Capacity is inventory that perishes when it is not used. It is precisely this characteristic that makes yield management relevant. It is because capacity that is not utilized is lost forever, that service organizations are willing to sell it cheaply, so that at least some marginal revenue is earned.

What about no-shows and overbooking?

Airlines allow customers to cancel unpaid reservations with no penalty. Even after having purchased a ticket, passengers are allowed to cancel their flights and receive at least partial refunds. On average, about half of all reservations made for a flight are cancelled or become no-shows. American Airlines estimates that about 15 per cent of the seats on sold-out flights would be unused, if reservations sales were limited to aircraft capacity.[23]

As a result, airlines, like hotels, have very little choice but to set reservation levels higher than their capacity. Of course, the problem is how high the overbooking level should be. If the level is too low, there will be a large number of empty seats; if the level is too high there is the prospect of disappointed and often angry customers who have made reservations but are being turned away. The airline or hotel must compensate them for the inconvenience and accommodate them on other flights or in other hotels.

Determining the overbooking level can again be based on the marginal analysis described above. To illustrate this approach, let us consider the case in Exhibit 15.6.

Exhibit 15.6

The Gates Hotel, San Francisco

The Gates Hotel,[24] a very popular business traveller's luxury hotel in San Francisco, found that it frequently turned down the rental of a room that was being held for a no-show reservation. Mr Barnes, the manager, felt that the hotel's policy of overbooking should be examined. He wondered how much extra capacity should be maintained to cover these commitments.

The average lost contribution for a room was $20 per night if a customer reserved the room and the hotel was unable to honour the reservation. About 10 per cent of the guests who showed up with reservations that could not be honoured could be placated without cost. Another 30 per cent were satisfied with being 'walked' (or transferred) to another hotel at a cost to the Gates of $3 per reservation. The remaining guests were so upset by this situation that the Gates could expect a loss of future business with an expected value in terms of contribution of approximately $50.

Mr Barnes reviewed his records and found that, when it was operating around full capacity, the Gates Hotel had the no-show experience summarized in Table 15.6.

Let us assume that the hotel accepts five more customers than it can accommodate. The cost of having one room unoccupied at the end of the day (C_o) is $20. The expected cost of having one room short (C_s) can be calculated as follows:

$$C_s = 0 \times 0.1 + 3 \times 0.3 + 50 \times 0.6 = \$30.9$$

As long as five or more customers do not show up, there will be no cost of overbooking, but the hotel will have to carry the cost of reduced occupancy. From Table 15.6 we can see that the probability of this happening is 27 per cent. Therefore, the marginal expected cost of unoccupancy is 0.27 × 20 = $5.40. On the other hand, if four or fewer

Table 15.6 The Gates Hotel no-show experience

No-shows	% of experiences	Cumulative % of experiences
1	10	10
2	21	31
3	19	50
4	13	63
5	10	73
6	5	78
7	6	84
8	4	88
9	3	91
10	2	93
11	1	94
12	2	96
13	2	98
14	1	99
15	1	100

customers do not show up, the hotel will have an overbooking cost. The probability of this happening is 63 per cent (see Table 15.6), so the marginal expected cost of overbooking is 0.63 × 30.9 = $19.50. Given that this latter cost is higher than the first cost, the hotel should overbook a lower number of customers. It can be proven that the optimal overbooking level (L) is such that:

$$P(D > L) = \frac{C_s}{C_s + C_o} = \frac{30.9}{30.9 + 20} = 0.61 \text{ or } 61\%$$

where D is the number of people that do not show up. $P(D > L)$ is then the probability that the number of people that do not show up is greater than L. We can see from Table 15.6 that the optimal level L is somewhere between 2 and 3. We would probably advise the hotel to keep its overbooking level to 2.

In reality, determining the overbooking level is usually more complex. First of all, it can seldom be approached in a static manner. The overbooking level changes over time. The earlier a passenger or guest has made a reservation on an airline, the higher the probability that he or she will cancel. This means that the overbooking levels must be higher a month before the departure than a week before the departure. Furthermore, the cost of overbooking is usually not in proportion to the number of passengers. When overbooked, American Airlines offers vouchers to passengers willing to give up their seats. It works something like an auction: the value of the voucher increases until enough willing passengers are found. The higher the number of oversales, the higher the average value of the voucher the company has to offer.

THE PSYCHOLOGY AND MANAGERIAL CONSEQUENCES OF WAITING

Waiting is not waiting

Table 15.2 illustrated what most of us have experienced personally. We do not like to wait. The amount of time we have to wait before being served affects our satisfaction level and our repurchase behaviour.

We saw from Figure 15.3 that there is a strong relationship between waiting and the capacity level provided. When faced with a waiting problem, it seems very logical for the service organization to change (i.e. increase) the capacity level. However, increasing the capacity might not always be a possible, adequate, or the most effective alternative. If waiting is a problem, then there are various other alternatives at a manager's disposal. Improving the customer's perception of the waiting experience can be as effective as reducing the actual length of the wait. In other words, we should focus on managing perception as much as managing capacity.

Before considering such actions, managers should be aware of how people perceive waiting and what the factors are that influence people's perception of waiting. David Maister[25] refers to this as the 'psychology of waiting'.

The psychology of waiting

Most of us have probably had similar experiences when travelling to an unknown destination. The first time you drive your car to visit a colleague or friend who lives in a place you have never been to, the drive towards the unknown destination always seems longer than the return drive. This impression disappears as you become more acquainted with the road. If you have experienced this, you have witnessed one of 'Maister's laws'.[26] David Maister, at that time a Harvard Business School professor, formulated a number of laws (without proving them, however) that express experiences many of us have had in waiting situations. We will briefly describe (an adaptation of) this list of laws.

Most people tend to overestimate the actual waiting time

Various studies indicate that customers cannot accurately estimate how long they have waited and usually think that they have waited much longer than they actually have. For instance, in the telephone study at Florida Light and Power referred to earlier,[27] 41 per cent of the customers who had actually waited less than

30 seconds, thought they had waited between 30 seconds and 1 minute, while 28 per cent even thought they had waited more than 1 minute. More generally, the study indicated that the following relationships existed between real waiting time (expressed in seconds) and the subjective or perceived waiting time:

$$\text{Real time} = 11.9 \text{ seconds} + 0.276 \text{ Subjective time}$$

Other studies, at least for waits of 5 minutes or less, point to the same conclusion. In a supermarket study, the average percentage differences between the perceived waiting time was found to be between 21 and 40 per cent.[28] A third study in a bank came to the conclusion that customers overestimated the waiting time by about 30 per cent (4.7 minutes *versus* 3.6 minutes) with 78 per cent of the customers overestimating the waiting time.[29] There is clearly an element of time distortion in all these situations. There are many factors that might explain this time distortion ranging from the fact that people generally are very poor at estimating time, to the fact that waiting is an anticipatory stage and therefore draws attention to itself and to the circumstances under which it takes place. Whatever the reason, however, such distortion exists and there is little point in arguing about the subject of a customer's estimate.

Unoccupied time feels longer than occupied time

There is an anecdote reported by Sasser *et al.*[30] about a hotel where customers complained about the waiting times at the lifts. Not being able to immediately increase the capacity of the lift facilities, the management of the hotel installed mirrors next to the lift doors. The result was that the number of complaints dropped significantly, despite the fact that the actual waiting time had not changed. The conclusion is that when people are distracted, they are less aware of the waiting time or are more tolerant of waiting. In the bank study referred to earlier, for instance, the bank installed an electronic news board. This board displayed fifteen minutes of up-to-date news and information, interspersed with ads for the bank. As a result, customers found waiting much more tolerable. When asked to describe their waiting experiences on a scale from one to ten (from very boring to very interesting) the interest level increased significantly. In the supermarket study,[31] Jones and Peppiatt found that when customers were distracted by a television screen at the check-outs, the average difference between actual and perceived waiting time dropped from 71.8 to 48.1 seconds.

Pre-process waits feel longer than in-process waits

Maister states that 'people waiting to make their first human contact with the service organisation are much more impatient than those who have "begun".' This is closely related to the 'anxiety' level of people when waiting. Generally speaking, a person's anxiety level is much higher while waiting to be served than it is when being served. Imagine entering a crowded café or tearoom, where waiters appear to be very skilled at ignoring your presence and avoiding your signals. You are probably very anxious for fear of being forgotten or being leap-frogged by customers who entered later. Your anxiety will magically disappear after the waiter has made eye contact with you and has somehow assured you that you have been noticed. Your tolerance for waiting increases as soon as you have the feeling of being 'in the system', rather than being 'in front of the system'.

The walk-in medical clinic at Harvard University noticed a significant drop in dissatisfaction levels due to waiting after they installed a triage system, despite the fact that the actual average waiting time increased after the installation of the system. This contradiction was resolved after observing the fact that in the new system the average time a walk-in visitor waited before he or she saw a medically qualified person (the triage nurse) attending to his or her problem decreased. In the new system the average time was 19.7 minutes, while in the old system, without the triage nurse, it took an average of 23 minutes before a first contact with a nurse or a physician took place. In addition, in the new system, the distribution of this time was much narrower than in the old system.

Anxiety makes waiting feel longer

That a trip to an unfamiliar destination seems longer than the return trip has a lot to do with the anxiety we feel about the unknown, the fear of being late. Anxiety about whether or not one has been forgotten is also the reason why pre-process waits feel longer than in-process waits, as noted above. Another source of anxiety might be the uncertainty of the length of the waiting and service time. The impatience of many motorists waiting in a traffic jam is surely more closely related to the uncertain length of the waiting than to the waiting time itself. There is also the fear of being unfairly treated as other customers pass you in the queue. All of us have had the experience of choosing a queue at a supermarket or a lane on a motorway, and then worrying whether or not we have made the right choice. Doesn't the other queue always move faster?

The supermarket study supports this hypothesis. It was found that the less familiar customers were with a supermarket, the more they overestimated the waiting time. Frequent visitors overestimated the waiting time by about 28 seconds, while infrequent visitors overestimated the same time by 167 seconds. Uncertain waits always feel longer than known, finite waits.

Unexplained waits are less tolerable than explained waits

In addition to not knowing how long you will have to wait, not knowing *why* you are waiting makes the waiting less tolerable and makes the perceived waiting time longer. Passengers waiting to board an aeroplane will be less angry when they are told that the plane is late because of weather conditions, than when they are told only that the plane is late. You will perhaps forgive your doctor's lateness when you are informed that he or she has been held up by an emergency.

The lower the degree of personal control, the less tolerance there is for waiting

While it is true that knowing why you have to wait is beneficial for the particular waiting experience, the impact of the information on the customer's overall and long-term satisfaction will depend very much on how customers attribute the cause of waiting. This is determined by two factors:

1. *The customer's perception of his or her role.* Customers who know the peak hours of a service delivery system (i.e. the motorway, the bank), but still decide to come during those hours, have only themselves to blame for the waiting and delay, certainly if they had the opportunity to come at a different time. Generally speaking, the more the customers perceive themselves as having control (even while waiting), the more tolerant they are of waiting. This aspect was also illustrated in the walk-in clinic referred to earlier. In the new system there was not only a triage, but a choice of doctor or nurse, while previously patients had been

assigned to a doctor or a nurse on a first-come, first-served basis. This, together with a faster first contact, explains why patients were more satisfied with the changed system despite the fact that the objective waiting times were longer.

2. *Whether or not the reason for waiting is within the service delivery system*. Most people will be tolerant of waiting when the cause of the delay is beyond the control of the service organization. When a tour bus pulls into a restaurant, customers that follow will probably understand and accept that waiting is inevitable. On the other hand, when the same restaurant has accepted a wedding party and uses this as an excuse to other customers for long delays, such an excuse will not be accepted. A reservation has been made for the wedding party well in advance and the restaurant should have made arrangements to cope with the increased demand. We are more tolerant when an aeroplane is late due to weather conditions than when it is late due to maintenance failure.

Unfair waits are longer than equitable waits

An otherwise very quiet waiting room with very civilized citizens can be transformed all of a sudden into a mob of angry people, when somebody has successfully 'skipped the queue'. Even the most patient customer becomes furious in such a situation. Some of us might even have witnessed fights between motorists in the street after one motorist has cut in front of another while not obeying the traffic rules.

In waiting situations, where there is no visible and/or enforced order, or when people can easily violate the 'first-come first-served' order, instead of being able to relax, the customer remains in a state of nervousness about whether his or her place in the queue is being preserved.

The more valuable the service, the higher the tolerance for waiting

When you go to a supermarket to buy a newspaper or a loaf of bread, you are not willing to wait ten minutes behind other customers whose carts are fully loaded with groceries. Supermarkets have recognized this problem and have installed express checkouts. Airlines provide special counters for passengers that do not have any luggage to check in. There is not only a value-for-money expectation – that is, where you pay a high price, you expect high values – but also a value for waiting time. This principle not only applies to the value of the service itself, but also to the perceived 'value' of the service provider. A customer is more tolerant of waiting in a bank when waiting to see the manager or being served by the manager, than when dealing with a clerk. Maister illustrates this principle by referring to an old rule in academia that 'you wait five minutes for an assistant professor, ten for an associate professor and fifteen minutes for a full professor.'

An interesting consequence of this principle is the intolerance involved in waiting after the service is over. Post-process waits are perhaps even less tolerable than pre-process waits. When the service is over, there is no further expected added value. This explains the haste of airline passengers to disembark and find their luggage once the plane has landed or the impatience of hotel guests to check out, or restaurant visitors to pay the bill.

Solo waits feel longer than group waits

The supermarket study referred to earlier is one of the few studies that tested the proposition that waiting alone seems longer than waiting in a group. In this study it was found that people who queued alone perceived the waiting time to be on average 75.6 seconds higher than the actual waiting time. This was significantly higher than for people who queued together with one or more other persons. In this category the average difference between perceived and actual waiting time was 49.3 seconds. This is partially explained by the fact that in group waits, customers are 'occupied' and also perhaps less anxious. There is also the phenomenon that the customers, even if they do not know each other, turn to each other when the delay is announced and express their exasperation. There is some form of comfort in group waiting rather than waiting alone.

Sometimes, more positively, a sense of group community develops in queues, and as Maister states:

> 'the line turns into almost a service encounter in its own right: part of the fun and part of the service'.

However, sometimes groups can amplify feelings of discomfort and therefore be the cause of dissatisfaction.

Managing perception of waiting times

Each of the propositions introduced above can help managers to actively influence a customer's perception of the waiting time, and by so doing influence the customer's satisfaction. The various propositions are interdependent, however, and acting on each of them separately could even be counter-productive. Take, for instance, the idea of installing television screens in queues. A Dutch hospital did just that, but had to conclude afterwards that it had no effect at all on customers' satisfaction. Most people did not watch the TV and those who did, did so only after some time, once they had finished browsing through magazines or had run out of small talk with other people. It is possible that those watching TV were those who had to wait the longest or those who were the most impatient – that is, with the lowest tolerance for waiting.

It is therefore necessary to develop an integrated view of the problem. Two Dutch researchers, Smidts and Pruyn,[32] have developed and tested such a model (*see* Figure 15.13). This model attempts to explain customers' dissatisfaction with certain services. According to the model, overall satisfaction or dissatisfaction is influenced by satisfaction or dissatisfaction with the wait. Of course, this is influenced by the actual waiting time, but there are other factors that come into play here. The first factor is what the customers consider to be the acceptable waiting time – his or her 'zone of tolerance'. The second is the 'posterior predicted waiting times'. The third factor is the perceived waiting environment.

The acceptable waiting time

It is beyond question that customers consider zero waiting times to be ideal. They recognize, however, that this is not always possible, because the price would be too high. Figure 15.13 describes some of the factors that have an influence on the acceptable waiting time.

1. *Factors which are temporary and individual.* When you are in a hurry to catch a train, you will be less tolerant of people who cause traffic jams; when you are hungry you will be more impatient towards the waiter who fails to take your order immediately. Certain persons are by nature more impatient than others. In their banking study,[33] Katz and her colleagues classified customers into three categories: the *watchers*, the *impatients* and the *neutrals*. Watchers enjoyed observing people

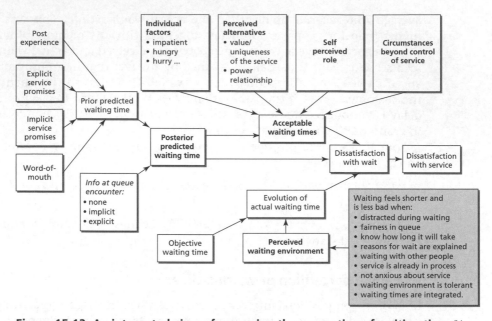

Figure 15.13 An integrated view of managing the perception of waiting times[34]

Source: Pruyn, A. T. H. and Smidts, A. (1993) *De Psychologische Beleving van Wachtrijen*. Erasmus Universiteit, Management Report Sciences, 126.

and events at the bank, while impatients could think of nothing more boring than waiting in a queue. Neutrals fell somewhere in between.

2. *Factors related to the perception of alternatives*. If the service is very valuable and unique, tolerance for waiting will be higher. Certain restaurants, certain medical doctors and even certain management consultants work with waiting lists measured in months. In other circumstances, the same customers who in the above situations wait patiently become very impatient if they have to wait more than 30 seconds for someone to answer the telephone, or if they have to stand in a queue for more than five minutes at the supermarket. Uniqueness and value have of course something to do with power relationships. If you as a customer are clearly in a subordinated position, your tolerance for waiting will be higher. That is why, at least in Belgian universities, students have to respect the academic quarter, meaning that the professor is allowed fifteen minutes of grace before students can leave a class. Would any student dare to act likewise and come fifteen minutes late for an exam?

   Similar conclusions could be drawn for monopolistic situations, as in many government or government-controlled systems. However, the fact that the customer has no other choice and therefore is 'forced' to be tolerant does not mean that his or her satisfaction level will not be influenced by waiting time. The extent to which the customer feels forced to use a certain service provider should be considered.

3. *Factors related to the 'self-perceived role'*. The zone of tolerance will be smaller when a customer perceives his or her control to be very small. This is one of the reasons why the multiple queuing system is preferable to a single queuing system: customers pick a queue and at least can blame themselves if their queue seems to be moving more slowly that the others.

4. *Factors that are due to circumstances beyond*. These concern the perception that waiting is caused by circumstances beyond the control of the service provider, such as weather conditions or strikes.

Posterior predicted waiting times

As illustrated in Figure 15.13, a further important factor that influences tolerance of waiting is what Smidts and Pruyn call the *posterior predicted waiting time*. However, this factor has a more direct influence on the satisfaction level and demands special attention.

The posterior predicted waiting time is a prediction of the expected waiting time once you have entered the service system. It is a 'will' expectation, not a 'should' expectation (i.e. not a norm). It is a combination of the prior predicted wait and the specific queue information at the service encounter. For example, before setting out to the post office you might make an implicit or explicit prediction of the expected waiting time. When you arrive, you see a large number of cars and bikes parked outside the post office. You will probably adjust your expected waiting time immediately. In this example, you are receiving implicit information about the waiting time. In some circumstances, you receive explicit information about the expected queue. This happens at Disney parks, where at various points in the queuing space, boards are erected indicating the length of the queue in front of you, expressed in minutes. Some call centres do the same. They not only tell you the number of customers in front of you, but will also sometimes tell you the expected waiting time.

The prior expected waiting time

The prior expected waiting time – that is, the time you expect to wait before receiving specific situational information – is first of all based on past experience with similar or 'verisimilar' situations. By 'verisimilar' we mean situations which are not exactly the same, but from which we can extrapolate. Based on our experience in the bank, we can extrapolate waiting time expectations at the post office, for instance. Even if you have no experience of the immigration service at, for instance, Kennedy Airport in New York, you will have a prior expectation of a waiting time, based on your immigration experience in other countries or, even more generally, with the customs service when crossing borders by car.

A second factor is the explicit service promise, either because the time has been explicitly advertised or promised when making reservations. Some supermarkets, for instance, promise that there will never be more than four customers waiting at the checkout. A pizza restaurant makes very explicit promises about the time it will take before you can pick up your pizza. Even if there are no explicit promises, quite often there are implicit promises. As is generally the case for other quality dimensions, price is often an implicit promise with respect to waiting. If you are booked in an expensive hotel, you expect short check-in and check-out times, and, more generally, short servicing times. The same is true for airlines. People who pay a more expensive fare expect shorter check-in times and expect to be able to leave the aeroplane before the other passengers.

A final factor influencing an individual's prior expected waiting time is the word-of-mouth information by friends, relatives, consumer reports, and so on.

Perceived waiting environment

A final factor in the model in Figure 15.13 is the perceived waiting environment. In this category we include all the factors that influence your perception of waiting time, while waiting, apart from the actual waiting time. It is here that the so-called 'Maister's laws' apply. They are summarized in Figure 15.13.

CONCLUSION

In this chapter we have discussed various issues that need to be addressed, when managing the capacity of a service delivery system, in such a way to ensure that capacity and demand match as far as possible. We emphasized that in service industries, to a greater extent than in industrial firms, management has to look at both sides of the equation: supply (i.e. capacity) and demand. Capacity management is therefore not only an 'operational' problem, but also a marketing problem. Capacity is part of the product, as we have seen.

While there are many rational approaches to managing capacity, it is important to take into account how the results of capacity management are perceived by the customer. The customer is not always a rational human being. There are many subjective elements in the way customers perceive capacity management effects, such as waiting times.

Review and discussion questions

- State the capacity of a highway with the following characteristics:
  - One lane, marked with 'kilometers' markers.
  - Speed limit 120 km/h.
  - All cars drive at the speed limit.
  - Average length of a car 5 meter.
  - Average distance between cars: 40 meters (including the length of the car).

- How will the use of a number-taking system influence your waiting experience?

- Discuss the advantages and disadvantages of a snake like entry system which you find at a Disney Park versus the 'funnel' entry you might find at other places?

- Apply the model of Figure 15.2 to a (non-fast food) restaurant. How will capacity and capacity management influence your perception of the service offered?

- In the bank example (see Figure 15.5), what is the reason that, despite an utilization rate lower than 95 per cent, the customers are waiting for 30 minutes? How could you reduce the working time without increasing the number of employees?

- In the St. Luke's hospital there are four lifts for visitors. While the average capacity of the four lifts is sufficient to transport the visitors during the day, visitors have to wait about 3 minutes on the average to get in the lift. Installing a fifth lift would reduce the waiting time to 1 minute 30 seconds. Knowing that the yearly depreciation and operational costs of a fifth lift is 30 000 euro and knowing that there are about 70 000 visitors a year, would you recommend the hospital to install a fifth lift?

- Is the demand for cashier resources in a supermarket dependent, independent, quasi-dependent or quasi-independent?
  What is the implication for managing these resources? Develop a resource planning system for a supermarket.

- Explain how the planning system at McDonald's described in Exhibit 15.2 can be seen as a pull system. What is the pull signal?

- Apply the demand management policies to a postal service.

Technical note

Queueing systems in service environments and various forms of queuing theory are analysed in Technical Note 2. The role of simulation as a tool when designing services is discussed in Technical Note 3. These notes appear at the end of the book.

Notes and references

[1] *See* 'Queuing for flawed services', *Financial Times*, 14 June 1992, p. 13 and *EuroDisney Case* (1981) Harvard Business School, 9–681–044.

[2] Belmont case in Hill, A. (1991) *Minnesota Pollution Control Agency*. University of Minnesota.

[3] This figure was inspired by Jaime Ribeca at IESE, Spain.

[4] Pruyn, A. and Smidts, A. (1992) *De Psychologische Beleving van Wachtrijen* (The psychological experience of waiting lines) Erasmus Universiteit, Management Report Sciences, no 126.

[5] Graessel, B. and Zeider, P. (1993) 'Using quality function deployment to improve customer service', *Quality Progress*, Nov, 39–63.

[6] Based on simulation.

[7] *See* Davis, M. (1991) 'How long should a customer wait?', *Decision Sciences*, Vol 22, 421–34.

[8] In normal distribution tables we can see that the z-value corresponding with 20 per cent is equal to 0.85. Therefore the additional number of rooms above the average should be equal to: 0.85×20, or 17.

[9] This description is based on the McDonald's Corporation Case, pp. 156–74 in Sasser, W. E., Clark, K. B, Garvin, D. A., Graham, M. B. W., Jaikumar, R. and Maister, D. H. (1982) *Cases in Operations Management*. Homewood, Illinois: Richard D. Irwin.

[10] Based on an article of Wacker, J. (1985) 'Effective planning and cost control for restaurants', *Production and Inventory Management*, Vol 26, 55–70.

[11] For further information on the MRP concept the reader is referred to J. Orlicky (1975) *Materials Requirements Planning*. New York: McGraw Hill.

[12] Khoong, C. M. (1996) 'An integrated system framework and analysis methodology for manpower planning', *International Journal of Manpower*, Vol 17, No 1, 26–46.

[13] Siferd, S. P. (1991) The Ohio State University Hospital Nurse Staffing and Scheduling Survey Results, a document sent to the respondents, June.

[14] *Source*: Khoong, C. M. (1996), op. cit.

[15] Pue, R. O. (1996) 'A dynamic theory of service delivery: implications for managing service quality', non-published dissertation, Sloan School of Management, MIT, June.

[16] *See*, for instance, for a review of these models, Smith-Daniels, V. L., Schweikhart, S. B. and Smith-Daniels, D. E. (1988) 'Capacity management in health care services', *Decision Sciences*, Vol 19, 898–919.

[17] Siferd, S. P. (1991), op. cit.

[18] Marriner-Tomey, A. (1992) *Guide to Nursing Management*, p. 238.

[19] Easton, F. F., Rossinm, D. F. and Borders, W. S. (1992) 'Analysis of alternative scheduling policies for hospital nurses', *Production and Operations Management*, Vol 1, No 2, Spring, 159–74.

[20] Smith, B., Leimkuller, J. and Danon, R. (1992) 'Yield management and American Airlines', *Interfaces*, Vol 22, No 1, Jan–Feb, 8–31.

[21] *See* Sasser, W. E. (1970) 'Match supply and demand in service industries', *Harvard Business Review*, Nov–Dec, 113–41.

[22] Some of the commonly used fare restrictions are: advanced purchase requirements, required Saturday night's stay over, and so on.

[23] Smith, B., Leimkuller, J. and Danon, R. (1992), op. cit.

[24] 'The Gates Hotel', p. 101, in Sasser, W. E., Olsen, R. P. and Wyckoff, D. D. (1978) *Management of Service Operations: Text, cases and readings*. Boston, MA: Allyn and Bacon.

[25] Maister, D. H. (1988) 'The psychology of waiting lines', in Lovelock, C. H. (ed.) *Managing Services: Marketing, operations and human resources*. London: Prentice-Hall.

[26] Ibid.

[27] Graessel, B. and Zeider, P. (1993), op. cit.

[28] Jones, P. and Peppiatt, E. (1996) 'Managing perceptions of waiting times and service queues', *International Journal of Service Industry Management*, Vol 7, No 5, 44–61.

[29] Katz, K., Lawson, B. and Lawson, R. (1991) 'Prescription for the waiting-in-time blues: entertain, enlighten and enjoy', *Sloan Management Review*, Winter, 44–53.

[30] Sasser, W. E. *et al.* (1982), op. cit.

[31] Jones, P. and Peppiatt, E. (1996), op. cit.

[32] Pruyn, A. and Smidts, A. (1992), op. cit.

[33] Katz, K. *et al.* (1991), op. cit.

[33] Pruyn, A. and Smidts, A. (1992), op. cit.

Suggested further reading

Crandall, R. E. and Markland, R. E. (1996) 'Demand management – today's challenge for service industries', *Production and Operations Management*, Vol 5, No 2, Summer, 106–20. This article provides an overview of demand management strategies which can be used by service firms. A comparison is made between the use of different strategies in different service sectors.

Davis, M. (1991) 'How long should a customer wait?', *Decision Sciences*, Vol 22, 421–34. This article attempts to quantify the cost of waiting for the customer.

Kimes, S. E. (1989) 'Yield management: A tool for capacity-constrained service firms', *Journal of Operations Management*, Vol 8, No 4, Oct, 348–63. This article gives a review of the literature regarding the concept of yield management. Several techniques are presented along with the managerial implications of yield management.

Maister, D. H. (1988) 'The psychology of waiting lines', in Lovelock, C. H. (ed.) *Managing Services: Marketing, operations and human resources*. London: Prentice Hall, pp. 176–83. Everybody reading this article will certainly have encountered many if not all, of the scenarios or feelings described when waiting. It is the definitive article on how to influence the customer perception of waiting.

Makane, J. and Hall, R. W. (1983) 'Management specs for stockless production', *Harvard Business Review*, May–June, 84–91.

Orlicky, J. C. (1975) *Materials Requirements Planning*. New York: McGraw Hill.

Smidts, A. and Pruyn, A. T. H. (1993) 'Customer reactions to queues: towards a theory of waiting and delay', in Chias, J. and Sureda, J. (eds) *Marketing for the New Europe: Dealing with complexity*, Vol 2. Barcelona: ESADE, pp. 1383–402. This article provides an excellent discussion on how customer satisfaction is influenced by customers' evaluation of waiting, and which factors mediate these evaluations.

CHAPTER 16

Facilities management

Roland Van Dierdonck · Paul Gemmel · Steven Desmet

INTRODUCTION

A University of Leicester study found that in-store music had a significant effect on purchasing and in particular on product choice. The results were published in *Nature*,[1] a respected scientific journal.

Royalty payments for non-broadcast commercial uses of music in 1995 amounted to £53.8 million in the UK alone.[2] However, research on music and consumer behaviour[3] has almost completely ignored the potential effect of in-store music on purchasing and particularly on product choice. By investigating the purchasing of German and French wines, the researchers found that musical 'fit' has a profound influence on product choice.

Specific musical pieces may activate superordinate knowledge structures,[4] suggesting how in-store music could influence product choice. For example, stereotypical French music should activate superordinate knowledge structures concerning France, so priming the selection of products such as French wines. Similarly, stereotypical German music should activate related knowledge and prime selection of products such as German wines.

To test this, four French and four German wines were displayed in a supermarket drinks section. The wines were matched between the countries for their price and dryness or sweetness. Each of the four shelves contained one French and one German wine and appropriate national flags. The position of the wines on the shelves was changed halfway through the two-week testing period. French accordion and German Bierkeller pieces were played on alternate days from a tape deck situated on the top shelf. Shoppers buying wines from the display were asked to complete a questionnaire by two experimenters, with 44 shoppers consenting.

French wine outsold German wine when French music was played, whereas German wine outsold French wine when German music was played ($P < 0.001$) despite an overall bias in favour of French over German wine sales (*see* Table 16.1). Questionnaire responses indicated that the French music made them think of France ($P < 0.001$). Respondents did not differ in their general preference for wines from these two countries ($P > 0.05$), and only six respondents answered 'yes' to the question, 'Did the type of music playing influence your choice of wine?' Customers did not seem aware of the effect that music had on their selections.

Table 16.1 Summary of results by type of music*

	When French music was played		When German music was played	
Bottles of French wine sold	40	(79.9%)	12	(23.1%)
Bottles of German wine sold	8	(26.7%)	22	(73.3%)
Extent to which music made respondents think of France (0 = not at all; 10 = very much)	6.25	+/− 3.34	2.5	+/− 3.68
Extent to which music made respondents think of Germany (0 = not at all; 10 = very much)	1.52	+/− 2.08	6.08	+/− 3.73

* Ratings from the questionnaires were on a scale of 0 to 10. Mean ratings +/−s.d. are given.

Source: Reprinted by permission from *Nature* (1997) No 390, p. 132. Copyright © Macmillan Magazines Ltd.

'There are three important things in retailing: location, location, and location', stated Lord Seif, the chief executive of the UK-based retail company, Marks & Spencer. This quote highlights the importance of one major element of facilities management for service organizations. The anthropologist E. Hall, in his book, *The Silent Language*,[5] stated, 'Space speaks' – highlighting another aspect, namely that the physical environment in which the service takes place is observed by the customer and 'speaks' to him or her about what to expect and how to behave. The physical environment (or the *'servicescape'* as Mary Jo Bitner[6] calls it) in which the service process takes place, is not only part of the service delivery system, but is actually part of the product, which is the service itself.

In this chapter we deal with the important issues, particularly those that are specific to service sectors, which result from the two major characteristics of services – their intangibility and simultaneity. We begin by discussing the nature of facilities management and how this task is different for service businesses as compared to businesses in industrial sectors. We then focus on the fundamental decision about which activities can and should take place in the back office, and which can and should take place in the front office. We then discuss the location decision, taking a look at some examples of models that help us decide where to locate individual service units. Finally, we deal with facilities management issues within a given service unit: the so-called servicescape.

Objectives

By the end of this chapter, you should be able to discuss:

- the nature of facilities management in services and, in particular, how facilities management decisions influence the customer
- how facilities management is not a purely technical or even operational decision but should involve marketing and HRM aspects as well
- the distinction between back-office and front-office processes
- the various considerations in locating a service unit and some basic location concepts
- the notion of servicescape and which factors to take into consideration when designing the servicescape

THE NATURE OF FACILITIES MANAGEMENT IN SERVICES

Facilities management is concerned with all the physical aspects of the service delivery system, ranging from such major strategic decisions as where Disney should build its next theme park down to very detailed decisions such as posting the signs to the ladies' toilets in a restaurant. In a manufacturing environment, facilities management belongs in the domain of production or operations management and includes decisions such as plant location, process choice and design, automation, layout and task design. In a service organization, however, it is more difficult to assign the responsibility to one of the traditional functional departments as the activities of facilities management cross the boundaries between organizational structuring, marketing, organizational behaviour, product development and operations management. Decisions in these domains affect human resources goals (e.g. the motivation of workers), operational goals (e.g. the quality and efficiency of the service processes) and marketing goals (consumer attraction and customer retention).

Issues relating to facilities management decisions were among the first to be studied in the so-called scientific management movement. At the beginning of the twentieth century, Frederic Taylor and Frank Gilbreth concerned themselves with task and process design, including time and motion studies. Somewhat later, Roethlisgberger studied the impact of environmental factors on human aspects such as motivation and productivity. Plant and warehouse location models were among the first applications of operations research models developed during the Second World War, and layout studies have traditionally attracted the attention of many researchers and practitioners, especially in the industrial engineering field. Ergonomics is another related field, where the impact of the work environment on workers' psychological and physiological needs is studied.

This research has produced insights, concepts and models which can be usefully applied to solve facilities management problems in service sectors. However, in these traditional approaches little or no concern is given to the customer. This is perfectly acceptable in manufacturing environments where the customer is not involved in, interested in, or even aware of decisions related to facilities. However, this is not the case in service operations where, as we discussed earlier, there is always some simultaneity between production and consumption. The customer is present in the 'service factory' and participates in the service delivery process. When making decisions related to location, physical setting and process design, a company has to take the customer and his or her explicit and implicit needs and expectations into consideration and has to realize that the outcome of these decisions is actually part of the product. Almost all researchers in the field of service management refer to the importance of 'tangibles' in the total service package (*see* Chapter 1). In addition to this direct effect, the facilities also have indirect effects on other elements of the service package such as convenience (in particular, accessibility) or functionality.

Product, promotion and place constitute three of the four Ps (the fourth being 'price') in the traditional marketing mix. Obviously facilities management will have a direct impact on the 'place' element. Facilities also have an impact on both the product and, as can be inferred from the quote 'space speaks', on the communication or promotion elements of the mix. It is no wonder that marketers have not only discovered the importance of facilities management, but recently have added some interesting dimensions that help to take the customer into account.

The intangibility of services also makes facilities management in this context different to that experienced in an industrial context. As explained earlier, many services are high in experience and credence attributes. They have fewer intrinsic features upon which to base an evaluation of quality. Therefore, the building, decor, employees' attire, background music, physical surroundings and locations are all used by the customer to infer quality.

The conclusion is very clear. In services, an important additional element must be introduced into facilities management: the customer. Of course, this generally makes those decisions more complicated. Too much attention to operational priorities frequently runs counter to achieving customer satisfaction (and vice versa). As Lovelock[7] noted, the goals of operations in facilities management include:

- controlling costs;
- improving efficiency by ensuring proximity of operationally related tasks in layout decisions;
- achieving economies of scale or logistics efficiency in location decisions; and
- enhancing safety, security and standardization in work design decisions.

However, quite often this results in a customer:

- becoming confused;
- being shunted around unnecessarily;
- finding the facilities unattractive and inconvenient; and
- finding employees unresponsive to individual customer needs.

This was exactly the situation Jan Carlzon discovered on his appointment as president of SAS. In his book, *Moments of Truth*,[8] he describes many facilities management decisions, such as the layout of the Copenhagen air terminal and choice of airplane type, which were the result of an internally and operationally oriented culture at SAS. The cultural change which he had to effect was best expressed by his well-known slogan, 'We fly people, not airplanes'.

BACK OFFICE VERSUS FRONT OFFICE

Not all service activities should be performed in the presence of the customer. Given that the customer brings an additional element of complexity to the facilities management decisions, it is useful to make a distinction between the 'back office' and the 'front office'.

- The *back office* consists of the activities which can be physically and/or temporally separated from the customer.
- The *front office* consists of the activities which have to be, or which an organization wants to be, performed while the customer is present.

Facilities management decisions regarding back-office operations can differ greatly from those for front-office operations, as illustrated in Table 16.2. We can conclude from this table that designing the back office is 'easier', at least from an operations management point of view. One of the major reasons for this is that customer objectives do not have to be directly taken into account in making facilities management decisions regarding back-office activities:

Table 16.2 Major design considerations for back office and front office

	Back office	Front office
Location	Operations may be placed near the supply of skilled or cheap resources and facilities	Operations must be near the customer
Process design	Focus on efficiency through economies of scale	Focus on the needs and wants of the customer
	Support of a smooth service delivery process	Use the customer as co-producer
Design of the physical setting	Make the factory appealing to the employees	Make the factory appealing to the customer and the employees
Operations strategy	Low-cost strategy	Differentiation strategy

- Location can be decided based on the availability of skilled or cheap (human) resources.
- Economies of scale can be achieved by centralizing activities; this makes computerization viable since the transaction volume necessary for making such an investment can be more easily reached.
- The labour force does not have to possess the social and communication skills necessary to interact with the customer.
- The company does not have to deal with demand fluctuations to the same extent – that is, production can be more level.
- The often considerable additional investments needed to make the 'factory' appealing to the customer are unnecessary.

Generally speaking, the operations manager has more freedom when the customer does not have to be taken into account, and thus does not have to sacrifice customer satisfaction in the name of operational efficiency and employee satisfaction (or vice versa).

Furthermore, in the back office a major source of uncertainty – the customer (behaviour, arrival pattern, processing times, and so on) – is eliminated from most of the activities. In other words, the 'technical core' can be isolated from environmental fluctuations. Therefore, traditional efficiency can be aimed for in the back office, which supports a *strategy of cost leadership*.

The benefit of the front office, however, is that it quite often supports one form or another of a *differentiation strategy*. It is in the front office that the service can be adapted to the particular customer needs. The front-office personnel interact with customers and, by doing so, can make a difference in customer satisfaction. It is also in the front office that the physical setting can be used to influence customer expectations, as we will see later in this chapter. The customer's behaviour can also be influenced more effectively from here. A final point is that the customer's perception of quality can be affected, not only before, but, more importantly, also during and after the actual process.

The distinction between back office and front office, however, should not only be seen as a choice between a low-cost strategy *versus* a differentiation strategy. Having the customers serve themselves, for instance, may mean enlarging the front office, but can also help to reduce costs. On the other hand, the back office itself can be a source of differentiation. In the Brussels restaurant 'Comme chez Soi' – one of the few restaurants outside France to have three Michelin stars – VIP guests are invited to eat in the kitchen, which they consider a special privilege. This is a subtle and creative use of the back office.

The low-cost strategy in the back office should be in line with the differentiation strategy in the front office. It is important for a service firm to avoid its back office and front office becoming separate worlds with different rules and different service cultures. For instance, a billing department sending out the wrong bills can have a negative impact on the company's image. One study reported how telecom firms' back-office chaos was hurting customers.[9] The main problem was the lack of integration in the information systems, with the result that no one had complete customer information. A clear service concept (*see* Chapter 2) should guarantee consistency between front-office and the back-office activities.

The size of the front office relative to the back office – i.e. the relative number of activities which are performed in direct contact with the customer – is a major variable which has to be carefully analysed when designing processes and the physical setting. The high-contact services (those with a high number of activities performed in direct contact with the customer) are subject to different rules than low-contact services.

LOCATION

Exhibit 16.1

Determining the site of EuroDisney[10]

In Chapter 15, we described how the Walt Disney Corporation's top management was confronted in the 1980s with the decision whether or not to open a new theme park in Europe. Besides its world-famous theme park in California, it had already opened theme parks in Florida and Japan, both of which had proved to be successful. Although an estimated two million Europeans visited the US sites each year, Disney felt that the European market had much more potential. The population of Europe exceeded that of the United States by 150 million people, in roughly half of the land mass (*see* Figure 16.1, p. 323). However, the distance between the two continents was seen as the major obstacle. If Disney wanted to access this huge market, then Disney would have to come to Europe.

Once the decision was made to pursue the European market, a second and equally important decision had to be made. Like the US, Europe is a huge territory, with many possible sites to be considered. Where would EuroDisney be built?

What kind of parameters would Disney's management take into account in this decision? Some factors remain the same even if this decision were about where to locate a manufacturing plant: for example, the quality of the transport infrastructure, the degree of government support or the available space for such a large compound. However, since this decision involved a service, one very important new parameter came into play: the customer. Since the customer would be travelling to EuroDisney, a central location would be advantageous. Locating EuroDisney in a far corner of Europe, such as the south of Greece or the north of Finland, would mean a far greater travel distance for most of its customers. Undoubtedly, analyses were made and models used to roughly estimate the optimal location, taking into account the geographical distribution of the potential visitors.

The weather was clearly another important factor in determining the location. Since walking around Disneyland would be much more pleasant in a warm and sunny climate, many countries were dropped from the list of possibilities, such as those located in Scandinavia or Central Europe. Ultimately, the choice came down to two sites – one in Spain and one in France. Although Spain had the advantage of better weather, the French site was eventually chosen due to its proximity to a mass market of customers, better transport infrastructure and government inducements.

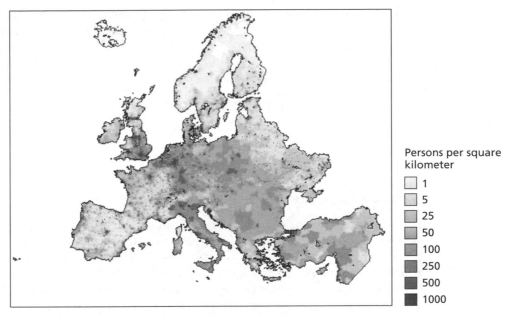

Figure 16.1(a) Population density of Europe, 1995

Source: Center for International Earth Science Information Network (CIESIN), Columbia University; International Food Policy Research Institute (IFPRI); and World Resources Institute (WRI), 2000. Gridded Population of the World (GPW), Version 2. Palisades, NY: CIESIN, Columbia University. Available at *http://sedac.ciesin.columbia.edu/plue/gpw*. Copyright © 2003 The Trustees of Columbia University in the City of New York.

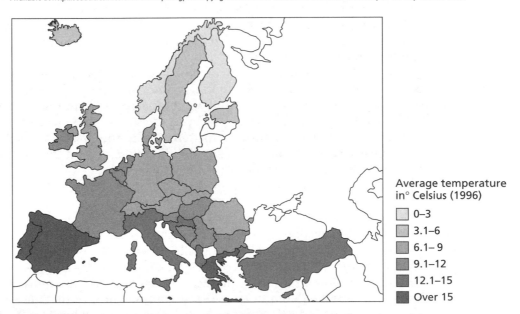

Figure 16.1(b) Average temperature in selected European countries, 1996

Source: Royal Meteorological Institute, Belgium.

Exhibit 16.1 illustrates how locating a service facility differs from locating a manufacturing firm: the customer has to be taken explicitly into account. In services, the customer and service provider have to be brought together in a service environment. A large goods-producing facility can be set up in one country and the goods exported to another country, but this is not possible for services. Services are intangible and can neither be stored nor transported. As a result, either the consumer has to go to the service provider (for example, in going to a restaurant), or the service provider has to go to the customer (as in at-home pizza delivery).

A different location for the same service may lead to a totally different service experience, such as the difference between EuroDisney in a warm climate *versus* EuroDisney in a cold and rainy one. This highlights the fact that the surroundings and the atmosphere in which the service takes place are an integral part of the service itself, as will be discussed further in this chapter.

We will now explore the question of how a service company decides where to locate its service facility.

Factors influencing the location decision

The location problem can be dealt with on several levels. A location for a service facility might have to be found on another continent, country, state, city, block or street. Depending on the size of the area under consideration, the importance attached to factors that determine the final choice of location will change. Remember the factors that Disney's management considered in deciding where to locate a new theme park in Europe. How different will they be for McDonald's when it considers where in Paris it should open a new drive-through restaurant? Disney's management was considering such factors as the availability of an adequate labour force and transport infrastructure, the climate and the degree of government support, but McDonald's local management will be thinking of quite different things. Factors such as traffic density, location of the competition, legal considerations including zoning and building regulations, available space and easy access will be of greater importance.

The next step is the domain of *micro-scale location*, dealing with the precise position within the chosen city centre, regional shopping centre, inner city arterial, secondary shopping district or retail warehouse park.[11] At this level of detail, factors such as the presence of magnet or attractor stores, the effect of exit and entry points on consumer circulation patterns, and the maximal walking distance between stores play a role. This micro-level leads us beyond the scope of this book, so we will limit our discussion to the higher levels.

A large-scale survey in 1994 among 926 service firms in five mid-western US states, representing almost 100 000 employees, investigated which factors could influence the location decision, first when choosing a general area and then, more specifically, when choosing the particular site (*see* Table 16.3).[12]

The most important factors influencing the location decision at a more general level were the availability of a good infrastructure (for example, available roads and communication), ability to attract labour and proximity to customers. However, several differences emerge in the importance of these factors depending on the type of industry. Sectors such as hospitals, education and social and personal services attach in general relatively less importance to the location factors than sectors such as transportation, warehousing and wholesaling, indicating that they are relatively immune to many of the general area factors. For instance, since customers are generally less willing to travel greater distances for more common services, it is clear that services such as food retailers or banks attach more importance to being located close to their customers than professional or educational services.

Table 16.3 Factors influencing the location decision

	General area			Particular site	
Factors (in order of importance)	Services for which higher than average influence	Services for which lower than average influence	Factors (in order of importance)	Services for which higher than average influence	Services for which lower than average influence
Good infrastructure	Transportation – warehousing, Wholesaling	Education – social	Adequate parking	Restaurant – retailing	Construction Wholesaling
Proximity to consumers and buyers	Auto sales-service Banking Hospitals Retailing Wholesaling	Education – social Professional service Utilities	Attractive building	Banking Insurance – real estate	Construction Utilities
Ability to attract good labour	Hospitals Personal-business services	Retailing Utilities	Attractive rent cost	Retailing	Banking Construction Hospitals Hotels Utilities
Attractive place to live	Personal-business services		Specialized space needs met here	Transportation – warehousing	Retailing
Low rents, building costs		Banking Hospitals Utilities	Easy commute for employees	Professional service	Auto sales-service Education – social Hotels
Favourable taxes	Auto sales-service	Banking Education – social Hospitals Personal-business services	High customer traffic in area	Auto sales-service Banking Hotels Restaurants Retailing	Construction Professional service Utilities Wholesaling
Favourable governmental policies	Transportation – warehousing	Personal-business services	Easy commute for managers and owners	Professional service	Auto sales-service Education – social Hospitals
Proximity to suppliers and services	Transportation – warehousing	Retailing	Favourable governmental policies (zoning, traffic, etc.)	Restaurants – wholesaling	Professional service
Labour costs	Transportation – warehousing, wholesaling	Amusement Personal-business services Utilities	Favourable taxes at site	Auto sales-service wholesaling	Hospitals Professional service
Labour 'climate'	Personal-business services Restaurants Wholesaling	Amusement Utilities	Proximity to suppliers and services		Utilities
Proximity to competitors	Auto sales-service Banking	Amusement Education – social Personal-business services Utilities	Proximity to competitors	Auto sales-service Banking	Amusement Education – social Personal-business services Utilities
Being near other company facilities		Hospitals Personal-business services	Being in fully developed site	Wholesaling	Construction Insurance – real estate Restaurant Utilities

Source: Schmenner, R. W. (1994) 'Service firm location decisions: Some midwestern evidence', International Journal of Service Industry Management, Vol, 5, No 3, pp. 49 and 52.

At the level of choosing a particular site, more specific and practical factors come into play. Adequate parking emerged as the most important factor, followed by three factors related to the building and its costs. Again, the more retail-oriented services such as stores, banks and restaurants attach more importance to these location factors, while hospitals and utilities assigned less weight to them.

Clearly the nature of the service has a key influence on the relative importance of factors determining the location choice. A service company, providing a maintenance-interactive type of service which relies on customers passing by, cannot afford to pay too much attention to labour factors or the degree of government support in its location decision. Since convenience and comfort are keywords, such a company often has no choice but to locate itself where the customers are. However, services such as most professional services do not need to be located right beside the customer and have more freedom in their choice of location.

A company has to ask the question 'what is the value of the service to the customer?' and, more importantly, 'what is the extra value of that service compared to the competition?' It would be unreasonable to expect a customer to drive an hour to reach a certain fast-food restaurant when another chain is just five minutes away, no matter how good the cheeseburger tastes. However, that same customer might be willing to drive for an hour to a distinctive three-star restaurant. Thus, the freedom of locating a facility will be influenced by the perceived value of the service.

As already mentioned, however, advances in IT also play a role. IT can sometimes create a substitution for transportation, which means that the customer and service provider need not always have physical contact. These advances do not have the same impact on all service sectors. The impact will be greater for the more maintenance-interactive type of services, such as banks with their ATMs and phone banking, or the retail sector and its home shopping network, than for the task- or personal-interactive services, such as architects and physiotherapists.

Location models

A number of models, with a varying degree of complexity, have been developed to aid companies in decisions regarding the optimal location. As it is not our intention to give a complete overview of all these models, we will limit ourselves to three examples of service environments where location techniques and models have been used.[13]

Location models can basically help companies in answering two simple questions: 'How many sites should I build?' and 'Where should I build them?'

How many sites?

Since a service facility can cover only a certain geographical area, a service provider wants to reach the maximum number of customers with a minimal number of service facilities. Just what this number should be is difficult to determine. It depends on such things as the type of service offered to the customer, the infrastructure required to deliver that service and the strategy of the service firm.

In order to find the optimal number of sites, a balance must be struck between the number and cost of facilities, on the one hand, and the transportation costs of bringing service provider and consumer together, on the other (see Figure 16.2). Transportation costs decline when the number of sites increases, since the distance

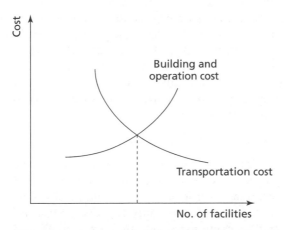

Figure 16.2 Determining the optimal number of service facilities

between the provider and consumer of the service decreases. Furthermore, revenues will probably rise since a company can expect customers to visit the facility more frequently when the distance is shorter. On the other hand, the cost of building and operating facilities increases with the number of facilities.

We have already seen that there is a correlation between the value of a service to the customer and the efforts that customer is willing to make to purchase that service. Hence, a company cannot expect to serve a whole metropolitan area with just one fast-food outlet, while one Rolls-Royce garage might suffice.

A single-site service facility location problem can easily be solved mathematically in most cases. The problem becomes much more complicated when models for locating multiple sites are involved. The process of data collection itself is also more difficult, since the visiting patterns become more complex.

Where?

Proximity to the customers was obviously one of the prime determinants of location in the survey in Table 16.3. Many models are based on this principle. They define the best location of a service facility as one which minimizes the distances between the customers and the facility. Other models – the so-called 'gravity models' – are more profit-oriented; they examine the sites with the highest potential for attracting customers. Before we can use any of these models, however, we will first look at two questions that arise:[14]

- How should we optimize our model? Should we use a minimization of distance, a maximization of profits or some other criteria?
- How should the geographical demand for the service be estimated (or where can an estimate be obtained)?

1. Optimization criteria

Two criteria immediately come to mind. One is *minimal transport distance or time* – for instance, in the case of a courier service company building a new distribution centre for package handling. The other is *maximal profit* – for instance, in the case of a retail outlet trying to find an area with the highest market potential.

More social considerations can also be used, especially in the public sector. For example, a public hospital might aim to have all patients be able to reach the hospital within

30 minutes, or a fire department might want to locate fire boxes in such a way that the maximum distance that any person must travel to the closest fire box is minimized.

The choice of criteria is an important decision, since different criteria may point to different optimal locations. For instance, using only the minimum total travel distance criterion might point to a centrally located site, while the maximum reach of customers approach might recommend the choice of a densely populated area, not necessarily closest to all of its customers.

2. Determination of geographical demand for the service

As stated before, locating a facility so that it is in the vicinity of the target population is important in almost all service sectors. The ability to estimate the potential of customers in an area is crucial to the accuracy of the location analysis, and also to the service firm's success. It would probably be very unwise to open a trendy new discotheque in a rural area populated mainly by retired people, or to locate a motel alongside a road with little overnight traffic.

Thorough market research should be undertaken to determine who the customers are, and where they are located and how they will reach the facility. The guiding principles relevant to identifying customers have already been touched upon in Chapter 2. Locating the customers involves several options. One of the most extensive sources of customer information is, of course, the Census data, which gives information on variables such as age, marital status and number of children for a whole country. Other possible sources include magazines or journals which release annual surveys on the buying power of the population or computerized databases which are available from private firms.[15]

A central location close to the customer was an important parameter in Disney's location decision. Disney had estimated that 17 million people lived within two hours of the Paris site by car; 109 million lived within six hours of the site by car; and 310 million could reach the site by plane in less than two hours. On top of that, the opening of the Eurotunnel in 1994 made EuroDisney accessible from the UK in four hours by car.[16] The fact that it was accessible to such an enormous market was one of the primary reasons why Disney decided to locate its theme park near Paris.

Several facility location techniques and models exist. The appropriate one to use will depend on the nature of the facility location problem. The three examples which follow illustrate several concepts of location theory.

A simple qualitative model to locate a restaurant[17]

Consider the example of a restaurant manager having to choose between four possible sites for a new restaurant (*see* Table 16.4). The manager has made up a list of factors which are important to his decision, such as the view from the terrace, the available parking space and the proximity to the customer. He attaches weights to these factors to depict relative differences in importance. Each site under consideration is then scored on these factors (*see* Table 16.4) and, finally, a weighted average score for each site is calculated. For instance, site A gets a score of:

$$\frac{(5 \times 7) + (10 \times 7) + (15 \times 9) + (20 \times 9) + (30 \times 8) + (20 \times 7)}{(5 + 10 + 15 + 20 + 30 + 20)} = 8$$

In this case, site A is clearly the best potential site of the four.

Table 16.4 Choosing a restaurant site

Factor	Weight	Site A	Site B	Site C	Site D
Visibility from the street	5	7	8	8	6
Available parking space	10	7	9	8	4
Closeness to suppliers	15	9	6	7	8
Accessibility by car	20	9	5	6	8
View from the terrace	30	8	7	5	8
Closeness to customer	20	7	6	7	8
Total score		8	6.5	6.35	7.5

While this model has the advantage that the location decision takes multiple factors into account, it is clear that it is rather general and simplistic and that other models are required to make a more complex location decision.

The use of trading areas in the location of bank branches

People in Belgium sometimes joke that there is a bank branch on every street corner. Sustaining such a large network of branches not only costs a lot of money, but also leads to an intensive competition between banks. Being near the customer seems to be an essential credo of banks. But how do we define being near? What is the relationship between distance and the willingness of customers to go to a particular bank branch?

A survey of 246 rural customers of one Belgian Bank in a region with seven small towns, provided some more information.[18]

If we consider the marketing mix (price, product, place and promotion), location is the single most important factor in the selection of a bank: 88 per cent of the 246 respondents go to the bank with a branch in their town. The distance between home and the bank branch is under 10 minutes for more than 90 per cent of the customers. In terms of distance this means less than 5.5 km. Seventy-three per cent of the customers are located at a travel distance of less than 5 minutes. It is also interesting to see that 78 per cent of the customers go by car to their branch. Most customers do not accept a travel time of more than 10 minutes to their branch for a standard transaction, or more than 15 minutes for a specialized transaction.

The probability that the customer living at a certain distance from a branch also travels to this branch, can be calculated using the Huff formula. This formula states that the expected number of customers at demand point i travelling to service facility j is equal to the total number of customers at demand point i multiplied by the probability that the consumers go to the facility j:[19]

$$E_{ij} = P_{ij} \times C_I$$

or

$$P_{ij} = E_{ij}/C_i$$

Table 16.5 shows the expected number of customers for each category of travel time (based on the survey of the 246 customers). If the travel time is 0–5 minutes, 100 per cent of the customers will still come, and 72.4 per cent are willing to come to the bank branch if the travel time is between 5 and 10 minutes. This means that 27.6 per cent of the customers do not accept a travel time of more than 5 minutes.

Table 16.5 Probabilities

Travel time (minutes)	Standard transactions	Specialized transactions
0–5	100%*	100%
5–10	72.4%	90.4%
10–15	25.4%	66.0%
15–20	5.6%	33.9%
20–25	2.8%	17.2%
>25	0.9%	6.2%

* = % of customers still willing to come to the bank branch.

Table 16.6 The current trading areas of the seven branches

Branch (town)	<5 minutes	5–10 minutes	10–15 minutes
A	96.0%*	4.0%	0.0%
B	96.3%	3.7%	0.0%
C	78.2%	16.4%	5.4%
D	62.0%	30.0%	8.0%
E	69.3%	29.9%	0.8%
F	83.9%	16.1%	0.0%
G	64.2%	26.8%	9.0%

* = % of customers living x minutes from the bank branch.

The trading area of bank branches can be determined using the probabilities in Table 16.5. A trading area is

'a geographically delineated region, containing potential customers for whom there exists a probability greater than zero of their purchasing a given class of products or services offered for sale by a particular firm or by a particular agglomeration of firms'.[20]

The current trading area is shown in Table 16.6. The overwhelming majority (83.9 per cent) of the customers of branch F (at location F) are living less than 5 minutes (by car) from the branch, while 16.1 per cent of the customers are willing to travel between 5 and 10 minutes. Other aspects which can be considered in determining the trading area of a bank are the kind of product (e.g. standard transactions versus specialized transactions), and degree of competition (the presence of branches of other banks). In other service environments (such as retail), the breadth and depth of the services offered at the facility are also considered important elements. How several of these elements can be combined in a quantitative model to determine the optimal location is illustrated in the next example of location in retail.

Once the trading area has been determined, thorough analysis of the demographic and socio-economic characteristics of the customers can be performed. Geomarketing can be useful here. Promotion and other publicity efforts can be oriented towards the right geographical area.[21]

Gravity models in retail management

Gravity models are widely used in retail management. These models are based on the premise that the probability that a given customer will shop in a particular store or shopping centre becomes larger as the size of the store or shopping centre grows and the distance or travel time to the store or centre diminishes.[22] The most frequently used model is the Huff model.[23] This model determines the probability (P_{ij}) that a customer, located in a certain area (i), will shop at a particular store or shopping centre (j).

$$P_{ij} = \frac{\dfrac{S_j}{T_{ij}^b}}{\displaystyle\sum_{j=1}^{n} \dfrac{S_j}{T_{ij}^b}} \tag{1}$$

where

P_{ij} = probability of a consumer at a given point of origin i travelling to a particular store or shopping centre j

S_j = size of the facility j (expressed in square footage)

T_{ij} = travel time (or distance) from consumer i's location to facility j

b = parameter, empirically estimated on the basis of market research, which reflects the effect of travel time or distance on the shopping likelihood for various types of facilities

According to this model, the probability that a site will attract customers depends on three factors:

1. The larger the size of the shopping centre (S_j) compared to the size of competing shopping centres, the higher the probability that a particular customer will come to the shopping centre. From the customer's point of view, a larger size is more attractive since it means a larger selection and more variety.
2. The longer the travel time or the greater the distance between the customer and the shopping centre, compared to the competition, the smaller the chance that the customer will shop at the site.
3. The parameter b can attach more or less weight to the travel distance or time. As already mentioned, there is a relationship between the value of a service and the time or distance a customer is willing to travel in order to purchase a service. A distance which would be acceptable for you if you want to buy clothes would probably be considered unacceptable if you just want to buy a newspaper. In general, travel distance is more important with convenience goods than with luxury goods. Therefore, stores specializing in convenience goods receive a higher value for b which reflects the reduced attraction for the customer due to the distance.

This model can also be used to forecast the sales of a facility at a certain location, by multiplying the probability that a customer will shop at the site by an estimation of the customer's expenditure. Comparing the forecast sales of different potential sites can help companies to make a choice.

This model therefore makes a trade-off between the size of the facility, reflecting the selection and variety, and the proximity to the customer. A simple example will clarify this.

Imagine that you are the manager of a popular chain of clothing stores. You are thinking of opening a new store near a university campus, which you consider to be your prime market. There are already two similar stores in the vicinity (B and D) and you have a choice of two possible sites (A and C). Which one would you choose?

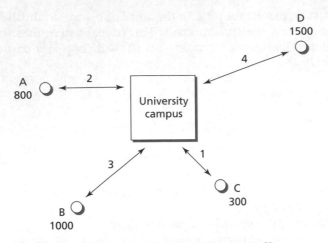

Figure 16.3 Location model according to Huff

Source: From *Journal of Marketing,* published by the American Marketing Association, Huff, D. L., 1964, Vol. 28, pp. 34–38.

Since shops A, B and C are quite similar in the nature of their offering, we assume b to be the same for all three – for instance, 2. Shop D, however, has a larger range of more upmarket clothes; thus, we presume b for this store to be smaller, say 1, since customers will be more willing to travel a greater distance.

Figure 16.3 depicts the size in square metres and the distance in kilometres from the university campus for each store. Using formula (1), it is possible to calculate the probability that a customer will visit site A or C. Since B and D are already in the market and the manager is deciding between A and C, ultimately only three shops will be competing for the customers of the university. Therefore, the denominator consists of only three stores.

$$P_{iA} = \frac{\dfrac{800}{2^2}}{\dfrac{800}{2^2} + \dfrac{1000}{3^2} + \dfrac{1500}{4^1}} = 29\% \text{ or } P_{iC} = \frac{\dfrac{300}{1^2}}{\dfrac{1000}{3^2} + \dfrac{300}{1^2} + \dfrac{1500}{4^1}} = 38\%$$

If we assume that the university has 10 000 students, each spending an average of $400 a year on clothes, the annual forecast sales for sites A and C will be:

$$\text{Site A } 0.29 \times 10\,000 \times \$400 = \$1\,160\,000$$
$$\text{Site C } 0.38 \times 10\,000 \times \$400 = \$1\,520\,000$$

If the shops only attracted customers from the university, then site C would be most profitable. However, although the university represents the largest market, other potential demand areas do exist, for which this analysis should be repeated. An exact decision can only be made when the forecast sales are added up for all these areas.

DESIGNING THE SERVICESCAPE

The 'service factory' environment has a strong impact on the customer's perception of the service experience. Before even entering the service facility, consumers commonly look for clues about the firm's capabilities and quality. Observe your own behaviour on your next trip to an unfamiliar city when you are looking for a place to eat. Since services are so intangible, the physical environment outside and inside is very influential in communicating an image and in shaping your expectations. As we mentioned earlier, services afford fewer clues from which an idea can be formed about not only the product's quality but sometimes the product itself, particularly in initial purchase decisions. Customers are therefore looking for surrogate indicators.

Moreover, the 'environment' in which the service is delivered becomes part of the service (i.e. the product). While the customer is in the servicescape, the service provider is addressing not only his or her 'substantive' need, but also the entire person with all his or her needs and senses. A certain meal, for instance, will be perceived entirely differently when served on the sunny, quiet terrace of a family-owned and -operated restaurant in Provence, from when the same meal is served in the restaurant of a busy international hotel in Paris. The passenger flying from London to New York in business class receives exactly the same 'core service' element as the tourist class passenger – that is, transportation from London to New York in a certain amount of time – but the business class passenger is willing to pay two or three times more, mainly due to the difference in 'servicescape'.

For these reasons it is clear that the physical setting influences the customer's 'ultimate satisfaction' with the service. When designing this environment, therefore, a company should explicitly take the customer into consideration. The environment should support the needs and preferences of the customer. Bitner[24] was one of the first marketing specialists to discover the importance of the physical setting and its interaction with the customer. She developed a model that enables us to see how the environment is perceived by the customer and how it affects his or her behaviour, degree of satisfaction, and in turn loyalty – that is, return behaviour. Figure 16.4 illustrates this conceptual model.

In this model, recognition is not only given to the customer, but also to the employee. The response of the employee is important because, as indicated earlier, employee satisfaction is important for the success of a service. In addition, the physical setting will directly affect the nature and quality of the interaction between the customer and the service provider, which, as was mentioned, is an important element of the service 'bundle'. As the sociologists Bennett and Bennett[26] stated:

> 'all social interaction is affected by the physical container in which it occurs.'

Ideally, the physical environment should support the needs and preferences of not only the customers, but also the needs and preferences of the employees. We will focus here, however, on the customer side.

Elements of the servicescape

Bitner defines the servicescape as:

> 'all objective physical factors that can be controlled by the firm to enhance (or constrain) employees' and customers' activities'.

The customer perceives the servicescape holistically. While distinct stimuli are perceived, it is the total configuration of stimuli that determines responses. When enjoying the dinner in the restaurant in Provence, we will probably notice the

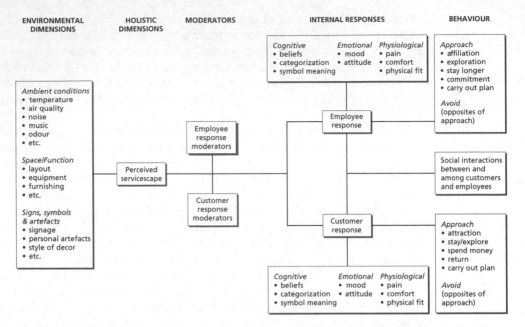

Figure 16.4 A framework for understanding environment-user relationships in service organizations[25]

Source: Bitner, M. J. (1992) 'Servicescapes: The impact of physical surroundings on customers and employees', *Journal of Marketing*, Vol 56, April, 57–71.

various individual elements such as the sunset, the lavender fragrance, the quiet landscape and the temperature, but we will also have an overall perception. The wine experiment described in our introductory case study is an excellent illustration of this point. However, when designing the servicescape we have to take a more analytical point of view. The model in Figure 16.4 suggests three (composite) dimensions: the ambient conditions, what we call spatial layout and process, and signs, symbols and artefacts.

- *Ambient conditions* refer to largely background characteristics such as noise, temperature, scent, lighting, aesthetics and colour – in short, all the elements of our environment that affect our five senses. The background music in shopping malls or the clatter of dishes if we are sitting too close to the kitchen in a restaurant, the aroma of freshly baked croissants in a French bakery or the polluted river we smell from the café terrace in an old city on a hot day, the coolness of the air in the hotel lobby of an international hotel in Barcelona in the summer, or the cold when we are walking around in Disneyland Paris in the winter are all examples of positive or negative ambient conditions.
- *Spatial layout and process* includes the elements of the environment that are closely related to the core element of the service. It includes items such as machinery, equipment and furniture that are necessary to deliver the service. This dimension refers to the way they are arranged and the physical and psychological (indirect) effects they have on the customer. A lift that is out of order, tables placed too close together in a Parisian bistro, the uncomfortable chairs in a waiting room and obviously disorganized and inefficient routines are all examples of processes that can have a negative impact on the customer. This is the

traditional domain of operations management, but it is important to note that these elements not only affect the efficiency of the process and the quality of the output, but also have a direct impact on the customer.

■ *Signs, symbols and artefacts* are the many items in the physical environment that serve as explicit or implicit communications to its users about the place. Signs such as labels on doors or instructions on how to proceed are used for directional purposes (e.g. to show the way to the toilets), or to communicate rules of behaviour (e.g. to reserve parking spaces for disabled persons). Signs, of course, also communicate indirectly to customers such things as the firm's degree of professionalism or its respect for the customer.

Other elements in the environment – such as the look and feel of the furniture in the reception area of the hotel, the decoration in the bank manager's office, the floor covering in the consultant's office, the tablecloths in the restaurant, the plastic utensils in the fast-food restaurant, and diplomas on the wall of the lawyer's office – communicate less directly, but are no less effective in communicating the value of the service, norms and expectations for behaviour or the trustworthiness of the service provider.

How does a customer respond?

As indicated in Figure 16.4, the customers' (and similarly the employees') response to the environmental stimuli can be found to consist of a *cognitive* response, an *emotional* response and a *physiological* response.

A cognitive response

This refers to the effect the environment has on the customers' understanding, beliefs and convictions. Stimuli have to be seen as a form of non-verbal communication. The floor coverings, the dress of the receptionist or clerk and the language used on the telephone 'tell' the customer something about the firm and the expected outcome. These stimuli influence the customer's perception of, for instance, how successful or cosmopolitan the company is. For example, Bitner found that a travel agent's office decor affected customer perception of the travel agent's behaviour. The fact that stimuli from the servicescape help customers to mentally categorize the service firm is also indicative of a cognitive response. People always try to label objects or other people. Elements of the servicescape help customers to classify and 'recognize' the firm and the expected quality. For most people in Belgium, the aroma of freshly baked pastry or bread is an unmistakable sign of what is called a warm baker – that is, a baker who bakes the bread himself. A bit of dirt on the vegetables helps people to perceive them as fresh. A waiter in fancy dress helps us to classify the restaurant as 'chic' and elegant.

An emotional response

This is perhaps less rational, but no less effective in influencing a customer's behaviour. It appears that as far as emotional responses are concerned, environments can be characterized by two qualities. The first is the extent to which the environment is perceived as being '*pleasant or unpleasant*'. Obviously, people want to spend more time in pleasant environments, and want to leave unpleasant ones as soon as possible, or avoid them entirely. The second quality is *the degree of arousal* – that is, the amount of excitement the environment generates. Research indicates that arousing environments are viewed positively unless the excitement is combined with unpleasantness. This means that unpleasant environments that are also high in arousal are particularly avoided. The key here seems to be the extent to which customers perceive themselves as having personal control. People like crowded marketplaces as long as they do not feel they 'have to go' there. Particular to understanding customers' emotional responses to an environment is that environment's complexity and coherence. According to Bitner, *complexity* (visual richness, ornamentation, information rate) has been found consistently to increase emotional arousal, whereas *coherence* (order, clarity, unity) has been found to enhance positive evaluation.

A physiological response

The servicescape also affects customers in concrete physiological ways. People will stay in a restaurant longer if the seats are comfortable. Noise might cause physical discomfort in a hotel. The temperature and humidity in a classroom will have an impact on the students and their behaviour. Putting pure comfort or discomfort aside, physiological responses also influence unrelated beliefs and feelings. When the temperature is too hot or humid, for example, customers are more aware of feeling crowded. Feelings of discomfort will be transferred to the rest of the service system. For instance, it is difficult to enjoy a meal or show when there is an unpleasant odour.

As indicated in Figure 16.4, these responses are not automatically or deterministically related to the stimuli. We described earlier that the tolerance for waiting is modified by situational or individual personal characteristics of the customer. The same is true for the servicescape stimuli. In other words, there are *moderating factors*. The mood of the individual customer when he or she enters the servicescape, the perceived degree of control and the plan or purpose for being in the environment are all situational factors that may affect the response. Personality characteristics, such as arousal-seeking versus arousal-avoiding behaviour, and certain cultural factors will influence, for instance, how people respond to noise, odours,[27] temperature and other stimuli.

Social interactions

The responses which have been described so far are individual responses of customers. However, the servicescape might also have an impact on the social interaction among the customers and between the customers and the employees. This is obvious in the case of space and layout. When social interaction between customers is an important aspect of the service concept, the physical setting should encourage interactions and discourage people's natural tendency to isolate themselves from 'strangers'. A U-shaped setting in the classroom stimulates interaction between participants and also makes it clear from the very beginning that people should be active and interactive. A high window in a bank protected with bullet-proof glass makes it very clear that long conversations are not wanted.

However, the other elements of the environment such as the ambient conditions or signs, may have a similar effect. A yellow line in the front section of a bus makes it very clear that interaction between the driver and the passenger should be strictly limited to functional conversation. The noise and lighting in discos does not invite people to have long conversations. Establishing office hours as a university professor might improve the professor's efficiency, but will certainly also give the message to students that conversation should be short and kept strictly to business. If coaching students is an important part of the service concept, the professor should be seen as more accessible.

Servicescape and business results

As we have already noted, the servicescape will affect not only the customer's initial purchase behaviour, but also the perception of the final quality of the experience, and thus the degree of customer satisfaction (*see* Exhibit 16.2). Given the relationship between customer satisfaction (and employee satisfaction) and profit established in the service profit chain, the link between servicescape and business results seems obvious. However, more direct evidence is available about the relationship between the servicescape and business results. As suggested in Figure 16.4, individuals generally react to physical settings with one of two opposing behaviours: approach or avoidance. *Approach behaviours*, according to Mehrabian and Russell,[28] 'include all positive behaviours that might be directed at a particular place, such as desire to stay, explore, work and affiliate. *Avoidance behaviours* reflect the opposite – in other words, a desire not to stay, explore, work or affiliate.

Such behaviours and their impact have been studied in detail in retail stores where a clear relationship was found between the perception of the environment and approach/avoidance behaviour as evidenced by shopping enjoyment, returning, spending money, time spent browsing, and exploration of the store – all factors that have a positive effect on business results. Approach/avoidance behaviours have two subcomponents: attracting or deterring entry by the customer, on the one hand, and influencing the degree of success of the customer in experiencing plans once inside.

Exhibit 16.2

Terminal decline[29]

It may be better than New York's airports, but arriving at London's Heathrow can still be a grim experience, on time or not. Passengers are confronted with poky terminal buildings, long corridors, smelly toilets and a cramped baggage hall. Travel into central London is either expensive or slow. This is not what passengers expect from one of the world's 'great' airports.

But airlines are right to be concerned about BAA's (British Airport Authority) commitment to improve facilities. The regulator should ensure that it delivers, especially now that a fifth terminal at Heathrow has been given the go-ahead. Otherwise BAA may need to be broken up to allow greater competition, smarter airports and happier passengers.

Source: Financial Times, 21 August 2002.

CONCLUSION

The importance of facilities management is underestimated in most service organizations. It is frequently dealt with at a too superficial level or in a too technical manner which ignores the customer. In some sectors, such as retailing, the location decision is given some top management attention, but in others, even this decision is not handled properly, let alone other facilities management decisions.

Hopefully, this chapter has made two messages clear. The various facilities management decisions are strategic decisions, since they have an impact on the business – that is, the type of product offered to the customers and the type of customers it attracts. When making facilities management decisions, a company should have a clear understanding of the desired service concept and the target market it wants to serve. These decisions also have an impact on such competitive strategic variables as the perceived quality and cost-effectiveness of the service.

The second message we hope to have conveyed is that no single department or function should make these decisions alone. Facilities management requires an interdisciplinary approach. Therefore, marketing and operations specialists, architects, organizational behaviour experts and others should be included in these decisions.

Review and discussion questions

- What are the differences in operations management, marketing and human resources management between back-office and front-office activities?

- What are the most common elements used in determining a specific location of a service firm? What are the decision variables in the location models for service firms?

- What is the meaning of 'Space speaks' in services?

Notes and references

1 North, A., Hargreaves, D. and McKendrick, J. (1997) 'In-store music affects product choice', *Nature*, 13 Nov, p. 132.

2 *The Value of Music*. London: National Music Council, 1996.

3 North, A. C. and Hargreaves, D. J. (1997) in Hargreaves, D. J. and North, A. C. (eds) *The Social Psychology of Music*, Oxford University Press, pp. 268–89; and Areni, C. S. and Kim, D. (1993) *Advanced Consumer Research*, Vol 20, 336–40.

4 Martindale, C. and Moore, K. J. (1988) *Exp.Psycholo.Hum.Percept.Perform.*, Vol 14, 661–70.

5 Hall, E. (1959) *The Silent Language*. New York: Doubleday and Co, p. 158.

6 Bitner, M. J. (1990) 'Evaluating service ecounters: The effects of physical surroundings and employee responses', *Journal of Marketing*, Vol 54, April, 69–82; and Bitner, M. J. (1992) 'Servicescapes: The impact of physical surroundings on customers and employees', *Journal of Marketing*, Vol 56, April, 57–71.

7 Lovelock, C. (1988) *Managing Services: Marketing, operations and human resources*. London: Prentice Hall.

8 Carlton, J. (1989) *Moments of Truth*. London: Harper Collins.

9 Adshaed, A. (2002) 'Telecoms firms' back office chaos is hurting customers', *Computer Weekly*, 06/06/2002, p. 4.

10 Based on 'Euro Disney: The first 100 days', *Harvard Business School case study*, 9–693–013.

11 Brown, S. W. (1994) 'Retail location at the micro scale: Inventory and prospect', *The Service Industries Journal*, Vol 14, No 4, Oct, 542–76.

12 Schmenner, R. W. (1994) 'Service firm location decisions: Some midwestern evidence', *International Journal of Service Industry Management*, Vol 5, No 3, 35–56.

[13] For the reader interested in a comprehensive overview of location models, we refer to Brandeau, M. L. and Chiu, S. S. (1984) 'An overview of represented problems in location research', *Management Science*, Vol 35, No 6, June, 645–74.

[14] This paragraph is in part based on Fitzsimmons and Fitzsimmons (1994) *Service Management for Competitive Advantage*, McGraw-Hill.

[15] The magazine *Sale and Marketing Management* annually releases a survey of buying power which measures the overall retail demand in an area as a percentage of total demand in the US. CONSU-DATA is an example of a computerized database. It contains information data such as social class, type of car or house, composition of the household and so on of more than four million Belgian households.

[16] 'Euro Disney: The first 100 days', op. cit., p. 8.

[17] Waters, D. (1996) Chapter 19 in *Operations Management: Producing goods and services*. Harlow, Essex: Addison-Wesley Longman.

[18] This part is based on a student project on location in services performed by Mieke Van Oostende under the supervision of Roland Van Dierdonck, Faculty of Economics and Business Administration, University of Ghent, 1997–1998.

[19] Huff, D. Z. (1964) 'Defining and estimating a trading area', *Journal of Marketing*, Vol 28, 34–8.

[20] Ibid.

[21] Berman and Evans (1983) *Retail Management: A strategic approach*. London: Macmillan.

[22] Levy, M. and Weitz, B. (1992) *Retailing Management*. Homewood, Illinois: Irwin, pp. 364–9.

[23] Huff, D. L. (1964) 'Defining and estimating a trade area', *Journal of Marketing*, Vol 28, 34–8; and Huff, D. L. (1966) 'A programmed solution for approximating an optimum retail location', *Land Economics*, Aug, 293–303.

[24] Bitner, M. J. (1992), op. cit.

[25] Ibid.

[26] Bennett and Bennett (1970) 'Making the scene', in Stone, G. and Farberman, H. (eds) *Social Psychology Through Symbolic Interactionism*. Waltham, MA: Ginn Blaisdell, pp. 190–6.

[27] Victor (1992) makes a distinction between olfactory cultures and non-olfactory cultures. In non-olfactory cultures, like most of the western cultures, 'smell' is not considered a major source of messages. Odours are masked as much as possible. In olfactory cultures, including most Arabic societies for instance, smells communicate emotions, such as fear and tension, relaxed friendliness. *See* Victor, D. A. (1992) *International Business Communication*. New York: Harper Collins.

[28] Mehrabian, A. and Russell, J. A. (1974) *An Approach to Environmental Psychology*. Cambridge, MA: MIT.

[29] *Source*: *Financial Times*, 21 August 2002.

Suggested further reading

Bitner, M. J. (1992) 'Servicescapes: The impact of physical surroundings on customers and employees', *Journal of Marketing*, Vol 56, April, 57–71. Bitner is the founder of the servicescape notion, so this is a definitive article on the impact of the environment on the customers' and employees' perception of the service.

Brandeau, M. L. and Chiu, S. S. (1984) 'An overview of representative problems in location research', *Management Science*, Vol 35, No 6, June, 645–74. For readers wanting to dig deeper into the mathematical location models, this is an excellent paper. It includes a literature review on the most relevant models indicating which models are best suited for which situations.

CHAPTER 17

IT developments and their impact on services

Tim Duhamel · Bart Van Looy · Wilfried Grommen · Wim Grielens
Niels Schillewaert · Pedro Matthÿnssens

INTRODUCTION

> *'Computers in the future may weigh no more than 1.5 tons.'*
> Popular Mechanics, 1949

> *'There is no reason anyone would want a computer in their home.'*
> K. Olson, 1977

Services are processes characterized by both simultaneity and intangibility; they are also rich in terms of information exchange. As such they are highly affected by developments related to information technology, as has been demonstrated many times throughout this book. In this chapter we explore in greater detail the role information technology can have in managing service transactions.

We begin with a general introduction to the different stages in the development of information technology and we will discuss the economic implications of the network era as it manifests itself today. Next we examine the impact IT developments can have on service transactions: replacing and/or complementing the traditional, physical 'marketplace' by its virtual counterpart, the 'market space'. We will argue that the impact these IT developments will have on service transactions depends on a number of factors: the behaviour of customers and service providers as well as the nature of the service transaction itself. Maintenance-interactive services are most easily 'digitalized'; this will be more difficult for task-interactive services and the process will be least viable for personal-interactive services. This is explained by the notion of 'media richness' – that is, new technologies are often less rich in terms of interaction possibilities than face-to-face meetings. Hence complex service transactions will continue to involve a great deal of direct contact between service provider and customer.

At the same time, it is important to keep in mind the complex social adaptation processes surrounding every technological evolution. We will examine past technological developments (during the nineteenth century the hottest thing around was the bicycle) and learn by relating these to the actual IT developments.

Finally, ingredients for relevant action strategies which allow combining market place and market space activities into coherent service delivery systems will be discussed.

Objectives

By the end of this chapter, you should be able to discuss:

- why information technology is important for services

- what is meant by 'virtual value creation' and what the implications are of working in the market space

- the factors that will influence the degree and extent to which combining marketplace and market space might be relevant

- relevant action strategies that might be deployed when shifting into the direction of virtual service transactions

THE NETWORK ERA – WHERE DO WE STAND?

As became clear in Chapter 1, the service sector is the largest and most rapidly growing segment of the economy for most of the industrialized world. In terms of technology, information technology is dominant: IT accounts for more than 80 per cent of the technology purchased by service sector firms and is the predominant focus of service sector R&D staffs.[1] This does not imply that other technology is not relevant; just think about the technologies deployed by medical staff for diagnosis or intervention. It does however justify this book's focus on information technology and the way in which it may affect service delivery processes. And here we have been witnessing some turbulence during recent years, directly related to the explosive growth and diffusion of Internet technologies. This growth has been so spectacular that, with hindsight, the burst of the bubble even seems inevitable. Let us briefly look at what the network era implies and how it is being used today; this sets the stage for a more in depth examination of the impact of information technology on service delivery processes.

The network era

After the batch era, the time sharing era, and the still ongoing client/server era, a new episode in the development of IT has begun. *Network computing* – that is, the increasing range of possibilities for doing transactions by means of electronic media – is becoming an integral part of most organizations. Workstations such as servers, mainframes or PCs are being linked by means of networks of wires, satellite or infrared connections permitting transactions on an ever-larger scale (*see* Figure 17.1).

Batch work involved processing only one, often very complex, 'batch' of transactions at the same time. *Time sharing* introduced possibilities for switching between jobs. Still, the three different logics that can be discerned in any computer application – presentation, application and data logic – were still heavily concentrated

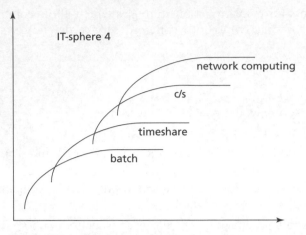

Figure 17.1 Network computing

in each operating unit.[2] *Client/server systems* started to 'disconnect' these different logics. It became possible to have data, applications and presentation devices on different workstations. The scale on which exchange took place was still rather limited, however. Network computing reduces these limitations.

Basically, network computing extends the range of transactions (communication, publicity, solution definition, ordering, solution delivery or fulfilment, payment, satisfaction analysis and follow-up business) that can be executed or enabled electronically, reducing the time required to initiate, execute and conclude them. In addition, network computing extends the reach of the players, permitting them to establish these interactions with partners independent of distance and time constraints. In short, it expands the market for providers and buyers from local to global, at a fraction of the cost of traditional market development.[3] This evolution results from an alignment on the interface issues underlying this network computing breakthrough. Over the years, many initiatives have been developed towards standardizing communication between information devices to create *platform independence*. The adoption of the TCP/IP protocol suite has accelerated these developments. This 'suite' bundles agreements (made between the main players within the industry as well as governments) related to information device interface standards. HTML[4] is perhaps one of the best-known protocols. This protocol, together with many others, has fuelled the spectacular growth of the Internet over the last few years. HTML conventions define the 'electronic' standards for presenting texts and figures including 'links' with other texts.[5]

The *Internet* in its incarnation as the World Wide Web (WWW) can be considered as a specific form of network computing. One of the distinguishing characteristics of the WWW has been its universal standard browser interface to a world of on-line textual and pictorial resources. This is currently being extended to sound and moving images (video-like data streams). In addition to the increase in media types, the Internet offers an increasing number of possibilities of real on-line transactions, where dynamic and customized responses to individual requests become possible. As a network resource, the Internet offers organizations not wishing to invest in a private network infrastructure the capability to establish a linkage with their target partners.

The Internet: fact and fiction

'It is impossible for old prejudices and hostilities to exist any longer, now that such an instrument has been created for the exchange of thought between all the nations of the earth.'

(Victorian enthusiasts acclaiming the arrival of the first transatlantic cable in 1858)

As observed by the Economist a while ago, the Internet does certain things extremely well, while not doing other things at all, or at best very partially.[6] Bringing world peace undoubtedly fits the latter category, although several leading scholars have made this claim in the recent past. Similar expectations have been voiced about the Internet technologies helping to reduce energy consumption and its related pollution, and reducing inequality while simultaneously fostering democracy. And although Internet technology may contribute to the development of solutions for some of these problems, it still implies complex and multifaceted trajectories in which technological developments are only one of the actors on stage, as we will show in this chapter.

This does not mean, however, that the recent developments in information technology in general and of network technology in particular should be trivialized. The Internet has already changed many things. It can be said that for a lot of individuals in the industrialized world e-mail is the most important new form of personal communication since the advent of the telephone. And although at this point there is still great variation in the diffusion of the Internet – in some countries (e.g. Norway, Singapore, US) over 50 per cent of all households have Internet access at home, whereas for the majority of the industrialized world these figures fluctuate between 15 and 50% – its popularity is still clearly increasing. Also, an enormous number of firms have linked their systems directly with those of their suppliers and partners, allowing them to do business around the clock. At the same time, several firms heavily use Internet technology to reach and to conduct transactions with end consumers, Dell being the most well-known example in this respect.

As for e-commerce, at the beginning of the new millennium (2001),[7] on-line sales accounted for about one per cent of US retail sales. The economic value within the business-to-business realm is estimated at several times the volume being realized in business-to-consumer environments. Within two to three years this volume is expected to triple within the industrialized world.

It is clear, however, that e-commerce has not lived up to the expectations voiced during the mid-1990s. One of the major reasons for this can be found in confusing the use of the Internet – for commercial purposes – with actual purchasing by means of the Internet. An example clarifies this point: while only 2.7 per cent of new car sales in America in 1999 took place over the Internet, as many as 40 per cent of all new car sales involved the use of the Internet at some point. Consumers use it to obtain information and compare prices, but not for actually purchasing the vehicle. Likewise, research conducted by Forrester (second quarter of 2000) reveals that about half of the on-line households in North America use the Internet weekly to search for information directly related to purchasing decisions. Purchasing over the net is done in only about 25 per cent of all on-line households.

Moreover, while using the Internet for shopping has some interesting advantages (such as a considerable expansion of the range offered, combined with increasing opportunities for time-price comparisons[8]), one should be aware that Internet transactions do not succeed in replicating the social function of shopping. Neither does on-line purchasing generate the serendipity and impulse purchases that come from visits to a shopping centre.[9] In addition, the Internet does not offer the instant gratification sought by many consumers buying 'physical' goods, as the separate delivery process entails delays. Also, a majority of people prefer physical contact for what have been called 'high touch' products: goods like shoes or clothes, as well as vegetables or meat, that one likes to see, feel, fit or even taste before buying. This is far less the case for products like books, computers or CDs. It could even be argued that the more 'digital' products or services are, the more relevant the Internet will be for their delivery. We will develop this logic somewhat in the next pages.

At the same time one observes that all is not well on this front. Music, for instance is easily delivered over the Internet, at a reasonable quality, and as the astounding growth of Napster (a file sharing site) showed, there is plenty of demand. But the record companies have not found a way of getting people to pay for music distributed in this way. The music, consumer-electronics and software industries are struggling to agree on an encryption system for protecting copyright owners.

Getting people to pay for content is a problem for other business too. The on-line editions of several newspapers started off charging subscriptions, but most of them have abandoned that model. They found that too many rival services are available for free at this point. On the other hand, it is clear that offering services or goods for free isn't exactly a sustainable business proposition. So in one way or another, agreements will be worked out between consumers, content providers and network and other service providers to arrive exactly at more sustainable value propositions. Such arrangements will become more feasible to the extent that enabling technologies (related to security, payments, and identification, including geolocation) become available. Notice that while several of these technologies are already available, their present form is often not being perceived as fair or convenient for – and by the majority – of consumers.[10]

What do these observations teach us?

First of all, as the last examples clarify, information technology in general and Internet technology in particular are still technologies 'under development'. Not only does this mean that technology is sometimes unstable or even just clumsy,[11] it also implies that in a number of cases clear business models and rules are lacking. The current situation with respect to intellectual property right illustrates our point. Although everyone agrees that the current situation is not feasible in the long run, no clear scenarios – or business models – are emerging yet. So, being active in Internet technology requires being able to address the ambiguity or 'interpretative flexibility' (a notion that we will explain in detail in the following pages) which characterizes the actual deployment of the Internet.

Secondly, the emerging picture seems to suggest that we should use Internet technology for what it does well. In certain instances this might imply a full transactional cycle, in which information technology is used in all stages of the service delivery process,[12] ranging from orientation to closing (buying) and evaluation. In many cases, however, information technology will only be useful for certain parts of the service delivery process. This observation inspires us to plead for combining both the market space and place. In addition, when deciding upon an appropriate mix of both, we will stress the importance of taking into account the nature of the service delivery process as well as the specific context of use.

THE IMPACT OF IT DEVELOPMENTS ON SERVICE ENCOUNTERS

Exhibit 17.1

IT and the stockbroking industry

In 1974, Charles Schwab[13] founded a stockbroking firm intended to take advantage of the scrapping of fixed commissions in securities trading in the US. He believed that customers would be enticed by discount dealing. The firm used high-tech remote service-delivery means and cut prices thanks to its lower cost base. Schwab was the first of a new class of stockbrokers in the mid-1970s which undercut the high charges imposed by established full-service firms with an army of brokers and expensive research. The stockbroking industry seemed destined to transform itself in an unpredictable way.

Wall Street giants, such as Merrill Lynch and Smith Barney, suddenly seemed threatened by this retail stockbroking industrial revolution.[14] A new class of entrants in retail stockbroking with a much lower cost base seemed destined only to increase as one remote service-enabling technology evolution followed another: faster communication, PCs, modems, voice recognition and, finally, the Internet. Stock price information and analytical software, formerly the privileged domain of giant old-style firms, were given away free of charge and in 1996, the new generation of brokers raced to offer on-line electronic share-dealing services through virtual discount-broking – for example, e.Schwab, e.trade and Lombard.

Competition and technological improvements are sparking innovators to discover new, more efficient ways to fulfil such basic financial service functions as executing trades and providing price information. Did these companies overthrow their old-fashioned colleagues in retail stockbroking? Did they gain dominant market share? At first sight, there appeared to be no reason why they should not eventually dominate the retail stockbroking marketplace.

As it happened, the new generation of stock-brokers failed to take over the retail market after their entry into the market. Two decades later, discounters like Schwab have a share of the retail market of only 25 per cent and on-line accounts represent only around 1 per cent of the total US brokerage market.[15] This relative failure had nothing to do with technological shortcomings; what happened is that they misunderstood the nature of the customer–service provider interaction, or at least underestimated the information poverty of their technology-heavy service process. They focused on stockbroking as a commodity service, executing trades and providing price information. The commodity service, as defined by Schwab and the others, appealed only to a minority of investors. Most of the investors did not simply want to execute a trade, but wanted some advice and help in execution. That is why they remained with their traditional, much more expensive, service medium. The high-profile stockbroker, backed up by investment research and ensuring a personal relationship with the client, has proven very resilient. Plenty of investors still prefer traditional methods for making a trade.

Discounters like Schwab and Quick & Reilly are now repositioning their service offering, incorporating:

- a more substance-rich service, with analysis and advice via the computer; and
- a mix of distribution channels, including telephone links, computer links, and even offices(!).

The innovative discounters now compete directly with their more traditional counterparts. In response, however, the traditional, full-service rivals, such as Merrill Lynch and Prudential Securities, are extending their service with on-line capabilities to review accounts, check price information, and send e-mail to stockbrokers. The traditional packages of services offered by these companies are becoming more and more transparent because of this differentiation in service media: low-value commodity elements of their service are gradually unbundled from the high-value elements like research (e.g. investment ideas) and superior products (e.g. proprietary funds) and are distributed through distinct channels. The difference between the new and old generations is blurring.

The next question then might be what each of the service elements of the full-service brokers is worth in itself. And this in its turn might lead to the fragmentation of traditional institutions and the spinning off of services to focus on a smaller number of high-value services.

Market space: value creation in the virtual world

As Exhibit 17.1 illustrates very clearly, the introduction of new information technologies can shape the service transaction process and hence influence the ways in which business is being carried out. Nowadays, the global deployment of the Internet has led many to believe that their business may run into trouble without a presence on that medium. We will look in more detail at what doing business in the 'virtual' world, or the market space, implies.

Virtual value creation: three stages

Value creation in the 'virtual world' involves working with information; it is information that flows through new media. Globally, working with information can be depicted in three ways; often they present themselves in consecutive stages.[16]

1. In the first or the '*visibility*' stage, companies acquire an ability to 'see' physical operations more effectively through information. At this stage, large-scale information technology systems are put into place to monitor and co-ordinate activities in the physical value chains. Here information is treated as a supporting element of the value-adding process, not as a source of value itself. In other words, managers use information to monitor or control their processes, but they rarely use information to create new value for their customer.
2. In the second stage, called '*mirroring*', companies replace physical activities with virtual ones. They start to create a parallel value chain in the market space. These activities, however, mirror the ones that were taking place in the physical world. An example is the offering of opportunities to listen to new CDs, which previously was only possible at the local music store, but now can also be done via the Internet. Here disintermediation, involving intermediaries being removed from the value chain, will often be the case; mirroring will imply in most cases a cost advantage for 'virtual' distribution systems (*see* below).
3. In the third stage, information is used to establish new services as well as new customer interactions and relationships. Managers draw on the flow of information in their virtual value chain to deliver value to their customers in new ways by looking for '*virtual value creation*' – virtual in the sense that it is performed through and with information. Creating value within a virtual value chain involves a sequence of five activities: gathering, organizing, selecting, synthesizing and distributing information.[17]

A nice example of rethinking and combining information as to create new services, is Pacific Pride, a company that sells diesel fuels for trucks.[18] They have created a distribution system that includes ATMs at local gas stations, allowing truckers fast and efficient access to fuel. At the same time, the information gathered in this way is used to provide the transport companies with detailed information on fuel purchase, and with accounting reports as specified by the customer. This creates added value for the customer in terms of higher quality information that helps them control their transport activities and that enables them to improve the efficiency of their activities. Pacific Pride even offers a credit line for some customers. These new service offerings allow them to charge prices that correspond with margins twice as high as the industry standards.

In fact, working in this way with information allows us to rethink the way we offer services, and possibly the services themselves. A service offering can be seen as a mixture of content, context and infrastructure.[19] What the new information technology offers us are new ways of configuring our service offerings: content, context and infrastructure can be mixed differently. These new possibilities are allowing us to reconfigure service offerings and design new services. Federal Express understood that their customers wanted immediate and accurate feedback on the packages they delivered and therefore built an easy-to-use and very effective service on the Web. FedEx customers can now track their packages at every stage of the delivery and check the signature of the recipient, if necessary. FedEx saves a considerable amount of toll-free phone charges, but their biggest benefit seems to be customer loyalty. Customers will not run to the competition with such impeccable service at their fingertips.[20]

Doing business in the market space or by means of the virtual value chain thus implies new ways of combining and distributing information. It also requires a thorough knowledge of the actual marketplace, as well as seamless information flows.

Value creation in the virtual world assumes a thorough knowledge of the 'real' world; it is the actual behaviour and preferences of your customers that allow a successful design of new service offerings. Just think back to the Schwab case described in Exhibit 17.1. The monitoring service offered by the trucking company (described in point 3 above) would never have been offered if the company had not been aware that such a service would add value. However, this knowledge should not be seen as a starting point for only mirroring the physical activities of the classical marketplace. Instead, this knowledge can be used as a starting point for designing new complementary activities.

A good understanding of the company's value chain and customers' situation is not enough; there must also be a seamless flow of information. The recent advent of middleware messaging products and data-warehousing and data-mining software allows a company to integrate islands of information and to structure this information into more than a by-product. The next step would then be to look for new opportunities to create value.

Dis-intermediation or re-intermediation?

The introduction of the market space will have implications for the way in which business will be done. One of the most debated issues is centring around the notion of *dis-intermediation*. Cynthia Moore describes dis-intermediation as:[21]

> '...the removal of intermediaries from the industry value chain. In other words, it is cutting the middleman out of the loop.'

This implies an imminent threat to certain job categories. Commodities such as books, CDs, certain off-the-shelf financial products and airline travel will no longer require the services of a middleman or broker. Unless the customer perceives the activity of the intermediary as an added value, this position will be under scrutiny. Recent IT developments will urge many intermediaries to look for more added value in their offerings, otherwise their profession could be forced into obsolescence.

However, the intermediary could follow a more drastic approach and seize the opportunity of new IT developments to create additional or new value for customers. This is called *re-intermediation* – the creation of new value between producers and consumers by exploiting the new information technologies, such as the Internet. An example of this is portal sites such as those developed by Yahoo.

Marketplace or market space? The driving forces

No one can deny that market spaces are more present everyday and that, in a number of occasions, they replace existing marketplaces.

The extent of, and speed at which, this replacement takes place will not be the same for all types of services, however. In this section we will provide a framework that can help us to assess the impact of the recent information technology developments. We will examine the different forces that are at play:

- the customer's preferences and actual behaviour;
- the service provider; and
- the nature of the service process.

Customers' preferences and behaviour

New technologies will be adapted by customers to the extent that they fit their needs better. However, new technologies also entail new ways of acting and behaving. As such, they imply a learning and development phase characterized by uncertainty. Predicting the outcomes of such an adaptation and learning process is always a hazardous enterprise. One has only to recall the predictions of the paperless office made some decades ago. Rather than formulating absolute predictions, we shall discuss some major trends that are already visible. These trends will exert their influence on the ongoing adaptation and development process.

The changing preferences of the consumer: in search of convenience

In a rapidly changing world, consumers are changing their lifestyles: the notion of free time is more differentiated in character,[22] more of that time is spent on doing things they really want to do (instead of queuing in a supermarket), communicating with the rest of the world and the environment. Furthermore, customers have a wide variety of choices in brands, stores, shopping methods and communication channels. Companies are now offering the customer more convenience because the customer is asking for it. The customer's new attitudes are most prevalent in the following four domains:

- *Instant satisfaction.* When a customer buys a new product today, he or she wants it delivered 'yesterday'. The success of distributors like IKEA is a shining example. You buy a new dining-room table on Saturday morning and invite your friends to dine from it the same evening. Car manufacturers that can deliver a car in less than three weeks have a huge competitive advantage. The pre-selection of products or services will in the near future become more and more virtual. The pre-selection of goods will take place in a market space. The final selection and delivery, however, will continue to occur in a market place. This phenomenon may put 'hybrid' configurations combining both market place and market space in an advantageous position. This phenomenon may also lead to situations where the market place 'triumphs' over the market space. For instance, 'fun shopping' on a Saturday afternoon is only fun if you come home with new stuff. Only in as far as the underlying products can be digitalized, will Internet technology be able to meet this requirement.
- *Consumer control.* Customers want to decide when the interaction with others (and other companies) should take place. Pay-TV channels without advertising are increasingly successful. Customers are demanding privacy (and the law is on

their side). Customers decide whether they want to be in a database or not. The locus of control for interactions is shifting in favour of the customer.

■ *A more personal interaction, back to nature.* The knowledge of individual customers' needs that companies can gather through technology harks back to the days when the butcher and the baker knew their clientele personally. In that setting, customer service relationships were built in face-to-face transactions.[23] Bringing back the individual transaction with the help of technology not only gives a competitive advantage because of the personal approach, it is also a channel through which market information can be gathered.

The changing needs of customers, as discussed above, provide indications about the things companies will have to focus on in the near future. Those companies that do not take into account customer needs will undoubtedly lose market share. As we look at the changing needs of the customer, we notice that IT can provide solutions to these needs. Increasingly, accurate information can be delivered from the company to the customer and vice versa. What is important, however, is that this information at a certain point in time becomes value, for which people are willing to pay. This will become clear further on in this chapter.

Developing new behaviour: dealing with uncertainty about the offer and the medium

As we mentioned earlier, in a buying process customers show a certain amount of uncertainty related to the product or service itself. Buying a product or service in many cases means taking a risk. The lower the perceived risk of buying a product or service is, the greater the chance the customer actually buys the product. During the decision phase, all kinds of questions appear in the mind of the customer. Does this product fit my specific needs? Is the service quality guaranteed? Is the product damaged in any way?

When providing services or products in the market space as opposed to the marketplace, uncertainty about the product is an even bigger problem, because of the lack of risk-reducing factors. In the market space, the customer cannot touch, feel, smell or even see a product sufficiently. We could say that when buying products or services in a market space there is a higher risk perception than in a marketplace.

Of course, the nature of the offer is of extreme importance. Buying CDs, for instance, is a relatively low-risk process. The quality of the product is very much the same world-wide; there are no compatibility problems because the disc plays just as well on a Chinese player as it does on an American one and, except for the imperfections of live recordings, the quality of the music on the disc is guaranteed. Buying a CD in the market space is far less risky than, for example, buying a CD player in the market space. There is more quality uncertainty with the latter. You can buy a Philips or a Sony player, but even then you do not know if the player will arrive at your home in one piece.

When using new media such as the Internet or other on-line computer media for communication or distribution purposes, therefore, we have to deal with the acceptance and use of the new media by the customer. Indeed, the average customer is not aware of the possibilities and richness of a computer-mediated environment. Moreover, even if the customer is aware of the characteristics and capabilities of a medium, it does not guarantee an awareness of its convenience and timeliness. One has to be aware of the features before knowing the benefits of the service.

The uncertainty about the delivered product or service, then, is higher in the market space. The challenge here is to provide risk-reducing elements to eliminate the customer's risk perception – for example, by delivering information, branding, or providing service guarantees.[24]

Service providers looking for cost effectiveness

Many services can be delivered through multiple media. It is impossible to separate distribution media from service. In most cases, the distribution channel is a part of the service, both from the viewpoint of the medium's share of the total service cost, and from the customer's viewpoint.

All distribution channels have an initial fixed cost (investment) and an operational cost. Innovations in service delivery over the past two decades have dramatically lowered the cost of setting up and running a distribution channel. Starting and running a virtual service company that uses the Internet as a medium is tremendously cheap in comparison with a company that distributes its services in offices with marble halls and well-paid employees. As a result, the economics of services distribution has changed radically over the last two decades and is likely to change in the coming decade. Many service suppliers that have been around for a while have built diverse and extensive distribution systems with different cost structures.

Often a small percentage of customers subsidizes the cost of the more expensive distribution medium for the majority of the consumers – that is, most of the consumers are not really worth the expensive distribution medium from a profitability perspective, but only enjoy the channel because a small minority of the consumers make the channels profitable overall.

Such a distribution pattern is untenable, especially as competitive wars swirl through an industry. Competitors start undercutting each other's media costs. New entrants only use low-cost media to offer services. High-cost media are thrown on the defensive. Profitable customers will not tolerate the large channel cost that is factored into their service cost, and will go looking for more economical alternatives rather than subsidizing the channel for non-profitable consumers. The inattentive service provider will be left with a distribution medium that loses money.

In addition, many service industry players do not know what return they are receiving on service delivery investments. This is where modern cost/benefit ratio diagnostics come into play. Even when good statistical information is available, however, the complexity of the supplier–medium–consumer relationship described here does not allow for simple remedies. Although cost structure is important in the choice of the service medium, it cannot be the only basis for action but has to be regarded as part of a holistic view of service consumers and their unique behaviour, needs and profitability dynamics.

A look at banking today reveals the complexity banks face in realigning their retail distribution systems. Customers can do business with their banks through multiple channels: branches, kiosks, call-centres, telephones, personal computers, automated teller machines (ATMs), digital televisions, electronic purses, smart cards, and so on. The number of media is steadily increasing. Electronic transactions are much cheaper than people- or paper-based ones. This is no simple basis for action, however. Banks realize that what drives their costs is how customers behave and not the cost of a service transaction. The first step to making the most of service delivery media is understanding the evolving behaviour of customers – how the customer changes and what those changes mean for retail banks. Furthermore, adding a new, cheaper electronic distribution channel does not cut total distribution costs *per se*; customers will start using the cheaper distribution channel but will not necessarily make less use of the more expensive one. As banks make more media available, they experience an increase in overall activity. Clients are tending to make vigorous use of the entire range of delivery channels at their disposal. Additionally, a service transaction in one service medium might translate into multiple service transactions in another medium. For example, instead of making a single large withdrawal when the customer visits the branch, ATM customers make many more visits to the machine, withdrawing much smaller amounts, and checking their balance more frequently. The increase in activity, in general, conceals the substitution of activities across channels. Often banks invest in every delivery channel in order not to risk losing the customer rather than having a cost-based justification for their investments.

Although adding cheaper service delivery channels is therefore likely to cause a reduction in the use of a bank's more expensive delivery channels in the long run, it is difficult for many reasons to predict the pace and volume of the reduction. Accordingly, banks prefer to focus on optimizing the use of their service media by the consumer rather than deciding not to invest in or close down a channel.

Banks should focus on customer segments which use multiple distribution channels and cost more than the revenue they represent for the bank. The banks should then define these customers' service needs and the ways to meet them in a manner that is less detrimental to the bottom line. The bank can then begin creating a service delivery system consisting of the right media mix which works for the customer and the shareholder.[25] The type of service – that is, the nature of the service delivered – will have to be taken into account as well, as we will demonstrate in the next section.

Nature of the service process

Of course, not all services will be affected to the same extent by the fact that the market space is taking over some of the traditional marketplace activities. If you are looking for advice on a way to carry out a re-organization, if you need some personal counselling and advice on how to develop your career, or if you are looking for support to improve the relationship with your spouse, you will probably want to have a face-to-face meeting with a counsellor. On the other hand, you will not be looking for a profound personal discussion when you want to rent a VCR or when checking your bank account.

Services vary, then, in terms of the extent to which they require close and in-depth interaction between the customer and service provider. It is clear that this dimension – the degree and nature of interaction between service provider and customer – will correlate with the degree to which the information technology developments affect the way services are delivered and consumed. Services that imply short, standardized information transactions will be more easily delivered by new media than services that require a more complex type of interaction. As a matter of fact, in the more complex cases, the medium is part of the service. Delivering the service by another medium is changing the product itself.

To see this differential effect, it is useful to re-examine the typology of services that was developed by Mills and Margulies and has been discussed in Chapter 1.[26] Here a distinction was made between three basic types of services and service organizations: maintenance-interactive services, task-interactive services and personal-interactive services.

- *Maintenance-interactive* service operations can be found in financial institutions such as banks and insurance companies. The direct interaction between provider and customer is usually rather predictable and standardized (e.g. the interaction between a bank teller and a customer). The service is based on the provider seeing to the maintenance of some goods or assets for the customer.
- Examples of *task-interactive* types of service can be found in engineering and advertising. Here the interaction between customer and provider is based on technical problem solving, related to finding ways to obtain or accomplish something. Customers ask for assistance and interact with service providers in order to have specialized knowledge and skills at their disposal. Complex financial engineering can also be an example of task-interactive services: companies will often offer a variety of services. The bank not only performs a number of maintenance-interactive services but also delivers task-interactive services.
- The third type of service operations can be described as *personal-interactive*. Here service providers work with customers who are not only unsure exactly how to solve their problems or satisfy their needs but also want to know how best to serve their own interests. An example here is, of course, a psychotherapist, but this type might also include a whole range of professional services, like lawyers or consultants.

The type of interactions between service providers and customers will vary between these three types of service transactions (*see* Figure 17.2). The complexity of interaction will be greater in task- or personal-interactive types of services than in maintenance types of services. This will in turn affect the sensitivity towards the recent information technology developments; it is far easier to substitute 'physical' maintenance interactions for their 'virtual' counterpart.

The basic idea behind this model is the so-called '*information richness theory*'. However, this framework does not explain everything. We need to go one step further and position the characteristics of new media within their context of use; this will bring us to the notion of *virtual communities*. We will examine both ideas more in depth in the next section.

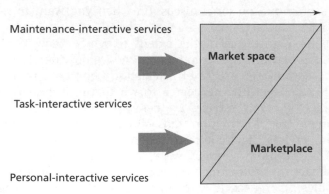

Figure 17.2 Relationship between nature of service and relevance of the market space

Linking service transactions and media channels

Information richness theory was developed in the 1980s[27] to help companies to prescribe the appropriate channels, given certain information-processing requirements. Information-processing requirements should be understood as the degree of uncertainty or equivocality reduction that an individual is looking for in the interaction. Communication channels can differ in terms of richness; face-to-face communication is richer than, for instance, EDI (electronic data input) transactions. For instance, if you only need to know the status of your bank account, you do not need a face-to-face meeting with the local bank manager; an ATM or an electronic bank link will provide you with all the necessary information. On the other hand, if you want to discuss possible ways of investing your money, taking into account the fiscal situation and so on, a face-to-face meeting can be the most effective way to proceed.

So let us examine more closely both factors: types of interaction and media richness.

Defining and linking types of interaction and media richness

As already argued, interaction may imply uncertainty or ambiguity. Uncertainty can be seen as the 'difference between the information required and the amount of information already possessed'.[28] However, this definition implies an ability to assess the degree and content of the information required. This is not the case for equivocal or ambiguous situations – that is, situations characterized by the existence of multiple and possibly even conflicting interpretations. Given a certain situation, it is impossible to decide what input is necessary. Uncertainty, then, is seen as a measure of the ignorance of a value of a variable, whereas equivocality is a measure of the ignorance of whether a variable exists. Whereas uncertainty relates to answering well-defined questions, equivocality or ambiguity implies that the right questions are still being sought.

If you want to know the status of your bank account, you find yourself in a situation of uncertainty: you know the variable, the question, and you are looking for a precise answer to that question. However, if you are looking for advice on how best to manage your deposits, you do not know all the different elements that are involved – for instance, the range of possible products and their rates of return, or the effects of tax legislation. Not only are you looking for answers, you are not even sure what questions should be asked. This situation involves equivocality or ambiguity.

Media differ in their ability to transfer rich information. If you meet someone in a face-to-face setting you will obtain more information, not only from their voice, but also from gestures or facial expressions. Thus, more information can be transferred in a face-to-face meeting than with e-mail or a fax. As such, a face-to-face meeting is seen as a richer medium. The richness of an information handling medium can be expressed by the following characteristics:

1. the opportunity for timely feedback;
2. the ability to convey multiple cues;
3. the tailoring of messages to personal circumstances; and
4. language variety.[29]

Based on these criteria, different media can be classified on a scale of low to high richness (*see* Figure 17.3).

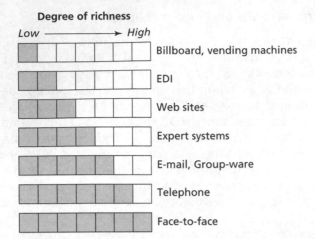

Figure 17.3 Degree of richness of task-interactive services

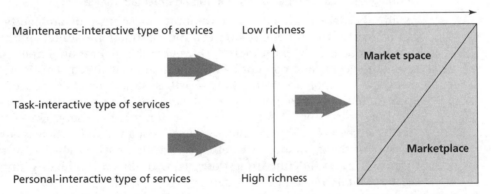

Figure 17.4 The relationship between the nature of a service, information richness demands and the relevance of the market space

Information richness theory teaches us that effective communication or interaction will occur when there is a fit or a match between the media characteristics (richness level) and the information-processing requirements (uncertainty or equivocality). Thus, when we need to pass on simple information required for uncertainty reduction, we can use a lean medium. Complex, vague or ambiguous information demands rich media such as a telephone call or a face-to-face meeting – the media most suited for equivocality reduction.

This framework can be linked with the previous one, where the nature of services was linked with the relevance of the market space. Figure 17.4 depicts the relationship between the nature of a service, demands in terms of information richness, and thus the relevance of the market space.

Does this framework allow us to predict which services will become virtual and which will not? Of course it provides us with good insights. However, it should be noted that one-to-one relationships, like those depicted in this simplifying framework are seldom as straightforward in practice; life is more complicated.

Information richness theory starts from the assumption that rational knowledge of the characteristics and the applicability of the various media will eventually drive their use. However, people's actions or interactions are not necessarily based on 'rational' considerations alone. Situational constraints, as well as symbolic considerations, will also influence the selection and use of certain media. People will use certain media because these are the only ones available, to show that they have mastered them, because they attach a certain symbolic meaning or emotion to them, or because they are allowed to use them, and not just because they are the most effective. Just think about the e-mails you receive every day. How many of the messages you receive are relevant or accurate? Some might just be better put on a database, so you could look for the information when you need it, instead of muddling through a list of relevant messages every day. Others are so delicate in content that they only raise questions and are probably better suited to a meeting or discussion.

Most importantly, it is becoming increasingly clear that everyday practice is rooted in social behaviour, and hence the use of media will also be strongly influenced by the social practices surrounding these media. Effectiveness will in one way or another always connote effectiveness within a certain social community.

It is of no use to have telephones and e-mail connections everywhere in order to speed things up if people are slow to adopt them or do not use them at all. This observation stems directly from the fact that interaction is a two-way street. A caller or sender cannot complete a communication via certain media successfully unless the intended recipient uses them as well.[30] When deciding on a certain media channel, it is important to take into account not only the appropriateness of a certain medium to a communication task, but also whether the intended recipients are likely to use, react and respond to messages in that medium within the desired time frame. This brings us to the notion of *communities of practice*. The development of new technologies can be seen as a process that is situated within a context of use, with actors shaping and also being shaped by the possibilities of technological characteristics. This is clearly illustrated in the work of Bijker *et al*. An examination of their findings and concepts can add to this discussion.

Technology's social dimension: the example of the bicycle

It is very difficult to assess today what current IT developments imply for the future. Making predictions, and hence establishing actions and strategies based exclusively on technological characteristics, can be a hazardous way to progress. This does not mean, however, that we should sit around waiting to see what happens. Much can be learned from recognizing the nature of technology development. This process can be understood not only as a 'technology' story, but also as an inherent social negotiation and construction process.

It would be a mistake to look at IT developments and their impact only from a technical or rational point of view. Technological developments can follow strange patterns. Our PC keyboards still follow an Azerty or Querty logic designed specifically to *avoid* fast typing, which jammed the keys and levers in the first typewriters. Designs for improving both speed and accuracy have been developed during the intervening years, but none has succeeded in replacing the 'good old-fashioned' keyboard.[31] Closer to home, we only need to look at the case of Apple and Microsoft. In the 1980s, Apple was already offering the devices that made user-friendliness a reality and allowed intuitive manipulation of the PC functions.

These features were only offered by Microsoft with the release of Windows 95, but it is Microsoft that has emerged as one of the biggest success stories of the last decades.

Introducing the social dimension will bring us to a view of technology development that is richer because it takes into account the concept of social practice and user groups. Including this social dimension will create a greater generative potential in terms of action strategies regarding individual roles and positioning in the evolving stream of events. However, it will not always lead to clear-cut answers, as technology is not the only consideration. This will be illustrated later on, when we develop the notion of virtual communities. However, before we start looking at possible action strategies, let us first examine what we mean when we describe technological development as a social negotiation and construction process. We will do this by going back to the end of the nineteenth century, when bicycles were the 'hottest' thing around.[32]

Bijker[33] reconstructs the development of the bicycle by tracing it back to the earliest known drawings of a bicycle, made by a pupil of Leonardo da Vinci. (Exhibit 17.2 covers the historical analysis in greater detail.) In this account of the development process it becomes clear that technological characteristics are not the only drivers of the use and the evolution of the bicycle. First came the low-wheeled ancestors, then the appearance of high-front-wheeled vehicles and the final stabilization of, once again, low-wheeled bicycles. How can we explain this evolution process?

A first element to be taken into account is the notion of relevant social groups. Relevant groups can be initial users, producers, non-users, or 'would-be' users. In the history of the bicycle, the initial users were young, healthy, upper-class sportsmen. The first vehicles had no cranks or pedals but were propelled by the feet pushing the ground, which, given the average road conditions, had some severe safety drawbacks and posed some serious problems for one's shoes. The initial users were interested in the first bicycles as an elegant pastime which could be exploited to impress the ladies with their athletic prowess. This group was especially interested in speed, so producers made the bicycle faster by increasing the size of the front wheel. The high front wheel also situated the driver above his fellow citizens, which was another part of the thrill for this social group. Safety was not a primary concern, since mastering such a high-risk piece of machinery was a challenge in the first place. However, other people started to notice the new technology and were affected by it, not least because the first cyclists were using the pavement and not the road. Exhibit 17.2 contains some references to colourful discussions around issues such as safety, women's dress and price.

What is striking here is that the same piece of machinery was perceived differently by different social groups. Different groups held different views on what the bicycle meant, its use, and its problems and possible solutions. As a result, there was no single unambiguous view on what the bicycle was. The aspects of speed, safety, dress and the like were seen and experienced differently by sport cyclists, touring cyclists, elderly men and women.

As Bijker states, this condition can be referred to as '*interpretative flexibility around the technical artefact*', i.e. the bicycle. Problems and solutions were seen and experienced differently depending on the viewpoint, situation and context of use. This interpretative flexibility around the same technical device is central to the social construction and negotiation process. In consecutive steps, opinions are articulated, actions undertaken and adaptations to the technical design are worked out and examined by the different groups. Producers try to create a 'dominant' design by announcing and promoting the one best vehicle they have produced. The design of the bicycle ultimately stabilized, as did its use among various social groups.

Finally, the *closure* and *stabilization* stage occurred. The introduction of the air tyre created closure and stabilization for the bicycle. The air tyre was conceived as a solution for the vibration problem, and thus was only relevant for the users of the low-wheeled bicycle. For the group of sporting cyclists using high-wheelers, vibration was an inherent part of the game and not seen as a problem. However, when the new tyre's implications for speed became apparent, the perceptions of sporting cyclists started to change. The whole issue of air tyres was redefined in such a way that it solved the problems of several social groups. Sportsmen were pleased with the high speed, and the broader public was pleased with the anti-vibration solution. This eliminated the safe low-wheeled bicycle's most serious drawback.

It is clear that during this social process, consensus was realized at a certain point. This closure led to a decrease in interpretative flexibility. In addition, consensus among the different relevant social groups about the dominant meaning and uses of the technology emerged. Closure mechanisms can be *rhetorical* (by claiming that one has the perfect solution or by massive promotion and advertising, although in the case of the bicycle this was not quite successful), or can take the form of a *redefinition* of the problem (as was the case here). Different groups could thus take advantage of the same technological solution. Power will also have an impact upon this social negotiation process. Once there is closure, it can be difficult to understand or even see the diversity that was present in the first stages.

What this tale teaches us is that we must not only take into account technological features, but that we should look at the different social groups involved, their use of the technology and the range of preferences, problems and solutions. This diversity of actors, preferences and problems will result in periods of 'interpretative flexibility' moving towards closure and stabilization through a complex social construction and negotiation process. It is risky to look only at the technology without taking into account the different players, their problems, preferences and their context of use. Just think of all the predictions made a decade ago about how with the introduction of computers and communication media, the 'paperless office' would put an end to the paper industry. There has never been so much paper around as there is today.

Perhaps within ten years people will wonder how it was possible during the 1980s (and even now) that people were producing text by means of a word processor (digital medium), then transmitting it by means of a fax (analogue medium), while at the other end of the fax machine the information coming through often was stored (read typed in again) using a computer. Another example that clarifies our argument can be found in today's banking industry. At the beginning of the 1980s, banks in Europe were exploring new distribution channels that had become available through the different IT developments. At the same time, the ATMs were developed, as were opportunities for home banking, telebanking and self-banking.

- *Home banking* requires some hardware at home, usually a terminal and a modem.
- With *telebanking*, the customers only need a telephone, albeit a digital one: they can interact by using the number keys to indicate commands, numbers of bank accounts, and amounts of money.

■ In *self-banking*, the customers access a (small) branch of the bank which has no personnel at all. However, it can be accessed at almost any hour of the day and the customers can perform all the operations they wish to by means of the available terminals.

What has happened with these different types of new information technology? Up to now, self-banking has proved to be the most successful in Belgium. However, only one of the major banks adopted this kind of distribution channel right from the start. Other banks misjudged their customers' preferences and the context of use. In the case of home banking, only a limited number of customers have a personal computer at home. Several banks miscalculated the speed with which users would pick up the new technologies and integrate them into their daily routines. In the case of telebanking, customers often feel insecure about typing in all the different numbers (which involve their own money) without getting any visible feedback on their accuracy. This immediate feedback can be received, even on paper, in the case of self-banking. Thus, although self-banking can be described as less convenient for customers (one has to go to the 'self-bank') and more expensive for the banks, it seems to best suit the concerns and habits of a majority of the customers today.

Exhibit 17.2

The development of the bicycle: a socio-technological tale[34]

'The bicycle: the awakening of a new era... Cyclisation: the era of the bicycle, that is the new time with richer, broader and more mobile civilisation ...[35]

The bicycle started off as 'prince of the parks'. Aristocratic young men drove high-wheeled bicycles in Hyde Park to show off to their lady friends in the 1870s and 1880s. The 'safety' bicycle, a low-wheeled vehicle with a diamond frame and a chain drive on the rear wheel (similar to the one we know today), did not emerge until the following decade. As Bijker illustrates, the bicycle's evolution shows an increase and subsequent decrease of the front-wheel diameter, beginning and ending at about 22 inches and reaching a peak at 50 inches.

All the technical elements needed to modify the very first bicycle – the so-called 'running machine' – into the bicycle we know today were available right from the start. Why did it take so long, and why did inventors and builders make this 'strange detour from the sure path of technological progress'? Bijker explains this evolution by demonstrating that it was not only a 'technical' story: it involved people – users as well as non-users – playing different roles and affecting

the chain of events related to the bicycle's development. In short, the evolution of the bicycle should be understood as a social construction process of technology. Here is what happened.

A pupil of Leonardo Da Vinci made a drawing of a bicycle as early as 1493, but the idea remained dormant until 1791, when eccentrics were observed riding in Parisian parks on something resembling an ancestor of the modern bicycle. This 'célirifère' was shaped like a wooden horse, had two wheels arranged in a line, and was pushed by the feet. The first steering mechanism was added in 1817 by Karl von Drais. The 'Draisienne', as his vehicle was called, was fast but was very demanding on shoes, and it remained difficult to steer. In 1839 Macmillan added cranks, driven by a back-and-forth motion, to the rear wheel, so that the feet could be raised off the ground. During the 1860s in France, Michaux added several improvements to the Draisienne and started to mass-produce this improved vehicle. His 'vélocipède' became a commercial success, although Michaux himself was not the first to either produce the vélocipède or invent its best features. His success was related to frequent minor improvements and an active promotion policy.

Exhibit 17.2 continued

The Franco-German war of 1870–1 halted the vélopicède's development in France and Germany, and the English took the lead. Rowley Turner, an agent in Paris for his uncle's company, Coventry Sewing Machine Company, brought a vélocipède back to Coventry and convinced his uncle to start manufacturing them.

It should be noted that the original vélocipède's wheels differed only slightly in size. When Starley and Hillman in England (working at that time for the Coventry Sewing Machine Company) patented the 'ariel' model in 1870, it reflected the trend of enlarging the front wheel. As the vélocipède had front-wheel cranks, this increased its speed. To promote their bicycle, Starley and Hillman made a memorable trip from London to Coventry, travelling 96 miles in a single day. This remarkable ride boosted the bicycle's image as a sport machine. Records were set and contested all over England, and track racing started on the continent as well. Cycling had always been seen as an athletic pursuit, since driving a Draisienne or vélocipède demanded both energy and acrobatic skills. As it was not easy to mount a high-wheeled bicycle, enlarging the front wheel only added to the challenge. Once seated, however, riding was experienced as pleasant and comfortable. The rider sat upright, high above the ground. Cycling had an element of showing off, but also was associated with progress and modern times.

The only social group actually riding bicycles at that time were young men, but this does not mean that other people had no opinion of the bicycle or influence upon its evolution. Anti-cycling sentiment escalated. One of the reasons was the satisfaction with which bicyclists elevated themselves above their fellow citizens. Their presence was also seen as a threat to pedestrians. Confrontations between bicyclists and pedestrians or coach drivers, frequently ending in insults, were commonplace.

Two problems remained. First, many people could not afford to buy a bicycle, and second, the safety problem was a barrier, especially for older people. The bicycle's design at that time implied a serious risk, as the centre of gravity was situated above the front wheel. Riders were prone to going head over heels after encountering a small obstacle like a stone or a hole in the road.

Women faced additional problems, typified by the following passage written in the *Münchner Zeitung* in 1900, reporting on a man and woman riding a two-seater bicycle:

'The numerous public walking in the Maximilian Strasse yesterday at noon witnessed an irritating spectacle that gave rise to much indignation… Unashamed, proud as an amazon, the graceful lady displayed herself to men's eyes. We ask: is this the newest form of bicycle sport? Is it possible that common decency is being hit in the face without punishment in this manner? Finally: is this the newest form of advertising for certain female persons? Where are the police?'

While this article reports on an unassuming low-wheeled two-seater in 1900, you can imagine the atmosphere in Victorian England two decades earlier. Some bicycle producers tried to solve the 'dress problem' by installing both pedals on one side of the bicycle and modifying the handlebars (making one longer than the other) so it could be 'side-ridden'. Other, less 'technical' solutions were tried and had greater success: changing the design of women's clothing led to new standards of fashion.

The safety problem was solved in several ways. One consisted of the invention of the tricycle, which had two front wheels. This also helped to solve the problem of women's dress, especially after Queen Victoria described the performance of a female tricyclist as 'really very graceful and one which by no stretch of the imagination could be termed unladylike'. The introduction of tricycles allowed women and older men to engage in cycling, and many proceeded to do so. This made bicycle producers acutely aware of other potential markets and they began to produce new and different bicycles in addition to the tricycles. Although it was easier to keep one's balance on a tricycle, it retained or even introduced several safety problems. Having three tracks made a tricycle more subject to the perils of the road. The lack of effective brakes (the rider had to 'reverse the action of the machine') also caused serious problems. Attempts to solve the safety problems consisted of efforts to improve the bicycle's basic design. This was mainly done by moving the saddle backward and modifying the size of the wheels. Other attempts included the replacement of the pedals with a lever mechanism, the introduction of gears, the addition of a chain drive linked only to the front wheel, and

▶

Exhibit 17.2 continued

even the reversing of the front and rear wheels, with the latter becoming the larger one.

In 1879, H. Lawson patented a bicycle more similar to the one we know with the drive, which included a chain, moved to the rear wheel. This machine, called the 'bicyclette', was promoted heavily but never became a commercial success, although many bicycle historians describe the bicyclette as 'ahead of its time'. As it still had a larger front wheel, it was perceived as 'grotesque' and compared with a crocodile because of its elongated frame. Starley, a nephew of the pioneer of the same name, was more successful in 1884. Together with his partner, Sutton, he launched the 'Rover', which had 36-inch front and rear wheels and a chain drive to the rear wheel. Sales started to boom when the Rover started beating records and winning races.

In 1888, it was written that:

'no radical changes have been made in the construction of cycles during the past year, and the tendency is to settle down to three types of machines: the ordinary bicycle [which at that time had a larger front wheel], the rear driven safety bicycle [like the "Rover"] and the direct front-steering tricycle.'[36]

However, before the end of that year, Dunlop had patented[37] his air tyre and applied it immediately to the design of his own bicycle. Although the text of the patent stressed its anti-vibration effects, in practice the air tire also considerably increased a bicycle's speed. Pneumatic tyres won races, and thus commercial production of air tyres for bicycles began. The first tyres were very expensive (a quarter of the cost of an entire bicycle or tricycle), easily punctured, and made cyclists vulnerable to side-slipping. However, the air tyre's success on racetracks was enormous, and within a year, no serious racing man bothered to compete on anything else.

Thus the 'safety' bicycle was born. It combined safety with speed, while the dominant design up till that time was fast, due to its large front wheel, but not at all safe. Improvements in the following years included solving the problems of the chain drive by constructing effective chain casings, an agreement on the best kind of foot motion (up-and-down *versus* rotary), and the emergence of the diamond frame. A period of closure and stabilization around the new dominant design started and the large-front-wheel bicycle faded very quickly into obscurity.

ACTION STRATEGIES FOR THE NEW MEDIA

So far we have explored recent IT developments and have seen that value creation is more and more a question of working with information – gathering, organizing, selecting, synthesizing and distributing information. This creation process assumes a thorough knowledge of the 'real' world. Opportunities for new service offerings can be found here. A second argument is related to the suitability of the recent IT developments for managing the service delivery process. We suggested that the relevance of virtual value creation will vary depending on the type of services. However, it is important to note that what eventually will happen depends on the actions of customers, producers, and authorities. Even the implementation of 'hard' technology is embedded in a social negotiation and construction process.

We can now start thinking about action strategies. These can be divided into those which mirror action strategies already existing in the 'physical' world, and those that are specific to the new technology available. In the latter case, virtual value creation will be essential; the new technology and media will be used to develop new forms of interaction with the customer resulting in 'new' services as new forms of co-ordination and co-production come into place. For example, in the case of the use of network computing for providing 'distant shopping' services (whereby the customer can choose what he or she wants to buy from home instead of going to the supermarket), supermarkets are experimenting with screens where the customer can 'virtually' walk through the store. However, this leads to time lost in front of the screen. An alternative approach involves the customer asking directly what he or she is looking for. Helping the customer to make choices and providing different kinds of advice, recipes and so on, mean that a whole new form of shopping becomes possible for supermarkets.

We shall discuss action strategies that explore new 'virtual' ways of creating value. These involve new forms of distribution, often based on the idea of bundling or unbundling services into their components, and the development of learning relationships. We will argue that all these 'new' concepts and approaches will only work as long as they are able to create value which is also perceived as such. And while this might sound like stating the obvious, the impression remains that especially as far as Internet initiatives are concerned, the value equation has been out of balance, i.e. much more has been spent than can be justified by the resulting value creation afterwards. Hence we will devote specific attention to approaches which restore the balance in this respect. And here, the 'old' knowledge we already have about developing a relevant market approach will turn out to be extremely important. In fact, the idea of segmenting and targeting (and branding), pointed out in the discussion of the service concept in Chapter 2, remains as relevant as ever. So we will start with a brief discussion of these strategies.

Segmenting and targeting

Segmenting has many advantages, and targeting even more. By targeting a specific segment, a company can upgrade the level of service offered to the customer. The smaller the segment, the more customized the market approach to the customers in that specific segment can and to an extent must be. Very small and well-defined market segments, known as *hypersegments*, offer the advantage of treating the customer on a very personal basis. However, targeting a very small segment by definition means offering a product or service to a small number of customers, implying that there is not a lot of money to be made. IT can help solve this problem. Very small local (hyper)segments are becoming large global segments. For example, one major financial corporation in the US has set up a banking service targeted at women in the process of divorce, offering a number of services directed to their specific needs. Offering this banking service in one local area would never be affordable, but if they can offer this service on the Internet, they can deliver it throughout the entire country.

Branding

A brand can be defined as:

> *'a name, term, sign, symbol or design, or a combination of them, which is intended to identify the goods or services of one seller or group of sellers and to differentiate them from those of competitors.'*[38]

Branding will become more important as the amount of information around us increases. Customers drowning in information will develop a tendency to choose speed, convenience and/or easy accessibility, which for many will mean choosing the provider they know or have already heard of. Established brands will thus have a certain advantage with regard to the new media. Furthermore, branding will take away some of the customer's inherent uncertainty about an offer or service provider. As we look for news or current affairs on the Internet, we shall end up at the CNN site, since it is known for providing information and news services. However, this advantage should not be seen as absolute. In the end, the services provided by means of the new media will make the difference. Also, branding is an essential cornerstone when it comes down to develop trust between service providers and customers. Finally, an important point here relates to extending the idea of branding towards the new media. For example, creating an attractive Internet site will entice certain groups of 'surfers' to regularly check out the site. People will log on not only because of the product or service offerings, but also to experience the site in and of itself.

Developing learning relationships[39]

A company aspiring to give its customers exactly what they want must look at the world through new eyes. It must use technology to assume two roles: a mass customizer that efficiently provides customized goods and services, and a one-to-one marketer that elicits information from each customer about his or her specific needs and preferences. These two concepts bring producer and customer together in what we call *a learning relationship*. This is a relationship that becomes more responsive over time as the two parties interact with each other, collaborating to meet the consumer's needs.

In learning relationships, individual customers teach the company more and more about their preferences and needs, giving the company an enormous competitive advantage. The more customers teach the company, the better it becomes at providing exactly what they want in the way they want it, and the more difficult it will be for a competitor to entice them away. Even if a competitor were to have precisely the same capabilities, a customer already involved in a learning relationship with the first company would have to spend an inordinate amount of time and energy teaching the competitor what the company already knows. A company that can cultivate learning relationships with its customers should be able to retain their business virtually forever.

Learning relationships is not the same as database marketing. Mass marketers use information technology to define the most likely buyers of the products they sell. For the most part, the information comes from simple transactional records and public information compiled by specialist firms. The mass marketer generates a list, based upon this data, of the most likely prospects and solicits them with offers or messages. Companies only guessing at the tastes of potential customers often flood them with information. By contrast, the one-to-one marketer conducts a dialogue with each customer, one at a time, and uses the increasingly detailed feedback to find the best products or services for that customer. Bank of America offers the 'Build Your Own Bank' feature to its customers on the Internet. Customers can develop their own bank site tailored to their specific needs. They do not need to go through all the data and features on the BofA Website; they receive only what they are interested in.

Although many companies are moving toward this model, few have fully implemented it or combined it with mass customization.

Bundling or unbundling products and services

'Product bundling is used in almost every industry, but frequently it is not part of a specific and intentional strategy. Unfortunately, failing to consider bundling as a strategic marketing variable may unnecessarily reduce the performance of the firm.'[40]

The electronic travel desk is a service delivered via the Internet where businessmen can make reservations for business trips. Not only does the travel desk reserve the airplane tickets, but through the travel desk menus you can reserve your hotel room, rental car and concert tickets, and indicate that you are a vegetarian so that you are given appropriate meals. Bundling products and services in the travel industry can go even further. If you are interested in going on an adventurous holiday, this 'extended' service can mean that the travel agency decides where you should go, makes reservations for the different hotels, flights, water-ski and/or rafting facilities, and even buys appropriate vacation clothes for you.

By bundling products and services, you upgrade the level of delivered service, but you downgrade the level of possibilities for the customer to choose from. Interactive media are ideal not just for offering the customer a broad array of possibilities, but also for knowing ahead of time which possibilities the customer might want; as such, *tailor-made bundling* (and hence *un-bundling*) becomes a possibility for many services, as the Bank Of America example above clearly illustrates.

New forms of distribution

With the rapid growth of interactive media, consumers are being offered a broad range of possibilities for buying products or services. As we have already seen, an increasing number of different forms of distribution channels are offering a wide range of products to the customer.

Distributors, traditionally, fulfil different functions for their customers:

- bridging the distance between producer and consumer;
- setting the time of delivery;
- adjusting the form of the product;
- setting quantity;
- offering assortment;
- providing information;
- post-sales activities;
- the sale itself.

Many of the functions cited above can be provided in a market space rather than a marketplace. The question is whether the retailer or the producer will carry them out. Consider, for instance, home delivery, which bridges the distance gap as well as the time gap. Three principal parties can deliver this service: the retailer ready to change his processes, the producer who eliminates links in the value chain, or a third party who specializes in distribution. Hence, what can be expected in the near future is the emergence of new value configurations, whereby providing relevant information to customers will be an important competitive issue.

Providing information by means of the market space is in one way the easiest, and in another way the most difficult function to achieve. Providing advice via electronic media is probably better and more efficient in the eyes of the consumer, who wants the locus of control. However, electronic media can only deliver to two of our senses, which eliminates smelling, feeling and tasting from the selection process. For certain customers, this might lead to a dual use of both place and space: a pre-selection of possible deliverers of services or products is made via electronic media, and the selection of the final supplier can take place in the 'real' world.

Avoiding the commodity magnet: Value, value, value

As became clear above, there is a danger that companies will not meet the expectations put forward when drawing up their Internet deployment action plans. And although the number of customers ready to engage in certain web enabled service transactions has been overestimated in several cases, it seems that the most common mistake lies in a phenomenon called 'commoditizing'. Figure 17.5 depicts products or services on two axes: price, i.e. a reflection of the value of a certain service given prevailing market circumstances, and 'cost to serve', which relates to the amount and costs of the actual resources an organization needs to deliver the service at hand.

The commodity magnet, a concept advanced by Rangan and Bowman,[41] reflects the idea that forces are pulling 'high value, high cost' services away towards areas in which the cost to serve actually exceeds the market prices asked for. Such forces include competition, the presence of demanding customers who are unwilling to pay for additional services and options and the presence of low/no cost alternatives provided by competitors. The Internet has been particularly guilty of flirting with so-called 'new economic laws' which in the end turned out to be a form of wishful thinking.[42] On a company level, at certain points this 'new economics' implied an almost complete absence of attention to metrics that actually assessed the value creation of companies, like profit. Instead growth, especially in terms of the customer base, became emphasized. Recall the famous quote by Jeff Bezos, CEO of Amazon, who only a few years ago claimed that if 'Amazon were profitable anywhere in the near future, it would be purely accidental'. This one-sided emphasis on growth metrics, as opposed to value creating indicators, surely contributed to fuel the growth of the 'magnet'. And while selling at prices below the 'cost to serve'

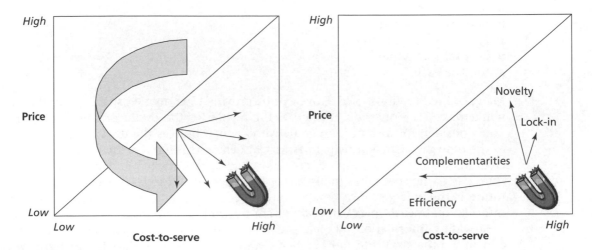

Figure 17.5 The commodity magnet and how to handle it

threshold makes sense for a certain phase of growth,[43] it is clear that in the longer run someone needs to pay for the service delivered. And it is exactly this longer perspective, which includes considering the resources required to accomplish this 'skimming strategy' successfully that seems to be absent. Companies made huge investments in back-office infrastructure, personalization software and the like without addressing the value equation: who is willing to pay what for what kind of services? Instead, services were offered for free, based on the premise that one should grab customers first and once this was accomplished, thinking about revenues and margins could start; 'the "lock in customers first, ask questions later" premise'. Thus, and this will come as no surprise at this stage, value creation should be a central idea not only when defining and designing the service concept (*see* Chapter 2), but also when considering the use of Internet technology within your service delivery system. And there is some good news in this respect: value creation through deploying Internet technology is indeed feasible. Recently, Amit and Zott pointed out four ways to create 'e-value'.[44] They arrived at these four models by analysing actual practices that are profitable today! These four ways relate to enhanced levels of efficiency; bundling resulting in superior value, increasing customer retention and finally the production of novelty. Efficiency, the first strategy, is straightforward; to the extent that Internet technology results in efficiency enhancements relative to offline business (or other on-line initiatives), it will flourish. Efficiency can be obtained by customers because they experience improved search and bargaining processes; but also service providers can achieve considerable savings. Low-cost airlines such as Virgin Express and Ryan Air rely heavily on the Internet to sell tickets for exactly these reasons. The case of Cisco is well known in the business-to-business environment; by installing an extranet which connects 32 suppliers, Cisco was able to redeploy 50 agents who had been busy in the past collecting information on components. Moreover, Cisco is now able to make in hours supply chain decisions which took almost a week in the past.[45]

We already discussed the idea of bundling; let us add here the idea that bundling does not limit itself to on-line offerings alone. One can easily define packages that combine elements of the market space with marketplace ingredients, like ordering on-line while picking up goods at a physical store. Likewise newspapers and magazines are starting to offer bundles of subscriptions for printed copies with on-line access and services. Increasing customer retention implies finding ways to motivate customers to engage in repeat transactions and/or to improve their associations. The most obvious way to enhance customer retention takes on the form of introducing special bonuses for repeat purchases. The familiarity with the interface of a website may also contribute to retention. Using a certain interface implies learning, and once this has begun, it creates incentives to continue the interaction, especially if the savings in doing so are considerable. For instance, once all your shipping and payment details have been entered into a certain shopping site, you will tend to check there first. Needless to say, this type of lock-in behaviour is only interesting in so far as opportunities for customizing and personalizing are actually being exploited in a mutual beneficial way. Finally, novelty can be traced back to the third stage discussed earlier in this chapter, that of virtual value creation. Here one tries to create value by offering complete new services which would not be feasible without Internet technology; examples include the 'reverse markets' introduced by Priceline.com; or the customer-to-customer auction formula introduced by E-bay which allowed to successfully auction low-value items successfully.

CONCLUSION

In this chapter we started off with a brief overview of technological developments related to the emergence of network computing. We then looked at what can be described as the transition from marketplace to market space, as more and more services are delivered by means of electronic media. As a first step, we discussed the particularities of this virtual value chain; handling and combining information in new ways is crucial. That this transition is not as general as one is sometimes led to believe became clear when we discussed the driving forces that influence the extent and speed with which this transition is taking place. Customer preferences and behaviour, cost considerations on the part of service provider, and finally the nature of the service process all play their part here. To clarify the role the nature of the service process plays in this respect, we introduced some insights on information richness. Here it became clear that maintenance-interactive services will be affected to a larger extent than task- and personal-interactive services. We also argued that the social side of technology development and diffusion processes should also be acknowledged. Finally, we sketched some relevant action strategies that could be deployed when companies are starting to move in the direction of virtual transactions.

Review and discussion questions

- It is clear that certain business models actually do work on the Internet and that there are even companies who make a profit using them. Notable examples include E-bay (auctioning) and Yahoo (portal/e-media). Amazon.com (e-tailing) has also reported operating profits recently. Can you come up with other profitable companies that rely heavily on Internet technology? What makes them distinctive? How do they avoid the 'commodity magnet'? To what extent do these companies combine the market space with the market place?

- Sceptics might argue that e-commerce will never be more than a phenomenon like mail order sales, appealing to certain segments of the market, but all in all a modest phenomenon. Would you agree? Why and/or in which cases?

- Some futurologists indicate that what is happening now on the Internet is just the beginning of the 'digital age'; within a couple of decades, we will be surrounded by 'ambient intelligence' and ubiquitous computing will make the way we work and live today as very much 'outdated'? Would you agree with such viewpoints? What kind of technologies would be needed? And how would it alter human behaviour specifically? Why?

Notes and references

1 *The Economics of a Technology-Based service Sector*. NIST Report prepared by TASC, Inc., January 1998.

2 Within every computer application or program, one can always make a distinction between three different 'logics': presentation, application and data. Presentation logic involves all

'dialogue' features and codes that allow for interaction between machine and user: the user interface. Think about all the screens you have seen passing when entering data into a certain program; you were interfacing with the presentation 'logic'. With application logic the build-in intelligence of a program is referred to; all 'algorithms' that make computations or transactions within a particular program possible. Data logic finally refers to all codes applied to handle and manage the data used within the program.

3 The network era has become possible because certain discrete developments started to combine. There is increasing compatibility among the main players in the field, especially with regard to interfacing issues. Bandwidth is expanding and more and more actors are becoming linked by integrating the development of networks with new and complementary developments in the fields of processors, security technologies and the like.

4 Hyper Text Mark-up Language.

5 Likewise, the more recent XML, Extensible Markup Language, is an open standard that allows to extend the use of 'tags' so that content and form can become transmitted in a much more refined way.

6 *The Economist*, August 19, 2000.

7 Notice, however, that this figure varies heavily from industry to industry; the online share in 1999 for toys amounted to less than 0.5% (US & Europe), and for travel varied between 0.5% (Europe) and 1.5% (US), but the online share for services like financial brokerage amounted to over 14% (US) and 5% (Europe). Likewise, online shares for computer hardware and software went to nearly 10% (US). *Source*: 'First America, then the world. E-Trends', *The Economist*, 2001.

8 Armstrong, A. and Hagel, J. (1996) The real value of on-line communities, *Harvard Business Review*, Vol 74, No 3, 134.

9 Of course, using electronic catalogues has advantages as well. One can bring different products to the attention of customers in a customized manner, while at the same time other items of interest can be pointed out. This can be done by preferences expressed by customers themselves, or derived from analysing purchasing behaviour of other customers.

10 Look at, for example, 'Digital Rights Management' systems. Several of them imply some kind of 'box' which contains both the content (e.g. a software package or music) and the rights you have acquired on this content (e.g. installing it once, or playing it endlessly). In order to actually enjoy the use of the content, consumers need specific software that allows decoding. Few customers are willing to install such systems, especially when the same content can be acquired relatively easy by walking a different route.

11 Just imagine introducing cars on the market with as many 'bugs' as software packages include upon launch.

12 *See* Figure 5.5 as discussed within the chapter on promotion.

13 *See* www.software.ibm.com/eb/schwab:schwab-fullstory.html.

14 Whereby big professional customers dealing with full-service firms would get discounted prices.

15 'Turning digits into dollars, a survey of technology in France', *The Economist*, 26 Oct., 1996.

16 Rayport, J. F. and Sviokla, J. V. (1994) 'Managing in the market space', *Harvard Business Review*, 141–50.

17 Rayport, J. F. and Sviokla, J. V. (1995) 'Exploiting the virtual value chain', *Harvard Business Review*, Nov.–Dec.

18 *See* Rayport, J. F. and Sviokla, J. V. (1994), op. cit.

19 The newspaper provides us with an example: here the information (content) can be consumed by reading it at home, or at the office (context), and is delivered via a complex infrastructure, involving typesetting, printing, distribution, and so forth.

[20] Rayport, J. F. and Sviokla, J. V. (1995), op. cit.

[21] Moore, C. (1996) 'Disintermediation: Communications technologies are having some impact', *Dataquest*, June.

[22] For some people less free time tends to be the case, for others free time becomes the rule (e.g. the elderly).

[23] McKenna, R. (1995) Real-Time Marketing, *Harvard Business Review*, Vol 73, No 4, 87–95.

[24] Still one has to realize that adaptation will not happen overnight. In this respect, the well-known distinction between innovators (about 2.5% of the market), early adopters (13.5%), early majority (34%), late majority (34%) and laggards (16%) as developed by Rogers in the 1960s can be kept in mind: it takes time to get the majority of customers to make the shift.

[25] Here cost considerations should be matched with the customers' perceptions of value; *see also* Chapter 8 on pricing. However, as a service provider, every sound policy starts with a clear insight on the cost structure of the activities contained in each service transactions.

[26] For a full discussion of this service classification, *see* Mills, P. and Margulies, N. (1980) 'Towards a core typology of service organisations', *Academy of Management Review*, Vol 5, No 2, 255–65.

[27] Leading authors here were Daft, R. H. and Lengel, R. H. (1986) 'Organisational information requirements, media richness and structural design', *Management Science*, Vol 32, No 5, 554–71.

[28] Galbraith, J. (1977) *Organisational Design*. London: Addison-Wesley.

[29] *See* Huber, G. P. and Daft, R. H. (1987) 'The information environments of organisations', in Jablin, F., Putnam, L., Roberts, H. and Porter, L. (eds) *Handbook of Organisational Communication: An interdisciplinary perspective*. Newbury Park: Sage Publications, pp. 135–48.

[30] *See* for a more extended discussion Lee, A. (1995) 'Electronic mail as a medium for rich communication; an empirical investigation using hermeneutic interpretation', *MIS Quarterly*, June, 143–57; and Markus, M. L. (1994) 'Electronic mail as the medium of managerial change', *Organisation Science*, Vol 5, No 4, 502–27.

[31] For an account on the historical developments here, *see* David, P. (1985) 'Clio and the economics of Qwerty', *Economic History*, Vol 75, 227–32. The original Qwerty and Azerty formats were developed so that typing would not go too fast as this might lead the mechanical devices to run into trouble. Despite the change from mechanical to electronic technology, more efficient formats have not been able to replace the Qwerty and Azerty formats.

[32] The following illustration is adapted from the work of Pinch, T. and Bijker, W. For a complete overview of this view on technology development, *see* Pinch, T. and Bijker, W. (1987) 'The social construction of facts and artefacts: or how the sociology of science and the sociology of technology might benefit each other', in Bijker, W., Hughes, T. and Pinch, T. (eds) *The Social Construction of Technological Systems*, MIT Press; and Bijker, W. E. (1995) *Of Bicycles, Bakelites and Bulbs*. Cambridge, MA: MIT Press.

[33] *See* Bijker (1995, 1987), op. cit.

[34] This tale is based on the extensive descriptions as given by Bijker. Interested readers can find the 'full' story as well as an extensive discussion of the development process of bakelite and bulbs in Bijker, W. (1995), op. cit.

[35] Ibid. p. 40.

[36] *Engineer* (1888) in Bijker, W. (1995), op. cit.

[37] In 1845 in fact William Thomson had already patented a form of air tyre. They were used on carriages at that time but never became a success, as they were expensive and other anti-vibration alternatives were available. However, it meant that Dunlop's patent was invalid, as he was informed in 1890. Using complementary patents, Dunlop and his company prospered after all.

[38] Kotler, P. (1983) *Principles of Marketing* (2nd edn). Englewood Cliffs, NJ: Prentice-Hall.

[39] Pine II, B. J., Peppers, D. and Rogers, M. (1995) 'Do you want to keep your customers forever?', *Harvard Business Review*, Mar./Apr., 103–14.

[40] Paun, D. (1993) 'When to bundle or unbundle products', *Industrial Marketing Management*, Vol 22, 29–34.

[41] Ranga, V. K. and Bowman, G. (1992) 'Beating the commodity market', *Industrial Marketing Management*, Vol 21, No 3, 215–24.

[42] Whether or not 'new' economic laws prevail in the information or knowledge society remains a highly-debated issue. The authors of this chapter are doubtful. For a recent overview of the debate, see for instance 'New Economy? What's left?' Special Report, *The Economist*, May 2001.

[43] *See* Chapter 6 on pricing strategies for new products/services.

[44] Amit, R. and Zott, C. (2001) 'Value creation in e-business', *Strategic Management Journal*, Vol 22, 493–520.

[45] *See* 'Trying to connect You: A supply side revolution'. *The Economist*, E-trends (2001).

Suggested further reading

Amit, R. and Zott, C. (2001) 'Value creation in E-business', *Strategic Management Journal*, Vol 22, 493–520. This article discusses in depth a variety of strategies one can deploy to use Internet technology in a sustainable way.

Rayport, J. F. and Sviokla, J. V. (1994) 'Managing in the market space', *Harvard Business Review*, Vol 72, No 6, 141–50.

Rayport, J. F. and Sviokla, J. V. (1995) 'Exploiting the virtual value chain', *Harvard Business Review*, Vol 73, No 6, Nov–Dec.

These articles provide an excellent overview of what the market space implies.

Daft, R. H. and Lengel, R. H. (1986) 'Organisational information requirements, media richness and structural design', *Management Science*, Vol 32, No 5, 554–71.

Markus, M. L. (1994) 'Electronic mail as the medium of managerial change', *Organisation Science*, Vol 5, No 4, 502–27.

People interested in information richness theory and its (social) extensions are advised to read these two works.

Bijker, W. E. (1995) *Of Bicycles, Bakelites and Bulbs*. Cambridge, MA: MIT Press.

We highly recommend this work on the, often neglected, social side of technology development.

Pinch, T. and Bijker, W. (1987) 'The social construction of facts and artefacts: or how the sociology of science and the sociology of technology might benefit each other', in Bijker, W. E., Hughes, T. and Pinch, T. *The Social Construction of Technological Systems*. Cambridge, MA: MIT Press.

An integrated approach

Roland Van Dierdonck · Paul Gemmel · Bart Van Looy

In Part Five we address issues of a more integrated nature: How can you set up an integrated performance measurement system that allows you to achieve the defined service concept? What is crucial to bear in mind when rejuvenating the service concept (i.e. innovation) or when extending it beyond cultural boundaries (i.e. internationalization)? Finally, we discuss in depth the notion of service strategy, which is the starting point of it all. As such, the goal of this final part is to return to practice and apply some of the insights gained through reading this book.

Dynamic changes in the environment and heterogeneity in the service delivery process continuously confront service firms with the danger of losing focus. Therefore, it is important to define a clear service concept as described in Chapter 2. However, defining a service concept is only one part of the story. Making sure that the employees in the organization underwrite and sustain the service concept is the other (more difficult) part. A fundamental requirement for actualizing the service concept is the design and implementation of a performance measurement system. If a performance measurement system can guide the organization in the right direction, equally it can misguide it to the same extent when the performance measures chosen are not aligned with the service concept. Because of its far-reaching implications, the first chapter of Part Five (Chapter 18) concentrates on the design and implementation of such performance measurement systems.

An important 'booby trap' to avoid in the service concept by means of a performance measurement system, is sole reliance on financial performance measures. Throughout the book we have repeatedly stressed that financial performance is simply the consequence of the satisfaction and loyalty of both employees and customers, which are in turn intertwined with the design of the services delivery system. In Chapter 18 we shall sketch the outlines of a service-specific performance measurement system that acknowledges these dynamic relationships. Since attention to the implementation process is equally vital, we shall focus on important issues in this area too.

However, no single-service concept is made to last forever, thus in Chapter 19 we discuss the process of rejuvenating services or innovation. Here we introduce the concept of value constellation in order to place the customers and the solutions to their problems at the heart of the innovation process. While this seems to be the most natural approach, it implies a shift from strict, linear processes of innovation towards more iterative and broader views of the innovation process. In addition, we discuss specific points of attention related to managing and anchoring the innovation process within the service firm.

Another aspect which might contribute to the long-term survival of service firms is their ability and willingness to work internationally. In Chapter 20, we describe in more detail the impetus towards internationalization as well as the things service firms need to bear in mind when developing an international strategy. It will come as no surprise that such basic characteristics of services such as intangibility and simultaneity play a crucial role here.

In the last chapter, we discuss the notion of service strategy as a coalescing framework, linking operations, human resources, and marketing to the service concept. While the more traditionally oriented approaches provide us with meaningful insights for developing a service strategy, the more recent competence-based approaches seem to be especially valuable for looking at the particular strategic challenges faced by service firms today: the need for tangibility, the use of intangible resources in creating and sustaining competitive advantage, mastering the dynamics of value creation and value perception in delivering services, using technology, and managing continuity in creating competitive advantage in time and space.

We could not think of a more fitting chapter to end this book: translating the insights presented here into daily practice starts with the question of what you want to be on the market, which means defining a service strategy, including an appropriate service concept. Only then can you start designing an adequate operational system (Part 4), creating the right atmosphere and approach towards employees (Part 3) and establishing loyal relationships with customers (Part 2), taking into account the specific nature of services (Part 1). We hope reading this book is helpful in getting it right in practice; a task as complex as designing the appropriate service strategy.

CHAPTER 18

Performance measurement systems in service firms

Paul Gemmel · Kurt Verweire · Gino Van Ossel · Werner Bruggeman
Roland Van Dierdonck · Bart Van Looy

INTRODUCTION

Today, organizations are competing in complex and rapidly changing environments, which makes an accurate understanding of their goals and the methods for attaining those goals critical to their survival. To ensure that the organization moves in the direction of the proposed goals – i.e. realizing its service concept – a performance measurement and reporting system must be developed. Such a system plays an important role in motivating managers to take actions that are in line with the organizations strategy and that further its goal. The performance measurement and reporting system quantifies the degree to which managers achieve their objectives and it is the basis of the reward system. As a result, the measurement system has a significant impact on management behaviour. It is also an important communication tool about those goals and how to achieve them. It is said that 'you get what you measure'.[1]

Obviously, the measurement of performance is only a means to an end – the enhancement of organizational performance. This enhancement is only possible when the performance measures and the service concept are closely linked. Aligning performance measures with the service concept is extremely important in service organizations because of the danger of losing focus. Without a good insight into the service concept, the customer can build up expectations and ultimately demand a service delivery which does not fit the service concept. This may encourage service workers to disregard this concept. In the same way, when the internal service worker does not know what the goals are, divergence in behaviour – for instance, between back office and front office – is highly probable. Performance measurement and control is part of strategic performance management and is a crucial tool for helping the organization to keep focused.

While it is clear that performance measurement is important in services, its success depends totally on the way that the measurement system is designed and how it is implemented. In the first part of this chapter we will argue that an integrated and balanced approach is necessary in designing a performance measurement system. Then we will look at some service-specific aspects of performance measurement. We will go on to show how a performance measurement system as part of performance management must be implemented if the service concept is to be achieved.

Objectives

By the end of this chapter, you should be able to discuss:

■ the design of a performance measurement system and its alignment with the strategy, goals and the service concept

■ the need for a 'balanced' performance measurement system – that is, one that includes measures on several performance areas

■ the use of the balanced scorecard and the European Foundation for Quality Management Excellence model as a starting point for the design of a performance measurement system

■ the importance of customers, employees and processes as the performances areas which are particularly relevant for the service firm

■ the significance of throughput time, quality and productivity as the most important process measures

■ the steps involved in implementing a performance measurement system

DESIGNING PERFORMANCE MEASUREMENT SYSTEMS FOR SERVICES

In many organizations, the performance measurement system discourages managers and employees from taking actions in the desired strategic direction. Sometimes, the measurement system points them in the wrong direction. Consider, for instance, the example of a service company where the key message of the service strategy is quality and customer satisfaction, but the performance report focuses only on costs. As a result, employees focus on improving productivity in order to reduce costs, neglecting the possible negative consequences on the quality of the service delivered. It is said that such a performance report is *not aligned with the service concept*.

The starting point in designing integrated performance measurement systems is therefore the definition of the service concept (*see* Chapter 2). The service concept is a formulation of the fundamental reason for the existence of a service firm, and thus goals must be defined in line with this concept. The definition of the service concept does not guarantee that the service concept is being successfully implemented. Many companies do not even know if they do what they intend to do. A company striving to become the world leader should report on a regular basis the degree to which the company is actually becoming a world leader. An organization intending to delight its customers should measure and report the level of customer delight.

Far too many organizations lack performance measurements that are anchored within the service concept and goals. They rely too heavily or – even worse – exclusively on financial figures to measure how well they are doing. There are many reasons for this. Companies listed at the stock exchange are judged by their quarterly financial results. However, unlisted organizations also consider profit and/or financial stability to be their main objective, and therefore their management control system emphasizes financial measures. Moreover, it is much easier to measure the financial situation than the more qualitative degree of employee satisfaction. However, relying on financial measures to manage an organization is like steering one's car by using only the rear mirror. Indeed, while today's financial results are the result of yesterday's performance, they are a poor indicator of tomorrow's success.[2]

The performance measurement system should be capable of giving advance warning of potential financial decline. Remember the basic idea behind the service profit chain: employee satisfaction drives customer satisfaction which ultimately influences financial performance. Non-financial figures, such as employee satisfaction and customer satisfaction, will not only give a company additional information regarding its performance but may also present it with a warning light of a possible financial decline. This way, preventative actions can be taken – something which would not be possible if only financial performance were to be considered. We therefore need measurement systems that give a more balanced view of performance. An important question here is which performance measures need to be included in a scorecard in order for it to be 'balanced'. Some inspiring general frameworks can be used as a starting point to design a balanced performance measurement system. In the next section, we will discuss two frequently used models which reflect an integrated and balanced view – namely, the *balanced scorecard* and the *European Foundation for Quality Management's (EFQM) Excellence model*.

These two models are designed in general terms, however: they do not always reflect the specific issues service firms are confronted with. We will therefore go on to develop some service-specific issues in designing a performance measurement system.

The balanced scorecard

The balanced scorecard (BSC), a framework developed by Kaplan and Norton, helps managers translate their organization's mission, goals and strategy into a comprehensive set of performance measures aimed at achieving competitive success.[3] Thus, the BSC is primarily a mechanism for strategy implementation. Figure 18.1 illustrates an example of the BSC for a large US healthcare system[4].

The BSC is organized around four different perspectives:

- financial;
- customer;
- internal business processes; and
- innovation, learning and growth.

These four perspectives both provide an integrated balance between measures of current, short-term operating performance and drive future competitive performance and growth. The BSC perspectives should be considered a template and not a 'straitjacket'. Although there is no mathematical theorem proving that four perspectives are both necessary and sufficient, the four perspectives make sense for many companies, since shareholders, customers and employees are very important stakeholders in each and every company. Depending on industry circumstances and the company's strategy, one or more additional perspectives may be needed to incorporate the interests of other important stakeholders such as suppliers, the community and the environment.

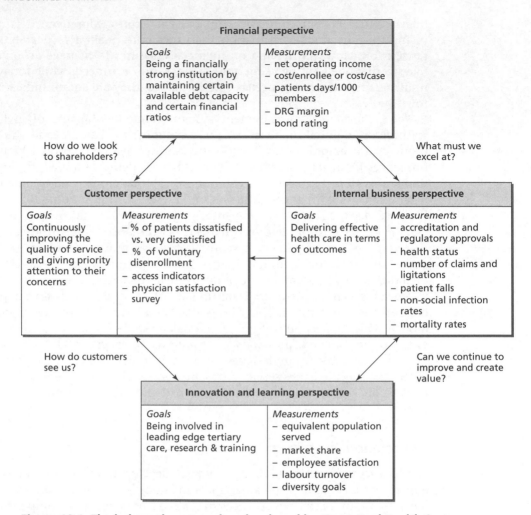

Figure 18.1 The balanced scorecard as developed by Henry Ford Health System

Source: General framework of the balanced scorecard based on 'The balanced scorecard – measures that drive performance', Kaplan, R. S. and Norton, D. P., *Harvard Business Review*, Jan.–Feb., 1992. Reprinted by permission of *Harvard Business Review*.

The key in developing a BSC is to construct the multiple scorecard measures so that they are properly linked together and directed towards achieving a single, integrated strategy. The set of objectives and measures should be internally consistent and mutually reinforcing. The linkages should incorporate the complex cause-and-effect relationships that exist among the critical measures in the four perspectives. For example, a chain of cause-and-effect relationships can be established between improving employee skills (in the learning and growth perspective), which has a positive effect on the quality and efficiency of internal processes (in the internal business process perspective), leading to on-time delivery of orders and as a result, a high degree of customer loyalty (in the customer perspective), which eventually influences the financial performance. The BSC thus 'tells the story of the strategy', starting with the long-term financial objectives, and linking them to the actions that must be taken in terms of customers, internal processes, employees, and systems to deliver the desired value.

Although the BSC was originally devized as a strategic tool at the business unit level, it can be implemented at the corporate and functional levels, and on the level of corporate support functions and shared services as well. A functional scorecard translates the functional strategy (e.g. marketing, human resources and operations) into a coherent set of performance measures. A BSC of a shared service unit (e.g. a HRM department) links the performance measures of the service unit with its goals and strategies, and aligns them with the service concept of the firm (or business unit). Because many of these shared service units are in the back office, the deployment of the BSC at unit level will guarantee a better fit between back-office and front-office activities.

The BSC framework provides a balance between:

- quantitative outcome measures and more subjective, non-financial measures of the drivers of performance;
- external measures for shareholders and customers, and internal measures of critical business processes, innovation, and learning and growth.

The full power of the BSC will only be apparent when it is embedded in an approach which implements the service organization's policy of becoming strategy-focused[5] (*see* also Chapter 21).

The EFQM Excellence Model for Total Quality Management

A second model that can be used to design an integrated performance measurement system is the *EFQM Excellence Model*, underlying the European Quality Award and proposed by the European Foundation for Quality Management (EFQM). This award is similar to Japan's Deming Award and America's Baldridge Award. As the EFQM award is the most recent, it is based on the American and Japanese experiences, and is thought to be the most comprehensive model.

The EFQM excellence model is based on nine criteria, divided into two major groups: enabler criteria and results criteria (*see* Figure 18.2).[6] The five enabler criteria are Leadership, Policy and Strategy, People, Partnerships and Resources,

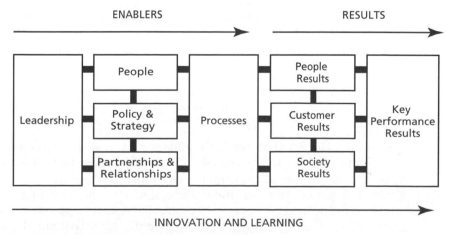

Figure 18.2 The EFQM Excellence Model[7]

Source: The EFQM Excellence Model has been reproduced with the permission of EFQM, Avenue des Pleiades 15, 1200 Brussels.

and Processes. The RADAR approach is central to the use of the enablers in the EFQM excellence model. According to this four-step approach, an organization needs to:

- determine the Results it is looking for
- plan and develop sound Approaches to attain the results
- deploy the approaches in the proper way and
- finally, Assess and Review the approaches.[8]

The four results criteria are Customer Results, People Results, Society Results and Key Performance Results. In terms of the results, the questions of the EFQM model aim at defining the organization's actual performance as well as comparing the organization's performance against its own targets and, if possible, its performance compared to competitors and 'best in class' organizations.[9]

There is a dynamic relationship between the enablers and the results: excellence in the enablers will be visible in the results. An organization using the scoring profile of the EFQM model can earn up to 1000 points distributed among the nine categories.

The EFQM Excellence Model is a non-prescriptive framework of criteria. In other words, it recognizes that there are many approaches to achieving excellence. In 2001, in line with this observation that organizations can follow diverse paths to excellence, EFQM introduced different levels of recognition of the efforts and progress of organizations towards quality management. Whereas only the European and National Quality Awards were available before, organizations can now apply for the Recognition of Achievement in Excellence and the Recognition of Commitment in Excellence awards.[10] The European Quality Award is the key stimulator of excellence for role model organizations. The Recognition of Achievement in Excellence is designed for organizations that aspire to become best in class. The application procedure for this recognition scheme takes less time and the assessment is modified. Finally the recognition of commitment is designed for organizations at the beginning on the path to excellence. The emphasis is on helping to understand their current level of performance and to establish improvement priorities.

During the development of the EFQM Excellence Model, several questions were raised about the relationship of this model to other 'models' such as the balanced scorecard and ISO 9000. While the Balanced Scorecard is designed to communicate and assess strategic performance, the EFQM model focuses on encouraging the adoption of good practice across all management activities of the organization:[11]

> 'A self-assessment by the EFQM model seeks to establish **how well** an organisation defines and manages the process of strategic planning. The Scorecard on the other hand **tests the validity** of the strategy and monitors the organisation's performance against its delivery on a regular and frequent basis.'[12]

The use of ISO 9000 in service companies as a quality assurance system was discussed in Chapter 14. Traditionally ISO 9000 has mostly focused on the Process area of the EFQM model. The major difference between ISO and EFQM is that the former is prescriptive and the latter is not. The openness of the EFQM model introduces more room for creativity and its holistic approach makes it more complex. Conversely, ISO procedures can be deployed without the complexity of a holistic approach.[13] In business practice, EFQM and ISO are considered rather complementary:

'The EFQM Model and ISO procedures are both used as management tools. ISO enables better management of production processes, while the Excellence Model is used for self-assessments and long-term orientation.'[14]

The new ISO 9001:2000 includes some major new features also covered by the EFQM model. These new features include customer feedback, business improvement, ideas from the Deming Cycle (Plan-Do-Check-Act) and new requirements for management when dealing with customers and suppliers.[15] As such the new ISO 9001:2000 is a step further towards an integrated performance management system.

All these different models stimulate the search for a comprehensive approach and inspire the development of concrete performance indicators that reflect the different aspects of performance a company wants to improve.

Designing a service-specific performance measurement system

While both the balanced scorecard and the EFQM Excellence Models undoubtedly have their merits, neither was developed specifically for service industries. Now that we know that a good performance measurement system must be linked to the service concept and needs to be balanced, we can start asking ourselves what the crucial ingredients are for a service-specific performance measurement system.

The service profit chain should inspire us to design a performance measurement system for service firms. We have already discussed how the service profit chain implies various cause-and-effect links between the following elements: the service concept and organizational capabilities impact on employee satisfaction, which in turn affects employee retention as well as service productivity and quality, resulting in value created for customers. Creating value for customers will eventually result in customer satisfaction and lead to customer loyalty and profitability. This framework highlights which areas of attention – besides profitability – should be included in a balanced scorecard for services:

■ organizational capabilities which include skills, technology and operations;
■ employees;
■ customers and the value which is created for them (*see* Figure 18.3).

In Fig. 18.3, we emphasize the notion of service concept, which implies a focus using certain capabilities. These elements should not be measured as such; they need however to be clearly defined – or designed in the case of capabilities – and will determine the relevance of specific measurements related to employees, customers and processes.

Once we understand the service concept and the focus on the target markets (*see* Chapter 2), we can start to think about the required capabilities the 'service delivery system' should possess.

The major resources enabling a firm to deliver services are technology and people (skills and knowledge). Knowledge workers are the key resource in today's service firms, and getting the most from these knowledge workers is the major challenge for the twenty-first century.[16] Although many years have been spent in getting better insight into the performance and more specifically productivity of physical labour, only limited attention has been paid as yet to the performance (productivity) of knowledge workers. Productivity of knowledge is much more

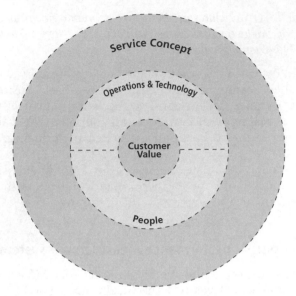

Figure 18.3 Service concept as a guiding framework

difficult to measure because it is intangible and because quality is more important than quantity.[17] A management professor should be evaluated not by how many students are taking his course, but by how many students have learned something. This is a question of quality. In Chapter 21 we will look more at the issue of managing intangible resources such as knowledge.

Once the capabilities have been defined, the design of the performance measurement system can begin. In designing a performance measurement system for services, special attention needs to be paid to employees, customers and processes.

Assessing employees and customers

The importance of employees cannot be stressed enough in service operations as became clear in Chapter 9. Different elements relating to employees can be given a place in an integrated performance measurement system. *Employee satisfaction* is an absolute must. Scales are widely available on the market.[18] *Employee-retention indicators* can be easily derived from looking at seniority figures. It is advisable to document more than these two elements, however. The notions of competencies and empowerment are the next dimensions to be included. In the case of *competence development*, the efforts employed in this area as well as the progress made should be documented. While assessing performance might often take on a more descriptive and qualitative form in this context, indices can also be relevant – for instance, the number of people trained to perform certain new tasks, the speed and number of apprentices that grow out of this status and so on. *Empowerment* can be assessed on two levels: the degree to which a company is engaging in employee involvement and the level of empowerment at the level of the individual employee. Both notions have been discussed extensively in Chapter 12 so we will not repeat them here.[19]

From a customer point of view, a core concept is customer (perceived) value (*see* Figure 18.3):

'Customers will derive value according to the utility provided by the combination of attributes less the disutility represented by the final price paid.'[20]

Value seems to have a moderating role between service quality and customer satisfaction.[21] Higher levels of service quality will only result in more customer satisfaction to the extent that customers believe that value is being enhanced. Customers can be very satisfied with a lower-priced package holiday, compared to a higher-priced holiday to the same destination, as long as the value received is high.

With regard to *customer satisfaction* and *retention*, a wide range of tools and approaches for measurement is available. The key issues have been discussed at length in Chapter 7.

Customers and employees interact with each other during the process of service delivery. It is quite clear that the performance of the service delivery process will strongly influence the satisfaction (and hence retention) of customers and employees. Therefore it is important to measure and assess the process performance.

Assessing process performance

Employees perform activities which constitute the service process. It is clear that the performance of the processes is determined by the performance of the employees in this process. However, focusing on the individual employees is not enough: organizations should also consider how people interact in the process. This is also a function of the other resources: tangible resources such as equipment or building, but also the information provided. It is also a function of the way the various activities interact, how the processes are improved and how the processes are perceived by the customers. The evaluation of processes has been discussed in Chapter 14. It seems to us that, generally speaking, the processes can and should be evaluated in terms of throughput time, productivity and quality.

Measuring throughput time

Throughput time is an important performance measure, as the speed with which the service is delivered determines the competitive position of the service firm. It is *the* measure of, for example, fast-food restaurants and exhaust repair centres, but sectors like insurance companies, financial institutions or even consulting firms can also gain competitive advantage, if they can provide a short 'delivery time'.

There are some particular developments in the service sector which make short throughput time one of the basic needs of many customers:[22]

■ Customers want to be served at the time and place, and in the way they prefer. Technologies such as PC banking make it possible for today's customers to be served at whatever time (and place) they prefer. Customers are becoming 'nomads in time and space'.

■ At the same time, customers increasingly ask for fast responsiveness in the service delivery. Fast responsiveness does not necessarily mean that the service must be delivered immediately, but that a 'time contract' is made with the customer, indicating the time by which the service must be delivered. Many examples of these 'time contracts' can be found in field service agreements, stating in what time frame the repair of a machine will be performed.

■ Service firms are increasingly required to be permanently available for the customer. Computer firms, for instance, sell back-up room capacity to customers. If the computer system in the customer's firm fails, the customer can immediately be installed in these back-up rooms and can continue their activities.

The role of employees changes completely in these time-based service delivery environments. Managing the customer contact time becomes a major point of attention in the service delivery. Managing the customer contact time includes the following action points:[23]

■ making waiting times as short as possible;
■ measuring time from the customer's point of view;
■ defining a service contract (guarantee or agreement) in terms of time performance (*see* Chapter 8);
■ indicating what the payout will be if the firm is not able to keep the promise in the service contract;
■ matching opening hours to the times customers are able to visit the service firm;
■ spending some extra attention on the first and the last contact point in the service delivery;
■ matching the level of service delivery to the customer requirements;
■ paying attention to who accompanies the customer during the service delivery;
■ anticipating defects in the service delivery process;
■ guaranteeing that every moment in the service process is perceived by the customer as a quality experience.

As a result, lead time or delivery time can be included as an element of quality. However, even if the customers are not aware of or do not value short throughput times, it might be worthwhile measuring the throughput time of the processes or, more specifically, the ratio between the sum of the operating times of the steps in the process that really add value to the total time spent in the process. A ratio of less than 1 per cent is not rare, as was the case with an insurance company where the actual time it took to process a life insurance policy was ten days, of which only 7 minutes (= 0.16 per cent) was actual added value time. The rest was (mainly) waiting time, transportation time, time necessary to inspect somebody's work, etc. According to the theory of time-based competition, reducing the throughput time will help companies to simultaneously:[24]

1. reduce costs;
2. improve quality dependability;
3. increase flexibility;
4. improve delivery dependability;
5. improve innovativeness by shortening the time to market for new products.

Throughput time appears therefore to be a universal measure encompassing a number of performance criteria. At the same time it is an important lever for change. By insisting on a 50 per cent reduction in throughput time, for instance, companies have to radically change their processes.

Measuring productivity

Productivity is the ratio of output to input. Services are at least partially intangible which makes defining, let alone measuring, output much more difficult. Moreover, in many service organizations, there is no one output measure which summarizes the whole activity. The output of a professor at a business school can be measured in terms of number of publications, the number of teaching hours, the quality of the teaching itself, the success of the management training programs, etc. It is really impossible to reduce these measures to one (financial) output figure.

In addition, the presence of the customers in the process brings heterogeneity. The customer, with his or her specific needs and behaviour, introduces a high level of variability into the service process, which will make reaching uniform productivity standards difficult. Are nurses productive when they provide care to five patients per hour? Although no absolute productivity standard can be put forward in this example, the productivity of several nurses can be compared under the assumption that they treat similar kinds of patients. The absence of an absolute productivity standard has made relative efficiency benchmarking very popular in service environments. The requirement of working with multiple output measures (and eventually multiple input measures) in such benchmarking has created new techniques for relative efficiency benchmarking such as Data Envelopment Analysis (DEA). DEA is a linear-programming-based technique which allows to rank service units in terms of performance by comparing several output and input measures simultaneously. Exhibit 18.1 shows an example of the use of DEA in a bank to measure the relative performance of counter operators in 24 branches. The reader who wants to have some more technical insight into the DEA technique should first read Technical Note 4.

Exhibit 18.1

Benchmarking employee performance in a bank using DEA

This study was performed by a Belgian bank. Like most banks, this bank (and more specifically its network of branches) are confronting a number of developments in service delivery to its customers.

The increasing use of automated distribution channels such as ATMs, home banking and phone banking led to a decrease in the number of transactions taking place in the branches. On the other hand, there was a shift in the nature of the customer visits towards increasingly complex interactions with the counter personnel. The focus shifted towards advice and sales, from low-contact to higher contact.

The bank was not sure what the net effect of these two developments would be. Management first assumed that a drop in the number of transactions would lead to a lower workload for the personnel, making it possible to free up personnel to handle the more complex interactions. However, this was contrary to the feeling of the branch staff that their workload had increased significantly. A number of

explanations were given: a number of relationship-building activities such as advising customers were not registered as transactions; the decreasing number of transactions may have only slightly increased the free time of the staff so that that free time could not always be used effectively, and so on. In other words, the developments started a discussion on staffing patterns, more specifically re-allocation of the available personnel.

Given the increasing importance of relationship banking in the banking industry, this was an important discussion. Taking into account the notion of strategic HRM, this trend towards relationship banking implies a change in HRM policies within the bank.

The bank wanted to investigate the impact of these developments in greater detail. While all branches experienced these developments, some branches were better able to cope with them than others. It was clear that a detailed insight was required into the practices of each branch and more specifically into the division of work, the allocation of personnel resources and the

▶

383

Exhibit 18.1 continued

staffing performance in terms of the effectiveness, efficiency and quality.

To do this, bank management started a project, collecting data for 24 bank branches in order to compare the performance of these branches (pilot study). Three input measures were used:

1. The number of full-time equivalent employees (FTE), working at the counter and having customer contact.
2. The amount of FTE doing administrative work for counter operations.
3. The infrastructure, being the sum of the number of terminals, ATMs, statement printers and money dispensers in the branch.

The output measures are transaction-based measures and include the number of transactions, the number of investments, and the number of loans granted (to individuals, professionals and small firms). Because management was particularly worried about the productivity of their counter employees, they excluded the commercial activities in the first stage. Table 18.1 shows the data as collected. Data envelopment analysis has been used to produce the results in Table 18.2. Technical note 4 gives some more technical information about the technique.

The results table shows us that branch 1 is 96.60 per cent efficient as compared with a reference set of three other branches (branch 10, 18, and 21), which are always 100 per cent efficient. By reducing the number of FTEs by 1 unit, the efficiency of branch 1 will improve by 34.80 per cent. However, branch 1 only needs an increase of 3.4 per cent to become 100 per cent efficient. This is only one tenth of 34.8 per cent. Then, it suffices to reduce the number of FTEs by 0.1.

Table 18.1 Input of the 24 branches for the DEA analysis

Branch	ACCOUNTS	GRCUST_9596	GGM_9596	FTE_COOP	FTE_COAD	INFRASTR
1	917	184	6278.85	0.79	1.10	6
2	585	124	3830.21	1.49	0.85	4
3	1088	130	3339.95	1.48	1.34	9
4	918	231	4026.29	2.02	1.23	5
5	1469	129	5783.78	2.42	1.54	8
6	1309	139	1262.69	2.27	0.67	8
7	1417	303	6656.47	2.66	2.00	8
8	1058	265	−981.52	2.71	1.25	8
9	460	75	304.81	0.91	0.22	3
10	1023	297	4608.12	1.75	0.66	5
11	1254	199	4514.81	2.20	0.65	5
12	880	173	3793.39	1.44	0.69	7
13	231	79	5027.55	0.81	0.40	3
14	1589	359	7568.34	3.71	3.04	10
15	948	44	577.46	1.50	0.80	4
16	786	102	7987.37	2.10	1.39	7
17	663	105	1369.14	1.57	0.67	7
18	388	95	3552.80	0.98	0.61	2
19	500	146	2746.54	1.05	0.39	2
20	1344	256	6767.75	3.50	2.08	8
21	720	162	8792.14	1.63	1.37	7
22	597	161	4366.91	1.21	0.41	5
23	868	195	−2014.65	2.48	1.01	8
24	472	113	3893.03	1.16	0.69	6

ACCOUNTS: number of accounts in 1995 in the branch.
GRCUST_9596: growth of the number of customers between 1995 and 1996 (in absolute number).
GRGRM_9596: growth of the gross margin between 1995 and 1996 (in absolute number, 000).
FTE_COOP: time spent on counter operations with customer contact (such as money transfers).
FTE_COAD: time spent on counter operations administration (except for sales).
INFRASTR: sum of the number of terminals, ATMs, statement printers and money dispensers in the branch.

▶

Exhibit 18.1 continued

Table 18.2 Data Envelopment Analysis for 24 bank branches

Branch	Efficiency score (%)	Efficiency reference set	FTE Coop (%)	FTE Coad (%)	Infrastructure (%)
1	96.60	10, 18, 21	34.80	0.00	6.30
2	78.60	10, 18, 21	45.10	0.00	8.20
3	100				
4	81.70	10, 11, 19	23.90	0.00	10.40
5	99.44	10, 15	32.40	0.00	2.70
6	100				
7	91.61	3, 10, 21	32.10	0.00	1.80
8	65.63	3, 10, 15	30.90	0.00	2.10
9	100				
10	100				
11	100				
12	100				
13	100				
14	76.32	10, 18, 19	16.70	0.00	3.80
15	100				
16	85.21	10, 13, 18, 21	29.20	1.00	5.30
17	69.60	3, 6, 10	52.10	27.10	0.00
18	100				
19	100				
20	73.94	10, 11, 19	18.70	0.00	4.30
21	100				
22	100				
23	58.57	3, 6, 10, 11	33.00	16.80	0.10
24	81.20	10, 12, 21, 22	74.00	20.00	0.00

FTE Coop: Time spent on counter operations with customer contact (such as money transfers).
FTE Coad: Time spent on counter operations administration (except for sales).
Infrastructure: Sum of the number of terminals, ATMs, statement printers and money dispensers in the branch.

In general, service firms have an advantage over manufacturing firms when performing internal efficiency benchmarking because they have a much larger network of service delivery sites. DEA is a very popular tool for internal and external efficiency benchmarking in multi-site service environments, which are confronted with multiple inputs and outputs.[25] Examples of such environments are banks, hospitals, courts and university departments.

The conclusion is that measuring productivity is more problematic and complex in a service environment than in manufacturing. Nevertheless, it is obvious that they should still be measured. Service productivity cannot be left out of an integrated performance measurement system.

Measuring quality

How to measure quality has already been discussed extensively in Chapters 7 and 14. The main points discussed in these chapters can be summarized as follows:

■ Several service quality dimensions can be identified in a particular service environment, and a distinction can be made between expected service quality and perceived service quality. A tool such as Servqual helps to measure this gap in terms of different service quality dimensions. Service firms should try to understand why the gap between expectations and perception exists.

■ It is important to identify the moments of truth and potential fail points in the service delivery process. Service blueprinting can be the start for this analysis. More advanced methods such as critical incident technique and Service Transaction Analysis can be used to learn more about why the organization has these particular fail points.

■ There is a need to measure process variability.

Integrating the different performance measures

In the previous paragraphs we identified many different performance measures related to employees, customers and operational capabilities. As already indicated at the start of this chapter, integrated performance measurement means that these different performance measures are looked at simultaneously and more insight is obtained into the relationship between these different performance measures. Although the service profit chain gives a conceptual model of the relationship between performance measures such as employee satisfaction, value, customer satisfaction, etc., operationalization of each of the conceptual performance measures is necessary to really get an integrated view for a particular service organization. Table 18.3 shows how this operationalization is done for a bank.

The next challenge is to collect data on each of the performance measures in Table 18.3. Having a large sample data set encompassing all of these measures, from internal service quality to financial performance, is the main obstacle for an integrated performance measurement allowing the relationships between these performance measures to be seen. Some references to studies of empirical testing of the link between performance measures, carried out in different service environments such as after-sales services and banking, are given in the suggested reading list.

The importance of the different performance measures depends on the kind of services delivered. The value of personal-interactive services is generally higher than for maintenance-interactive services. This means that customers are more willing to wait for the former than for the latter, or in other words, that personal-interactive services are less time-sensitive than maintenance-interactive services.

In maintenance-interactive services, productivity is also a major issue. Better productivity is considered to be positively correlated with better quality. In these service environments internal benchmarking studies using DEA are well accepted. The relationship between productivity and quality in task-interactive and personal-interactive services is much less clear. Higher nursing productivity in terms of number of patients treated per hour can lead to lower service quality, because nurses no longer have enough time for each patient. In personal-interactive services, the productivity of knowledge can be considered the major challenge of the next century.

Once the service concept has been translated into very concrete performance measures, as in Table 18.3, it can be implemented through the introduction of an integrated and balanced performance measurement system. Before discussing the implementation of such a system, we should consider the story of John Brown at G-Mart in Exhibit 18.2. Why does he not succeed in turning the firm around?

Table 18.3 An integrated set of performance measures and their operationalization for a bank[26]

Conceptual performance measure	Subcategory	Operationalization
Profitability measures		Revenue per full-time equivalent per household
		Revenue per household
Customer loyalty measures	Checking retention	Number of customers with checking accounts who stayed with the bank from year 1 to year 2
		Percentage change in the number of customers with checking accounts who stayed with the bank from year 1 to year 2
	Deposit retention	Number of customers with deposits who stayed with the bank from year 1 to year 2
		Percentage change in the number of customers with deposits who stayed with the bank from year 1 to year 2
	Average investable assets	Average percentage of customer investable assets held at the bank
		Percentage change in the average percentage of customer investable assets held at the bank from year 1 to year 2
	Cross-sell	Average number of services purchase per household
		Percentage change in the average number of services purchased per household (year 1 to year 2)
Customer satisfaction measures		% ranking branch 6 or 7 (on a scale from 1 to 7)
		% ranking bank 6 or 7
		Average branch rating
		Average bank rating
Employee loyalty measures		Manager full-time average service months
		Average employee tenure (years)
		Percent of employees surveyed who are 'committed to regional's success'
		Ratio of employees surveyed who would 'leave if offered same pay elsewhere'
Employee satisfaction measures		Average of responses to 'how would you rate this organization as a place to work?'
		Average of responses to 'how would you rate your job – the type of work you do?'
Internal service quality (percent of employees rating bank a 6 or 7 in the following categories)		Communications
		Teamwork
		Training
		Reward/opportunity
		Available resources to perform job well
		Top corporate management
		Business line management
		Geographic market management
		Immediate supervisor

Source: Based on Loveman, G. W. (1998) 'Employee satisfaction, customer loyalty and financial performance: an empirical examination of the service profit chain in retail banking', *Journal of Service Research*, Vol 1, No 1, pp. 18–31.

IMPLEMENTING AN INTEGRATED PERFORMANCE MEASUREMENT SYSTEM

Exhibit 18.2

Performance measurement at G-Mart

John Brown was taking his first day off since accepting the position of CEO at G-Mart about three years before, but the day was not a gratifying one. He had decided to resign the week before, after much reflection, having failed to put the drifting ship of G-Mart on a new course heading for improved customer satisfaction and regained profitability.

G-Mart operates over 100 supermarkets, making it the second largest grocery retailer in the country. But for almost a decade, G-Mart's profit margins had gradually been eroded because of a slow but steady loss of market share. The entrance of hard discounters, combined with the poor economic climate, had made all the major market players suffer, but G-Mart had turned out to be the biggest loser. Long queues at check-outs, frequent out-of-stocks, unfriendly staff, a messy store – in short, a generally unpleasant shopping atmosphere – caught G-Mart in a difficult competitive position: it was perceived both as being more expensive than the hard discounters and as offering a lower quality service than the so-called 'value retailers'.

As a result, about three years before, the board of G-Mart, in search of a turnaround, invited John Brown to become CEO. Brown accepted the challenge, considering it to be that once-in-a-life-time opportunity, and gave himself three years to put G-Mart back on track.

The first step in this major endeavour was to redesign G-Mart's service strategy. After a period of six months of intense consulting with senior management, it was agreed that the first priority should be to increase customer loyalty and retention in order to stop the crumbling away of G-Mart's market share. It was also accepted that G-Mart should position itself as a value retailer rather than as a discounter. This strategy was based on the view that the hard discounters carried a less deep product range, resulting in a structural cost advantage. G-Mart would thus be a benchmark against the other value retailers. All senior managers agreed that only by offering world-class service could the company be given a competitive edge. The objective would be to increase customer loyalty through increased customer satisfaction.

As a second step, Brown launched a major internal communication campaign. Before the campaign actually started, he held a survey of all employees, which would later show whether or not his efforts were paying off. The objective was to measure both staff motivation and involvement, as well as to assess the staff's view of G-Mart's strategy and service concept. Future surveys would then show the impact of the internal communication campaigns. Not surprisingly, the first survey showed that the perception of what strategy G-Mart should adopt was highly diffuse. Some believed G-Mart should lower its prices immediately, while others wanted to take some type of 'value' path. However, the staff did express their belief in the company's future. There seemed to be a true sense of urgency and the survey's results clearly indicated that John Brown had the staff's support.

After his first year as CEO, he wanted to assess his progress. To do this he ordered a second internal survey, which showed that awareness of the new strategy was very high. Almost all employees strongly agreed that G-Mart wanted to offer its customers world-class service. Brown also organized a preliminary customer satisfaction measurement. A survey was held exclusively among G-Mart's active loyalty-card owners, as sales to card holders accounted for over 82 per cent of all transactions and for over 90 per cent of all sales. The results showed that the overall satisfaction index was 7.2 on a scale of ten. More alarming was that 14 per cent of respondents could be defined as dissatisfied, having rated G-Mart a six or less. Furthermore, both market share and profitability were down.

With these results in mind, John Brown wanted to stabilize G-Mart's market share during his second year as CEO. Aware of the staff's motivation and its high awareness of the importance of quality service, customer satisfaction and customer retention, he was fully convinced that the customer satisfaction index would go up and that business results would start to improve. Throughout that year he and his staff meticulously

Exhibit 18.2 continued

monitored the progress of sales, market share and costs, at the level of both individual stores and product categories. Store managers and store department heads alike were closely monitored on their business results.

In spite of all these efforts, however, it soon became clear that the fall in market share had not been stopped. At the end of his second year as CEO, G-Mart's profitability was at an all-time low. This was reflected in the third employee survey, which showed that employees were still supporting the world-class service strategy, but their belief in the organization's future had decreased dramatically. On the other hand, the customer satisfaction index was up from 7.2 to 7.5, while the number of dissatisfied customers had slightly decreased from 14 per cent to 12 per cent of the sample.

During his third and final year at G-Mart, Brown had to drink the cup of bitterness to the dregs. The disappointing financial results forced management to take drastic measures, including

both a substantial wage cut and major layoffs, which resulted in strikes at several stores. The social unrest was reflected in that year's employee and customer satisfaction surveys. Customer satisfaction was down from 7.5 to 7.1 points, while the number of dissatisfied customers had increased from 12 per cent to 16 per cent. Moreover, employee motivation was at a record low and the staff's commitment to the world-class service strategy had decreased dramatically. Finally, the strikes had caused an additional loss of market share. Investors seemed to have lost their trust in G-Mart's future, as the price of the company's stock had decreased by over 30 per cent during the previous six months.

John Brown could not help but admit that he had failed. He resigned and decided not to accept any new assignment or job offer for at least six months. He wanted a sabbatical leave to try to assess where he had gone wrong and what he could have done differently.

Like G-Mart, many companies claim in their mission statements that they are striving for 'customer and employee satisfaction'. Customer-focus programmes are being set up everywhere, and employee satisfaction measurement systems are being conceived. However, all is not well. While some companies have experienced early improvements, most campaigns do not get beyond the stage of mere lip service. Furthermore, the established measurement systems often produce nothing more than attractive reports. It has thus become clear that sloganeering and heightened awareness can only marginally improve actual customer and employee satisfaction, and eventually profitability. Unless a measurement system, aimed at realizing the desired service concept, is linked to the company's business practice and processes, it will not affect the way the company runs its business, and consequently cannot have a significant impact on the actual satisfaction of its customers, employees' morale or longer term profitability.

Figure 18.4 shows the steps involved in implementing an integrated and balanced performance measurement system.[27] We shall now discuss each of these steps in greater detail.

Step 1 Defining the service concept in actionable terms

The first challenge is to make the service concept actionable. This is particularly relevant if the service concept is rather general in its wording. If this is the case, there is ample room for interpretation, which may result in ambiguity and differences of opinion as to what the service concept actually means. It also makes it difficult to judge to what degree the organization is delivering the service concept and thereby achieving its strategic goals.[28]

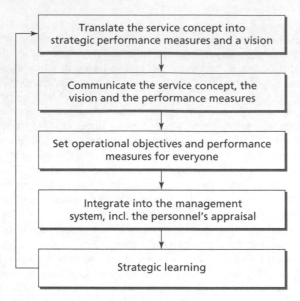

Figure 18.4 The implementation process of a performance measurement system

It is of key importance, therefore, that senior management selects a limited number of strategic performance measures. If all senior managers are committed to the same goals and measures, they are ready to deploy the service concept throughout the organization. This often involves writing down what is called a *vision statement*.

The general wording of service concepts

If we look at the mission statement and/or service concept of most organizations, they all express the intent to excel. Service providers want to be the best, offer superior quality and service, be innovative, and employ the best people. The problem, however, is that many service concepts lack a precise description of what is actually meant by being the best. A clear example of different interpretations of a service strategy can be found in Exhibit 18.3.

Exhibit 18.3

Internationalization at Vlerick

In the 1950s, Belgium's leading business school, the Vlerick School of Management, was founded by Professor André Vlerick. He wanted to assist Flemish businessmen in their working with American managers and found that the Europeans eagerly adopted the ready-made techniques of their American counterparts. Seeing a lack of European methods, Professor Vlerick decided to work on establishing European management training. To that end he founded one of the first business schools on the European continent, the Seminar for the Study and Research of Productivity (SPSO), through

which he wished to establish and foster a management culture within Flanders. Several decades later this vision was translated into a formal mission statement indicating that the Vlerick School – as the SPSO was renamed – should focus its resources on management development in Flanders.

However, in the early 1990s the Vlerick School was experiencing the effects of the rapid internationalization of the in-company management training market, one of its core activities. The board of the School adjusted the mission statement, agreeing that the School should

Exhibit 18.3 continued

aim to be recognized as being an international, not just a Flemish, leader in management development. Almost all staff members supported the idea of 'internationalization', as the new stream of thought was being called. However, while the first initiatives in the internationalization effort were being implemented, it turned out that board members – and consequently also employees – had varying opinions as to what was actually meant by 'being internationally recognized'. Some considered Wallonia to be the prime target market for the school's training programmes, as the French-speaking part of Belgium was not being serviced by the school's (then) Dutch-only curriculum. Others stressed the opportunity of tackling the Dutch market, as it was a neighbouring country with the same mother tongue as Flanders. A third group believed that the prime target group should be the thousands of expatriates working at the

numerous European headquarters located in Belgium, the home country of the European Union's capital city. Finally, some believed that the school should target all European or even all global managers and markets, as the most prestigious business schools recruited their students and participants from all over the world.

Similar discussions arose as to the degree to which the faculty was to become international. Some felt the school should limit itself to seeking close co-operation with other business schools, while sending its own doctoral students for at least one year abroad to a school with an international faculty. Others wanted to internationalize the school's faculty itself. Eventually it became clear that the first step in the internationalization process had to be achieving agreement among the board members as to what internationalizing the school actually meant.

Measures of long-term strategic performance

Making the service concept concrete can be achieved by establishing long-term strategic performance measurements. Achieving such objectives by using these measurements means that the organization is realizing its service concept.

A fine example of this approach is the management accounting system at Rank Xerox, the first winner of the EFQM award. Rank Xerox states that customer and employee satisfaction enables the company to increase market share, which drives the financial results. The company's balanced scorecard consists of four strategic performance measures:

- *Personnel satisfaction*. Rank Xerox surveys its staff annually on their overall satisfaction. A total of 110 questions measure, among other things, the employees' relationship with their superiors and their peers, and satisfaction with their wages and salaries. The anonymous survey is mailed to the home address of the white-collar workers and achieves a response rate of about 80 per cent. The blue-collar workers fill out the survey during working hours – for instance, in the dining hall – so that the response rate is close to 100 per cent.
- *Customer satisfaction*. Rank Xerox mails a customer-satisfaction questionnaire to its customers and gathers the responses by telephone. This combines the completeness of a written survey with the high response rate of a telephone survey. The measurement is executed by an independent research agency on behalf of Rank Xerox. Satisfaction data are available for a broad range of customer impacting processes, both for Rank Xerox and for its competitors.
- *Market share*. This is considered to be one of the key drivers of profitability.
- *Return on assets*. This completes the strategic management control system by adding the financial perspective.

Senior management at Rank Xerox stress that during their visits to middle and junior managers, 'business results are only discussed when there is time left'.

Absolute priority is given to customer satisfaction and personnel satisfaction. By stressing the strategic performance measures, while coaching their staff, Rank Xerox's senior management turn their strategy into action.

Translating the service concept into a vision

Conciseness is one of the characteristics of a good service concept. Many formulations of the service concept are too long to be easily communicated to and remembered by all personnel. Therefore many organizations have benefited from translating the more comprehensive and elaborate service concept into a short and inspiring vision.

A good vision statement focuses the attention on lofty aims with which everyone can identify. As such the vision turns the bare essentials and the key strategic priorities and directions of the service concept into guiding beliefs.[29] As a communication tool, the wording should be easy to understand, clear, concise and easy to remember. The contents should be ambitious and challenging yet achievable. In short, a vision statement has to be inspiring.

Probably one of the strongest vision statements ever is the late president John Kennedy's vision for the US space programme:

'Before the turn of the decade, we will put a man on the moon.'

Similar examples are abundant in service organizations. We already mentioned DHL's service concept:

'DHL will become the acknowledged global leader in the express delivery of documents and packages.'

Although this message was not a lengthy one, DHL learned that it was not easy to convey it to all employees. Consequently, DHL crafted a simple yet very clear vision:

'To achieve 100% next-day delivery.'

The service division of Asea Brown Boveri (ABB) also experienced that it was having trouble making everyone within the organization aware of its already concise service concept:

'Increased customer satisfaction through service which is professional, close to the customer, comprehensive, and all from one ABB Service organisation.'

Like DHL, ABB came up with a short vision statement to get the message across, both internally and externally:

'ABB Service wants to be the world-wide experts in industrial maintenance.'

Once everyone agrees on what is essentially meant by the vision, the organization is ready to kick off its internal communication effort, which is the second step in implementing customer focus.

Step 2 Communicating the service concept, the performance measures and the vision

As part of a customer-focus programme, a major airline decided to empower its cabin crew to distribute money for dry cleaning whenever food or drinks were spilled accidentally on a passenger's clothes during a flight.[30] The objective of the empowerment exercise was twofold:

1. The airline wanted to retain customers who might otherwise be dissatisfied. The compensation for the damages would minimize the customer's hassle and consequently might create some goodwill.
2. The initiative was conceived as a means of communicating to all staff that customer satisfaction and retention was a major priority. Staff had to realize that the old days of filing formal service recovery requests were over: whenever the airline made an error, it would try to make it up to its customers.

The first time one of the crew members actually paid a passenger for dry cleaning, she obviously had to hand in the passenger's receipt. The manager accepting the receipt killed the initiative by asking one simple question:

'Was there any way you could have avoided paying the compensation?'

This example illustrates the key role of middle management in any customer focus initiative. No matter how much an organization invests in internal communication efforts, eventually it is the immediate supervisors who will give a concrete meaning to whatever message is being communicated to their subordinates.

Experience has taught us time and time again that middle managers can make or break any programme. If middle managers are committed to the service concept and vision, they will set an example by communicating and supporting it through junior management to all personnel. However, if they disapprove of the concept or do not clearly understand what is actually meant by it, they will convey the wrong message to junior management, both in their deeds and in their words. In these circumstances, middle management functions as a terrorist squad fighting a guerrilla war from the inside.

Middle management's role is particularly vital in geographically decentralized organizations, with a high personnel turnover and a high percentage of low-skilled and/or part-time workers. The important role of middle management is clearly illustrated in the case of Belgium's leading fast-food chain of hamburger restaurants, Quick (*see* Exhibit 18.4).

Exhibit 18.4

'Living the vision' at Quick

The vast majority of the staff of Quick are part-timers – for instance, students trying to earn extra money. Thus the contact personnel consider working in a Quick restaurant to be a temporary job rather than a career. This situation confronts Quick's management with the major challenge of creating a feeling of belonging among these employees. Investing heavily in training and internal communication targeted at the part-timers is not a solution because of the high personnel turnover rate: too many employees leave the organization before the investments start to pay off.

Quick recognizes the key role of its middle management, and therefore focuses its internal communication on its restaurant managers. The underlying hypothesis is that the manager should fully understand and be committed to the Quick organization's service concept and culture. Managers will thus act according to Quick's service strategy and communicate its meaning to their staff on the job. By 'living the vision', they act as a role model for all other employees and have made an important contribution to Quick's overwhelming success.

It is obvious, and yet sometimes overlooked, that any internal communication plan should take middle management's key role into account. This has consequences both for the timing and contents of internal communication efforts.

1. Since subordinates will always turn to their superiors for an interpretation of the service concept, managers deserve a more in-depth approach. While the communications targeting other staff may consist mainly of impersonal media, managers should go through an intense briefing effort. There should be ample time for asking questions and discussion. Only then will it be possible for senior management to make sure that the message is not only clearly understood but also accepted.
2. The distribution of any internal communication effort should follow the hierarchy, as managers should always be informed ahead of their subordinates. This will avoid having managers argue about and/or reject the service concept in the presence of those who are not their peers. This should be particularly avoided in larger organizations.

Some companies devise different training programmes for middle and for junior management; others do not. The latter argue that submitting middle and junior management to the same training programme simultaneously helps to build the team spirit and creates consensus among the managers. Others train the middle managers first and then have them sit in on the training programme of the junior managers. The same principle is often applied to the contact personnel, with junior management participating in the training programme to give support to the delivered message.

Step 3 Set operational performance measures for everyone

With the exception of senior management, employees do not perceive themselves as having any impact on or direct responsibility for the strategic performance measures, as defined in the organization's balanced scorecard. Operational objectives which are in line with the strategic objectives should therefore be set for each individual and/or team. The resulting *personal scorecards*[31] complement the strategic balanced scorecards.

In developing these personal scorecards it is recommended that the organization's key priorities are defined. Deploying these priorities from the top down, while developing the personal scorecards from the bottom up, means that all efforts are integrated into the organization's endeavour to implement its strategy.

We will first discuss the personal scorecard and then the importance of setting priorities.

The personal scorecard

A balanced scorecard, containing the organization's strategic performance measures, helps top management to monitor the degree to which it is achieving its goals and objectives. All other employees in the organization cannot be held responsible for reaching those goals, as they only have a minor impact on the organization's processes and output. Overall, the lower one is in the hierarchy, the less one's involvement is with comprehensive performance measures.

That is why leading companies invite all their staff to translate those strategic performance measures into their own operational performance measures. All employees have to specify what actions they will undertake to help the organization reach its goals. The actions have to be linked to quantifiable objectives, deadlines and performance measures.

This process is called *policy deployment* (also referred to as *management by objectives* (MBO)).[32] Again, Rank Xerox provides us with a good example. As mentioned earlier, the company uses four strategic performance measures: customer satisfaction, employee satisfaction, market share and return on assets. These measures also function as the key indicators of senior management's performance, as it can and should be held responsible for how well the organization is doing. In the case of individual employees, however, it is difficult for them to see how their performance is linked to Rank Xerox's overall performance measures. Yet this overall performance depends entirely on the effort of all individuals. The challenge is to integrate all these efforts.

That is why each individual or team within Rank Xerox is invited to work out for themselves how they can contribute to the overall strategic objectives. They have to devise their own action plans, their own objectives and their own performance measures (*see* Figure 18.5).

For instance, a manager whose direct subordinates' satisfaction falls below average, can set up an action plan which should result in the increased satisfaction of his own staff. The manager will be held responsible for achieving his own objective and not for the organization's overall employee satisfaction.

Setting priorities

The policy deployment process yields the highest results when the action plans are developed in line with set priorities. These priorities are determined top-down, whereby each manager sets his priorities in line with those of his direct supervisor. Top management sets the strategic priorities and then the priorities are cascaded

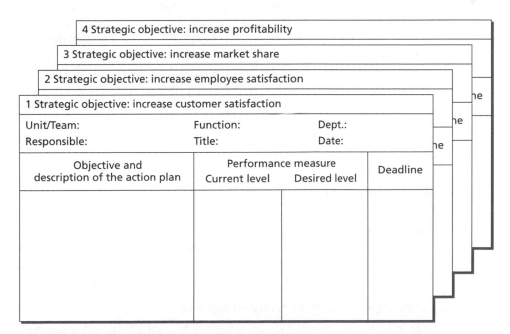

Figure 18.5 The balanced scorecard at Rank Xerox

down the organization, developing priorities for each level. Rank Xerox strongly believes that focus on the 'vital few' priorities is far more desirable than diluting the efforts by working on the 'useful many'.

Setting these priorities has a double integrating effect:

- *Horizontally*. All people working at the same level within the organization have to confer with one another when setting their own priorities. Their supervisors can function as moderators. As such, all priorities at a single level are integrated.
- *Vertically*. Each manager is making sure that his subordinates set priorities in line with his own. As such, the cascading process guarantees that all set priorities are in line with the vital few strategic priorities of top management.

Furthermore, the top-down approach allows for both process improvement and process re-engineering. If the approach were bottom-up, re-engineering would be almost impossible within the policy deployment effort. Indeed, in a bottom-up situation, every manager or team at the lowest level would come up with projects aimed at improving their own processes according to the Kaizen philosophy of continuous improvement, excluding projects which go beyond the scope of one single team or manager. With the top-down approach, however, any manager can decide whether he considers a re-engineering effort desirable for the group of processes for which he is responsible or whether he wants to leave it up to the managers below him to work independently on the sub-processes for which they are responsible.

If setting the priorities is basically a top-down effort, developing concrete action plans should be more of a bottom-up process. The involvement of employees largely depends on the degree of freedom they are given to conceive their own actions, performance measures and objectives. It is extremely important in a professional service environment to ensure that a balance can be found between the personal development plans and the set priorities.

Not setting priorities can only be justified when the policy deployment technique has just been introduced. At that point in time, the first objective is to mobilize energy, so that everyone becomes involved in designing and implementing action plans. To maximize the chances of success, employees are simply invited to participate, without being steered towards set priorities. It is only after employees have mastered the philosophy and practice of policy deployment, that vital few priorities are used to focus the individual action plans on the implementation of the strategy.

Step 4 Integrate the personal scorecards into the management system

Once the organization has set up a system of policy deployment, it is essential to integrate the personal scorecards into the management system. We will explain why changing the criteria for personnel appraisal is essential before going on to give a brief overview of the most important elements of employee appraisal and the risk inherent in this step.

Changing the criteria for personnel appraisal

All too often organizations are reluctant to change the way they evaluate their staff. The internal communication programme, sometimes strengthened by the policy deployment effort, stresses customer satisfaction and customer focus as the number one priority. Yet at the same time the old criteria for appraising staff are being used; as a result ambiguous signals are being sent out.

In the last decade, several car manufacturers have developed customer-focus initiatives, resulting in kick-off meetings, training efforts and other types of internal communication efforts as well as extensive customer satisfaction surveys. The letter accompanying the survey of one manufacturer stated:

> 'In the 1990s it is no longer sufficient to build excellent cars. Customers expect outstanding service from their dealers.'

As a general rule, manufacturers trained their regional dealer supervisors to coach the dealers in analysing and using the customer satisfaction results. The objective was to encourage dealers to start service quality improvement projects in order to increase customer satisfaction.

Many car manufacturers learned the hard way that not adjusting the appraisal system undermined customer satisfaction efforts. The further use of sales volumes as the key strategic performance measure and of promotions in an attempt to boost sales volume lead to a focus on short-term sales results, at the expense of long-term customer satisfaction. One car manufacturer learned, for instance, that customers were extremely disappointed in the attention they received when their new car was delivered. Before the signing of the sales contract, the sales people gave them the royal treatment. They wanted to close a deal, because their bonus depended on it. However, when the customers came to collect their new cars several weeks later, the person who had sold the car hardly paid them any attention at all but was giving the royal treatment to a new prospect.

Time and again it has been proven that companies have to change their personnel appraisal system so that it reflects the emphasis on customer satisfaction. Otherwise they may become entangled in the 'what's it gonna be this year' syndrome, in which top management regularly launches a new programme, which employees perceive as the latest in a long line. They do not change their behaviour, as they think the newly launched programme will not last.

By changing the appraisal system, management can prove it means business.

The most important elements of personnel appraisal

There are several means at management's disposal for proving that the organization is going to be run differently. We will briefly discuss the advantages and disadvantages of the most important appraisal elements.

- *Management by wandering around.* Managers are judged by their deeds, not by their words. Therefore, the most important tool of personnel appraisal are the comments and the proper behaviour of managers in their everyday contacts with their subordinates. This is essentially why all customer focus programmes have to start from the top. Indeed, middle managers will mirror senior management's comments and behaviour.
- *Bonus schemes.* A bonus system can be a very powerful tool to steer people's behaviour. Setting up bonus schemes linked to customer satisfaction is therefore an absolute prerequisite. The reluctance to install extensive variable remuneration systems is very high, particularly among Europeans. When the company is already using a bonus scheme, however, not changing the

criteria – that is, not including customer satisfaction measures – will endanger the programme.

■ *Periodical appraisal talks.* Many organizations make use of periodical, formal appraisal talks. Typically, the employee is invited to assess his or her own performance over the past period, to indicate the areas for improvement and to set objectives for the next period. This self-assessment results in a memo, which is discussed by the employee's managers. Finally, employee and direct supervisor sit together and try to come to an agreement. The appraisal talk can function as an input for bonus schemes and/or pay increases and/or promotions.

Traditionally, the appraisal talks have not been linked to the strategic objectives. However, by integrating the personal scorecard into the system, the employee becomes aware that his or her 'official' appraisal is linked to the customer focus criteria. Furthermore, the appraisal talks are typically limited to managers; the system should be expanded to all staff.

British retailer, ASDA, for instance, organizes periodical appraisal talks for all staff, including those on the shop floor. To simplify the process, the lowest skilled workers do not have to write a self-assessment memo, but they are invited to complete a self-assessment questionnaire. The questionnaire contains closed-ended questions, providing two columns for the actual answers. For example:

	Self	Agreed
I am helpful to customers.	always usually sometimes rarely	always usually sometimes rarely

The first column is completed by the employees themselves. The second column is completed by the supervisor and the employee together, reflecting the 'agreed' performance.

The questionnaire lists all criteria which are important for the employee's performance. Again, the objective is to assess the strengths and the weaknesses, as well as to come up with action plans to tackle the areas for improvement.

■ *Criteria for promotion.* By clearly communicating that the criteria for selecting people to be promoted have changed, management can communicate that it means business. Obviously, this approach is only credible if the new criteria are applied rigorously.

An example of this approach can be found in the acquisition of a Belgian company by an American competitor. The American parent wanted the newly acquired 'daughter' to adopt English as the official company language. To that end, all employees who had not mastered English were invited to take intensive training courses. However, some diehards simply refused to learn the language. As some of them were highly rated within the organization, they did not feel vulnerable. Eventually, management decided that anyone not passing a test of English could no longer be promoted. Gradually, everybody complied with the new rule and studied English.

■ *Non-financial rewards.* Instead of or complementary to a bonus scheme, companies can use non-financial rewards to stimulate customer-focused behaviour.

Sometimes these are linked to a competition among employees – for example, the 'employee of the month' reward. There is a risk that only the most motivated will participate, as the others will feel they can never win. Furthermore, the more motivated employees are bound to win regularly. This may turn out to be counter-productive, as others may become demoralized. This demoralization can be exacerbated if the employees question the objectivity of the jury giving the rewards. A possible way to overcome this problem is to invite customers to reward staff.

Another way of avoiding demoralization and ensuring everybody's participation is to select more than one winner – that is, to distinguish between different levels of rewards. All those who meet the top criteria can earn the platinum reward; all those who fall into the middle category earn the gold reward; and all those meeting the lowest criteria earn a silver medal.

Non-financial rewards are not necessarily merely symbolic; they can also take the form of small gifts. Certain companies offer training as a reward. They typically distinguish between two types of training. Training which is required for job performance is given to anyone – for example, all secretaries being invited to attend a course on the upgrade of a word processor. The second type of training is not required for an employee's current job, but it will allow him or her to grow within the organization. As such, being invited to attend such training opens opportunities for promotion.

It should be obvious that, by linking these rewards to the strategic performance measures and to the personal scorecards, people will start adjusting their behaviour. Although this is the objective, there is an important danger inherent in this approach. People will now alter their behaviour in order to obtain a positive appraisal. If the criteria are not correct, the outcome can be disastrous.

The biggest danger is that the criteria used to appraise people are wrong – either the strategic direction is wrong, or the set objectives are not in line with the strategy. In both cases, the consequences can be dramatic.

A more common problem is that the criteria are correct but not in balance. Companies can become customer obsessed instead of customer focused. Secretaries who can earn a bonus by improving their responsiveness on the telephone may end up picking up the telephone very quickly, but performing less well in all other aspects.

Step 5 Strategic learning

A final step in implementing the service concept consists of the systematic analysis of the relationship between the various performance measures. This process of strategic learning allows the organization to assess the soundness of the strategy and to optimize the chosen path. A company can try to improve its understanding of the relationship between each of these elements:

- Does improved employee satisfaction result in higher productivity, lower staff turnover and higher customer satisfaction?
- Does improved customer satisfaction result in less attrition, more retention and more referrals?
- Do improved employee satisfaction and customer satisfaction result in more revenue and lower costs, and consequently in better business results?
- How strong are these relationships?

In a study in the Netherlands on the role of after-sales services in developing relationships with customers of a large office equipment firm,[33] it was found that technical quality (the quality of the end result, i.e. repairing the machine properly) has a direct effect on affective commitment, but the functional quality (i.e. the quality of the process, the way in which it happens) has an indirect effect on affective commitment through customer satisfaction. So the way that the field engineer interacts with the customer has an impact on satisfaction, as well as on commitment and thus on customer retention.

In the same study the authors also tried to find the elements explaining customer perceptions of quality. High role conflict and high role ambiguity leads to lower job satisfaction for the employee and thus to lower quality. Role conflict means that the expectations of management are different from the expectations of the customers. The field engineer is confronted with this clash. For example, a superior might expect a service employee to serve as many customers as possible, while each of those customers is demanding personal attention. Role ambiguity occurs when a person does not have access to sufficient information to perform his or her role as a service employee adequately. New projects (for instance with wireless communication) can experience role conflict if not managed in the right way.

The relationship between the personal scorecards and the balanced scorecard should be monitored. If all employees implement their action plans and meet their objectives – for instance, regarding the improvement of customer satisfaction – does overall customer satisfaction go up?

These analyses will help organizations to adjust their priorities and to fine-tune the set strategy. Calculating the results of improvement projects becomes possible.

Exhibit 18.2 continued

John Brown had spent a great deal of time thinking about his three years as CEO at G-Mart. He was beginning to understand what had gone wrong. The programme had started pretty well, as all employees had a strong feeling of urgency. Furthermore, the chosen strategy had been the right one. Through internal communication he had convinced all staff that delivering world-class service was the only way to regain momentum.

Where he had failed was in setting up a system to improve the service according to clearly defined priorities. In his eagerness to regain market share, he had only discussed sales figures, turnover, number of transactions conducted and market share with his subordinates. They had repeated the same message to their people. Eventually, G-Mart became a sales-driven organization. The customer who either wanted a low price or a good service was receiving neither.

Obviously, customer satisfaction had gone up, because dissatisfied customers simply stopped doing business with G-Mart. The remaining customers seemed to be happy doing their shopping with G-Mart, but their numbers decreased.

Eventually, employees who had had their expectations raised – probably too high – saw no real improvement, so that the initial motivation and overwhelming energy turned against John Brown and G-Mart. The resulting strikes scared off the customers and finally resulted in his resignation.

He now knew what had gone wrong: his approach had been built on enthusiasm, but it had lacked an integrating system to direct the mobilized energy to the set goals.

CONCLUSION

The requirements of integration and balance in designing a performance measurement system for services form the basis of most of the content of this book: operations, marketing and human resources cannot be separated from each other in managing services. They are the components that make up the engine of a ship and are given orientation by a compass – that is, the service concept. We have also made clear that it is not enough to have a compass. It must be used to move the ship in the right direction. We therefore need a captain and a crew. If they don't understand the ship, or do not know what the ultimate destination is, the ship will not proceed in an efficient and qualitative way. The motivation of people and the alignment of their personal scorecard with the organization's balanced scorecard are crucial in implementing the service concept. The service concept must therefore be communicated in a straightforward way and attention must be paid to the system of personnel appraisal; these are the most important steps in the implementation of an integrated and balanced performance measurement system.

Review and discussion questions

- What are the similarities and the differences between integrated performance models such as the Balanced Scorecard, the EFQM Excellence model and ISO 9000:2000?

- Using Table 18.1 verify that the efficient branches have better output/input ratios than the inefficient branches. How can the inefficient branches in Table 18.2 become efficient? Which branches are used most frequently as reference?

- Using Table 18.3, develop hypotheses about the relationship between the different operational performance measures. Read the article by Loveman as indicated in the suggested reading list, and evaluate to what extent your hypotheses are supported by their research.

- What is the importance of a service concept in the implementation of an integrated performance measurement system?

Technical note

Technical Note 4 relates to this chapter. It describes in more detail the technique of Data Envelopment Analysis.

Notes and references

[1] Bruggeman, W., Bartholomeeusen, L. and Heene, A. (1988) 'How management control systems can affect the performance of service operations', *International Journal of Operations and Production Management*, Vol 8, No 3.

[2] Kaplan, R. S. and Norton, D. P. (1993) 'Putting the balanced scorecard to work', *Harvard Business Review*, Sep–Oct, 134–47.

[3] *See* the following articles and books of Kaplan, R. S. and Norton, D. P. (1992) 'The balanced scorecard – measures that drive performance', *Harvard Business Review*, Jan–Feb, 71–9; (1993) 'Putting the balanced scorecard to work', *Harvard Business Review*, Sep–Oct, 134–47;

(1996a) 'Using the balanced scorecard as a strategic management system', *Harvard Business Review*, Jan–Feb, 75–85; (1996b) *The Balanced Scorecard: Translating strategy into action*. Boston: Harvard Business School Press; (1996c) 'Linking the balanced scorecard to strategy', *California Management Review*, Vol 39, No 1, Fall, 53–79.

4 Based on Griffith, J. R., Sahney, V. K. and Mohr, R. A. (1995) *Reengineering Health Care: Building on CQI*. Ann Arbor, Michigan: Health Administration Press.

5 Kaplan, R. S. and Norton, D. P. (2001) 'Building a Strategy-Focused Organisation', *Ivey Business Journal*, Vol 65, No 5, May–June, 12–19.

6 European Foundation for Quality Management (1999) *The EFQM Excellence Model*, Pabo Prestige Press.

7 *Source*: EFQM.

8 European Foundation for Quality Management, 1999.

9 Porter, L. J. and Tanner, S. J. (1996) *Assessing Business Excellence – a guide to self-assessment*. Oxford: Butterworth-Heinemann.

10 EFQM (2001a) 'The EFQM in action', European Foundation for Quality Management.

11 Lamotte, G. and Carter, G., 'Are the Balanced Scorecard and the EFQM Excellence Model mutually exclusive or do they work together to bring added value to a company'? prepared for the EFQM Common Interest Day, 17 March 2000.

12 Lars-Erik Nilsson and Peter Samuelsson, 2000, Self-assessment for Business Excellence in Large Organisations: the EFQM Excellence Model as a tool for continuous improvement, Masters Thesis, Chalmers University of Technology, Sweden.

13 EFQM (2001b) 'ISO 9001:2000: a new stage on the journey to excellence', *Excellence Network, European Foundation for Quality Management*, Vol 1, Issue 2, Feb–March, pp. 4–7.

14 Hans-Friedrich Bühner, Manager of Business Excellence, and Klaus-Peter Bastian, Vice-President of Processe & Corporate Culture, Infineon Technologies, as quoted in EFQM, 2001.

15 EFQM (2001b), op. cit.

16 Drucker, P. F. (1999) 'Knowledge Worker Productivity: The Bigger Challenge', *California Management Review*, Vol 41, No 2, pp. 79–94.

17 Ibid.

18 Readers interested in job satisfaction scales that were developed rigorously and according to scientific standards are referred to Miller, D. (1991) *Handbook of Research Design and Social Measurement*. Sage; as well as Ferry, D. and Van de Ven, A. (1979) *Measuring and Assessing Organisations*. New York: John Wiley.

19 Relevant references for assessing levels of empowerment are Spreitzer (1996) and Van Looy *et al.* (1998b). *See* Spreitzer, G. (1996) 'Social structural characteristics of psychological empowerment', *Academy of Management Journal*, Vol 39, No 2, 483–504; Van Looy, B., Desmet, S., Krols, K. and Van Dierdonck, R. (1998b) 'Psychological empowerment in a service environment', in Swartz, T., Bowen, D. and Brown, S. (eds) *Advances in Services Marketing and Management*, Vol 7, JAI Press.

20 Caruana, A., Money, A. H. and Berthon, P. R. (2000) 'Service quality and satisfaction – the moderating role of value', *European Journal of Marketing*, Vol 34, No 11/1, 1338–53.

21 Ibid.

22 Fessard, J. and Meert, P. (1994) *De tijd van de klant* [The customer time], Roularta, 216 pp.

23 Ibid.

24 Stalk, G. and Hout, T. (1990) *Competing Against Time*. Free Press.

25 The following article gives a very good insight into the technique of DEA and also shows that DEA is frequently used in efficiency benchmarking of banks and bank branches all over the world: Avkiran, N. K. (1999) 'An application reference for data envelopment

analysis in branch banking: helping the novice researcher', *International Journal of Bank Marketing*, Vol 17, No 5, 206–20.

[26] Based on Loveman, G. W. (1998) 'Employee satisfaction, customer loyalty and financial performance: an empirical examination of the service profit chain in retail banking', *Journal of Service Research*, Vol 1, No 1, 18–31.

[27] The overall thinking in this section is inspired by Kaplan, R. S. and Norton, D. P. 'How the balanced scorecard changes your management system', *Harvard Business Review*, Jan–Feb.

[28] Heene, A. (1995) *Bruggen Bouwen naar de Toekomst*. Tielt: Lannoo.

[29] Belasco, James A. (1990) *Teaching the Elephant to Dance*. New York: Plume, pp. 99–104.

[30] Project Klachten & Luchtvaart (Complaints and Aviation Project).

[31] We first came across personal scorecards at Rank Xerox, but the name itself was found in Kaplan, R. S. and Norton, D. P. (1996b), op. cit.

[32] *See*, for an excellent and systematic account on MBO, Reddin, B. (1989) *The Output-oriented Manager*. Gower Publications.

[33] Martin Wetzels, doctoral dissertation, Maastricht University, The Netherlands.

Suggested further reading

Loveman, G. W. (1998) 'Employee Satisfaction, customer loyalty and financial performance', *Journal of Services Research*, Vol 1, No 1, 18–31. In this article, Loveman tests empirically the relationships between the different components of the services profit chain. Table 18.3 is based on this article.

Soteriou, A. and Zenios, S. A. (1999) 'Operations, quality and profitability in the provision of banking services', *Management Science*, Vol 45, No 9, 1221–38. In this article a series of efficiency benchmarking models is developed guided by the service-profit chain. The efficiency benchmarking models are based on the technique of Data Envelopment Analysis. The use of the models is illustrated using data from the branches of a commercial bank.

Van Looy, B., Gemmel, P., Desmet, S., Van Dierdonck, R. and Serneels, S. (1998) 'Dealing with productivity and quality indicators in a service environment: Some field experiences', *International Journal of Service Industry Management*, Vol 9, No 4, 359–76. In this article, a service-specific approach to performance measurement is described using process mapping, activity-based management and quality function deployment. The approach is used to develop a balanced scorecard for two case sites: a hospital and a health insurance company.

Wetzels, M., De Ruyter, K. and Lemmink, J. (1999) 'Role stress in after-sales service management', *Journal of Services Research*, Vol 2, No 1, 50–67. Martin Wetzels has written a doctoral dissertation where he empirically tests the service profit chain in an after-sales service environment. In this article, the first part of the relationship (starting with internal service capability and ending with quality) is investigated. The managerial recommendations are very interesting.

CHAPTER 19

Managing innovation in a service environment

Koenraad Debackere · Bart Van Looy

INTRODUCTION

'Virtual' banks and stockbrokers are emerging. They are not much more than a logo. They consist only of an electronic network and its customers. Other financial service companies supply the products. Buildings, headquarters, branches disappear.

A small family-owned hotel chain in Europe forms a network with other small, family-owned colleagues to develop a reservation system on the Internet to circumvent the fees they now have to pay to the institutional reservation systems like Sabre. A multi-media company develops the system. Customers will be able to make reservations by phone without the intervention of agents.

A publisher formed alliances with major suppliers of EDI tools. He acquired and internalized the necessary multimedia capabilities and applications in order to become a provider of digitized information. Today, the former publisher manages the information and marketing databases of its major customers. He prints the personalized mail-order catalogues at the request of the customers, and handles the mailing and distribution via the information carrier preferred by the customers of its customer.

The ever-increasing pace of change is well-known to any of today's managers. Technological, competitive and cultural pressures collide. Innovation's ability to fundamentally change the rules of competition is becoming generally recognized and appreciated. Management is caught in this vortex. Sometimes management creates the change, but all too often, management is reacting to it, or still worse, is hurt by the eternal gale of creative destruction whipped up by competitors that were not even part of the incumbents' strategic industry horizon.

We begin the chapter with a plea for a more holistic view of the innovation process. Innovation processes have been traditionally viewed as being rather linear and sequential. Shifting toward more iterative and spiral approaches fully supports the trend towards managing the value constellation of the company instead of 'merely' managing its value chain. This shift from the value chain towards value constellation deserves special attention for service firms as the notion of value constellation places customers and the solutions to their problems at the heart of the innovation process. Looking at innovations in this manner brings the dynamics of innovation into line with the notion of the service concept: everything starts from addressing a specific customer need and approaching these needs in an integrated manner. Moreover, in services the involvement of the customer in the innovation process is not limited to explaining needs; the intangibility and simultaneity of services implies a real involvement of customers in design and development phases as well. Given the crucial importance of approaching innovation from a value-constellation perspective for services, we shall start with this idea in the first section.

Innovation is perhaps the single most destructive force in an industry.[1] Both research and practice have highlighted the paradoxical nature of the innovation process. On the one hand, innovation fosters endogenous firm growth through the development of competence-enhancing products, processes, and services. These competence-enhancing innovations are important since they consolidate and optimize existing commercial and technological capabilities, both at the level of the firm and at the industry level. These are the well-known incremental innovations that extend and rejuvenate existing product and service platforms. On the other hand, though, innovation can be highly disruptive, destroying a firm's commercial and technological capabilities. The advent of desk-top publishing, for instance, has signalled the destruction of many well entrenched capabilities in the traditional pre-press industry.

The dual nature of the innovation process therefore necessitates careful managerial attention. Companies need to balance the competence-enhancing and the competence-destroying forces with their innovation endeavours. Innovation portfolios provide a powerful tool for managing this strategic paradox. The concept of the innovation portfolio and the process of portfolio management will therefore be major issues in this chapter.

The fact that innovations can both be competence-enhancing and competence-destroying of course raises another issue: how should this dual challenge be addressed, given the existing technological and market capabilities of the firm? Should internal developments ('make') be sought or should partners be found that embody the desired new capabilities ('buy')? We shall argue that a well-balanced innovation approach implies both making and buying.

We end this chapter by discussing some major insights and guidelines regarding the management of innovation projects at an operational level and by considering how the innovation project can be anchored within the broader organization.

Objectives

By the end of this chapter, you should be able to discuss:

- innovations as spiral processes whereby the value constellation is taken into account
- why this idea is especially relevant for services
- how the portfolio approach is beneficial in balancing the contradictory forces present within the innovation process
- how 'make' and 'buy' are both relevant for organizing the innovation portfolio
- how to approach the innovation process at the project level and how to anchor it within the organization

INNOVATIONS AS SPIRAL PROCESSES: THE VALUE-CONSTELLATION APPROACH

Early models of innovation activities took a rather linear view of the nature of the innovation process. Innovation was viewed as a sequence of phases or activities to be carried out in a rather sequential way. The linear process started with conducting research activities, followed by development and design activities, resulting in pilot production. Once the pilot production phase was finalized, large-scale production and commercialization could begin. However, research on the management of innovation in the 1970s and 1980s concluded that the process was in essence non-linear and iterative, incorporating many feedback loops between the different activities involved. Problems detected during the design phase, for instance, can trigger a new research activity. Engineering change orders are yet another (unwanted) illustration of the non-linearity of the process. They signal design changes, even when the product has already been commercially launched.

Even allowing for this non-linearity, however, approaches to managing innovation still rely on phase-based models during which the innovation gradually becomes refined and better articulated. Between the different phases or stages, important design review moments take place, resulting in crucial stop–go decisions. Various models[2] highlight the need to distinguish between the presence of different phases, stages, or activities during the innovation process. These are still managed in a rather sequential way – for example, the idea-generation phase, the concept-definition phase, the problem-solving phase, the prototype-design-test-correct cycles, the manufacturing ramp-up and commercialization phases. However, between the different phases, stop–go decision moments and evaluations are inserted to tunnel and filter uncertainty reduction.

Recently, the emphasis has been on the '*concurrency*' of the various phases, with the objective being to maximize feedback and iteration. Interdependence and overlap between the different activities and functions involved along the innovation journey are increased. However, limits to organizational as well as human resources experimentation and information processing capabilities have been important liabilities in the attempt to achieve full-blown concurrency.

This emergence of the 'concurrency' paradigm signals the need for a still more interactive and iterative way of developing and designing new products. The innovation process has now become much more dynamic and adaptive. This is best illustrated by the rise of interactive design methodologies for software development. New software is increasingly being developed in a sequence of short-cycle iterations where analysts, testers, programmers and users provide input, evaluation and monitoring of a sequence of rapidly developed prototypes. Instead of spending a long time studying a basic software design which is then followed by a detailed design, which is in turn programmed, tested and debugged, we are now being confronted with a quite different development approach. First of all, the software is increasingly being modularized. Then, for each module, small-scale prototypes are designed, quickly built, and upgraded towards full-scale applications. Specifications and functionalities are refined in a cycle of interactions between small module design groups and users. New meta-technologies – that is, technologies that support and enable the design of new technology – such as case-tools and object orientation, further foster this evolution.

As a consequence, we can start speaking of an *innovation spiral* instead of an innovation chain. The innovation spiral points to the continuous sequence of iterations refining and articulating the firm's product, service and process platforms with solutions to customers' needs being addressed in an integrated manner. In this way, they support the *value constellation* of the firm, rather than its *value chain*.[3] It seems to us that this interactive and iterative model for the development and design of new products is particularly relevant for services. Given the fact that services are intangible, prototyping, for example, is not possible; service providers have to move almost immediately from concept design to tests in the presence of customers. Moreover, by involving customers from the earliest stages in new and complementary development, ideas pop up, leading to an integrated solution for customers' needs instead of just a new product.

In the case of value-chain thinking, there is a tendency to focus on the activities in the value chain upstream or downstream from those conducted at present by the firm. Integrating or eliminating steps along the value chain proves an important source of innovation for many firms. For instance, an important service innovation in the airline industry is the elimination of the ticketing and seat reservation activity. These types of innovations are important, of course, although they are still the result of a rather linear analysis of the value chain along which the firm operates.

The *value constellation* takes a much more holistic view of the way in which the innovation process creates value for the final customer. The value constellation inspires innovation managers to fully understand and articulate how the products and services developed by their organization, in interaction with other (complementary) products and services, create value for the customer. This analysis can lead to the integration of activities across value chains (rather than along the value chain) into new product and service offerings. As a consequence, a service organization (e.g. an automobile association) might realize that, for their next service innovation, not only should they focus on their traditional activities along the value chain of providing automobile assistance, but, they might start integrating complementary activities from related value chains with their traditional automobile assistance offerings. This might result, for example, in the (co-)development of smart cards that can be used in combination with a car radio to obtain the latest traffic and automobile assistance. Value-constellation thinking thus stimulates innovation both across and within service lines (*see* Exhibit 19.1).

Exhibit 19.1

Dream ticket for truck transport[4]
A French inventor's idea could save time and money, writes *Arkady Ostrovsky*

Idly staring out of the school window can be extremely productive, according to Sebastian Lange, a 26-year-old French inventor. For it was while staring at trains and trucks stuck outside his school that Lange started thinking about putting trucks on top of trains.

The result is claimed to be a breakthrough in transport design that could reduce congestion on European highways. Earlier this month, the development won Mr Lange a prize at a European inventions competition in Monaco.

Mr Lange has come up with a way of overcoming one of the biggest problems of carrying trucks by train – how to get wagons carrying lorries through narrow, low-roofed tunnels. The system, which he has licensed to De Dietrich, a small

Exhibit 19.1 continued

French rolling stock company, could give new impetus to the slowly developing market for 'intermodal' freight transport, which combines road and rail. Several European and US rail companies have been developing intermodal transport. English, Welsh & Scottish Railway, the largest UK rail freight operator, for example, is currently testing so-called 'piggyback' trailers, which can be loaded on to specially designed wagons. However, the system is limited to carrying trailers, not trucks, and requires special lifting equipment. Swiss and Austrian rail companies cunningly use trains with smaller wheels to get wagons through tunnels in the Alps. Small wheels, however, reduce speed and increase maintenance costs.

Mr Lange's invention allows trucks and trailers to be transported on flatbed wagons with standard-size wheels and requires no lifting equipment. The invention involves lowering the middle part of the flatbed wagon on which a lorry is stationed, while the two ends remain higher to accommodate the wagon wheels. The system also allows the middle section of the wagon to be detached from the two ends so that it can be swung to the side, permitting lorries to drive on

and off. Mr Lange estimates 56 trucks can be loaded and unloaded in a train of 28 wagons in approximately 30 minutes.

Long-haul drivers in Europe are required to rest for ten hours between nine-hour shifts, but Mr Lange says his invention would allow drivers to rest on an accompanying sleeper wagon while their trucks are carried across Europe, saving time and money. The innovation, he says, would reduce a journey from the UK to Italy from two days to 24 hours.

But to build a life-size prototype of his invention, Mr Lange needs FFr 50 million (£5 million). 'De Dietrich says it has not enough cash for such a project, while big companies such as SNCF (the French state rail monopoly) do not like young graduates coming with ideas and telling them how to build trains,' says Mr Lange. 'People still have images of crazy inventors and do not believe you when you tell them your invention is practical.' Dan Hodges, of the UK's Road Haulage Association, says: 'This proposal allows a complete unit to be transported together and is by far the most efficient intermodal option available for our members. We hope to support and promote it in any way we can.'

Taking a closer look at the concept of an innovation spiral, we find that breakthrough innovations are often the basis of a whole range of new product and service families that are marked by an increase in functional variety and application possibilities. For instance, the innovative breakthrough of processing soya in food and relating this to health and physical well-being has triggered the development of a highly varied stream of product platforms, such as soya margarines, soya yoghurts, and soya drinks. The result has been a range of new product–market possibilities. Not only has the depth of the product–market assortments offered been augmented, but also the breadth and variety of product–market possibilities have dramatically increased thanks to underlying process innovations.

Although anyone would agree that, once such a breakthrough has been realized, harvesting the possibilities offered should be the next step, the paradoxical nature of the innovation emerges here yet again. Indeed, without active management intervention, what was once a breakthrough innovation will ultimately result in very incremental changes. For instance, in the longer run, innovations in the soya drink product range may end up by adding more and more varieties of flavours to the assortment. This type of incremental innovation, unfortunately, is strongly affected by imitative actions from competitors, eroding the firm's initial competitive advantage at increasing speed. Moreover, this trend often results in the incremental innovator being led by its customers and competitors, rather than it leading its customers and competitors.

As a consequence, management has to strike a continuous balance between the need for short-term incremental improvement to its existing product–market platforms and the more long-term need for fundamentally new business development.

Although the spiral model based on the analysis of value constellations allows for a more accurate modelling and understanding of the innovation process than the 'traditional' linear and value-chain oriented models, it still has one major drawback: if used inadvertently, it may once again lead to 'path-dependent' thinking. There is a risk that a company will become locked into the technical path chosen, a path which will inevitably be eroded over time.

In order to minimize the dangers of path-dependent thinking, the concept of the innovation portfolio can be used. The portfolio approach forces management to articulate its innovation efforts in several dimensions that are determinants of both the long-term and short-term survival and good health of the firm.

INNOVATION PORTFOLIO MANAGEMENT

Portfolio management forces management to make the mission and nature of the organization's innovation activity explicit. The framework developed by Kim Clark and Steve Wheelwright[5] at Harvard Business School distinguishes between *research, breakthrough, platform* and *derivative projects* (*see* Figure 19.1). These different types of projects support different missions entailed in the firm's innovation efforts.

The objectives of innovation strategy[6]

Portfolios thus first of all remind us of the fact that innovation activities serve several purposes. The most obvious (and also the one involving fewer risks) is to provide support to existing business. This, of course, is a short-term objective which results in mostly incremental improvements to existing products and services: the so-called *derivative* projects.

Besides this short-term objective, innovation efforts also aim at extending and expanding the existing product range of the organization (*platform* projects). This is achieved through the creation of new product generations for existing markets, or through the further extension, adaptation and modification of existing service families to new markets. Innovation activities also carry the seeds of creative destruction. *Breakthrough* innovations break or change the rules of the competitive game. They have the potential to fundamentally destroy and re-orient the technological capabilities as well as the market capabilities in an industry. For example, the Internet breakthrough will fundamentally re-orient the way we do business, both from an organizational perspective and from a technical and commercial perspective.

Finally, innovative companies also realize that they have to continuously rejuvenate and adjust their competence base. Hence, a final objective of an innovation strategy is the timely alignment of the firm's technical competencies (or knowledge economy) to its future product–market requirements.

The four objectives of a firms innovation strategy can therefore be summarized as:

- support to existing operations and products;
- extension and expansion of product range;

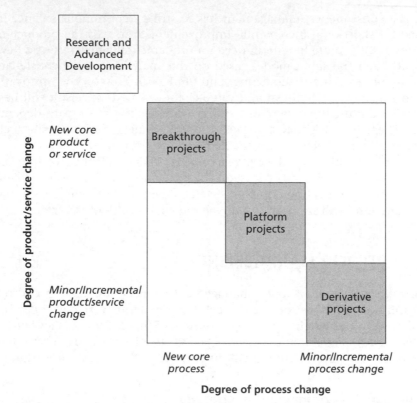

Figure 19.1 The innovation portfolio

Source: Adapted with the permission of the Free Press, a Division of Simon & Schuster, from *Revolutionizing Product Development: Quantum leaps in speed, Efficiency, and Quality* by Wheelwright, S. C. and Clark, K. B. Copyright © 1992 by Wheelwright, S. C. and Clark, K. B.

- creation of breakthrough products and processes;
- rejuvenation and alignment of the firm's competence base.

The strategic objectives of a firm's innovation efforts have to be balanced over time. The relative weight of each objective can vary over time and place in the firm's strategy process. For instance, competitive pressures may force the firm to (temporarily) focus the bulk of its innovation investment on support to and incremental improvement of its existing product range. However, senior management should be fully aware of this distribution of focus and assess the long-term consequences of not investing (or over-investing) in particular innovation objectives and outcomes.

The first two objectives (the support to existing operations and products as well as extension and expansion of the product range) attempt to exploit powerful learning-curve effects during the firm's innovation process. The other objectives (the creation of breakthrough product and service innovations as well as rejuvenating and aligning the competence base to future needs) are more disruptive, necessitating 'un-'learning and signalling the onset of new learning curves.

The project typology as developed by Wheelwright and Clark and shown in Figure 19.1, offers managers an instrument around which processes can be developed to ensure that the strategic objectives of the innovation process are in balance.

Types of innovation projects

As Figure 19.1 shows, the innovation project typology makes a distinction between the *service offering* and *the service delivery process*. Positioning the various types of innovation activity within the matrix highlights the fact that service offering and service process innovations are related.[7]

The creation of new service offerings to complement an existing line of service offerings is illustrated by the financial services sector. Over the last decade, the boundaries between banks and insurance companies have blurred. This has led to serious efforts by all players in the market to develop new services, resulting in new combinations of typical bank and insurance offerings. Innovations can also occur at the level of the service delivery process: banks invest in electronic banking facilities and supermarkets install optical readers linked to cash registers. Although these process innovations in some cases have not affected the basic services banks or supermarkets are offering, it has changed the delivery process and had a significant impact on the queues at check-outs. It has also given supermarkets a better understanding of customer preferences and allowed for more efficient direct marketing, stock control and purchasing strategy.

Combining both axes – the *content* of the service offerings and the service delivery *process* – allows us to define the three types of innovation projects with greater accuracy.

- *Derivative projects* imply small or incremental changes and improvements to either the services itself, the service delivery process, or both. For example, the development of a new savings account for loyal customers, or the development of express check-out counters in a supermarket.
- *Breakthrough projects* imply radical changes to existing services as well as to the delivery process. The offerings that result from a breakthrough innovation differ fundamentally from their predecessors. For example, second-hand cars are sold at several locations. During the second half of the 1980s, Japan witnessed the emergence of Aucnet. Aucnet was founded by Masataka Fujisaki and made use of a computer and satellite communications system. Each week, sellers can call Aucnet with a list of cars they are offering. Aucnet people then travel to the seller's lots, verify the information on the cars and collect pictures of them. All this information is then digitized and distributed to dealers who subscribe to the system. Consumers can access this system and choose from a larger variety of cars than ever before. This type of innovation has a dramatic impact both on the 'technology' used to sell second-hand cars and on the 'customer relations' through which the commercial transaction is organized.
- *Platform projects* fill the middle ground between breakthroughs and derivatives. Originating in breakthroughs, they imply significant product–market extensions and the developments of new services, both in terms of the service itself and in terms of the service delivery process, or both. For example, the breakthrough project of electronic banking led to the spin-off of a multitude of platform projects like electronic banking for larger companies, followed by electronic banking services for SMEs, and ultimately, electronic banking applications for the home. These electronic banking platforms were then further complemented with application platforms such as services to compute taxes, to prepare investment projects, etc.

From a strategic perspective, the distribution of the firm's innovation efforts into breakthrough, platform and derivative projects is crucial. Figure 19.1 shows that breakthrough projects imply fundamental changes both from a product/functional perspective and from an operations/process perspective. New core products and new core processes are created. They support the *long-term competitive position* of the company. Platform projects are positioned at the origins of the creation of new product families. They symbolize the degree of product–market differentiation and diversification the company is aiming for. As a consequence, platform projects are mostly *medium-term oriented*. Derivative projects, finally, point to incremental changes (both from a product perspective and a process perspective) that further enhance the performance (in terms of cost and/or functionality) of the firm's existing platforms. By their very nature, they are *short-term oriented*.

It is clear that the bulk of the firm's innovation efforts should go into the execution of platform projects as they represent the medium-term survival of the company. Typically, experience suggests that 50 to 60 per cent of the firm's innovation efforts should be devoted to the creation of new platforms. Derivative projects are important since they sustain existing market relationships. However, portfolio management should be aware of the dangers involved in placing too much emphasis on derivative project activities since they quickly degenerate into imitative behaviour (as they are often driven by short-term customer requests or by the moves of competitors).

In addition to the three types of projects described above, there are more fundamental research activities which can be labelled as *research and advanced development projects*. These involve, for example, the researcher taking on new scientific or technological leads, thereby exploring fundamental know-how and know-why that may ultimately lead to the development of new competence areas for the organization. These projects are not aimed at creating specific products yet. Nevertheless, companies are recommended to frame these research and advanced development activities within a context of value-oriented thinking. In other words, the potential to contribute to value creation (even if it is still defined according to rather abstract and often subjective dimensions) should not be neglected when defining, selecting and following up those research and advanced development projects. Research and advanced development projects or activities are singled out in this portfolio model. This is because their uncertain and unpredictable nature causes extreme difficulties for predicting specific outputs and results within a pre-defined time-frame and budget constraint. It is therefore advisable to consider them as a separate, long-term investment whose progress cannot be measured against well-defined and predetermined criteria and standards. This does not mean, of course, that the quality of the effort cannot be measured and monitored. In terms of future business performance, however, outcome predictability is low.

Creating a balanced portfolio

The benefits of this framework relate to the way in which it enables the firm to manage the collection of innovation activities it is carrying out. It allows for the design of a *balanced* innovation strategy, taking into account both the shorter- and longer-term imperatives of business strategy. It is therefore interesting to map the different projects that are proposed in the innovation portfolio along a number of dimensions that make their contribution to the firm's strategy even more explicit. Typical dimensions are the following:

■ *Distributions of reward expectations versus risk.* What are the potential rewards to be reaped when the new product is introduced in the marketplace (these rewards are often described in qualitative terms such as modest, acceptable and outstanding)? How do these compare with the risk that the project achieves a combined market and commercial success? The logic behind this type of criteria mapping is that more risky projects tend to be more promising in terms of rewards and benefits. This is typical of breakthrough projects. The balancing act then calls for an equilibrium between risky but potentially outstanding projects in terms of rewards and benefits on the one hand, and less risky but often also less rewarding projects on the other. Derivative projects are typical examples of projects involving little market and technology risk, while at the same time often offering limited rewards.

■ *Time-to-market distributions.* We do not want the portfolio to be too long-term oriented, neglecting the need to achieve short-term, bottom-line results. However, at the same time, we should refrain from having project distributions that are too heavily oriented towards the short-term, since they signal an incapacity to develop and sustain the long-term business development process of the firm. Hence, the need to carefully monitor the time-to-market distribution in the portfolio.

■ *The product and technology life cycles underlying the projects.* Product and technologies typically show S-curve life cycles. After a start-up (*embryonic*) phase, they often tend to develop rapidly, as shown by dramatic increases in sales (*product life cycles*) or technological performance (*technology life cycles*). However, there are limits to performance growth, both from a product and technology perspective. The result is that (inevitably) *maturity* sets in. Mature products and services are subject to margin erosion and sales stagnation. Mature technologies are marked by diminishing marginal returns on technological performance. Mature products and technologies are either replaced by newer ones, or rejuvenated by 'enabling' breakthrough innovations – for example, the punctuated leaps in performance increases in silicon technology as a result of breakthroughs achieved in silicon processing technologies, despite the long predicted 'maturity' of silicon-based semiconductor products. It is therefore necessary to monitor the maturity distribution of the technologies and products captured by the development projects in the portfolio. Mature portfolios are vulnerable to substitution and other competitive pressures. Portfolios that have a disproportionate presence of embryonic technologies, products or services contain a high degree of risk. Once again, there is a need to balance maturity distributions.

■ *The degree of familiarity with the market and the technology.* The less the organization is familiar with the technological capabilities to be deployed in the project and/or markets to be served by the project, the higher the risk involved and the greater the need for collaboration with external partners. The market/technology familiarity distributions therefore provide yet another insight into the nature of the firm's innovation portfolio.

So far, we have discussed some of the considerations related to portfolio management in innovative environments. As was suggested during the discussion on the familiarity criterion, the portfolio also highlights weaknesses with respect to the technological and/or market capabilities of the firm. These can be solved through the management of 'make' and 'buy' decisions.

ORGANIZING THE INNOVATION PORTFOLIO: THE MAKE-OR-BUY DECISION

The development of new business activities via the portfolio approach and methodology can be achieved through:

1. internal development activities (the 'make' decision);
2. reliance on other partners to conduct part of the development activity (the 'buy' decision); or
3. joining internal and external development capabilities (the 'co-operate' decision).

Table 19.1 reflects the spectrum along which the make-and-buy decision should be situated.

Roberts and Berry[8] point out that the relevance of the different approaches will depend on the degree of familiarity with both the technical requirements and the market requirements of the new business. Familiarity has to be interpreted from the perspective of the company analysing its portfolio. For instance, a bank may not yet be familiar with a certain new chip card technology; however, this technology may already have been around for a long time, and thus, it may not be 'new to the world' at all. Hence, familiarity points to the extent to which competencies (both market- and technology-related) are present within the firm.

By stressing both technology and market familiarity, the distinction between breakthrough, platform and derivative projects can be further enriched:

- Breakthrough projects imply increasing degrees of newness and hence will often imply less familiarity.
- Derivative projects are minor extensions of the existing competence base; the company will be familiar with both the market and the underlying technology.
- Platform projects are situated inbetween.

As a consequence, there is a direct link between familiarity and risk: the less the company is familiar with the market or technical aspects of the new business, the higher the risk of failure.

So Table 19.1 can now be linked to the familiarity concept in the following way. The more the company is familiar with the technology and/or the market, the more it can rely on internal mechanisms (such as 'making' the technology using internal development and internal ventures) or disembodied modes of technology transfer and acquisition (such as 'buying' the technology via licensing) to develop the new product or service. These modes can be deployed because the level of familiarity ensures that the organization is able to understand and to handle both the technical and the functional (or market-related) parameters involved in the project.

However, when this capacity is underdeveloped (either from a market or a technology perspective), the project will only succeed if this situation can be rectified. In other words, innovation projects can only succeed if, within the organization carrying out the project, there are well-developed market and technical

Table 19.1 The make-or-buy decision spectrum[9]

Internal developments	This implies the use and development of existing resources, meaning also that the time lag for breaking even tends to be long, especially when these new developments are related to breakthrough projects.
Internal ventures	Existing resources are grouped into a new entrepreneurial unit. Although it allows the company to hold on to talented entrepreneurs, one often observes a mixed record of success. Organizational culture is a critical element in creating and sustaining a successful internal venture process.
Licensing	Licensing allows rapid access to proven knowledge, systems, processes or technology, and reduces the financial exposure. However, the licensee remains dependent upon the licenser throughout the entire process.
Venture capital investments	By providing venture capital to small start-up firms working on relevant new developments, the firm can obtain a 'window on technology'. While this strategy allows for (initially) low levels of commitment, this type of buy decision is not without its problems. The agreement of time horizons between the capital provider and the receiver of funds is not easy, balancing financial and non-financial objectives often causes tensions, and legal problems related to property rights often surface.
Joint ventures or alliances	The competence base of the firm is linked to another company, preferably one with complementary assets. Whereas this approach allows a company to balance risks during the innovation effort, it also requires investments in developing a common infrastructure for the venture as well as establishing operational relationships at the level of the innovative staff belonging to the venture partners.
Acquisitions	In this mode, a company acquires new competencies through the acquisition of another company. In doing so, it gains access to technical capabilities and market competencies it does not possess. However, the challenges of becoming familiarized with the new competence areas and of establishing co-operative relationships between the parent and the newly acquired organization are often high. All too often, core competencies disappear during the transition period. The inability of the parent to accommodate the acquisition, often results in core staff members leaving the newly acquired company. A special form of acquisition is the 'educational' acquisition. Here, the emphasis is on gaining access to the people familiar with the new business. While this allows for rapid familiarization with the technical and market aspects of the new business, the success of this approach depends to a large extent on the ability to retain the key people involved.

Source: Reprinted from Roberts, E. B. and Berry, C. A. (1985) 'Entering new business: Selecting strategies for success', *Sloan Management Review*, Vol 23, No 3, by permission of the Publishers. Copyright (1998) by Sloan Management Review Association. All rights reserved.

competencies relevant to the successful completion of the project. If this is not the case, the company will have to acquire and develop these competencies. When there is a serious lack of familiarity, the organization will have to engage in an *embodied technology transfer mode*, implying not only a black box transfer of technical or market results, but also a more intense and co-operative mode of transfer involving fluxes of people as the major carriers of the competencies needed. Hence,

Table 19.2 Portfolio management and the make-and-buy decision

Objective	Type of innovation	Transfer mechanism	Emphasis is on
Developing new competence	Research/advanced development	Embodied buy mode	Exploring
Creating new product and service generations	Breakthrough project	Embodied as well as disembodied buy mode	Strategic business development
Expanding actual product	Platform project	Disembodied buy mode as well as make mode	Sustaining current competitive position Exploitation
Improving/adjusting existing product and service offerings	Derivative project	Make mode	Quick market response and diffusion

as familiarity decreases, we witness a rise in the use of such mechanisms as acquisitions and joint ventures.

In all cases, however, the familiarity discussion demonstrates that, in order to successfully 'buy' and integrate 'new' competencies, the company also has to possess or develop a base of internal competencies. This internal competence base characterizes the absorptive capacity of the company. Therefore, we cannot speak any longer of the make-or-buy decision; rather, we should refer to the *make-and-buy* decision. Indeed, competencies can only be successfully bought when they are supported and complemented by internal capabilities.

It is also obvious that the ways or sequences in which the different make-and-buy mechanisms are deployed, evolve over time. When entering a new business, the emphasis will be on embodied transfer modes. The more competencies are developed internally, the more the company can engage in disembodied transfer modes and fully supported internal development approaches. Hence, the deployment of the various mechanisms discussed in Table 19.1 will change as well, involving the use of different organizational approaches as the internal competencies co-develop and co-evolve. This co-evolution, and its link to portfolio management, is further illustrated in Table 19.2.

Now that we have achieved a better understanding of portfolio management as a tool to support the process of strategic decision making regarding product and service innovations, including the need to balance the internal and external development of competencies, we can start looking at the operational paradoxes in the management of innovation.

THE OPERATIONAL MANAGEMENT OF INNOVATION

In Figure 19.2, we provide a summary overview (simplified) of the key performance variables relevant to the innovation processes at the operational level. The critical influence of information flows and communication patterns on the performance of innovation activities has been well documented and is the subject of major research attention. Not only are intense intra-organizational and cross-functional information flows and communication patterns necessary during the innovation

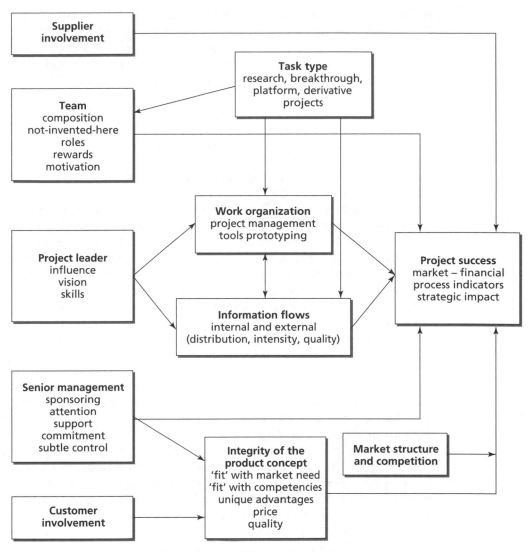

Figure 19.2 Performance determinants of innovation projects[10]

Source: Debackere, Van Looy and Vliegen, 1997. Reprinted with permission of Blackwell Publishers Ltd.

process, but, the innovative organization must also be closely linked to its broader (external) technological environment. This close relationship is symbolized by the presence of special 'network' roles during the innovation process, among which the gatekeeper figures prominently. Related studies that have their origins in the development and the marketing of new products have further pointed to the importance of the design and the application of appropriate work organization techniques and approaches for achieving innovative performance.[11] These include:

■ the use of flowchart-based decision and monitoring models of the innovation process;

■ the application of project management techniques;

■ the introduction of creativity and idea-generation techniques, like brainstorming;

- the development of selection methodologies that respond to the innovation's need for tolerating and handling uncertainty and ambiguity;
- the use and the design of grid-methodologies and techniques to define and to monitor innovation opportunities (e.g. product maturity grids, business growth matrices, quality function deployment matrices).

The interaction and co-evolution of work organization techniques and information flows is at the very heart of the operational management of the innovation process. Information flows are to be initiated and supported by an appropriate work-organization methodology. However, in order for these work methods to be deployed successfully, the necessary informal as well as formal information flows and communication patterns have to be developed.

As shown in Figure 19.2, the innovation performance is complex and multi-dimensional. Performance relates to such rational, financial indicators as market shares and revenues that accrue from innovative activities. However, market shares and revenues only present one dimension of the performance concept. A second type of performance dimension relates to perceptual measures as the innovation's contribution to the strategic mission of the organization. The third route towards measuring performance refers to the internal efficiency of the innovation process. It considers the extent to which the innovation process is efficiently managed in terms of, for instance, throughput times during the various phases of the innovation trajectory (e.g. time-to-concept, experimental problem-solving cycle times, time-to-ramp-up).

These dimensions of innovative performance (often operationalized at the project-level and aggregated at the portfolio-level) are influenced by a myriad of parameters, as is further shown in Figure 19.2. Communication patterns, information flows and work organization techniques are at the heart of this framework. In addition, there are important roles to be assumed. Senior management attitudes and commitment, project leader traits and behaviour, as well as team member characteristics, all exert a strong influence on the performance of innovation activities. Moreover, these have to be embedded in an appropriate motivational context, using incentive mechanisms that foster 'project ownership' rather than performance 'control'. Incentive mechanisms encouraging entrepreneurship and 'ownership' in innovative contexts therefore have to be related to the realization of project outcomes as well as to the overall success of the project in the eyes of its customer – for example, by providing substantive bonus schemes for project members if they achieve a successful project result. Of course, as suggested in Figure 19.2, the complexity of the project (research, breakthrough, platform or derivative) has an important impact on the relationships just described. More specifically, in the case of derivative or incremental projects, these performance relationships can be managed in a much more structured and formalized way than in the case of a research activity or a breakthrough project. For instance, in a breakthrough project, creating ownership may involve the development of highly visible bonus schemes that give the project members significant stakes in the project's success. For derivative projects this should not be the case. Here the incentive system should evaluate such 'classic' performance control criteria as responsiveness and timeliness of the project members' activities.

The involvement of external parties, more specifically suppliers and customers, is yet another well-known determinant of innovation success.[12] The relative importance of their impact varies depending on the party that obtains the highest returns from investing in the innovation. Although this is a simple criterion, it may be difficult to determine who will benefit most from a particular innovation, certainly when it pertains to emerging industries.

For example, the telecommunications industry is in a state of flux. Product and service innovations are increasingly intertwined and have a dramatic impact on our daily lives. However, it is unclear so far who will reap the most benefits from these innovations. Five years ago, MCI was a big innovator in the industry. Today, it has been acquired by WorldCom, who are is much smaller than MCI but are now one of the most admired service innovators in the industry. However, it is still unclear whether a company like WorldCom will ultimately be able to reap the benefits from those innovations, or whether they will accrue to another as yet unknown player in the industry. It is only when the value constellation can be articulated, that we can start to analyse who should benefit most from involvement in the innovation process. In emerging industries, this value constellation is most often unclear, and hence the relative importance of users and suppliers is difficult to establish.

As can be seen in Figure 19.2, the structure of the market or the degree of competition in the marketplace are other important parameters influencing success along the innovation journey. Turbulent market structures, marked by high degrees of monopolistic competition, strongly moderate the 'optimal' organization of the innovation process. Examples abound, such as the case of Quantum Corporation.[13] Quantum, active in the area of computer disk drives, experienced a turbulent, fast-evolving marketplace with fierce competition based on slightly differentiated product characteristics. This competitive environment necessitated an innovation function highly responsive to frequent changes in the marketplace. As a solution, Quantum based the organization of its innovation process on flexible lateral (team-based) structures, state-of-the-art functions or competencies and appropriate incentive systems. These required each team member to act as a 'cross-functional specialist' who had to strike a balance between team performance and individual performance, as well as between expertise and experience. Appropriate incentive systems were developed and implemented.

This need for 'cross-functional specialists' points to the dilemma or the tension present in the matrix structure – a tension which is characteristic of most innovative organizations. An innovator always needs to balance the development of competencies (i.e. the development of a satisfactory absorptive capability) with the imperative to achieve the results expected from the projects and programmes in the portfolio. This dilemma is often captured by creating a matrix form of organization structure, in which competence areas and project teams are intertwined and balanced. As Figure 19.3 shows, successful innovation efforts require 'strong' matrix structures.

In order for competencies to be allocated to and deployed in a breakthrough or platform project, they need to be up-to-date and state-of-the-art (we intentionally leave out derivative projects, since they often require only minimal forms of project organization). Hence, successful breakthrough and platform projects will have to be embedded in well developed competence areas. This calls for a 'strong' matrix structure, where competence areas and project management are allies in resource accumulation and deployment, rather than the one being dominated by the other. Both need to be state-of-the-art in their respective domains of expertise and experience.

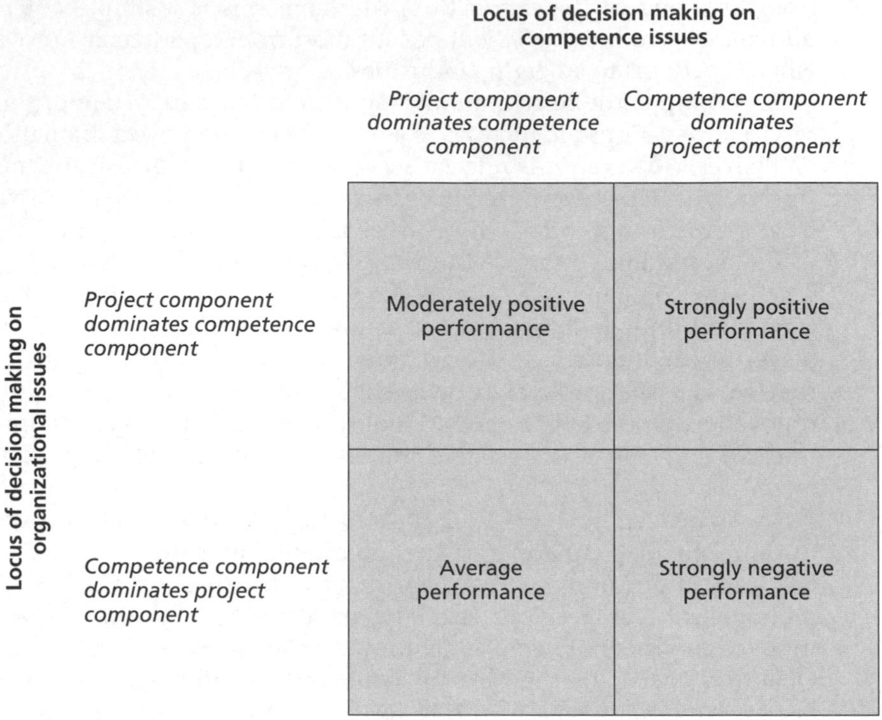

Locus of decision making on competence issues

	Project component dominates competence component	*Competence component dominates project component*
Project component dominates competence component	Moderately positive performance	Strongly positive performance
Competence component dominates project component	Average performance	Strongly negative performance

Locus of decision making on organizational issues

Figure 19.3 Project performance in the innovation matrix[14]

Source: Adapted from Katz, R. and Allen, T. (1985) 'The locus of control in the R&D matrix', *Academy of Management Journal*, Vol 28, No 1, 67–87.

Clearly, the presence of two strong components sows the seeds of a situation of conflict. However, this need not be a problem since a 'strong' matrix will certainly have some conflict between its project and competence components. What a 'strong' matrix certainly does have is an ability to solve those conflicts. In other words, these forms of organization handle the tensions that occur between their competence and project components not by being conflict-free, but through their ability to manage and resolve the conflicts that inevitably occur. This is a critical capability in managing innovation matrices. Certain companies, such as Intel, have become very good at it.

This argument is further corroborated by the research results reported in Figure 19.3. Two major dimensions that relate to decision making in an innovation matrix have to be addressed:

1. Decisions about competence issues will have to be made – for example, those relating to technical issues such as the telecommunication protocol to be used in the development of a new service. Will it be the Internet protocol TCP/IP or not?
2. Decisions have to be made with respect to organizational or managerial issues – for example, those relating to the allocation of (additional) resources to a project or the evaluation of the performance of project team members.

For each of these decision areas, we have to ask what should be the most influential component. Should it be the competence component of the organization, or should it be the project component? The summary research results reported in Figure 19.3 show that the highest performance is obtained when a balance is realized between the competence and the project component. The project component then dominates organizational/managerial decision making, while the competence component dominates competence-related or technical decision making. The lowest performance occurs when the competence component dominates both organizational/managerial decision making and technical decision making on the project. In the other instances (*see* Figure 19.3), project performance is average or moderately positive.

The tension in the innovation matrix therefore calls for competencies and projects to be both well managed and state-of-the-art, instead of one dominating the other. Unfortunately, the fact that organizations have – and always will have – only limited resources available, often obscures this important finding. Very often, the finite capacity problem is solved by allowing one component in the innovation matrix to control the other component on both dimensions of the decision-making process, resulting in sub-optimal performance, as demonstrated in Figure 19.3.

Even worse, all too often the finite capacity constraints are resolved by making the traditional functional (i.e. the competence-based) organization dominate decision making in both dimensions. As is demonstrated in Figure 19.3, this is the worst-case scenario. Typically, in such a situation, it becomes impossible for a company to grow and to retain strong project management skills and leadership. The overall result is a portfolio which underperforms and does not achieve its objectives in terms of strategic support to the growth of the company.

Now that we are acquainted with innovation and its translation into practice, the issue can be raised of whether and to what extent innovation management is different within service environments.

A first observation that must be made in this respect relates to the amount of R&D spending. In general, this is lower for services than for manufacturing firms.[15] Recent OECD figures indicate that about 15 per cent of all business expenditure on R&D (BERD) takes place within service industries. Given that these same industries count for about 70 per cent of GDP, it seems that manufacturing industries are 'outperforming' services in this area. There are several reasons for this difference. The first relates to the character of innovations in services. The majority of these innovations are non-technical and involve small and incremental changes, which often require little R&D. In addition, innovation surveys have made clear that R&D expenditure is only one element of a firm's innovation expenditure. Spending linked to changes in processes, organizational arrangements and training of staff seems to represent a larger share of expenditures for innovation in service environments.[16] Also, one frequently observes within services 'ad hoc' innovations stemming directly from a particular request from a customer,[17] which seldom result in the formation of a 'centralized' R&D department. Hence, within service environments, R&D activities tend to be more 'hidden' and their extent less well documented. It is nevertheless clear that during the last few decades, more R&D activity has taken place in manufacturing industries. Service industries have thereby tended to play the role of 'lead user', whereby ideas and requests for new ways of delivering services resulted in the service firms' suppliers developing new technology, instead of these technologies being developed by the service firms 'in house'. A crucial role in this respect is played by the IT industry, as became clear in Chapter 17.

While this might give a rather 'passive' view of innovation within service companies some serious nuances can and should be made. First of all, over the last decade, R&D expenditures have steadily increased within service firms, bringing them closer to the ranges observed in manufacturing industries.[18] Secondly (and this phenomenon has already been discussed in Chapter 3), the boundaries between manufacturing and service industries are tending to fade. Servitization implies that manufacturing companies will to an ever-increasing extent offer bundles of products and services; similarly, service firms are often very interested in complementing their offerings with products (*see* Chapter 21). As a consequence, the distinctions in the ways in which innovation is organized between services and manufacturing are tending to disappear.

In addition, considerable differences can be observed between industries, and even between firms within an industry, in the role and importance of innovation, and thus of R&D activities. It seems that these differences no longer correspond to boundaries between services or manufacturing industries. Industries such as engineering and telecommunications outperform a lot of manufacturing industries in terms of R&D intensity. In this respect, taking the nature of the service delivery process itself into account might be more relevant for explaining the R&D intensity of a service firm (or industry). We will illustrate this idea with the service classifications advanced by Mills and Margulies and discussed in Chapter 1. Maintenance-interactive services, given their predictable and routine character, are most susceptible to standardization (*see* Part 3) and are most easily translated into technology (*see* Chapter 17); it will therefore come as no surprise that the R&D intensity of such service firms is tending to resemble that of manufacturing firms.[19] As for task-interactive services, the specialized knowledge involved in their delivery means that two types of technologies play a central role. These are specialized equipment (such as medical), and more generic, knowledge-supporting technologies such as databases, expert systems and communication technologies that allow for information exchange between experts (*see also* Chapters 11 and 17). Finally, personal-interactive services seem to benefit mainly from this last type of technology; the ambiguous nature of at least part of the service transaction itself makes it extremely difficult to introduce tools or technology that complement the competencies embodied by the service provider as a person. Thus it could be said that organizing R&D activities as outlined above might be somewhat less relevant for personal-interactive services. For task- and maintenance-interactive services, organizing innovation becomes a process very similar to the processes taking place within manufacturing environments.

Two important points need to be stressed in this respect. First of all, getting organized with respect to innovation requires an explicit R&D *investment* strategy. As demonstrated above, translating an innovation project portfolio into a range of new services will require resources, which will more often than not be human. As will be illustrated in Chapter 21, services can suffer from 'limits to earnings due to restrictions on selling capacity'. This simply means that what you can earn may be limited by the time (capacity) available within the service organization. For instance, if you are a consultant, your earnings amount to the number of hours you work, multiplied by the earnings per hour. If you decide to invest in R&D projects, this might imply that you forego short-term revenue in the hope that it will be compensated by future revenues from the new projects. The intangibility of services (since they consist mainly of know-how) poses specific problems, however; the problematic nature of intellectual property rights arrangements for services has been pointed out by several scholars. While patents offer many manufacturing industries a solid ground for safeguarding the future benefits resulting from the investments made, the intangible nature of services makes effective protection less straightforward.[20] And whereas trademarks and copyrights do exist, they are generally much easier to circumvent than patents. Hence, within services, short-term-oriented R&D projects, which entail fewer resources, tend to be favoured over projects with extended time frames and requiring considerable resources. Stated otherwise, in order to arrive at an effective realization of any innovation strategy, service firms will have to come up with a well designed plan that addresses the way in which the results of these investments will be appropriated. We will discuss this issue in more depth in the chapter on service strategy.

Secondly, a particular phenomenon in relation to innovation and services has been advanced by Barras (1986):[21] the idea of the 'reversed product cycle'. Whereas manufacturing environments are dominated by the idea that product innovations are followed by process innovations, the opposite may hold true for services. Within manufacturing environments, the so-called Abernathy-Utterback model,[22] named after the authors who proposed it, is considered highly valuable. This model illustrates how the nature of a company's innovation activity changes as it grows and matures. During a first phase, a novel product design is subject to major changes; since product characteristics are underdetermined, product innovations are numerous. These innovations are focused on improving the functional per-formance of the product, rather than on reducing its (production) costs. After a while (often as a result of frequent interaction with lead users) a 'dominant' design tends to emerge, implying a stabilized product concept. The product becomes standardized and production systems become more and more efficient and reliable, precisely because the product design doesn't change fundamentally. Innovation during this second stage focuses on process improvements and adaptations. What Barras has been suggesting with respect to services is that the order of these stages is reversed. In certain services, like banking, insurance and administration, Barras observed a product life cycle opposite to the traditional industrial cycle. At the beginning, there is the adoption of an item of a new technology, for instance computer equipment. This first triggers the emergence of incremental process inno-vations resulting in efficiency improvements of the services provided. In a next step, one arrives at more radical improvements in terms of service quality, to finally arrive at the emergence of new products based on these new technologies. A case in point here is the introduction of home banking, in which PCs and networks are used to connect the bank's customers to its services. Although this initially results in less expensive distribution channels, it also implies new quality achievements (availability, speed). Nowadays, the Internet banking platform is being used more and more to introduce new services (e.g. tax simulation). While it is true that this process might not hold for all service industries to the same extent,[23] it again draws our attention to the design of specific innovation trajectories – including relevant roadmaps – that fit with the specific nature of services.

CONCLUSION

In this chapter, we have provided an overview of the major strategic and opera-tional imperatives that come into play during the development of new products and services. Innovation efforts should be aimed at providing solutions for customers' needs and problems. In services, it is especially crucial for companies to bear in mind the notion of value constellation; innovation efforts should in a sense be in line with the service concept the company is striving to achieve.

Moreover, innovation is a paradoxical process; both competence-enhancing and competence-destructive forces need to be balanced. We deliberately focused on products as well as services since recent trends in innovation in service industries show that the two have become increasingly intertwined. Thus, the development of combined product/service offerings becomes imperative to successful innovation practice in service industries.

In order to develop these product/service platforms, firms will have to balance their portfolios. This balancing act has a cross-sectional dimension as well as a longitudinal one. From a cross-sectional perspective, portfolio management requires a balance to be struck between the longer term (breakthrough projects) and the shorter term (derivative projects). Management thus has to develop a strategic vision as to the sequence and the timing of the development of new product and service platforms.

Given the dual nature of the innovation process, both make and buy actions will be relevant for acquiring new capabilities.

Next, we discussed the operational issues of managing innovation projects and the organizational structure in which this strategic innovation portfolio becomes embedded. As we have suggested, this structure has to be 'strong', enabling and sustaining a 'strong' project component as well as a 'strong' competence component. This balancing act is at the heart of the operational performance of the innovative service organization. Finally we discussed differences between manufacturing and services environments in terms of defining and implementing an adequate innovation strategy.

Review and discussion questions

- How important is innovation for the long-term survival and growth of service firms? Why? Can you give examples? Would you consider this importance the same for all sorts of service industries? Why/why not?

- Suppose you are a successful R&D manager within a large manufacturing company. You are asked to develop the R&D activities of a large international bank. While the offer is very interesting, you still have your doubts; do you have all the relevant experience and do you know how to succeed? Stated otherwise, what might be different in terms of managing an R&D department within a large service firm, as opposed to managing such a department within a manufacturing firm? Would you consider these to be differences of degree?

Notes and references

[1] *See*, for instance, Kay, J. (1993) *Foundations of Corporate Success*. Oxford: Oxford University Press.

[2] *See*, for instance, Saren, M. (1984) 'Models of the innovation process', *R&D Management*, Vol 14, No 1, 11–24; Roberts, E. B. and Frohman, A. (1978) 'Strategies for improving

research utilisation', *Technology Review*, Vol 80, No 5; Wheelwright, S. C. and Clark, K. B. (1992) *Revolutionising Product Development*. New York: The Free Press; and Twiss, B. C. (1992) *Managing Technological Innovation*. London: Pitman Publishing.

[3] *See* Normann and Ramirez (1996) 'From value chain to value constellation: Designing interactive strategy', in Champy, J. and Nohria, N. (eds) *Fast Forward: The Best Ideas on Managing Business Change*. Boston, MA: Harvard Business School Press, pp. 39–60.

[4] *Source*: Ostrovsky, A. (1997) 'Dream ticket for truck transport', *Financial Times*, 23 Dec.

[5] *See* Wheelwright, S. and Clark, K. (1992), op. cit.

[6] Ibid.

[7] However, both process and product innovations do not have to coincide. Just think back to the issues discussed in relation to information technology. Here we have seen that process innovations (e.g. self-banking facilities) do not necessarily imply new services; they simply mirror an existing bank office. However, in practice, new processes will often lead to new services as well; just think about the extensions of services made possible through self-banking (e.g. tax calculations).

[8] Roberts, E. B. and Berry, C. A. (1985) 'Entering new businesses: selecting strategies for success', *Sloan Management Review*, Vol 26, No 3, 3–17.

[9] Ibid.

[10] *Source*: Debackere, K., Van Looy, B. and Vliegen, J. (1997) 'Quality as a process during the creation of technical innovations: Lessons from field research', *R&D Management*, Vol 27, No 3, 197–211.

[11] We refer to the work of Bergen, S. A. (1986) *R&D Management: Managing new projects and new products*. Oxford: Basil Blackwell; Cooper, R. G. and Kleinschmidt, E. J. (1995) 'Benchmarking the firm's critical success factors in new product development', *Journal of Product Innovation Management*, 12, 374–91; Crawford, C. M. (1983) *New Products Management*. Boston, MA: Irwin; Souder, W. E. (1987) *Managing New Product Innovations*. Lexington, MA: Lexington Books; Twiss, B. C. (1974) *Managing Technological Innovation*. London: Longman; or Wheelwright, S. and Clark, K. (1992), op. cit.

[12] For instance, von Hippel's research has documented well the important role played by lead users and suppliers. *See* von Hippel, E. (1988) *The Sources of Innovation*. New York: Oxford University Press.

[13] Quantum Corporation (1992) *Business and Product Teams*. Harvard Business School Case 9-692-023.

[14] Adapted from Katz, R. and Allen, T. (1985) 'The locus of control in the R&D matrix', *Academy of Management Journal*, Vol 28, No 1, 67–87.

[15] Although differences are considerable between industries.

[16] Pilat, D. (2001) 'Innovation and Productivity in Services', Paris, *OECD Proceedings*.

[17] As such, a consequence of the simultaneity and heterogeneity that characterizes services.

[18] For exact figures, *see* Edwards, M. and Crocker, M. (2001) *Innovation and Productivity in Services: major trends and issues*. OECD Report.

[19] Whereby for services, suppliers will take care of the development of technology more often.

[20] For a more in-depth discussion on this topic, *see* Howells, J. (2001) 'The nature of innovation in services'. *OECD Proceedings on Innovation and Productivity in Services*; and Andersen, B. and Howells, J. (2000) 'Intellectual property rights shaping innovation in services', in Anderson *et al.* (eds) *Knowledge and Innovation in the new Economy*, Edward Elgar Publishers.

[21] Barras, R. (1986) 'Towards a theory of innovation in services', *Research Policy*, 15, 161–73.

22 Abernathy, W. and Utterback, J. (1975) A dynamic model of product and process innovation. Omega, Vol 3, No 6, 639–656.

23 See for instance the arguments outlined above with respect to the relevancy of organizing R&D in relation to the nature of the service delivery process. *See* as well Gallouj, F. and Weinstein, O. 'Innovation in services', *Research Policy*, 26, 537–56, on this topic.

Suggested further reading

Champy, J. and Nohria, N. (1996) *Fast Forward: The best ideas on managing business change*. Boston, MA: Harvard Business School Press.

Kay, J. (1993) *Foundations of Corporate Success*. Oxford: Oxford University Press.

We recommend these two works as they discuss the crucial role of innovations for a firm's strategies and long-term survival.

Twiss, B. C. (1992) *Managing Technological Innovation*. London: Pitman Publishing.

Wheelwright, S. C. and Clark, K. B. (1992) *Revolutionising Product Development*. New York: The Free Press.

Readers looking for more details on the portfolio model should not hesitate to consult these books.

Allen, T. J. (1977) *Managing the Flow of Technology*. Cambridge, MA: The MIT Press.

Katz, R. and Allen, T. (1985) 'The locus of control in the R&D matrix', *Academy of Management Journal*, Vol 28, No 1, 67–87.

Worthwhile reading for people interested in issues related to the innovation process, and how it can be embedded within the organization.

Innovation and Productivity in Services. (2001) OECD Publications.

CHAPTER 20

Managing services across national boundaries

Roland Van Dierdonck

INTRODUCTION

The following report of Wal-Mart's entry into the European market appeared in 1997 in the *Financial Times*.[1]

Exhibit 20.1

Wal-Mart comes shopping in Europe

The legendary Sam Walton and his brother, Bud, opened the first Wal-Mart Discount City store in Rogers, Arkansas, in 1962. In the 35 years since, the mighty Wal-Mart Stores have conquered the US with its cut-price goods, becoming by far the country's biggest retailer.

Now, it's Europe's turn. This week Wal-Mart took its first step into the European retail market by buying the Wertkauf hypermarket company from Germany's Mann family for an undisclosed sum. In itself, the acquisition is not large: Wertkauf has only 21 stores and its sales last year were about $1.4 billion, a flea-bite next to Wal-Mart's $105 billion. But Wal-Mart left no doubt that it regarded the acquisition as just the start of its European expansion.

'When we enter new markets, our first priority is to learn more about the customers, introduce Wal-Mart concepts and philosophy, and prove ourselves,' said Bob Martin, chief executive of Wal-Mart's international division. 'When we serve our customers and exceed their expectations, growth in the business will follow.'

At the last count, Wal-Mart had 1904 out-of-town discount stores in the US and another 436 Supercenters selling groceries as well as general merchandise. Its success in the US is attributable to many factors, but high on the list is corporate culture that places heavy emphasis on something that should be every retailer's top priority: customer service.

Employees in the stores are bound by the so-called 'ten-foot rule' that requires them to approach any customer who comes within 10 feet of them, look them in the eye, welcome them with a smile, and ask them what they can do to help. Shoppers are met and greeted on entering the store, and when they ask where they can find certain goods, employees are required to escort them all the way to the right place instead of pointing or telling them.

Wal-Mart is also highly regarded for its advanced retail technology which enables it to have the right quantities of goods in the right place at the right time while keeping costly inventories at a minimum. The company was the first retailer in the US to equip all its stores with scanners at the check-outs. Nowadays, employees carry hand-held computers enabling them to re-order merchandise,

Exhibit 20.1 continued

while backroom computers link each store with a sophisticated satellite system.

Since starting its international expansion in 1991, Wal-Mart has already become the biggest retailer in Canada and Mexico. It has also dipped its toe into emerging markets, opening small numbers of stores in Argentina, Brazil, Indonesia and China. Yet retailing travels notoriously badly. Retailers that develop a successful concept in their home market usually find they need to adjust the formula to suit local conditions overseas: yet, in doing so, they risk undermining whatever it was that made them successful in the first place.

Previous US ventures into Europe have a mixed record. McDonald's and Toys 'R' Us may be growing, but Woolworth sold its UK stores, Sears Roebuck pulled out of Spain, J. C. Penney sold its Sarma stores in Belgium, and Safeway sold its UK supermarkets. If Wal-Mart's European venture is to succeed, then it will have to overcome the

obstacles that have discouraged other US retailers: much higher costs for real estate, labour and distribution than in the US, plus tastes that differ widely from one country to another.

However, European retail analysts say that Wal-Mart has probably made the right decision by starting in Germany. Although competition is intense, the market is large, and in some ways German retailing is not as advanced as it is in other countries. Nicholas Jones, an analyst at Goldman Sachs in London, says the depth and breadth of assortments are inferior in German hypermarkets, as are store lay-outs and visual presentation. And relatively few German retailers are equipped with the systems and logistics that are among Wal-Mart's biggest strengths. 'Wal-Mart's key challenge is to secure critical mass so it can offer attractive prices as soon as possible,' says Mr Jones. 'If they can combine that with their skills in merchandising, then they will differentiate themselves very distinctly.'

Exhibit 20.2

Overseas expansion is a graveyard

International expansion has been a graveyard of many prominent UK retailers, and none more so than Marks and Spencer. Now it must extricate itself from the businesses around the world that have never fulfilled its hopes.

That is likely to be a far from easy task. M&S first ventured abroad in 1972 when it formed a joint venture with a Canadian retailer, and opened stores similar to its UK branches.

The late Lors Sieff, then chairman, ruefully recalled in his autobiography: 'We thought we knew all about retailing and that M&S's principles and practices in the UK would apply to our Canadian operations.'

In spite of high hopes that it could be used as a springboard into to US, the Canadian operations made losses for 20 years. It was unpicked during the 1990s, with the last piece being closed in 1999.

European expansion has not proved much more successful. John Richards, a vetaran retail consultant who has followed the M&S story since the 1960s, says: 'They were besieged by French shoppers in the Dover store, so they thought there was a demand in France for M&S.'

In 1975 a store was opened in Paris on the Boulevard Haussmann. 'Business was excellent in the first week or two,' Lord Sieff wrote. But it soon transpired that shoppers were British expatriates stocking up on home comforts. After that 'business fell away sharply, but this did not deter us,' Lord Sieff added, and European expansion continued.

However, it was not until Lord Rayner became chairman in 1984 that M&S's expansion outside the UK became more determined.

In 1988 M&S bought Brooks Brothers of the US, a 47-store chain of somewhat stuffy mens outfitters, whose hallmark was the buttondown Oxford shirt. M&S paid $750 m for it, a figure that was widely criticized as excessive.

Lord Rayner said at the time that the deal was 'an important step in fulfilling our objective to become an international retailer'.

The same year M&S acquired Kings Super Markets for $108 m, of which Lord Rayner said, 'the acquisition of Kings will enable us to build a significant food retailing operation in the US'.

Exhibit 20.2 continued

But it was not to be and, in 1999, M&S appointed Morgan Stanley to try to sell the business. It is still trying.

According to Mr Richards, M&S's failures outside the UK are due to the 'insufferable arrogance' of management, which thought it could replicate its UK success internationally. But, says Mr Richards,

M&S's UK profits benefited from having prime sites, without high rents.

Outside the UK, they did not have that advantage nor did they understand how to adapt merchandise to non-British tastes.

Source: Financial Times.

In 2002, five years after the report in Exhibit 20.1 appeared, Wal-Mart successfully operated 95 stores in Germany with 16 500 employees. In the same year, Wal-Mart operated more than 12 000 stores in nine countries outside the US contributing $37.4 billion to its revenues and 1.4 billion to its operating profit, an increase of 33.1 per cent over previous years.

Wal-Mart success contrasts sharply with the difficulties of Marks & Spencer as described in Exhibit 20.2. In 2001, this British Company shut down the vast bulk of its overseas operations. Comparing the two cases one must conclude that the internationalization of a service firm is a tremendous opportunity but becomes at the same time a big risk. It appears that managing across national boundaries poses a serious management challenge.

Service businesses are becoming more and more international. Figure 20.1 indicates services' growing share of international trade as opposed to merchandise trade. This challenges the traditional belief that services by their very nature are local, not transportable, and therefore cannot be exported. Even if this belief is accepted, it does not mean that there cannot be an international trade, since customers can cross borders to 'consume' their services. An obvious example of this is, of course, tourism-related services. It comes as no surprise, therefore, that countries with a strong tourism base perform well in the international service trade.

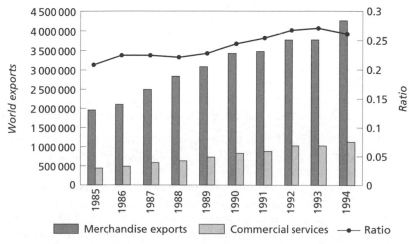

Figure 20.1 Ratio of exports in commercial services to merchandise trade, 1985–94 ($ million)[2]

Source: World Trade Organisation (1995).

Service providers can also cross borders in some cases. ABB, for instance, has maintenance expertise in a large variety of industries, but not in every country. When faced with a maintenance problem in a Dutch paper mill, they might call in an expert in Finland.

Internationalization is more than exports, however. Just as with manufacturing industries, exporting is only the initial phase of an internationalization strategy. In this chapter we shall explore various approaches to internationalization, while taking the specificity of services into consideration.

The simultaneity of consumption and production is one of the major characteristics of a service. This has three major consequences for the internationalization:

1. *The problem of customer accessibility to the service delivery system*. This means that export, although not excluded, can only be considered in a few instances or in a very limited way. Service firms will have to establish foreign operations much earlier in their life cycle than manufacturing industries. If Disney wants to grow in the theme park business it has little choice other than to set up theme parks in Japan and Europe.

2. *The need for personal contact between the customer and the service provider*. This does not only have logistical consequences as described in the previous point, but requires particular skills of the provider: language, cultural fluency, sensivity for and knowledge of local situation.

3. *The problem of difference in culture*. In most service 'encounters', there is an interaction, sometimes an intensive one, between the service delivery system and the customer. In certain service environments, for instance, customers are expected to behave in a certain way. This type of behaviour is often culture-dependent. For example, in a business school using interactive teaching methods, students are expected to participate and to defend their personal view. However, this may be in conflict with values and norms of non-Western cultures. In Western Europe, the attitude towards complaining is quite different from that in the United States. Therefore, quality-control systems which work well in the US might not work well in Europe. There is not only the culture (i.e. norms and values) of the customer to take into account, but also the culture of the personnel. For instance, the extent to which the behaviour of the personnel (an important part of the service) can be 'controlled' by the organization will vary from country to country. Europeans will more rapidly consider something as belonging to their private 'space' than, for instance, North Americans, and they will therefore reject too much control on something they consider to be private. This means that it will not always be possible to 'transfer' a service concept 'undamaged'. The behaviour of both customer and personnel is part of the service.

In the remainder of this chapter, we will first explore why companies would want to internationalize. We will see that, generally speaking, internationalization motives are of a strategic nature; companies internationalize because they hope to improve or defend the current competitive position. The need to internationalize and opportunities to internationalize are not the same for all service sectors. Before a service company decides to internationalize, it should first identify and analyse the extent to which the drivers towards internationalization are present in its sector. We will describe the most important drivers in a separate section.

As mentioned earlier, services are very cultural sensitive. We have included a framework to assess or at least understand cultural differences across countries or regions. Based on the insights gained in the previous sections, we will finally describe the application in the service sector of a model that describes various approaches to internationalization.

Objectives

By the end of this chapter, you should be able to:

- understand why and identify how services are becoming more and more international
- understand the drivers and the enablers of this internationalization trend in general and apply them to particular sectors
- understand the range of internationalization strategies and select an appropriate strategy, depending on the sector, the type of service and the local circumstances
- understand the cultural dimension of services, which necessitates an awareness on the part of service companies of ethnic and corporate cultural differences

WHY INTERNATIONALIZE?

The basic motives for internationalizing in service industries are not very different from those in manufacturing industries. Companies by nature want to grow and thus, instead of diversifying in their own country, they expand by going abroad. In many cases it is easier to sell the same product in another country than to make and sell another product in an existing market. The chances that the company will stay closer to the core business are greater in the former case than in the latter. In the case of Wal-Mart, there are few opportunities for expanding in North America.

Growth is not the only reason for companies to go abroad. Quite often, by becoming bigger they are better able to exploit static and dynamic economies of scale. The effort a company like SAP or Microsoft has to make to develop software is the same, whether or not they do this for their domestic market or a worldwide one. This is not very different from the motives that drive pharmaceutical companies to enter global markets, for instance. Dynamic economies of scale or learning curve advantages are as relevant to the McDonald's corporation (for instance, both in setting up and operating a new restaurant) than they are in an automotive factory.

More generally, it can be said that the usual motive for going international is leveraging a competitive asset. This asset can be a well-designed service concept and/ or a well-designed and -operated service delivery system, such as a Disney theme park or a Wal-Mart retail concept. It can be specific knowledge or know-how, as in the case of large consulting firms, such as McKinsey, or it can also be an image or reputation, such as Harvard Business School or, closer to home, INSEAD.

There are a number of other reasons why a company might want to go international.

- As we shall see later, there are trends, or drivers, which are making it easier for service companies to operate internationally. As a result, many foreign service companies are entering our home markets – for example, banks, law firms, maintenance organizations, business schools, and even universities. The Vlerick

Leuven Ghent Management School in Belgium until 1998 was primarily focused on the local market for its MBA programme, when it come to the conclusion that is was competing for the best (local) students not so much with (other) local business schools as with international business schools which recruited aggressively in the school's local market. These companies therefore quite often have no choice but to become international as well, in order to protect their own markets. This reason is of course more defensive in nature.

- Companies also become international to add value to their product. The more international a company such as Federal Express, Hertz, ABB Services or Ernst & Young Consulting becomes, the more attractive is its service. The Vlerick Leuven Gent Management School will also serve its regional market much better by becoming international and accepting foreign students. The other students in the class will perhaps learn more about foreign cultures and about doing business internationally by interacting daily with foreign students, than by taking a battery of courses in international business.

- Customers are becoming international. This is especially the case for service-to-business industries, such as consulting, accounting, market research and maintenance. However, it might also be the case for consumer services such as department stores (this was quite often the reason for Marks & Spencer to set stores like Brussels or Paris) or health care, even if such companies only cater to expatriate managers and their families.

- A company may wish to tap into cheaper or more valuable local resources. One of the traditional reasons why manufacturing companies have set up plants in countries with low labour wages is to take advantage of cheap labour resources. This trend is found increasingly in information-intensive service organizations such as software development (in India) and insurance back-office processing (in Ireland or even the Philippines). Companies set up foreign operations not only to tap into cheaper regions, but also into scarce resources. For instance, call centres and translation services are set up in Belgium because of its available pool of multilingual people. Likewise, most banks have an office in financial centres such as London and New York, because of the expertise and information available there.

- A company may want to learn something from foreign operations. This trend is becoming more and more prevalent in manufacturing industries. Companies set up and manage a network of plants with opportunities for exchange and transfer of learning across plants. While it is rare, if not unknown, for a service organization to set up a foreign operation with this as the initial reason, there are quite a few organizations that extensively transfer knowledge, experience and practices across 'offices' in various parts of the world. Food Lion, the American subsidiary of Belgium's second biggest supermarket chain, Delhaize, is an interesting outpost for Delhaize to learn firsthand about innovative practices in supermarkets in the US.

DRIVERS TOWARDS INTERNATIONALIZATION[3]

The fact that more and more service companies are operating internationally is no coincidence. There are some factors which (often in conjunction with each other) stimulate or at least enable service companies to become international. Some of these factors are common to all types of industries, and others are more specific to service industries. These factors, which we call drivers towards internationalization, will be described below.

The increase and homogenization of disposable income

As was mentioned in Chapter 1, the emergence and growth of the service sector in our economies is linked to general economic development. Services as structured activities appear in the more developed economies of the world. Therefore, the more countries there are which have reached a certain stage of economic development, the more service activity there will be, and also the more room there will be to 'import' services. Not only do more countries enjoy a higher standard of living, but this standard of living is shared by more and more people in these countries. Forty years ago in most European countries, going to a restaurant was a rare activity limited to the upper income class. There simply was no 'culture' of eating outside the home and therefore no market for restaurants, let alone international restaurants.

Socio-economical changes

There are other socio-economical changes that have led to greater demand in services in a variety of countries and therefore to a spread of demand for services over various countries. There is the aging world population which leads to greater demand for services in the health sector, this coupled with a greater international mobility of this segment of the population. There is also the more extensive participation of women in the workforce stimulating the need for all kinds of household and day-care services.

The homogenization of customer needs

Not only have markets for service products grown with increasing economic development, but these markets have also become more and more homogeneous – that is, customers' needs across various countries have come to have more and more in common. Demand patterns are converging all over the world. This global 'standardization' (or 'globalization' as some would like to call it) of customer needs and tastes is obvious in such products as soft drinks (e.g. Coca Cola), cigarettes (Marlboro), chocolates (Godiva), and clothing (Levi Strauss), but is doubtless also occurring within service sectors like restaurants (McDonald's), television series (X-files, Neighbours), advertising (Saatchi & Saatchi) or accounting (the big 5). The more 'de-personalized' the service becomes, the more this standardization occurs, since an intensive interaction between the customer and the service delivery system offers less possibility for standardization. It is therefore not surprising to see that the more a service organization is positioned towards the top of the service triangle (see Chapter 1), the more internationalized the sector is, because the 'product' usually lends itself to more standardization. Furthermore, service organizations positioned towards the right-hand bottom corner of the service triangle (e.g. professional service firms) are sometimes among the first to internationalize, because the needs which they address are quite often universal (such as management advice or medical treatment).

Global customers

The reason why many professional service firms are international in both their markets and their operations has probably much to do with the fact that their clients are becoming international. These types of service firms often have little choice other than to follow their customers. As large corporate customers become global, they often seek to standardize and simplify the service they consume. The success of SAP-software is claimed to be due to a great extent to the fact that multinational companies want to standardize software and information processing at various sites around the world. Telephone companies such as British Telecom and MCI are becoming international because multinational companies do not want to be dependent on the various national telephone operating companies for something which is becoming increasingly critical. The more the trend towards outsourcing internal services persists in many multinational companies, the more opportunities there will be for service companies which not only provide these services (such as maintenance, catering, cleaning and recruitment) but do so on an international scale.

It is not only businesses which are becoming more global, but also individual consumers, who quite often work for these globalizing international organizations. Health care, insurance, removal companies, banks, schools and other organizations are therefore tracking business services very closely, especially travel-related services. These start with transportation (e.g. airlines or car rental) and extend to credit, communication, emergency support, restaurants, hotels and many other fields, and are becoming international on an exponential scale.

Global channels

Many services have substantial information-processing components (*see* Chapter 17). Given the revolution in information-processing technologies, the services can be easily distributed worldwide and can therefore be provided on a nearly global scale. An American citizen can withdraw funds or transfer money from his American bank account at any ATM in Japan coupled to, for instance, the CIRRUS network. The Internet allows us to consult the American Library of Congress or the Harvard Business School case catalogue on-line. In addition, the Internet gives many of us access to service providers all over the world. For example, if we are planning a vacation to Australia, we can not only book a plane seat to Australia from our home or office, but even make hotel and rental-car reservations and obtain information on tourist attractions and sites, planning our visit more quickly (and perhaps cheaply) than any travel agent could do before.

These trends ensure that many services can be distributed immediately, or at least can be accessed, on a worldwide basis.

Favourable logistics

Information technologies have had little effect, as we explained earlier, on personal-interactive services like health care or recreation although experiments with, for instance, remote-controlled heart surgery have recently taken place. However, falling transportation costs, especially in the case of air travel, can make even this type of business more global. One analyst, for instance, claims that the strongest competition for Disneyland Paris is not so much other European or French theme parks, but Disneyland in Orlando, Florida. Travel packages to Florida from London or Amsterdam are becoming so cheap that some people might prefer the 'real' thing in Florida to the 'copy' in Paris. Hospitals in London are attracting Middle Eastern and Asian patients, just as Miami hospitals are attracting an increasing number of Latin American patients. The 'Chunnel' has made London Christmas shopping very popular for the Belgians, French and Dutch.

Information technology

The tremendous evolution in information-processing technologies has fuelled several trends. This is clear for information-intensive services as described, but it is also true for services with less information processing. Information about new services can be disseminated much more quickly than ever before. Besides the Internet, there are also satellite television and global news stations like CNN, which make global marketing easier.

One important trend is that information-processing technologies permit the uncoupling of the various stages of the service processing chain. Back-office activities can take place in different locations far away from the front-office activities without any loss of time. Banks or insurance companies can have their central office processes in countries with much lower labour wages. Maintenance companies can have their call centres in places more fiscally attractive or where multilingual skills are abundant. India's success in attracting call centres that serve global markets is to a large extent due to the low wages. Employees are paid $3000 a year compared with the $30 000 their US counterparts are paid.[4]

Global segmentation

Earlier, we indicated that the markets are generally becoming more global, which makes it worthwhile to offer a service in other countries. However, there is another similar but somewhat different phenomenon, which we call global segmentation. By this we mean that for certain services, there exist in different countries small segments of (potentially) interested customers, but which are each on their own too small to approach separately. However, if all those small local segments can be approached in the same or similar way, it might be worthwhile to do so. The previous three trends, alone or combined, often enable such a joint approach. CNN is a good example: the market for 24-hours news broadcasting is small.

Changing government policies and regulations

Government has more control of service industries than manufacturing industries. Either the government itself is an active operator – for example, in transportation, information provision and health care – or it heavily controls and/or subsidizes certain services. In addition, there are frequently restrictions in foreign investments in some sectors in order to protect local firms or enhance national security. However, there is an undeniable trend towards privatization and deregulation. The Uruguay Round, for instance, has focused on the creation of free markets for services. It is believed that the current economy of the EU is suffering huge losses because the EU has failed to build a single market for services. It is realized that 'EU will miss its target of becoming the world's most competitive economy by 2010 unless it removes the maze of national barriers to the cross-border provision of services.'[5] The European Commission is therefore pushing hard to abolish all kinds of state monopolies, and many governments are realizing that national monopolies like airlines are too small to be efficient. As a result, we can expect more mergers, joint ventures, and network organizations among companies active in such diverse fields as air travel, telephone services, TV and other media, electrical utilities and banking.

Outsourcing

Outsourcing is to 'private' companies and other organizations what privatization is to governments. Applying 'back to basics' or 'core business' philosophies, organizations are outsourcing many service activities which had previously been done internally – for example, maintenance, cleaning, PC network support, human resource management and catering. This trend creates opportunities for service companies, in particular for those which convey an image of trustworthiness and professionalism. Given that in some countries service firms are often 'underdeveloped', firms with experience in this type of service in one country have an opportunity to move quickly into these countries. Moreover, when multinational firms are outsourcing, they want to reduce the complexity and uncertainty of dealing with many local service companies, and therefore will actually prefer to work with companies that can provide these services on a global scale.

The motives and drivers described in the previous sections help a service company to decide whether or not there is a strong pull or push to internationalize. However, before companies develop action strategies, they should be aware of culture differences across various regions in the world.

CULTURE AND CULTURAL DIFFERENCES

Services, especially personal-interactive services, are experiences and therefore neither culture-free nor culturally neutral. The transaction is often much more than a specific exchange at a certain moment in a certain place. A service concept expects not only that employees will act or behave in a certain way, but also that customers act or believe in a certain way. The Club Méditerranée experience would not be a Club Med product if the employees ('*les gentils organisateurs*' or GOs) and the customers ('*les gentils membres*' or GMs) did not behave in the 'Club Med' way. Not only would customers damage the quality of the experience for themselves, but also the quality of the experience for the other visitors. Behaviour, people's actions and interaction between people are all governed by culture – that is, values, beliefs and implicit assumptions.

For example, in the US housewives are used to having their groceries packed by supermarket personnel. Belgians resent this, because they interpret it as an invasion of their privacy. How can a stranger pack a customer's groceries if he or she does not know when and how the customer is planning to store the various items? In France, a car-rental agent addressing a customer by his or her first name is considered rude. On the other hand, the practice in some French restaurants of men and women using common toilets is unheard of for American visitors, as is allowing dogs in a restaurant. Disney's policy of requiring its employees to adhere to certain hygiene and dress standards is considered to be an intrusion on the (French) employees' privacy and is therefore resisted by them. It is impossible for French customers and employees to understand how a dinner (or even lunch) experience can be complete without wine. Lovelock and Yip[6] explain that 'McDonald's' has a different meaning for Americans than for non-Americans. When an American goes to a McDonald's restaurant in a foreign country it means 'us', something to be trusted, a piece of back home. For the non-American, going to the local McDonald's means 'them', a foreign experience, something different.

An employee working in a call centre in Tiruchchir in the South of Tamil Nadu (in India) talking to an American in Texas complaining about his gas bill from his local utility company, should not only have an American if not Texas accent, but should also know something about the outcome of yesterday's superbowl.[7]

Service organizations wanting to set up foreign operations should be more culturally aware for all these reasons. We shall now describe a framework to help companies understand and analyse various cultures.

The concept of culture

When we refer to culture in this chapter, we don't mean so much the concept of corporate culture but rather national, or more accurately ethnic culture. (As a matter of fact, the concept of corporate culture is derived from the notion of ethnic culture as anthropologists have defined it.) Probably the best-known of these anthropologists is Margaret Mead,[8] who defined culture as 'a shared pattern of behaviour', and later refined this to 'a system of shared meaning or understanding that drives behaviour'. This of course comes very close to what has been defined earlier as 'corporate' culture – that is, 'a pattern of beliefs and expectations shared by the members of a group'. In any group, these beliefs and expectations produce norms which powerfully shape the individual members' behaviour.

Culture is visible and observable via *people's artefacts and behaviour*. Artefacts can be pieces of art such as music, poetry, painting or architecture (Culture with a capital C), but can also be a decorated Christmas tree, a cuckoo clock, a strict gun-control law, garlic sauce, or eating french fries with ketchup. Another visible aspect is human behaviour – for instance, driving on the left-hand side of the road, eating with one hand on one's lap or saying 'yes' while thinking 'no'.

Figure 20.2 illustrates how the same hand movement is interpreted differently in three different countries.

Artefacts and behaviour are the things we notice immediately when we arrive in a foreign country. They can be a source of either amusement, irritation or confusion for visitors. When questioned about this, the insiders quite often do not know why they are behaving the way they do, or do not see anything particularly strange about the artefacts. As a matter of fact, they are surprised and sometimes irritated by the series of seemingly stupid questions they may be asked about their culture.

Delving a little deeper, it can be seen that the artefacts are based on *fundamental beliefs and values or norms* that people have. Beliefs are statements of facts – the way things are. Values are expressions of the preferred status about what should be, or about ideas. The Japanese say yes, despite the fact that they mean no, because they find this the proper thing to do (i.e. a value), as they do not want to offend others or to make them lose face. That the French cannot imagine having dinner without wine is based on values they hold with respect to wine.

EGYPT
Be patient

ITALY
What exactly do you mean?

GREECE
That's just perfect

Never underestimate the importance of local knowledge.

To truly understand a country and its culture, you have to be part of it.

That's why, at HSBC, all our offices around the world are staffed by local people. In fact you'll find we've got local people in more countries than any other bank.

It's their insight that allows us to recognise financial opportunities invisible to outsiders.

But those opportunities don't just benefit our local customers.

Innovations and ideas are shared throughout the HSBC network, so that everyone who banks with us can benefit.

Think of it as local knowledge that just happens to span the globe.

HSBC
The world's local bank

Figure 20.2 The same hand movement interpreted differently in three different countries

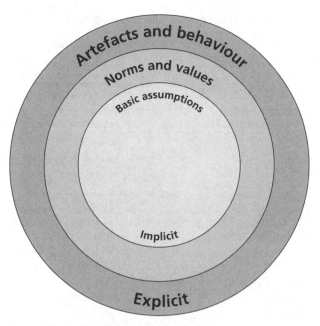

Figure 20.3 The structure of culture[9]

Source: From Organisational Culture and Leadership. 1st Edition, Schein, Edgar H., Jossey-Bass Publishers, Copyright © 1985 Edgar H. Schein, this material is used by permission of John Wiley & Sons, Inc.

These beliefs and values can only be understood, however, when one is aware of the basic underlying assumptions, what some call the *underlying world view*. These underlying assumptions prescribe ways of perceiving, thinking and evaluating the world, oneself and others. They are often implicit. Thus, when we talk about culture, we should be aware of this complex construction (*see* Figure 20.3). If we really want to appreciate culture we should therefore try to understand the inner core. It is here that cultures are fundamentally different. It is also at this level that cultural changes are difficult to bring about. People might be persuaded to change their behaviour, or even change beliefs, but to change fundamental assumptions is much more difficult, if not impossible.

Dimensions of cultural differences

In what way do these underlying assumptions differ from group to group? Various researchers have used different, albeit related, dimensions to describe these differences. We shall describe the dimensions defined by F. Trompenaars[10] (for other authors, we refer the reader to the literature). These dimensions are summarized in Table 20.1.

1. The first dimension concerns how a society deals with its rules. Does one believe that there is a universal truth, or does it all depend on the particular instance or situation? On these dimensions, North Americans and perhaps also the Dutch, score at one end of the scale (the universal truth), while the more one moves South, on both the American and European continents, the more one tends to move towards the particularistic view. The original decision not to serve wine at Disneyland Paris was probably based on the universal view of North Americans that wine (or alcohol in general) is bad, certainly in relation to children. As Trompenaars explains:

Table 20.1 Dimensions to characterize underlying assumptions

1 Universalism	Particularism
Apply rules and procedures universally to ensure equity and consistency	Encourage flexibility by adapting to particular situations
2 Individualism	**Collectivism**
Encourage individual freedom and responsibility	Encourage individuals to work for consensus in the interest of the group
3 Affective neutral	**Affective**
We must control the expression of our emotions so that we can consider issues objectively	Be able to express whatever we think or feel openly and freely
4 Specific	**Diffuse**
It is important to keep business separated from other aspects of life	Recognise that the integration of different aspects of the total person can stabilise and deepen relationships
5 Achievement	**Ascription**
We need to appreciate and reward the things our people do and achieve based on skills and knowledge	Respect 'who' our people are, based on their own experience and past record
6 Future	**Present – Past**
We can get the present of our business into focus by relating it to a desired future	The present of our business is building on the learning of the past

Source: Trompenaars, F. and Hampden-Turner, C. (1998) *Riding the Waves of Culture: Understanding cultural diversity in business.* London: Nicholas Brealy.

> *'universalist societies tend to feel that general rules and obligations are a strong source of moral reference. Universalists tend to follow the rules even when friends are involved and look for the one best way of dealing equally and fairly with all cases. They assume that the standards they hold here are the right ones and attempt to change the attitude of others to match. Particularist societies are those where particular circumstances are much more important than the rules. Bonds of particular relationships (family, friends) are stronger than any abstract rules and the response can be made according to the circumstances and the people involved.'*

2. In an individualistic society, the primary orientation is towards the 'self'. In a collectivist society, the orientation is towards common goals and objectives. In individualistic societies, the fundamental belief is that individual freedom and responsibility should be encouraged. In collectivist societies, the fundamental belief is that individuals should be encouraged to work for consensus in the interest of the group. North Americans again would probably be put at the individualistic end of the scale, while many Far Eastern societies (Japanese, Koreans) would probably be at the other end.

3. This dimension is related to the extent one displays or is allowed to display emotions. This dimension rates societies from 'affective-neutral' at one end to 'affective-relationships' at the other end. In the affective-neutral societies, there is a fundamental belief that relationships should be governed by reason and not by emotions. 'We must control expression of our emotions so that we can consider issues objectively' is the unwritten rule. On the other end is the belief that we

should 'be able to express whatever we think or feel openly and freely'. Again, in our North/Western world we tend to lean towards the affective-neutral end of the scale. In the South/Eastern world there is often more room for emotions.

4. This dimension is a bit more complicated, and has to do with how deeply we become involved with others, distinguishing between specific and diffuse cultures. In specific-oriented cultures, the relationship a person has with somebody else is segregated and dependent on the 'task' or business dealing the person might have with that person. Private and professional relationships are strictly separated. In other countries, every life space and every level of personality tend to permeate all the others. Somewhat related to this dimension is the size of private space. How far do we let others penetrate our private space? Who is allowed to use our first name? When people visit our house, do we show them our bedroom? Generally, we believe that the North American's private space is smaller (i.e. public space is larger). However, the public space is compartmentalized (i.e. specific). In the more Southern countries, the space is much more diffuse. In Belgium there is perhaps a more restricted space, but it is perhaps more diffuse than the Nordic nations.

Based on this dimension, but also the previous dimensions, is the differentiation between low-contact and high-contact cultures. In high-contact cultures people don't mind standing close to one another and engaging in frequent touching. People in low-contact cultures on the other hand prefer to stand apart and touch less.

5. A fifth dimension is related to the significance of status, or better put, the attitude towards status: 'Do you work for it or is it given?' In some societies, status is accorded to people on the basis of their actual achievements. In other societies, status is ascribed to them by virtue of age, gender, education or class. Trompenaars makes a distinction between achieved status and ascribed status. In the *achievement orientation*, people are appreciated and rewarded for the things they do and achieve, based on skill and knowledge. In the *ascription orientation*, people are respected for who they are, based on their experience and past record.

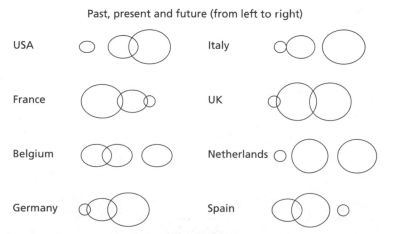

Past, present and future (from left to right)

Figure 20.4 International views of the past, present and future[11]
Source: Trompenaars, F. (1993).

6. The final dimension is the way time is organized. This includes first of all the relative importance given to the past, present and future. In Figure 20.4 the importance of each of these three elements is expressed by the size of the circle symbolizing it. In the US, according to Trompenaars, the past is of relatively little importance; the future is what counts. This is in contrast with, for instance, France. Note the relative importance in Spain of the present, and the 'mañana' attitude symbolized by the little importance given to the future. A second element of this dimension is how people consider the past, present and future are related. The view of time can be sequential, a series of passing events, or it can be synchronic, 'with past, present and future all interrelated'. The latter view means that both ideas about the future and memories of the past shape actions in the present.

Trompenaars' six dimensions help us to understand the fundamental assumptions in different cultures. However, it is important to exercise care in applying these dimensions. A first reason for caution is that while there appears to be a broad consensus on the existence of cultural differences, the same consensus does not exist when it comes to the dimensions themselves. Geert Hofstede, another well-known researcher in this field, uses different dimensions.[12]

There is also a danger of stereotyping people. We tend to look at the extremes and extrapolate these extremes to the whole population. The real situation is much more like Figure 20.5, with a wide distribution within one population on a certain dimension and a great deal of overlap between various populations. It should also be noted that people will not always behave consistently according to one of the extreme positions. They fluctuate between various positions, depending on the situation at hand, and try to find a balance between the extremes.

Implication for service industries

As has been argued by many researchers, an appropriate and strong culture is a very important factor for success in service organizations. The 'customer service' culture at Wal-Mart, symbolized by the 'ten-foot' rule, is an example of a strong culture. Organizational culture – that is, shared beliefs and values – is a way to 'control' people's behaviour. As we have already stated, the personnel's activities or behaviour are not always easy to prescribe, and therefore contact personnel should be given more discretion and empowerment. The more the need to customize the service grows, the more this will apply. A service organization's management

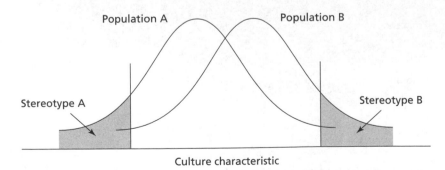

Figure 20.5 The relationship between cultural characteristics and stereotypes

should perhaps devote more attention to culture than their colleagues in industrial organizations. Not only should they make sure that a strong culture is developed, but they should also ensure that the right kind of culture exists – that is, the so-called *service culture*. In addition, they should be aware of the (ethnic) culture of both personnel and customers. Organizations therefore should not only look for a sufficient amount of culture-related consensus from the employees, but also on the part of the customers. The latter task is not easy for a service organization operating in an international environment.

Differences in ethnic cultures reflect the way customers perceive an otherwise identical service and in particular the servicescape. Serving wine (or not serving wine) in a family theme park will affect the perception of the service differently in France than it will in the US. The same is true for queuing and the extent to which queues are managed. A Belgian will react differently to a car salesman calling him by his first name during his first visit than an American will. A German will perhaps have difficulties sharing a table in a Japanese restaurant with total strangers. Students in certain parts of the world will react differently to being invited to participate in class discussions than in others. French and American employees will react differently to being told to take a shower every morning and change their underwear every day. Managing by objectives will be less effective in Asian countries than it is in the US, and so on. When we described the servicescape, we discussed how colour may play a determining role in how an environment is perceived; but a certain colour has a different meaning in different cultures. Yellow, for instance, is associated in China with royalty, in Greece with age, in Italy with prostitution and in Egypt with famine.

The examples described above are differences in behaviour or artefacts, but they are based on the fundamental assumptions we have explained. The decision not to serve wine in Disneyland Paris was perhaps an expression of the 'universalism' found in American culture, while for the French not having wine with dinner is a major quality mistake. They simply expect wine at the table. The acceptability of queuing is without a doubt influenced by people's attitude towards time. Willingness to participate is influenced by the individualism-*versus*-collectivism dimension, or by the importance of hierarchy in a society. Standing close to the customer in front of you who is being served in a bank or public service, is considered to be impolite in most Northern countries but not so in middle eastern countries. American cinemas keep the temperature in the theatre at 20 °C or below, so that people do not feel the bodyheat of their (strange) neighbour. Perhaps more important for services is the 'affective-neutral versus affective-relationships' dimension. The service culture, as described earlier, requires a much more affective type of relationship – a more 'feminine' society according to Hofstede – than is perhaps the norm in many more 'masculine' cultures.

Management implications for international service operations

When setting up international service operations, a company should be aware that there may be a conflict between corporate culture and the employees' ethnic culture. Such a conflict not only will prevent the company from developing a strong corporate culture, but will influence the service concept, i.e. the product itself. A company should therefore examine its service concept and its service delivery system for cultural biases. Another implication relates to the conflict between corporate culture and the 'ethnic' culture of the customers. The same advice as in the previous points can be given here. The service concept and the service delivery system should be scrutinized to allow for cultural biases. It is clear that the Disney concept is very American, which is all right as long as it is not in conflict with fundamental values and underlying assumptions of the host country.

In the case of a conflict, the service concept and the service delivery system must be adapted. McDonald's serving beer in Belgium is a good example. The important question here, however, is how far a company can and should go in this adaptation process. There are some general core values or some company-specific values which cannot or should not be compromised. Doing so runs the risk of losing the essence of the service concept or sacrificing the fundamental characteristics of the service process (*see* Chapter 2). This may lead to the conclusion that certain services simply cannot be transferred unless we target a specific market segment which shares some of the original market's cultural characteristics. For instance, Marks & Spencer's decision to internationalize was fundamentally based on the existence of a British or Anglophile segments in foreign countries.

INTERNATIONALIZATION STRATEGIES

When a service company decides to internationalize, it should understand that various strategies are possible. The best strategy of course depends on the objective the company is trying to achieve, but also depends very much on the type of product, i.e. service. Bartlett and Goshal[13] have developed a general framework which classifies various internationalization strategies and relates these strategies to various conditions. This framework is generally applicable to any type of industry, but it especially applies to service organizations (*see* Figure 20.6).

There are two fundamental forces that one should take into account when considering an internationalization strategy: a force towards *global integration* and a force towards *local responsiveness*. The appropriate internationalization strategy will depend on the strength of these two forces, as indicated in Figure 20.5.

Figure 20.6 A general framework of internationalization strategies[14]
Source: Bartlett, C. A. and Ghoshal, S. (1989).

- The force towards global integration has been described in previous sections of this chapter. This force refers to such factors as the presence of economies of scale, or opportunities to globally exploit certain assets, competencies or competitive advantages. The drivers towards globalization described earlier stimulate the move towards global integration or remove barriers to it. An increasing number of service organizations will be driven towards global integration as a result of this force. We are referring to industries such as airlines, film studios and electrical utilities.

- At the other end is the force towards local responsiveness. The more personalized and/or customized a service is, the more necessary it will be to adapt it to local needs. This is especially the case for services which are culture-dependent – for example, having a high language content, or involving local taste or traditional habits. Although there are no doubt some 'universal' theatre plays, most plays and actors will be local since they involve almost all the responsiveness factors mentioned. While there may be organizations that address universal educational needs, most educational systems will remain local as well. The need for local responsiveness may also result from a high level of government control. Governments often demand local content not only from companies manufacturing goods such as automobiles, but also for instance in television and radio broadcasting.

A global strategy

When the need for local responsiveness is low and the force towards global integration strong, companies will develop a purely *global strategy*. The characteristics of a global strategy are summarized in Table 20.2. The world is basically seen as one large market, which can and should be approached in a homogeneous way, or at least integrated across countries. The company's position in one country is evaluated not on its own merit, but on its contribution to the global competitive position. There are few examples of service businesses using purely global strategies. Given the need for accessibility and the almost certain presence of interactions, there will always be some local content. However, international airlines such as British Airways, Singapore Airlines, or KLM, fast-food restaurants such as McDonald's, and express package delivery services such as Federal Express come very close. The international business schools such as INSEAD or IMD also come close to this position. All these types of services address a universal and homogeneous need and are very much scale-intensive. Citibank has positioned itself, according to Lovelock and Yip,[15] as a uniquely global consumer bank, its objective being to allow its customers to do their banking 'anyway, anywhere, anytime'.

Ikea,[16] the international retailer of furniture, follows a strategy which tends to be global. Country managers at Ikea assume control for day-by-day activities, and are allowed some discretion in augmenting the basic range of Ikea products to meet local tastes. The responsibility for product development and purchasing lies with Ikea of Sweden, the original company that pioneered the 'blond' style of Nordic furniture and furnishings. The group's international headquarters in Denmark oversees investment in new markets and the refurnishment or expansion of existing stores. Ikea has strong centrally imposed formats and procedures. It has a single logistics system, funnelling the products from its bulk-buying operation into individual stores.

Table 20.2 Organizational models

	Global	International	Multi-domestic	Transnational
Dominant strategic capability	Global efficiency	World wide learning	Local responsiveness	Global efficiency, local responsiveness learning
Configuration of assets and capabilities	Centralized and globally scaled	Sources of core competencies centralized, others decentralized	Decentralized and nationally self-sufficient	Dispersed, interdependent and specialized
Role of international operations	Implementing parent company strategies	Adapting and leveraging parent company competencies	Sensing and exploiting local opportunities	Differentiated contributions of national units to integrated worldwide operations/supply chain
Development and diffusion of knowledge	Knowledge developed and retained at the centre	Knowledge developed at the centre and transferred to overseas operations	Knowledge developed and retained in each unit	Knowledge developed jointly and shared worldwide

Source: Bartlett, C. A. and Goshal, S. (1989).

A multi-domestic strategy

When the need for local responsiveness is high, on the other hand, and there is little drive towards global integration, the best internationalization strategy might be a *multi-domestic* one. This is actually a situation in which very few international companies will operate in the first place. While there are many international law firms which serve international companies, law services to individuals in most countries are very localized and few international 'chains' exist. The same is true today for health-care providers. These sectors are dominated by small local organizations. Even the big international law firms are usually much more domestic in nature. The characteristics of such a strategy are summarized in Table 20.2. If there is a headquarters, then control by the headquarters is very weak. The offices are staffed and managed by local people, and form a very loose confederation of very autonomous units. Each local unit contributes little more than profit, and at most prestige, to the whole.

A transnational strategy

In certain services, there is a simultaneous need for both local responsiveness and global integration. The service and the service delivery system must be adapted to local needs, but at the same time, there are important advantages to be gained from becoming bigger or from leveraging certain corporate assets. In this case, there is a need for an integrated network strategy, or what others call a transnational strategy. This is the somewhat uneasy position of, for instance, the Vlerick Leuven Ghent Management School and many other regionally strong business schools. The only way out for these schools is for them all to form a consortium. However, the difficulties of doing so become obvious if one looks at the characteristics of this strategy in Table 20.2. Some global co-ordination is necessary; there has to be sharing of experience; there has to be an agreement on fundamental values and approaches; and so on. This is perhaps an impossible task for formerly independent institutions. There are, however, examples of companies that have successfully implemented such strategies. Companies like ISS which has acquired many small local service companies, has succeeded in moving from the multi-domestic to the transnational situation. It has taken tremendous cultural changes in most local companies to achieve this. However, management of those companies has succeeded in highlighting the advantages of global integration: worldwide accessible expertise in many industries and professional management. Some companies are moving away from the global strategy position and towards the transnational position, in some cases in order to be able to compete against strong local companies. McDonald's, for example, serves beer in Belgium, and in India serves a vegetarian sandwich instead of a hamburger.

A good example of a company that appears to be following such a strategy is Toys 'R' Us, in contrast with Ikea's strategy, for instance. As described in the *Financial Times*:[17]

'The fickle nature of children's choices requires more latitude for local managers. Toy tastes vary significantly between different cultures. For example, Asian families like educational toys, while American children are heavily influenced by Saturday morning television programmes.'

Managers are given great latitude in the management of their business. Like Ikea, Toys 'R' Us also has common store lay-outs and distribution procedures, but these are flexible to suit local markets. In Japan, some items are delivered directly to the stores and the delivery of all items is more frequent than in the US to take into account the limitation and cost of big warehouses in Japan. To keep in touch with local needs, the headquarters management of Toys 'R' Us travels frequently to the local stores. Mr Staley, president of the company's International Division is quoted as saying:

'We believe it's far better for our headquarters organisation to be able to meet on their own turf, dealing with their day-to-day problems, than to try to rationalise their business issues sitting here in Paramus, NJ.'

An 'international' strategy

Finally, there is the lower left quadrant of Figure 20.6. It is difficult to describe a strategy here. It may be that the '*de facto*' strategy of service organizations is such that they belong to this quadrant. This is an unstable situation. Companies in this position should seriously consider moving towards the right and being more locally responsive by adapting their service and service delivery system. By doing this, they may be able to protect themselves against foreign competitors who are following the global strategy. If this is impossible or unfeasible, then they should consider a move upwards towards the global strategy position. This means that they should carefully analyse their service delivery systems and look for elements that can be leveraged by exploiting them on an international scale.

Choosing the right strategy

The three strategies that we have described above (the 'international' strategy is not considered a viable option) are broad generic orientations for a service company. However, this general framework should be applied to the various parts of the service and service delivery system at a more detailed level. For instance, it is possible to use a global strategy for the back office and a multi-domestic strategy for the front-office activities. We have already mentioned that many service-based businesses need a local presence for their downstream activities because of the need for accessibility. Therefore, there is an opportunity to build local responsiveness into the local operations. The critical balance here is how much should be controlled centrally by centrally designed operating procedures and/or by creating a common corporate culture, and how much leeway should be given to local offices, without sacrificing the 'integrity' of the service concept.

The applicability of each of the three strategies is very much dependent on the situation. It is clear, however, that in certain service sectors, certain strategies are more applicable than in others. Lovelock and Yip,[18] for instance, make a distinction between people-processing, information-processing and possession-processing services. They state that global strategies are most appropriate for the latter two, more impersonal, types of services, while for the people-processing type of services, the multi-domestic or the transnational approach is more appropriate. Translated to the service classifications with which we are familiar, we could say that the more the service is situated towards the interactive side, the more a global strategy will be appropriate. While in the case of services of a more personal-maintenance interactive nature, a more multi-domestic or transnational strategy will be called for.

The same authors also make a distinction between various services, using the weight given to the service core in relation to the weight given to the more peripheral elements of the service. The more weight given to the service core, the more a global strategy is appropriate. This explains why, for instance, many service-to-business sectors follow a global strategy.

Somewhat deeper insights into internationalization strategies are provided by two other researchers, Välikangas and Lethinen.[19] They make a distinction between three types of international ('marketing') strategies for services: *standardization, specialization* and *customization* (*see* Table 20.3). Such strategies involve five elements:

1. *Service conceptualization*: definition of the service concept. This means providing an answer to the three basic business definition questions: who (markets), what (functions) and how (technology).
2. *Service differentiation*: how the service is different from the competitor's, i.e. the service characteristics that the firm is competing with.
3. *Market focus*: a more detailed description of the target customer (defined in point 1) of the firm.
4. *Service availability*: opting for broad or selective availability of the service.
5. *Mode of international operations*.

The three internationalization strategies differ with respect to each of the five elements, as summarized in Table 20.3. The authors link these strategies to different types of services which they call *generic* or *standardized, specialized* and *customized*

Table 20.3 Elements of internationalization strategies

	Internationalization strategy		
	Standardization	Specialization	Customization
1 *Service conceptualization*	Procedure/ Technology-based conceptualization	Service function/ Expertise-based conceptualization	Consumer-based service conceptualization
2 *Service differentiation*	Consistency in service performance	Superior in unique service performance	Personalized service performance
3 *Market focus*	Broad market focus	Narrow/broad market focus	Narrow market focus
4 *Availability*	Extended availability	Selective availability	Limited/exclusive availability
5 *Mode of international operations*	Network of production units (e.g. licensing franchising)	International expertise network with high costs (e.g. subsidiaries, joint ventures)	International service netrwork with partnership character

Source: Välinkangas, L. and Lehtinen, U. (1994).

services. We can, however, link these strategies to frameworks which have been developed before.

It is very clear that the *standardization strategy* is close to the global strategy discussed before. Referring back to the service triangle concept (*see* Chapter 1), what this strategy basically calls for is a strategy of investment in the top of the triangle. As economies of scale are an important factor here, fast and broad availability is crucial. The service is marketed to a broad and/or un-segmented market, and therefore the international operations have to be developed as a network of production units. The necessary speed of growth requires formulae such as licensing or franchising. These formulae are feasible since the critical competitive competence is at the top of the triangle and control of the franchise unit is relatively easy, given the emphasis on standardization.

The *specialization strategy* also tends to come close to a global strategy, but rather than looking for economies of scale, a company tends to exploit the uniqueness of a particular type of service, expertise or skill which is superior to that available to the competitors in the international environment. Typically, the service concept has been developed in a more advanced market with more demanding customers or a specific combination of environmental factors (for example, hotel service in the US, or restaurant services in Western Europe). This development may indeed be necessitated by more advanced customers, as is often the case for US corporate services (but also consumer services, as the Wal-Mart example illustrates), or in conjunction with a factor such as the high labour cost in 'continental' Europe. The latter could lead to more automation and more technology-intensive service delivery systems in Europe. The service is offered in the segmented market, usually implying a narrow market focus. The availability quite often has to be selective to ensure an adequate pool of knowledgeable and adequately trained service personnel. The firm therefore may want to exercise a relatively high degree of control over its international network, and thus it will tend to internationalize by establishing foreign subsidiaries. The corporation's name and image are heavily promoted to make the service well known and to create credibility in an international environment. While the flow of knowledge initially will be from corporate to subsidiaries, in order to keep the network growing the company should make sure that knowledge is also effectively transmitted across the various units.

Referring back to the service triangle concept, this strategy also implies heavy investment at the top, but not so much in systems or procedures as in knowledge and expertise development. A corporate 'R&D' centre and/or training is important, as is the development of the corporate image and the representation and building of corporate culture. Corporate, however, must not always be seen as 'central'. Quite often it means a network of decentralized units, interacting with each other so that learning also can take place literally between the units. In other words, it looks much more like a network of equal computers working together than a central computer or server linked to other smaller units. International consulting firms typically follow this strategy. Part of ABB Services World-wide would fit into this category, with various types of its expertise distributed throughout numerous countries worldwide. Other geographical units can call on this expertise and learn from it.

The third strategy, *customization*, falls much more to the right-hand side of the Bartlett and Goshal framework (*see* Figure 20.6). The service is conceptualized around the needs of the target customer, and long-term relationships are cultivated. International service networks sometimes remain limited in scope (i.e. they fit the multi-domestic strategy). However, sometimes a loose network of formally independent units will form chains, sharing some of the service delivery activities (e.g. hotels linked in common reservation networks). Service is sometimes exported by having the service provider travel to the customer. Referring to our service triangle, it is clear that this strategy applies to organizations positioned towards the bottom left side of the triangle.

CONCLUSION

The view that services are by their very nature local and therefore cannot be internationalized is increazingly contradicted by what we see all around us. As a matter of fact, there are a number of reasons why services are becoming increasingly international. Service companies should therefore develop an internationalization strategy. The appropriate strategy depends on the particular situation and on the type of service that the company offers.

In this chapter we have described the various strategies and the factors which determine the appropriate strategy. In developing an appropriate strategy, companies should give particular attention to potential cultural differences, since services are not culturally neutral. In designing the service and the service delivery system, companies should be careful to avoid conflicts between corporate culture and (implicit) cultural biases in both the service concept and the culture of the employees and customers. This chapter has described some useful dimensions that might help us understand and evaluate such potential conflicts.

Review and discussion questions

■ Based on the description of the Wal-Mart and Marks and Spencer cases at the beginning of the chapter. Identify the drivers for internationalization in the retail sector. Contrast the two cases. Why was Wal-Mart successful and why did Marks and Spencer fail?

■ Analyse the challenges opportunities faced by the sector of call centres with respect to internationalization. See the report in *Financial Times* 'India learns language of customer service', *Financial Times*, 4 Apr, 2001.

Notes and references

[1] Tomkins, R. (1997) 'Wal-Mart comes shopping in Europe', *Financial Times*, 21 Dec, p. 23.

[2] World Trade Organisation (1995) *International Trade: Trends and statistics*.

[3] This part has been inspired to a large extent by an article written by Lovelock, C. H. and Yip, G. S. (1996) 'Developing global strategies for service businesses', *California Management Review*, Vol 38, No 2, Winter, 64–86.

[4] For more information on call centres in India *see* Merchant, K. (2001) 'India learns Language of Customer Service', *Financial Times*, 4 April, p. 11.

[5] For more information see the recent report by the European Commission on this topic. *See also* the article by Guerrer, F. (2002) 'EU Economy hit by lack of single market in services', *Financial Times*, 31 July, p. 1.

[6] Ibid. *See also* Roberts, J. (1999) 'The internationalisation of business service firms: a stages approach', *The Service Industries Journal*, Vol 19, No 4, 68–88.

[7] *See* Merchant, K. (2001), op. cit.

[8] Mead, M. (1978) *Culture and Commitment: The new relationships between the generations in the 1970s*. New York: Columbia University Press.

[9] *Source*: Schein, E. (1985) *Organisational Culture and Leadership*. San Francisco: Jossey-Bass Publishers.

[10] Readers who want to know more about this are referred to Trompenaars, F. and Hampden-Turner, C. (1998) *Riding the Waves of Culture: Understanding cultural diversity in business*. London: Nicholas Brealy.

[11] Ibid.

[12] The four dimensions used by Hofstede are power distance, uncertainty avoidance, individualism and masculinity. The main difference is that Hofstede limits his framework to work-related values:

■ *Power distance* is the extent to which a society accepts that the power in institutions and organizations is distributed unequally.

■ *Uncertainty avoidance* is the extent to which a society lacks tolerance for uncertainty and ambiguity.

■ *Individualism* is the extent to which a society believes that people are supposed to take care of themselves and remain emotionally independent from groups, organizations and other collectivities.

■ *Masculinity* is the extent to which 'masculine' or ego values of assertiveness, money and things prevail in a society, rather than 'feminine' or social values of nurturing, quality of life, and people.

For more information, *see* Hofstede, G. (1980) *Culture Consequences: International differences in work-related values*. Beverly Hills: Sage Publications.

[13] Bartlett, C. A. and Ghoshal, S. (1989) *Managing Across Borders: The transnational solution*. Hutchinson Business Books.

[14] Ibid.

[15] Lovelock, C. H. and Yip, G. S. (1996), op. cit.

[16] Burt, T. and Tomkins, R. (1997)'Case Study: Ikea and Toys 'R' Us', *Financial Times*, 8 Oct.

[17] Ibid.

[18] Lovelock, C. H. and Yip, G. S. (1996), op. cit.

[19] Välikangas, L. and Lethinen, U. (1994) 'Strategic types of services and international marketing', *International Journal of Service Industry Management*, Vol 5, No 2, 72–84.

Suggested further reading

Hofstede, G. (1980) *Culture Consequences: International differences in work-related values*. Beverly Hills: Sage Publications. Basic book on internationalization.

Lovelock, C. H. and Yip, G. S. (1996) 'Developing global strategies for service businesses', *California Management Review*, Vol 38, No 2, Winter, 64–86. This excellent study provides a framework for developing global strategies for service businesses. It integrates existing, separate frameworks on globalization and on service businesses and analyses which distinctive characteristics of service businesses affect globalization and which do not.

Trompenaars, F. and Hampden-Turner, C. (1998) *Riding the Waves of Culture: Understanding cultural diversity in business*. London: Nicholas Brealy. Basic book on internationalization.

CHAPTER 21

Defining a service strategy

Aimé Heene · Bart Van Looy · Roland Van Dierdonck

INTRODUCTION

In this chapter we explore the issues involved in defining a strategy for a service firm. We start off by taking a broader look at what strategy is all about. What is the nature of strategic management? What questions have to be answered when defining an organization's strategy? What are the relevant frameworks and recent insights? Equipped with this background we shall be able to discuss some of the specific challenges involved in defining a service strategy: managing intangible resources, looking at added value carriers and the dynamics of value creation, managing for continuity, and finally the role of technology.

Objectives

By the end of this chapter, you should be able to discuss:

- the basic questions or themes that have to be dealt with when defining a service strategy
- the notion of competitive advantage and how competitive forces erode this advantage
- how recent insights from resource- and competence-based views on strategies enhance our insights into the strategy process
- specific issues and challenges faced by service firms: tangibilization, the use of intangible resources, the dynamics of value creation and perception, the role of technology and ways of managing for continuity in time and space

THE NATURE OF STRATEGIC MANAGEMENT

The basic themes in defining a strategy

We start from the assumption that it is a fundamental objective of an organization to safeguard its longevity. In some industries, such as the dot.com industry currently and the airline industry at certain moments in time, this might mean

453

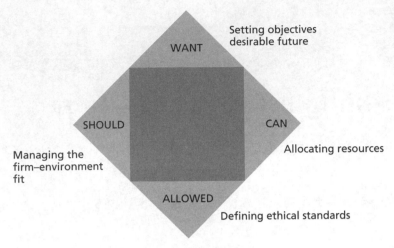

Figure 21.1 The field of strategy making[1]

Source: Reprinted from *Long Range Planning*, Vol 30, No 6, Heene, A., 'The nature of strategic planning', p. 934 (1997), with permission from Elsevier Science.

simple survival, however, generally longevity implies being successful or even gaining 'above average rents', as economists express it. In order to safeguard its longevity each firm has to define a strategy which requires decisions regarding four basic elements: the firm's objectives, its environment, its resources and patterns of resource allocation, and finally its corporate values, norms and ethics. These elements are summarized in Figure 21.1. To be effective, a well-balanced strategy needs to address all these elements in a consistent manner.

The objectives: What do we want to do?

Developing a strategy consists first of decisions regarding what it is that the company wants to do and wants to become. This means that the management has to define a desirable future for the company. This desirable future will usually be summarized in the firm's objectives, its 'business definition', its mission statement and its vision on the future.

Let us take Ikea as a first example. The desirable future as Ikea defines it reads like this:[2]

> 'We'd like to help you improve your home and create a better everyday life. We do this by offering a wide range of quality home furnishings in our stores that combine good design and function with prices so low that as many people as possible can afford them.'

The environment: What should we do?

Strategy, of course, is more than a simple wish list of what management wants. A company should consider whether what it wants to do is in line with what is going on in the market, and so strategy will also imply an analysis of the firm's environment, leading to a definition of what the firm, given its environment, should achieve.

Within environmental analysis, customers and their needs and preferences will be a central focus of attention. Other elements include the existing competition, possible substitutes, the bargaining position towards suppliers, as well as regulatory elements.[3] Environmental analysis allows the firm to be connected to its environment and guarantees the alignment between the company and its environment, be it through adapting the firm to its environment or through a process of 'changing' the environment so that the needs of the environment better fit the firm's objectives and capabilities.

In the case of Ikea, this alignment exists. Large segments of the market are interested in furniture that is cheap, functional and attractive at the same time. Notice too that Ikea's offering to its customers actually shapes the market as well. The conception of furniture and how it fits into people's purchasing behaviour becomes altered. In the past, buying furniture was more a twice-in-a-lifetime event: a cheaper set of furniture at the beginning of adult life, followed by a more luxurious design intended to last for decades once careers work out well and the children have outgrown their 'creating-damage-all-over' phase. Now flexibility and more frequent changes in interior have become an option within the grasp of a large group of customers.

Resources and resource allocation patterns: What can we do?

A company has to take into consideration what it can do, given limited resources. Whether a firm will be able to successfully pursue the course of actions defined depends on its resources and the deployment of these resources. Resources and their deployment determine what the firm can achieve. If we look at Ikea again, we should not forget that, behind the rather simple objective stated above, hides a complex resource allocation pattern. Ikea has contracts with about 2000 suppliers, selected to meet the manufacturing standards required. The low price is built into the production process; the flat packs used for shipping allow for a rational distribution; selling surfaces are designed in such a way that self-service and immediate take-away becomes possible for the majority of the products.

In terms of resources, it is important to notice that – besides the classical tangible resources like facilities, plants and so on – two types of resources are becoming more crucial everyday: the intangible resources (such as knowledge, aptitudes, attitudes, reputation, image and brand equity) and the 'firm-addressable resources'. The latter are resources which are not legally owned by the firm but are used within the processes of product design, development, service delivery, or marketing and sales. This notion of firm-addressable resources is becoming more and more important as firms are starting to operate in networks. Strategy then does not limit itself to *one isolated* company but needs to address the network as a whole. Good examples are the so-called virtual business schools. Such schools do not have a faculty of their own, but are able to 'address' a group of (visiting) faculty members employed elsewhere, to teach their courses. This is of course also the essence of supply chain management: 'controlling' the entire supply chain without owning it.

Corporate values: What are we allowed to do?

A further element defining the firm's strategy which under the influence of corporate scandals over the last two years, has gained importance and therefore needs to be addressed up front, concerns the company's values. This includes corporate norms and values and 'business ethics' through which management decides what is allowed to be achieved by the company's associates.

'Thrift, inventiveness, and hard work. Modesty and willpower. Our relationships with each other and the world around us. Co-operation and sharing, and the knowledge that we are in this together and we all need each other.'

These are the values of Ikea: it inspires the company to pay attention to eco-logical considerations, to work with manufacturers all over the world (in more than 60 countries) and to develop appropriate HR practices.

Such values should not be seen as something that merely scratches the surface. Situations where values are at stake are abundant and the position a company takes influences its daily operations. Consider what happened with the Barings bank, or more recently Enron or World.com.

Addressing potential conflicts

Any strategy for any company, including service firms thus needs to address four different issues: what is desirable, and what should and can be realized, in a man-ner that is in line with the organization's values. While these four levels sound rather simple, dealing with them in a consistent way is often complex in practice. In particular, in defining the content of strategy, many potential conflicts between the four constituting issues of strategy need to be resolved.

Conflict with the environment

One of the typical conflicts in defining the content of strategy is the tension between the objectives of the firm and the value that the environment attaches to the services offered – that is, at the price at which the firm wants to sell a service, the market might not be interested in the service concept offered. An interesting example can be found in the Belgian history of fast food. The concept, brought over from the US, started to present itself in European streets in the late 1960s. During the early 1970s the results of the first hamburger chains were disastrous. The price at which hamburgers were offered simply was perceived as too high by customers. Just when some of the major local players in Belgium were considering abandoning this market, a form of last-chance marketing plan was launched by one of the major distribution chains. This plan consisted in essence of strong price reductions, and if sales went up, the installation of larger scale operations. The rest is history: it is impossible to visit a single town in Belgium that does not have its own hamburger restaurant.

Conflict with available resources

Another 'classical' field of conflicts arises out of the tension between what the avail-able resources allow the firm to do and the direction in which the company wants to go. New business development may for instance be constrained by past history and the assets that have been built up over time. Larger organizations in particular tend to have difficulties in changing when the times demand it. What were once assets might become liabilities. As discussed in Chapter 17, new forms of distribu-tion become possible for financial services: a bank with a large network of branches should be aware that this network could become a liability in the future when customers start to use electronic banking devices on a large scale. Competitors with a less costly distribution network might start to outperform more traditional banks. Other illustrations of the fact that changes or transformations are difficult to realize, can be found everywhere: think of the difficulties the flag carriers in the airline industry have had and still have to survive. Organizational structure and culture, the routines and technologies developed over time, are all elements very resistant to change. For more than a decade now, national railways in Europe have been talking about changing into a customer-oriented service company, but very few have succeeded in doing so. Indeed, changing direction to realize objectives is in practice a rough job compared to defining these objectives. This type of strategic change remains one of the most difficult challenges managers face.[4]

The key to long-term survival and profitability: competitive advantage

The challenge in defining a sound and sustainable strategy is thus to come up with a consistent and integrated answer to the basic strategic questions of what management wants to do, should do, can do, and is allowed to do. This answer will result in longevity when it implies the creation of a competitive advantage.

A competitive advantage first of all refers to the 'distinctive capability' of the firm. A firm creates competitive advantage if it succeeds in becoming different from its competitors in a way that is recognized and appreciated by its (potential) clients. IKEA unquestionably has a competitive advantage: the firm succeeds in clearly distinguishing its product offer from competing product offerings, and customers assign value to IKEA's product offering as it clearly addresses their needs and preferences.

A competitive advantage also has to be sustainable. It has to create a 'time window' which lasts long enough to allow the firm to harvest the benefits of the differences, in terms of both financial profits and opportunities for building and leveraging resources to create a 'new' competitive advantage.

It is now recognized in strategy theory that a firm may pursue three types of strategy:[5]

- a cost leadership strategy;
- a differentiation strategy; or
- a focus strategy.

The cost leadership strategy aims at minimizing the costs of products or services delivered to the marketplace. Discount retailers such as Aldi and Lidl apply this generic strategy, as does Easyjet or Ryan Air. Policies such as limiting the product range, offering non-branded or privately branded goods or services, formalizing, standardization, automation or harvesting economies of scale, and simplification of business processes perfectly fit this strategy.

Differentiation strategies aim at creating competitive advantage not by striving for the lowest possible cost structure, but by maximizing value created for the customer. Companies like Marks & Spencer and Delhaize pursue a differentiation advantage in the retail sector, while Lufthansa and Singapore Airlines do the same in the airline industry. The rationale behind the strategy is that the higher value that has been created will be rewarded in the marketplace by means of a price premium that is sufficiently large to cover the higher costs that may have been necessary to create the added value and to bring this higher value to the attention of the (potential) customer. Within this strategy, typical policies include extending the product range, offering branded goods, highly personalized 'on-the-spot' procedures and harvesting economies of scope.[6]

With a focus strategy, the firm applies a cost-leadership or a differentiation strategy within a particular market segment in a specialized way, and as a result of this focus, gains competitive advantage over firms applying their generic strategy on a wider market. Local retail shops often apply this kind of strategy. Specialized hospitals apply a focus strategy and can as a result gain competitiveness over general hospitals. This brings to mind the Shouldice Hospital we looked at when discussing HR practices. By concentrating on one type of medical intervention and organizing the whole hospital accordingly, Shouldice was able to become the leader in hernia treatment, with the lowest price, the highest service quality and the shortest throughput time. In the Belgian financial industry, Bank van Breda focuses on 'entrepreneurs' and develops specific products for this market segment.

Competition: eroding the competitive advantage to a competitive requirement

One can observe that in almost any industry products and services become better, more fitted to customer needs, are delivered in a more reliable way and even become cheaper over time. Cars for instance have clearly advanced technologically over time and at the same time have become cheaper. Just consider how the prices of PCs are dropping at an ever-increasing pace, while performance is continuously increasing.

This all is the result of competition that makes competitive advantages erode to competitive requirements, definable as the minimal threshold that companies have to maintain in order to remain in business. The distinction between a competitive advantage and a competitive requirement is similar to the distinction which some people make between order winners and qualifiers.[7] Four mechanisms are used to erode or destroy competitive advantage: imitation, substitution, resource mobilization and resource paralysis.[8]

■ *Imitation* is undoubtedly the best-known erosion mechanism and has become reinforced in the past by practices such as 'benchmarking'. Take distribution, for example: over the past decade, Aldi has introduced a low-cost approach, attracting a significant number of customers. By offering a well-balanced but at the same time rather restricted line of products, introducing a very sober surface lay-out and minimizing the number of staff, Aldi has been able to offer products at very low prices. At the moment, Aldi is suffering from competition not so much from the classical distribution players, but from companies applying the same logic but trying to push it even further: fewer products, less 'comfort' within the shop, and so on.

■ *Substitution* often involves product innovation whereby existing products or services are replaced by new ones. The essence of substitution is that the same function with the same customer group is fulfilled by a new product or service based on a new or different technology. Examples in the manufacturing industries abound: digital *versus* mechanical watches, electronic type writers, etc. In the service industry, one could refer to the substitution of traditional surgery methods by endoscopic methods. It is interesting to note that substitution can also be the result of 'process innovation' which can eventually lead to 'changing the rules of competition'.[9] This is the route many on-line stock brokers took by completely redesigning the distribution channel.[10] It is interesting to note that in service industries what some see as a process innovation is actually at the same time a product innovation as the customer is confronted with the new process. Think for instance at the electronic delivery of courses (a process innovation) which is for the student distance learning (a product innovation).

- Some forms of *resource mobilization* such as headhunting are widespread and well known. The mechanism of resource mobilization is at work whenever resources contributing to a competitive advantage start to move or when ownership over them is changed. Resource mobilization can have different causes. It can result from an internal loss – for example, when an important employee having an important body of knowledge leaves the firm. It can also result from external causes involving a competitor's action – for instance, when an employee leaves the firm to join the competitor after having been invited by the competitor to do so.

- *Resource paralysis* is a direct attempt by competitors to reduce the value-creating potential of the firm's resources. Resource paralysis is a frontal attack which takes the form of competitors spreading rumours, provoking false complaints, using negative comparative advertising, or lobbying for the enforcement of laws that prevent their competitor from using its resources – for instance, through import barriers, standards enforcement or environmental regulations. The way Easyjet is frontally attacking Go (British Airway's low cost carrier) in its advertisements perfectly illustrates resource paralysis. Government regulation (e.g. accreditation) in the educational field is effectively paralysing distance learning competencies of the UK open university courses in many fields.

The quest for sustainability

The fundamental purpose of strategy is not just to build competitive advantage, but is to build 'sustainable' competitive advantage. Apple computer had a competitive advantage in the PC market throughout most of the 80s, but it did not appear to be sustainable. Therefore, one of the important issues in defining and implementing strategy is to define actions that eliminate the erosion mechanisms or that at least slow down their deployment or effects. Counter-erosion actions are aimed at extending the time window during which the competitive advantage 'exists' and allow the firm to earn the profits that it needs to safeguard its longevity.

Over time, strategic management theory has developed several frameworks for conceptualizing and developing such counter-erosion decisions. The first approach that has been developed is based on the competitive forces model[11] discussed earlier. Based on this model one can argue that creating and sustaining a competitive advantage implies: building barriers to entry, keeping track of possible substitutes, reducing the intensity of rivalry and building a stronger structural negotiation position towards both buyers and suppliers.

- Barriers to entry can be created by different means:

  1. *Employing economies of scale* – e.g. as in car rental.
  2. *Product differentiation* – e.g. Harvard Business School's emphasis on case research and case methodology in its programmes.
  3. *Capital requirements* – e.g. Disney who through his model parks, enormously increased the need for working capital.
  4. *Switching costs* – (costs for the client when switching from one supplier to another) – e.g. the (mainly psychological) costs that a consumer is facing when switching from his traditional hairdresser to a new one.

5. *Access to distribution channels or generally location* – e.g. with the fierce competition going on for space on the supermarket shelf, introducing a new product will require serious investment if traditional distribution channels are to be persuaded to incorporate the new product.

6. *Property rights* – e.g. technological patents, exclusive access to certain resources or licensing agreements and even favourable locations as in the case of McDonald's.

7. *Government regulations and policies* – e.g. in the case of energy supply in large parts of Europe.

■ Possible substitutes should also be monitored. For security brokers, insurance companies or real estate agents are competitors and the services provided are to a certain extent exchangeable: they all offer longer-term investments with a certain return. Security companies were confronted in the 1980s with the development of ever more sophisticated electronic alarm systems technology that could take over the work of guards at a much cheaper rate. Security firms had no choice but to develop service packages combining guards and electronic systems whereby the guards become highly skilled operators.

■ Working on the intensity of competition itself implies complicated strategies and actions very much like a game of chess. Deciding what actions are the most relevant – working on advertising or price, or trying to increase market share by acquiring smaller competitors – depends heavily on the specific industry – that is, the number of competitors, the life cycle stage of the industry, the overall cost structure prevailing within the industry, and so on.[12]

■ Sources of competitive advantage – and hence also threats to it – can also lie in the relationships with customers and/or suppliers. The relative power balance between parties – the firm, the customers, the suppliers – will influence the strength and the sustainability of competitive advantage. A limited number of customers means vulnerability in terms of profit rates as well as long-term results; as soon as something happens within such a customer base, you feel it.

An alternative view on how to defend against processes that erode competitive advantage can be found in the resource- and competence-based strategic management theory.[13] These theories basically argue that the complexity of the system of resources used to create competitive advantage determines the sustainability of the competitive advantage created. Co-ordinated resources can by their nature be protected against erosion because of three characteristics: they include a certain degree of intangibility; they are time-dependent; and they are co-ordinated and hence complex.

Tacit knowledge, brands, reputation, networks (social capital), and organizational climate and corporate culture are all examples of resources that are difficult to imitate given their highly intangible nature. McKinsey (the consulting firm), Wal Mart or Club Med offer examples here. Characteristics such as culture, reputation and more implicit ways of working are built up over time. It is not only by bringing together a few highly intelligent people that a new McKinsey is born; equally, just throwing together a bunch of enthusiastic young people in an attractive resort by the seaside doesn't mean Club Med has to start worrying about its long-term future. It may take years if not decades for a distibutor to make his employees behave as the Wal Mart employees do. Moreover, often a complex process of different kinds of co-ordination of resources is involved, making it extremely difficult to imitate. This is an issue we shall discuss further when looking in greater depth at managing intangible resources.

We now have a taste of the issues involved in establishing a consistent strategy. Let us turn to some specific challenges faced by service firms.

THE CHALLENGES OF STRATEGIC MANAGEMENT FOR SERVICES

The general issues of strategic management in service industries are not fundamentally different from those in manufacturing industries. However, there are some issues which are specific to service industries, given the specific nature of a service – in particular, intangibility and simultaneity.

The identification of the 'added value carriers'

Creating a sustainable competitive advantage means creating distinctive added value for the firm's clients in a sustainable way and 'embedding' this added value in the firm's outputs: its products. According to this line of reasoning, products can be regarded as 'carriers of added value'. As we argued earlier (*see* Chapter 3) most products are a combination of goods and services, i.e. a package of tangible and intangible elements. From this point of view the firm has to decide:

1. What added value will be embedded in the tangible components of its offering to the marketplace.
2. What added value will be embedded in the pure service (i.e. intangible) component of its offering to the marketplace.
3. How synergy can be created between the added value in the tangible component and intangible component.
4. Whether and how the mix of tangible and intangible components itself can become an added value for its customer.

As stated, this is and should be a concern for any type of firm. However, the reason for doing so differs for service firms as opposed to manufacturing firms. Manufacturing companies may add service components to their product in reacting to the price-erosion that takes place due to competitive dynamics. Service companies may do the reverse and add tangible elements; by doing so they may overcome the earning limitations that service companies have to face in selling 'capacity'. Moreover, by acting in this way, the service offer becomes anchored in the service company and so-called 'switching costs' for customers are built in.

Limits to earnings due to restrictions on selling capacity

Capacity management is an important concern in service companies. As has been argued before, balancing and co-ordinating the supply of capacity and market demand is one of the core problems in capacity management in service companies; it also determines in many cases the chance of survival of service companies.

One of the critical factors is the extent to which a service organization in general, and a professional service organization in particular, is able to 'leverage' its available capacity. Given the need for interaction between the service provider and the customer, the available time of the provider is the 'scarce' resource limiting the earning potential of the firm.

The earnings of a service firm can be expressed as follows:

Total earnings = Units of time available in service delivery
× Earnings per unit of time.

If a firm wants to raise earnings it can increase the units of time available in service delivery or raise the earnings per unit of time. The first alternative means increasing the available capacity, which of course is an option at least as long as there are positive economics of scale. The other alternative, however, to increase capacity, is to increase the productivity of the service process (that is, to get more out of one unit of time) or to increase the value of one unit of time for the customer – that is, leveraging capacity.

One way of leveraging capacity is what we call the tangibilization of the product. Tangibilization in fact means that 'goods' are substituted for 'time sold' so that the embedded value is less dependent on time. This will lead the service company to take a new position on the goods–services continuum (*see* Figure 21.2). In fact, with the tendency towards servitization discussed in Chapter 3, one could speak of the phenomenon of 'productization' here. An excellent example of this tangibilization process can be observed in software companies, in the case of 'body-shopping activities', i.e. commercial activities whereby personnel are supplied to a customer by the service provider. Here activities which are highly subject to the limit on earnings are substituted by selling software packages.

The added value for the customer is then the sum of the added value in the tangible components, the added value in the service component and the added value by combining both types of components.

The added value of software packages is less constrained by time than body shopping and thus allows the software company to raise earnings per head and to maximize the earnings of time spent. Similarly, in the maintenance services, diagnostic tools provided to the customer can replace the intervention of the technicians.

It goes without saying that extending one's offerings by adding components – whether tangible or not – should be accompanied by adequate pricing. Far too often, extensions take place – in order to differentiate – without charges to customers for the additional value creation. This approach (not charging for additional offerings) is risky in two ways.

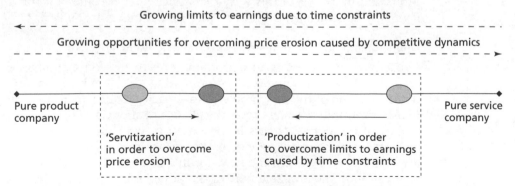

Figure 21.2 **Product companies and service companies moving towards each other**

1. Customers do not perceive the additional value or start to find it normal that it is free; they become 'spoiled' and start to ask for more.
2. Resources are required to deliver additional services: so someone has to pay the bill in the end. By not acknowledging this, the chances are high that the company is mortgaging the future developments of the organization.

Of course, adequate pricing will demand a thorough understanding of what value means to the customers; it will imply adequate information systems and policies (for instance, activity-based costing) and might imply some efforts in educating customers.

Finally, it is important to note that the tangibilization of services constitutes a move upwards in the service triangle. By doing so, the service – and also the service company – becomes somewhat more independent of its employees and their loyalty (or lack thereof) towards the organization. This leads us to the second consequence of tangibilization, the issue of anchoring the service in the firm.

Anchoring the service offer within the firm

A growing number of companies extend their service components in order to raise competitiveness and to fight against the 'standardization' or even 'banalization' of their products resulting from the competitive battle. For instance, a growing number of banks are evolving towards financial consulting. It is expected that adding this service component will contribute to the competitiveness of the firm and will help the firm overcome erosion processes caused by the competitive pressures.

Added service components have to be 'anchored'

Although this line of reasoning seems to be acceptable at first sight, the practice is highly questionable. Raising competitiveness through adding service components can indeed only be successful if one can 'anchor' the service component within the firm and prevent customers from using the service component delivered by the firm to obtain better conditions from a competitor that may be inclined to supply these better conditions due to the fact that it did not have to deliver the service (the advice) offered.

If clients can 'consume' the (additional) service component offered and use this to obtain better prices or slightly better products from competitors, the strategy of extending services in order to raise competitiveness risks raising the competitor's competitiveness. Raising competitiveness through adding or extending can only be successful if the firm is able to 'anchor' the service within the firm itself and if the firm as a result is able to 'lock in' customers.

Two forms of anchoring the service in the firm

Anchoring the service delivered within the service firm can take different forms. In all cases of anchoring, switching costs for clients are raised and, as a result, the firm succeeds in 'locking in' clients: if the client uses the service delivered to bargain for better conditions from the competitor, the client will have to overcome additional costs for doing so.

A well-known example is the pharmacist. In most European countries a pharmacist is a highly skilled professional. The added value of the pharmacist is his or her knowledge about various types of medicines and expertise in preparing special prescriptions. The service component is without doubt very important in this 'product'. However, preparing prescriptions is becoming less important given that more and more standardized medicines are prescribed by doctors. As a result, the added value of the pharmacist (real or perceived) is decreasing, with price erosion the inevitable result. The pharmacist, however, can limit this erosion by making sure that all medicines can only be distributed by pharmacists. In other words, his or her service as a pharmacist is linked to a product which is anchored in a pharmacy. The customer is not tempted to use the service at one place and buy the drug elsewhere, as the price is the same everywhere, and the drug can in any case only be found in other pharmacies, the number of which is limited by law.

Generally speaking, at least two strategic approaches to anchoring are worth considering:

- raising the uniqueness of the product component sustained by service delivery;
- creating causal ambiguity for the client.

If the firm succeeds in connecting the service offered (advice) and the unique goods, the value of the service component delivered can only be harvested in the firm itself while the added value of the service component can only be 'consumed' through consuming the product that 'materializes' the service component. This is actually what our pharmacist is doing. Whereas at first sight services are or can be used to 'upgrade' and 'de-banalize' goods, in fact the opposite happens here: the added value and de-banalization of services can only be sustained if these are connected to and sustained by unique goods or services. Let us take investment advice as an example. No matter how good the advice is, not being able to deliver the necessary stock transactions in a timely manner will remain a major drawback for investment consultants. Customers will try to get the advice free and spend the money (transaction costs and broker's fee) elsewhere. Harvesting the value of the additional service offered will be far easier when offering both services (transactions and advice) especially when they are blended in such a way that they create 'causal ambiguity'.

The second approach, creating causal ambiguity, implies that the service company does not reveal the component to which additional services will be connected. Clients are not given any insight into the specifics that will be used to solve the problem; the service delivered only reveals the problem-solving potential without revealing the characteristics of the components themselves. Let us look again at the situation of financial advisers: when an investment consultant talks to a potential customer about which bonds he or she should invest in, the customer can 'take' this advice and after a few such discussions decide for himself or herself what transactions to pursue and where. When no such clear indications on the product are offered, but instead information is given about the approach, the customer base or previous results, customers are not able to make decisions on the 'components'. As a result, uncertainty on how to achieve results is created in the client's mind. This prevents him or her from 'joy-riding'.

Of course, despite the fact that introducing tangibles in the service offering can be a visible way to create a competitive advantage and/or create higher earnings, it is important to pay careful attention to the intangibles in services, which brings us to the next topic.

Managing intangible resources

Intangibles and competitive advantage

Intangible asset stocks are central for the creation of sustainable competitive advantage in a service firm. Distinctive characteristics of tangibles and intangibles for the process of creating competitive advantage are summarized in Table 21.1.

Building competitive advantage by using intangible assets protects competitive advantage against imitation, mainly due to the intangibility of the assets and the resulting causal ambiguity. It becomes unclear to an outsider which assets are precisely used to create competitive advantage and how the creation of competitive advantage by using these assets is achieved. It is for instance difficult to precisely and completely understand where the competitive advantage of Disney comes from. One can argue that this competitiveness is the result of the working together of many resources of a tangible and an intangible nature: location, the attractions themselves, the atmosphere, the employees' behaviour, etc.

Whereas it is rather obvious that intangibles are highly protected against imitation, it is at the same time true that they are not necessarily equally well protected against 'resource mobilization'. Knowledge, for instance, can easily 'leave' the firm when 'key employees' are mobilized and leave the firm due to internal or external causes. Many professional service firms, such as law firms, are for this reason very vulnerable to key personnel leaving the firm accompanied often by customers who are loyal to the service provider and not to the service firm.

The challenge for 'knowledge management' in this context is then:

- reducing the mobilization itself;
- safeguarding the firm's knowledge stock when mobilization takes place;
- preventing the deployment of mobilized knowledge stocks outside the firm that is subject to mobilization. Firms may take actions that limit the possibilities of key employees to leave the firm legally, they may articulate knowledge and embed it in large databases as consulting companies do and they may split up knowledge over groups of people as is happening in development teams.

Reducing the process of resource mobilization

How can, for instance, a business school or a law firm prevent or discourage its 'knowledge carriers', mainly personnel, from leaving the organization? Two approaches can be followed here:

- raising the dependency of the personnel;
- raising the attractiveness of the firm for the personnel.

Table 21.1 Distinctive characteristics of tangibles and intangibles

Tangible assets	Intangible assets
Build-up time rather predictable	Build-up time less predictable
Rather easy to imitate	Difficult or impossible to imitate
Fixed reproduction costs	Economies of scale on reproduction
Depreciates through use	Grows through use
Remains if not used (leveraged)	Disappears if not used
Easy to appropriate	Difficult to appropriate
Easy to control	Difficult to control; difficult to deny access to others

Raising the dependency can be achieved through legal measures such as contracts that prevent knowledge carriers from leaving the firm. However, it should be noted that this approach has limited value: making people dependent by contracts (and their enforcement) often does not enhance motivation. Increasing the firm's attractiveness is in this respect much more advisable. It is clear that human resource policies play a key role in creating such an attractive internal environment – for instance, by offering career opportunities that cannot be obtained from the competitors or by creating a corporate culture that highly motivates employees and invites them to demonstrate loyalty towards their firm. In short, HRM's crucial role in the service company's strategy must focus primarily on raising to express it in economic terms, 'switching costs' for personnel through the creation of a highly attractive internal environment.

Safeguarding the knowledge stock

It will never be possible to completely prevent personnel from leaving the firm. It is therefore necessary to work out measures to safeguard the knowledge present in the firm when personnel is leaving the company. Measures to safeguard the knowledge of the firm can involve:

- the spread of the knowledge over personnel;
- articulation and codification of (mainly tacit) knowledge – for instance, in schemes, manuals, drawings, procedures and databases. This is common practice in the major consulting firms where huge databases are built to accumulate experience and knowledge that has been developed by the consultants.

Spreading knowledge over personnel of course guarantees that the firm can go on using the knowledge stock in its processes of product and value creation when resource mobilization has taken place. Spreading knowledge means setting up learning processes within the firm and thus managing the firm as a 'learning organisation'.[14]

Articulation and codification of knowledge are processes through which (mainly tacit) knowledge is made explicit and as a result made 'apprehensible'.[15] This is exactly what the SOP (standard operating procedures) manuals at McDonald's do. At first sight, it might seem that articulated and codified knowledge has major disadvantages compared to 'tacit' knowledge, as one could argue that the more knowledge is articulated and codified, the more it becomes 'observable' by an outsider and thus more easily imitated by competitors. One can however argue that the articulation and codification of knowledge does not necessarily imply that the value of the knowledge for creating sustainable competitive advantage is affected:[16]

- If an individual's knowledge is articulated within an organization, the ability of outsiders to apprehend the full meaning of the articulated knowledge cannot be presumed.
- Even when articulated knowledge can be fully apprehended by the outsiders, causal ambiguity about the importance of the knowledge to create competitive advantage may obscure the value of the knowledge to the outsiders.
- The value of knowledge, whether tacit or articulated, is time-dependent and erodes over time.
- Tacit knowledge is very hard to spread throughout and transfer within the organization.
- Tacit knowledge is much harder to leverage than articulated and codified knowledge.

One could thus argue that articulating and codifying knowledge has serious advantages over leaving knowledge tacit and that it should be recommended even if the imitability of articulated knowledge might seem to be higher than the imitability of tacit knowledge.

Preventing knowledge deployment and knowledge leveraging outside the firm

Knowledge should not only be spread, articulated and codified, but also 'anchored' within the company as well. Anchoring knowledge prevents the deployment or leveraging of knowledge outside the firm. This can only be achieved if 'knowledge stock' within the firm is managed as part of the system of resource stocks and flows that make up the company.

'Anchoring' in this sense, for instance, means that knowledge of technologies is connected both to tangibles such as computer hardware and software that are put at the development engineer's disposal, and to organizational structures – for example, structures that define interfaces between the engineering and the marketing departments.

Looked at from this point of view, 'organizational knowledge management' becomes a meaningful concept differing significantly from 'individual knowledge management'. A strategic approach to knowledge management does not only incorporate managing the knowledge base of individuals, but also considers 'individual knowledge management' to be part of a much larger management issue.

Mastering the dynamics of value creation and value perception in delivering services

The reader will understand by now, that strategic management in any firm is about creating value for the customer. As we know, services imply that customers are actively involved in the service delivery process. This phenomenon poses some specific value related challenges.

- Service companies have to address specific problems that might result from taking over one or more of the value-creating activities of their clients. These problems relate to interdependencies stemming from 'interweaving' value systems but pertain as well to the situation that clients may be in a bad position to assess the added value delivered by the service company. An in depth knowledge of the clients value systems as well as the appropriate use of value signals will turn out to be highly relevant.

- Service companies also have to define whether and how the involvement of the client in the process of service delivery creates added value for the client. This implies that service companies will have to manage the 'actual use' of the service by the client, a process which starts when defining the service concept.

Taking over value-creating activities: dealing with interdependencies and ensuring that clients are able to assess the added value of the service

The nature of the interaction that service companies build with their clients differs significantly from that of industrial companies. Whereas industrial companies deliver inputs to the 'value system'[17] of their clients (raw materials, subassemblies, etc.), service companies take over one or more of the value-creating activities and thus become interwoven with their client's value system. In many cases service companies 'take over' value-creating activities for which clients do not have sufficient resources, such as knowledge.

The fact that service companies are involved in the value system of their clients and may perform activities which are not 'mastered' by the client has serious consequences for the competitiveness of the service firm and for the perception of this competitiveness:

- Since performances of a value-creating activity in the value system are affected by the other activities in the same value system, the performance of the service company may be affected by the performance of the client in other value-creating activities.

- Clients with little or no knowledge about the value-creating activities that the service company is performing may be in a bad position to assess the added value that the service company is creating.

In order to overcome the first consequence, it can be advised that service companies aim for a very broad and deep involvement in the client's value system. A private banker offering services in wealth management has to have a complete understanding of the total assets of the customer, including his real estate position, his risk profile, family situation, life style, etc. If not the banker might risk ending up in a situation where he advises the wrong investment. The competitive service company should be able not only to take over a limited part of the value-creating activities of its client, but should be able to take over the interconnected value-creating activities as well or should at least be able to 'manage the interfaces' between the value-creating activities taken over and the interconnected value activities that the client continues to perform itself. At the very least, service companies can undertake a very detailed and in-depth analysis of their clients' value systems so that it becomes clear to the service company and to the clients how they should both co-operate to maximize the added value.

This is without any doubt a major point of concern for any service company that takes over activities that used to be done internally by its client, such as payroll administration, IT services, etc. For this type of service, it is undoubtedly important to establish clear arrangements on how information should be passed on.

Secondly, it may be difficult or even impossible for clients to assess the value the service company is offering and thus the competitiveness of the firm base on that value proposition, especially when the client lacks knowledge about the value-creating activities performed by the service company. As was described in Chapter 1, this is typically the case in the so-called task and personal interactive service sectors. In these cases it is advisable to define in advance the performance criteria and norms as precisely and in as much detail as possible and to agree on an 'output'-based assessment of the service the company delivered. We refer to the practice of agreeing on service level agreements discussed earlier. The emergence of 'no cure no pay' contracts fits an extreme example of this. This might require some effort, but in these cases clients should be prevented from assessing the service company's competitiveness based on the service process alone (as they may lack the knowledge to do so). In addition, it might be relevant to compensate for the client's 'lack' of individual perception of the service company's value by introducing 'inter-subjective assessments'. 'Word of mouth' marketing is in this respect a tremendously valuable strategic tool for service companies, and building 'image' (as an intangible resource stock) within a relation network that sustains the perception of competitiveness of the service company is becoming a necessity for the service firm.

A consequence of the above is that service companies should also steer the client's perception of the added value created in delivering the service by the extensive use of 'value signals'. These value signals can and should be embedded in the service firm's physical elements of the service offering, its tangible resources or its outputs. For instance, good-looking and well-written reports for a consulting firm or clean trucks for a transport company are important value signals; nice, cozy branches may be important value signals for a bank; or smartly dressed technicians for a maintenance firm.

By means of value signals, the service company influences the client's perceptions of the value of the service provider. By becoming deeply involved in the client's value system, the service company can guarantee the competitiveness of its service and can guarantee that the 'actual use' of the service provided equals the 'intended use'.

Added value results from the involvement of clients in the service delivery process

It will not come as a surprise that we argue that the value the service firm offers results directly from having the client involved in the service delivery process. This is clearly the case in business schools where students have the opportunity to actively participate in the learning process. Also in the Shouldice hospital the active participation of the patients in their recovery process is creating extra value for the patient. Hence, the competitiveness of any service firm will depend on how this involvement is being organized. As a general rule one could state that in delivering services, a detailed 'knowledge and expertise analysis' should be undertaken and used to determine which activities are to be offered by the service company and which ones conducted by the client. This should be done while defining the service concept as discussed in Chapter 2. Service companies can gain competitiveness by working out a service concept in which the service company creates the most favourable conditions for the client to apply its own knowledge and expertise.

So defining the service concept should address the roles performed by both parties – customer and provider – and hence implies the following activities:

- analysing which knowledge is needed to maximize added value in the service delivery activities;
- defining which party has the knowledge;
- creating conditions for successfully applying the knowledge.

This again underscores the importance of knowledge management in a service firm. It also indicates that knowledge management includes the customer as well.

The role of technology in safeguarding the longevity of the service firm

Often service delivery is highly 'human-factor driven'. However, it can be argued that humans in service delivery not only add value to the process, but can 'subtract' value as well. The major disadvantages of human-driven service delivery from a competitive point of view can be summarized as follows:

■ The involvement of a human deliverer limits the availability of the service in time and space as service delivery implies the physical presence of the human service deliverer at the time and place of the service consumer. This point has been raised before when discussing the relevancy of 'tangibilization' for overcoming capacity limitations. Computer software as a substitute for 'human' teaching activities allows the student to 'consume' the teaching where and when this is most suitable to his or her needs.

■ Unless highly structured and steered by strictly applied procedures, the repeatability of the service delivery process is in danger of being harmed by the human service deliverer – that is, by his or her 'on-the-spot' degree of initiative and creativity. This will be the case when this initiative results in 'sub-optimal' outcomes. In the future one might expect artificial intelligence and expert systems intended to solve problems to become more widespread. Such systems allow problem-spotting and problem-solving independent of the specific (and limited) knowledge of a human trouble-shooter and thus will lead to the same corrective measures in all equal-problem situations. A case in point are the expert systems to be found more and more in surgery environments; these enable one to have the most advanced know how available in all surgery rooms.

■ 'On-the-spot' creativity and initiative on the part of the human service deliverer can affect the cost effectiveness of the service delivery. The introduction of technology allows the client to be involved in the service delivery process in a cost-effective way. For example, home- and phone-banking, which can be fully automated, can be cost-saving.

Substituting technology for the human factor encourages the company to clearly define in what respect and to what extent the involvement of the human service provider adds value to the service delivery process, and how and where the 'personal touch' that only the human service provider can deliver adds value to the service provided. Any service firm should therefore thoroughly question when and how the personal touch that can be delivered by the human factor can add value to the service. All characteristics of the service delivery process in which this 'personal touch' does not add value should lead the service provider to investigate whether and how the substitution of the human factor by technology can contribute to the competitiveness of the service delivered. From a strategic point of view, then, technology can play a major role in safeguarding the longevity of the service firm through its impact on building and sustaining competitive advantage. Generally speaking, technology can add to the firm's competitiveness by lowering the service firm's costs or improving its competitive performance. The introduction and application of technology (such as information technology) in service delivery allows a company to:

■ optimize the service delivery process;
■ standardize the service delivery process and as a result guarantee the quality reliability of the services offered;
■ guarantee the deliverability of the service, independent of space and time.

Through the introduction of technology, service delivery becomes an activity in which the 'human factor' is sometimes less involved, and in all cases differently involved. This redefinition of the involvement of the human factor in service delivery adds value for customers if technology leads to reducing or even eliminating the non-value-adding characteristics of the involvement of the human factor in service delivery.

The foregoing reasoning does not necessarily imply that the service firm should adopt a industrialization approach. Introducing technology might allow the service firm to redefine the role and impact of the human factor to the point were it can really add value to the process of service delivery. Such a redefinition would then result not in reducing staff levels, but rather in the creation of superior value by allocating resources differently.

The fundamental strategic issue raised by extending the technological base of the service firm is the identification of the contribution of both technology and the human factor to the creation of value and based on this sustainable competitive advantage. Clearly defining the role of technology and of the people delivering services in a complementary and mutually reinforcing way can enhance the competitiveness of the service firm and thus its growth, prosperity and, consequently, its potential to safeguard the employability of its people.

Managing for continuity by creating sustainable competitive advantage

As has been repeatedly demonstrated in the foregoing sections, managing knowledge is highly relevant to service companies, since it allows them to manage for continuity by creating a competitive advantage over time. It is crucial that competitiveness shows such continuity.

However, service companies not only have to guarantee the continuity of their competitiveness in time. For many service companies, it is at least as important to guarantee the continuity of competitiveness in space. Fast-food restaurants, cleaning companies, banks, consulting companies, transport companies and in general all service companies with a geographically distributed service delivery, have to make sure that all their geographically spread associates deliver the service in a comparable way and on an equal level of competitiveness, even though they may be acting and delivering the service in quite different circumstances and with totally different customers. Continuity of service delivery in space can be achieved through:

■ standardization of the service delivery process;
■ standardization of the service delivery output.

In the first case, the delivery of the service is made independent of the particular circumstances in which the service is delivered. Processes and procedures are standardized and do not take particular circumstances into account or only allow for minor adjustments to these particular circumstances. This approach can be highly effective for implementing a differentiation strategy in the service delivery, and at the same time can produce economies by reducing and even eliminating uncertainty and fluctuation. Process standardization in service delivery can be applied in any case where the client is not actually involved in the service delivery – for example, cleaning companies – or where standardizing the interaction with the client adds value to the client – for instance, by guaranteeing quality reliability. Fast-food chains are perfect examples of this. Generally speaking, this approach could be regarded as suitable for all maintenance-interactive types of services (*see* Chapter 1). For this type of service growth becomes the more easy as licensing and franchising become more viable. In the case of standardization of output, continuity of competitiveness of the service delivery is not achieved at the level of the delivery process itself, but rather at the level of the result of the delivery process. This is possible if the service company succeeds in explicitly and clearly expressing the service concept in terms of results produced for the customer. In this approach, 'service quality' is described in terms of criteria that will be used to assess the performance of the service delivered and in terms of norms to be achieved in order to judge the quality to be 'good' or 'competitive'. Take, for instance, the maintenance of lifts: the maximum duration of breakdown allowed or the intervals between lift failure and repair can be agreed. How to organize the service delivery process is a challenge for the provider and as such not stipulated within contracts.

Standardizing output will often be necessary if the service delivery process involves a high degree of unpredictable involvement on the part of the client. Teaching is one of the best examples. It is difficult – if not impossible – to standardize the process of service delivery in this case due to the unpredictable and particular circumstances in which teaching has to take place. Every group of students has its own particularities. In order to guarantee continuity of competitiveness in this kind of service process, it makes sense only to standardize the output; what are students supposed to master in terms of knowledge and/or skills at the end of the course. This 'output standardization' often goes hand-in-hand with an emphasis on 'input' competencies and empowerment. Teachers need a comparatively long period of training and apprenticeship in order to develop adequate didactic insights and skills. Equipped with these skills, they are allowed considerable discretion in how to teach. Another example is physicians: here standardization with 'skills' is matched by decision latitude on how to handle a specific patient. Generally speaking, for task- and personal-interactive services there will often be a combination of input and output standardization, while the process is far less 'determined'.

CONCLUSION

In this chapter we started with an overview of relevant strategic questions and issues which needed to be addressed. Strategy is about finding answers on what to do in order to safeguard the firm's longevity and how to do this. Crucial to long-term survival and profitability is the creation of a distinctive and sustainable competitive advantage. Recently emerging resource- and competence-based theories offer new insights here: sustainability can be realized by configuring complex constellations that create value for customers.

Services are confronted with specific strategic challenges resulting from the intangibility and simultaneity inherent in the service process. We looked at these challenges systematically: how to overcome limits to earnings due to capacity constraints, how to anchor the intangible offer within the service company, how to use the intangible nature and technology to create and sustain competitive advantage over time and space and how to deal with the role of the customer in the value-adding process.

What becomes clear over and over again in this context is the need for an integrated approach towards service management. Customers, employees and the whole operational system have to be combined into a coherent service concept or value constellation. Strategy is as simple and as difficult as that.

Review and discussion questions

- What are the themes to be included in a service firm's strategy statement?

- Why do flag carriers in the airline industry create separate ventures in order to compete with the low cost carriers? Why don't they integrate the low cost strategy in their traditional high service strategy?

- What is the best defence against imitation by competitors? Illustrate using three concrete examples.

- What are three typical strategic issues for service firms?

- Companies like McDonald's or Disney have developed so-called universities to train their employees. How does this fit within concerns which have been described in this chapter?

- Identify and document in your environment three retail companies that follow one of the three generic strategies (cost leadership, differentiation and focus) described in this chapter. How have they implemented their strategic choices?

- An increasing number of business schools develop web based MBA programmes (i.e. using the distance learning concept). How would you look at this from the perspective of a traditional business school? Use the concepts developed in this chapter.

- Recall the service typology we have been using throughout the book and which makes a distinction between maintenance, task and personal interactive services. Would you expect differences between these types of services in terms of the strategic challenges outlined in this chapter (e.g. the issue of resource mobilization, or managing for continuity across time and space)? Which ones? And why? What strategies can firms follow to handle these issues? How would you see the – differentiated – importance of the human factor in this respect? And what about the way in which a firm interacts with its customers and how it designs its service delivery system (processes, facilities, operations management)?

Notes and references

[1] *Source*: Heene, A. (1997) 'The nature of strategic planning', *Long Range Planning*, Vol 30, No 6, p. 934.

[2] *See* www.ikea.com.

[3] For a systematic framework for analysing environments in relation to defining strategy, *see* Porter, M. E. (1980) *Competitive Strategy: Techniques for analysing industries and competitors*. New York: Free Press.

[4] For a more comprehensive discussion on strategic change, we recommend Pettigrew, A. and Whipp, R. (1992) *Managing Change for Competitive Success*. Oxford: Blackwell Business.

[5] Porter, M. E. (1980), op. cit.

[6] If value is defined as the ratio between (perceived) quality and price, it could be said that both of the above strategies result in 'similar' value propositions, but cost leaders and differentiators work for different segments (D'Aveni, R. (1994) *Hyper-Competition: Managing the dynamics of strategic manoeuvring*. New York: Free Press). The trouble starts when a company deviates from the 'value line' and becomes 'stuck in the middle'. Being stuck in

the middle means that for the same price someone else offers more quality or that the same quality can be found elsewhere at lower prices, which is not a very stable starting point for sustainable competitive advantage. Of course, a company can deviate from the value line in an opposite direction as well; this involves 'changing the rules of the game'. By introducing new ways of working – often involving new technologies – a company starts to offer the same or higher quality at lower prices than previously available. Ikea is a good example: the firm's operations managed to completely change the market of furniture distribution and sales. By combining production processes that allow for flexibility with, among other things, well thought out distribution practices and a specific surface layout, Ikea is able to offer what in the past seemed an impossible marriage between opposites: a broader range of furniture characterized by an appealing design at reasonable prices. In this way, Ikea started to break the industry rules, offering more value in comparison with other low-price producers. The price comparison with producers of more exclusive designed furniture is favourable, and so Ikea even attracts customers from this segment.

[7] *See* T. Hill's work on manufacturing strategy.

[8] Rotem, Z. and Amit, R. (1997) 'Strategic defence and competence-based competition', in Heene, A. and Sanchez, R. (eds) *Competence-Based Strategic Management*. New York: Wiley, pp. 169–91.

[9] *See*, for example, Hamel, G. and Prahalad, C. K. (1995) *Competing for the Future*. Boston: Harvard Business School Press.

[10] See as well the work of Barras in this respect as discussed in Chapter 19.

[11] Porter, M. E. (1980), op. cit.

[12] For a more detailed overview of possible relevant action strategies, *see* Porter, M. E. (1980), op. cit.

[13] For more details, *see* Technical Note 5.

[14] Senge, P. (1990) *The Fifth Discipline*. New York: Doubleday.

[15] Sanchez, R. and Heene, A. (1997) 'A competence perspective on strategic learning and knowledge management', in Sanchez, R. and Heene, A. (eds) *Strategic Learning and Knowledge Management*. New York: Wiley, p. 7.

[16] Sanchez, R. (1997) 'Managing articulated knowledge in competence-based competition', in Sanchez, R. and Heene, A. (eds) *Strategic Learning and Knowledge Management*. New York: Wiley, pp. 166–9.

[17] The chain of activities by which the firm builds value.

Suggested further reading

For readers interested in the recent insights related to resource- and competence-based models of the firm and their particular relevance to service firms, we recommend the following works:

Hamel, G. and Prahalad, C. K. (1995) *Competing for the Future*. Boston: Harvard Business School Press.

Heene, A. and Sanchez, R. (eds) (1997) *Competence-Based Strategic Management*. New York: Wiley.

Porter, M. (1980) *Competitive Strategy: Techniques for analysing industries and competitors*. New York: The Free Press. This book is very worthwhile reading, when discussing strategy in general.

Sanchez, R. and Heene, A. (eds) (1997) *Strategic Learning and Knowledge Management*. New York: Wiley.

TECHNICAL NOTES

The following notes contain supplementary material of a more technical nature which should be used in conjunction with the text.

1 How to collect customer satisfaction data

2 Analysing queuing systems in service environments

3 Simulation as a tool in designing services

4 Data envelopment analysis

5 Insights stemming from emerging resource and competence-based strategic management theories

How to collect customer satisfaction data

Gino Van Ossel

This technical note should be read in conjunction with Chapter 7

In Chapter 7, we have been discussing the measurement of customer satisfaction and how to set upon integrated customer satisfaction measurement system. Once we have decided what we want to measure, for which organizational unit and with which customers, the final step in conceiving the customer satisfaction performance measure is deciding how to collect the data. As measuring customer satisfaction is simply a particular type of market research, the data collection methods are in many ways very similar. In this section we shall describe the basic elements of a system of data collection and shall highlight those details that are particular to a system of satisfaction measurement. We shall discuss the following areas:

- the communication method by which the data can be collected;
- the format of the questions, including what scale to use;
- the frequency with which to survey;
- the make-or-buy decision.

(For a more in-depth discussion of data collection, you should consult the numerous excellent books on market research.) (*See* Suggested further reading at the end of Chapter 7.)

THE COMMUNICATION METHOD

Customers can be surveyed by telephone, by mail, in person or with a combination of the three. The main criteria for deciding on the communication method are:

- the nature and amount of information that has to be collected;
- control of the sample and supervision of the field work;
- response rates;
- time and cost considerations.

By telephone

The telephone is a very good means by which to collect a limited amount of relatively simple information quickly. This makes it a very good instrument for customer satisfaction performance measurement. However, it also has some disadvantages:

- Open-ended questions, inviting the customer to comment on how the organization might improve its service offering, usually result in short and rather superficial answers. We shall discuss later in this section how these questions are an important complement to the actual performance measure.
- The survey is never really anonymous. Even if the interviewer guarantees the respondent that the company will not know his or her personal opinions, the respondent knows that the interviewer by definition knows his or her identity. Obviously this is only a problem if anonymity is required.

Controlling the sample and field is also relatively easy by using Computer Assisted Telephone Interviewing (CATI). The telephone numbers are selected automatically by the computer and in case of non-response, the computer redials the number several times. Furthermore, if the call is answered, but the respondent is not present or does not have time at the moment, the interviewer can also instruct the computer to redial at another time. The questions and the possible answers are being displayed on a computer screen. The interviewer simply has to read them off and enter the respondent's answers into the computer. The computer automatically keeps track of the time a call takes and of the hit rate of each interviewer.

Problems related specifically to telephone interviews include:

1. Most people are not at home during office hours, which makes the method more expensive.
2. People do not like to be disturbed during their free time and may perceive it as an invasion of their privacy. This may not only result in a refusal to co-operate and consequently in a lower response rate, but it may even damage the customers' satisfaction.
3. Not all individuals have a telephone. In particular, elderly people, people with a low educational level and low-income families will be under-represented in the sample.
4. Different problems arise when surveying companies. It may take several calls before targeted respondents are present, assuming they are willing to answer the questions.

On the other hand, response rates are fairly high since only customers are being interviewed. Their interest in your product or service is usually relatively high. In our overall experience, the telephone is best used in a business-to-business context and is far less useful in assessing the customer satisfaction of individuals.

By mail

The major advantage of mail surveys is that it is possible to question all types of people at a relatively low cost. Compared to telephone surveys, it is not only possible to ask a larger number of questions but also more complex ones.

Promising anonymity and asking open-ended questions is perfectly feasible. Another advantage is that controlling the field is relatively easy. As field workers do not really intervene, except for entering the answers into the computer, the company has good control over the sample. Furthermore, standardized surveys being used over a long period of time can be processed automatically. Scanning becomes economically feasible if the number of questionnaires is high enough.

The major challenge is the response rate. Even when surveying one's own customers, response rates can be extremely low, particularly when surveying companies. The response rate is typically related to the effort that is required of the respondent and his or her involvement with the service and/or company. This effort largely depends on the length and complexity of the questionnaire. In our consideration of what information to collect, we discussed the disadvantages of over-lengthy questionnaires. Enclosing a return envelope also lowers the effort required of the respondent. Affixing a stamp, or printing on the envelope that no stamp is needed, has a positive impact on the response rate, particularly when surveying individuals. An alternative to including a return envelope is to design the survey as a fax. Although the advantage of anonymity is removed, companies are tending to return their questionnaires to a growing degree by fax.

The involvement level with the service and/or company is always relatively high as the questionnaire is being sent only to customers; but not always high enough to trigger good response rates. One Belgian fast-food chain has received response rates of about 5 per cent. Car distributors mailing their customers achieve response rates ranging from 25 to 50 per cent. There are two main reasons for this variation:

1. It seems that more expensive makes achieve lower response rates than other makes. Possible explanations are that expensive cars are often company cars (resulting in a lower involvement) and that they are driven by business people who are busier and generally confronted with more surveys.
2. Response rates differ depending on the timing of the survey. Car distributors typically question their customers shortly after they have bought a car about the buying process and the delivery of the car. A couple of years later, they send out a second survey about the after-sales service.

A very important factor in increasing the involvement and consequently the response rate is the letter accompanying the questionnaire. The letter should state the objective of the survey, as well as identify the company undertaking it, and explain why and how the respondent will benefit from the survey and how much (or hopefully how little) time it will take.

If the company can manage to achieve an acceptable response rate by taking the above considerations into account, then sending out a survey by mail is the best option. Experience has shown that this is more often the case with individuals than with companies. Short questionnaires taking the form of a fax can yield high response rates with companies.

Finally, the nature of the service and the relationship with the service provider will also affect the response rate. Increasing the response rate is possible but very expensive. Announcing the survey in advance by mail or telephone and sending out reminders when people do not respond have proven their effectiveness. However, as customer satisfaction measurement is by nature ongoing, this option may prove to be too expensive.

In person

The most powerful data collection method is the personal interview. Lengthy surveys with complex questions, including open-ended questions, will trigger high response rates and elaborated answers. However, as customer satisfaction performance measurement typically uses relatively simple and concise questionnaires, this is largely a theoretical advantage. Given the disadvantage of their relatively high cost, true personal interviews are rarely used.

Personal interviews fall into four categories of location: interviews inside a service location, street interviews, interviews at a third party's location, and interviews at the respondent's home or office. Interviewing customers inside the service location is the only commonly used technique, as the high concentration of customers helps to keep costs under control. If the surveyor simply hands over the questionnaires and collects the answers afterwards, the cost is relatively low. If, on the other hand, the interviewer actually has to go through the questions with the customer, costs will increase, depending on the length of the interview and the response rate. In certain service industries this is a very common approach, particularly for individuals with low involvement. Its feasibility depends on the nature of the service. In a fast-food restaurant, for instance, this is often not a good option, as these customers by definition usually have little time to spare. Those who do have time to spare are not necessarily representative of the customer population. Surveying customers in this situation is only justified when the questionnaire is very short. An alternative in this situation is to hand out the questionnaire together with a return envelope reading 'postage paid'.

Certain service locations, such as trains or aeroplanes, are perfectly suited to questioning customers in person. Another example is a hotel chain which asks its guests in the evening if they would care to answer a limited number of questions while having breakfast the following morning. By announcing the interview in advance, very high response rates are achieved. This is the most common way to measure participants' customer satisfaction in management training programmes.

It should be clear that in all the above examples the interviewer's role is mostly to distribute a written survey in order to increase the response rate. The opportunity to ask a greater number of, or more complex questions, is rarely used.

An important disadvantage of this technique is that it is difficult to control the sample and the field. In aeroplanes, the cabin crew has to distribute and collect the surveys. If their evaluation hinges on the results of the survey, they may be tempted to manipulate the results. They can fill out some forms themselves, throw away forms with unfavourable answers, give the forms to different passengers, or simply look over the passengers shoulders in order to influence them. In shops or restaurants, the sample is unlikely to be random, unless the interviewers ask screening questions. Interviewers will always be inclined to select respondents who appeal to them – for example, people of the same age group.

Techniques other than interviewing inside the service location are rarely used for customer satisfaction performance measurement. Street interviews are a very inefficient sampling technique, as the percentage of targeted customers walking the street tends to be limited. Interviews at a third party's location (often the offices of a market research agency) or at the customer's location are extremely expensive. The customer has to be convinced to go to the third party's location, which typically results in high recruitment costs and low response rates. Interviewing at the respondent's home or office involves transportation costs for the interviewer.

These methods do offer important opportunities for more qualitative and unstructured or semi-structured surveys (*see* later). However, for quantitative customer satisfaction performance measurement, which does not go beyond simple and concise questionnaires, these techniques are far too expensive.

Combining different media

While discussing the personal interview techniques, we indicated that the interviewer's role can be limited to distributing and/or collecting written questionnaires. This could be considered as combining different data collection methods. Other more advanced combinations are also possible. For instance, companies have experimented with calling respondents to notify them in advance that a written survey was going to be sent to them. The response rates can increase significantly, but unfortunately this is an expensive solution.

Rank Xerox is using the reverse combination. They mail a questionnaire to the respondents, explaining that they will be calling them to assist them in answering the questions. The actual data collection is done by telephone, but the respondent can see and read the questions and alternative answers. Rank Xerox has chosen this method because it allows them to combine the length of a written survey with the higher response rate of telephone interviews in a business-to-business context.

Response rates

When discussing the issue of response rates, managers always express their concern about whether the participants in the survey are representative of the whole population. In other words, they wonder if the outcome would have been different if the people who did not respond had done so. Their concern is only partly justified. In fact, it is necessary to distinguish between the *representativeness* and the *stability* of the measurement.

Customer satisfaction measurement is rarely representative if the response rate is not close to 100 per cent. As we explained earlier, the more involved people are, the more they tend to participate in a survey. By definition, the dissatisfied and the delighted are more involved than the somewhat satisfied, who we have described as being 'indifferent' vis-à-vis the service and its provider. Consequently, it is safe to assume that the dissatisfied and the delighted are over-represented among those who respond. Therefore the answer to the managers' concern has to be: yes, the people who do not respond will probably give a different opinion from those who do. This means that it is dangerous to treat the results of such a measurement as absolute fact. Stating that the customer satisfaction score of a company is 8.2 on a scale of 10 denies the simple fact that the score would almost certainly have been different had the response rate been different. Similarly, comparing scores across companies should be carried out with the utmost care. Even if the wording and the scale of the questions are identical, differences in response rates can account for differences in calculated scores.

Of course, measuring customer satisfaction by telephone may yield high response rates, so that representativeness can be obtained, but without these high response rates there can be no true representativeness.

In their concern for representativeness, managers often overlook the true objective of performance measurement. As we explained at the beginning of this chapter, performance measures can only be interpreted if they are compared to a benchmark. Therefore the stability of the measurement is more important than its representativeness. Stability means that the same results would be obtained if the survey were duplicated. Sending out the same survey to a different sample should give the same result. The issue should not be whether or not there is a measurement error, but whether or not the measurement error is constant.

Decentralized service organizations therefore have to monitor whether the response rates are the same across all organizational units. A retail bank, for instance, does not simply report the results of its measurement for each branch, but also its response rates. Typically these will be about the same for all branches. Any exceptions to this rule are studied with the utmost care, because differing response rates are usually a symptom of some underlying phenomenon. Similarly, in comparing results over time or across competitors, stable response rates are an indication of a stable measurement error. Consequently, benchmarking the results is justified, which is ultimately the objective of the performance measurement.

In our experience the true challenge is not to obtain representative or stable results. Neither is it to convince the managers directly involved in the satisfaction measurement, or those responsible for organizational units performing well, that representativeness is less of an issue than obtaining stable results. Managers responsible for organizational units which do not perform well will always question the representativeness and validity of the measurement tool, and will remain blind to their own inability to meet their customers' expectations. This is particularly tragic as it is precisely these managers who would benefit most from the measurement, as their opportunities for improvement are the greatest. The challenge lies in making these managers see the opportunities for improvement in their unit. The greater the importance attached to the customer satisfaction performance measure when evaluating managers, the more the representativeness will be contested. By linking the appraisal to the performance measure, managers are offered only two alternatives: they can either leave the organization or give up their resistance and focus on improving their performance.

THE FORMAT OF THE QUESTIONS

The format of the questions has to reflect the communication method through which the data will be collected. The questions should be kept as simple as possible, particularly in telephone surveys. Two basic choices have to be made with regard to the format of the questions:

1. It is possible to list service aspects and ask the respondents to rate their satisfaction, or, alternatively, it is possible to describe service aspects and ask the respondent whether or not they feel the provider's service meets that description.
2. More importantly, the scale has to be selected. We recommend using a balanced seven-point scale, with verbal labels at the extremes only and with the numerical value '0' denoting the neutral point. If the organization wants to limit its analysis to calculating averages, an unbalanced five-point scale can be used.

We will now discuss the wording of the questions and the scaling of the answers in more detail.

The wording of the question itself

The most common way to measure customer satisfaction is to ask directly:

How do you feel about the quality of the meal?   satisfied/dissatisfied

Sometimes the question is made more precise by replacing the words 'satisfied' and 'dissatisfied' with other descriptive words:

How do you judge the quality of the meal?   good/bad

Finally, it is possible to turn the question into a descriptive statement and to ask the respondents whether they agree with the statement:

The quality of the meal is good.   agree/disagree

Some argue that asking for the satisfaction directly is the most neutral and consequently the best option. Others prefer the descriptive statements as they are more specific. They would claim that, in our example, describing the quality of the food as simply good or bad is inadequate, but words such as tasty or fresh are far more useful. By asking those more specific questions, the collected information becomes more relevant. It is, however, also possible to ask for the respondent's satisfaction with the freshness or the tastiness of the food. Consequently, the real point is not so much which format gets chosen, but rather the degree of detail needed (what to ask rather than how to ask it). It should be clear that the questions have to be worded very carefully to obtain the desired results. As long as that is the case, the only concern should be that the exact wording is standardized across several surveys, so that benchmarking will be possible. Finally, we must stress that testing a questionnaire before actually using it on a large scale is absolutely essential.

The scaling of the answers

The scaling of the answers is as important as the wording of the questions. In fact, the chosen scale largely affects what analysis will be possible afterwards. In deciding on the scale, one has to take into account the fact that the average customer is satisfied. The percentage of dissatisfied customers will always be limited because in the long run dissatisfied customers defect, becoming former customers, and are no longer part of the surveyed population. Obviously this is not the case in monopoly situations, where no alternatives are open to the customer. In the light of this, decisions regarding the following features have to be made:

- a numerical, verbal or graphical scale
- many or few points on the scale
- an odd or even number of points
- balanced or unbalanced scales.

A numerical, verbal or graphical scale

A *numerical scale* means that the answer categories carry a number, so that the respondent has to give a quantitative rating. The advantage is that applying statistics becomes possible. In particular, using so-called interval scales, where the distance between each point is equal, allows for calculating averages or performing a correlation or regression analysis, in order to indirectly assess the importance of service aspects. The disadvantage is that the same score may have a different meaning for different respondents.

How would you rate the quality of the food?

| 1 | 2 | 3 | 4 | 5 |

A *verbal scale*, on the other hand, describes the answer categories without assigning a number to them, which offers the advantage of clarity to the respondents. However, statistics can only be applied if the distance between each point is the same (interval scale). In the example below, it is hard to tell whether the distance between 'very bad' and 'bad' is exactly the same as the distance between 'bad' and 'neutral'.

How would you rate the quality of the food?

| very bad | bad | neutral | good | very good |

The third option is a *graphical scale*. These scales are appealing to the respondents, which may yield higher response rates. For certain groups of respondents, such as children or foreigners, they may be the only feasible scales. For instance, Air France uses graphical scales, since their surveys are not available in all their passengers' native languages. The disadvantage is that it is difficult to make scales containing very many points.

How would you rate the quality of the food?

Obviously it is possible to combine these scales, that is, to add numbers to the labels or graphs and vice versa. Although this may seem an easy way to turn a verbal scale into an interval scale, strictly speaking the distance between each of the verbal labels has to be identical, as if no numerical labels were being used:

How would you rate the quality of the food?

very bad	bad	neutral	good	very good
1	2	3	4	5

This problem can be solved by only adding verbal labels to the extreme categories. Sometimes, a verbal label is also attached to the centre category:

How would you rate the quality of the food?

very bad		neutral		very good
1	2	3	4	5

Many or few points on the scale

Using a limited number of points on a scale – for instance, two or three – requires less effort from the respondent. This can affect the response rate positively. The major disadvantage, however, is that such scales offer limited possibilities when analysing the results. Not only should they not be treated as interval scales, since respondents do not see the distance between points one and two as equal to the distance between points two and three, but also the spread of the answers will be limited.

How would you rate the quality of the food?

bad	neutral	good
1	2	3

How would you rate the quality of the food?

bad	good
1	2

As we have explained, the average customer is satisfied, so that the '3' or 'good' category will probably attract the most answers on a three-point scale, and '1' or 'bad' will trigger only a limited number of answers. These scales thus only allow the percentage of dissatisfied customers to be monitored, and are not, or are at best poor, indicators of the percentage of delighted customers. As a result, three-point scales are rather uncommon in customer satisfaction measurement.

Two-point scales are being used more frequently, but usually only as part of more detailed and temporary questions. They also help to break the monotony of the questionnaire by reinforcing the respondent's concentration and discouraging their automatic piloting. These scales are rarely used for important questions.

Using too many points is not a valid alternative. Customers using, for instance, an 11-point scale may use an '8' in the beginning of the questionnaire and a '7' later on to express exactly the same feeling. Obviously these scales cannot be considered interval scales.

In the light of these considerations, most scales in customer satisfaction measurement contain at least four and at most ten points. Such scales can be used as interval scales and will generate a sufficient spread of answers.

An odd or even number of points

When faced with a scale with an even number of points, respondents cannot give a neutral answer as they are forced to mark either the satisfied or dissatisfied category. The justification for using an even-numbered point scale is that it discourages respondents from marking the neutral answer out of laziness, which can happen with an odd-numbered scale. This can also be a disadvantage. Some respondents do have a neutral opinion and by making them take sides, you do not get a correct reflection of their opinion.

Unlike other types of market research, this tendency to mark the neutral answer out of laziness is far less common in customer satisfaction measurement. As explained earlier, the average customer is at least satisfied, so he or she will tend to give a higher than neutral score. This phenomenon is exacerbated by the so-called *leniency effect*. Some respondents who know a product or service and make use of it do not want to say anything negative about it. In a satisfaction survey, the neutral answer can be interpreted as being slightly negative.

For these reasons, odd-numbered scales are more commonly used. If an odd-numbered scale is chosen, it is common to assign a numerical value of zero to the neutral position. Dissatisfaction is indicated by a negative number, which supports the 'image' of dissatisfaction. Furthermore, the interval stability is greater, as the scale contains fewer absolute values. Compare the following examples:

How would you rate the quality of the food?

very bad				very good
1	2	3	4	5

How would you rate the quality of the food?

very bad				very good
−2	−1	0	+1	+2

Balanced or unbalanced scales

As we know, customers are on the average satisfied, and, as we have just explained, most of them are somewhat reluctant to mark the 'neutral' answer. Consequently, on a balanced five-point scale most answers will fall into the categories '+1' or '+2':

How do you feel about the quality of the food?

very dissatisfied				very satisfied
−2	−1	0	+1	+2

If most answers fall into only two categories, the spread is rather limited. This can be exacerbated by the so-called *central tendency effect*, which refers to respondents' reluctance to take extreme positions. They want to see themselves as 'normal' and therefore may not readily mark '+2'. In that case the average score will probably be around '+1' with a relatively small standard deviation.

This is why it is more common to use unbalanced scales in customer satisfaction measurement – that is, with the middle of the scale not being the neutral point:

How do you feel about the quality of the food?

dissatisfied	neither satisfied nor dissatisfied	somewhat satisfied	satisfied	very satisfied
1	2	3	4	5

The problem is, of course, that all the above considerations in constructing the best possible interval scale have been ignored. The neutral point is not indicated by zero, with positive and negative values representing the satisfied and dissatisfied categories and also, verbal labels, formerly only at the extremes and on the neutral position, are now at every position.

If the analysis is limited to calculating averages, this will probably not result in making the wrong management decisions. If, however, the organization wants to perform correlation and regression analyses to assess the relative importance of the various service aspects indirectly, we recommend using a seven-point scale. This combines the best of both worlds – that is, a sufficient spread of the answers and an interval scale:

How do you feel about the quality of the food?

very dissatisfied			neither satisfied nor dissatisfied			very satisfied
−3	−2	−1	0	+1	+2	+3

Open-ended questions

In research which is carried out on an *ad hoc* basis and relates to a specific management problem, the 'other' category is often added to a list of suggested answers in closed-ended questions in order to allow the respondent to give a non-standard answer. If the questionnaire is well designed and reflects the insights of the qualitative research, very few respondents will choose the 'other' category since (almost) all relevant answers will already be listed.

However, ongoing research which is carried out more regularly cannot achieve the same degree of detail as *ad hoc* research, and therefore questions may be asked at a rather general level. The solution to this problem is to include several open-ended questions throughout the questionnaire. For instance, if a respondent indicates in a closed-ended question that he or she is dissatisfied with his airplane meal, a clarifying open-ended question (such as 'What did you or did you not like about the food?') may reveal more details. Another typical open-ended question is 'What can we do to serve you better in the future?'

THE FREQUENCY OF SURVEYS

Once the questionnaire has been designed, the respondents can be surveyed. How often this should be done is another important decision that has to be made. This decision should be based on the following considerations:

- *The size of the population.* The growing number of surveys being taken may result in customer saturation. They may end up being surveyed very frequently, particularly if their numbers are limited. Eventually, they may not only refuse to co-operate, but their customer satisfaction may be negatively affected. For instance, if a company has 500 customers and it wants to survey 200 customers on a yearly basis, each customer will be surveyed on average every 2.5 years. If the number of customers is smaller or if the frequency is higher, the survey may make excessive demands of the customers.

  This phenomenon is exacerbated when the customer base is being segmented. If 100 of those 500 customers are considered to be key accounts, they may end up being surveyed at a much higher frequency. The choice of organizational unit for which the satisfaction is measured may have a similar effect. At first glance, an organization servicing 2000 customers should have no problem surveying different customers with a relatively high frequency. If these customers are being serviced through four different service centres, however, obtaining statistically significant results for each service centre will necessitate increasing the total sample, since the population of each service centre will have been reduced to 500 customers.

Similarly, researching internal customer satisfaction may not be easy. In a retail bank with 500 branches, a department at headquarters should be able to send out a customer satisfaction survey to customers of a few branches on a yearly basis. However, often all departments at headquarters take the same initiative, which damages the overall effort as the branch offices receive an internal customer satisfaction survey.

Obviously, the opposite can also be the case. Branches of a retail bank serving several thousands of customers can easily send out their own surveys in the context of improvement projects at the same time as standardized surveys are being sent out by the head office.

- *The frequency with which the service is being used.* The more a customer makes use of a service, the more likely his or her satisfaction can or will change. As the survey frequency should follow the volatility of the customer satisfaction itself, the intensity with which the service is being used will affect the frequency.

- *The reliability and/or the rate of improvement of the service quality.* Similarly, customer satisfaction is more likely to change when improvement projects are taking place or, in the worst case, when the quality of the service is unstable. In those circumstances the frequency of the measurement should be high. However, if the service quality is highly reliable and no improvement projects are in the works, it is very unlikely that customer satisfaction will change overnight, even if the customer uses the service with a high frequency.

- *The customer's involvement with the service and its provider.* The more a customer is involved, the more he or she is willing to participate in a customer satisfaction survey. Unfortunately, key accounts are not always involved with their suppliers. This is because often the concept of the key account paradoxically takes the supplier's point of view. It is not just that a key account is an important customer for the supplier, the reverse is true as well – that is, that the supplier is an important one for that customer.

  If the key account considers you to be a key supplier, he or she will not only be interested in a highly frequent customer satisfaction survey, but will feel neglected if you do not show enough concern for his or her interest.

  It is not the relationship with the service provider alone which determines whether a high frequency is possible and/or desirable. The type of service in itself will play a role. Customers will be more inclined to fill out a customer satisfaction survey for their doctor than for their plumber.

- *The cost.* Obviously sending out surveys costs money. The higher the frequency, the more up-to-date, but unfortunately the more expensive the customer satisfaction information will be.

As a general rule, companies try to survey their key accounts in a business-to-business context exhaustively on a yearly basis. Of course, that is only possible if they themselves are considered to be key suppliers. For all other customers, an annual or biannual survey is very common. An interesting alternative is to make the measurement ongoing, but to split the yearly sample into smaller groups. Every month one-twelfth, or every three months one-quarter, of the customers can be surveyed. By calculating moving averages, the information is always up to date, without raising the budget.

THE MAKE-OR-BUY DECISION

In conceiving and executing customer satisfaction surveys, a company has to decide whether to make use of a market research agency or not. Unless the company has its own market research specialists, using outside help is desirable. Even if those in-house specialists are available, however, the peculiarities of satisfaction may justify hiring outside consultants. However, selecting an outside consultant is not easy. Even excellent market research agencies do not necessarily have the required skills to construct customer satisfaction surveys.

Not all market research agencies are experts in ongoing research in general, and in satisfaction measurement in particular. For ongoing research, the distinction between conceiving and executing the survey is extremely important.

Conceiving *versus* executing the survey

Conceiving an ongoing survey requires brainpower, while executing an ongoing survey (including analysis) is largely operational. Therefore, any request for a quote from a market research agency should stress the distinction between these two elements.

The company must also demand copyright over the survey and the questionnaire. This will give it the flexibility to hire another agency to execute the survey if this is necessary, or even to execute it itself.

In the conception stage, in-depth knowledge of the ongoing research in general and of customer satisfaction measurement in particular, is essential. If in-house research specialists are available, the hired outsiders should be able to demonstrate great expertise in customer satisfaction measurement.

In the executional stage, however, efficiency is important. We have come across companies who were paying an agency a fortune to simply repeat the same research over and over again. The agency could virtually process the survey automatically, but was still charging for its brainpower. Moreover, the contract stated very clearly that the agency was the intellectual owner of the survey, so that the company was bound to that agency.

It should be clear that conceiving the survey with the help of outside experts will not automatically result in excellent surveys. On the other hand, executing the survey can be handled by any good field agency, since mail, telephone or written customer surveys require limited field control and are relatively easy to sample. Cost considerations are important here.

Ad hoc versus ongoing research and customer satisfaction measurement

In *ad hoc research*, a specific management problem is translated into a series of research questions. For the in-depth study of that management problem, a custom-made research design is developed. That particular design is usually executed only once. Both the field and the analysis are unique and will probably not be duplicated again. As a result, the cost implications of each question are more or less limited. Furthermore, it is almost impossible to detach the conception from the execution (particularly the analysis) of the research.

In its most typical form, the *ad hoc* research consists of two stages. The first or qualitative stage aims at inventorying all possible views and aspects of the research questions. The second or quantitative stage sums up all those views and aspects and comes up with a representative answer.

Ongoing research, however, is different in many respects. The survey has to be executed several times and often over a very long period of time. This has many consequences:

- From a budgetary point of view, the execution and analysis stage is much more important in ongoing research than it is in *ad hoc* research. Since the same research will be executed several times, the total field work is much greater. Consequently, with ongoing research, the cost of the field work is more carefully planned during the conception stage. This usually results in relatively short surveys which can be processed as automatically as possible. Sometimes the survey is designed for CATI (computer-assisted telephone interviewing) and sometimes the written surveys can be scanned into a computer.

- The analysis itself is also standardized. The same calculations are performed so that the bare facts and figures are also generated automatically. Interpreting the facts and figures is also much easier as a learning effect occurs.

- Finally, the questionnaire itself should be generic enough to be useful over a relatively long period of time.

Furthermore, customer satisfaction measurement is ongoing research of a very specific nature. It is important to reiterate the need for unbalanced scales, the issue of which organizational unit to measure, and the importance of the percentage of dissatisfied and delighted customers rather than the average satisfaction score.

Analysing queuing systems in service environments

Paul Gemmel

This technical note should be read in conjunction with Chapter 15

QUEUING SYSTEMS AND THEIR CHARACTERISTICS

At many moments in our daily lives we wait for some type of service. At the supermarket, the post office, the bank, we join queues, waiting to be served. In services, queues are a mechanism to match supply with demand. Like inventories, queues are a kind of buffer, but instead of keeping products in stock, customers are kept waiting. Queues must be avoided; they benefit neither the customer nor the organization providing the service. 'Time spent queuing is time wasted forever.'[1] Let us examine the behaviour of queues more closely.

In the example of the supermarket, queues are formed when the time taken to serve a shopper at the check-out exceeds the time between two subsequent arrivals. In the same way, at a telephone call centre, queues are formed when the calls come in more quickly than they are handled. This is equally true of traffic jams and of doctors' surgeries. In other words, we can distinguish some common elements in the different queuing situations. There is a *server*, providing the service at a certain pace, on the one hand, and *customers*, arriving at a certain pace, on the other. In the case of the server, we speak of *the service delivery process* and in the case of the customer, of *the arrival process*. Queues are formed at the intersection of the arrival and the service delivery processes. The customer and his or her arrival process, the server and its service delivery process, and the resulting queues are the basic but common elements of every queuing situation. Recognizing these basic components means that queuing situations can be considered as a system and that analytical models can be developed to describe such a system. We term this '*queuing*' (or 'waiting-line') *theory*.

Arrival characteristics

Let us consider the example of the supermarket. After selecting their goods, clients arrive with their shopping trolleys at the check-outs. The time between two subsequent arrivals is the *interarrival time*. This interarrival time can be measured and an average can be calculated. Table TN2.1 shows the registration of arrival times and interarrival times for 12 shoppers. The first shopper arrives four minutes after the opening of the supermarket. The second shopper arrives ten minutes after the opening. There is a six-minute time-lag between the first and second customer. This time-lag is the interarrival time. The average interarrival time for the 11 customers is equal to five minutes; this also means that one shopper arrives every

Table TN2.1 Arrival time, interarrival time and service time of 12 shoppers

Arrival	Time of arrival in minutes from time 0	Interarrival time	Service time
1	4	6	3
2	10	3	5
3	13	6	6
4	19	1	4
5	20	9	7
6	29	2	3
7	31	3	6
8	34	9	7
9	43	4	2
10	47	4	3
11	51	8	3
12	59	–	8
Total		55	58
Average		5	4.8

five minutes, or twelve shoppers per hour. The indication of x number of customers per time period is called arrival rate λ and is used to indicate the average arrival rate. It must be taken into account that the arrival process and thus the average interarrival time can be influenced by daily, weekly or even seasonal patterns. In a supermarket, Saturday is traditionally the busiest day of the week and Friday evening busier than the rest of the day.

The arrival of the shoppers in the supermarket cannot be scheduled and thus cannot be controlled. Scheduling patients in a hospital is one example of controlling the arrival pattern. Although most shoppers arrive alone, they may arrive in a group (e.g. a family). *Batching behaviour* can have an important impact on the performance of the queuing system. For instance, in many university restaurants, students arrive in large batches depending on what time courses finish.

Finally, the population from which arrivals are drawn can be infinite or finite. The calling population of a supermarket is *infinite* (or very large). A population is infinite when the probability of the arrival of the next customer is independent of the number of shoppers already present in the supermarket. If a small shop has only ten regular customers, the chance that a customer will arrive is highly dependent on how many customers are already present in the shop (*finite*).

Server characteristics

Table TN2.1 also shows the time it takes to serve customers. In the example of the supermarket, serving encompasses the whole process of scanning goods, computing the bill, and placing the items in bags. The average service time in the example is 4.8 minutes. This means that on average one shopper is served every 4.8 minutes – 12.5 shoppers per hour. An M notation is used to indicate the average service rate of one shopper each 4.8 minutes or 12.5 shoppers per hour. The service rate can vary among customers. For instance, Figure TN2.1 shows the relationship between method of payment and billing time. Certainly when a combination of vouchers and electronic funds transfer (EFT) is used, the billing time is significantly higher. Another characteristic of the service process is the number of servers available and

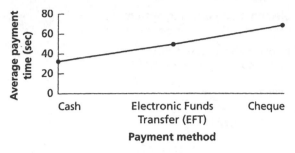

Figure TN2.1 The relationship between method of payment and payment time in a supermarket

whether servers are in a parallel or serial position. In a supermarket, servers are considered to be serial when the acts of scanning and registration are separated into two subsequent workstations.

Queue characteristics

In supermarkets, several check-outs are available for the shoppers. This also means that several queues are formed. In some other service organizations such as banks, there is only one queue for multiple servers. These are different examples of the organization of servers. In banks there is an ongoing discussion about how to organize queues. The multiple-server/one-queue situation seems to work faster than the same number of servers each with its own queue. The former is also perceived as the most fair by customers and enhances the privacy of the service. On the other hand, with multiple-servers/multiple-queues, a company is able to differentiate services and assign more experienced servers to lines with more difficult transactions. Customers may be able to select their favourite server.

In any queuing situation, attention must be paid to the order in which customers are served (*queue discipline*). In the case of a single check-out, a *'first-in first-out'* (FIFO) system is used. When an additional counter is opened, this rule may be violated as shoppers who were last in the queue switch first to the newly opened counter. Impatient shoppers may switch queues (*jockeying*). If queues are exceedingly long, some customers may leave a queue before being served (*reneging*) or may decide not to join the queue (*balking*). The lower the value of the purchases in the shopper's trolley, the higher the chance that reneging or balking will take place. That is why express lanes are created for customers with only a limited number of items. When an express lane is used, different customers receive different priorities.

In summary, all queuing problems can be broken down, as shown in Table TN2.2.[2]

Linking arrival pattern, service pattern and queuing

The proportion of the arrival rate λ to the service rate M is the *average utilization* or occupancy of the server. We use the symbol σ. In our example of the supermarket, the average utilization of the check-out is 96 per cent.

$$\sigma = \frac{\text{Arrival rate}}{\text{Service rate}} = \frac{12 \text{ shoppers per hour}}{12.5 \text{ shoppers per hour}} = 96\% \qquad (1)$$

493

Table TN2.2 Different elements of a queuing system

1	***Arrival characteristics***
	1.1 Arrival rate or time between arrival statistics
	1.2 Controlled or uncontrolled
	1.3 Grouping (single or batch)
	1.4 Infinite or finite calling population
2	***Service characteristics***
	2.1 Service rate or service time/server
	2.2 Number of servers
	– one
	– multiple
	– serial
3	***Queue characteristics***
	3.1 Queue organization
	– one or more queues
	– queues with limited or unlimited capacity
	3.2 Queue discipline
	3.3 Queuing behaviour of customers
	– reneging
	– balking
	– no action

As we shall see next, the average utilization determines the length of the queues. In order to have a stable system, σ must be lower than 1.[3]

QUEUING THEORY

As previously mentioned, analytical models have been developed to analyse queuing systems. Analytical models are always subject to, sometimes stringent, assumptions. In queuing theory the basic assumptions are summarized in an *a/b/c/d* notation – that is, the so-called *Kendall notation* – where:

a = the distribution of the interarrival times

b = the distribution of the service times

c = the number of servers

d = the maximum number of customers in the queue

The M/M/1/∞ system

The M/M/1/∞ system is a queuing system where:

a = M = a negative exponential distribution of the interarrival times, indicated by M

b = M = a negative exponential distribution of the service time, indicated by M

c = 1 = one server

d = ∞ = an infinite queue capacity

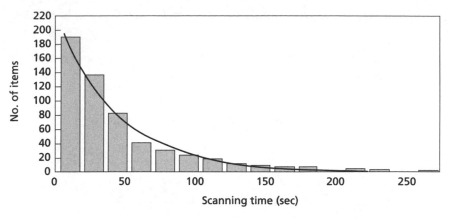

Figure TN2.2 An example of the negative exponential distribution

A frequently used distribution in queuing modelling is the *negative exponential 'M'* *distribution* (*see* Figure TN2.2). An important property of the exponential distribution is that it is memoryless. This means that the time until the next event (arrival) does not depend on how much time has already elapsed since the last event (arrival).[4] Interarrival times can be modelled as a negative exponential distribution when the arrivals of customers in a service organization are independent of each other. For instance, emergencies in a hospital arrive independently of one another and their interarrival time can be modelled through a negative exponential distribution. In contrast, scheduled patients do not arrive independently of one another and in this case the exponential distribution cannot be used. Nonetheless, many service situations are memoryless.

An interesting characteristic of the exponential distribution is that it is a one-parameter distribution: mean and standard deviation are equal. It is also important to indicate that an exponential distribution of interarrival times means that the distribution of the number of arrivals per time period is a *Poisson distribution*. A Poisson distribution arises from the *Poisson process*. A Poisson process can be viewed in terms of its calling population (i.e. the group of potential customers). If the calling population is large (infinite), the probability that customers arrive independently is larger than in the case of a finite calling population, and the probability that a particular customer arrives during any small time interval is small and constant.[5] In this case, a Poisson probability distribution can be used.

For an M/M/1/∞ queue system, it can be proved that the probability of having n customers in the system is equal to:[6]

$$P(n) = (1 - \sigma)\, \sigma^n$$

with $n = 0, 1, 2$ \hfill (2)

In our example the chance that there are three shoppers in the system is:

$$P(3) = (1 - 0.96) \times (0.96)^3$$

$$P(3) = 0.035 \text{ or } 3.5\%$$

The mean ('expected') number of customers in the system is equal to:

$$L_s = \frac{\sigma}{1 - \sigma}$$

$$L_s = \frac{0.96}{1 - 0.96} = 24 \qquad (3)$$

The mean number of customers in the queue is equal to:

$$L_q = \frac{\sigma^2}{1 - \sigma}$$

$$L_q = \frac{0.96^2}{1 - 0.96} = 23 \qquad (4)$$

It is quite clear that in our example the queue is large (on average 23 customers per hour), mainly due to the high occupancy rate (96 per cent). Assuming an occupancy rate of only 70 per cent, the mean number of customers in the queue will be equal to an average of 1.6 using formula (4).

The expected time in the queue and time in the system are not uniquely defined by σ; they also depend on the arrival rate. In fact, there is an important relationship between the mean number of customers in the system (L_s) and the mean time in the system (W_s), and between the mean number of customers in queue (L_q) and the mean time in queue (W_q):

$$W_s = \frac{L_s}{\lambda} \qquad (5)$$

$$W_q = \frac{L_q}{\lambda} \qquad (6)$$

In our basic example (occupancy rate of 96 per cent) this means that the mean time in the system is equal to two hours and that the mean time in the queue is equal to 1.9 hours:

$$W_s = \frac{24}{12} = 2 \text{ hours}$$

$$W_q = \frac{23}{12} = 1.91 \text{ hours}$$

This relationship between L_s (L_q) and respectively W_s (W_q) is the so-called *Little's Formula* and means that W_s and W_q are a direct function of the arrival rate $1/\lambda$ as the utilization σ is considered constant.

OTHER QUEUING SYSTEMS

What happens if the average time between arrivals and the average service time are not negatively exponentially distributed or if more than one server is available?

Queuing theory has developed some more advanced analytical solutions or approaches which take into account deviations from the M/M/1 queuing system. We refer readers who wish to use one of these models to the more specialized literature on queuing systems (*see* reference).

Notes and references

[1] Hall, R. W. (1991) *Queuing Methods for Services and Manufacturing*. Englewood Cliffs, New Jersey: Prentice-Hall, p. 3.

[2] Partially based on Chisman, J. A. (1993) *Introduction to Simulation Modelling Using GPPS/PC*. Englewood Cliffs, New Jersey: Prentice-Hall, p. 9.

[3] A system is not stable if a queue continuously grows over time.

[4] Hall, R. W. (1991), op. cit., p. 61.

[5] Ibid., p. 54.

[6] Readers who wish to know how P(n) is calculated are referred to Appendix 2.

Suggested further reading

Hall, R. W. (1991) *Queuing Methods for Services and Manufacturing*. Englewood Cliffs, New Jersey: Prentice-Hall. This is a reference book on queuing. The different queuing models and the application of queuing in manufacturing and services are extensively discussed. Several strategies to avoid queuing or to reduce waiting lines are suggested.

Simulation as a tool in designing services

Paul Gemmel

This technical note should be read in conjunction with Chapter 15

DISCRETE-EVENT SIMULATION

In the supermarket example several checkouts (servers) are available. When customers arrive at the counters, some will choose the express lane because they have fewer than ten items in their trolley. Other shoppers will be jockeying from one queue to another. The service time for each customer is a function of the number of items purchased and the payment method used. It is not possible to approach this (more complex) queuing system analytically and to determine, for instance, the average waiting time using the formulas of queuing theory. In fact, pure M/M/1, M/M/n and M/G/1 queuing systems are relatively rare in daily life. When an analytical solution is not available, computer simulation can be used to evaluate the queuing system numerically.

Computer simulation models dealing with queuing problems in service environments are stochastic, time dependent, and discrete-event.

- In a *stochastic* model, the exact value of some variables cannot be estimated, but the probability of the occurrence of each possible value can be determined. For instance, the service time at a checkout is not known with certainty. Service time is in this case a stochastic variable and can be described by a distribution.
- In a queuing example, the *passing of time* is crucial. There is a sequence of events in time such as the arrival of the shopper at the supermarket, the checkout and the departure.
- In a *discrete-event* time model, time jumps from one event to another. If the first shopper arrives at 9.00 a.m. and the second shopper arrives at 9.05 a.m. and no other relevant event occurs between these two events, a discrete-event simulation model jumps in time from the arrival of the first customer to the arrival of the second customer. In other words, the simulation is event-driven.

In service organizations, there are many examples of problems which can be studied using such models. Discrete-event simulation is a necessary tool to compare and evaluate the design alternatives for a service process.[1] The building blocks of service design are the 'product', the facilities, the process and the interaction between the server and the customer. An example of the simulation of alternative product designs is to analyse the impact on the delivery performance of bank tellers when ATMs take over several kinds of banking transactions. Problems of service facility design which can be solved by simulation include, for instance, the question of how many checkouts the supermarket manager needs in order to keep checkout queues below five people each. A similar problem can be found in the banking sector. Service process design questions, for example, deal with the lift operations policy in a large building. An example of a design study which has an important impact on the interaction between the customer and the server is the study of the layout of a university student restaurant. Does the restaurant choose a continuous line layout or a free-flow layout? In each of the examples, waiting time is (partially) determined by how the service delivery is designed.

Components of discrete-event simulation models

In the example of the supermarket, the number of people in the queue (before each checkout) and the number of servers available are variables which tell something about the system state. Anything that occurs and that changes the state of the system is an event. The arrival of a shopper at the checkout or the departure of a client from the checkout are events because they change the state of the checkout from idle to busy and *vice versa*.

Each simulation model contains a timing routine and a time clock which allows jumps from one event to another. Note that the time increments between consecutive events are variable.[2] The scheduling of events at certain points in time drives the system. At the moment a shopper arrives at a checkout, a simulation programme immediately schedules the next event for this shopper – his or her departure. If no subsequent event is scheduled in the simulation logic with variable time increments, the system will shut down. Without the arrival of new shoppers, the dynamics of the supermarket will stop.

To obtain output from the simulation model, statistical counters must be defined. Statistical counters operationalize the performance measures which must be defined in order to design services which exceed customer expectations. Two kinds of counters are possible: *observation-based* and *time-integrated*. Average waiting time is an observation-based counter. It is the average of the 'observed' waiting time of each shopper. Time-integrated counters take into account how long a certain state lasts. For instance, the length of the queue is a state variable that changes over time. In order to measure the average length of the queue, it is necessary to know the length of time when one or more shoppers are queuing. A queue of three shoppers lasting three minutes has a larger impact on the average length of queue than a queue of three shoppers lasting two minutes. Using a report generator, the final value of the statistical counters can be presented in a mathematical or a graphical way.

As in any programme, it is necessary to initialize the system. This means, for instance, that the number of checkouts which are open at the beginning of the day is fixed.

Finally, all stochastic simulation models require random numbers. They therefore use a random-number generator which produces a stream of figures by chance so that the stochastic variables are not influenced in any way by past values.[3] This is because all discrete simulation modelling languages use the Monte Carlo approach for generating arrivals, service times, and other input variables.[4]

In summary, the most important components of a discrete-event stochastic and dynamic simulation model are:

1. variables which track the state of the system;
2. a list of events;

3. a mechanism (timing routine) to schedule events;

4. a time clock;

5. statistical counters;

6. a report generator;

7. an initialization routine; and finally

8. a random-number generator.

In order to show the concept of a random-number generator and to illustrate how the Monte Carlo approach works, we shall manually work out the supermarket case. Let us assume that there is a supermarket with one checkout. The interarrival and service-time distributions are described respectively in Tables TN3.1 and TN3.2. Random numbers can now be assigned to each distribution directly proportional to the respective probabilities in each frequency class. For instance, we assign random number '00' to the first frequency class to represent the event that the time between arrivals is zero seconds. In other words, if we draw a number from a two-digit uniform random number table (numbers ranging from 0 to 99 (*see* Table TN3.3)), we have one chance out of 100 (or a probability of 1 per cent) of drawing one of these numbers. The numbers '01–40' represent a 40 per cent chance of a time between arrival being 20 seconds. The same reasoning has been used for the service time distribution.

To generate arrivals, we shall start (randomly) in column 2 of table TN3.3 and move down. The generation of service times will start in column 9. The first event is an arrival of a shopper. The random number of 92 (i.e. the first number in the second column of Table TN3.3) represents a time between arrivals of 80 seconds, since 92 lies between 91 and 99 (*see* Table TN3.1). Hence, the first shopper arrives at the counter 80 seconds after the opening of the doors. In order to determine the service time of this shopper, we pick the first number in column 9 of Table TN3.3. '41' lies between 05 and 59. This corresponds with a service time of 40 seconds.

Table TN3.1 Interarrival distribution

Time between arrivals	Probability	Cumulative probability	Random numbers
0 sec	0.01	0.01	00
20 sec	0.40	0.41	01–40
40 sec	0.30	0.71	41–70
60 sec	0.20	0.91	71–90
80 sec	0.09	1.00	91–99

Table TN3.2 Service-time distribution

Required service-time	Probability	Cumulative probability	Random numbers
20 sec	0.05	0.05	00–04
40 sec	0.55	0.60	05–59
60 sec	0.20	0.80	60–79
80 sec	0.15	0.95	80–94
100 sec	0.05	1.00	95–99

Table TN3.3 A two-digit random number table

26	92	96	04	84	03	48	38	41	35
44	46	47	20	04	71	81	44	07	58
75	41	72	88	54	33	06	87	63	59
71	13	45	61	26	53	27	37	89	30
15	91	81	39	86	41	43	46	57	34
18	11	80	97	33	16	75	26	93	29
50	56	19	00	95	88	00	70	90	93
10	15	33	70	05	13	08	29	75	43
72	69	75	95	56	15	73	27	72	99
10	02	26	69	12	64	99	18	78	19

The second random number in column 2 of Table TN3.3 is 46. This means that the second shopper will arrive 40 seconds after the first one. The time on arrival is then 120 seconds (after opening the doors). Note that at this time the first shopper leaves the checkout, so there is no waiting time for the second shopper. Using the second random number '07' of column 9 in Table TN3.3, it can be deduced that the service time for this second shopper is 40 seconds. This procedure is repeated for a total of ten shoppers in Table TN3.4.

The random number table is an essential component of Monte Carlo simulation. Random numbers cannot be reproduced (by definition), and so some mathematical models have been defined to imitate random behaviour. This explains the term 'pseudo-random number', used in simulation. The validity of the simulation results depends greatly on the quality of the pseudo-random number generator.[5]

Tools for discrete-event simulation modelling

Generally, there are three categories of tools for discrete-event stochastic and dynamic simulation:[6] general programming languages, simulation languages and simulators.

Table TN3.4 Monte Carlo simulation of the bank-teller problem

No.	TBA[a]	TOA[b]	ST[c]	WT[d]	Idle[e]	Queue[f]
× 1	80	80	40	0	80	0
× 2	40	120	40	0	0	0
× 3	40	160	60	0	0	0
× 4	20	180	80	40	0	1
× 5	80	260	40	40	0	1
× 6	20	280	80	60	0	2
× 7	40	320	80	100	0	2
× 8	20	340	60	160	0	2
× 9	40	380	60	180	0	3
×10	20	400	60	220	0	4

[a] Time between arrivals
[b] Time on arrival
[c] Service time
[d] Waiting time
[e] Time during which server is idle
[f] The position in the queue that the arriving shopper takes

Compared with the general programming languages, simulation languages and simulators have some specific built-in functions:[7]

1. a mechanism for advancing simulated time;
2. methods of scheduling events;
3. statistical counters;
4. methods of representing constrained resources;
5. a report generator;
6. debugging and error detection facilities;
7. random-number generators and related sets of tools;
8. a general framework for model creation.

While a programming code is still necessary in the case of simulation languages, this is no longer necessary for simulators. Simulators offer the user a number of building blocks which represent, for example, the arrival or the service process.

To select a specific tool, two important criteria have to be taken into account: flexibility offered and modelling effort.[8] The programming languages require more modelling effort than simulation languages because, for example, the timing mechanism (which is a normal feature of a simulation language) has to be modelled. The basic characteristic of a simulator is that it decreases the modelling effort. By using predefined constructs, the user is guided throughout the development of a simulation model. This decreases the flexibility to build in some specific or uncommon features. Most simulation software packages link the flexibility of a simulation language with the modelling efforts of a simulator. They work with different levels. On the first level, very aggregate building blocks are defined. This is the simulator level. On a lower level, a simulation language can be used. The interesting point is that these levels can be combined.

In selecting a simulation tool, other parameters such as price and the quality of the random-number generator must be considered. It should also be noted that some simulators are designed for specific applications.

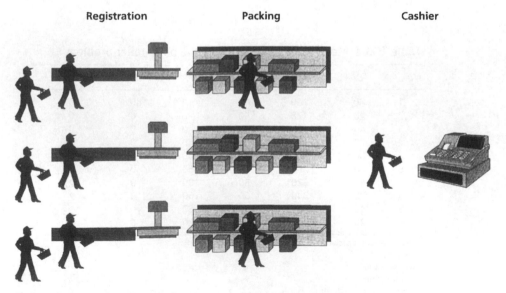

Figure TN3.1 Animation of the supermarket

There are more than 100 simulation languages and simulators on the market today. Examples of simulators are ARENA[9] and Entreprise Dynamics. We must stress that several of these simulators are typically made for a manufacturing situation. Our experience with ARENA in simulating service environments is positive. Moreover, ARENA combines a simulator and a simulation language (SIMAN).

Most simulators and simulation languages have a built-in module for animation of the computer model.[10] Animation is the use of a graphical interface on the computer to present entities and activities in a dynamic way. The advantage of animation is that it can be used to enhance the confidence in the model (*face validity*). At the same time, the danger of animation is that too much confidence is granted to the model without thorough statistical analysis. An example of animation of the supermarket example is shown in Figure TN3.1.

SIMULATING THE SERVICE ENCOUNTER IN A SUPERMARKET

As indicated before, simulation can be used to design service processes in order to improve the service encounter. In the supermarket example, the manager wondered whether the productivity of the clerks at the checkouts could be improved without decreasing the quality of the service encounter. Several productivity improvement strategies have been proposed, such as the use of a professional 'packer', the uncoupling of registering and billing where several scanning points are served by one cashier, the differentiation of a checkout, based on the payment method (for instance, only a few counters would accept EFT-payment). The supermarket manager wants to know whether the use of a professional packer will lead to a reduction of the throughput time at the checkout and consequently an increase in the potential throughput. The manager has observed that sometimes the process of scanning was blocked because the shopper could not bag the registered products fast enough.

In order to see whether a packer could make the difference, a simulation study is set up. The first step in the study is to define the system to be modelled. The components of the system, their interrelationship and the system's boundaries must be defined.

To reduce the complexity of the model, we limit the study to one standard checkout and one overflow counter which is opened and closed in a dynamic way in order to manage the queue at the standard checkout. Shoppers arrive at the checkout with their shopping trolley filled with food and/or non-food products. If the regular counter is busy, they will wait in the queue at the checkout. As soon as possible, a shopper places his or her products on the checkout. The scanning time is a function of the number of products. Then the shopper puts the products in the bag. The packing time is a function of the number of products, the kind of products and the experience of the shopper. After packing, the shopper pays and the payment time is related to the payment method used. It may happen that the customer continues packing after paying. The clerk delays scanning the products of the next customer until the current shopper has left the checkout.

When defining the system, it is also important to indicate the performance measures to be used. In this case, we are interested in the throughput time of shoppers or the average throughput within some predetermined time period (for instance, one hour). The performance of only the standard checkout is registered.

Table TN3.5 Summary statistics for different variables (in seconds) in the situation with and without packers

		Number of articles	Packing time	Payment time	Customer time*	Scanning time*	Purchasing time**
Without packers	Average	20	12	29	41	74	115
	Standard deviation	16	10	13	17	57	69
With packers	Average	21	5	29	34	65	99
	Standard deviation	18	6	17	20	51	65

* The average customer time is the sum of average packing time and the average payment time.
** The average purchasing time is the sum of the average customer time and the average scanning time.

To model the system, we also need some data on the arrival pattern of shoppers, the scanning time, the packing time, and the payment time. An experiment is set up. Over eight hours, data on the different time components are collected in a situation as described above and in a situation with a professional packer. In the latter experiment, a student starts packing as soon as products are scanned. Meanwhile, the shopper can get his or her money ready for payment. No data are collected on the arrival pattern. It is decided to use a 'theoretical' Poisson distribution with an average number of arrivals per time unit which allows a continuous flow of customers at the checkout. If the queue at the regular checkout is longer than ten persons, the eleventh person is sent to the overflow counter. Table TN3.5 shows the results of these experiments. Note that the packing time decreases by 50 per cent when a professional packer is used.

In the simulation study, we use the purchasing time, which is defined as the sum of scanning time, packing time and payment time. To be able to use the data in the simulation, we need to describe the distributions as in Table TN3.6. While it

Table TN3.6 Comparison of the frequency distribution of the variable purchasing time respectively in the situation with packer and without packer

Category (sec)	Frequency in the case without packer (%)	Frequency in the case with packer (%)
0–27	4	5
27–54	13	19
54–81	16	23
81–108	21	21
108–135	15	10
135–162	10	6
162–189	6	5
189–216	5	5
216–243	5	1
243–270	1	1
270–297	1	2
297–324	2	1
324–351	1	0
351–378	0	1
Total	100	100

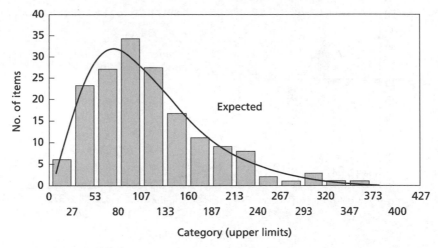

Figure TN3.2 The fitting of a gamma distribution to the variable purchasing time (without a packer)

is possible to use the empirical distribution (as described in Table TN3.6) in the simulation model, we prefer to 'fit' an existing theoretical distribution (such as the normal distribution or the exponential distribution) to the empirical data. The main reason is that an empirical distribution is 'limited' to the observations, in this case for eight hours in each experiment. It is highly probable that many different values are not caught by this empirical distribution. If we can prove that there is a high probability that the empirical distribution looks like a theoretical distribution, we have a greater certainty that all values are covered. Moreover, most of the theoretical distributions are pre-programmed in a simulation language or simulator so that it is sufficient to determine the relevant parameters of the distribution such as the mean and the standard deviation in the case of the normal distribution. Figure TN3.2 shows the fitting of the theoretical gamma distribution to the empirical distribution of purchasing time in the base case without professional packer. The Kolmogorov-Smirnov test as well as the chi-square test examine the goodness of fit of the gamma distribution to the empirical data. Most simulation languages or simulators have some input module which allows the user to fit theoretical distributions to the empirical data and to determine the parameters of the distributions. Figure TN3.3 shows the fitting of the log-normal distribution to the empirical distribution of purchasing time when a professional packer is used.[11]

Before going on, we must be sure that the previous data are adequate and precise and that the assumptions underlying the model are acceptable. Does the clerk wait until a shopper has left before continuing the scanning of the next customer's products? If this is not the case, what is the impact of this assumption on the results of the study? Is a gamma distribution a well-fitting distribution? If not, the results are not valid. This process is called *validation*. There are several ways to increase the validity of the model such as observing the real system or talking to experts.

Once the model has been defined and validated, it must be translated to a computer program using one of the simulation tools which have been presented above. It is important that this translation is carried out accurately. Therefore, we need to carefully document the program and use techniques of structured programming.

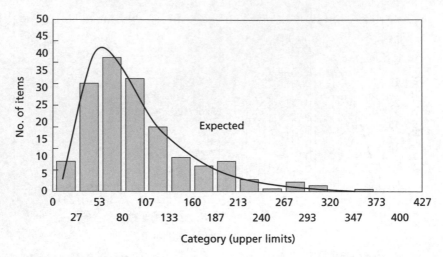

Figure TN3.3 The fitting of a log-normal distribution to the variable purchasing time (with a packer)

Once the program is finished, we must be able to check the path which is followed during the programming. Does the customer wait on a first-come-first-served basis? Does scanning precede packing? Animation can be helpful in studying this behaviour. In summary, we need to verify the program carefully.

In a next step, we make some pilot runs to further validate the model. At this point, we study the output of the pilot runs in the light of the goal of the simulation study and to verify whether the simulation output changes adequately if the input is changed. For instance, when the arrival pattern in the supermarket is such that the occupancy of the regular checkout is only 50 per cent, the throughput must be much lower than in the case of 100 per cent occupancy. The clerk has a lot of idle time in the 50 per cent case.

If a similar 'real' system exists, the input/output of the simulation model can be compared with the input/output of the real system.

After validating and verifying, we start the production runs. There are two important decisions to make:

1. the number of times the simulation must run to deliver confident results; and
2. the length of the simulation run.

It is essential to be aware that each experiment must be replicated several times to obtain valid results. By sampling from a distribution (using the Monte Carlo method), random behaviour is introduced into the model. This means that the output of any single production run is not the exact value to be considered. It is probable that the results will lie within some confidence interval. Several replications are necessary to obtain a smaller confidence interval.

To determine the length of one simulation run and to analyse the output, it is important to make a distinction between different types of simulation:[12] the simulation of a terminating system or the simulation of a non-terminating (or steady-state) system. A *terminating system* is one with a clearly identifiable event beyond which no useful information can be obtained or with a time point at which the system is cleaned out. For instance, a supermarket closes at a given time; this is

Table TN3.7 Results in terms of numbers of customers served by the clerk in an eight-hour day

Mean interarrival time	Without packer	With packer
50 seconds (occupancy rate of 100%)	317	353
200 seconds (occupancy rate of 50%)	177	176

the moment at which the system is clearly cleaned out. In a *non-terminating system*, such an event does not exist. For instance, since hospital beds are continuously occupied, the start-up of a new hospital, when all beds are empty, is not representative of the working of the system. Therefore, the output collected during the start-up of the system must be excluded for further analysis.

Table TN3.7 shows the results of the simulation experiments. In each situation, we have run the simulation five times. Each run simulates an eight-hour workday. If there is no professional packer, the average throughput through the regular checkout is 317 customers during an eight-hour workday. The standard deviation is nine customers. With a professional packer, the mean throughput is 353 clients and a standard deviation of ten clients.

We have repeated both experiments for a situation where the occupancy of the checkout is approximately 50 per cent. In this case, both situations have a throughput of approximately 180 customers. This means that using a professional packer is only meaningful if the occupancy of the checkout is high.

The study concludes that using a professional packer leads to a significantly higher throughput in the case of high occupancy.

CONCLUSION

Simulation is a very powerful tool for solving operational or queuing problems in a service organization. It allows experimentation with new concepts or a new configuration without intervening in the real system. It is possible to answer many different 'what if' questions, as in the example of the supermarket. Nonetheless, simulation is not the panacea for every operational problem in services. Remember that 'garbage in' means 'garbage out'. When it is impossible to collect precise input data, the output data must be studied with a great deal of caution. In any case, no single simulation model gives exact results. That is the main weakness of simulation modelling as compared to queuing theory. Consequently, it is preferable to use the analytical model (if it can be applied).

The most important steps in performing a simulation study are:

1. defining and describing the system, its components, and its boundaries;
2. defining performance measures;
3. setting up an experimental design – i.e. describing the alternatives required to achieve better performance in the service design;
4. collecting and validating data for the input variables;
5. preparing the collected data for use in the simulation model;
6. validating the assumptions underlying the model;
7. translating the conceptual model into a computer program;

8. verifying the computer program;
9. making pilot runs to further validate the model;
10. making production runs;
11. analysing the output;
12. making a report.

This chapter shows that performing a simulation study is not easy. There are many booby traps which can completely compromise the results of the simulation study. For instance, it is essential to conduct multiple production runs for each experiment. Generally, the modelling stage is much more important than the programming stage. Before starting a simulation study, a serious amount of time must be invested in acquiring simulation and modelling skills. Selecting a good simulator can support this learning process in many ways. A good simulator is one which minimizes the modelling effort and maximizes the flexibility to adapt to a specific situation.

The current evolution in simulation tools allows individuals to simulate systems without being an expert in simulation. Furthermore, in order to design service delivery processes in such a way that they exceed customer expectations, several design alternatives must be considered, especially in a service environment which is characterized by high arrival and process uncertainty. Simulation is a practical tool which allows companies to perform such evaluations before deciding whether to commit large amounts of money to an untested design.

Notes and references

[1] Ramaswany, R. (1996) *Design and Management of Service Processes*. Engineering Improvement Series. Massachusetts: Addison-Wesley.

[2] There are discrete-event simulation models with fixed time increments, although they are not so common.

[3] McHaney, R. (1991) *Computer Simulation: A practical perspective*. San Diego, California: Academic Press, p. 92.

[4] Chisman, J. A. (1993) *Introduction to Simulation Modeling Using GPPS/PC*. Englewood Cliffs, New Jersey: Prentice-Hall, p. 27.

[5] For a discussion on the different methods of generating (pseudo-) random numbers, we refer to Kleijnen, J. P. C. and Van Groenendaal, W. (1992) *Simulation: A statistical perspective*. Chichester: John Wiley & Sons.

[6] Chaharbaghi, K. (1990) 'Using simulation to solve design and operational problems', *International Journal of Operations and Production Management*, Vol 10, No 9, 89–105.

[7] McHaney, R. (1991), op. cit., p. 19.

[8] Chaharbaghi, K. (1990), op. cit.

[9] Systems Modeling Corporation (1994) *Arena Getting Started Guide*.

[10] McHaney, R. (1991), op. cit., p. 27.

[11] A gamma distribution is characterized by a shape and a scale-parameter. The shape parameter is in this case 2.83 and the scale parameter is 40.49. This is the same as a mean purchasing time of 114.66 seconds and a standard deviation of 68.13 seconds. A log-normal distribution is characterized by a mean and standard deviation. In the example of Fig. TN2.3, the mean is 100.26 seconds and the standard deviation is 73.32 seconds.

[12] Thesen, A. and Travis, L. E. (1992) *Simulation for Decision Making*. St. Paul, MN: West Publishing Company, pp. 158–9; *see also* Law, A. M. and Kelton, W. D. (1991) *Simulation Modeling and Analysis*. New York: McGraw-Hill, p. 527.

Suggested further reading

Chaharbaghi, K. (1990) 'Using simulation to solve design and operational problems', *International Journal of Operations and Production Management*, Vol 10, No 9, 89–105. Different applications of simulation in changing processes are discussed. Some insights are given on how to select an appropriate simulation tool.

McHaney, R. (1991) *Computer Simulation: A practical perspective*. San Diego, California: Academic Press. This book is written for practitioners. It describes very clearly the different steps which must be performed in order to develop a simulation model.

Data envelopment analysis

Paul Gemmel

This technical note should be read in conjunction with Chapter 18

Several techniques are available for relative efficiency benchmarking of service units. The most basic technique is the ratio-analysis, where the ratio of one output to one input is compared between several units. In the case of the example of bank branches, efficiency is defined as:

$$\text{Efficiency (branch 1)} = \frac{\text{Output}}{\text{Input}}$$

So, the relative efficiency of branch 1 is the result of the comparison of the efficiency of branch 1 to the efficiency of another branch (e.g. branch 2):

$$\text{Relative efficiency} = \frac{\text{Efficiency (branch 1)}}{\text{Efficiency (branch 2)}}$$

If branch 2 is a best practice (i.e. in this case branch 2 produces more output with the same amount of input than branch 1), branch 2 forms the frontier for branch 1 and the frontier efficiency of branch 1 is determined. Depending on how much shape is imposed on the frontier, a distinction is made between non-parametric and parametric frontiers. Non-parametric approaches, such as data envelopment analysis (DEA), do not impose any particular functional form that presupposes the shape of the frontier.

Using DEA, a best-practice function is empirically built from observed inputs and outputs. Linear programming is used to derive this best practice function. The objective is to maximize a service unit's efficiency – expressed as a ratio of outputs to inputs – by comparing a particular unit's efficiency with the performance of a group of similar units delivering the same service. Some of the units are evaluated as 100 per cent efficient as compared to the other units. These 100 per cent efficient units are said to lie on the efficient production frontier. Other units have an efficiency rating of less than 100 per cent and are considered to be relatively inefficient. DEA further indicates how an inefficient service unit can improve its performance. By identifying a reference set of efficient service units for each inefficient unit, one can determine how the amount of some of the input factors must be reduced to attain the same level of output in an efficient way. In this way, the efficient production frontier represents a standard of performance that the units not on the efficient frontier could try to achieve. In other words, the efficient frontier envelopes (encloses) all the data points. This is the origin of the term 'data envelopment analysis' (DEA).

The most basic DEA model was developed by Charnes, Cooper and Rhodes (CCR) in 1978.[1]

The CCR model allows that each unit adopts a set of weights which shows it in the most favourable light in comparison to the other units. Suppose that there are k branches j involved in the study. Each branch uses different amounts of n inputs to produce m outputs. For each branch j, y_{rj} and x_{ij} indicate respectively the observed amount of output r and input i. The efficiency of a target unit j_0 can be described in the following algebraic model (adapted from Charnes *et al.*, 1994[2]):

$$\text{Max } E_0 = \frac{\sum_{r=1}^{m} u_r y_{rj_0}}{\sum_{i=1}^{n} v_i x_{ij_0}} \tag{1}$$

$$\text{subject to } \frac{\sum_{r=1}^{m} u_r y_{rj}}{\sum v_i x_{ij}} \leq 1 \text{ for each unit } j = 1, 2, 3, ..., k$$

$$\text{and} \quad u_r \geq \varepsilon \text{ for } r = 1, 2, ..., m$$

$$v_i \geq \varepsilon \text{ for } i = 1, 2, ..., n$$

$$x_{ij} \geq 0, y_{rj} \geq 0$$

The above model (1) is a fractional model trying to look for a set of weights (u_r, v_i) which gives the target unit j_0 the highest possible efficiency rating. 'Highest possible' means that when these same weights are used in the other units j, $j = 1, 2, ..., k$, the efficiency ratings of the other units cannot be higher than 1. Furthermore all input and output weights need to be greater or equal to an infinitismal small value ε. This guarantees that each input and output variable is included in the model. Nonetheless the positive value ε is so small that it cannot disturb any solution involving only real numbers.

Because it is not always possible to solve non-linear fractional models such as stated in (1), Charnes and Cooper propose to convert it into a linear non-fractional model that can be solved with linear programming (adapted from Charnes *et al.*, 1994).[3]

$$\text{Max } \omega_0 = \sum_{r=1}^{m} \mu_r y_{rj_0} \tag{2}$$

$$\text{subject to} \quad \sum_{i=1}^{n} v_i x_{ij_0} = 1$$

$$\sum_{r=1}^{m} \mu_r y_{rj} - \sum v_i x_{ij} \leq 0; \text{ for } j = 1, 2, ..., k$$

$$\mu_r \geq \varepsilon \text{ for } r = 1, 2, ..., m$$

$$v_i \geq \varepsilon \text{ for } i = 1, 2, ..., n$$

$$x_{ij} \geq 0, y_{rj} \geq 0$$

Because model (2) is a typical linear programming model, there exists also a dual problem formulation (adapted from Charnes *et al.*, 1994):

$$\text{Min } z_0 = \theta - \varepsilon\left(\sum_{r=1}^{m} S_{rj_0}^{+} + \sum_{i=1}^{n} S_{ij_0}^{-}\right) \tag{3}$$

$$\text{subject to} \quad \sum_{j=1}^{k} \lambda_j y_{rj} - S_{rj_0}^{+} = y_{rj_0}; \; r = 1, 2, \dots, m$$

$$\sum_{j=1}^{k} \lambda_j x_{ij} + S_{ij_0}^{-} = \theta_{j_0} x_{ij_0}$$

$$\lambda_j \geq 0; \; j = 1, 2, \dots, k$$

$$S_{rj_0}^{+} \geq 0; \; r = 1, 2, \dots, m$$

$$S_{ij_0}^{-} \geq 0; \; i = 1, 2, \dots, n$$

In this dual model (3), $S_{rj_0}^{+}$ and $S_{rj_0}^{-}$ denotes slack variables and λ_j are intensity weights defining the linear combination of best practices to be compared with branch j_0. The primal model (2) is referred to as the multiplier form, while the dual problem (3) is referred to as the envelopment form. The duality theorem of linear programming can be used to guarantee that $z_0^* = \varpi_0^*$ where the superscript* denotes an optimal value with intensity weight λ_j^*. The optimal value of the intensity weight is based on the composition of a hypothetical efficient branch with output $\Sigma\lambda_j^* y_{rj}$ and input $\Sigma\lambda_j^* x_{ij}$ so that the composite branch level has input levels that do not exceed those of branch j, and output levels that are at least as high as those of branch j_0. The optimal value z_0^* yields an efficiency rating that measures the distance that j_0 lies from the frontier. Thus j_0 is efficient if and only if $z_0^* = \varpi_0^* = 0$. j_0 is not efficient if any component of the slack variables in the optimal solution, $S_{rj_0}^{+*}$ and $S_{rj_0}^{-*}$, is not zero. The values of these nonzero components identify the sources and amounts of inefficiency in the corresponding outputs and inputs.[4] The variable θ_{j_0} indicates how all inputs of branch j_0 must be proportionally reduced in order to become efficient. When the focus in the model is on the maximal movement toward the frontier through proportional reduction of inputs, we speak about an input oriented CCR model. It is also possible to focus on maximal movement via proportional augmentation of outputs. In this case, we speak about an output-orientation.

Notes and references

[1] Charnes, A., Cooper, W. and Rhodes, E. (1978) 'Measuring the efficiency of decision making units', *European Journal of Operational Research*, Vol 2, 429–44.

[2] Charnes, A., Cooper, W., Lewin, A. Y. and Seiford, L. M. (eds) (1994) *Data Envelopment Analysis: Theory, metholodogy and application.* Kluwer Academic Publishers.

[3] In transforming the fractional programming model (1) into a linear programming model (2), μ_r is set equal to tu_r and $v = tv_i$, where $t^{-1} = \sum_i v_i x_{ij_0}$.

[4] Charnes *et al.* (1994), op. cit., p. 26.

Insights stemming from emerging resource and competence-based strategic management theories

Aimé Heene

Within competence-based strategic management, firms are modelled as open systems consisting of hierarchically interdependent resource-stocks, connected through resource-flows as can be seen in Figure TN5.1.

The open systems model basically argues the following:

1. Within the firm's resources different levels can be defined whereby resources at these different levels influence each other reciprocally. This influence can move in two directions: from top to bottom and bottom to top.
2. 'Top-down' interdependencies can be described as follows:

   ■ Products are the result of (four) operations: product design, product development, manufacturing and marketing.
   ■ Operations are determined by tangible resources such as buildings, equipment and plant investment goods.
   ■ Intangible resources such as knowledge are applied to these tangible resources.

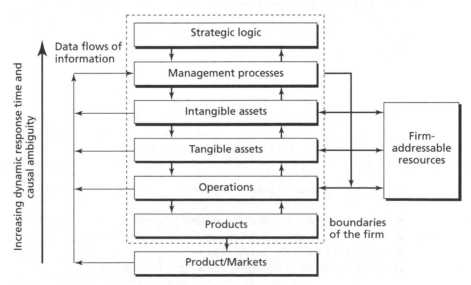

Figure TN5.1 The firm modelled as an open system[1]

Source: Copyright © John Wiley & Sons Ltd. Reproduced with permission.

- Management processes organize data flows and information processing structures and processes.
- The firm's strategic logic represents the rationale as to how this arrangement of resources will help the firm achieve its goals.

3. Adjusting the different resource-stocks or flows to changing internal or external environments is subject to growing 'causal ambiguity' and increased 'dynamic response times'. Adjusting the firm's strategic logic implies and leads to much more debate and discussion in management teams and takes a considerably longer time than adjusting the firm's products or its operations.[2] As a result of increased causal ambiguity and dynamic response times, firms are inclined to adjust the 'lower level' systems elements before they adjust the higher level systems elements and as a result may end up with outdated strategies reducing their chances of survival. This phenomenon becomes particularly visible when new disruptive changes occur in the market. How long did it take for companies like Philips, IBM, Digital or Apple to abandon the logic that made them big, but which was suddenly outdated if they were to compete in today's markets? This phenomenon, also labelled as path dependency, will imply specific challenges. While companies have to create an intertwined configuration – as described in Figure TN5.1 – to create a sustainable competitive advantage, it should not be forgotten that the assets of today might become the liabilities of tomorrow. Management therefore faces the challenge of not only building resources in an intertwined way, but also re-configuring or even replacing (parts of) them. We have already discussed this issue in far more detail in Chapter 20.

4. Firms are in a process of constantly 'exchanging' resources with their environment. Within the context of co-operative agreements (such as alliances) firms share their knowledge base with the client's (or even competitor's) knowledge base and in this way create (new) products or services.

5. Connecting and co-ordinating resource deployment throughout different or all 'levels' of resource-stocks builds barriers to the erosion mechanisms. 'Competence' is defined as 'the ability of an organization to sustain co-ordinated deployments of resources in ways that promise to help that organisation achieve its goals.'[3]

6. Strategic decisions within the open system model concern decisions to build resource-stocks or flows, decisions to leverage resource-stocks or flows, and decisions to replace resource-stocks and flows so as to avoid the risk of becoming locked in. It is through the processes of building, leveraging and replacing resources that the firm achieves its longevity.

7. Strategy within the open systems model thus involves decisions relating to:

- which resources to build;
- how to organize the building process;
- how to connect resources and how to configure resource-arrays;
- which resources to leverage (up to the level of product/markets);
- how to organize the leveraging process;
- how and when to reconfigure or even replace resources.

Notes and reference

[1] Adapted from Sanchez, R. and Heene, A. (eds) (1997) Strategic Learning and Knowledge Management, New York, Wiley.

[2] Empirical evidence for this was presented at the 1996 Strategic Management Society Conference: Heene, A., Sanchez, R. and Bartholomeeusen, L. (1996) 'Managing dynamic response times and causal ambiguities in the firm's strategy', *Proceedings of the Strategic Management Society 16th Annual International Conference*, Nov.

[3] Sanchez, R. and Heene, A. (1997), op. cit., p. 7.

Importance of informational elements in ads – comparing goods and services

The following detailed results – discussed in Chapter 5 of this book – were obtained by Butler and Abernethy in their 1994 study 'Information consumers seek from advertisements: are there differences between advertisements for goods and services?', published in the *Journal of Professional Services Marketing*, 10 (2), 75–91.

Informational elements	Services Mean (stand. deviation)	Goods Mean (stand. deviation)	t-test for significant differences between services and goods (p-value)
1 Phone number	6.37 (1.30)	5.79 (1.67)	S > G (.001)
2 Opening hours	5.86 (1.36)	5.59 (1.55)	S > G (.002)
3 Different services	5.60 (1.28)	5.23 (1.53)	S > G (.001)
4 Capable personnel	5.60 (1.28)	4.70 (1.86)	S > G (.001)
5 (Years of) experience	5.38 (1.57)	4.36 (1.88)	S > G (.001)
6 Concerned personnel	5.35 (1.66)	4.80 (1.85)	S > G (.001)
7 Helpful employees	5.12 (1.70)	4.91 (1.89)	S > G (.030)
8 Independent qualifications	4.93 (1.73)	4.02 (1.96)	S > G (.001)
9 Safety/security	4.56 (1.90)	4.33 (2.18)	S > G (.030)
10 Ability to solve problems	4.51 (1.79)	4.08	S > G (.001)
11 Price	5.04 (1.82)	6.32 (1.91)	G > S (.001)
12 Quality	5.88 (1.45)	6.21 (1.13)	G > S (.001)
13 Special promotions	4.02 (1.90)	5.70 (1.44)	G > S (.001)
14 Guarantees	4.97 (1.91)	5.66 (1.63)	G > S (.001)
15 Performance	5.19 (1.40)	5.45 (1.72)	G > S (.001)
16 Method of payment	4.96 (1.88)	5.31 (1.78)	G > S (.001)
17 Detailed explanations	3.86 (1.77)	4.22 (1.89)	G > S (.002)
18 Comparison with competitors	3.96 (1.87)	4.13 (1.71)	G > S (.060)
19 Home delivery	3.55 (1.93)	3.82 (2.19)	G > S (.020)
20 Illustrations	2.72 (1.74)	3.65 (2.15)	G > S (.001)
21 Address	6.26 (1.21)	6.32 (1.08)	S = G (0.180)
22 Speed of delivery	4.92 (1.67)	4.84 (1.83)	S = G (.250)
23 Free sample/trial	4.42 (2.05)	4.45 (2.13)	S = G (.420)
24 Financing	4.67 (1.88)	4.75 (2.02)	S = G (.270)
25 Components	4.21 (1.77)	4.16 (1.89)	S = G (.320)

APPENDIX 2

The state probability (P(n))

The probability of having n customers in the system is called the state probability P(n). To find the state probability P(n), it is necessary to formulate and solve a set of balance equations that equate the rate at which transitions occur into the state to the rate at which transitions occur out of the state. The rate into a certain state must be equal to the rate out of this state to reach a situation of steady state. A situation of steady state is necessary to solve a M/M/1/∞ queuing system analytically. In setting up these balance equations it is important to remember that only one customer can arrive at a time and that only one customer at a time can leave the server. The transition rate into P(2) (the probability of having two customers in the system) can be obtained either by multiplying the probability that there is one customer in the system P(1) with the arrival rate λ or by multiplying the probability that there are three customers in the system P(3) and that one customer is leaving after being served. The transition rate out of the state P(2) is the consequence of an arrival or a departure. Balancing the transition in and out of the state P(2) leads to the following equation:

$$\lambda P(2) + \mu P(2) = \lambda P(1) + \mu P(3)$$

If we repeat the previous reasoning for different states, we obtain the following set of balance equations:

State
0     $\mu P(1) = \lambda P(0)$
1     $\lambda P(0) + \mu P(2) = \lambda P(1) + \mu P(1)$
2     $\lambda P(1) + \mu P(3) = \lambda P(2) + \mu P(2)$
...   ...
n $\lambda P(n - 1) + \mu P(n + 1) = \lambda P(n) + \lambda P(n)$

It is easy to transform the above set equations to the following set:

State
0     $\mu P(1) = \lambda P(0)$
1     $\mu P(2) = \lambda P(1)$
2     $\mu P(3) = \lambda P(2)$
...   ...
n $\mu P(n + 1) = \lambda P(n)$

This gives the following general relationship between two state probabilities:

$$P(n) = \lambda/\mu P(n - 1) = \rho P(n - 1)$$

When this relationship is worked through until the single state probability P(0) is reached, this gives:

$$P(n) = \rho^n P(0)$$

To determine P(0), another characteristic of a proper probability distribution is used, i.e. that the sum of the state probabilities must be 1:

$$\sum_{n=0}^{\infty} \rho^n P(0) = 1$$

This is the sum of a geometric series. Using the standard equation for the sum of a geometric series, we can write:

$$P(0)\frac{1}{1-P} = 1$$

or

$$P(0) = 1 - \rho \text{ with } \rho < 1$$

This results in:

$$P(n) = (1 - \rho)\rho^n \text{ with } \rho < 1.$$

INDEX